Valid Forms of the Categorical Syllogism

Any syllogistic form is completely determined by the combination of its mood and figure. There are exactly 15 valid forms of the categorical syllogism, each with a unique name:

In the first figure:

AAA–1	Barbara
EAE–1	Celarent
AII–1	Darii
EIO–1	Ferio

In the second figure:

AEE–2	Camestres
EAE–2	Cesare
AOO–2	Baroko
EIO–2	Festino

In the third figure:

AII–3	Datisi
LAI–3	Disamis
EIO–3	Ferison
OAO–3	Bokardo

In the fourth figure:

AEE–4	Camenes
IAI–4	Dimaris
EIO–4	Fresison

Rules governing every valid Aristotelian categorical syllogism:

(Note: A term is *distributed* when the proposition in which the term appears refers to *all* members of the class to which the term refers. Thus, in the proposition "All humans are mortal" the term "humans" is distributed, but the term "mortal" is not.)

1. The syllogism must contain exactly three terms, used consistently.

2. The middle term of the syllogism must be distributed in at least one premiss.

3. If either term is distributed in the conclusion, it must be distributed in the premisses.

4. A valid syllogism cannot have two negative premisses.

5. If either premiss of the syllogism is negative, the conclusion must be negative.

6. If the conclusion of the syllogism is negative, at least one premiss must be negative.

INTRODUCTION TO LOGIC

Eleventh Edition

Irving M. Copi
University of Hawaii

Carl Cohen
University of Michigan

Prentice
Hall

Upper Saddle River, New Jersey 07458

Library of Congress Cataloging-in-Publication Data
Copi, Irving M.
   Introduction to logic / Irving M. Copi, Carl Cohen. — 11th ed.
     p. cm.
   Includes bibliographical references and index.
     ISBN 0-13-033735-8
        1. Logic   I. Cohen, Carl (date) - II. Title.
BC108.C69 2001
160—dc21   2001021441
                                                CIP

Editorial Director: *Charlyce Jones Owen*
Acquisitions Editor: *Ross Miller*
Editor-in-Chief of Development: *Susanna Lesan*
Development Editor: *Carolyn Smith*
Media Editor: *Deborah O'Connell*
Media Development Editor: *David Chodoff*
Website Editor: *Matthew Krack*
Marketing Manager: *Christopher Ruel*
Creative Design Director: *Leslie Osher*
Art Director: *Nancy Wells*
Interior & Cover Designer: *Lisa A. Jones*
Cover Art: *Conceptual colorful quarter cylinder shapes. Natural Selection Stock Photography, LLC.*
Interior Art:
Part One and Chapters 1-4:
Colorful nautilus shell. Orion Press/Natural Selection, Stock Photography, LLC.

Part Two and Chapters 5-10:
Fossilized spiral shell of an ammonite, an extinct squid-like cephalopod animal related to the living nautilus. Photographer: *Martin Bond/Science Photo Library/Photo Researchers, Inc.*
Part Three and Chapters 11-14:
Spiral pattern in sand. Source: *Pictor.*
AVP, Director of Production and Manufacturing: *Barbara Kittle*
Manufacturing Manager: *Nick Sklitsis*
Prepress and Manufacturing Buyers: *Sherry Lewis & Mary Ann Gloriande*
Production Editor: *Jean Lapidus*
Copy Editor: *Stephen C. Hopkins*
Indexer: *Murray Fisher*
Formatting & Art Manager: *Guy Ruggiero*
Artist: *Mirella Signoretto*

This book was set in 10.5/12.5 Palatino by Carlisle Communications, LTD.
and was printed and bound by Courier Companies, Inc.
The cover was printed by Phoenix Color Corp.

 © 2002, 1998, and 1994 by Pearson Education, Inc.
Upper Saddle River, New Jersey 07458

Printed in the United States of America
10 9 8 7 6 5 4 3 2 1

Student ISBN 0-13-033735-8

Professional Copy ISBN 0-13-096869-2

PRENTICE-HALL INTERNATIONAL (UK) Limited, London
PRENTICE-HALL of Australia Pty. Limited, Sydney
PRENTICE-HALL Canada Inc., Toronto
PRENTICE-HALL Hispanoamericana, S.A., Mexico
PRENTICE-HALL of India Private Limited, New Delhi
PRENTICE-HALL of Japan, Inc., Tokyo
PEARSON EDUCATION Asia Pte. Ltd., Singapore
EDITORA PRENTICE-HALL do Brasil, Ltda., Rio de Janeiro

We dedicate this eleventh edition of
Introduction to Logic
to our children

David M. Copi
Thomas R. Copi
William A. Copi
Margaret R. Copi

Jaclyn Z. Cohen
Noah J. Cohen

CONTENTS

PART TWO   DEDUCTION   179

CHAPTER 5   CATEGORICAL PROPOSITIONS   181

FOREWORD

*In a republican nation, whose citizens are to be led by reason
and persuasion and not by force, the art of reasoning
becomes of the first importance.*

—Thomas Jefferson

When we need to make reliable judgments—to decide what we ought to do in some complicated circumstances, or to know what is true where the truth has been in doubt—*reason* is the instrument upon which we most wisely depend. Nonrational instruments—hunches and habits and the like—are commonly employed, we know. But when the chips are down, when much depends upon the judgment we make, success is most likely if we reason the matter out. There are well-tested methods—*rational* methods—-for determining what really is the case, what really is true, and there are well-established principles to guide us in drawing inferences from what is known.

Our ignorance is vast, of course, so we are often forced to resort to authority in reaching judgment. But even when that is so, we cannot escape the need for reason, because then we must decide *which* authorities are to be respected, and why they deserve that respect. In every serious intellectual pursuit, we come to rely ultimately upon reasoning because there is nothing that can successfully replace it.

Logic is the study of reasoning. In this study we learn to have confidence in our own native powers, and with practice we strengthen those powers. All of us have at least a partial grasp of logical principles. When these principles are brought to the surface, formulated and recognized and understood, we develop the ability to distinguish good reasoning from bad. The study of logic helps one to reason well by illuminating the principles of *correct* reasoning, explaining them, justifying them, and exhibiting their effective use.

Correct reasoning is useful in every sphere of knowledge. College courses are often criticized for being too "academic," not clearly relevant to the affairs of everyday life. This complaint cannot be fairly brought against the study of logic. Whether in science, or in politics, or in the conduct of personal life, we use logic in reaching defensible conclusions. The study of logic helps us to identify arguments that are good, and the reasons why they are good. It also helps us to identify arguments that are bad, and the reasons why they are bad. No study is more widely relevant than this.

Democratic ideals are now professed almost universally. To realize these ideals, citizens must be able to participate effectively in their common affairs. But effective participation requires that citizens evaluate claims presented by leaders or those who would be leaders. So the success of democracy depends upon the reliability of the judgments we citizens make, and hence upon our capacity to weigh evidence and arguments rationally. Logic, therefore, is critical in advancing not only our personal aims, but those democratic aims we share with others.

Nothing more useful can be learned in formal study than the principles of accurate thinking: how to acquire reliable information and how to evaluate competing claims. Ideally, every college course should contribute to this end, but we know that many do not. It is squarely within the province of logic to focus on these supremely important tasks.

Much that is taught in college classes grows soon out of date. But the skills of correct reasoning never become obsolete. To the readers of this book we give our considered assurance: Command of the principles of logic can make a permanent and deeply satisfying contribution to the intellectual lives of all those who devote the time and energy necessary to master these principles.

PREFACE TO THE ELEVENTH EDITION

Many changes will be found in this new edition of *Introduction to Logic*, but instructors who have used previous editions may be assured that the integrity and spirit of this book have been retained. Much of the detail of previous editions and most of the exercises also have been retained. The changes introduced—of five different kinds—are designed to make this well-tested volume more accessible, and thus more effective as an instrument in the teaching of elementary logic. We recount these changes briefly here, addressing this report mainly to those acquainted with previous editions.

A Revised Chapter 1.

Structural changes have been made in the first part of the book. The expansion of the opening chapters in the preceding edition was found by many users to hinder student progress along what may be called "the main line" of instruction in logic. We have therefore compressed the material of what was Part One into a single opening chapter in which the same topics are addressed, but more crisply, and in ways likely to provide a better base for the more advanced material in the later chapters of the book. Chapter 1 has now become very hefty as a result—but it is also richer, more clearly formulated, and more fun to read.

Exposition—Rules and Definitions.

The most pervasive of the changes in this edition, and most important too, we think, are the very many adjustments in the ways in which theoretical matters are explained and expressed. We have long prided ourselves on the logical accuracy of *Introduction to Logic*, and of course we would do nothing to injure our hard-earned reputation for reliability. But our colleagues around the country have advised us, on many occasions, that our efforts to be exact, and to cut no corners, have in some parts of the book resulted in formulations rather difficult to digest—especially for beginning students.

This is not an easy matter to address. We have worked hard to ameliorate this problem—and if we have succeeded in this edition many of the resultant changes will be hardly noticeable. Explanations should be formulated in language that is transparent and thoroughly perspicuous, and (we hope) that will cause few brows to wrinkle.

Some illustrations of the kind of changes we have made are worth noting. Several of our colleagues observed that, where a set of rules or criteria have been put forward (as, for example, those to test the validity of categorical syllogisms, or to appraise the merit of analogical arguments), our exposition relied too heavily, in referring to a rule, upon the number assigned to it rather than to the substance of the rule itself. We have reformulated such exposition, consistently referring now to the rule itself.

Another example of reformulation will be noted in the chapter on definition. Previously, in explaining methods of defining, we caused needless confusion by using that much misunderstood word "connotation." The terms "connotation" and "denotation" were not employed erroneously, but to avoid confusion, we now rely fully upon the terms "intension" and "extension" in explaining techniques of definition.

Even format can serve to confuse, or to clarify. It was and remains our practice, in presenting deductive exercises in symbols, to mark the conclusion of an argument with the three triangular dots (∴) that commonly represent "therefore." But in earlier editions we had sometimes placed this sign on the same line as the last premiss of the argument, after a slash; and sometimes we had placed this sign on a separate line of its own. This proved to be a source of distraction if not confusion, so we now consistently place the three-dot "therefore" sign of conclusion on a separate line. This format enables students to see more sharply the claim that the argument is making, and what the target of a needed proof must be.

Many such adjustments appear in this edition, far too many to permit their identification in this Preface. In some cases the change is no more than the clarification of a transition, in others the tightening of a paragraph in which the prose was blurred. A textbook in logic ought to be concise, but it must also be precise; precision and clarity we have prized above all.

Along with such adjustments we have sought, where feasible, to strike a lighter and more friendly tone in this edition, to introduce illustrations or observations that may amuse as they instruct. The study of logic is sometimes laborious, but it need not be forbidding.

Sidebars.

Those who study logic with the help of this book differ very greatly in the range of their interests and in the degree of their preparation. We will not be satisfied if we fail to challenge those who are most well prepared and most acute; but those coming to systematic logic for the first time also deserve support and guidance appropriate for them. To this end, we have introduced a device that is wholly new to *Introduction to Logic:* We have sought to distinguish some portions in some chapters that may, for good reasons, be omitted in some learning contexts, or may be treated by instructors as tangential to "the main line." These portions can serve to challenge some students who feel ready for additional work.

Finding a way to do this without injury to the whole is problematic. We have adopted the simple device of a sidebar. These sidebars take two forms, "Advanced Material" and "For Enrichment." We emphasize that this contrivance is not meant to depreciate the passages so marked off, which are often especially interesting and demanding. But such sidebar material, we hope, will make it easier for instructors to guide their own students to a mastery of the elements of theory most critical for them—and perhaps to avoid some complexities not essential for their solid grasp of elementary logic. Many instructors will simply ignore these markings, and may do so without damage to the understanding of their students.

Technical Changes.

Some technical changes have been introduced into this edition of *Introduction to Logic*—changes that we think reduce ambiguity and thus support instruction.

For example, we have responded to the frequently expressed concern of colleagues by expanding the discussion of logical equivalence in Chapter 8, now more sharply emphasizing the differences between material equivalence as a truth-functional connective, and logical equivalence as a logical relation that justifies the rules of replacement. An entirely new section on this topic (section 8.6) has been inserted, and in this section we have introduced a new symbol for logical equivalence as well.

In earlier editions we allowed the equivalences expressed by the rules of replacement—the last 10 of the 19 Rules of Inference—to be symbolized by the same three-bar symbol ($\equiv$) with which material equivalence ("if and only if") is symbolized throughout. This practice had some justification, but it surely led to student confusion when, for example, rules of replacement were formulated in which the three-bar symbol appeared more than once, with more than one meaning. A distinct symbol was needed.

Selecting that symbol has been a matter of long-continuing deliberation. Many alternatives were considered and rejected for reasons pedagogical or theoretical or aesthetic. We have chosen to retain the three-bar symbol, *over* which a small T indicates that the equivalence confronted is a tautology. This achieves the teaching aim, we think, with a minimum of disruption. Students are rarely called upon to write the symbol for logical equivalence—but can (with this notation) recognize it unambiguously when it appears in the list of the rules of replacement that natural deduction employs.

Elsewhere in the treatment of deduction, we have changed the design of Venn diagrams in representing Categorical Syllogisms. Where previously we had used simple shading to mark off what the premises of the argument rule out, we have in this edition used slanted lines. This permits the impact of each of the two premises of a syllogism to be distinguished, and because their lines are slanted in opposite directions, a cross-hatching results when the logical impacts of the two premises overlap. Different colors we chose not to use, not wanting to convey the suggestion that students would need anything more than an ordinary pencil to employ Venn diagrams for themselves.

Revised Exercises.

Finally, exercise sets provided at the close of many sections have been enriched. Many exercises have been added, some removed. As in previous editions of *Introduction to Logic,* we have sought to provide a wide array of illustrative passages, where possible on controversial issues likely to be of genuine interest to college students. Some contrived exercises are still used, or course, but we take pride in the fact that the exercises are for the most part extracted from worthy books and periodicals of very great variety. We have not excluded the writing of classical, and even ancient philosophers—but we greatly favor arguments and illustrations produced in the push and pull of discourse in the twentieth and twenty-first centuries.

As in the past, we have scrupulously avoided partisanship in selecting these materials. When some passage provides a telling example of some mistake in reasoning, or a fine illustration of some argumentative technique, we have included it whatever our judgment of its conclusion might be. What we wrote in the Preface to the preceding edition we again affirm: The argumentative chips must be allowed to fall where they may.

Finally, we draw attention to the substantial influence of criticisms and suggestions received from colleagues, senior and junior—whose names and institutions are noted elsewhere in these pages. We strive to make *Introduction to Logic* a teaching instrument ever more finely tuned, and the responses of readers around the world have given us splendid help in spotting errors and identifying deficiencies. We earnestly welcome this thoughtful engagement—and for this continuing and widespread support we express here, not for the first or the last time, our heartfelt appreciation.

ACKNOWLEDGMENTS

The loyal support of instructors and students of logic has been a major factor in the steady improvement of *Introduction to Logic* over the years. This widespread (and sometimes critical!) participation of our readers has proved to be a mighty strength. To all of those who have had some role, large or small, in molding this eleventh edition, we convey our hearty thanks. Readers who offer their suggestions (email: *ccohen@umich.edu*) receive our direct response, of course; but we also take satisfaction in listing here the names of some of those to whom we are indebted.

Prof. John M. Abbarno, of *D'Youville College, Buffalo, New York*

Prof. Benjamin Abellera, of the *University of the Dsitrict of Columbia*

Dr. Gerald Abrams, of the *University of Michigan, Ann Arbor*

Mr. Russell Alfonso, of the *University of Hawaii, Honolulu*

Ms. Amelia Bischoff, of *Ithaca College, Ithaca, New York*

Mr. Nicholas Bratton, of the *University of Michigan, Ann Arbor*

Mr. Matthew Bronson, of the *University of Michigan, Ann Arbor*

Prof. Keith Burgess-Jackson, of the *University of Texas at Arlington*

Prof. Sidney Chapman, of *Richland College, Dallas, Texas*

Prof. Zoe Close, of *Grossmont College, El Cajon, California*

Prof. William S. Cobb, of the *University of Michigan, Ann Arbor*

Prof. Keith Coleman, of the *University of Kansas, Lawrence*

Prof. Malcolm S. Cohen, of the *University of Michigan, Ann Arbor*

Mr. Eric Dyer, of the *University of Michigan, Ann Arbor*

Prof. Kevin Funchion, of *Salem State College, Salem, Massachusetts*

Prof. Faith Gielow, of *Villanova University, Villanova, Pennsylvania*

Prof. Joseph Gilbert, of the *State University of New York at Brockport*

Mr. Anand Giridharadas, of the *University of Michigan, Ann Arbor*

Dr. Robert A. Green, of the *University of Michigan, Ann Arbor*

Ms. Janice Grzankowski, of *Cheektowaga, New York*

Prof. Warren Harbison, of *Boise State University, Boise, Idaho*

Mr. Abdul Halim B. Abdul Karim, of the *National University of Singapore*

Prof. Royce Jones, of *Illinois College, Jacksonville*

Prof. Richard T. Lambert, of *Carroll College, Helena, Montana*

Mr. James Lipscomb, of *New York, New York*

Prof. Charles Lambros, of the *State University of New York at Buffalo*

Mr. Andrew LaZella, of *Hamline University, St. Paul, Minnesota*

Prof. Gerald W. Lilje, of *Washington State University, Pullman*

Ms. Linda Lorenz, of *Ann Arbor, Michigan*

Prof. Krishna Mallick, of *Bentley College, Waltham, Massachusetts*

Prof. Edwin Martin, of *North Carolina State University, Raleigh*

Prof. Michael J. Matthis, of *Kutztown University, Kutztown, Pennsylvania*

Prof. George Mavrodes, of the *University of Michigan, Ann Arbor*

Prof. Leemon McHenry, of *Wittenberg University, Springfield, Ohio*

Mr. David A. Mihaila, of *Honolulu, Hawaii*

Ms. Erin Moore, of *Ohio State University, Columbus*

Mr. David Nelson, of the *University of Michigan, Ann Arbor*

Dr. Sumer Pek, of the *University of Michigan, Ann Arbor*

Prof. Howard Pospesel, of the *University of Miami, Carol Gables, Florida*

Ms. Deborah Pugh, of *New York, New York*

Mr. Roberto Picciotto, of *Gastonia, North Carolina*

Prof. Ray Perkins, Jr., of *Plymouth State College, Plymouth, New Hampshire*

Prof. Dennis P. Quinn, of *Saint Vincent College, Latrobe, Pennsylvania*

Prof. Lee C. Rice, of *Marquette University, Milwaukee, Wisconsin*

Prof. Blaine B. Robinson, of the *South Dakota School of Mines and Technology, Rapid City*

Prof. Edith Schipper, of the *University of Miami, Carol Gables, Florida*

Mr. Milton Schwartz, Esq., of *New York, New York*

Prof. Emeritus Albert C. Shaw, of *Rowan College, Glassboro, New Jersey*

Prof. Edward Sherline, of the *University of Wyoming, Laramie*

Dr. Barbara M. Sloat, of the *University of Michigan, Ann Arbor*

Ms. Lauren Shubow, of the *University of Michigan, Ann Arbor*

Mr. Jason A. Sickler, of the *University of North Dakota, Grand Forks*

Ms. Stefanie Silverman, of the *University of Michigan, Ann Arbor*

Prof. Michael Slattery, of *Villanova University, Villanova, Pennsylvania*

Mr. Matthew Spivak, of the *University of Michigan, Ann Arbor*

Prof. James Stuart, of *Bowling Green State University, Bowling Green, Ohio*

Mr. James Sullivan, of the *University of Michigan, Ann Arbor*

Prof. Paul Tang, of *California State University, Long Beach*

Mr. Andrew Tardiff, of *North Kingstown, Rhode Island*

Mr. J. A. Van de Mortel, of *Cerritos College, Norwalk, California*

Prof. Roy Weatherford, of the *University of South Florida, Tampa*

Prof. Allen Weingarten, of *Morristown, New Jersey*

Prof. Phillip H. Wiebe, of *Trinity Western University, Langley, British Columbia, Canada*

Mr. Michael Wingfield, of *Lake Dallas, Texas*

We acknowledge a special debt to those penetrating scholars who have scrutinized *Introduction to Logic* meticulously, and whose many suggestions have resulted in the marked improvement of this eleventh edition. These reviewers are: Jeffery Borrowdale and Allan Hancock, Cuesta College Polytechnic State University; Clare Swift Heiller, Bakersfield College; Paul Tang, California State University-Long Beach; Elmer H. Duncan, Baylor University; Dr. Patrick Rardin, Appalachian State University; Neil Manson, University of Aberdeen, UK; Rebecca Carr, George Washington University; Gale Justin, California State University-Sacramento; and Warren Weinstein, California State University, Long Beach.

Finally, we express heartfelt thanks to our editors at Prentice-Hall, Dr. Ross Miller and Ms. Jean Lapidus, and their many colleagues, whose patience and intelligent support throughout have been as admirable as they are precious.

Irving M. Copi
University of Hawaii, Honolulu

Carl Cohen
University of Michigan, Ann Arbor

NEW TO THE 11TH EDITION OF *INTRODUCTION TO LOGIC* IS A COMPELLING ONLINE TUTORIAL PROGRAM...

eLOGIC

Combining a concise version of the text with animated examples, interactive exercises, and a toolkit to use for solving logic problems, **eLOGIC** will help you master the study of logic!

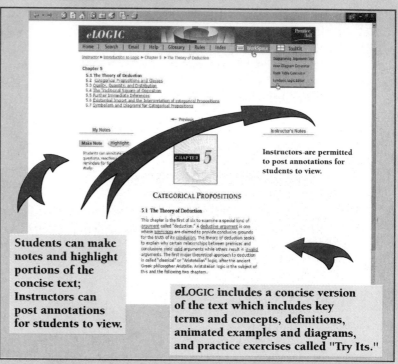

Instructors are permitted to post annotations for students to view.

Students can make notes and highlight portions of the concise text; Instructors can post annotations for students to view.

eLOGIC includes a concise version of the text which includes key terms and concepts, definitions, animated examples and diagrams, and practice exercises called "Try Its."

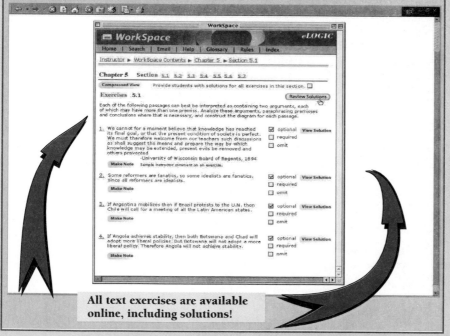

Instructors can assign *any* text exercise and make *any* solution available. **Students** solve exercises online and save their work for instructors to assess.

All text exercises are available online, including solutions!

The *Workspace* in **eLOGIC** provides students with a toolkit, a series of interactive tools which are used to solve exercises. The toolkit contains a *Diagramming Arguments Tool*, a *Truth Table Generator*, a *Venn Diagram Generator* and a *Symbolic Logic Editor*. Two tools are illustrated here.

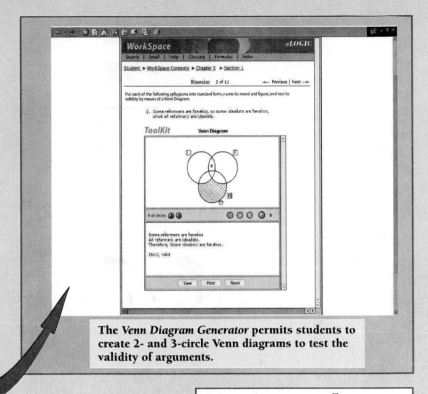

The *Venn Diagram Generator* permits students to create 2- and 3-circle Venn diagrams to test the validity of arguments.

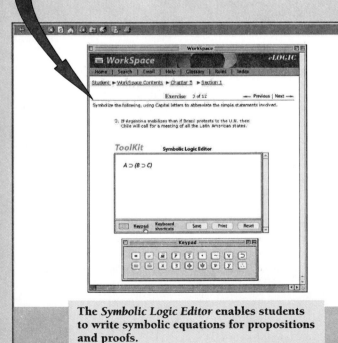

The *Symbolic Logic Editor* enables students to write symbolic equations for propositions and proofs.

How do I use **eLOGIC** now?

1 Connect to **www.prenhall. com/copi,** and select *Introduction to Logic,* 11th edition.

2 Locate the link to **eLOGIC** and click on it.

3 Locate you instructor's course and click on the link. If it is not listed, select the first option to use your copy of **eLOGIC** without a course.

4 Complete student registration and click on 'proceed to checkout'. Enter the access code provided with your new textbook. If your text book does not include an access code card, contact your bookstore to order one.

eLOGIC - Logic for the next generation...

PART ONE

LOGIC AND LANGUAGE

All our lives we are giving and accepting reasons.
Reasons are the coin we pay for the beliefs we hold.
—Edith Watson Schipper

Come now, and let us reason together.
—Isaiah 1:18

. . . this we do affirm—that if truth is to be sought in every division of Philosophy, we must, before all else, possess trustworthy principles and methods for the discernment of truth. Now the Logical branch is that which includes the theory of criteria and of proofs; so it is with this that we ought to make our beginnings.
—*Sextus Empiricus*

. . . everyone knows the distinction of cogent reasoning from fallacy. The study of logic appeals to no criterion not already present in the learner's mind.
—*C. I. Lewis*

CHAPTER 1

BASIC LOGICAL CONCEPTS

1.1 WHAT LOGIC IS

Logic is the study of the methods and principles used to distinguish correct reasoning from incorrect reasoning. There are objective criteria with which correct reasoning may be defined. If these criteria are not known, then they cannot be used. The aim of the study of logic is to discover and make available those criteria that can be used to test arguments, and to sort good arguments from bad ones.

The logician is concerned with reasoning on every subject: science and medicine, ethics and law, politics and commerce, sports and games, and even the simple affairs of everyday life. Very different kinds of reasoning may be used, and all are of interest to the logician. In this book arguments of many varieties, on very many topics, will be analyzed. Our concern throughout will be not with the subject matter of those arguments, but with their *form* and *quality*. Our aim is to learn how to test arguments and evaluate them.

It is not the thought processes called reasoning that are the logician's concern, but the outcomes of those processes, the *arguments* that are the products of reasoning, and that can be formulated in writing, examined, and analyzed. Each argument confronted raises this question for the logician: Does the conclusion reached *follow* from the premises used or assumed? Do the premises *provide good reasons* for accepting the conclusion drawn? If the premises do provide adequate grounds for accepting the conclusion—that is, if asserting the premises to be true does warrant asserting the conclusion also to be true—then the reasoning is correct. Otherwise it is incorrect.

It would be a mistake to suppose that only the student of logic can reason well or correctly, just as it would be wrong to suppose that only the athlete who studies physiology can run well. Athletes unaware of the processes going on in their bodies often perform excellently, and some advanced students of physiology, although knowing much about the way the body functions, nevertheless perform poorly on the athletic field. Similarly, the study of logic does not give assurance that one's reasoning will be correct.

But a person who has studied logic is more likely to reason correctly than one who has never thought about the principles involved in reasoning. Partly this is because the student of logic will acquire methods for testing the correctness of reasoning, and the more easily errors are detected, the less likely they are to be allowed to stand. Among the errors detected will be those common fallacies, or "natural" mistakes in reasoning, that can be readily avoided when fully understood.

The study of logic is likely to improve the quality of one's reasoning for another reason: It gives one the opportunity to *practice* the analysis of arguments and the construction of arguments of one's own. Reasoning is something we *do* as well as understand; it therefore is an art as well as a science, with skills to be developed and techniques to be mastered. To this end this book provides an abundant supply of exercises through which those skills and techniques may be strengthened.

There are affairs in human life that cannot be fully analyzed by the methods of logic, and issues that cannot be resolved by arguments, even good ones. The appeal to emotion sometimes is more persuasive than logical argument, and in some contexts it may be more appropriate as well. But where judgments that must be relied upon are to be made, correct reasoning will in the long run prove to be their most solid foundation. With the methods and techniques of logic we can distinguish efficiently between correct and incorrect reasoning. These methods and techniques are the subject matter of this book.

1.2 PROPOSITIONS AND SENTENCES

We begin by examining *propositions,* the building blocks of every argument. **A proposition is something that may be asserted or denied.** Propositions in this way are different from questions, commands, and exclamations. Neither questions, which can be asked, nor commands, which can be given, nor exclamations, which can be uttered, can possibly be asserted or denied. Only propositions assert that something is (or is not) the case, and therefore only they can be true or false. Truth and falsity do not apply to questions, commands, or exclamations.

Moreover, every proposition *is* either true or false—although we may not know the truth or falsity of some given proposition. The proposition that there is life on some other planet in our galaxy is one whose truth or falsity we do not know; but either it is true that there is such extraterrestrial life, or it is not true. In short, an essential feature of propositions is that they are either true or false.

It is customary to distinguish between propositions and the *sentences* by means of which they are asserted. Two sentences that consist of different words differently arranged may in the same context have the same meaning and be used to assert the same proposition. For example,

Leslie won the election.
The election was won by Leslie.

are plainly two different sentences, for the first contains four words and the second six, and they begin differently, and so on. Yet these two declarative sentences have exactly the same meaning. **We use the term *proposition* to refer to what declarative sentences are typically used to assert.**

A sentence, moreover, is always a sentence in a particular language, the language in which it is used. But propositions are not peculiar to any language; a given proposition may be asserted in many languages. The four sentences

> It is raining.
> Está lloviendo.
> Il pleut.
> Es regnet.

are certainly different, for they are in different languages: English, Spanish, French, and German. Yet they have a single meaning, and all may be uttered to assert the same proposition.

The same sentence can be used, in different contexts, to make very different statements. For example, the sentence

> The largest state in the United States was once an independent republic.

would have been a true statement about Texas during the first half of the twentieth century, but it is now a false statement about Alaska. A change in the temporal context, plainly, may result in very different propositions, or statements, being asserted by the very same words. (The terms "proposition" and "statement" are not exact synonyms, but in the context of logical investigation they are used in much the same sense. Some writers on logic prefer "statement" to "proposition," although the latter has been more common in the history of logic. In this book, both terms are used.)

The propositions illustrated thus far have been simple: "Leslie won the election"; "It is raining"; and so on. But propositions are often *compound,* containing other propositions within themselves. Consider the following passage from an account of the last days of Hitler's Third Reich in 1945:

> The Americans and Russians were driving swiftly to a junction on the Elbe. The British were at the gates of Hamburg and Bremen and threatening to cut off Germany from occupied Denmark. In Italy Bologna had fallen and Alexander's Allied forces were plunging into the valley of the Po. The Russians, having captured Vienna on April 13, were heading up the Danube.[1]

Several propositions contained in this paragraph are compound. "The British were at the gates of Hamburg and Bremen," for example, is the *conjunction* of two propositions: "The British were at the gates of Hamburg," and "The British were at the gates of Bremen." And that conjunctive proposition is itself one component of a larger conjunction, that "the British were at the gates of Hamburg and Bremen and [the British] were threatening to cut off Germany

---

[1] William L. Shirer, *The Rise and Fall of the Third Reich* (New York: Simon and Schuster, 1960).

from occupied Denmark." Every proposition in this passage is asserted; that is, it is stated as true. Asserting the conjunction of two propositions is equivalent to asserting each of the component propositions themselves.

But there are other kinds of compound propositions which do not assert the truth of their components. For example, in *alternative* (or *disjunctive*) propositions, such as

>   Circuit Courts are useful, or they are not useful.[2]

neither of the two components is asserted; only the compound "either-or" disjunctive proposition is asserted. If this disjunctive proposition is true, either of its components could be false. And in compound propositions that are *hypothetical* (or *conditional*), such as

>   If God did not exist, it would be necessary to invent him.[3]

again neither of the components is asserted. The proposition that "God does not exist" is not asserted here; nor is the proposition that "it is necessary to invent him." Only the "if-then" proposition is asserted by the hypothetical or conditional statement, and that conditional statement might be true even though both of its components were false.

In the course of this book we shall analyze the internal structure of many kinds of propositions, both simple and compound.

1.3 ARGUMENTS, PREMISSES, AND CONCLUSIONS

Propositions are the building blocks with which arguments are made. **The term** *inference* **refers to the process by which one proposition is arrived at and affirmed on the basis of one or more other propositions accepted as the starting point of the process.** To determine whether an inference is correct, the logician examines the propositions with which that process begins and ends, and the relations between them. This cluster of propositions constitutes an *argument,* and therefore there is an argument corresponding to every possible inference.

It is with arguments that logic is chiefly concerned. As logicians use the word **an** *argument* **is any group of propositions of which one is claimed to follow from the others, which are regarded as providing support or grounds for the truth of that one.** The word "argument" is often used in other senses also, of course, but in logic it has strictly the sense just explained.

In this strict sense, it is clear that an argument is not a mere collection of propositions; a passage may contain several related propositions and yet contain no *argument* at all. For an argument to be present, the cluster of propositions must have a structure. In describing this structure, the terms "premiss" and "conclusion" are commonly used. **The** *conclusion* **of an argument is the proposition that**

---

[2]Abraham Lincoln, annual message to Congress, 3 December 1861.
[3]Voltaire, *Épitre à l'Auteur du Livre des Trois Imposteurs,* 10 November 1770.

is affirmed on the basis of the other propositions of the argument, and these other propositions, which are affirmed (or assumed) as providing support or reasons for accepting the conclusion, are the *premisses* of that argument.

The simplest kind of argument consists of one premiss and a conclusion that is claimed to follow from it or be implied by it. The premiss and the conclusion, in that order, may each be stated in a separate sentence, as in this argument that appears on a sticker affixed to biology textbooks in the State of Alabama:

> No one was present when life first appeared on earth. Therefore any statement about life's origins should be considered as theory, not fact.

Or both the premiss and the conclusion may be stated in the same sentence, as in the following argument:

> Since it turns out that all humans are descended from a small number of African ancestors in our recent evolutionary past, believing in profound differences between the races is as ridiculous as believing in a flat earth.[4]

Even in simple arguments, the statement of the conclusion may *precede* the statement of the single premiss. When it does, the two propositions may appear in separate sentences or in the same sentence. An example of separate statements in which the conclusion is stated first is this:

> The Food and Drug Administration should stop all cigarette sales immediately. After all, cigarette smoking is the leading preventable cause of death.[5]

And an example of a combined statement in which the conclusion comes first is this:

> Every law is an evil, for every law is an infraction of liberty.[6]

Most arguments are much more complicated than these, and some arguments, containing compound propositions with several components, are exceedingly complicated, as we shall see. But every argument, whether simple or complex, consists of a group of propositions, of which one is the conclusion and the others are the premisses offered to support it.

Since an argument is made up of a group of propositions, no single proposition can, by itself, be an argument. But some compound propositions closely resemble arguments. Care must be taken not to confuse such propositions with arguments. Consider the following hypothetical proposition:

> If life evolved on Mars during an early period in its history when it had an atmosphere and climate similar to Earth's, then it is likely that life evolved on countless other planets that scientists now believe to exist in our galaxy.

---

[4]David Hayden, "Thy Neighbor, Thy Self," *New York Times,* 9 May 2000.
[5]"Ban Cigarettes," *Orlando Sentinel,* 27 February 1992.
[6]Jeremy Bentham, *Principles of Legislation,* 1802.

Neither the first component of this proposition—"life evolved on Mars during an early period in its history when it had an atmosphere and climate similar to Earth's"—nor the second component—"it is likely that life evolved on countless other planets that scientists now believe exist in our galaxy"—is asserted. The proposition asserts only that the former implies the latter, and both could very well be false. No inference is made in this passage, no conclusion is claimed to be true. This is a hypothetical proposition, not an argument. But now consider the following passage:

> It is likely that life evolved on countless other planets that scientists now believe exist in our galaxy, because life very probably evolved on Mars during an early period in its history when it had an atmosphere and climate similar to Earth's.[7]

In this case we *do* have an argument. The proposition that "life very probably evolved on Mars" is here asserted as a premiss, and the proposition that "life likely evolved on countless other planets" is here claimed to follow from that premiss and to be true. Thus, a hypothetical proposition may *look* very much like an argument, but it never can *be* an argument, and the two should not be confused. Recognizing arguments is a topic discussed below in section 1.5.

Finally, it should be emphasized that while every argument is a structured cluster of propositions, not every structured cluster of propositions is an argument. Consider this passage from a recent account of travel in Africa:

> Camels do not store water in their humps. They drink furiously, up to 28 gallons in a ten-minute session, then distribute the water evenly throughout their bodies. Afterward, they use the water stingily. They have viscous urine and dry feces. They breathe through their noses and keep their mouths shut. They do sweat, but only as a last resort….They can survive a water loss of up to one-third of their body weight, then drink up and feel fine.[8]

There is no argument here.

Exercises

Identify the premisses and conclusions in the following passages, each of which contains only one argument.[9]

Example:

1. A well regulated militia being necessary to the security of a free state, the right of the people to keep and bear arms shall not be infringed.

    —*The Constitution of the United States*, Amendment 2

---

[7] Richard Zare, "Big News for Earthlings," *New York Times*, 8 August 1996.
[8] William Langewiesche, *Sahara Unveiled: A Journey Across the Desert* (New York: Pantheon Books, 1996).
[9] Solutions to the starred exercises may be found at the back of the book.

Solution:

> PREMISS: A well regulated militia is necessary for the security of a free state.
>
> CONCLUSION: The right of the people to keep and bear arms shall not be infringed.

2. We can avert a majority of cancers by prevention efforts, even if we never get straight on the causes; more research on prevention and less on cure makes increasing sense.

    —Daniel Callahan, "Lab Games,"
    New York Times Book Review, 9 April 1995

3. Good sense is of all things in the world the most equally distributed, for everybody thinks himself so abundantly provided with it that even those most difficult to please in all other matters do not commonly desire more of it than they already possess.

    —René Descartes, *A Discourse on Method,* 1637

4. Of all our passions and appetites the love of power is of the most imperious and unsociable nature, since the pride of one man requires the submission of the multitude.

    —Edward Gibbon, *The Decline and
    Fall of the Roman Empire,* vol. 1, chap. IV

*5. Forbear to judge, for we are sinners all.

    —William Shakespeare, *Henry VI, Part II,* act 3, scene 3

6. In preparing for the national census of 2000, intense disagreement arose over whether the U.S. Constitution requires an actual head count of the population, or whether a sophisticated sampling technique might reasonably replace the head count. A letter to the *New York Times* on 6 September 1998 contained the following argument: With the "head count" method, the Census Bureau cannot succeed in counting all the people in the United States. Therefore the 'head count' system is itself a sampling method, in which the sample is the portion of the population that actually returns the questionnaire.

    —Keith Bradley, "What Did the Founders Expect
    From the Census?"

7. The essence of our admirable economic system is to create wants as fast as, or faster than it satisfies them. Thus the improvement of living conditions, meaning greater consumer satisfaction, is, by definition, impossible.

    —J. Maher, "Never Better," *New York Times,* 1 January 1993

8. Because they clear the way for pathogens bio-chemically, as well as giving them a free ride, ticks are among the most pernicious disease vectors in the world.

    —Cynthia Mills, "Blood Feud," *The Sciences,* April 1998

9. He that loveth not knoweth not God; for God is love.

—1 John 4:8

*10. Because light moves at a finite speed, looking at objects that are millions of miles away is actually looking at light that was emitted many years ago.

—D. Richstone, "University of Michigan Joins Magellan Project," *Ann Arbor News*, 13 February 1996

11. What stops many people from photocopying a book and giving it to a pal is not integrity but logistics; it's easier and inexpensive to buy your friend a paperback copy.

—Randy Cohen, *New York Times Magazine*, 26 March 2000

12. Some live to 100 without ever contributing to the improvement of humankind. Some die young in an undertaking that improves humankind. So it is absurd simply to concentrate on some scientific means to extend longevity."

—William J. Cousins, "To a Long Life! But How Long?" *New York Times*, 25 December 1999

13. The theoretical justification of our argument [that the legalization of abortion in the 1970s substantially reduced crime in the 1990s] rests on two simple assumptions: 1) Legalized abortion leads to fewer "unwanted" babies being born, and 2) unwanted babies are more likely to suffer abuse and neglect and are therefore more likely to be criminally involved in later life.

—Steven Levitt, *www.slate.com/dialogues/*, 23 August 1999

14. Today's first year college students have lived the external appearances of an adult life for many more years than their counterparts 50 years ago did. [Therefore], what we have traditionally associated with the intellectual awakening during the college years must now occur in the high school."

—Leon Botstein, *Jefferson's Children: Education and the Promise of American Culture*, 1998

*15. The institution of public education thrives on its own failures. The more poorly its charges perform, the more money it asks for (and gets) from the public and the government. The more money it gets, the more it can grow itself.

—Ian Hamet, "School for Scandal," *The Weekly Standard*, 23 August 1999

16. The ideal audience [for the magician] is one comprising mathematicians, philosophers, and scientists, because a logical mind, receptive to a connection between each apparent cause and its ap-

parent effect, is more prone to surprise when an illusion reaches its
'illogical' climax.

> —Martyn Bedford, *The Houdini Girl,* Pantheon Books, 1999

17. Accusations [of sexual harassment] are based on "impact" not intention; therefore the accused is guilty if the accuser believes him
to be guilty.

> —Herbert London, New York University Dean,
> quoted in Alan Kors and Harvey Silverglate,
> *The Shadow University,* The Free Press, 1998

18. It is wrong to tax people on the income they make while they are
living and to double-tax them when they die and want to pass
their life savings on to their children, grandchildren, or the charity
of their choice. The death tax, otherwise called the estate tax, is
unfair and should be abolished.

> —Representative Bill Archer,
> Chairman of the U.S. House Committee
> on Ways and Means, 3 July 1998

19. Standardized tests have a disparate racial and ethnic impact;
white and Asian students score, on average, markedly higher
than their black and Hispanic peers. This is true for fourth-grade
tests, college entrance exams, and every other assessment on the
books. If a racial gap is evidence of discrimination, then all tests
discriminate.

> —Abigail Thernstrom, "Testing, the Easy Target,"
> *New York Times,* 15 January 2000

*20. Unquestionably, no more important goal exists in medical research
today than the development of an AIDS vaccine. Last year (1998)
AIDS, caused by HIV (Human Immunodeficiency Virus) was the
infectious disease that killed the most people around the world,
and the epidemic is not abating.

> —David Baltimore, President of the
> California Institute of Technology, in
> *The Chronicle of Higher Education,* 28 May 1999

1.4 ANALYZING ARGUMENTS

Many arguments are simple, but some are quite complex. The premises of an
argument may support its conclusion in different ways. The number of premises and the order of the propositions in an argument may vary. We need
techniques to analyze argumentative passages and clarify the relations of premises and conclusions within them.

Two techniques are common. We may *paraphrase* an argument, setting forth its propositions in clear language and logical order. We may also *diagram* an argument, exhibiting its structure using spatial relations in two dimensions. Both techniques can be useful; we choose the one that helps most in the context given.

A. Paraphrasing

Consider the following argument, in which there are more than two premisses and the conclusion is stated first:

> Upright walking therapods, the group that includes Tyrannosaurus rex, could not have evolved into modern birds, for three main reasons. The first is that most fossils of bird-like therapod dinosaurs originated 75 million years *after* the fossilized remains of the first bird....The second is that the ancestors of birds must have been suited for flight—and therapods are not. A third problem is that ...every therapod dinosaur has serrated teeth, but no bird has serrated teeth.[10]

To clarify it we may *paraphrase* it, listing each premiss, restating the conclusion, and simplifying the language for the sale of clarity:

1. Fossils of bird-like therapod dinosaurs originated long after the fossilized remains of the first bird.
2. The ancestors of birds must have been suited for flight, but therapod dinosaurs were not so suited.
3. Every therapod dinosaur has serrated teeth, but no bird has serrated teeth.
   Therefore therapod dinosaurs could not have evolved into modern birds.

Paraphrasing an argument often assists our understanding of it because in doing so we must bring to the surface what is assumed in the argument but is not fully or explicitly stated. The great mathematician G. H. Hardy argued thus:

> Archimedes will be remembered when Aeschylus is forgotten, because languages die and mathematical ideas do not.[11]

To paraphrase this argument fully we would spell out what it takes for granted:

1. Languages die.
2. The great plays of Aeschylus are in a language.
3. So the work of Aeschylus will eventually die.

---

[10]Adapted from Alan Feduccia, *The Origin and Evolution of Birds* (New Haven, CT: Yale University Press, 1996).

[11]G. H. Hardy, *A Mathematician's Apology* (Cambridge University Press, 1940).

4. Mathematical ideas do not die.

5. The great work of Archimedes was with mathematical ideas.

6. So the work of Archimedes will not die.

   Therefore Archimedes will be remembered when Aeschylus is forgotten.

The paraphrase enables us to see that several arguments, with disputable premisses, have been compressed into Hardy's one short sentence.

B. Diagramming

Sometimes it is useful to *diagram* an argument to exhibit its structure. To do this we number each proposition in the order in which it appears, circling the numbers. We then exhibit the logical relations of premisses and conclusion using arrows between the numbers. This avoids the need to restate the premisses. Consider this argument:

> ① Contrary to what many people think, a positive test for HIV is not necessarily a death sentence. For one thing, ② the time from the development of antibodies to clinical symptoms averages nearly ten years. For another, ③ many reports are now suggesting that a significant number of people who test positive may never develop clinical AIDS.[12]

Without restating the propositions of this argument we can use the circled numbers to represent the propositions and diagram the argument as follows:

   If an argument is straightforward, we may not need a diagram to understand it fully. But arguments often are not straightforward, and the diagramming technique[13] is helpful because it displays the structure of the argument *visually* in space. We place the conclusion in the space below the premisses, while the premisses of a given argument will all appear on the same horizontal level.

   Unlike a paraphrase, a diagram can readily exhibit the *way* in which the premisses support the conclusion. In the argument above, for example, each of the premisses, (2) and (3), supports the conclusion (1)—that a positive test for HIV is not necessarily a death sentence—*independently*. That is, each premiss by itself supplies some reason for accepting that conclusion and gives such sup-

---

[12]R. S. Root-Bernstein, "Misleading Reliability," *The Sciences,* March 1990.

[13]The technique was first developed and perfected decades ago by several distinguished logicians: Monroe C. Beardsley, in *Practical Logic* (Prentice-Hall, 1950); Stephen N. Thomas, in *Practical Reasoning in Natural Language* (Prentice-Hall, 1973); and Michael Scriven, in *Reasoning* (McGraw-Hill, 1976). We follow their lead.

port even in the absence of the other premiss. This separate support is visually exhibited in the diagram.

But in some arguments the premisses serve their purpose only when combined. For example:

> ① If an action promotes the best interests of everyone concerned and violates no one's rights, then that action is morally acceptable. ② In at least some cases, active euthanasia promotes the best interests of everyone concerned, and violates no one's rights. Therefore ③ in at least some cases active euthanasia is morally acceptable.[14]

An accurate diagram of this argument will exhibit the fact that its premisses work only because they are *joined together*, thus:

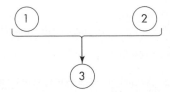

We bracket the premisses here because in this case neither premiss supports the conclusion independently. If the principle expressed in the first premiss were true, but there were no case in which active euthanasia promoted everyone's best interests, the conclusion would be given no support at all. And if there were cases in which active euthanasia did promote everyone's best interests, but the principle expressed in the first premiss were not true, the conclusion would remain without support.

Diagrams are particularly useful when the argument has a complicated structure. What cannot be easily said can sometimes be easily shown. Consider the following argument:

> ①Desert mountaintops make good sites for astronomy. ② Being high, they sit above a portion of the atmosphere, enabling a star's light to reach a telescope without having to swim through the entire depths of the atmosphere. ③ Being dry, the desert is also relatively cloud-free. ④ The merest veil of haze or cloud can render a sky useless for many astronomical measures.[15]

In this argument proposition ① is plainly the conclusion, and the other three provide support for it—but they give that support in different ways. The single statement ② by itself supports the claim that mountaintops are good sites for telescopes. But statements ③ and ④ must work together to support the claim that *desert* mountaintops are good sites for telescopes. A diagram exhibits this relationship neatly:

---

[14]James Rachels, cited in T. A. Mappes and J. S. Zembaty, eds., *Social Ethics*, 3d ed. (McGraw-Hill, 1987).

[15]Blanchard Hiatt, University of Michigan Research News, September 1979.

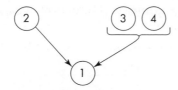

But some kinds of complications are revealed more efficiently using paraphrase. For example, when an argument has a premiss that is not explicitly stated, a paraphrase allows us to simply add the tacit premiss to the list. A diagram would require us both to formulate the tacit premiss and to represent it visually in some form—usually a broken circle—that indicates that it has been added to the original passage. Thus the argument

> [I]t is only when it is believed that I could have acted otherwise that I am held to be morally responsible for what I have done. For a man is not thought to be morally responsible for an action that it was not in his power to avoid.[16]

may be more readily clarified by paraphrase in which its tacit premiss is made explicit, thus:

1. A man is not thought to be morally responsible for an action that it was not in his power to avoid.
2. Only when I could have acted otherwise was the action one that was in my power to avoid.

   Therefore only when it is believed that I could have acted otherwise am I held responsible for what I have done.

C. Interwoven Arguments

When a passage contains two or more arguments and a number of propositions whose relations are not obvious, a diagram may prove particularly useful. Here, for example, is a passage from one of the letters of Karl Marx to Friedrich Engels:

> ① To hasten the social revolution in England is the most important object of the International Workingman's Association. ② The sole means of hastening it is to make Ireland independent. Hence ③ the task of the "International" is everywhere to put the conflict between England and Ireland in the foreground, and ④ everywhere to side openly with Ireland.[17]

The number of arguments in a passage is generally agreed to be determined by the number of conclusions. Thus, because there are two conclusions in this

---

[16]A. J. Ayer, "Freedom and Necessity," *Polemic*, no. 5.
[17]Karl Marx, Letter #141, 9 April 1870, *Karl Marx and Friedrich Engels Correspondence, 1846–1895* (International Publishers, 1936).

passage, it contains two arguments. Here, however, both conclusions are inferred from the same two premises. A diagram exhibits this structure nicely:

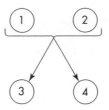

In some passages two conclusions, and hence two arguments, have a single stated premiss. Here is an example:

> Older women have less freedom to fight sexual harassment at their jobs or to leave a battering husband, because age discrimination means they won't easily find other ways of supporting themselves.[18]

The single premiss here is that older women cannot easily find alternative ways of supporting themselves. That premiss supports two conclusions: that older women have less freedom to fight sexual harassment at their jobs, and that older married women have less freedom to leave a battering husband. Ordinarily, by a "single argument" we mean an argument with a single conclusion, regardless of how many premisses are adduced in its support.

When there are two or more premisses in an argument, or two or more arguments in a passage, the order of appearance of premisses and conclusions may need to be sorted out. The conclusion may be stated last, or first, or it may be sandwiched between the premisses offered in its support, as in the following passage:

> The real and original source of inspiration for the Muslim thinkers was the Quran and the sayings of the Holy Prophet. It is therefore clear that the Muslim philosophy was not a carbon copy of Greek thought, as it concerned itself primarily and specifically with those problems which originated from and had relevance to Muslims.[19]

Here the conclusion, that "Muslim philosophy was not a carbon copy of Greek thought," appears after the first premiss of the argument and before the second.

The same proposition that serves as a conclusion in one argument may serve as premiss in a different argument, just as the same person may be a commander in one context and a subordinate in another. This is well illustrated by a passage from the work of Thomas Aquinas. He argues

> Human law is framed for the multitude of human beings.
> The majority of human beings are not perfect in virtue.
> Therefore human laws do not forbid all vices.[20]

---

[18]Boston Women's Health Book Collective, *Our Bodies, Our Selves* (Simon and Schuster, 1984).
[19]C. A. Quadir, *Philosophy and Science in the Islamic World* (London: Croom Helm, 1988).
[20]Thomas Aquinas, *Summa Theologiae,* I, Question 96, Article 2, circa 1265.

The conclusion of this argument is used immediately thereafter as a premiss in another, quite different argument:

> Vicious acts are contrary to acts of virtue.
> But human law does not prohibit all vices....
> Therefore neither does it prescribe all acts of virtue.[21]

A cascade of arguments in which the conclusion of one serves as the premiss of another may be so compressed that a full paraphrase can be very helpful. Consider the following set of arguments:

> Because ① the greatest mitochondrial variations occurred in African people, scientists concluded that ② they had the longest evolutionary history, indicating ③ a probable African origin for modern humans.[22]

We might diagram the passage thus:

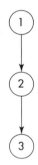

A paraphrase of the same cascade, though clumsier, is more complete:

1.   The more mitochondrial variation in a people the longer its evolutionary history;
2.   The greatest mitochondrial variations occurred in African people.
       Therefore African people have had the longest evolutionary history.

1.   African people have had the longest evolutionary history.
2.   Modern humans probably originated where people have had the longest evolutionary history.
       Therefore modern humans probably originated in Africa.

Such combinations make it evident that a proposition taken in isolation is neither a premiss nor a conclusion. It is a premiss where it occurs as an assumption in an argument. It is a conclusion where it is claimed to follow from other propositions assumed in an argument. In other words, "premiss" and "conclusion" are *relative* terms.

---

[21]*Ibid*, Article 3.
[22]From *Science*, 26 May 1995.

Multiple arguments may appear in forms other than cascades; they may be interwoven in unusual patterns that require thoughtful analysis. The diagramming technique is particularly well suited to such cases. For example, in John Locke's influential *Second Treatise of Government*, two arguments are combined in the following passage:

> It is not necessary—no, nor so much as convenient—that the legislative should be always in being; but absolutely necessary that the executive power should, because there is not always need of new laws to be made, but always need of execution of the laws that are made.

The component propositions may be numbered thus: ①It is not necessary or convenient that the legislative [branch of government] should be always in being; ②it is absolutely necessary that the executive power should be always in being; ③there is not always need of new laws to be made; ④there is always need of execution of the laws that are made. The diagram for this passage is:

which shows that the conclusion of the second argument is stated between the conclusion and premiss of the first argument, and that the premiss of the first argument is stated between the conclusion and premiss of the second argument. The diagram also shows that both conclusions are stated before their premisses.

The same diagram exhibits the logical structure of two related arguments of the Roman philosopher Seneca in support of the deterrence theory of punishment:

> ① No one punishes because a sin has been committed, ② but in order that a sin will not be committed. [For] ③ what has passed cannot be recalled, but ④ what lies in the future may be prevented.

That "we do not punish because a sin has been committed" is the conclusion of one argument; its premiss is that "what has passed cannot be recalled." That "we do punish in order that a sin will not be committed" is the conclusion of a second argument, whose premiss is that "what lies in the future may be prevented."

In sum, diagramming and paraphrasing are useful tools with which we can analyze arguments so as to understand more fully the relations of premisses to conclusions.

Exercises

The following passages—all appearing recently in the *New York Times*—concern important matters of public policy. Analyze the arguments they contain, paraphrasing propositions where that is needed, and diagramming the argument where you find that helpful.

Example:

1. Genes and proteins are discovered, not invented. Inventions are patentable, discoveries are not. Thus, protein patents are intrinsically flawed.

   > —Daniel Alroy, "Invention vs. Discovery,"
   > *New York Times,* 29 March 2000

Solution:

PREMISES: Proteins are discovered, not invented.
    Discoveries are not patentable, although inventions are.
CONCLUSION: Protein patents are intrinsically flawed.

2. Why decry the wealth gap? First, inequality is correlated with political instability. Second, inequality is correlated with violent crime. Third, economic inequality is correlated with reduced life expectancy. A fourth reason? Simple justice. There is no moral justification for chief executives being paid hundreds of times more than ordinary employees.

   > —Richard Hutchinsons, "When the Rich Get Even Richer,"
   > *New York Times,* 26 January 2000

3. Wall Street, where prices were sinking, saw the recent employment numbers as fresh evidence of a rising inflation rate, if not right away, then by early spring. The concern is that a shortage of workers forces employers to pay higher wages, and then to raise prices to cover the added labor costs.

   > —Louis Uchitelle, "387,000 New Jobs"
   > *New York Times,* 5 February 2000

4. Married people are healthier and more economically stable than single people, and children of married people do better on a variety of indicators. Marriage is thus a socially responsible act. There ought to be some way of spreading the principle of support for marriage throughout the tax code.

   > —Anya Bernstein, "Marriage, Fairness and Taxes,"
   > *New York Times,* 15 February 2000

*5. If you marry without love, it does not mean you will not later come to love the person you marry. And if you marry the person you love, it does not mean that you will always love that person or have a successful marriage. The divorce rate is very low in many countries that have prearranged marriage. The divorce rate is very high in countries where people base their marriage decisions on love.

   > —Alex Hammoud, "I Take This Man, For Richer Only,"
   > *New York Times,* 18 February 2000

6. Our entire tax system depends upon the vast majority of taxpayers who attempt to pay the taxes they owe having confidence that they're being treated fairly and that their competitors and neighbors are also paying what is due. If the public concludes that the IRS cannot meet these basic expectations, the risk to the tax system will become very high, and the effects very difficult to reverse.

    —David Cay Johnston, "Adding Auditors to Help IRS Catch Tax Cheaters," *New York Times,* 13 February 2000

7. Since 1976, states (in the United States) have executed 612 people, and released 81 from death row who were found to be innocent. Is there any reason to believe that the criminal justice system is more accurate in *non*-capital cases? If the criminal justice system makes half the mistakes in non-capital cases that it makes in capital cases, thousands of innocent people live in our prisons.

    —Philip Moustakis, "Missing: A Death Penalty Debate," *New York Times,* 23 February 2000

8. The divergent paths taken by New York and Texas in the 1990s illustrate the futility of over-reliance on prisons as a cure for crime. Texas added more people to prisons in the 1990s (98,081) than New York's entire prison population (73,233). If prisons are a cure for crime, Texas should have mightily outperformed New York from a crime-control standpoint. But from 1990 to 1998 the decline in New York's crime rate exceeded the decline in Texas's crime rate by 26%.

    —Vincent Schiraldi, "Prisons and Crime," *New York Times,* 6 October 2000

9. In most presidential elections in the United States, more than half the states are ignored; voters who don't live in so-called swing states are in effect bystanders in these quadrennial events. An Amendment to the U.S. Constitution should replace the archaic electoral vote system with a direct vote. Only in this manner will citizens in all 50 states be able to take part fully in selecting our nation's leaders.

    —Lawrence R. Foster, "End the Electoral College," *New York Times,* 27 September 2000

*10. Petitioners' reasoning would allow Congress to regulate any crime so long as the nationwide, aggregated impact of that crime has substantial effects on employment, production, transit, or consumption. If Congress may regulate gender-motivated violence [on these grounds], it would be able to regulate murder or any other type of violence since gender-motivated violence, as a subset of all violent crime, is certain to have lesser economic impacts than the larger class of which it is a part.

    —Chief Justice William Rehnquist, U.S. Supreme Court, *U.S. v. Morrison,* Decided 15 May 2000

*11. For discussion:

In a recent murder trial in Virginia, the judge instructed the jury that: "you may fix the punishment of the defendant at death" if the state proved beyond a reasonable doubt at least one of two aggravating circumstances: that the defendant would continue to be a serious threat to society, or that the crime was "outrageously or wantonly vile, horrible or inhuman." The jury, deliberating the sentence after finding the accused guilty, returned to the judge with this question: If we believe that the state has satisfied one of these alternatives, "then is it our duty as a jury to issue the death penalty?" The judge, in response, simply told them to re-read the instructions already given on that point. The jury returned two hours later, some of its members in tears, with a death sentence for the defendant.

This death sentence was appealed, and the case was ultimately reviewed by the U.S. Supreme Court [*Weeks v. Angelone*, No. 99-5746, decided 19 January 2000]. The issue that Court confronted was whether, in the circumstances of this case, the death sentence should be nullified on the ground that the jury had been confused about the instructions they had been given. What arguments would you construct in support of either side of this controversy?

1.5 RECOGNIZING ARGUMENTS

A. Conclusion- and Premiss-Indicators

As we have seen, the order in which propositions appear in an argumentative passage cannot be relied upon to identify the conclusion or the premisses. What then may we use to make this identification? Certain words or phrases, called "conclusion-indicators," are helpful because they typically serve to introduce the conclusion of an argument. Here is a partial list of *conclusion-indicators:*

therefore	for these reasons
hence	it follows that
thus	we may infer
so	I conclude that
accordingly	which shows that
in consequence	which means that
consequently	which entails that
proves that	which implies that
as a result	which allows us to infer that
for this reason	which points to the conclusion that

Other words or phrases typically serve to mark the premisses of an argument and hence are called premiss-indicators. Usually, but not always, what follows any one of these will be the premiss of some argument. Here is a partial list of *premiss-indicators:*

since	as indicated by
because	the reason is that
for	for the reason that
as	may be inferred from
follows from	may be derived from
as shown by	may be deduced from
inasmuch as	in view of the fact that

B.   Arguments in Context

The words and phrases listed above may help us recognize the presence of an argument or identify its premisses or conclusion. But it is not necessary for these terms to appear; the fact that an argument has been presented may be indicated by the setting or by the meaning of the passage. For example, one author extends her sharp criticism of smoking with the following statements:

> Whether or not to smoke is a conscious decision, made in the light of an abundance of information on the lethal effects of tobacco. Surely those who choose unwisely should bear the cost of any resulting ill health.[23]

No premiss or conclusion indicators are used here, yet the argument is unmistakable. Similarly, the following passage contains an argument that is immediately recognizable from the sense of the propositions themselves:

> The deterrence argument has been refuted in recent years. Eighteen of the twenty states with the highest murder rates have and use the death penalty. Of the biggest cities with the highest murder rate, seventeen are in death penalty jurisdictions. Texas has executed more people during the last decade than any other state, but still has three cities with murder rates among the top twenty-five. Over nearly two decades two neighboring states, Michigan, with no death penalty, and Indiana, with a death penalty, have had indistinguishable homicide rates.[24]

The argumentative functions of such passages are exhibited by their contexts and their meanings—just as, if I said that I am taking a lobster home for dinner, you would have little doubt that I intended to eat it, not feed it.

Another argument without conclusion- or premiss-indicators appears in a recent defense of proportional representation:

> The single-member-district system of elections is seen to have a number of serious drawbacks. It routinely denies representation to large numbers of voters, produces legislatures that fail to reflect accurately the views of the public, discriminates against third parties, and discourages voter turnout.[25]

---

[23]Lois Taylor, "Is Smoking About Choice?," *New York Times,* 5 September 2000.

[24]D. C. Leven, "Deterrence Fails," *New York Times,* 3 March 1995.

[25]D. J. Amy, "Elections in Which Every Vote Counts," *The Chronicle of Higher Education,* 12 January 1996.

Although this passage might be regarded as *stating* a widely understood truth and then *illustrating* it with various consequences of the single-member-district system, it can be equally well understood as an argument whose conclusion is stated first and followed by the premises offered in its support.

A somewhat more intricate example of an argument in which neither conclusion-indicators nor premiss-indicators appear is the following passage from a Supreme Court opinion concerning the desegregation of public schools:

> That there was racial imbalance in student attendance was not tantamount to a showing that the school district was in noncompliance with …its duties under the law. Racial balance is not to be achieved for its own sake. It is to be pursued when racial imbalance has been caused by a constitutional violation. Once the racial imbalance due to the *de jure* violation has been remedied, the school district is under no duty to remedy imbalance that is caused by demographic factors.[26]

The first sentence of this passage presents the conclusion of its argument, which may be paraphrased as "the presence of racial imbalance does not show that the school district violated the law." How do we know this? Context is crucial here: the sentences that follow the first one offer reasons for what has gone before. We see that it is the conduct of "the school district," referred to in the first sentence, that is at issue; we discern that the sentences following that one express more general propositions that bear upon the conduct of the school district. The words chosen also give clues; although the phrase "was not tantamount to a showing" is not a conclusion-indicator, it does convey the suggestion that the first sentence is the logical endpoint of the passage.

Passages containing arguments often contain additional material that serves neither as premiss nor conclusion. Sometimes that material supplies background information that enables the reader (or hearer) to understand what the argument is about. In the following passage an argument appears in the concluding sentence, but it would not be intelligible if we had not grasped the sentence before it:

> As the government spends increasingly less on student financial aid, many leading colleges and universities are using a greater percentage of tuition revenues for scholarships. Just as income tax breaks are given for charitable contributions, this portion of tuition should be tax deductible.[27]

Strictly speaking the first sentence in this passage is not part of the argument, but without it we would not understand that "this portion of tuition" is the portion used for scholarships. With that understanding, we can paraphrase the argument as follows:

1.　Charitable contributions to the needy are tax-deductible.
2.　Substantial portions of tuition revenue are used by colleges as a charitable contribution to scholarships for needy students.

---

[26]*Freeman v. Pitts,* 503 U.S. 467, 1992.

[27]D. Goldin, "Some College Costs Should Be Tax Deductible," *New York Times,* 18 April 1992.

Therefore, that portion of tuition used for scholarships to needy students should be tax-deductible.

Understanding cross-references within the context may thus be essential for understanding the argument itself. An argument by the philosopher Arthur Schopenhauer in defense of suicide illustrates this reliance upon cross-reference:

> If the criminal law forbids suicide, that is not an argument valid in the Church; and besides, the prohibition is ridiculous; for what penalty can frighten a person who is not afraid of death itself?[28]

The material before the first semicolon in this passage is neither premiss nor conclusion—but without it we would not know that in the conclusion of the subsequent argument ("the prohibition is ridiculous"), the "prohibition" referred to is the prohibition of suicide by the criminal law.

C.   Premisses Not in Declarative Form

In the preceding illustration, the premiss of the argument appears in the form of a question: "What penalty can frighten a person who is not afraid of death itself?" But as we saw in section 1.2, questions assert nothing; they do not express propositions. How then can a question function as a premiss? It can do so when the question is *rhetorical*. That is, a question may suggest or assume a premiss when the question is one whose answer the author believes to be obvious or inescapable. In our illustration, Schopenhauer thought the obvious answer to his question was "none." Thus, though framed in the form of a question, the premiss of Schopenhauer's argument was the implied proposition that "there is no penalty that can frighten a person who is not afraid of death itself."

Arguments in which one of the premisses is a question whose answer is assumed to be evident are very common; they also can be rhetorically effective, as in the following argument of Socrates:

> If there is no one who desires to be miserable, there is no one, Meno, who desires evil; for what is misery but the desire and possession of evil?[29]

Using questions in this way is risky, however. Strictly speaking, the question can be neither true nor false. If the answer that is assumed to be obvious or inescapable is *not* so, the argument is defective, and its defect may be obscured by the question. Was Socrates correct in assuming that misery *is* the desire and possession of evil? The answer to his question is not obvious.

The conclusions of arguments that depend on rhetorical questions are suspect. To avoid responsibility for the forthright assertion of their premisses, authors sometimes ask a question whose answer is supposed to be obvious when that assumed answer actually is dubious or even false.

---

[28] A. Schopenhauer, "On Suicide," 1851.
[29] Plato, *Meno*, 78a.

The use of a genuinely rhetorical question as a premiss can be a very clever technique, however. By suggesting the desired answer and leading readers to provide that answer for themselves, one can augment the persuasiveness of the argument. Consider the use of rhetorical questions in the following two examples. In the New Testament we find this passage:

> If a man say, I love God, and hateth his brother, he is a liar: for he that loves not his brother whom he hath seen, how can he love God whom he hath not seen?[30]

And in a recent critique of the defense of euthanasia, the following argument appears:

> If a right to euthanasia is grounded in self-determination, it cannot reasonably be limited to the terminally ill. If people have a right to die, why must they wait until they are actually dying before they are permitted to exercise that right?[31]

In both examples the supposed answers (that "one who does not love his brother cannot love God," and that "people need not wait until they are actually dying before they are permitted to exercise their right") are assumed to be perfectly evident. These answers serve as premisses that support the conclusions intended: "that one who loves God cannot hate his brother," and that "if there is a right to euthanasia grounded in self-determination it cannot be limited to the terminally ill."

Sometimes the conclusion of an argument takes the form of an imperative, or command. After reasons have been offered to persuade us to perform a given action, we are *directed* to act thus-and-so. In Proverbs, for example, we read:

> Wisdom is the principal thing; therefore get wisdom.

And in *Hamlet*, Polonius gives famous advice to his son, Laertes:

> Neither a borrower nor a lender be;
> For loan oft loses both itself and friend,
> And borrowing dulls the edge of husbandry.[32]

Since a command, like a question, cannot express a proposition, it cannot be (strictly speaking) the conclusion of an argument. But for the sake of simplicity it is useful to regard commands, in these contexts, as no different from propositions in which hearers (or readers) are told that they *should,* or *ought to,* act in the manner specified in the command. The conclusions in the two arguments above may then be rephrased as: "Getting wisdom is what you should do," and "You ought to be neither a lender nor a borrower."

---

[30]1 John 4:20.
[31]Ramsey Colloquium of the Institute on Religion and Public Life, "Always to Care, Never to Kill," *Wall Street Journal*, 17 November 1991.
[32]William Shakespeare, *Hamlet*, act 1, scene 3.

Almost everyone will agree that assertions of this kind can be true or false. Exactly what difference, if any, there is, between a command to do something and a statement that it should be done is a difficult problem that need not be explored here. By ignoring that difference (if there really is one) we are able to deal uniformly with arguments whose conclusions are expressed in this form.

Our aim is to understand arguments more fully. Reformulation can help by clarifying the roles of the argument's constituent propositions while depending as little as possible on context. We want to focus on the propositions themselves; we want to know whether they are true or false, what they imply, whether they are implied by other propositions, and whether they are serving as premiss or as conclusion in some argument. We seek to grasp the substance of the propositions relied on, whatever their grammatical form.

Some reformulations are merely grammatical. Arguments are built of propositions, but the words that express a proposition (and hence a premiss) may take the form of a phrase, rather than a declarative sentence. This is well illustrated in a passage discussing the possibility of extraterrestrial life.

> Is there life beyond the earth? The jury is still out. But with planets aplenty; with creatures that can live without the energy of a nearby star; with abundant cosmic sources of cosmic hydrogen and oxygen to make water; with several natural ways for planets to generate internal heat; with the possibility that life could originate in undersea volcanoes and propagate varieties hardy enough to spread their seeds to other worlds; and with rocky meteorites that could serve as vehicles for interplanetary exchange, the idea that life has evolved elsewhere in the universe seems less daunting than it did just a few years ago.[33]

The conclusion here—that life beyond our earth is a notion at least more acceptable now than it used to be—is supported by six distinct premises, each calling attention to recently discovered facts or possibilities, and each rendering extraterrestrial life somewhat more plausible. When these premises are rephrased as declarative sentences, *e.g.,:* (1) There are plenty of other planets; (2) there are creatures that can live without the energy of a nearby star; and so on, the argument expressed in this passage becomes evident.

D. Unstated Propositions

The analysis of an argument may become yet more complicated when one or more of its constituent propositions is not stated but is assumed to be understood. An example arose at the U.S. Supreme Court in April 2000, involving the famous *Miranda* rules (which prohibit confessions from being admitted at trial unless a suspect in custody has been first advised that he has the right to remain silent, and the right to have an attorney). Defenders of the *Miranda* rules argued thus:

> If the *Miranda* decision is reversed, police will no longer be compelled to give those warnings [of the right to remain silent, etc.]; and if they aren't compelled to give them,

---

[33]Peter G. Brown, "Stardust," *The Sciences,* August 1988.

> they won't give them. But because police interrogations take place out of public view, the integrity of such interrogations can be safeguarded only if those *Miranda* warnings are invariably given.[34]

The conclusion of their argument—that those warnings must always be given and that the Supreme Court should *not* reverse the *Miranda* decision—did not need to be stated in that context.

In a very different context, the distinguished novelist Anais Nin described one of her fictional characters by saying that "The dreamer rejects the ordinary. Jay invited the ordinary."[35] We infer what the author sought to convey—"Jay was no dreamer"—even though it is not stated.

One of the premisses of an argument may be left unstated because the arguer supposes that it is common knowledge or that it will be readily granted for other reasons. In Shakespeare's *Julius Caesar,* while Marc Antony is delivering his famous speech about Caesar's ambition, one of the listening citizens remarks about Caesar:

> He would not take the crown;
> Therefore 'tis certain he was not ambitious.[36]

This is an argument, but part of it is missing; plainly it relies upon the plausible, but unstated, premiss that "one who would not accept the crown must not have been ambitious." Arguments in everyday discourse often rely on some proposition that is not stated. Such arguments are called **enthymemes.**[37]

Sometimes it may not be obvious just how one would formulate the proposition on which the speaker relies, even though, once formulated, it is readily accepted. In a recent account of the historical controversy over slavery in America and the role of moral argument in that controversy, the author writes:

> If one doesn't believe that moral arguments make any difference, then one doesn't believe in republican government.[38]

In this enthymeme the unstated premise is the claim that "believing in republican government entails that one does believe that moral arguments make a difference"—a claim that most of us would grant.

On the other hand, the unstated proposition on which an enthymeme relies may not be obvious, but disputable—and the absence of an explicit statement of that proposition may serve to shield it from attack. For example, medical

---

[34]The case before the Court was *Dickerson v. United States* (No. 99-5525). The central issue (at oral argument on 19 April 2000) was whether Congress has the authority to overturn *Miranda* by statute.

[35]Anais Nin, *Cities of the Interior* (Denver, CO: Swallow Press, 1959).

[36]William Shakespeare, *Julius Caesar*, act 3, scene 2.

[37]Discussed from another perspective in section 7.5, below.

[38]William L. Miller, *Arguing About Slavery: The Great Battle in the United States Congress* (Knopf, 1995).

research using embryonic stem cells (the undifferentiated cells found in the human embryo that can develop into other types of cells and most types of tissue) is highly controversial. One U.S. senator used the following enthymeme in attacking legislation that would permit government financing of such research:

> This research [involving the use of embryonic stem cells] is illegal, for this reason: The deliberate killing of a human embryo is an essential component of the contemplated research.[39]

The stated premiss is true; if the embryo were not destroyed, research of that kind would be impossible. But the conclusion that such research is illegal depends on the unstated premiss that the killing of a human embryo is illegal—a claim that is very much in dispute.

Enthymemes depend heavily on context, and often on the listener's knowing that some stated proposition is false. When the aim is to emphasize the falsity of some *other* proposition, it is not uncommon for the speaker to construct a hypothetical proposition of which the target component is the antecedent (the "if" component) and a proposition generally known to be false is the consequent (the "then" component). Thus one of the great Bavarian organ-builders of the 18th century, Karl Josef Reipp, was known to express pride in his organs by saying that "If better organs can be found in Europe, then my name is Jack." Since everyone understands intuitively that in a true hypothetical statement the antecedent cannot be true if the consequent is false, the assertion of that hypothetical proposition serves as an enthymematic argument that ridicules the antecedent, the supposition that better organs can be found in Europe. Both the conclusion (No better organs can be found in Europe) and one of the premisses (My name is not Jack) are left unstated.[40]

Exercises

I. In each of the following passages, identify the premisses and conclusions of any argument it contains. Paraphrase arguments, or diagram them, as you deem necessary for thorough analysis.

  *1. The Supreme Court will only uphold federal racial set-asides in light of convincing evidence of past discrimination by the federal government itself; but, for almost 20 years, the federal government has been discriminating in favor of minority contractors rather than against them. Therefore, federal minority preferences in procurement are doomed.

  —Jeffrey Rosen, cited by Ian Ayres, "Remedying Past Discrimination," *Los Angeles Times*, 26 April 1998

---

[39]Senator Sam Brownback, of Kansas, at a Senate hearing in April 2000, on a bill designed to permit such funding, introduced by his Republican colleague Senator Arlen Specter of Pennsylvania.

[40]And Bruno Bettelheim, a distinguished psychiatrist and survivor of the death camps at Dachau and Buchenwald, wrote: "If all men are good, then there never was an Auschwitz."

2. Science studies the natural. That is all we ask of it. If there is any fact or truth beyond nature, science knows nothing about it and has nothing to say on the subject.

    > —Richard W. Metz, "Don't Throw Crackpottery at Haunted Houses," *New York Times*, 1 August 1996

3. In the *Crito*, Plato presents the position of the Athenian community, personified as "the Laws," speaking to Socrates or to any citizen of the community who may contemplate deliberate disobedience to the state:

    > He who disobeys us is, as we maintain, thrice wrong; first, because in disobeying us he is disobeying his parents; secondly, because we are the authors of his education; thirdly, because he has made an agreement with us that he will duly obey our commands.

4. The black-power movement's fundamental problem was that it focused essentially on *power*. We found out that we cannot organize and sustain the organization with just power talk, because we don't have the principles around which to organize. We must now combine the political and the moral.

    > —Maulana Ron Karenga, "After the Revolution," *The New Yorker*, 29 April 1996

*5. The *New York Times* reported, on 30 May 2000, that some scientists were seeking a way to signal back in time. A critical reader responded thus:

    > It seems obvious to me that scientists in the future will never find a way to signal back in time. If they were to do so, wouldn't we have heard from them by now?

    > —Ken Grunstra, "Reaching Back in Time," *New York Times*, 6 June 2000

6. There could be no such thing as a first event, looked at from a strictly physical perspective. If things had to begin . . . (a big bang?) the question is, "Why only then, why not earlier?" The answer has to be: "Conditions were not yet right." What was it for "conditions to become right"? Something had to happen first (*i.e.*, before the big bang). Thus there is always an event presupposed by any posited "first event." The big bang, even if it is science and not mere "literary conception," is only an interesting event.

    > —Lawrence Dewan, "Big Bang, If There Was One, Was No Big Deal," *New York Times*, 7 May 1990

7. I reject the argument . . . that the white journalist featured in your series on race should not have written about black drug addicts in Baltimore because it was not "his story to tell." This assumes that only black people can or should write about black people, and

implies that there exists a single, unanimous perspective that all black Americans hold.

—Ian Reifowitz, in a letter to the
New York Times, 19 June 2000

8.   There can be no resolution of the conflict between the autonomy of the individual and the putative authority of the state. Insofar as a man fulfills his obligation to make himself the author of his decisions, he will . . . deny that he has a duty to obey the laws of the state *simply because they are the laws.* In that sense . . . anarchism is the only political doctrine consistent with the virtue of autonomy.

—Robert Paul Wolff, *In Defense of Anarchism,* 1970

9.   Space contains such a huge supply of atoms that all eternity would not be enough time to count them and count the forces which drive the atoms into various places just as they have been driven together in this world. So we must realize that there are other worlds in other parts of the universe with races of different men and different animals.

—Lucretius, *De Rerum Natura,* (1st century B.C.)

*10.   The Internal Revenue Code is inordinately complex, imposes an enormous burden on taxpayers, and thus undermines compliance with the law. Repeated efforts to simplify and reform the law have failed. We have reached the point where further patchwork will only compound the problem. It is time to repeal the Internal Revenue Code and start over.

—Shirley D. Peterson, "Death to the Tax Code,"
New York Times, 29 July 1995

II.   Each of the following passages can be interpreted as containing two arguments, each of which may have more than one premiss. Analyze these arguments, paraphrasing premisses and conclusions where you find that helpful, and exhibit the diagram for each passage.

Example:

1.   In a recent attack upon the evils of suburban sprawl, the authors argue as follows:

The dominant characteristic of sprawl is that each component of a community—housing, shopping centers, office parks, and civic institutions—is segregated, physically separated from the others, causing the residents of suburbia to spend an inordinate amount of time and money moving from one place to the next. And since nearly everyone drives alone, even a sparsely populated area can generate the traffic of a much larger traditional town.[41]

---

[41]Paraphrased in part from Andres Duany, Elizabeth Plater-Zyberk, and Jeff Speck, *Suburban Nation: The Rise of Sprawl and the Decline of the American Dream,* (North Point Press, 2000).

Solution:

① The dominant characteristic of sprawl is that each component of a community—housing, shopping centers, office parks, and civic institutions—is segregated, physically separated from the others, caus- ing ② the residents of suburbia to spend an inordinate amount of time and money moving from one place to the next. And since ③ nearly everyone drives alone, ④ even a sparsely populated area can generate the traffic of a much larger traditional town.

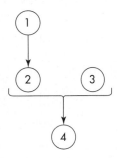

2. The biggest advantage of compulsory voting is that, by enhancing voter turnout, it equalizes participation and removes much of the bias against less-privileged citizens. It also has two other signifi- cant advantages. One is that mandatory voting can reduce the role of money in politics, since it does away with the need for candi- dates and political parties to spend large sums on getting voters to the polls. Second, it reduces the incentives for negative advertising.

   —Arend Lijphart, "Compulsory Voting Is the Best
   Way to Keep Democracy Strong," *The Chronicle
   of Higher Education,* 18 October 1996

3. Life is not simply a "good" that we possess. Our life is our person. To treat our life as a "thing" that we can authorize another to terminate is profoundly dehumanizing. Euthanasia, even when requested by the competent, attacks the distinctiveness and limita- tions of being human.

   —Ramsey Colloquium of the Institute on Religion
   and Public Life, "Always to Care, Never to Kill,"
   Wall Street Journal, 27 November 1991

4. All of the positive contributions that sports make to higher education are threatened by disturbing patterns of abuse, particularly in some big-time programs. These patterns are grounded in institutional indif- ference, presidential neglect, and the growing commercialization of sport combined with the urge to win at all costs. The sad truth is that on too many campuses big-time revenue sports are out of control.

   —*Keeping Faith with the Student-Athlete: A New Model for
   Intercollegiate Athletics,* Knight Foundation Commission
   on Intercollegiate Athletics, Charlotte, NC, March 1991

*5.   The distinguished economist, J. K. Galbraith, long fought to expose and improve a society exhibiting "private opulence and public squalor." In his classic work, *The Affluent Society* (1960), he argued as follows:

> Vacuum cleaners to insure clean houses are praiseworthy and essential in our standard of living. Street cleaners to insure clean streets are an unfortunate expense. Partly as a result, our houses are generally clean and our streets generally filthy."

—cited by John Cassidy in "Height of Eloquence,"
The New Yorker, 30 November 1998

6.   Back in 1884, Democratic nominee Grover Cleveland was confronted by the charge that he had fathered an out-of-wedlock child. While Republicans chanted, "Ma, Ma, where's my Pa," Cleveland conceded that he had been supporting the child. No excuses, no evasions. One of his supporters—one of the first spin doctors—gave this advice to voters:

> Since Grover Cleveland has a terrific public record, but a blemished private life, and since his opponent, James G. Blaine, has a storybook private life but a checkered public record, why not put both where they perform best—return Blaine to private life, keep Cleveland in public life.

7.   As force is always on the side of the governed, the governors have nothing to support them but opinion. It is therefore on opinion only that government is founded.

—David Hume, cited in Keith Thomas, "Just Say Yes,"
The New York Review of Books, 24 November 1988

8.   Cognitive function depends on neuro-chemical processes in the brain, which are influenced by enzymes. These enzymes are made by genes. It would be dumbfounding if intellectual functioning were without genetic influence.

—Dr. Gerald E. McClearn, "Genes a Lifelong Factor
in Intelligence," *New York Times,* 6 June 1997

9.   [C]ontemporary standards of decency confirm our judgment that such a young person [15 years old] is not capable of acting with the culpability that can justify the ultimate [death] penalty. Inexperience, less education, and less intelligence make the teenager less able to evaluate the consequences of his or her conduct while at the same time he or she is more apt to be motivated by mere emotion or peer pressure than is an adult.

Juvenile executions could not be expected to deter people under 16 from committing murder, because the likelihood that the teenage offender has made the kind of cost-benefit analysis that attaches any weight to the possibility of execution is so remote as to be virtually nonexistent.

> —Justice John Paul Stevens, *Thompson v. Oklahoma*, 487 U.S. 815, 1988

*10. This dichotomy between the "best" and the "best black" is not something manufactured by racists to denigrate the abilities of professionals who are not white. On the contrary, it is reinforced from time to time by those students who demand that universities commit to hiring some pre-set number of minority faculty members . . . saying [in effect] "Go out and hire the best blacks." And it is further reinforced by faculty members who see these demands as nothing more than claims for simple justice.

> —Stephen L. Carter, "The Best Black, and Other Tales," *Reconstruction*, vol. 1, Winter 1990

11. Does the past exist? No. Does the future exist? No. Then only the present exists. Yes. But within the present there is no lapse of time? Quite so. Then time does not exist? Oh, I wish you wouldn't be so tiresome.

> —Bertrand Russell, *Human Knowledge*, 1948

12. Tipping does not improve service; if it did, taxi drivers would be more courteous than flight attendants. Furthermore, tipping is undignified, since blurring the line between a fee and a gift puts both patron and server in a vulnerable position.

> —George Jochnowitz, "Let's Dispense with Tipping Altogether," *New York Times*, 24 January 1997

13. Without dust there would be no twilight, no blue skies, no gorgeous sunsets, none of the ethereal color effects that hold landscape painters in thrall. If light were not scattered by myriad minute dust particles in the air, the sun's heat would be unbearable. Without dust to serve as nucleation sites, rain clouds would not readily form, and so the days would be intensely hot and the nights intensely cold. Dust, in sum, makes life possible on this planet.

> —Ivor Smullen, "Homage to a Speck," *The Sciences*, April 1992

14. The lower strata of the middle class—the small tradespeople, shopkeepers, and retired tradesmen generally, the handicraftsmen and peasants—all these sink gradually into the proletariat, partly because their diminutive capital does not suffice for the scale on which modern industry is carried on, and is swamped in the competition with the large capitalists, partly because their specialized

skill is rendered worthless by new methods of production. Thus the proletariat is recruited from all classes of the population.

> —Karl Marx and Friedrich Engels,
> *The Communist Manifesto,* 1848

*15. Because I had decided, right off, that I liked Nolan Myers, what I heard in his answer was toughness and confidence. Had I decided early on that I didn't like him, I would have heard in that reply arrogance and bluster. The first impression becomes a self-fulfilling prophesy: we hear what we expect to hear. The interview is hopelessly biased in favor of the nice.

> —Malcom Gladwell, "The New-Boy Network,"
> *The New Yorker,* 29 May 2000

16. No one means all he says, and yet very few say all they mean, for words are slippery and thought is viscous.

> —Henry Adams, *The Education of Henry Adams* (1907), chapter 31

17. Natural selection is interested in behavior and isn't so involved in the content of what goes on in the mind. This means that the chance of natural selection supplying people with true beliefs is low, and therefore people have ample reason to doubt the beliefs held in any mind produced by natural selection alone.

> —Prof. Alvin Plantinga, quoted in "Science and
> Sensibility," *Insight,* 18 August 1997

18. Cuts in tuition can reduce institutional income from government-financed aid programs, which in certain cases are based on total expenses charged, so there is a built-in disincentive to lower prices.

> —David Spadafora, "Don't Expect Many Colleges
> to Lower Tuition," *New York Times,* 29 January 1996

19. The most powerful tax reform of all is this: cut the capital gains tax rate. Less money and energy would be spent seeking ways to defer capital gains taxes and more effort would be dedicated to entrepreneurial investing. Funds locked into mature investments with a low cost basis would be freed for new risk-taking. Both government tax receipts and new investment would rise, benefiting investors, government, and entrepreneurs all.

> —Bruce C. Lueck, "Cut the Capital Gains Tax,"
> *New York Times,* 2 December 1996

*20. Native American beliefs about the past and the dead certainly deserve respect, but they should not be allowed to dictate government policy on the investigation and interpretation of early American prehistory. If a choice must be made among competing theories of human origins, primacy should be given to theories based on the scientific method. Only scientific theories are built on empirical evidence; only scientific theories can be adjusted or over-turned.

> —R. Bonnichsen and A. L. Schneider,
> "Battle of the Bones," *The Sciences*, August 2000

1.6 ARGUMENTS AND EXPLANATIONS

Many passages, both written and spoken, that appear to be arguments are in fact not arguments but explanations. The occurrence of certain premiss-or con-clusion-indicators such as "because," "for," and "therefore" cannot settle the matter, since those words may be used in both explanations and arguments.[42] What we need to know is the *intention* of the author of the passage.

Compare the following two passages:

1. Lay up for yourselves treasures in heaven, where neither moth nor rust consumes and where thieves do not break in and steal. For where your treasure is, there will your heart be also.

> —Matthew 7:19

2. Therefore is the name of it [the tower] called Babel; because the Lord did there confound the language of all the earth.

> —Genesis 11:19

The first passage is clearly an argument. Its conclusion, that one ought to lay up treasures in heaven, is supported by the premiss (here marked by the word "for") that one's heart will be where one's treasure is laid up. But the second passage, which uses the word "therefore" quite appropriately, is not an argu-ment. It *explains* why the tower (whose construction is recounted in Genesis) is called Babel. The tower was given this name, we are told, because it was the place where humankind, formerly speaking one language, became con-founded by many languages.[43] The passage assumes that the reader knows that the tower had that name; the intention is to explain why that name was given to it. The phrase, "Therefore is the name called Babel" is not a conclusion but a completion of the explanation of the naming. And the clause "because the Lord did there confound the language of all the earth" is not a premiss; it could not serve as a reason for believing that Babel was the name of the tower, since the fact that that *was* the name is known by those to whom the passage is

---

[42]The premiss-indicator "since" often has a *temporal* sense as well. Thus, in the lyric of the famous old song "Stormy Weather," the line "Since my man and I ain't together, keeps rainin' all the time" is deliberately ambiguous, and richly suggestive. (Music by Harold Arlen, words by Ted Koehler, 1933.)

[43]The name "Babel" is derived from the Hebrew word meaning "to confound"; that is, to confuse by mixing up or lumping together in an indiscriminate manner.

addressed. In this context "because" indicates that what follows will *explain* the giving of that name, Babel, to that tower.

The two passages illustrate the fact that passages that are superficially similar may have quite different functions. Whether any given passage is an argument or an explanation depends upon the *purpose* to be served by that passage. If our aim is to establish the truth of some proposition, Q, and to do that we offer some evidence, P, in support of Q, we may appropriately say "Q because P." We are in this way presenting an argument *for* Q, and P is our premiss. But suppose, instead, that Q is known to be true. In that case we don't have to give any reasons to support its truth—but we may wish to give an account of *why* it is true. Here also we may say "Q because P"—but in this case we are giving not an argument *for* Q, but an explanation *of* Q.

In responding to a query about the apparent color of quasars (celestial objects lying far beyond our galaxy) one scientist wrote:

> The most distant quasars look like intense points of infrared radiation. This is because space is scattered with hydrogen atoms (about two per cubic meter) that absorb blue light, and if you filter the blue from visible white light, red is what's left. On its multibillion-light-year journey to earth, quasar light loses so much blue that only infrared remains.[44]

This is not an argument; it does not seek to convince the reader that quasars have the apparent color they do, but rather aims to give the causes for this being so.

Similarly, in discussing the early growth of British influence in Africa, a historian wrote:

> Sierra Leone became a crown colony in 1808 not because it flourished, but because it failed. Burdened by war and stagnant trade, the private Sierra Leone Company could not cover its costs, and a Government that had just abolished the slave trade felt obliged to adopt it.[45]

No argument is given here for the conclusion that Sierra Leone became a crown colony in 1808. It *did* become a crown colony then. But why? Because . . . In this and in the previous example, "because" is plainly the mark of an explanation, not an argument.

How can we tell whether a passage is intended to explain or to convince? Usually we can do so by asking, with reference to the form, "Q because P," what the status of Q is for that author. Is Q a proposition whose truth needs to be established? Then "because P" is probably offering premiss(es) in its support, and hence "Q because P" is an argument. Or is Q a proposition whose truth is known, or at least not in doubt in the context? In that case, "because P" is probably offering some account of why Q has come to be true, and therefore "Q because P" is an explanation.

In an explanation one must distinguish *what* is being explained from what the explanation *is.* In the explanation from Genesis given above, what is being

---

[44]Jeff Greenwald, "Brightness Visible," *New York Times Magazine,* 14 May 2000.

[45]Andrew Porter, in a review of Lawrence James's *The Rise and Fall of the British Empire* (1995), in the *New York Times Book Review,* 14 January 1996.

explained is how the tower came to have the name Babel; the explanation is that it was there that the Lord did confound the language of all the earth. In the historical example just given, what is being explained is Sierra Leone's becoming a British crown colony; the explanation is the failure of the Sierra Leone Company and the British government's response to that failure.

What is called an explanation may in fact be an argument, and vice versa. Not long ago the *New York Times* was criticized by a reader for treating the sexes unequally because it commented on the increased weight of a prominent actress but not on the increased weight of a prominent businessman referred to in the same report. Another reader then responded:

> Ellen R. Fox's complaint—that you noted that Catherine Deneuve was "perhaps not as slender as she once was" but that you did not mention Donald Trump's growing girth— is easily explained. Mr. Trump never appeared nude in a movie that made his shape a matter of interest.[46]

This is not really an explanation but an argument. Its premises are, first, that nude appearance in a movie makes one's appearance a matter of interest, and second, that Mr. Trump never made such an appearance but that Ms. Deneuve did. It was therefore reasonable (this writer contends) for the newspaper to comment on the shape of the prominent person who did so appear while ignoring the shape of the prominent person who did not. Therefore, the complaint that the sexes had been treated unequally was not justified.

To distinguish explanations from arguments, we must often be sensitive to context, and there will always remain many passages whose purpose cannot be determined. A problematic passage may need to be given alternative, equally plausible "readings"—viewed as an argument when interpreted in one way and as an explanation when interpreted in another.

Exercises

Some of the following passages contain explanations, some contain arguments, and some may be interpreted as either an argument or an explanation. What is your judgment about the chief function of each passage? What would have to be the case for the passage in question to be an argument? To be an explanation? Where you find an argument, identify its premises and conclusion. Where you find an explanation, indicate what is being explained and what the explanation is.

Example

1. There is no mystery to why the idea of a flat tax is appealing. The existing tax system can be maddeningly complicated and expensive to comply with. It rewards consumption and penalizes savings, exactly the opposite of economic common sense. And in many cases

---

[46]Andy Rooney, *New York Times*, 29 April 1996.

it is clearly unfair—for example many working couples pay substantially higher taxes on their joint return than do unmarried couples who live together and file separate returns.

—David E. Rosenbaum, "Panel Calls for a Flat Tax,"
New York Times, 18 January 1996

Solution:

On the surface this passage is an explanation of why the flat tax is appealing: It is appealing because of the deficiencies of the existing tax system, several of which are identified. But the passage may also be viewed as an argument in support of the flat tax. The deficiencies of the present tax system are the premises, and the conclusion (not explicitly stated) is that the present system ought to be replaced by a flat tax.

Which of these interpretations is closer to the intentions of the author depends on the context of the passage. If the context had been an impartial weighing of alternative tax systems, the passage would have served chiefly as an explanation. But since the passage appeared in the report of a panel *calling for* a flat tax, we may conclude that it served in fact mainly as an argument in support of that position.

2. It would be immoral and selfish not to use animals in research today, given the harm that could accrue to future generations if such research were halted.

—*Science, Medicine, and Animals*
(Washington, DC: National Academy of
Sciences, Institute of Medicine, 1991)

3. Animals born without traits that led to reproduction died out, whereas the ones that reproduced the most succeeded in conveying their genes to posterity. Crudely speaking, sex feels good because over evolutionary time the animals that liked having sex created more offspring than the animals that didn't.

—R. Thornhill and C. T. Palmer, "Why Men Rape,"
The Sciences, February 2000.

4. Changes are real. Now, changes are only possible in time, and therefore time must be something real.

—Immanuel Kant, *Critique of Pure Reason* (1781),
"Transcendental Aesthetic," section II

*5. A black hole is an object with so much gravity that nothing can escape it—not even light, the fastest thing in the universe. Anything approaching a black hole gets pulled into the object and disappears as if it fell into a hole. Because even light cannot escape, the hole appears black.

—Ken Croswell, "The Best Black Hole in the Galaxy,"
Astronomy, March 1992

6. To name causes for a state of affairs is not to excuse it. Things are justified or condemned by their consequences, not by their antecedents.

    —John Dewey, "The Liberal College and Its Enemies,"
    The Independent, 1924

7. Because he is my son and because I love him more than anything else in the world, more than I can imagine loving anyone else, more even than I loved his mother, I crawl in beside him, my torso jammed deep into the closet, with my legs stretched over a hooked rug.

    —Michael G. Jaffe, *Dance Real Slow*
    (New York: Farrar, Straus, & Giroux, 1996)

8. I like Wagner's music better than anybody's. It is so loud that one can talk the whole time without people hearing what one says.

    —Oscar Wilde, *The Picture of Dorian Gray,* 1891

9. Every President from Herbert Hoover through Jimmy Carter has donated his Presidential records to the public. Only Nixon sued for payment for such records. For years, Nixon's lawyers argued against any public access to the tapes for privacy reasons. It is absurd for the estate to argue now [1999] that it should be compensated for the tapes, along with the other materials, because Nixon might have cashed in on the evidence that drove him from office.

    —"A Curious Claim by the Nixon Estate,"
    New York Times, Editorial, 22 February 1999

*10. Love looks not with the eyes but with the mind;
    And therefore is wing'd Cupid painted blind.

    —William Shakespeare, *A Midsummer Night's Dream,*
    act 1, scene 1

11. Members of the primate order have especially long periods of infant dependency compared with other mammals, because, it is believed, juveniles need the time to learn the ropes of their uniquely intricate social world.

    —Meredith F. Small, "Political Animal,"
    The Sciences, March 1990

12. That appellate advocacy is largely a written art has two consequences: First, making heads or tails of Supreme Court arguments without having read the briefs is often difficult. Second, the decision in any Court case may bear no relation to the questions asked at oral argument; the decision reflects the arguments made in the briefs. Rather than demystify the process, televising Supreme Court arguments may only contribute to misunderstandings about how the Court operates.

    —Andrew C. Mergen, "Where Words Are Worth
    1,000 Pictures," *New York Times,* 8 May 1996

13.   U.S. Presidents have always been more likely to be killed or disabled by assassins than by diseases, and the Secret Service thus has more to do with the President's health and safety than the President's physicians.

> —George J. Annas, "The Health of the President
> and Presidential Candidates," *New England
> Journal of Medicine*, 5 October 1995

14.   People often think of inflammation as merely an annoying symptom. But inflammation doesn't just signal injury; it can—in a vicious cycle—perpetuate injury. That's why disorders like arthritis can be so crippling, chronic, and hard to treat. And that's why patients are willing to risk serious side effects for drugs that offer even a temporary respite.

> —Jerome Groopman, "Superaspirin,"
> *The New Yorker*, 15 June 1998

*15.   How do girls become afraid to ask questions in science class? How do they come to think of science as less useful or interesting than boys do? Such attitudes are learned, and parents and teachers teach them.

> —"Why Are There Fewer Women?"
> *Michigan Alumnus*, October 1995

16.   Increasing incarceration rates do not result in decreasing crime rates because few crimes result in imprisonment or arrest. This is not because judges are soft on criminals but because 90 percent of crimes are either not reported or go unsolved.

> —Elizabeth Alexander, "Look to More Cost-effective
> Antidotes than Prison," *New York Times*, 25 January 1996

17.   One may be subject to laws made by another, but it is impossible to bind oneself in any matter which is the subject of one's own free exercise of will. . . . It follows of necessity that the king cannot be subject to his own laws. For this reason [royal] edicts and ordinances conclude with the formula, "for such is our good pleasure."

> —Jean Bodin, *Six Books of the Commonwealth*, 1576

18.   The resistance of the bourgeoisie is increased tenfold by its overthrow (even if only in one country), and its power lies not only in the strength of international capital and the international connections of the bourgeoisie, but also in the force of habit in the strength of small production. For, unfortunately, small production is still very, very widespread in the world, and small production engenders capitalism and the bourgeoisie continuously, daily, hourly, spontaneously, and on a mass scale. For all these reasons the dictatorship of the proletariat is essential, and victory over the bourgeoisie is impossible without a long, stubborn and desperate

war of life and death, a war demanding perseverance, discipline, firmness, indomitableness, and unity of will.

—V. I. Lenin, *"Left Wing" Communism: An Infantile Disorder*, 1920

19. Neither the Federal Communications Commission nor the New York State Public Service Commission receives many complaints about the problem of inaccurate telephone directory assistance. This is because when looking at their bills, people don't realize that they are charged for a mistaken "no listing" answer. And directory assistance providers, paid whether or not they have up-to-date information, have no incentive to improve service.

—Bradley F. Taylor, "No Listing? Dial M for 'Maddening,' " *New York Times*, 29 August 2000

*20. By any standard one wants to set, Americans are not learning science. All too often what is taught as science is better not taught at all. All too often the mind-set against science and the fear of mathematics are solidly installed in grade school. All too often science can be skipped in high school and in most colleges. As for most American college students, the science requirement is a sad joke.

—Leon M. Lederman, "Science Education, Science, and American Culture," *The Key Reporter*, Winter 1992

21. All animal populations fluctuate in size from year to year, in response to the good conditions (gentle weather, abundant food) and the bad conditions (drought, harsh winters, famine) they encounter; and small populations are more likely to fluctuate to zero when conditions are bad, since zero is never far away. With less margin of security, a small population is also more vulnerable to the various forms of human persecution and natural catastrophe that can deliver a coup de grace. Therefore, small populations face a greater risk of extinction than big populations. And island populations—including those trapped within ecological islands, such as a park surrounded by development—tend to be small.

—David Quammen, "National Parks: Nature's Dead End," *New York Times*, 28 July 1996

22. Because gravity increases with the mass of an object, heavy objects exert more pull. And gravity grows stronger the closer you get to an object, so objects with small diameters wield greater force. That's why white dwarfs—collapsed stars with a mass about that of the sun packed into a sphere the size of the Earth—exert such strong gravity.

—Marcia Bartusiak, "To the Edge of Space," *Astronomy*, July 1998

23. George Mason, one of my ancestors, urged the abolition of slavery at the Constitutional Convention, calling it "disgraceful to

mankind." Failing in this attempt, he urged that his Declaration of Rights be enacted as a bill of rights. It too was turned down. Thus, Mason refused to sign the Constitution.

—Thomas C. Southerland, Jr., "A Virginia Model,"
New York Times, 5 July 1997

24. Mother rats give birth to very different ratios of sons and daughters depending on how they are faring. When the rats are doing well and mating with vigorous dominant males, they give birth to an excess of sons. When times are hard, or when they have recently lost a litter, they give birth to more daughters.

Daughters, it seems, are the "cheaper" sex to raise: mothers spend less time licking and nursing them, and they are smaller than sons at weaning. They are also the safer sex, almost assured of having some offspring and thus keeping their mother's genetic legacy alive. Sons, by contrast, are considered the jackpot sex, who in theory could do brilliantly by their mother come their sexual maturity, spawning far more offspring than their sisters ever could manage. Hence there is evolutionary justification for mothers to bear more expensive sons when they have the energy and resources to do so, and opting for fail-safe females when prospects are dim. Somehow the mothers extract relevant information from their habitat and translate it into a changed birth ratio.

—"How Biology Affects Behavior and Vice Versa,"
New York Times, 30 May 1995

*25. Black or white, rich or poor, male or female, conservative or liberal: we are willfully blind to the 700,000 black men incarcerated in 1994 (up from 25,000 in 1960) and to the 11,000 killed as a result of homicide in 1993 (both figures from the Bureau of Justice Statistics), to unemployment and life expectancy that lags far behind every other racial and gender classification. This class of Americans doesn't have think tanks, political parties or lobbyists. To paraphrase writer Ralph Wiley, that's why black boys tend to shoot.

—Bill Stephney, "Rap Star's Death Highlights Harsher Reality," *New York Times*, 18 September 1996

1.7   DEDUCTION AND VALIDITY

Every argument makes the claim that its premises provide grounds for the truth of its conclusion. Indeed, that claim is the mark of an argument. But there are two major classes of arguments: *deductive* and *inductive*. These two classes differ fundamentally in the *way* in which their conclusions are supported by their premises. In this section we give a brief account of deduction.

A deductive argument makes the claim that its conclusion is supported by its premises *conclusively*. In contrast, an inductive argument does not make such a claim. If, in interpreting a passage, we judge that such a claim is being made, we treat the argument as deductive; if we judge that such a claim is not being made, we treat it as inductive. Since every argument either makes this claim of conclusiveness or does not, every argument is either deductive or inductive.

When an argument makes the claim that its premisses (if true) provide irrefutable grounds for the truth of its conclusion, that claim will be either correct or not correct. If it is correct, that argument is **valid.** If it is not correct (that is, if the premisses when true fail to establish the conclusion irrefutably), that argument is **invalid.**

For logicians, therefore, the term *validity* is applicable only to deductive arguments. To say that a deductive argument is valid is to say that it is not possible for its conclusion to be false if its premisses are true. Thus we define "validity" as follows: **A deductive argument is valid when, if its premisses are true, its conclusion** *must* **be true.**

Every deductive argument makes the claim that its premisses guarantee the truth of its conclusion, but not all deductive arguments live up to that claim. Deductive arguments that fail to do so are *invalid.*

Since every deductive argument either succeeds or does not succeed in achieving its objective, every deductive argument is either valid or invalid. This point is important: if a deductive argument is not valid, it must be invalid; if it is not invalid, it must be valid.

The central task of deductive logic (treated at length in Part II of this book) is to discriminate valid arguments from invalid ones. Through the ages logicians have devised powerful techniques to do this. But the traditional techniques for determining validity differ from those employed by most modern logicians. The former, called *classical logic* and rooted in the analytical works of Aristotle, are explained in Chapters 5, 6, and 7 of this book. The techniques of *modern symbolic logic* are presented in detail in Chapters 8, 9, and 10. Although logicians of the two schools differ in their methods and in their interpretations of some arguments, all agree that the fundamental task of deductive logic is to develop the tools that enable us to distinguish arguments that are valid from those that are not.

1.8 INDUCTION AND PROBABILITY

Inductive arguments do not claim that their premisses, even if true, support their conclusions with certainty. They make a weaker but nonetheless important claim that their premisses support their conclusions with *probability,* which always falls short of certainty. What was said above about validity and invalidity therefore does not apply to inductive arguments: Inductive arguments are neither valid nor invalid.[47] We can still evaluate them of course. Indeed, the

---

[47] In everyday speech the terms "valid" and "invalid" have taken on much wider and looser meanings. One hears it said, for example, that a fine motion picture "makes a valid statement," or that some emotional response to an act or event is a "valid reaction," and so forth. English is beautifully rich. But as logicians we use the terms *valid* and *invalid* far more narrowly; they indicate nothing more than the success, or lack of success, of a deductive argument in making its claim that if its premisses are true its conclusion must be true.

appraisal of inductive arguments is one of the leading tasks of scientists in every sphere. The premises of an inductive argument provide some support for its conclusion, and the higher the level of probability the premises confer on the conclusion, the greater the merit of the argument. In general, we say that inductive arguments may be "better" or "worse," "weaker" or "stronger," and so on. But even when the premises are all true and provide very strong support for the conclusion, in an inductive argument the conclusion is never certain. The theory of induction, techniques of inductive reasoning, methods for appraising inductive arguments, and methods for quantifying and calculating probabilities are presented at some length in Part III of this book.

The difference between inductive and deductive arguments is deep. Because an inductive argument can yield no more than some degree of probability for its conclusion, it is always possible that additional information will strengthen or weaken it. Newly discovered facts may cause us to change our estimate of the probabilities, and thus may lead us to judge the argument to be better (or worse) than we thought it was. In the world of inductive argument—even when the conclusion is thought to be very highly probable—*all* the evidence is never in. It is this possibility of new data, perhaps conflicting with what was believed earlier, that keeps us from asserting that any inductive conclusion is absolutely certain.

Deductive arguments, on the other hand, cannot gradually become better or worse. They either succeed or do not succeed in exhibiting a compelling relation between premises and conclusion. The fundamental difference between deduction and induction is revealed by this contrast. If a deductive argument is valid, *no* additional premises could possibly add to the strength of that argument. For example, if all humans are mortal, and if Socrates is human, we may conclude without reservation that Socrates is mortal—*and that conclusion will follow from those premises no matter what else may be true in the world, and no matter what other information may be discovered or added.* If we come to learn that Socrates is ugly, or that angels are immortal, or that cows give milk, neither those findings nor any other findings can have any impact on the validity of the original argument.

In the case of every valid deductive argument, the conclusion that follows with certainty from its premises follows from any enlarged set of premises with the same certainty, regardless of the nature of the additional premises. If an argument is valid, nothing in the world can make it more valid; if a conclusion is validly inferred from some set of premises, nothing can be added to that set to make that conclusion follow more strictly, or more logically, or more validly.

But this is not true of inductive arguments, in which the relationship claimed between premises and conclusion is much less strict and different in kind. Consider the following inductive argument:

Most corporation lawyers are conservatives.
Angela Palmieri is a corporation lawyer.
Therefore Angela Palmieri is probably a conservative.

This is a pretty good inductive argument; its first premise is true, and if its second premiss also is true its conclusion is more likely to be true than false. But in this case (in contrast to the argument about Socrates' mortality) new premisses added to the original pair might weaken or (depending on the content of the new premisses) strengthen the original argument. Suppose we also learn that

> Angela Palmieri is an officer of the American Civil Liberties Union (ACLU).

and suppose we add the (true) premiss that

> Most officers of the ACLU are not conservatives.

Now the conclusion (that Angela Palmieri is a conservative) no longer seems very probable; the original inductive argument has been greatly weakened by the presence of this additional information about Angela Palmieri. Indeed, if the final premiss were to be transformed into the universal proposition

> No officers of the ACLU are conservatives.

The opposite of the original conclusion would then follow deductively—that is, validly—from the full set of premisses affirmed.

On the other hand, suppose we enlarge the original set of premisses by adding the following additional premisses:

> Angela Palmieri has long been an officer of the National Rifle Association (NRA).

and

> Angela Palmieri was appointed a contributing editor of the conservative *National Review*.

The original conclusion would be supported by this enlarged set of premisses with even greater likelihood than it was by the original set.

In sum, the distinction between induction and deduction rests on the nature of the *claims* made by the two types of arguments about the *relations between their premisses and their conclusions*. We may characterize the two types of arguments as follows:

A deductive argument is one whose conclusion is claimed to follow from its premisses with absolute necessity, this necessity not being a matter of degree and not depending in any way on whatever else may be the case. In sharp contrast, an inductive argument is one whose conclusion is claimed to follow from its premisses only with probability, this probability being a matter of degree and dependent upon what else may be the case.

Inductive arguments do not always acknowledge explicitly that their conclusions are inferred only with some degree of probability. On the other hand, the mere presence of the word "probability" within an argument is no sure indication that the argument is inductive. This is so because there are some strictly deductive arguments *about* probabilities themselves.* Arguments of this kind, in which the probability of a certain combination of events is deduced from the probabilities of other events, are discussed in Chapter 14.

1.9 VALIDITY AND TRUTH

As noted earlier, a successful deductive argument is *valid.* Validity refers to a relation *between* propositions—between the set of propositions that serve as the premisses of a deductive argument, and the one proposition that serves as the conclusion of that argument. If the latter follows with logical necessity from the former, we say that the argument is valid. Since logical necessity is never achieved by inductive arguments, validity never applies to them. *Nor can validity ever apply to any single proposition by itself,* since the needed *relation* cannot possibly be found within any one proposition.

Truth and falsity, on the other hand, *are* attributes of individual propositions. A single statement that serves as a premiss in an argument may be true; the statement that serves as its conclusion may be false. That conclusion may have been validly inferred, but it makes no sense to say that any conclusion, or any single premiss, is itself valid or invalid.

Truth is the attribute of a proposition that asserts what really is the case. When I assert that Lake Superior is the largest of the five Great Lakes, I assert what really is the case, what is true. If I said that the largest of the Great Lakes is Lake Michigan, my assertion would not be in accord with the real world; therefore, it would be false. This contrast is important: **truth and falsity are attributes of individual propositions or statements; validity and invalidity are attributes of arguments.**

Just as the concept of validity does not apply to single propositions, the concept of truth does not apply to arguments. Of the several propositions in an argument, some (or all) may be true and some (or all) may be false. But the argument as a whole is neither "true" nor "false." Propositions, which are statements about the world, may be true or false; deductive arguments, which consist of inferences from one set of propositions to other propositions, may be valid or invalid.

The relations *between* true (or false) propositions and valid (or invalid) arguments lie at the heart of deductive logic. Part II of this book is largely devoted to the examination of those complex relations. However, a preliminary discussion of the relation between validity and truth is in order at this point.

We begin by emphasizing that an argument may be valid even if one or more of its premisses is not true. Every argument makes a claim about the relation between the premisses and the conclusion drawn from them; that relation may hold even if the premisses turn out to be false or the truth of the premisses is in dispute. This point was made effectively by Abraham Lincoln in

---

*If, for example, we learn that the probability of three successive heads in three tosses of a coin is ⅛, we may infer deductively that the probability of getting at least one tail in three tosses of coin is ⅞.

1858 in one of his debates with Stephen Douglas. Lincoln was attacking the *Dred Scott* decision, which obliged the return of slaves who had escaped into northern states to their owners in the South:

> I think it follows, [from the *Dred Scott* decision] and submit to the consideration of men capable of arguing, whether as I state it in syllogistic form the argument has any fault in it:
>
> Nothing in the Constitution or laws of any State can destroy a right distinctly and expressly affirmed in the Constitution of the United States.
>
> The right of property in a slave is distinctly and expressly affirmed in the Constitution of the United States.
>
> Therefore, nothing in the Constitution or laws of any State can destroy the right of property in a slave.
>
> I believe that no fault can be pointed out in that argument; assuming the truth of the premisses, the conclusion, so far as I have capacity at all to understand it, follows inevitably. There *is* a fault in it as I think, but the fault is not in the reasoning; but the falsehood in fact is a fault of the premisses. I believe that the right of property in a slave *is not* distinctly and expressly affirmed in the Constitution, and Judge Douglas thinks it *is*. I believe that the Supreme Court and the advocates of that decision [the *Dred Scott* decision] may search in vain for the place in the Constitution where the right of property in a slave is distinctly and expressly affirmed. I say, therefore, that I think one of the premisses is not true in fact.[48]

In the argument that he recapitulates and attacks, Lincoln finds the second premiss—that the right of property in a slave is affirmed in the U.S. Constitution—to be plainly false. The reasoning in the argument is not faulty, he points out; nevertheless, its conclusion has not been established. His logical point is correct: *An argument may be valid even when its conclusion and one or more of its premisses are false.* For the validity of an argument, we emphasize once again, depends only upon the *relation* of the premisses to the conclusion.

There are many possible combinations of true and false premisses and conclusions in both valid and invalid arguments. Consider the following illustrative arguments, each of which is prefaced by the statement of the combination it represents. With these illustrations before us, we will be in a position to formulate some important principles concerning the relations between truth and validity.

I. Some *valid* arguments contain *only true* propositions—true premisses and a true conclusion:

> All mammals have lungs.
> All whales are mammals.
> Therefore all whales have lungs.

II. Some *valid* arguments contain *only false* propositions:

> All four-legged creatures have wings.
> All spiders have four legs.
> Therefore all spiders have wings.

---

[48]Abraham Lincoln, in Roy R. Basler, ed., *The Collected Works of Abraham Lincoln,* vol. 3. (Rutgers University Press).

This argument is valid because, if its premises were true, its conclusion would have to be true also—even though we know that in fact both the premises *and* the conclusion of this argument are false.

III.   Some *invalid* arguments contain *only true* propositions—all their premisses are true, and their conclusions are true as well:

> If I owned all the gold in Fort Knox, then I would be wealthy.
> I do not own all the gold in Fort Knox.
> Therefore I am not wealthy.

IV.   Some *invalid* arguments contain *only true premisses* and have a *false conclusion.* This can be illustrated with an argument exactly like the previous one (III) in form, changed only enough to make the conclusion false:

> If Bill Gates owned all the gold in Fort Knox, then Bill Gates would be wealthy.
> Bill Gates does not own all the gold in Fort Knox.
> Therefore Bill Gates is not wealthy.

The premisses of this argument are true, but its conclusion is false. Such an argument *cannot* be valid because it is impossible for the premisses of a valid argument to be true and its conclusion to be false.

V.   Some *valid* arguments have *false premisses and a true conclusion:*

> All fishes are mammals.
> All whales are fishes.
> Therefore all whales are mammals.

The conclusion of this argument is true, as we know; moreover it may be validly inferred from the two premisses, both of which are wildly false.

VI.   Some *invalid* arguments also have *false premisses and a true conclusion:*

> All mammals have wings.
> All whales have wings.
> Therefore all whales are mammals.

From examples V and VI taken together, it is clear that we cannot tell from the fact that an argument has false premisses and a true conclusion whether it is valid or invalid.

VII.   Some *invalid* arguments, of course, contain *all false propositions*—false premisses and a false conclusion:

> All mammals have wings.
> All whales have wings.
> Therefore all mammals are whales.

These seven examples make it clear that there are valid arguments with false conclusions (Example II), as well as invalid arguments with true conclusions (Examples III and VI). Hence it is clear that *the truth or falsity of an argument's conclusion does not by itself determine the validity or invalidity of that argument.* Moreover, *the fact that an argument is valid does not guarantee the truth of its conclusion* (Example II).

Two tables (referring to the seven examples on the preceding pages) will make very clear the variety of possible combinations. The first table shows that invalid arguments can have every possible combination of true and false premisses and conclusions:

INVALID ARGUMENTS		
	TRUE CONCLUSION	**FALSE CONCLUSION**
TRUE PREMISSES	Example III	Example IV
FALSE PREMISSES	Example VI	Example VII

The second table shows that valid arguments can have only three of those combinations of true and false premisses and conclusions:

VALID ARGUMENTS		
	TRUE CONCLUSION	**FALSE CONCLUSION**
TRUE PREMISSES	Example I	
FALSE PREMISSES	Example V	Example II

The one blank position in the second table exhibits a fundamental point: *If an argument is valid and its premisses are true, we may be certain that its conclusion is true also.* To put it another way: *If an argument is valid and its conclusion is false, not all of its premisses can be true.* Some perfectly valid arguments do have false conclusions—but any such argument must have at least one false premiss.

When an argument is valid, *and* all of its premisses are true, we call it "sound." The conclusion of a sound argument obviously must be true—and only a sound argument can establish the truth of its conclusion. If a deductive argument is not sound—that is, if the argument is not valid, *or* if not all of its premisses are true—it fails to establish the truth of its conclusion *even if in fact the conclusion is true.*

To test the truth or falsehood of premisses is the task of science in general, since premisses may deal with any subject matter at all. The logician is not interested in the truth or falsehood of propositions so much as in the logical relations between them. By "logical" relations between propositions we mean those relations that determine the correctness or incorrectness of the arguments in which they occur. The task of determining the correctness or incorrectness of arguments falls squarely within the province of logic. The logician is interested in the correctness even of arguments whose premises may be false.

Why not confine ourselves to arguments with true premises, ignoring all others? Because the correctness of arguments whose premises are not known to be true may be of great importance. In science, for example, we verify theories by deducing testable consequences—but we cannot know beforehand which theories are true. In everyday life as well, we must often choose between alternative courses of action, deducing the consequences of each. To avoid deceiving ourselves we must reason correctly about the consequences of the alternatives, taking each as a premise. If we were interested only in arguments with true premises, we would not know which set of consequences to trace out until we knew which of the alternative premises was true. But if we knew which of the alternative premises was true, we would not need to reason about it at all, since our purpose in reasoning was to help us decide which alternative premise to *make* true. To confine our attention to arguments with premises known to be true would therefore be self-defeating.

Effective methods for establishing the validity or invalidity of deductive arguments are presented and explained in Part II of this book.

1.10 COMPLEX ARGUMENTATIVE PASSAGES

Advanced Material   Arguments can be very complicated. Passages in which several arguments are interwoven, with many propositions appearing, some of which serve only as premises and some of which serve as both premises and sub-conclusions, can be difficult to analyze. The diagramming technique is very helpful, but there is no mechanical way to assure that the diagram we construct represents the passage accurately. Moreover, because the passage may be subject to varying plausible interpretations, there may be more than one diagram that can reasonably be considered to exhibit the logical structure of the passage.

To analyze complex passages fairly we must strive to understand the flow of the author's reasoning and identify the role of each element of the passage. The examples that follow (in which component propositions have been numbered for purposes of analysis) exhibit the ways in which we can set forth the connections between premises and conclusions. Once we have identified the arguments within a passage and their relations, we can go about deciding whether the conclusions do indeed follow from the premises affirmed.

In the following set of arguments the final conclusion of the passage appears in the very first statement, which is not unusual. There are four premises directly supporting this conclusion; two of these are sub-conclusions, which in turn are supported in different ways, by other premises affirmed in the passage:

① It is very unlikely that research using animals will be unnecessary or poorly done. ② Before an experiment using a vertebrate animal is carried out, the protocol for that experiment must be reviewed by an institutional committee that includes a veterinarian and a member of the public, and ③ during the research the animal's health and care are monitored regularly. ④ Researchers need healthy animals for study in science and medicine, because ⑤ unhealthy animals could lead to erroneous results. This is a powerful incentive for ⑥ scientists to make certain that any animals they use are healthy and well nourished. Furthermore, ⑦ research involving animals is expensive, and because ⑧ funding is limited in science, ⑨ only high quality research is able to compete effectively for support.[49]

The following diagram exhibits the logical structure of this passage. In examining such diagrams, it is helpful to "read" them by replacing the numbers with the indicated propositions, beginning with those highest on the page and therefore earliest in the logical cascade. In this way one can follow each of the several paths of reasoning to the final conclusion.

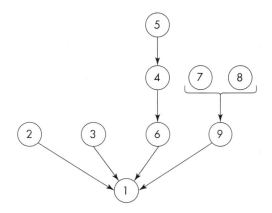

Within an argument, individual propositions are sometimes repeated in differently worded sentences, sometimes for emphasis and other times by oversight. This repetition complicates the task of analysis. Diagramming helps because we can assign the same number to different formulations of the same proposition. The following passage comprising three distinct arguments, exhibits this confusing duplication of propositions:

① The Big Bang theory is crumbling.... ② According to orthodox wisdom, the cosmos began with the Big Bang—an immense, perfectly symmetrical explosion 20 billion years ago. The problem is that ③ astronomers have confirmed by observation the existence of huge conglomerations of galaxies that are simply too big to have been formed in a mere 20 billion years.... Studies based on new data collected by satellite, and backed up by earlier ground surveys, show that ④ galaxies are clustered into vast ribbons that stretch billions of light years, and ⑤ are separated by voids hundreds of millions of light years across. Because ⑥ galaxies are observed to travel at only a small fraction of the speed of light, mathematics shows that ⑦ such large clumps of matter must have taken at least one hundred billion years to come together—five times as long as the time since the hypothetical Big Bang.... ③ Structures as big as those now seen can't be made in 20 billion years.... ② The Big Bang theorizes that matter was

[49]*Science, Medicine, and Animals*, National Academy of Sciences, Washington, DC, 1991.

spread evenly through the universe. From this perfection, ③ there is no way for such vast clumps to have formed so quickly.[50]

In this passage the premises that report observational evidence, ④, ⑤, and ⑥, give reasons for ⑦, the great length of time that would have had to elapse since the Big Bang. This passage of time is used to support the subconclusion (formulated in three slightly different ways) that ③ structures as big as those now seen are too big to have been formed in that period of time. From that subconclusion, combined with ②, a short statement (formulated in two slightly different ways) of the original symmetry and spread that the Big Bang theory supposes, we infer the final conclusion of the passage ①: that the Big Bang theory is crumbling—the proposition with which the passage begins. The following diagram exhibits this set of logical relations:

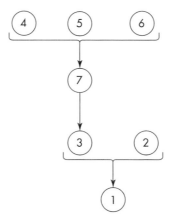

The analysis of an argument must take into account the fact that premises may appear in compressed form, sometimes as a short noun phrase. In the following argument the phrase, "the scattering in the atmosphere" serves as a premiss, ④, that may be reformulated as "the sun's energy is scattered in the atmosphere." This compression, along with repetition, makes it more difficult to analyze this argument:

① Solar-powered cars can never be anything but experimental devices. ② Solar power is too weak to power even a mini-car for daily use. ③ The solar power entering the atmosphere is about 1 kilowatt per square yard. Because of ④ the scattering in the atmosphere, and because ⑤ the sun shines half a day on the average at any place on earth, ⑥ average solar power received is 1/6 kilowatt, or 4 kilowatt hours a day....Tests on full-size cars indicate that ⑦ 300,000 watt hours are required in a battery for an electric car to perform marginally satisfactorily. So, ⑧ 40 square yards of cells would be needed to charge the car batteries, about the size of the roof of a tractor-trailer. ① It is not undeveloped technologies that put solar power out of the running to be anything but a magnificently designed experimental car. It is cosmology.[51]

---

[50]Eric J. Lerner, "For Whom the Bang Tolls," *New York Times,* 3 June 1991.
[51]Victor Wouk, "You Can't Drive Solar Cars to Work," *New York Times,* 15 July 1991.

The first proposition in this passage, asserting that "solar powered cars can never be more than experimental" is the final conclusion. It is repeated in more elaborate form at the end of the passage, as a diagram of the passage shows:

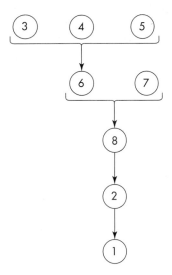

When we analyze complex argumentative passages, even ones that contain many premises and subconclusions, we often find them to be coherent and clear. Consider the following passage, by an editor defending her highly controversial editorial policy:

> The *Journal* [*New England Journal of Medicine*] has taken the position that ① it will not publish reports of unethical research, regardless of their scientific merit....
>
> There are three reasons for our position. First, ② the policy of publishing only ethical research, if generally applied, would deter unethical work. ③ Publication is an important part of the reward system in medical research, and ④ investigators would not undertake unethical studies if they knew the results would not be published. Furthermore, ⑤ any other policy would tend to lead to more unethical work, because, as I have indicated, ⑥ such studies may be easier to carry out and thus ⑦ may give their practitioners a competitive edge. Second, ⑧ denying publication even when the ethical violations are minor protects the principle of the primacy of the research subject. ⑨ If small lapses were permitted we would become inured to them, and ⑩ this would lead to larger violations. And finally, ⑪ refusal to publish unethical work serves notice to society at large that even scientists do not consider science the primary measure of a civilization. ⑫ Knowledge, although important, may be less important to a decent society than the way it is obtained.[52]

Again the final conclusion appears at the beginning of the passage, and the three major premises that support it directly, ②, ⑧ and ⑪, are themselves supported by various other premises arranged differently. But each of the

---

[52]Dr. Marcia Angell, "The Nazi Hypothermia Experiments and Unethical Research Today," *New England Journal of Medicine*, 17 May 1990.

many propositions in the passage has a clear logical role in leading to the conclusion that the passage aims to justify: reports of research done in unethical ways will not be published in the *New England Journal of Medicine,* regardless of their scientific merit. The following diagram exhibits the logical structure of this complicated but carefully reasoned passage:

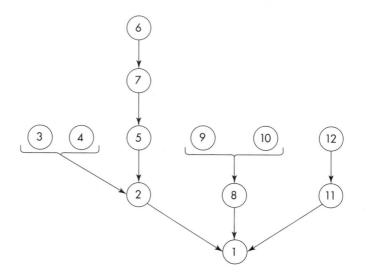

Arguments in everyday life often fall short of this standard. They may include statements whose role is unclear; connections among the statements in the argument may be tangled or misstated; even in the mind of its author the flow of the argument may be confused. Logical analysis, supported by diagrams, can expose such deficiencies. By exposing the *structure* of a reasoning process we can see how it was intended to work and what its strengths and weaknesses may be. The special province of logic is the evaluation of arguments; successful evaluation requires a clear grasp of the argument we are analyzing.

Exercises

Each of the following passages can best be interpreted as containing several arguments, whose premises and conclusions are arranged in a variety of ways. Analyze these passages, paraphrasing premises and conclusions where necessary, and construct a diagram for each passage.

*1.   Democractic laws generally tend to promote the welfare of the greatest possible number; for they emanate from the majority of the citizens, who are subject to error, but who cannot have an interest opposed to their own advantage. The laws of an aristocracy tend, on the contrary, to concentrate wealth and power in the hands of the minority; because an aristocracy, by its very nature, constitutes a minority. It may therefore be asserted, as a general proposition, that the purpose of a democracy in its legislation is more useful to humanity than that of an aristocracy.

> —Alexis de Tocqueville, *Democracy in America*, 1835

2. Paternal and maternal genes can be antagonistic to one another. Consider pregnancy. In most mammals, the mother's body regards the growing embryo as an intruder, and tries to limit the demands it places on her resources. The father, of course, does not bear the young and so is unaffected by such considerations. His genetic interest is unambiguous: to stimulate the embryo's growth and to shield it from the mother's defenses. Thus only males contribute the genes that foster the growth of the protective organ known as the placenta; females do not. Uniparental mouse eggs, created from the genes of the mother alone, develop into normal embryos, but the embryos lack a placenta and so do not flourish.

> —Laurence Marschall, in a review of *Genome*,
> by Matt Ridley (HarperCollins, 2000),
> appearing in *The Sciences*, August 2000

3. A question arises: whether it be better [for a prince] to be loved than feared or feared than loved? One should wish to be both, but, because it is difficult to unite them in one person, it is much safer to be feared than loved, when, of the two, one must be dispensed with. Because this is to be asserted in general of men, that they are ungrateful, fickle, false, cowards, covetous . . . and that prince who, relying entirely on their promises, has neglected other precautions, is ruined, because friendships that are obtained by payments may indeed be earned but they are not secured, and in time of need cannot be relied upon. Men have less scruple in offending one who is beloved than one who is feared, for love is preserved by the link of obligation which, owing to the baseness of men, is broken at every opportunity for their advantage; but fear preserves you by a dread of punishment which never fails.

> —N. Machiavelli, *The Prince*, 1515

4. Consider why the federal government is involved in student lending: it is in the national interest to have an educated populace. On average, college graduates earn almost twice the annual salary of high-school graduates. The cost of the nation's investment in the education of student borrowers is recouped many times over through increased productivity and greater earnings. By making a college education possible for millions of Americans, federally sponsored student loans produce a tremendous return for the U.S. Treasury and students, whose incomes—and tax payments—are greatly increased with their college degrees.

    But most college students are not creditworthy borrowers. The typical student is cash poor, owner of few if any assets that could be used as collateral, and often earns too little to be considered a good credit risk. If such a borrower could get a loan, in all likelihood it would carry a high interest rate—high enough to lead many students to decide not to go on to higher education. That is why student loans are backed by federal money and the interest charged on those loans is capped.

—Richard W. Riley, "Should Washington Have a Bigger Share of the Student-loan Industry? Yes!" *Insight,* 29 April 1996

*5. ". . . You appeared to be surprised when I told you, on our first meeting, that you had come from Afghanistan."

"You were told, no doubt."

"Nothing of the sort. I *knew* you came from Afghanistan. From long habit the train of thoughts ran so swiftly through my mind that I arrived at the conclusion without being conscious of intermediate steps. There were such steps, however. The train of reasoning ran, 'Here is a gentleman of medical type, but with the air of a military man. Clearly an army doctor, then. He has just come from the tropics, for his face is dark, and that is not the natural tint of his skin, for his wrists are fair. He has undergone hardship and sickness, as his haggard face says clearly. His left arm has been injured. He holds it in a stiff and unnatural manner. Where in the tropics could an English army doctor have seen much hardship and got his arm wounded? Clearly in Afghanistan.' The whole train of thought did not occupy a second. I then remarked that you came from Afghanistan, and you were astonished."

"It is simple enough as you explain it," I said, smiling.

—A. Conan Doyle, *A Study in Scarlet,* 1887

6. One of the most difficult problems associated with quantum research is how to observe subatomic particles in their natural states without affecting them—observing them non-destructively, so to speak. It's difficult for two reasons. First, atoms and subatomic particle are the smallest constituents of matter. Since any medium used to observe them emits energy of its own, that energy must affect the energy of the observed particles. Second, in isolation, atomic components exist in two quantum states simultaneously—particles and waves. It's as if they were packets of statistical probability. Only when they interact with other components do they display one manifestation or the other.

—"Skinning Schrodinger's Cat," *Insight,* 15 July 1996

7. Is there any room left at all in science for divine things? Michael J. Behe [in *Darwin's Black Box* (The Free Press, 1996)] contends that there is. He argues that the origin of intracellular processes underlying the foundation of life cannot be explained by natural selec-

tion or by any other mechanism based purely on chance. When examined with the powerful tools of modern biology, life on a biochemical level can be the product (this practicing biochemist believes) only of intelligent design.

The crux of his argument is that fundamental systems within the cell are "irreducibly complex"; they are composed of several specific, interacting components, each of which plays a vital role in the functioning of the system as a whole. Take out any step in the complex cascade of reactions that leads to the coagulation of blood, for example, and a wounded organism's lifeblood would leak out like water from a broken cup; but remove a single enzyme that limits the clotting process to the area of the wound, and the entire blood supply hardens up instead. Since either of these conditions would be fatal, the molecular components of clotting could not have come together gradually through natural selection and then assembled themselves into a functioning system.

8. In the U.S. Postal Service there is no straightforward mechanism to correct problems or force the agency to change. No citizens can own tradable shares. The income and security of managers and workers are guaranteed by the monopoly on first-class mail, public funding and the employees' political clout with Congress. The public cannot shift its business to more efficient competitors, because competition is prohibited. Consequently, the gross postal inefficiencies are not the result of the character or personality of the individuals who happen to occupy positions and jobs; they stem from the structure of the Postal Service itself.

> —Douglas K. Adie, "Privatizing Will Improve Mail Service Posthaste," *Insight*, 30 January 1995

9. Eliminating a tax on marriage sounds like a great idea. But it is also a sound idea to set higher rates on wealthier people and to tax families with the same total income the same no matter how their income is split between spouses. No tax code can satisfy these three goals simultaneously. Two people whose individual incomes are low enough to be taxed at 15 percent can, under a progressive code, hit the 28 percent bracket when their incomes are combined. Congress can eliminate the marriage tax, but only by sacrificing progressivity.

> —"Temptations of a Balanced Budget," Editorial in *New York Times*, 31 December 1997

*10. Nothing is demonstrable unless the contrary implies a contradiction. Nothing that is distinctly conceivable implies a contradiction. Whatever we conceive as existent, we can also conceive as nonexistent. There is no being, therefore, whose non-existence implies a contradiction. Consequently there is no being whose existence is demonstrable.

—David Hume, *Dialogues Concerning Natural Religion,*
Part IX, 1779 ∎

1.11 REASONING

∎ **For Enrichment** Logic, we have said, is the study of the methods and principles used to distinguish correct from incorrect reasoning. Reasoning is the process with which one advances, with arguments, from premises known (or affirmed for the purpose) to conclusions. Thus far we have been analyzing and evaluating the arguments of others. Arguments of our own we construct every day, of course, in deciding how we shall act, in judging the acts of others, in defending our moral or political convictions, and so on. Skill in building and applying good arguments is of enormous value.

This skill in reasoning can be improved with practice. To encourage such practice the various games of reasoning (chess, go, and Mastermind, for examples) are splendid instruments. But also quite useful are puzzles with which we may strengthen and test our logical skills. Reasoning is not only an essential activity, it is also an enjoyable activity—and the enjoyment it can yield is apparent when we solve logical problems designed both to stimulate and to entertain.

Contrived problems will be *neater* than those arising in real life, and usually simpler too. But solving them can be challenging, and often requires extended reasoning in patterns not very different from those employed by a detective, or a journalist, or a juror. Chains of inferences are likely to be needed, in which the sub-conclusions reached are used as premises in subsequent arguments. Insight may be called for too; finding the path to solution may require the creative recombination of information earlier given or discovered. Solving contrived problems can prove difficult, sometimes frustrating—but success, achieved through the successful application of reason, is very satisfying. Logical games and puzzles—in addition to being models for the employment of reason—are good fun. "The enjoyment of the doubtful," wrote the American philosopher, John Dewey, " is a mark of the educated mind."

One common type of reasoning problem is the brainteaser in which, using only the clues provided, we are asked to untangle and identify the names, or roles, or other facts about several specified characters. Here is a relatively simple example:

> In a certain flight crew, the positions of pilot, copilot, and flight engineer are held by three persons, Allen, Brown, and Carr, though not necessarily in that order.
> The copilot, who is an only child, earns the least.
> Carr, who married Brown's sister, earns more than the pilot.
> What position does each of the three persons hold?

To solve such problems we look first for a sphere in which we have enough information to reach some conclusions going beyond what is given in the premisses. In this case we know most about Carr: he is not the pilot, because he earns more than the pilot; and he is not the copilot because the copilot earns the least. By elimination we may infer that Carr must be the flight engineer.

Using that sub-conclusion we can determine Brown's position. Brown is not the copilot because he has a sister and the copilot is an only child; he is not the flight engineer because Carr is. Brown must therefore be the pilot. Allen, the only one left, must therefore be the copilot.

In addressing problems of this type (which can become very intricate) it is useful to construct a graphic display of the alternatives, called a *matrix,* which we fill in as we accumulate new information. To appreciate the helpfulness of such a matrix, consider the following puzzle:

> Alonzo, Kurt, Rudolf, and Willard are four creative artists of great talent. One is a dancer, one is a painter, one is a singer, and one is a writer, though not necessarily in that order.
> (1) Alonzo and Rudolf were in the audience the night the singer made his debut on the concert stage.
> (2) Both Kurt and the writer have had their portraits painted from life by the painter.
> (3) The writer, whose biography of Willard was a best-seller, is planning to write a biography of Alonzo.
> (4) Alonzo has never heard of Rudolf.
> What is each man's artistic field?

To keep the many facts asserted in these premises in mind, and also to remember the several subconclusions that may have been inferred from them, would be a demanding task. Writing our inferences down in the form of notes might prove helpful but could also result in a confusing clutter. We need a method for storing the information given and the intermediate conclusions drawn, a method that will keep what is known and what is inferred in order and available for use as the number of inferences increases and the chain of arguments lengthens. In the matrix we construct there will be room to represent all the relevant possibilities and to record each inference drawn.

The matrix for this problem must display an array of the four persons (in four rows) and the four artistic professions (in four columns) that they hold. It would look like this:

	DANCER	PAINTER	SINGER	WRITER
ALONZO				
KURT				
RUDOLF				
WILLARD				

When we conclude that the individual whose name is at the left of one of the rows cannot be the artist whose profession is at the top of one of the columns, we write an N (for "no," or a "−") in the box to the right of that person's name and in the column headed by that profession. We can immediately infer (from premiss 1) that neither Alonzo nor Rudolph is the singer, so we place an N to the right of their names, in the third (singer) column. Similarly, we can infer from premiss 2 that Kurt is neither the painter nor the writer, so we enter an N to the right of his name in the second (painter) and fourth (writer) columns. From premiss 3 we see that the writer is neither Alonzo nor Willard, so we enter N to the right of their names in the fourth column. The entries we have made thus far are all justified by the information originally given, and our matrix now looks like this:

	DANCER	PAINTER	SINGER	WRITER
ALONZO			N	N
KURT		N		N
RUDOLF			N	
WILLARD				N

From the information now available we can conclude by elimination that Rudolf must be the writer, so we enter a Y (for "yes," or a "+") in the box to the right of Rudolf's name in the fourth (writer) column, and we place an N in the other boxes to the right of his name. The array now makes it evident that the painter must be either Alonzo or Willard, and we can eliminate Alonzo in this way: Rudolf had his portrait painted by the painter (from premiss 2), and Alonzo has never heard of Rudolf (from premiss 4)—therefore Alonzo cannot be the painter. Thus we enter an N to the right of Alonzo's name under column two (painter).

We next conclude that Alonzo must be the dancer, so we enter a Y to the right of Alonzo's name in the first (dancer) column. Now we can enter an N in the dancer column for both Kurt and Willard. The only possible category remaining for Kurt is singer, and therefore we enter a Y in that box and an N in the singer column to the right of Willard's name. Again by elimination we conclude that Willard must be the painter and put a Y in the last empty box in the matrix. Our completed graphic display looks like this:

	DANCER	PAINTER	SINGER	WRITER
ALONZO	Y	N	N	N
KURT	N	N	Y	N
RUDOLF	N	N	N	Y
WILLARD	N	Y	N	N

From the filled-in matrix we can read off the solution: Alonzo is the dancer; Kurt is the singer; Rudolf is the writer; Willard is the painter.

Brainteasers of this general kind become more complicated when solutions on several dimensions are called for. Some such problems are very challenging and almost impossible to solve without using a matrix.[53]

Other reasoning problems present a different kind of challenge. Here is one that is elegant and amusing, but not very difficult. Try solving it before turning to the solution that follows.

You are confronted by six balls: two red, two green, and two blue. In each color pair you know that one ball is heavier than the other. You also know that all three of the heavier balls weigh the same, as do all three of the lighter balls. The six balls (call them R1, R2, G1, G2, B1, and B2) are otherwise indistinguishable. You have only a balance scale.

The Problem:

With no more than two weighings on the scale, how can one identify the heavier and the lighter balls in all three pairs?

Solution: First weighing: R1 + G1 // R2 + B1

If they balance: Of the pair R1 and R2, one is heavy and the other light. With the two red balls on opposite sides of the scale, we know that if the two sides balance there must be a heavy and a light ball on each side— because two heavies on one side would have to go down, and two lights on one side would have to go up. Therefore we know that either: G1 is heavy and B1 is light, or G1 is light and B1 is heavy.

If the two sides balance on the first weighing, the second weighing is: G1 // B1. Whatever the outcome of this weighing all balls will be identifiable:

If (on this weighing) G1 goes down:

— G1 is heavy (and G2 is light), and
— B1 is light (and B2 is heavy), and
— R1 is light (and R2 is heavy).

If (on this weighing) G1 goes up: the reverse is true.

But what if on the first weighing (R1 + G1 // R2 + B1) the two sides do not balance? Suppose R1 + G1 goes down. (If R1 + G1 goes up, the solution that follows is simply reversed.)

We know that in this case R1 (the red ball on the side that goes down) must be heavy; because if R1 were light, R2 would be heavy; and if R2 were heavy, R1 + G1 could not have gone down.

---

[53]Readers who find logical problems of this kind enjoyable will encounter a feast of such delights in a series entitled *Original Logic Problems,* and published by The Penny Press, Norwalk, CT.

Since R1 is heavy, one of the following three combinations must be the case:

(a) G1 is light   and B1 is light;   or
(b) G1 is heavy   and B1 is heavy;   or
(c) G1 is heavy   and B1 is light

If R1 + G1 go down on the first weighing, the second weighing is: R1 + R2 // G1 + B1.

We already know that R1 is heavy. On this second weighing, R1 + R2 (heavy + light) must either go down or go up, or the two sides will balance. Whichever the outcome, we can identify all the balls as follows:

(x) If R1 + R2 go down, G1 and B1 must both be light (since a heavy and a light can outweigh only two lights). In this case the combination must be pattern (a) above: G1 is light and B1 is light—and all are solved.

(y) If R1 + R2 go up, G1 and B1 must both be heavy (since heavy + light can be outweighed only by two heavies). In this case the combination must be pattern (b) above: G1 is heavy and B1 is heavy—and all are solved.

(z) If the two sides balance, G1 and B1 must also be heavy + light. In this case the combination must be pattern (c) above: G1 is heavy and B1 is light—and all are solved.

Before giving this problem to your friends, practice explaining the solution!

In the real world we are often called upon to reason from some present state of affairs to its causes, from what *is* to what *was*. Scientists—especially archeologists, geologists, astronomers, and physicians—commonly confront events or conditions whose origins are problematic. Reasoning that seeks to explain how things must have developed from what went before is called *retrograde analysis*. For example, to the amazement of astronomers, comet Hyakutake, streaking by the earth in 1996, was found to be emitting variable X-rays 100 times stronger than anyone had ever predicted a comet might emit. A comet expert at the Max Planck Institute in Germany remarked: "We have our work cut out for us in explaining these data—but that's the kind of problem you love to have."

We do love to have them, and because we do, problems in retrograde analysis are often devised for amusement. Such problems present a special difficulty, however: the logical framework that in the real world is supplied by scientific or historical knowledge must somehow be provided by the problem itself. Some rules or laws must be set forth within which logical analysis can proceed.

The chessboard is the setting for the most famous of all problems in retrograde analysis; the rules of chess provide the needed theoretical

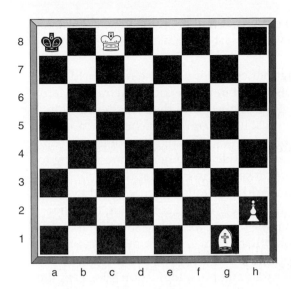

FIGURE 1-1

context. No skill in playing chess is required, but readers who are not familiar with the rules of chess may skip the illustration that follows.

Retrograde problems in chess commonly take this form: An arrangement of pieces on the chessboard is given; it was reached in a game of chess in which all the rules of the game were obeyed. What move, or series of moves has just been completed? An example of such a problem follows. The diagram presents a position reached in an actual game of chess, all moves in that game having been made in accordance with the rules of chess.

For the purpose of analysis the rows are numbered from bottom to top, 1 to 8, and the columns are lettered from left to right, a to h. Each square on the board then can be identified by a unique letter–number combination: the black king is on a8, the white pawn on h2, and so on. The problem is this: The last move was made by black. What was that move? And what was white's move just before that? Can you reason out the solution before reading the next paragraph?

Solution: The black king has just moved. Since the two kings may never rest on adjacent squares, it could not have moved to its present position from b7 or from b8; therefore, we may be certain that the black king has moved from a7, where it was in check.

That much is easily deduced. But what preceding white move could have put the black king in check? No move by the white bishop (on g1) could have done, it, because there would have been no way for that bishop to move to that square, g1, without the black king having been in check with white to move! Therefore it must be that the check was *discovered* by the movement of a white piece that had been blocking the bishop's attack and was captured by the black king on its move to a8. What white piece could have been on that black diagonal and moved from there to the white square in the corner? Only a knight that had been on b6. We may therefore be certain that before black's last move (the black king from a7 to a8) white's last move was that of a white knight from b6 to a8.[54]

The problems of reasoning that confront us in the real world are rarely as tidy as the puzzles discussed in this section, of course. Many real problems are not accurately described, and their misdescription may prove so misleading that no solution can be reached. In cases of that kind, some part or parts of the description of the problem need to be rejected or replaced. But we cannot do this when we are seeking to solve logical puzzles of the sort presented in this chapter.

Some problems in the real world, moreover, even when they are described accurately, may be incomplete in that something not originally available may be essential for the solution. The solution may depend on some additional scientific discovery, or some previously unimagined invention or equipment, or the search of some as-yet-unexplored territory. But in the statement of a logical puzzle, as in the writing of a good murder mystery, all the information that is sufficient for the solution must be given; otherwise we feel that the mystery writer, or the problem-maker, has been unfair to us.

Finally, the logical puzzle presents an explicit question (*e.g.,* Which member of the artistic foursome is the singer? What were black's and white's last moves?) whose answer, if given and proved, solves the problem definitively. But that is not the form in which many real-world problems arise. Real problems are often identified, initially at least, only by the recognition of some inconsistency or the occurrence of an unusual event, or perhaps just by the feeling that something is amiss—rather than by a well-formed question with a clearly defined answer.

In spite of these differences, problems designed to be solved through systematic reasoning are similar enough to problems in the real world to justify their use in the study of logic.

Exercises

The following problems require reasoning for their solution. To prove that an answer is correct requires an argument (often containing subsidiary arguments) whose premises are contained in the statement of the problem—and whose final conclusion is the answer to it. If the answer is correct, it is possible to construct a valid argument proving it. In working these problems, readers are urged to concern themselves not merely with discovering the answers but also with formulating arguments to prove that those answers are correct.

---

[54]Readers who find retrograde analysis enjoyable will take delight in a collection of such problems, compiled by the logician Raymond Smullyan and entitled *The Chess Mysteries of Sherlock Holmes* (New York: Alfred A. Knopf, 1979).

*1. In a certain mythical community, politicians never tell the truth, and nonpoliticians always tell the truth. A stranger meets three natives and asks the first of them, "Are you a politician?" The first native answers the question. The second native then reports that the first native denied being a politician. The third native says that the first native *is* a politician.

   How many of these three natives are politicians?

2. Of three prisoners in a certain jail, one had normal vision, the second had only one eye, and the third was totally blind. The jailor told the prisoners that, from three white hats and two red hats, he would select three and put them on the prisoners' heads. None could see what color hat he wore. The jailor offered freedom to the prisoner with normal vision if he could tell what color hat he wore. To prevent a lucky guess, the jailor threatened execution for any incorrect answer. The first prisoner could not tell what hat he wore. Next the jailor made the same offer to the one-eyed prisoner. The second prisoner could not tell what hat he wore either. The jailor did not bother making the offer to the blind prisoner, but he agreed to extend the same terms to that prisoner when he made the request. The blind prisoner said:

   > I do not need to have my sight;
   > From what my friends with eyes have said,
   > I clearly see my hat is _____ !

   How did he know?

3. On a certain train, the crew consists of the brakeman, the fireman, and the engineer. Their names listed alphabetically are Jones, Robinson, and Smith. On the train are also three passengers with corresponding names, Mr. Jones, Mr. Robinson, and Mr. Smith. The following facts are known:
   a. Mr. Robinson lives in Detroit.
   b. The brakeman lives halfway between Detroit and Chicago.
   c. Mr. Jones earns exactly $20,000 a year.
   d. Smith once beat the fireman at billiards.
   e. The brakeman's next-door neighbor, one of the three passengers mentioned, earns exactly three times as much as the brakeman.
   f. The passenger living in Chicago has the same name as the brakeman.
   What is the engineer's name?

4. The employees of a small loan company are Mr. Black, Mr. White, Mrs. Coffee, Miss Ambrose, Mr. Kelly, and Miss Earnshaw. The positions they occupy are manager, assistant manager, cashier, stenographer, teller, and clerk, though not necessarily in that order. The assistant manager is the manager's grandson, the cashier is the

stenographer's son-in-law, Mr. Black is a bachelor, Mr. White is twenty-two years old, Miss Ambrose is the teller's step-sister, and Mr. Kelly is the manager's neighbor.

Who holds each position?

*5. Benno Torelli, genial host at Miami's most exclusive nightclub, was shot and killed by a racketeer gang because he fell behind in his protection payments. After considerable effort on the part of the police, five suspects were brought before the district attorney, who asked them what they had to say for themselves. Each of them made three statements, two true and one false. Their statements were

> LEFTY: I did not kill Torelli. I never owned a revolver in all my life. Spike did it.
>
> RED: I did not kill Torelli. I never owned a revolver. The others are all passing the buck.
>
> DOPEY: I am innocent. I never saw Butch before. Spike is guilty.
>
> SPIKE: I am innocent. Butch is the guilty one. Lefty did not tell the truth when he said I did it.
>
> BUTCH: I did not kill Torelli. Red is the guilty one. Dopey and I are old pals.

Whodunnit?

6. Mr. Short, his sister, his son, and his daughter are fond of golf and often play together. The following statements are true of their four-some:
   (1) The best player's twin and the worst player are of the opposite sex.
   (2) The best player and the worst player are the same age.
   Which one of the foursome is the best player?

7. Daniel Kilraine was killed on a lonely road, two miles from Pontiac, Michigan, at 3:30 A.M. on March 17 of last year. Otto, Curly, Slim, Mickey, and the Kid were arrested a week later in Detroit and questioned. Each of the five made four statements, three of which were true and one of which was false. One of these persons killed Kilraine.

Their statements were

> OTTO: I was in Chicago when Kilraine was murdered. I never killed anyone. The Kid is the guilty one. Mickey and I are pals.
>
> CURLY: I did not kill Kilraine. I never owned a revolver in my life. The Kid knows me. I was in Detroit the night of March 17.

SLIM: Curly lied when he said he never owned a revolver. The murder was committed on St. Patrick's Day. Otto was in Chicago at this time. One of us is guilty.

MICKEY: I did not kill Kilraine. The Kid has never been in Pontiac. I never saw Otto before. Curly was in Detroit with me on the night of March 17.

THE KID: I did not kill Kilraine. I have never been in Pontiac. I never saw Curly before. Otto erred when he said I am guilty.

Whodunnit?

8. Picture a checkerboard (or chessboard like that on p. 63) having eight rows and eight columns of squares, alternately colored red and black. We are given a package of oblong dominoes, each one covering two of the squares of the chessboard, and asked to cover the chessboard completely. Obviously 32 dominoes are needed to cover the entire board.

But suppose we are given only 31 dominoes, so that, seeking to cover the chessboard, we must leave two squares empty. Suppose also that the upper-left-hand corner of the chessboard is left empty, so that one other square will also have to be left uncovered. Can the 31 dominoes be placed in such a way as to leave, as the other empty square, the square in the lower-right-hand corner? If so, how? And if not, why not?

9. In the same mythical community described in Exercise 1, a stranger meets three other natives and asks them, "How many of you are politicians?" The first native replies, "We are all politicians." The second native says, "No, just two of us are politicians." The third native then says, "That isn't true either."

Is the third native a politician?

*10. Imagine a room with four walls, a nail placed in the center of each wall, as well as in the ceiling and floor, six nails in all. The nails are connected to each other by strings, each nail connected to every other nail by a separate string. These strings are of two colors, red and blue, and of no other color. All these strings obviously make many triangles, since any three nails may be considered the apexes of a triangle.

Can the colors of the strings be distributed so that no one triangle has all three sides (strings) of the same color? If so, how? And if not, why not?

Challenge to the Reader

Here is a final reasoning problem whose solution requires the construction of a set of sustained arguments. It isn't easy—but solving it is well within your power and will give you great pleasure.

*11.   You are presented with a set of twelve metal balls, apparently identical in every respect: size, color, and so on. In fact, eleven of them are identical, but one of them is "odd": It differs from all the rest in weight only; it is either heavier, or lighter, than all the others. You are given a balance scale, on which the balls can be weighed against one another. If the same number of balls are put on each side of the balance, and the "odd" ball is on one side, that side will go down if the odd ball is heavier, or up if the odd ball is lighter; the two sides will balance if the odd ball is not among those weighed and the same number of balls are placed on each side. You are allowed three weighings only; any removal or addition of a ball constitutes a separate weighing.

Your challenge is this: Devise a set of three weighings that will enable you to identify the odd ball wherever it may lie in a random mixing of the twelve balls, *and* that will enable you to determine whether the odd ball is heavier or lighter than the rest. ∎

Summary of Chapter 1

In this chapter we introduced and illustrated the most fundamental concepts of logic.

In section 1.1 we defined logic as **the study of the methods and principles used to distinguish correct from incorrect reasoning,** and explained this definition.

In section 1.2 we explained **propositions**—which may be asserted or denied, and which are either true or false—and distinguished them from the sentences in which they may be expressed.

In section 1.3 we introduced and explained the concept of **an argument**—a cluster of propositions in which one is the **conclusion** and the other(s) are **premisses** offered in its support.

In section 1.4 we explained and illustrated **how arguments may be analyzed**—either by **paraphrasing,** in which the propositions are reformulated and arranged in logical order; or by **diagramming,** in which the propositions are numbered and the numbers are laid out on a page and connected in ways that exhibit the logical relations among the propositions.

In section 1.5 we discussed several aspects of the task of **recognizing arguments,** including conclusion- and premiss-indicators; the role of context in identifying premisses and conclusions; the nondeclarative forms in which premisses may appear; and arguments containing propositions that are not explicitly stated.

In section 1.6 we discussed the differences between **arguments** and **explanations.** We explained why it is often difficult to make this distinction, which depends on context and the purpose of the author of the passage.

In section 1.7 we discussed **deduction** and **validity.** We defined a deductive argument as one in which the conclusion is claimed to follow from the premisses with necessity, and a valid deductive argument as one in which the conclusion is necessarily true if the premisses are true.

In section 1.8 we discussed **induction** and **probability.** We defined an inductive argument as one whose conclusion has some degree of probability but in which the claim of necessity is not made. Inductive arguments, we explained, may be judged as better or worse but cannot be characterized as valid or invalid.

In section 1.9 we discussed some of the complicated relations between the **validity (or invalidity) of deductive arguments** and the **truth (or falsity) of propositions.**

In section 1.10 we discussed **complex argumentative passages,** showing how the diagramming technique is useful analyzing them.

In section 1.11 we discussed **problems of reasoning,** exhibiting the ways in which such problems can exercise and strengthen reasoning skills, while affording genuine intellectual pleasure.

*. . . the woof and warp of all thought and all research
is symbols, and the life of thought and science is
the life inherent in symbols; so it is wrong to say
that a good language is important to good thought,
merely; for it is the essence of it.*
—Charles Sanders Peirce

*Careful and correct use of language is a powerful
aid to straight thinking, for putting into words
precisely what we mean necessitates getting our
own minds quite clear on what we mean.*
—William Ian Beardmore Beveridge

CHAPTER 2

THE USES OF LANGUAGE

2.1 THREE BASIC FUNCTIONS OF LANGUAGE

Language is so subtle and complicated an instrument that we may lose sight of the multiplicity of its uses. We naturally seek to simplify, but without careful attention to the contexts of language use and the different purposes language serves, we may be led astray by the words or the forms of the discourse we encounter.

Words do not always serve the purposes they appear to be advancing. In casual conversation, the question "How are you?" is not really an inquiry about another's health. Although it might seem to be a request for information, we know that usually it is just a friendly greeting. Those who answer that question by describing the state of their health are likely to be thought obtuse. Requests, reports, and greetings are only some of the more obvious functions served by language.

The philosopher George Berkeley remarked in his *Treatise Concerning the Principles of Human Knowledge* (1710) that

> ...the communicating of ideas ...is not the chief and only end of language, as is commonly supposed. There are other ends, as the raising of some passion, the exciting to or deterring from an action, the putting the mind in some particular disposition; to which the former [communicating ideas] is in many cases barely subservient, and sometimes entirely omitted, when these can be obtained without it, as I think does not infrequently happen in the familiar use of language.

Twentieth-century philosophers have elaborated in great detail the variety of uses of language. In his *Philosophical Investigations* (1953), Ludwig Wittgenstein insisted rightly that there are "countless different kinds of use of what we call 'symbols,' 'words,' 'sentences.' " Among the examples suggested by Wittgenstein are giving orders, describing the appearance of an object or giving its measurements, reporting an event, speculating about an event, forming

71

and testing a hypothesis, presenting the results of an experiment in tables and diagrams, making up a story, play-acting, singing, guessing riddles, making a joke, solving a problem in practical arithmetic, translating from one language into another, asking, thinking, cursing, greeting, and praying.

Some order can be imposed on the staggering variety of language uses by dividing them into three very general categories: the *informative*, the *expressive*, and the *directive*. This threefold division is admittedly a simplification, perhaps an oversimplification, but it has been found very useful by many writers on logic and language.

1.   The **first** of these uses of language is **to communicate information.** Ordinarily, this is accomplished by formulating and affirming (or denying) propositions. Language used to affirm or deny propositions, or to present arguments, is said to be serving the *informative* function. Here we use the word "information" to include misinformation: false as well as true propositions, incorrect as well as correct arguments. Informative discourse is used to describe the world, and to reason about it. Whether the alleged facts are important or unimportant, general or particular, does not matter; in any case, the language used to describe or report them is being used informatively. A straightforward example of the informative use of language is the following passage from a recent report of facts by the Supreme Court of Florida:

> On Tuesday, November 7, 2000, the State of Florida, along with the rest of the United States, conducted a general election for the President of the United States. The [Florida] Division of Elections reported on Wednesday, November 8, that George Bush, the Republican candidate, had received 2,909,135 votes, and Albert Gore, Jr., the Democratic candidate, had received 2,907,351 votes. Because the overall difference in the total votes cast for each candidate [1,784 votes] was less than one-half of one percent of the total votes cast for that office, an automatic recount was conducted pursuant to Florida statutes.[1]

2.   Just as the clearest examples of informative discourse come from the reports of courts or laboratories, the best examples of language serving an *expressive* function come from lyric poetry. The lines of the poet, John W. Burgon, upon confronting the astounding ruins of the ancient city of Petra,

> Match me such marvel, save in Eastern clime—
> A rose-red city—"half as old as time"!

are not intended to inform us of any facts or theories concerning the world, but to manifest the poet's feelings of admiration and awe. With those lines we are told something about the scene before him, true, but their chief purpose was not to report information. The lines express emotions keenly felt by the writer and aim to evoke similar feelings in the

---

[1]*Palm Beach County Canvassing Board v. Katherine Harris*, decided 21 November 2000.

reader. Language serves the expressive function whenever it is used to vent or to arouse feelings.

The term *express* is used here in a somewhat narrower way than usual. It is natural to speak of expressing a feeling, an emotion, or an attitude. But ordinarily one speaks also of expressing an opinion, a belief, or a conviction. To avoid confusing the informative and expressive functions of language, we shall speak instead of *stating* or *declaring* an opinion or a belief and will reserve the term *express* in this chapter for revealing or communicating feelings, emotions, and attitudes.

Not all expressive language is poetry. We express sorrow by saying "That's too bad," or "What a pity," and enthusiasm by exclaiming "Terrific!" or "Fantastic!" Intense passion may be expressed by lovers murmuring private words of endearment. A worshiper's feeling of awe and wonder at the vastness and mystery of the universe may be expressed by reciting the Lord's Prayer, or the Twenty-third Psalm of David. Uses of language of this **second** kind are not intended to communicate information but **to express emotions, feelings, or attitudes.** Expressive discourse *as expressive* is neither true nor false. To apply only the criteria of truth or falsehood, correctness or incorrectness, to a piece of expressive discourse such as a lyric poem is to miss its point and to lose much of its value. One whose enjoyment of Keats's sonnet "On First Looking into Chapman's Homer" is diminished by knowing that it was Balboa rather than Cortés who discovered the Pacific Ocean is a "poor reader" of poetry. The purpose of the poem is not to teach history. Of course, some poems do have informative content that may be important. Some poetry may well be "criticism of life," in the words of a great poet. But such poems are more than *merely* expressive. Such poetry may be said to have a "mixed usage" or to serve a multiple function. This notion is discussed further in the following section.

Expression may be analyzed into two components. When one curses while alone, writes poems that are shown to no one, or prays in solitude, the language used functions to express the feelings of the speaker or writer, but it is not intended to evoke similar feelings in anyone else. On the other hand, when orators seek to move others, when a lover uses poetic language in courtship, and when the crowd cheers its athletic team, the language used not only expresses the feelings of its speakers but is intended to evoke similar feelings in the hearers. Expressive discourse, then, is used either to *manifest* the speaker's feelings or to *evoke* certain feelings in the auditor. Of course, it may do both.

3. Language serves the **third,** *directive* function when it is intended **to cause or to prevent overt action.** The clearest examples are commands and requests. When a parent tells a child to wash up for dinner, the intention is not to communicate any information or to express or evoke any particular emotion. The language is intended to get results. When a theatergoer says to the ticket seller, "Two, please," the language is again being used directively, to produce *action.* Between commands and requests the differences may be subtle—for almost any command can be converted into

a request with suitable changes in the tone of voice, or merely by the addition of the word "please." A question may also be classified as directive discourse when, as ordinarily, it is posed in order to request an answer.

In its nakedly imperative form, directive discourse is neither true nor false. A command such as "Close the window" cannot be either true or false. We may disagree about whether a command has been obeyed or disobeyed, but we never disagree about whether a command is true or false, because those terms simply do not apply to it. However, commands and requests have other attributes—reasonableness or impropriety—that are somewhat analogous to the truth or falsehood of informative discourse. We saw, in Chapter 1, that reasons can be given for an action to be performed, and that when the statement of those reasons accompanies the command, the whole may be regarded as an argument. For example:

> Drive defensively. Remember that the cemetery is full of law abiding citizens who had the right of way.[2]

In treating discourse of this kind as an argument, we regard the command that it contains as a proposition, one in which the recipients of the command are told that they should, or ought to, perform the action commanded. Exploring these issues, some writers have been led to develop a "logic of imperatives," but to discuss it is beyond the scope of this book.[3]

2.2 DISCOURSE SERVING MULTIPLE FUNCTIONS

The examples of informative, expressive, and directive discourse offered in the preceding section were chemically pure specimens, so to speak. This threefold division of communication is illuminating and valuable, but it cannot be applied mechanically, because almost any ordinary communication will probably exhibit all three uses of language. Thus a poem, which may be primarily expressive discourse, also may have a moral and thus also direct the reader (or hearer) to lead a different kind of life. Wordsworth wrote:

> The world is too much with us: late and soon,
> Getting and spending, we lay waste our powers:
> Little we see in Nature that is ours....

And of course, a poem may contain a certain amount of information as well.

On the other hand, although a sermon may be predominantly directive, seeking to bring about certain appropriate actions by members of the congregation (to abandon evil ways, or to contribute money to a good cause), it may evoke sentiments and manifest them, thus serving the expressive function, and may also include some information, such as the glad tidings of the Gospels. A scientific

---

[2] Ann Landers, "You Could Be Dead Right!", syndicated column, 26 August 1988.

[3] For an introduction to this topic, the interested reader can consult Nicholas Rescher, *The Logic of Commands* (London: Routledge & Kegan Paul, 1966).

treatise, although essentially informative, may express the writer's intellectual enthusiasm and may also, at least implicitly, bid the reader to verify independently the author's conclusion. Most ordinary uses of language are mixed.

When language serves mixed or multiple functions, the speaker or writer surely may not be doing so out of confusion. Rather, effective communication demands certain combinations of functions. Outside the context of clear and formal relationships—parent to child, employer to employee—one cannot simply issue an order and expect to have it obeyed; bald commands arouse resentment or antagonism and often are self-defeating. Consequently, a certain indirection must often be used. Normally, in order to cause the action we seek, we do not flatly issue an imperative; a more subtle method is generally required.

Actions often have very complex causes. Motivation is more properly the study of the psychologist than the logician, but it is common knowledge that actions usually involve both what the actor *wants* and what the actor *believes*. People who are hungry and desire food will not put what is before them into their mouths unless they believe that it is food; people who have no doubt that it is food may not touch it unless they are hungry.

Now, wants and desires are special kinds of what we have been calling "attitudes" or "feelings," and beliefs are commonly influenced by the information received. Consequently, we sometimes succeed in causing others to act by evoking in them the appropriate *attitudes*, and sometimes by giving them information that affects their relevant *beliefs*.

Suppose you aim to get your listeners to contribute to a particular charitable organization. Assuming your listeners to be benevolent in attitude, you may stimulate them to action by informing them of the good works done by that charitable organization. Your language is directive, its purpose being to cause action, but you advance this purpose by giving information rather than by issuing a naked command or a blunt request. Suppose, on the other hand, that your listeners are already fully persuaded that the charitable organization in question does accomplish benevolent results. A bold request for their money is still likely to fail—but you may succeed in causing them to contribute to that charitable organization by somehow arousing their benevolent feelings or emotions. In this case you achieve your end by using expressive discourse; you make a "moving appeal." Thus, again, your language naturally has mixed uses, functioning both expressively and directively.

Suppose, finally, that you are seeking a donation from people who have neither a benevolent attitude nor a belief that the charitable organization in question serves a benevolent purpose. You must then use language that is both expressive and informative, and the language used, aiming at action, will serve all three functions at once, not accidentally but deliberately and essentially, as necessary for successful communication.

The principal uses of language are three: the informative, the expressive, and the directive. But there are special uses of language in special contexts, worthy of note in passing, that do not fit neatly into this threefold division.

The *ceremonial* use of language is common, and in some cases it is a mixture of expressive and directive discourse. The expression of greetings of goodwill

■**For Enrichment**

and sociability, invitations to dinner, formal offers of employment—all may incorporate examples of ceremonial functions, and there are many other relatively insignificant uses that serve chiefly to lubricate human interaction. Also ceremonial are the solemn uses of language at religious rites. The impressive language of the marriage ceremony is intended both to emphasize the solemnity of the occasion (an expressive function) and to cause the bride and groom to perform in their new roles with a heightened appreciation of the seriousness of their marriage vows (a directive function).

Still other uses of language, akin to the ceremonial, are something more than mere mixtures of the principal uses. Suppose you are asked to attend a meeting at a certain time and place, and you reply, "I will, I promise." With those words you do more than report your attitude or predict your conduct. Your language in such cases serves to make the promise itself. And similarly, at the end of the marriage ceremony, when the minister or magistrate says, "I now pronounce you husband and wife," those words are much more than a mere report of what the speaker is doing. In some contexts the utterance of some words actually constitutes an important act. These are instances of the *performative* use of language.

A performative utterance is one that actually performs the act it appears to report or describe. Performative verbs are in a special class; they are verbs that denote an action that typically is accomplished (in the appropriate circumstances) by the use of that verb in the first person. Here are some other examples: "I congratulate you . . ."; "I apologize for my . . ."; "I suggest that . . ."; "I christen this ship . . ."; "I accept your offer . . ."; and so on.

These and other special uses of words and phrases exhibit the richness of every natural language, whose many complex functions are difficult to reduce to any single classificatory scheme. ■

2.3 THE FORMS OF DISCOURSE

A *sentence* is often defined as the unit of language that expresses a complete thought. In textbooks of grammar, sentences are commonly divided into four categories, called *declarative, interrogative, imperative,* and *exclamatory.* But these four grammatical categories do not coincide with those of assertions, questions, commands, and exclamations. We may be tempted to identify form with function, that is, to think that declarative sentences and informative discourse coincide, and that exclamatory sentences are suitable only for expressive discourse. Or we may think that directive discourse consists exclusively of sentences in the imperative or (regarding questions as always being requests for answers) the interrogative mood. Were such neat identifications possible, the problem of communication would be immensely simplified, for then we could tell the intended function of a passage simply by its form, which is open to direct inspection. But those who identify form with function may be led to misunderstand what is said, and perhaps to miss the point of much that is to be communicated.

It is a mistake to suppose that everything in the form of a declarative sentence is informative discourse, to be valued if true and rejected if false. "I had a very nice time at your party" is a declarative sentence, but its function need not be informative at all; rather, it may be ceremonial or expressive, expressing a feeling of friendliness and appreciation. Many poems and prayers are in the form of declarative sentences, even though their functions are not informative. To consider them simply informative and to evaluate them as simply true or false would be to shut oneself off from many valuable aesthetic and religious experiences. Again, many requests and commands are stated indirectly—perhaps more gently—by means of declarative sentences. The declarative sentence "I would like some coffee" should be taken by a waiter not as a mere report about the customer, but as an order or request for action. Were we invariably to judge the truth or falsehood of declarative sentences such as "I'd appreciate some help with this" or "I hope you'll be able to meet me after class at the library" and do no more than register them as information received, we should soon be without friends. These examples should show us that the declarative form is no certain indication of the informative function. Declarative sentences lend themselves to the formulation of every kind of discourse.

It is the same with other forms of sentences. The interrogative sentence "Do you realize that we're almost late?" is not necessarily a request for information about your state of mind; it may be a request to hurry. The interrogative sentence "Isn't it true that Russia and Germany signed a pact in 1939 that led to World War II?" may not be a question at all, but either an oblique way of communicating information or an attempt to express and evoke a feeling of hostility toward Russia, functioning informatively in the first instance and expressively in the second. Even a grammatical imperative, as in official documents beginning "Know all men by these presents that . . .," may be not a command but informative discourse in what it asserts and expressive discourse in its use of language to evoke the appropriate feelings of solemnity and respect. In spite of its close affinity to the expressive, an exclamatory sentence may serve a quite different function. The exclamation "Good Heavens, it's late!" may in context be a request to hurry. And the exclamation "What a beautiful view!", uttered by a realtor to a potential customer, may be intended to function more directively than expressively.

Much discourse is intended to serve two or possibly all three functions of language at once. In such cases, each aspect or function of a given passage is subject to its own proper criteria. A passage having an informative function may have that aspect evaluated as true or false. The same passage serving a directive function may have that aspect evaluated as proper or improper, right or wrong. And if an expressive function also is served by the passage, that component of it may be evaluated as sincere or insincere, as valuable or otherwise. To evaluate a given passage properly requires knowledge of the function or functions it is intended to serve.

For the logician, it is truth and falsehood, and the related notions of correctness and incorrectness of argument, that are most important. Hence, as students of logic, we must be able to differentiate discourse that functions informatively from discourse that does not. And further, we must be able to disentangle the informative function that a given passage serves from whatever other functions it may also be serving. To do this "disentangling," we must know what different functions language can serve and must be able to tell them apart. The grammatical structure of a passage often indicates its function, but there is no *necessary* connection between function and grammatical form. Nor is there any strict relation between function and content—in the sense of what might seem to be asserted by a passage. An illustration of this point was given by a great theorist of language in his discussion of "meaning":

> A petulant child, at bedtime, says *I'm hungry*, and his mother, who is up to his tricks, answers by packing him off to bed. This is an example of displaced speech.[4]

The child's speech here is directive—even though it does not succeed in procuring the wanted diversion. By the function of a passage, we generally mean the intended function. But that, unfortunately, is not always easy to determine.

When a passage is quoted in isolation it is particularly difficult to determine what function the passage is primarily intended to serve. The reason for this difficulty is that context is extremely important in determining function. What is imperative or flatly informative, by itself, may in its actual context function expressively, as part of a larger whole whose poetic effect is derived from all its parts in their arrangement. For example, in isolation,

> Come to the window,

is an imperative serving the directive function, and

> The sea is calm to-night.

is a declarative sentence serving an informative function. It might seem that neither of these has much expressive force—yet both appear, with great effect, in Matthew Arnold's poem "Dover Beach" and, in that context, chiefly serve the poem's expressive function. Many poems rely, similarly, on the expressive use of passages which, in other contexts, would be taken to have quite different functions.

It is also important to distinguish between the proposition that a sentence formulates and some fact about the speaker for which the utterance of that sentence is evidence. When a person remarks, "It is raining," the proposition asserted is about the weather, not about the speaker. Yet making the assertion is evidence that the speaker believes it to be raining, which is a fact about the speaker. It may also happen that people make statements that are ostensibly about their beliefs, not for the sake of giving information about themselves, but simply as a way of saying something else. To say "I believe that gold should not be used as a standard for currency" is ordinarily not to be construed as a psychological or autobiographical report about the beliefs of the speaker, but simply as a way of asserting that gold should not be so used. Similarly, when a speaker utters a command, it is reasonable to infer that the speaker wants something done; indeed, under some circumstances merely to assert that one has a specific desire is, in

---

[4] Leonard Bloomfield, *Language* (New York: Henry Holt, 1933).

effect, to give a command or make a request. An exclamation of joy gives evidence that the speaker is joyful, even though the speaker makes no assertion in the process. But to affirm, as a psychological report, that the speaker is joyful is to assert a proposition, something quite different from exclaiming joyously.

We noted in section 1.6 that the difference between an argument and an explanation often depends upon the intention of the speaker or writer of the passage. Our discussion of the different functions of language now permits a deeper examination of this matter.

When a speaker, addressing some controversial matter, says "I strongly oppose such-and-such," we understand that the intent of such a remark is not normally to give a report of that speaker's views (unless, perhaps, the remark is made by a candidate for public office, or by a public figure whose views are of popular interest). That "autobiographical" form of expression is, in fact, a common way of saying that such-and-such is a bad idea and we should all oppose it. When the speaker goes on to justify that point of view we get, not an explanation of his judgment, but an argument intended to persuade others that that judgment is correct. Opening the argument with a statement of one's own views on some disputable matter is not at all deceptive, even though, in such a case, the judgment and the biographical report are integrated.

The combination of more than one important function in a single passage can become problematic. The expression of ideas, protected by the First Amendment of our Constitution, may incorporate highly offensive language—and in such cases recognizing the *integration* of the informative and emotive functions in the offending utterance may be essential for the defense of free speech. Protesting the military draft during the Vietnam War by wearing in the Los Angeles County Courthouse a jacket on which a deliberate obscenity was emblazoned, a young man was convicted of "offensive conduct" under the California penal code. Reversing his conviction, the Supreme Court formulated this issue eloquently:

> [W]e cannot overlook the fact, because it is well illustrated by the episode involved here, that much linguistic expression serves a dual communicative function: it conveys not only ideas capable of relatively precise, detached explication, but otherwise inexpressible emotions as well. In fact, words are often chosen as much for their emotive as their cognitive force. We cannot sanction the view that the Constitution, while solicitous of the cognitive content of individual speech, has little or no regard for that emotive function which, practically speaking, may often be the more important element of the message sought to be communicated. . . . and in the same vein, we cannot indulge the facile assumption that one can forbid particular words without also running a substantial risk of suppressing ideas in the process.[5]

There is no mechanical method of distinguishing language that is informative and argumentative from language that serves other functions. In subsequent chapters we develop logical techniques that can be applied quite mechanically to test the *validity* of an argument, but there is no mechanical technique for recognizing the *presence* of an argument. Recognizing the different functions served in a given context requires careful thought and sensitivity to the flexibility of language and the multiplicity of its uses.

---

[5] *Cohen v. California*, 403 U.S. 15, at p. 26, 1971.

Principal Uses of Language	*Grammatical Forms of Language*
	Declarative
Informative	
	Interrogative
Expressive	
	Imperative
Directive	
	Exclamatory

Form often gives an indication of function—but there is no sure connection between the grammatical form and the use or uses intended. Language serving any one of the three principal functions (left column) may take any one of the four grammatical forms (right column).

Exercises

I.   Which of the various functions of language are exemplified by each of the following passages?

*1.   Check the box on line 6a **unless** your parent (or someone else) can claim you as a dependent on his or her tax return.

> —U.S. Internal Revenue Service, "Instructions," Form 1040, 1999

2.   'Twas brillig, and the slithy toves
Did gyre and gimble in the wabe;
All mimsy were the borogoves,
And the mome raths outgrabe.

> —Lewis Carroll, *Through the Looking Glass,* 1871

3.   What traveler among the ruins of Carthage, of Palmyra, Persepolis, or Rome, has not been stimulated to reflections on the transiency of kingdoms and men, and to sadness at the thought of a vigorous and rich life now departed . . .?

> —G. W. F. Hegel, *Lectures on the Philosophy of History,* 1823

4.   Of the five outer planets, Jupiter, Saturn, Uranus and Neptune are all vastly larger than Earth; but the outermost, Pluto, is the smallest planet of all, smaller even than Mercury.

*5.   I was a child and she was a child,
In this kingdom by the sea,
But we loved with a love that was more than love—
I and my Annabel Lee—

> —Edgar Allan Poe, "Annabel Lee"

6.   Reject the weakness of missionaries who teach neither love nor brotherhood, but chiefly the virtues of private profit from capital, stolen from your land and labor. Africa awake, put on the beautiful robes of Pan-African Socialism!

> —W. E. B. Dubois, "Pan-Africa," 1958

7. If I speak in the tongues of men and of angels, but have not love, I am a noisy gong or a clanging cymbal.

—I Corinthians 13: 1

8. I herewith notify you that at this date and through this document I resign the office of President of the Republic to which I was elected.

—President Fernando Collor De Mello, in a letter to the Senate of Brazil, 29 December 1992

9. American life is a powerful solvent. It seems to neutralize every intellectual element, however tough and alien it may be, and to fuse it in the native good will, complacency, thoughtlessness, and optimism.

—George Santayana, *Character and Opinion in the United States*, 1934

*10. The easternmost point of land in the United States—as well as the northernmost point and the westernmost point—is in Alaska.

II. What language functions are most probably *intended* to be served by each of the following passages?

*1. There is no caste here. Our Constitution is color-blind, and neither knows nor tolerates classes among citizens. In respect of civil rights, all citizens are equal before the law. The humblest is the peer of the most powerful.

—Justice John Harlan, dissenting in *Plessy v. Ferguson*, 163 U.S. 537, 1896

2. Judges do not know how to rehabilitate criminals—because no one knows.

—Andrew Von Hirsch, *Doing Justice—The Choice of Punishment*, 1976

3. When tillage begins, other arts follow. The farmers therefore are the founders of human civilization.

—Daniel Webster, "On Agriculture," 1840

4. The only thing necessary for the triumph of evil is for good men to do nothing.

—Edmund Burke, letter to William Smith, 1795

*5. They have no lawyers among them, for they consider them as a sort of people whose profession it is to disguise matters.

—Sir Thomas More, *Utopia*, 1516

6. Pleasure is an actual and legitimate aim, but if anyone says that it is the only thing men are interested in, he invites the old and legitimate reply that much of the pleasure they actually get would have been impossible unless they had desired something else. If men have found pleasure in fox-hunting, it is only because for the time they could forget about hunting pleasure, and hunt foxes.

—Brand Blanshard, *The Nature of Thought*, 1939

7. The bad workmen who form the majority of the operatives in many branches of industry are decidedly of the opinion that bad workmen ought to receive the same wages as good.

—John Stuart Mill, *On Liberty*, 1859

8. War is the greatest plague that can afflict humanity; it destroys religion, it destroys states, it destroys families. Any scourge is preferable to it.

—Martin Luther, *Table Talk*

9. Human history becomes more and more a race between education and catastrophe.

—H. G. Wells, *The Outline of History*, 1920

*10. The man who insists upon seeing with perfect clearness before he decides, never decides.

—Henri-Frederic Amiel, *Amiel's Journal*, 1885

11. Among other evils which being unarmed brings you, it causes you to be despised.

—Niccolò Machiavelli, *The Prince*, 1515

12. Eternal peace is a dream, and not even a beautiful one. War is a part of God's world order. In it are developed the noblest virtues of man: courage and abnegation, dutifulness and self-sacrifice. Without war the world would sink into materialism.

—Helmuth Von Moltke, 1892

13. Language! the blood of the soul, sir, into which our thoughts run, and out of which they grow.

—Oliver Wendell Holmes, *The Autocrat of the Breakfast-Table*, 1858

14. Over the past 133 years, more than 7,500 scientists, including social scientists, have been elected to the National Academy of Sciences. It appears that only three of them have been black.

—*The Journal of Blacks in Higher Education*, Summer 1996

*15. A little philosophy inclineth man's mind to atheism; but depth in philosophy bringeth man's mind about to religion.

—Francis Bacon, *Essays*

16. You'll never have a quiet world until you knock the patriotism out of the human race.

—George Bernard Shaw, *O'Flaherty, V.C.*

17. If [he] does really think that there is no distinction between virtue and vice, why, sir, when he leaves our houses let us count our spoons.

—Samuel Johnson, 1763

18. Man scans with scrupulous care the character and pedigree of his horses, cattle, and dogs before he matches them; but when he comes to his own marriage he rarely, or never, takes any such care.

    —Charles Darwin, *The Descent of Man*, 1871

19. The story of the whale swallowing Jonah, though a whale is large enough to do it, borders greatly on the marvelous; but it would have approached nearer to the idea of miracle if Jonah had swallowed the whale.

    —Thomas Paine, *The Age of Reason*, 1796

*20. The notion of race is the hydra-headed monster which stifles our most beautiful dreams before they are fairly dreamt, calling us away from the challenges of normative human interaction to a dissonance of suspicion and hatred in pursuit of a fantasy that never was.

    —C. Eric Lincoln, *Coming Through the Fire*, Duke University Press, 1996

21. White society is deeply implicated in the ghetto. White institutions created it, white institutions maintain it, and white society condones it.

    —The National Commission on Civil Disorders (Kerner Commission), 1968

22. An unhappy alternative is before you, Elizabeth. From this day you must be a stranger to one of your parents. Your mother will never see you again if you do *not* marry Mr. Collins, and I will never see you again if you do.

    —Jane Austen, *Pride and Prejudice*, 1892

23. Of this man Pickwick I will say little; the subject presents but few attractions; and I, gentlemen, am not the man, nor are you, gentlemen, the men, to delight in the contemplation of revolting heartlessness, and of systematic villainy.

    —Charles Dickens, *Pickwick Papers*, 1870

24. You praise the men who feasted the citizens and satisfied their desires, and people say that they have made the city great, not seeing that the swollen and ulcerated condition of the State is to be attributed to these elder statesmen; for they have filled the city full of harbors and docks and walls and revenues and all that, and have left no room for justice and temperance.

    —Plato, *Gorgias*

*25. The most inspiring and strengthening thing about the many open letters [to me] is that they show precisely the kind of will that is required to hold out against tyranny and vilification and murder: the will to win.

    —Salman Rushdie, *The Rushdie Letters*

III. For the following passages, indicate what propositions they may be intended to assert, if any; what overt actions they may be intended to cause, if any; and what they may be regarded as providing evidence for about the speaker, if anything.

*1. I will not accept if nominated and will not serve if elected.

—William Tecumseh Sherman,
message to the Republican National Convention, 1884

2. The government in its wisdom considers ice a "food product." This means that Antarctica is one of the world's foremost food producers.

—George P. Will

3. Criticism is properly the rod of divination: a hazel switch for the discovery of buried treasure, not a birch twig for the castigation of offenders.

—Arthur Symons, *An Introduction to the Study of Browning*, 1886

4. Without music, earth is like a barren, incomplete house with the dwellers missing. Therefore the earliest Greek history and Biblical history, nay the history of every nation, begins with music.

—Ludwig Tieck, quoted in Paul Henry Lang,
Music in Western Civilization, 1941

*5. Research is fundamentally a state of mind involving continual reexamination of doctrines and axioms upon which current thought and action are based. It is, therefore, critical of existing practices.

—Theobald Smith, *American Journal of Medical Science*, vol. 178, 1929

6. I have tried sedulously not to laugh at the acts of man, nor to lament them, nor to detest them, but to understand them.

—Baruch Spinoza, *Tractatus Theologico-politicus*, 1670

7. Of what use is political liberty to those who have no bread? It is of value only to ambitious theorists and politicians.

—Jean-Paul Marat

8. While there is a lower class I am in it, while there is a criminal element I am of it, and while there is a soul in prison I am not free.

—Eugene Debs

9. If there were a nation of gods they would be governed democratically, but so perfect a government is not suitable to men.

—Jean-Jacques Rousseau, *The Social Contract*

*10. There are three classes of citizens. The first are the rich, who are indolent and yet always crave more. The second are the poor, who have nothing, are full of envy, hate the rich, and are easily led by demagogues. Between the two extremes lie those who make the state secure and uphold the laws.

—Euripides, *The Suppliant Women*

11. I am convinced that turbulence as well as every other evil
    temper of this evil age belongs not to the lower but to the middle
    classes—those middle classes of whom in our folly we are so
    wont to boast.

    —Lord Robert Cecil, *Diary in Australia*

12. God will see to it that war shall always recur, as a drastic medicine
    for ailing humanity.

    —Heinrich Von Treitschke, *Politik*, 1916

13. I would rather that the people should wonder why I wasn't
    President than why I am.

    —Salmon P. Chase

14. He [Benjamin Disraeli] is a self-made man, and worships his
    creator.

    —John Bright

*15. We hear about constitutional rights, free speech and the free press.
    Every time I hear these words I say to myself, "That man is a Red,
    that man is a Communist." You never heard a real American talk in
    that manner.

    —Frank Hague, speech before
    the Jersey City Chamber of Commerce, 12 January 1938

16. Even a fool, when he holdeth his peace, is counted wise:
    And he that shutteth his lips is esteemed a man of understanding.

    —Proverbs 17:28

17. A word fitly spoken
    Is like apples of gold in ornaments of silver.

    —Proverbs 25:11

18. I have sworn upon the altar of God eternal hostility against every
    form of tyranny over the mind of man.

    —Thomas Jefferson, 1800

19. A free man thinks of nothing less than of death, and his wisdom is
    not a meditation upon death but upon life.

    —Baruch Spinoza, *Ethics*

*20. I have seen, and heard, much of Cockney impudence before now;
    but never expected to hear a coxcomb ask two hundred guineas for
    flinging a pot of paint in the public's face.

    —John Ruskin, on Whistler's painting "Nocturne in Black and Gold"

21. When people who are tolerably fortunate in their outward lot do
    not find in life sufficient enjoyment to make it valuable to them,
    the cause generally is, caring for nobody but themselves.

    —John Stuart Mill, *Utilitarianism*

22. A young man is not a proper hearer of lectures on political science; for he is inexperienced in the actions that occur in life, but its discussions start from these and are about these; and, further, since he tends to follow his passions, his study will be vain and unprofitable, because the end aimed at is not knowledge but action.

—Aristotle, *Nichomachean Ethics*

23. Men are never so likely to settle a question rightly as when they discuss it freely.

—Thomas Babington Macaulay, "Southey's Colloquies on Society," 1830

24. Mankind has grown strong in eternal struggles and it will only perish through eternal peace.

—Adolph Hitler, *Mein Kampf*, 1925

*25. But of the many falsehoods told by them, there was one which quite amazed me;—I mean when they said that you should be upon your guard and not allow yourselves to be deceived by the force of my eloquence. To say this, when they were certain to be detected as soon as I opened my lips and proved myself to be anything but a great speaker, did indeed appear to me most shameless—unless by the force of eloquence they mean the force of truth; for if such is their meaning, I admit that I am eloquent. But in how different a way from theirs!

—Plato, *Apology*

2.4   EMOTIVE WORDS

We now turn from our discussion of sentences and more extended passages to examine the *words* from which they are built. A single sentence, as we saw in section 2.2, can serve an informative and an expressive function simultaneously. To do the former, the sentence must formulate a proposition, and to do that, its words must have literal or descriptive meaning, referring to objects or events, and to their attributes or relations. When the sentence expresses an attitude or feeling, however, some of its words may also have emotional suggestiveness or impact. A word or phrase can have both a *literal* meaning and an *emotional* impact. The latter is commonly called the word's "emotive meaning."

The literal meanings and the emotive meanings of a word are largely independent of one another. For example, the terms "bureaucrat," "government official," and "public servant" have almost identical literal meanings—but their emotive meanings are very different. "Bureaucrat" tends to express resentment and disapproval, while the honorific "public servant" tends to express respect and approval. "Government official" is more nearly neutral than either of the others.

It is clear that the words we use to refer to things have a marked effect upon our attitudes toward those things. The actual fragrance of a flower is not altered by its name; a rose by any other name, as Shakespeare wrote, would smell as sweet. And yet our response to a flower may indeed be influenced if we were told that it is commonly called a "skunkweed." On Wall Street carefully chosen language can make any move in the stock market seem good. On some days there is a "rally," which means prices are rising. Other days see "profit taking," which means prices are falling because so many people are selling stocks, but it still sounds good. Big companies, moreover, rarely go "bankrupt" any more; they are "restructured," which sounds ever so much better.

This influencing of attitude explains the proliferation of euphemisms, gentle words for harsh realities. In wartime the defeat of one's own army is likely to be called, for popular consumption, a "temporary setback," and a massive retreat may be reported as an "orderly consolidation of forces." During the war in Vietnam, Senator Eugene McCarthy, campaigning for a presidential nomination, was caustic in his criticism of American military intervention and of the widespread unwillingness to be candid about it. "We don't declare war any more," he said, "we declare national defense."[6]

We are constantly inventing new phrases to replace old ones with which we are no longer comfortable. Undertakers become morticians, janitors become maintenance men, old people become senior citizens. But the replacements newly associated with the old realities eventually lose their appeal as well; "maintenance man" comes to be replaced by "custodian," and "mortician" by "funeral director," and so on. Germaine Greer wrote:

> It is the fate of euphemisms to lose their function rapidly by association with the actuality of what they designate, so that they must be regularly replaced with euphemisms for themselves.[7]

The story is told that President Harry Truman's wife, Bess, was asked by her friends to stop President Truman from saying "manure," to which she replied that it had taken her forty years to get him to *start* saying "manure."

Language does have a life of its own, independent of the facts it is used to describe. Certain physiological activities pertaining to reproduction and elimination can be unemotionally described by the use of medical vocabulary, without offending the most squeamish taste; yet the description of the same activities using four-letter vulgarisms may shock all but the most hardened listeners. Using our terminology, we may say that the two sets of words have the same literal or descriptive meanings but are moderately or sharply opposed in their emotive meanings.

Sometimes the emotive meaning of a word or phrase may arise, in the mind of a given person, not from the thing it literally refers to, but from the context in which it was first learned or encountered. One writer has reported

> . . . the illuminating story of a little girl who, having recently learned to read, was spelling out a political article in the newspaper. "Father," she asked, "what is Tammany Hall?" And her father replied in the voice usually reserved for the taboos of social communication, "You'll understand that when you grow up, my dear." Acceding to this adult whim of evasion, she desisted from her inquiries; but something in Daddy's tone had convinced her that Tammany Hall must be connected with illicit *amour*, and

---

[6] In a speech at the National Convention of the Democratic Party, in Chicago, July 1968.
[7] In *The Female Eunuch* (New York: McGraw-Hill, 1971).

> for many years she could not hear this political institution mentioned without expe-
> riencing a secret nonpolitical thrill.[8]

For many of us, certain words or phrases, because of some special association in our lives, carry a private emotional suggestiveness we may be reluctant to admit.

The contrast between literal and emotive meanings and the manipulative uses of their differences led the philosopher Bertrand Russell to devise an amusing and instructive word game. He "conjugated" an "irregular verb" thus:

> I am firm; you are obstinate; he is a pigheaded fool.

The London *New Statesman and Nation* subsequently ran a contest soliciting such irregular conjugations and picked among the winners the following:

> I am righteously indignant; you are annoyed;
> he is making a fuss about nothing.
>
> I have reconsidered it; you have changed your mind;
> he has gone back on his word.

The game confirms what common experience teaches: *One and the same thing can be referred to by words that have very different emotive impacts.*

Exercise

> Construct five original "conjugations of irregular verbs" in which literally the same activity is given a laudatory description in the first person, a fairly neutral one in the second person, and a derogatory one in the third person.

2.5 KINDS OF AGREEMENT AND DISAGREEMENT

To the extent that any thing or some activity can be described by using alternative phrases—one conveying approval, another disapproval, still another neutrality—different kinds of agreement and of disagreement may be communicated about anything.

Two people may disagree about whether something has in fact taken place, and when they do, they may be said to have *disagreement in belief.* On the other hand, they may agree that an event has actually occurred, thus agreeing in belief, and yet they may have different or even opposite attitudes toward that event. One may describe it in language that expresses approval; the other in terms that express disapproval. Here too there is disagreement, but it is not disagreement in belief. This disagreement is rather a difference in feeling about the matter, a *disagreement in attitude.*[9]

---

[8] Margaret Schlauch, *The Gift of Tongues* (New York: Viking Press, 1942).

[9] We are indebted to our late colleague and friend, Professor Charles L. Stevenson, for the terms agreement and disagreement "in belief" and agreement and disagreement "in attitude," and to him also for the notion of "persuasive definition," discussed in Chapter 4. See his *Ethics and Language* (New Haven, CT: Yale University Press, 1944).

Bearing these two kinds of disagreement in mind, we may identify four kinds of relations between two persons—let us call them A and B—discussing some given event or other matter of fact.

First, they may be in full harmony, agreeing in their beliefs regarding the occurrence of the event and in their attitude toward it.

Second, they may agree in their beliefs about the event, but disagree in their attitudes toward it, one thinking the event good, the other thinking it bad. Suppose the event in question were the change of a political candidate's position on some controversial issue. A and B may agree that the change did occur, but A thinks it splendid while B finds it dreadful. As A sees it, the candidate is to be commended for "listening to the voice of reason"; but as B sees it, the candidate is to be condemned for "opportunistic inconsistency."

Third, they may agree in attitude, yet disagree in their beliefs about facts giving rise to that attitude. Thus A and B may both approve warmly of the candidate in question, yet differ in their understanding of the candidate's actual position. A may think that, having "listened to the voice of reason," the candidate did change her position, while B may think she did not change her position at all, having "steadfastly refused to be swayed by blandishments." This third possibility may at first seem implausible, but on reflection will be recognized as common; in electoral politics we know that the same candidate often may be supported for reasons that are not only different but at times incompatible.

Fourth, the two may be in complete disharmony, disagreeing not only about the facts but also in their attitudes toward what they think the facts to be. A, believing that the candidate has *changed* a position, may very strongly *approve* of that change as a product of "wise reconsideration"; while B, believing that the candidate's position remains *unchanged,* may vigorously *disapprove* of the "stubborn refusal to admit error."

When the resolution of disagreement is our goal, we must attend not only to the facts in a given case, but also to the varying attitudes of the disputants toward those facts. Different kinds of disagreement call for different methods of achieving resolution. So, if we are unclear about what kinds of disagreement exist, we shall be unclear about what methods should be used. Disagreement in *belief* can best be resolved by ascertaining the *facts.* To decide them, if it is sufficiently important, witnesses could be questioned, documents consulted, records examined, and so on. When the facts are established and the issue decided, the disagreement is likely to be resolved. The methods of scientific inquiry are available here, and it will suffice to direct them squarely at the question of fact about which there is disagreement in belief.

On the other hand, if there is disagreement in *attitude* rather than disagreement in belief, the techniques appropriate for settling it are rather different, being more varied and less direct. To call witnesses, consult documents, and the like, to the end of establishing that the event did (or did not) take place, would be fruitless in resolving such a dispute because the facts of the case are not at issue; the disagreement is not over what the facts *are* but over how they are to be valued. Efforts to resolve this disagreement in attitude may involve reference to factual questions, but not the one about which there is attitudinal conflict. It may be fruitful to consider what happy (or unhappy) consequences would have been entailed had the event in question not occurred. Motives and intentions may also be of importance. These are factual matters, to be sure, but none of them is identical with what would be the issue if the disagreement were in belief rather than in attitude. Still other methods may sometimes resolve a disagreement in attitude. Persuasion may be attempted, with its extensive use of expressive language. Rhetoric may be effective in unifying the will of a group and in achieving unanimity of attitude—but of course, it is wholly worthless in resolving a question of fact.

Such words as "good" and "bad," "right" and "wrong," in their strictly ethical uses, tend to have a very strong emotive impact. When we characterize an action as *right* or a situation as *good* we express an attitude of approval toward it, whereas when we characterize it as *wrong* or *bad* we are expressing disapproval. That cannot be denied. Some writers on ethics contend, however, that these terms have *no* literal or cognitive meaning; only emotive meaning is allowed them. Other writers on ethics vigorously insist that such terms *do* have cognitive meaning, and refer to the objective characteristics of what is being discussed. In this quarrel, the student of logic need not take sides. But it is clear that not every attitude of approval or disapproval implies a moral judgment. There are aesthetic values too, and there are also personal values reflecting individual preferences or tastes. A negative attitude toward a thing—some food or item of dress, for example—need not involve either ethical or aesthetic judgment, yet it may be given strong verbal expression.

Where disagreement is in attitude rather than in belief, the most vigorous—and, of course, genuine—disagreement may be expressed in statements which are literally true. When two parties appear to disagree and formulate their divergent judgments in statements that are logically consistent with each other, it would be a mistake to say that the parties do not "really" disagree or that their disagreement is "merely verbal." They are not merely "saying the same thing in different words." They may, of course, be using their words to affirm what is literally the same fact, but they may also be using their words to express conflicting attitudes toward that fact. In such cases, their disagreement, although not "literal," is nevertheless *genuine.* It is not "merely verbal," because words function expressively as well as informatively. And if we are interested in resolving disagreements, we must be clear about their nature, since the techniques appropriate to the resolution of one kind of disagreement, as we have seen, may be hopelessly beside the point for another.

Determining whether a given disagreement is one of belief, or of attitude, or of both belief and attitude is sometimes difficult; it may depend on some interpretation of the words of the disputants. The distinction between differences of attitude and differences of belief may be obscured by the ways in which the conflicting opinions are expressed, the essential core of the dispute therefore remaining in doubt. When two persons disagree about whether one thing is "better" or "more important" than another, they are both likely to think that there are differences of belief that divide them, and that may well be true. But a dispute whose superficial form is that of a difference about alleged matters of fact may in some cases really be a dispute—a genuine dispute—about attitudes. This is especially true when what is in dispute are the *values* of things or acts.

One of the greatest sports writers and one of the greatest football coaches differed profoundly about the importance of winning. Wrote the journalist, Grantland Rice:

> For when the One Great Scorer comes
> To write against your name,
> He marks—not that you won or lost—
> But how you played the game.

Said the coach, Vince Lombardi:

> Winning isn't everything. It's the only thing.

Plainly the attitudes of these two men toward winning were in conflict. Do you believe that this disagreement of attitude was rooted in a disagreement of belief?

In spite of these inescapable difficulties, the distinction between disagreements of attitude and disagreements of belief is very useful; awareness of the different uses of language helps us to understand the kinds of disagreements we may be confronting. Drawing the indicated distinctions does not by itself solve the problem or resolve the disagreement, of course. But it clarifies the discussion and may reveal the kind and locus of the conflict. The more fully we understand the nature of a disagreement, the better able we will be to resolve it.

Exercises

Identify the kinds of agreement or disagreement most probably exhibited by the following pairs.

*1. **a.** Answer a fool according to his folly,
         Lest he be wise in his own conceit.

    —Proverbs 26:5

   b. Answer not a fool according to his folly,
         Lest thou also be like unto him.

    —Proverbs 26:4

 2. **a.** Native Abkhazians—a Turkic-speaking, mostly Muslim group—came under Georgian rule a millennium ago. Georgia itself was absorbed into the Russian Empire in the 19th century and its ethnic groups forcibly rearranged when Stalin, a Georgian-born communist, ruled the Kremlin. Last year [1991] Georgia regained independence. . . . And in July [1992] Abkhazian separatists declared independence, despite the fact that only 18 percent of the people living in Abkhazia are now ethnic Abkhazians.

    —Editorial, "Abkhazia: Small War, Big Risk,"
    New York Times, 8 October 1992

   b. Your description of native Abkhazians as a "Turkic-speaking, mostly Muslim" group is outrageous. The Abkhazian people have their own language, which the Turks know absolutely nothing about!. . . Your constant portrayal of Abkhazians as separatists and secessionists is quite wrong. Abkhazians are not claiming a territory that is not theirs. Abkhazia has been the territory of Abkhazians for many centuries. . . . If the Georgian people can claim independence, why can't the Abkhazians do the same? What makes self-determination a word that only Georgians can use?

> —Y. Kazan, letter to *New York Times*, 22 October 1992

3.   **a.** I want to make it clear that the two former faculty members to whom you refer, Professor David J. Ayers and Dr. John Jeffrey, were not "administratively suspended" as you suggest. Rather, they were given notices of the administration's intention not to recommend their reappointment and then released from having to fulfill further contractual obligations. . . . It is our considered judgment that there has been no abrogation of academic freedom or violation of academic due process in their cases.

> —Edward H. Pauley, Vice President for Academic Affairs,
> Dallas Baptist University, in a letter to the editor of *Measure*,
> August 1992

b. You state in your letter that, because Professors Ayers and Jeffrey received timely notice of the nonrenewal of their appointments, "due process" *was* followed in their cases. We disagree. There seems to be no dispute that Professors Ayers and Jeffrey had been issued contracts for the 1992–93 academic year and were scheduled to teach courses during the fall term. Accordingly, we continue to believe that the administration's action to separate Professors Ayers and Jeffrey from their professional responsibilities, followed neither by reinstatement nor opportunity for a hearing, constituted summary dismissal.

> —Jonathan Knight, Associate Secretary,
> American Association of University Professors,
> in a letter to Vice President Pauley, Dallas Baptist University,
> *Measure*, October 1992

4.   **a.** A stitch in time saves nine.
     b. Better late than never.

*5.   **a.** Absence makes the heart grow fonder.
     b. Out of sight, out of mind.

6.   **a.** The race is not to the swift, nor the battle to the strong.

> —Ecclesiastes 9:11

b. But that's the way to bet.

> —Jimmy The Greek

7.   **a.** For that some should rule and others be ruled is a thing not only necessary, but expedient; from the hour of their birth, some are marked out for subjection, others for rule. . . . It is clear,

then, that some men are by nature free, and others slaves, and that for these latter slavery is both expedient and right.

—Aristotle, *Politics*

b. If there are some who are slaves by nature, the reason is that men were made slaves against nature. Force made the first slaves, and slavery, by degrading and corrupting its victims, perpetuated their bondage.

—Jean-Jacques Rousseau, *The Social Contract*

8. a. War alone brings up to its highest tension all human energy and puts the stamp of nobility upon the peoples who have the courage to face it.

—Benito Mussolini, *Encyclopedia Italiana*

b. War crushes with bloody heel all justice, all happiness, all that is Godlike in man. In our age there can be no peace that is not honorable; there can be no war that is not dishonorable.

—Charles Sumner, *Addresses on War*, 1904

9. a. Next in importance to freedom and justice is popular education, without which neither freedom nor justice can be permanently maintained.

—James A. Garfield

b. Education is fatal to anyone with a spark of artistic feeling. Education should be confined to clerks, and even them it drives to drink. Will the world learn that we never learn anything that we did not know before?

—George Moore, *Confessions of a Young Man*, 1888

***10. a.** Belief in the existence of god is as groundless as it is useless. The world will never be happy until atheism is universal.

—J. O. La Mettrie, *L'Homme Machine*, 1865

b. Nearly all atheists on record have been men of extremely debauched and vile conduct.

—J. P. Smith, *Instructions on Christian Theology*

11. a. I know of no pursuit in which more real and important services can be rendered to any country than by improving its agriculture, its breed of useful animals, and other branches of a husbandman's cares.

—George Washington, letter to John Sinclair

b. With the introduction of agriculture mankind entered upon a long period of meanness, misery, and madness, from which they are only now being freed by the beneficent operations of the machine.

—Bertrand Russell, *The Conquest of Happiness*, 1930

12. **a.** Whenever there is, in any country, uncultivated land and unemployed poor, it is clear that the laws of property have been so far extended as to violate natural right.

    —Thomas Jefferson

    b. Every man has by nature the right to possess property of his own. This is one of the chief points of distinction between man and the lower animals.

    —Pope Leo XIII, *Rerum Novarum*

13. **a.** The right of revolution is an inherent one. When people are oppressed by their government, it is a natural right they enjoy to relieve themselves of the oppression, if they are strong enough, either by withdrawal from it, or by overthrowing it and substituting a government more acceptable.

    —Ulysses S. Grant, *Personal Memoirs,* vol. 1

    b. Inciting to revolution is treason, not only against man, but against God.

    —Pope Leo XIII, *Immortalie Dei*

14. **a.** Language is the armory of the human mind; and at once contains the trophies of its past, and the weapons of its future conquests.

    —Samuel Taylor Coleridge

    b. Language—human language—after all, is little better than the croak and cackle of fowls, and other utterances of brute nature—sometimes not so adequate.

    —Nathaniel Hawthorne, *American Notebooks*

* 15. **a.** How does it become a man to behave towards the American government today? I answer, that he cannot without disgrace be associated with it.

    —Henry David Thoreau, *An Essay on Civil Disobedience*

    b. With all the imperfections of our present government, it is without comparison the best existing, or that ever did exist.

    —Thomas Jefferson

16. **a.** Farming is a senseless pursuit, a mere laboring in a circle. You sow that you may reap, and then you reap that you may sow. Nothing ever comes of it.

    —Joannes Stobaeus, *Florilegium*

    b. No occupation is so delightful to me as the culture of the earth.

    —Thomas Jefferson

17. **a.** Our country: in her intercourse with foreign nations may she always be in the right; but our country, right or wrong!

    —Stephen Decatur, toast at a dinner in Norfolk, Virginia, April 1816

     b. Our country, right or wrong. When right, to be kept right; when wrong, to be put right.[10]

—Carl Schurz, speech in the U.S. Senate, January 1872

18.   **a.** A bad peace is even worse than war.

—Tacitus, *Annals* b.

     b. The most disadvantageous peace is better than the most just war.

—Desiderius Erasmus, *Adagia*

19.   **a.** It makes but little difference whether you are committed to a farm or a county jail.

—Henry David Thoreau, *Walden*

     b. I know few things more pleasing to the eye, or more capable of affording scope and gratification to a taste for the beautiful, than a well-situated, well-cultivated farm.

—Edward Everett

* 20.   **a.** Thought, like all potent weapons, is exceedingly dangerous if mishandled. Clear thinking is therefore desirable not only in order to develop the full potentialities of the mind, but also to avoid disaster.

—Giles St. Aubyn, *The Art of Argument*

     b. Reason is the greatest enemy that faith has: it never comes to the aid of spiritual things, but—more frequently than not—struggles against the divine Word, treating with contempt all that emanates from God.

—Martin Luther, *Table Talk*

2.6 EMOTIVELY NEUTRAL LANGUAGE

The expressive use of language is just as legitimate as the informative. There is nothing wrong with emotive language, and there is nothing wrong with language that is nonemotive, or neutral. Similarly, we can say that there is nothing wrong with pillows and nothing wrong with hammers. True enough; but we will not succeed in trying to drive nails with pillows, nor will we be comfortable resting our heads on hammers. We may preserve the literal meaning of a poet's romantic lines when we replace his or her emotive language with matter-of-fact speech, but we will lose a very great deal in doing so. In some kinds of poetry emotively colored language is properly preferred to neutral language. In other spheres, language that is neutral is preferable to language that is emotively colored.

    Which spheres are those? Neutral language is to be prized when factual truth is our objective. When we are trying to learn what really is the case, or trying to follow an argument, distractions will be frustrating—and emotion is a powerful

---

[10] On this kind of disagreement, G. K. Chesterton commented that " 'My country, right or wrong' is like saying 'My mother, drunk or sober.' "

distraction. The passions tend to cloud the reason; this truth is reflected in the usage of "dispassionate" and "objective" as near synonyms. Therefore, when we are trying to reason about the facts in a cool and objective fashion, referring to them in strongly emotive language is a hindrance rather than a help.

Language that is altogether neutral, completely free of emotional charge, may not be available when we deal with some very controversial matters. In discussions of the rights and wrongs of abortion, for example, the key terms used by one's opponent (whatever they may be) are very likely to be held emotionally distorting, and there may be no fully dispassionate terms acceptable as value-neutral to all parties. In such circumstances, if the genuine goal remains that of reaching the truth, the task is to reduce so far as possible the emotional loading of the terms used. The aim of emotive neutrality may not be fully achievable, yet we can at least try to use language that presupposes only those beliefs, of whatever kind, that are agreed to by the discussants. Language that is emotionally toned is bound to distract; language that is *loaded,* heavily charged with emotional meaning, is unlikely to advance the quest for truth.

In his essay "The Dilemma of Determinism," William James defended his "wish to get rid of the word 'freedom' " on the grounds that "its eulogistic associations have . . . overshadowed all the rest of its meaning." He rightly preferred to discuss "the freedom of the will" using the words "determinism" and "indeterminism" because, he said, "their cold and mathematical sound has no sentimental associations that can bribe our partiality either way in advance." We should do well to follow James's example.

Interviewers, conducting professional opinion polls, must be very careful not to prejudice the responses they receive by using emotive phrasing in the questions asked. When this caution is ignored the results may be worthless. In 1993 a large poll conducted by *Time* and the Cable News Network asked: "Should laws be passed to prohibit interest groups from contributing to campaigns, or do groups have a right to contribute to the candidates they support?" Of all respondents 40 percent said they would prohibit group contributions; 55 percent said groups had a right to contribute. That same year Ross Perot, a very wealthy candidate for the presidency, conducted his own poll, asking: "Should laws be passed to eliminate all possibilities of special interests giving huge sums of money to candidates?" Not surprisingly, 80 percent of those responding to this formulation of the question said yes, such contributions should be prohibited. Including phrases like "special interests" and "huge sums of money" plainly interferes with any effort to learn what people really do believe about such matters.[11] These two polls, it may be said, are not really asking the same question. But even if that is so, the logical point remains: If our aim is to communicate information, and if we wish to avoid being misunderstood, we should use language with the least possible emotive impact. Playing on emotion, rather than appealing to reason, is a common device of

---

[11] The 17 questions in the Perot poll, many of which contain emotionally loaded terms, appeared in full as a "referendum" ballot inserted in *TV Guide,* 20 March 1993, and were asked nationwide on NBC TV on 21 March 1993. The *Time*/CNN poll was reported in the *New York Times,* March 1993.

those who profit from the distortion of the truth. The most flagrant displays of such efforts to manipulate are in the world of advertising, where the overriding aims are always to persuade, to sell, and often to exploit. We must be constantly on our guard against these uses of emotionally charged language, and also guard against their uses in political campaigns, where almost every rhetorical trick is played and replayed. "With words," said Benjamin Disraeli, "we govern men." Our best defenses are thoughtful sensitivity to language and its different uses, as well as skill in recognizing the assorted efforts of unscrupulous persons to make the worse appear the better cause.

Exercise

Select a brief passage of highly emotive writing from some current periodical, and translate it in such a way as to retain its informative significance while reducing its expressive significance to a minimum.

Summary of Chapter 2

In this chapter, we have explained the multiple uses and forms of language, and the kinds of misunderstanding and abuse that may arise from the failure to recognize these complexities.

In section 2.1, three basic functions of language were distinguished: **informing, expressing,** and **directing.**

In section 2.2, we have exhibited the ways in which **a given linguistic passage may perform multiple functions**—two or even all three of the basic functions simultaneously.

In section 2.3, we showed that sentences in the standard grammatical forms—declarative, interrogative, imperative, and exclamatory sentences—do not always perform the functions associated with their names. Declarative sentences may serve a directive or expressive function; interrogative sentences may serve an informative or directive function, and so on. **Grammatical forms do not determine language function.**

In section 2.4, we examined the uses of the **words** with which sentences are built, and we discussed **emotive language.**

In section 2.5, we distinguished between **disagreements in belief** and **disagreements in attitude.** Parties in conflict may agree both about the facts and in their attitude toward what they think the facts to be, or they may disagree about both. They may agree about the facts and disagree in their attitudes toward those facts. They may disagree about what the facts are yet agree in their attitude toward what they believe the facts to be. To resolve disagreements, it is essential that their real nature be understood.

In section 2.6, we discussed the importance of reducing emotionally charged passages to **emotively neutral language,** so far as that may be possible, when the aim of discourse is to determine truth.

. . . familiarity with a notion [is] the first step toward clearness of apprehension, and the defining of it the second.
—Charles Sanders Peirce

Since all terms that are defined are defined by means of other terms, it is clear that human knowledge must always be content to accept some terms as intelligible without definition, in order to have a starting-point for its definitions.
—Bertrand Russell

CHAPTER 3

DEFINITION

3.1 DISPUTES, VERBAL DISPUTES, AND DEFINITIONS

Language is a very complicated instrument, the principal tool for human communication. But when words are used carelessly or mistakenly, what was our instrument becomes our burden. In section 2.5 it was explained that differences among conflicting parties may be of attitude as well as of belief, and we observed that differences of either kind may nevertheless be entirely genuine. But there are also circumstances in which apparent disagreements are in fact not genuine, but only the result of misunderstanding or the misuse of words. In the previous chapter we examined genuine disagreements of different kinds; here we turn to disputes of different kinds, of which some are genuine and some are not.

Three different kinds of disputes must be distinguished. The first is the **obviously genuine dispute,** in which the parties explicitly and unambiguously disagree, either in belief or in attitude. If A cheers while B sulks when the Yankees win the World Series, their disagreement in attitude (which nothing is likely to resolve) is plainly real, perhaps even intense, even though the identity of the winner is not at issue. In another context, if A maintains that the Pacific entrance to the Panama Canal is further east than the Atlantic entrance, while B denies this, attitudes are not at issue but the facts are, and a good map should settle the controversy.[1] Whether of attitude or of belief, disputes of this first kind always involve some genuine disagreement. What divides the parties is not a matter of language only; there is some real difference in their judgment of what the facts are or in their evaluation of the facts. Such genuine disputes therefore cannot be resolved by definitions, or by any merely linguistic adjustments.

Of course, there can be factual disputes *about* words—for example, how a word is correctly spelled or used—or factual disputes *about* attitudes—for

---

[1]A is correct; the Pacific entrance to the Panama Canal really is to the east of the Atlantic entrance!

example, whether some third party is unfriendly or only shy. Facts may be linguistic or psychological as well as physical or geographical, and the parties may disagree about facts of any kind. But the dispute remains genuine if it is indeed about some facts, and can be resolved by ascertaining facts of some kind.

There is, however, a second kind of quarrel, a **merely verbal dispute,** in which there is no genuine disagreement between the parties at all, and yet there appears to be disagreement. Misunderstanding or the misuse of language is likely to be the culprit here. Verbal disputes arise when some key term in the disputants' formulation of their beliefs is ambiguous, and the absence of real disagreement between the parties is concealed by that ambiguity. One party may be misusing an important term. Or some phrase or word central in the dispute may have different senses that may be equally legitimate but ought not to be confused, and the apparent conflict may arise because the parties, not realizing this, are each employing correct but different senses of that phrase or word.

Disputes of this kind are not always easy to spot, but once they are recognized they can be resolved fairly easily by specifying the different senses of the ambiguous phrase or word. In such contexts good definitions may prove to be critical for mutual understanding.

A now classic example of such a dispute was given by William James:

> Some years ago, being with a camping party in the mountains, I returned from a solitary ramble to find every one engaged in a ferocious metaphysical dispute. The *corpus* of the dispute was a squirrel—a live squirrel supposed to be clinging to one side of a tree trunk; while over against the tree's opposite side a human being was imagined to stand. This human witness tries to get sight of the squirrel by moving rapidly round the tree, but no matter how fast he goes, the squirrel moves as fast in the opposite direction, and always keeps the tree between himself and the man, so that never a glimpse of him is caught. The resultant metaphysical problem is this: *Does the man go round the squirrel or not?* He goes round the tree, sure enough, and the squirrel is on the tree; but does he go round the squirrel? In the unlimited leisure of the wilderness, discussion had been worn threadbare. Everyone had taken sides and was obstinate; and the number on both sides were even. Each side, when I appeared, therefore appealed to me to make it a majority.[2]

Of course it is not hard to see—and this was James's point in telling the story—that between the two parties in this dispute there was no genuine disagreement. Attitudes toward the squirrel and the tree were neutral, and all disputants fully understood and agreed on all the facts of the case given. What, then, was at issue? In this case—as in other cases, sometimes—no more than words. James continued:

> "Which party is right," I said, "depends on what you practically mean by 'going round' the squirrel. If you mean passing from the north of him to the east, then to the south, then to the west, and then to the north of him again, obviously the man does go round him, for he occupies these successive positions. But if on the contrary you mean being

---

[2] William James, *Pragmatism* (1907).

first in front of him, then on the right of him, then behind him, then on his left, and finally in front again, it is quite obvious that the man fails to go round him, for by the compensating movements the squirrel makes, he keeps his belly turned toward the man all the time, and his back turned away. Make the distinction, and there is no occasion for any further dispute. You are both right and both wrong according as you conceive the verb 'go round' in one practical fashion or the other."[3]

No new facts were required to resolve this dispute, and none could possibly have helped to do so. What was needed was just what James supplied: a distinction between different meanings of a key term in the argument. With alternative definitions of the term "go round," the dispute evaporated; the disagreement was never genuine. Wherever disputes are *merely* verbal, we can resolve them by supplying the definitions that eliminate the critical ambiguity. In such circumstances we are showing that the parties are not truly opposed to one another; they may simply be defending *different* propositions using the *same* word or words in different senses or with different meanings, or they may be defending the *same* proposition using *different* words. Once the different meanings have been identified, and with them the different propositions that result from using them, nothing remains at issue between the parties.[4]

A third kind of dispute is **apparently verbal but really genuine.** When the parties misunderstand one another's use of terms there is likely to be confusion, and that confusion may come to be recognized. But it sometimes happens that the quarrel really goes well beyond their differing uses of terms. In such circumstances, resolving only the ambiguity will not settle the dispute, because there remains some genuine disagreement—possibly in belief, more likely in attitude—between them.

To illustrate: Two parties may dispute whether a given film, in which explicit sexual activity is depicted, should be dealt with as "pornography." One party insists that its explicitness makes it pornography, and wicked; the other party insists that, in the light of its sensitivity and aesthetic merit, it is true art and not pornography at all. These parties apparently disagree about the meaning of the word "pornography," but if that verbal difference were fully understood and all ambiguity cleared up, it is very likely that the two parties would remain in genuine disagreement about the film. Their dispute is not really about the applicability of the term "pornography"; they disagree more deeply about whether the sexually explicit nature of the film makes it good or bad.

Disputes of this third kind are sometimes called "criterial" or "conceptual." The disputers have different *criteria* for the application of some key term; that is, different conceptions of what it is that is named by that term. And regarding the wisdom or correctness of the different sets of criteria, they are in

---

[3] *Ibid.*

[4] Words are on occasion deliberately used in two senses to *avoid* dispute by concealing a disagreement that is genuine. Rabbi A. J. Rudin explained that "interesting" is "arguably the most damning word in the English language," often used by members of a religious congregation to conceal the real opinion of the speaker. Rudin wrote, "When applied to a sermon, 'interesting' often means 'I had trouble staying awake,' or 'I counted light fixtures as you spoke.' At its most insidious, 'interesting' implies that the clergyperson had the temerity to . . . express a view with which the speaker disagrees." *Religious News Service,* January 1992.

sharp conflict. Thus, in the preceding example, even were the parties to understand that they had been using the term "pornographic" ambiguously, and even if the ambiguous meanings of the terms had been clarified and distinguished, each party would be likely to claim that its opponents erred in using their criteria to determine what is pornographic. If a film includes some scenes of explicit sexual activity (one party might contend), it is rightly classified as pornographic; that classification (the opponent might respond) is a conceptual mistake. The dispute is verbal only on the surface; beneath the surface, it is very real.

To aid one in recognizing and understanding these different kinds of disputes, a "flowchart" is of use. Once we determine that there is a dispute of some kind, we ask, "Is ambiguity present?" If the answer to this question is "No," we have a category-one (obviously genuine) dispute. If the answer is "Yes," we ask a second question: "Does clearing up the ambiguity eliminate the disagreement?" If the answer to this question is "Yes," then we have a category-two (merely verbal) dispute. If the answer to the second question is "No," then we have a category-three (apparently verbal but really genuine) dispute.

These three kinds of disputes can be summarily described as follows:

1.   In an obviously genuine dispute, **there is no ambiguity present and the disputers do disagree,** either in attitude or in belief.
2.   In a merely verbal dispute, **there is ambiguity present but there is no genuine disagreement** at all.
3.   In an apparently verbal dispute that is really genuine, **there is ambiguity present and the disputers disagree,** in attitude or in belief, either about facts or about the criteria for the application of some term(s).

Exercise

Identify three disagreements in current political or social controversy that exhibit the features described in this section:

  1.   A disagreement that is genuine.
  2.   A disagreement that is merely verbal.
  3.   A disagreement that is apparently verbal but really genuine.

Explain the disagreements in each case.

3.2 KINDS OF DEFINITION AND THE RESOLUTION OF DISPUTES

In the preceding section we saw that definitions, by exposing and eliminating ambiguities, can effectively resolve disputes that are merely verbal. Now we shall elucidate how definitions can serve to prevent or correct mistakes in reasoning. We begin by examining five *kinds* of definition.

Note first that definitions are always definitions of symbols, because only symbols have meanings for definitions to explain. The word "chair" we can define, since it has a meaning; but *a chair* itself we cannot define. We can sit on a chair, or paint it, or burn it, or describe it—but we cannot define it because the chair is not a symbol that has a meaning to be explained. Of course, in expressing definitions, we do sometimes talk about the symbol defined and sometimes about the thing referred to by the symbol. Thus we can equally well *say* either

> The word "triangle" means a plane figure enclosed by three straight lines.

or

> A triangle is (by definition) a plane figure enclosed by three straight lines.

Whichever the form of our expression, however, the definition can be a definition only of the symbol "triangle."

Two technical terms are common and useful. The symbol being defined is called the **definiendum;** the symbol or group of symbols being used to explain the meaning of the definiendum is called the **definiens.** It would be a mistake to say that the *definiens* is the meaning of the *definiendum*; rather, it (the *definiens*) is another symbol or group of symbols that, according to the definition, *has the same meaning* as the *definiendum.*

The principal use of definition in reasoning is the elimination of ambiguity, as we have seen. To eliminate ambiguity, two kinds of definition are commonly used: the *stipulative* and the *lexical.*

1.   Stipulative Definitions

One who introduces a new symbol has complete freedom to stipulate what meaning is to be given to it; **the definition that arises from the deliberate assignment of a meaning is properly called** *stipulative.* The term newly defined need not itself be entirely novel; it may be new only in the context in which the defining takes place. What are here called "stipulative definitions" have sometimes been referred to as "nominal" or "verbal definitions."

New terms may be introduced by stipulation for a variety of reasons. Convenience is one reason; a single word may serve as "short for" many words in a code or message. Secrecy is another reason; the stipulation may be understood only by the sender and the receiver of the message. Economy in expression is a third reason; in the sciences especially, new symbols often are introduced and defined, by stipulation, to mean what would otherwise require a long sequence of familiar words for its expression. The scientist thus economizes on the time and space required for writing reports and theories. More important than the time saved is the reduction in the amount of attention or mental energy then required, for when a sentence or equation grows too long its sense cannot easily be "taken in." The introduction of the exponent in mathematics illustrates this advantage vividly. What is now written briefly as "$A^{12} = B$" would, before the adoption of the special symbol for exponentiation, have had to be expressed either by "$A \times A \times A \times A \times A \times A \times A \times A \times A \times A \times A \times A = B$" or by a sentence of ordinary language instead of a mathematical equation. And numbers that are specially cumbersome are sometimes given names by stipulation. The number equal to a billion trillions (10^{21}) has by stipulation been named a "zetta," and that equal to a trillion trillions (10^{24}) is called a "yotta."[5]

New symbols are sometimes introduced by scientists having certain psychological objectives. On the negative side, some familiar words have emotional overtones that may prove disturbing; symbols stipulatively defined as having the same literal meanings as familiar ones free the investigator from the distraction of those emotive associations. In modern psychology, for example, Spearman's "g factor" is intended to convey the same descriptive meaning as the word "intelligence" but to share none of its emotional significance. On the positive side, a catchy name may add excitement and interest to an investigation that would seem dull if it used an established descriptive terminology. "Black hole," for example, was a term introduced to replace the awkward phrase "gravitationally completely collapsed star."[6] And the term "quark" was coined in 1963 by the physicist Murray Gell-Mann, to name an unusual type of subatomic particle about which he had been theorizing.[7] New terms that entice or charm may play a role in the acceptance of new theories. And for the new terminology to be learned and used, the meanings of the new symbols must be explained by means of definitions.

New words have sometimes been introduced into philosophy to facilitate a neutral analysis of controversial matters. In order to refer narrowly to the content of sensory experience, some recent philosophers have introduced the word "sensum" stipulatively, thus bypassing a venerable dispute over whether our experience of physical objects is direct or indirect. And the American philosopher Charles Sanders Peirce, one of the originators of the philosophical movement called Pragmatism, after becoming bitter about the careless way in which that word had been used, stipulated that his own view would henceforth be known as "pragmaticism"—which he said was a word ugly enough that no one would want to steal it!

A stipulative definition is neither true nor false, neither accurate nor inaccurate; in this respect, it differs sharply from a dictionary definition. A symbol defined by a stipulative definition did not have that meaning before being given it by the definition. Hence its definition cannot be regarded as a statement or report that the *definiendum* and the *definiens* have the same meaning. They actually do have the same meaning for anyone who accepts the definition, but that is a consequence of the definition rather than a fact asserted by it. **A stipulative definition should be regarded as a proposal or resolution to use the *definiendum***

---

[5] Defined stipulatively in 1991 by the Conférence Générale des Poids et Mesures (General Committee on Weights and Measures), the international body that governs in the realm of scientific units. At the other extreme, a billionth of a trillionth is called a "zepto," and a trillionth of a trillionth is called a "yocto."

[6] The new term was introduced in New York City by Dr. John Archibald Wheeler of Princeton University at a 1967 meeting of the Institute for Space Studies.

[7] "Quark" appears in James Joyce's novel *Finnegan's Wake,* in the line "Three quarks for Muster Mark," but Dr. Gell-Mann reported that he had chosen that name before he saw it there, relying on Joyce only for its spelling.

to mean what is meant by the *definiens,* or as a request or instruction to do so. In this sense a stipulative definition is directive rather than informative. Proposals may be rejected, requests refused, instructions disobeyed—but they are neither true nor false. So it is with stipulative definitions.

Of course, stipulative definitions may be evaluated on other grounds. A stipulation may be unusable because it is very obscure or too complex. The stipulation itself may be arbitrary. But whether that stipulation is clear or unclear, advantageous or disadvantageous in advancing the purposes for which it was introduced, is a matter of fact. Stipulative definitions normally are not productive in resolving genuine disagreements, but by clarifying informative discourse and by reducing the emotive role of language, they can help to prevent fruitless verbal conflict.

2.   Lexical Definitions

Where the purpose of a definition is to eliminate ambiguity or to increase the vocabulary of the person for whom it is constructed, then, if the term being defined is not new but has an established usage, the definition is *lexical* rather than stipulative. A **lexical definition** does not give its *definiendum* a meaning it hitherto lacked but **reports a meaning the** *definiendum* **already has.** It is clear that a lexical definition may be either true or false. Thus the definition

> The word "mountain" means a large mass of earth or rock rising to a considerable height above the surrounding country.

is true; it is a true report of how English-speaking people use the word "mountain" (*i.e.,* of what they mean by it). On the other hand, the definition

> The word "mountain" means a plane figure enclosed by three straight lines.

is obviously false. Of course most mistakes in word usage are not obvious, as when we say of muddy water that it is turgid when we mean that it is turbid—the lexical definition of "turgid" being "swollen" or "pompous." And some mistakes are downright funny, as when Mrs. Malaprop, an absurdly misspeaking character of the Restoration dramatist Richard Sheridan, gives the order to "illiterate him . . . from your memory" or uses the phrase "as headstrong as an allegory on the banks of the Nile." Not all such confusions are fictional, as was shown by students at an American university who gave the definition of "actuary" as "a home for birds," and the definition of "duodenum" as "a number system in base 2."[8] Amusing as these mistakes may be, they are mistakes, incorrect reports of how English-speaking people use these words.

Here lies the important difference between stipulative and lexical definitions. Because a stipulative definition's *definiendum* has no meaning apart from or before the definition introducing it, that definition cannot be false (or true).

---

[8] See *The Chronicle of Higher Education*, 30 May 1993.

But because the *definiendum* of a lexical definition *does* have a prior and independent meaning, its definition is either true or false, depending on whether that meaning is correctly or incorrectly reported.

What we are calling a "lexical definition" has sometimes been referred to as a "real" definition—the *definiendum* really does have that independent meaning identified. But whether a definition is stipulative or lexical has nothing to do with the question of whether the *definiendum* names any "real" or existent thing. The definition

> The word "unicorn" means an animal like a horse but having a single straight horn projecting from its forehead.

surely is a "real" or lexical definition, and a correct one, because the *definiendum* is a word with long-established usage and means exactly what is meant by the *definiens*. Yet the *definiendum* in this case does not name or denote any existent thing, since there are no unicorns.

A qualification must be made at this point. While many uses of words are flatly mistaken, other uses departing from what is normal may be better described as unusual or unorthodox. Word usage is a statistical matter, and inevitably subject to statistical variation. Hence, we cannot always specify "the" meaning of a term, but must often give an account of the various meanings of that term, as determined by the uses it has in actual speech and writing.

The effort to evade this variability by referring to "best" usage or "correct" usage cannot fully succeed because "best" usage also is a matter of degree, measured by the number of prominent authors or speakers whose usages of the given term are in agreement with that definition. Literary and academic vocabularies tend to lag behind the growth of a living language, so that definitions reporting only the meanings accepted by some academic aristocracy are likely to be out of date; usages at one time unorthodox may soon thereafter become catholic. Lexical definitions must not ignore the ways in which a term is used by sizable numbers of those who speak that language, or else they will not be true to actual usage and will not be entirely correct.

The notion of purely statistical definitions is utopian, of course, but good dictionaries move toward it by indicating which meanings of terms are "archaic" or "obsolete," and which are "colloquial," or "slang." With this qualification understood, we repeat that lexical definitions are in essence true or false, in the sense that they may be true to actual usage or not.

3.   Precising Definitions

Stipulative and lexical definitions serve to reduce ambiguity; **precising definitions serve to reduce vagueness,** also a source of confusion in argument. Vagueness and ambiguity are quite different. A term is **ambiguous** in a given context when it has more than one distinct meaning and the context does not make clear which is intended. A term is **vague** when there exist "borderline" cases, so that it cannot be determined whether the term should be applied to them or not. Of course any single term—for example, a phrase such as "right to life" or "right to choose"—may be both ambiguous and vague.

Every term is vague in some degree, but the difficulties created by excessive vagueness can assume great practical importance. For example: Facilities and funds for the treatment of mental illness are often in short supply; to determine in such circumstances which persons are most in need of treatment, a more precise definition of the term "serious mental illness" is needed. That need was met by the Federal Center for Mental Health Services in 1993, when it gave a rather precise account of which disorders are to fall under this heading. "Serious mental illness" must involve "functional impairment," that is, characteristics that substantially interfere with or limit role-functioning in one or more major life activities, including basic daily living skills such as "eating, bathing, and dressing," as well as "instrumental living skills" such as "maintaining a household, managing money, getting around the community, and taking prescribed medication."

Another example: Units of measurement have been notoriously vague in years gone by; many interests, scientific and mundane, can be better served when these units are defined more precisely. "Horsepower," for example, has long been used in reporting the power of motors, but consumers may be deceived when definitions of that unit are indefinite. "One horsepower" is now defined precisely as "the power needed to raise a weight of 550 pounds by one foot in one second"—calculated to equal 745.7 watts.[9]

A "meter," the internationally accepted unit of measure for distance, originally was defined, by stipulation, as one ten-millionth of the distance from one of the earth's poles to the equator, and this was long represented by a pair of very carefully made scratches on a metal bar made of platinum-iridium, kept in a vault near Paris. But scientific research has required a more precise definition; presently a meter is defined as "the distance light travels in one 299,792,458th of a second." A "liter" is defined precisely as "the contents of a cube having edges of one-tenth of a meter."[10]

In attempting to eliminate the troublesome vagueness of terms such as "serious mental illness" and "meter," it was not possible to appeal to ordinary usage. Ordinary usage was not sufficiently exact; if it had been, the terms would not have been vague. Decisions about borderline cases often must transcend ordinary language; definitions that help to resolve borderline cases will go beyond the report of normal usage. Such definitions may be called *precising definitions.*

A precising definition thus differs from both stipulative and lexical definitions. It differs from a stipulative definition in that its *definiendum* is not a new term, but one whose usage is established, although vague. The makers

---

[9] The power of one real horse weighing 600 kilograms (1,323 pounds) is far greater, and has been estimated at about 18,000 watts. A two-hundred-horsepower automobile, therefore, has approximately the power of 8 real horses.

[10] The unit of mass equal to that of the water contained in a liter measure was long accepted as the definition of a "kilogram." But a kilogram is now more precisely defined as a unit of mass equal to that of a block of metal in that same vault near Paris. Yet greater precision for "kilogram" is still being sought, a precising definition that will be based on the mass of a specific number of certain atoms.

of a precising definition, therefore, are not free to assign any meaning they choose to the *definiendum*. They must remain true to established usage so far as that is possible, making a known term more precise. At the same time they cannot give a simple report, but must go beyond established usage if the vagueness of the *definiendum* is to be reduced. Exactly how they go beyond it—how they fill the gaps or resolve the conflicts of established usage—may be partly a matter of stipulation.

When the judges of appellate courts, for example, are obliged to draw conceptual lines, making some common terms more precise, they commonly give reasons for the refinements introduced. Plainly they do not regard their precising definitions as mere stipulations, even when they go beyond precedent or established usage. They are guided in part by what they understand was intended by the authors of the words in question, and in part by how the general public may be expected to understand those words. The Fourth Amendment to the U.S. Constitution, for example, prohibits "unreasonable searches and seizures," and therefore evidence obtained through an unreasonable seizure is generally held to be inadmissible in court. But what is a "seizure"? Suppose a suspect, running from the police, throws away a packet of drugs, which is then confiscated. Have those drugs been seized? To resolve this matter, the U.S. Supreme Court needed a precising definition. A "seizure," they explained, must involve either the use of some physical force that restrains movement, or the assertion of authority such as an order to stop, to which a suspect yields. But so long as the suspect keeps running, the Court continued, no seizure has occurred. Hence anything discarded by a suspect while running from the police cannot be the product of an unreasonable seizure and will later be admissible as evidence.[11]

The importance of precising definitions in law is evident. Citizens must understand what the terms used in a law both include and exclude in order to obey it. Courts sometimes will strike down a statute simply because its terms are so vague that those who are governed by that law could not be expected to understand its limits, and therefore could not be expected to know how to act in order to comply with it. A federal law, making it illegal to transmit "indecent" or "patently offensive" material on the Internet was struck down on just such grounds in 1996. The court wrote:

> [T]he enforcer of statutes must be guided by clear and precise standards. In statutes that break into relatively new areas, such as this one, the need for definition of terms is greater, because even commonly understood terms may have different connotations or parameters in this new context. Words cannot define conduct with mathematical certainty . . . This rationale, however, [cannot] relieve legislators from the very difficult task of carefully drafting legislation tailored to its goal and sensitive to the unique characteristic of, in this instance, cyberspace.[12]

In order to avoid unacceptable vagueness, legislatures very commonly will preface the operative portions of a new statute with a section called "definitions," in which they specify precisely how the key terms used in that statute are

---

[11] *California v. Hodari D., 499* U.S. 621, 1991.

[12] *American Civil Liberties Union v. Reno,* 929 Fed. Supp. 824, 11 June 1996.

to be understood. The same practice is widely adopted in labor-management contracts, where the terms used in setting forth the agreed-upon rules of the workplace may be carefully defined. Precise definitions of the words used in criminal charges are of particular importance. Thus, "robbery," for example, is defined by the Federal Bureau of Investigation as "the taking, or attempted taking, of anything of value from one person by another, in which the offender uses force or the threat of violence." Precising definitions are conceptual instruments of wide and powerful use.

4.   Theoretical Definitions

When scientists, politicians, or philosophers dispute one another's definitions, there is usually more than precision or ambiguity at stake. They are seeking comprehensive understanding. The battle between Socrates and Thrasymachus over the definition of "justice" is recounted at length in Plato's *The Republic.* The battle among physicists over the definition of "heat" continued for generations. Disputants in such matters are seeking to develop a coherent theoretical account of the subject at hand. Part of such an account will be the definition of key terms, and so they ask: What *is* justice? What *is* heat? **A theoretical definition of a term is a definition that attempts to formulate a theoretically adequate or scientifically useful description of the objects to which the term applies.**

To propose a theoretical definition is tantamount to proposing the acceptance of a theory—and theories, as the name suggests, are notoriously debatable. As the knowledge and the theoretical understanding of some subject matter increase, one theoretical definition may be replaced by another. Thrasymachus defended a definition of justice as "the interests of the stronger." Socrates sought to replace that account with another that he thought more satisfactory. Physicists long defined "heat" to mean a subtle imponderable fluid; they now define it as a form of energy possessed by a body by virtue of the irregular motion of its molecules. Different theoretical definitions of "justice" and of "heat" have been given at different times because different *theories* of justice, and of heat, have been accepted at those different times.

The refinement of theory goes hand in hand with improved theoretical definitions in the world of biology and medicine. How is the disease we call "AIDS" to be defined? Almost all of those who are infected with HIV (human immunodeficiency virus) eventually succumb to life-threatening infections, and are then commonly said to be suffering from "AIDS" (autoimmune deficiency syndrome). But we need to know for important practical reasons, concerning disability benefits and other entitlements, who among those infected with HIV are to be counted as having actually contracted "AIDS." More deeply, we need to understand the nature and symptoms of HIV infection, for all of which we need a good *theoretical* definition of the disease to which that infection leads.

From 1987 to 1992, persons were declared sick with AIDS only after they had contracted certain opportunistic infections or other conditions. But scientists at the Federal Centers for Disease Control and Prevention revised the established theoretical approach to this terrible disease in 1992, defining AIDS in such a way that it will have been contracted not only when those opportunistic infections are present but, even if they are not yet present, when the immune system has deteriorated to a specified degree. Certain human cells, called CD-4 cells, are key components of the immune system that is gradually destroyed by HIV. Healthy people have about 1,000 of these CD-4 cells per cubic millimeter of blood. According to the revised theoretical definition of AIDS, an HIV–infected person has AIDS when that count of CD-4 cells has fallen to 200 or below. This change (as well as the identification of certain other infections that signal the presence of AIDS) resulted, in 1993, in a one-time surge in the number of new cases of AIDS reported. More important, the revised definition (now formally adopted by the Social Security Administration as well as by the Centers for Disease Control and Prevention) has proved very useful in understanding the advance of a fatal disease that, in some regions, has reached epidemic proportions.

The objectives of those who dispute over theoretical definitions go far beyond concern for the words involved. Socrates was not seeking a report about how people use terms like "justice" or "piety." Arbitrary stipulations of meanings for such general terms interested him not at all. Precising definitions were not his target either, since borderline cases were rarely emphasized by him. His aims were large; he sought—as philosophers and scientists seek today in their several fields of study—a theory within which a fully adequate definition of important terms could be stated.

Such quests remain compelling. Which countries today deserve to be called "democratic"? What is "gravity"? Is health care a "right"? When we debate topics like these, it is not merely verbal matters that trouble us. We too are seeking theoretical definitions; we are constructing theories—political, or scientific, or moral—through which our understanding may be enhanced.

5. Persuasive Definitions

Finally, **definitions may be formulated and used persuasively, to resolve disputes by influencing the attitudes, or stirring the emotions, of readers or hearers. These we call** *persuasive definitions.* We have seen in Chapter 2 that language can function both informatively and expressively. The kinds of definition discussed thus far are concerned with the informative use of language, but sometimes we define terms in ways deliberately calculated to affect feelings and, indirectly, to alter conduct.

A letter on the topic of abortion, distributed by staff members of the Hawaii State Legislature some years ago, illustrates the power of persuasive definition. The letter, proposed facetiously as a "general response to constituent letters on abortion," reads as follows:

> Dear Sir:
>   You ask me how I stand on abortion. Let me answer forthrightly and without equivocation.
>   If by abortion you mean the murdering of defenseless human beings; the denial of rights to the youngest of our citizens; the promotion of promiscuity among our shiftless

and valueless youth and the rejection of Life, Liberty and the Pursuit of Happiness—then, Sir, be assured that I shall never waver in my opposition, so help me God.

But, Sir, if by abortion you mean the granting of equal rights to all our citizens regardless of race, color or sex; the elimination of evil and vile institutions preying upon desperate and hopeless women; a chance for all our youth to be wanted and loved; and, above all, that God-given right for all citizens to act in accordance with the dictates of their own conscience—then, Sir, let me promise you as a patriot and a humanist that I shall never be persuaded to forgo my pursuit of these most basic human rights.

Thank you for asking my position on this most crucial issue and let me again assure you of the steadfastness of my stand.

Mahalo and Aloha Nui.[13]

Persuasive definitions are common in political argument. From the left, we encounter "socialism" defined as *democracy extended to the economic field,* and from the right we hear "capitalism" defined as *freedom in the economic sphere.* The manipulative intent of the emotive language in these definitions is obvious. But manipulation also may be subtle; emotive coloration may be slyly injected into the language of a definition that purports to be accurate and that appears on the surface to be objective. As we seek to distinguish good reasoning from bad, we must be on our guard against persuasive definitions.

Exercises

I.   Five types of definitions have been discussed in this section:

Lexical definitions
Stipulative definitions
Precising definitions
Theoretical definitions
Persuasive definitions

Find an example of each type and explain, in each case, the purpose it is intended to serve.

*II.   For discussion: Federal law imposes a five-year mandatory prison sentence on anyone who "uses or carries a firearm" in connection with a narcotics crime. In 1998, the U.S. Supreme Court faced this question: Does travelling in a car with a gun in a locked glove compartment or trunk—as opposed to carrying a gun on one's person—satisfy the meaning of "carry" in that law? Justice Breyer argued that Congress intended the word in its ordinary, everyday meaning, without the artificial limitation that it be immediately accessible. Quoting *Robinson Crusoe* and *Moby Dick,* he pointed to the common use of "carry" to mean "convey in a vehicle." The mandatory sentence, he concluded, is thus correctly imposed. Justice Ruth Bader Ginsburg found Breyer's literary evidence selective and unpersuasive; in response she offered quotations from Rudyard Kipling, the TV series "M.A.S.H.," and President Theodore Roosevelt's "Speak softly and carry a big stick" to show that "carry" is properly understood in the federal statute to mean "the gun

---

[13] "Defining Abortion a Tricky Business," *Honolulu Advertiser,* 14 February 1970.

at hand, ready for use as a weapon." [*Muscarello v. U.S.*, decided 8 June 1998] Which side, in this controversy, puts forward the better precising definition?

III. Discuss each of the following disputes. If it is obviously genuine, indicate each of the disputers' positions with respect to the proposition at issue. If it is merely verbal, resolve it by explaining the different senses attached by the disputers to the key word or phrase that is used ambiguously. If it is an apparently verbal dispute that is really genuine, locate the ambiguity and explain the real disagreement involved.

*1. DAYE: Pete Rose was the greatest hitter in the history of baseball. He got more hits than any other major league player.

KNIGHT: No, Hank Aaron deserves that title. He hit more home runs than any other major league player.

2. DAYE: Despite their great age, the plays of Sophocles are enormously relevant today. They deal with eternally recurring problems and values such as love and sacrifice, the conflict of generations, life and death—as central today as they were over two thousand years ago.

KNIGHT: I don't agree with you at all. Sophocles has nothing to say about the pressing and immediate issues of our time: inflation, unemployment, the population explosion, and the energy crisis. His plays have no relevance to today.

3. DAYE: Bob Jones is certainly a wonderful father to his children. He provides a beautiful home in a fine neighborhood, buys them everything they need or want, and has made ample provision for their education.

KNIGHT: I don't think Bob Jones is a good father at all. He is so busy getting and spending that he has no time to be with his children. They hardly know him except as somebody who pays the bills.

4. DAYE: Amalgamated General Corporation's earnings were higher than ever last year, I see by reading their annual report.

KNIGHT: No, their earnings were really much lower than in the preceding year, and they have been cited by the Securities and Exchange Commission for issuing a false and misleading report.

*5. DAYE: Business continues to be good for National Conglomerate, Inc. Their sales so far this year are 25 percent higher than they were at this time last year.

KNIGHT: No, their business is not so good now. Their profits so far this year are 30 percent lower than they were last year at this time.

6. DAYE: Ann is an excellent student. She takes a lively interest in everything and asks very intelligent questions in class.

KNIGHT: Ann is one of the worst students I've ever seen. She never gets her assignments in on time.

7.   DAYE: Tom did it of his own free will. No pressure was brought to
bear on him; no threats were made; no inducements were
offered; there was no hint of force. He deliberated about it
and made up his own mind.

KNIGHT: That is impossible. Nobody has free will, because everything anyone does is inevitably determined by heredity and
environment according to inexorable causal laws of nature.

8.   DAYE: Professor Graybeard is one of the most productive scholars
at the university. The bibliography of his publications is
longer than that of any of his colleagues.

KNIGHT: I wouldn't call him a productive scholar. He is a great
teacher, but he has never produced any new ideas or discoveries in his entire career.

9.   DAYE: Betty finally got rid of that old Chevy and bought herself a
new car. She's driving a Buick now.

KNIGHT: No, Betty didn't buy herself a new car. That Buick is a
good three years old.

*10.   DAYE: Dick finally got rid of that old Ford of his and bought
himself a new car. He's driving a Pontiac now.

KNIGHT: No, Dick didn't buy himself a new car. It's his room-
mate's new Pontiac that he's driving.

11.   DAYE: Helen lives a long way from campus. I walked out to see
her the other day, and it took me nearly two hours to get there.

KNIGHT: No, Helen doesn't live such a long way from campus. I
drove her home last night, and we reached her place in less
than ten minutes.

12.   DAYE: Senator Gray is a fine man and a genuine liberal. He votes
for every progressive measure that comes before the legislature.

KNIGHT: He is no liberal, in my opinion. The old skinflint contributes less money to worthy causes than any other man in
his income bracket.

13.   DAYE: The University of Winnemac overemphasizes athletics,
for it has the largest college stadium in the world and has
constructed new sports buildings instead of badly needed
classroom space.

KNIGHT: No, the University of Winnemac does not overempha-
size athletics. Its academic standards are very high, and it
sponsors a wide range of extracurricular activities for students in addition to its athletic program.

14.   DAYE: It was in bad taste to serve roast beef at the banquet. There
were Hindus present, and it is against their religion to eat beef.

KNIGHT: Bad taste, nothing! That was the tastiest meal I've had in
a long time. I think it was delicious!

*15.   DAYE: There are fewer than 8 million unemployed persons in this
country, according to the Bureau of Labor Statistics.

KNIGHT: Oh no, there are over fifteen times that number of unemployed. The President's Economic Report states that there are 160 million employed in this country, and the Census Bureau reports a total population of over 280 million. So the government's figures reveal that there are over 120 million unemployed persons in this country.

16.   DAYE: The average intelligence of college graduates is higher than that of college freshmen, because it takes more intelligence to graduate from college than to be admitted to college.

KNIGHT: No, the average intelligence of college graduates is not higher than that of college freshmen, because every college graduate was once a college freshman, and a person's intelligence does not change from year to year.

17.   DAYE: A tree falling in a wilderness with nobody around to hear will produce no sound. There can be no auditory sensation unless someone actually senses it.

KNIGHT: No, whether anyone is there to hear it or not, the crash of a falling tree will set up vibrations in the air and will therefore produce a sound in any event.

18.   DAYE: I see by the financial pages that money is much more plentiful than it was six months ago.

KNIGHT: That can't be true. I read a government report just yesterday to the effect that more old currency has been destroyed at the mint during the last half year than has been replaced. Money is therefore less plentiful, not more so.

19.   DAYE: Mr. Green is a real Christian. He speaks well of everyone and is never too busy to give friendly assistance to anyone who is in need.

KNIGHT: I wouldn't call Green a Christian. He spends his Sundays working in his yard or playing out on the golf course, never showing his face in church from one end of the year to the other!

*20.   DAYE: Don't ask your wife about it. You ought to use your own judgment.

KNIGHT: I will use my own judgment, and in my judgment, I should ask my wife.

3.3   EXTENSION AND INTENSION

A definition states the *meaning* of a term, but there are different senses of the word "meaning." Earlier we distinguished the descriptive or literal meaning of a term from its expressive meaning. Now we look more closely at literal meaning, and especially at the literal meaning of *general terms*, that is, class terms that may be applicable to more than one object. In reasoning, the definition of general terms is of special importance.

The general term "planet" applies in the same sense equally to Mercury, Venus, Earth, Mars, Jupiter, and so on. In one sense, these various objects are *meant* by the word "planet"; the collection of the planets constitutes its meaning. If I say that all planets have elliptical orbits, part of what I assert is that Mars has an elliptical orbit, and another part is that Venus has an elliptical orbit, and so on. The meaning of the term "planet"—in this important sense—consists of the objects to which the term may be correctly applied. This sense of "meaning" is called the *extensional meaning* of the term. Often it is said that a general term, or class term, *denotes* the several objects to which it may correctly be applied. **The collection of the objects to which a general term correctly applies constitutes the *extension* of that term.**

To understand the meaning of a general term is to know how to apply it correctly, but to do this it is not necessary to know all of the objects to which it may be correctly applied. All the objects within the extension of a given term have some common attributes or characteristics that lead us to use the same term to denote them. Therefore, we may know the meaning of a term without knowing its extension. "Meaning," in this second sense, supposes some *criterion for deciding,* of any given object, whether it falls within the extension of that term. This sense of "meaning" is called the *intensional meaning* of the term. **The set of attributes shared by all and only those objects to which a general term refers is called the *intension* of that term.**[14]

Thus we see that every general or class term has both an intensional meaning and an extensional meaning. The *in*tension of the general term "skyscraper" consists of the attributes common and peculiar to all buildings over a certain height. The *ex*tension of the term "skyscraper" is the class that contains the World Trade Center in New York, the Sears Tower in Chicago, the Shanghai World Financial Center, the Petronas Twin Towers in Kuala Lumpur, and so on—that is, the collection of the objects to which the term applies.

Sometimes it is alleged that the extension of a term changes from time to time, although its intension does not. The extension of the term "person," it is said, for example, changes continually as people die and babies are born. This claim flows from a confusion. The term "person," conceived of as denoting *all* persons, the dead as well as the unborn, does not have a changing extension. The varying extension is that of the term "living person." But the term "living person" has the sense of "person living now," in which the word "now" refers to the fleeting, changing present. Therefore the intension of the term "living person" is also different at different times. It is thus clear that any term with a changing extension must also have a changing intension. One is as constant as the other; when the intension of a term is fixed, the extension is also fixed.

Note that the extension of a term is determined by its intension, but that the reverse is not true. The intension of the term "equilateral triangle" is the

---

[14] Logicians sometimes use the term "connotation" in place of *intension,* and even more commonly the term "denotation" is used in place of *extension.* But "connotation" has other much more common uses in ordinary discourse; most often it refers to the emotive significance of a term—and therefore its introduction here is not helpful. Nothing is lost, and some confusion may be avoided, by dealing with this critical distinction using the terms intension and extension, as we do here.

attribute of being a plane figure enclosed by three straight lines of equal length. The extension of "equilateral triangle" is the class of all those objects and only those objects that have this attribute. Now, the term "equiangular triangle" has a different intension, the attribute of being a plane figure enclosed by three straight lines that intersect each other to form equal angles. Of course the extension of the term "equiangular triangle" is exactly the same as the extension of the term "equilateral triangle." Thus, to identify the extension of one of these terms leaves uncertain the intension of the class; intension is not determined by extension. But intension must determine extension. So terms may have different intensions and yet the same extension, but terms with different extensions cannot possibly have the same intension.

When attributes are added to the intension of a term we say that the intension *increases*. In the following sequence of terms, the intension of each is included within the intension of the term following it: "person," "living person," "living person over twenty years old," "living person over twenty years old having red hair." The intension of each is greater than the intension of those preceding it in the sequence; the terms are arranged in order of *increasing intension*. But if we turn to the extensions of those terms, we find the reverse to be the case. The extension of "person" is greater than that of "living person," and so on, and the terms are arranged in order of *decreasing extension*.

Some logicians have been led to formulate a "law of inverse variation," asserting that extension and intension always vary inversely. This assertion is suggestive, but not entirely correct. We could construct a series of terms in order of increasing intension, where the extension does not decrease but remains the same. Consider this series: "living person," "living person with a spinal column," "living person with a spinal column less than one thousand years old," "living person with a spinal column less than one thousand years old who has not read all the books in the Library of Congress." These terms are clearly in order of increasing intension, but the extension of each of them is the same, not decreasing at all. The correct, amended "law" asserts that, if terms are arranged in order of increasing intension, their extensions will be in non-increasing order; that is, *if* the extensions vary, they will vary inversely with the intensions.

Some extensions—such as that of unicorn, for example—may be empty, of course. Recognizing this, and using our distinction between intension and extension, fallacious arguments that play upon the ambiguity of the term "meaning" may be exposed. The following argument, for example, has been proposed to prove the existence of God:

> The word "God" is not meaningless; therefore it has a meaning. But by definition, the word "God" means a being who is all-powerful and supremely good. Therefore that all-powerful and supremely good being, God, must exist.

The equivocation here is on the words "meaning" and "meaningless," which refer in one sense to the intension, and in another sense to the extension, of the same term. The word "God" is not meaningless, and so there is an intension that is its meaning, to be sure. But it does not follow from the fact that a term has an intension that it denotes any existent thing.[15]

A similar fallacy is found in the following passage:

> Kitsch is the sign of vulgarity, sleaze, schlock, sentimentality, and bad faith that mark and mar the human condition. That is why utopia can be defined as a state of affairs in which the term has disappeared because it no longer has a referent.[16]

The fallacy of equivocation is committed here because the writer fails to distinguish between *meaning* and *referent*. Very many valuable terms—those naming the creatures of Greek mythology, for example—are without existing referent, but we do not want or expect such terms to disappear. Indeed, terms with intension but no extension are very useful; if utopia someday comes we may wish then to express our good fortune in having reduced or eliminated "kitsch" or "sleaze," and to do that we will need to be able to use those words meaningfully.

In earlier sections we have examined the *kinds* of definitions and their *uses:* lexical and stipulative definitions to eliminate or avoid ambiguity, precising definitions to diminish vagueness, and so on. In the sections that follow, we examine *techniques* for constructing definitions. Some definitions approach a general term through its extension, or denotation, while other definitions approach it through its intension. We shall see that each approach has both advantages and disadvantages.

Exercises

I.   Arrange each of the following groups of terms in order of increasing intension.

   *1. Animal, feline, lynx, mammal, vertebrate, wildcat.

   2. Alcoholic beverage, beverage, champagne, fine white wine, white wine, wine.

   3. Athlete, ball player, baseball player, fielder, infielder, shortstop.

   4. Cheese, dairy product, Limburger, milk derivative, soft cheese, strong soft cheese.

   *5. Integer, number, positive integer, prime, rational number, real number.

II. Divide the following list of terms into five groups of five terms each, arranged In order of increasing intension.

   Aquatic animal, beast of burden, beverage, brandy, cognac, domestic animal, filly, fish, foal, game fish, horse, instrument, liquid, liquor, musical instrument, muskellunge, parallelogram, pike, polygon, quadrilateral, rectangle, square, Stradivarius, string instrument, violin.

---

[15] The useful distinction between intension and extension was introduced and emphasized by St. Anselm of Canterbury (1033–1109), who is best known for his "ontological argument," to which the preceding fallacious argument has little resemblance. See Wolfgang L. Gombocz, "Logik and Existenz in Mittelalter," *Philosophische Rundschau* (1977).

[16] John P. Sisk, "Art, Kitsch and Politics," *Commentary*, May 1988.

3.4 EXTENSIONAL DEFINITIONS

Extensional definitions identify the collection of objects to which the general term being defined applies. The most obvious and effective way to instruct someone about the extension of a term is to give examples of objects denoted by it. This technique has certain limitations, however, that ought to be recognized.

It was noted in the preceding section (in the examples of "equilateral triangle" and "equiangular triangle") that two terms with different meanings—that is, different intensions—may have exactly the same extensions. Therefore, even if we could give a complete enumeration of the objects denoted by one of those two general terms, this extensional definition would fail to distinguish it from the other term that denotes the same objects. The two terms are not synonyms, but the extensional definition cannot make the distinction between them.

By itself this is not a troubling limitation, however, because very few terms can have their extensions completely enumerated. To enumerate all the numbers denoted by the term "number" is absolutely impossible. To enumerate all the literally astronomical number of objects denoted by the term "star," even if their number is finite, is a practical impossibility. And for most other general terms, complete enumeration is practically out of the question.

Thus extensional definitions must generally be restricted to partial enumerations of the objects denoted—and that is a limitation giving rise to serious difficulties. Any given object—say, the man John Doe—has many, many attributes and is therefore included in the extensions of many, many different general terms. Therefore, when given as an example in an extensional definition of one term, John Doe will be just as appropriately mentioned as an example in an extensional definition of many other terms. John Doe is an example of "man," of "animal," of "mammal"—perhaps also of "husband," and "father," and "student," and so on. Mentioning him, therefore, cannot help us to distinguish between the meanings of any of these terms. And even if we give two examples, or three, or four, the same difficulty is confronted. As another example, in defining the term "skyscraper," we may use the obvious examples of the Empire State, Chrysler, and Woolworth buildings, but these three serve equally well as examples of the extension of the terms "great structures of the twentieth century," "expensive pieces of real estate in Manhattan," or "landmarks in New York City." Yet each of these general terms denotes objects not denoted by the others, so by using partial enumeration, we cannot even distinguish among terms that have different extensions. Introducing "negative instances" (*e.g.,* "not the Taj Mahal" or "not the Pentagon") may help to specify the meaning of the *definiendum,* but the negative instances must also remain incomplete, and the basic limitation remains.

We may seek to provide examples not by mentioning one case at a time, but by mentioning whole groups of members. By using this technique—definition by subclasses—it is sometimes possible to achieve a complete enumeration. Thus we might define "vertebrate" to mean amphibians and birds and fishes and mammals and reptiles. Definition by enumeration—whether complete or partial, whether by individual class members or by subclasses—has some psychological merits, but it is logically inadequate to specify completely the meaning of the terms being defined.

A special kind of definition by example is called "ostensive" or "demonstrative definition." Instead of naming or describing the objects denoted by the term being defined, as in the ordinary sort of extensional definition, **an ostensive definition refers to the examples by means of pointing, or by some other gesture.** An example of an ostensive definition would be "The word 'desk' means *this*," accompanied by a gesture such as pointing a finger in the direction of a desk.

Ostensive definitions have all the limitations mentioned in the preceding discussion, as well as some limitations peculiar to themselves. There is a relatively trivial geographical limitation: One can indicate only what is visible, and so cannot ostensively define the word "skyscraper" in a country village and cannot ostensively define the word "ocean" in an inland valley. More serious, gestures are invariably ambiguous. To point to a desk is also to point to a part of it, and also to its color, its size, its shape, its material, and so on—in fact, to everything that lies in the general direction of the desk, including the wall behind it or the garden beyond.

This ambiguity can sometimes be resolved by the addition of some descriptive phrase to the *definiens,* the result being what may be called a **quasi-ostensive definition,** as for example, "The word 'desk' means *this* article of furniture" (accompanied by an appropriate gesture). But this sort of addition, because it supposes a prior understanding of the phrase "article of furniture," defeats the purpose that ostensive definitions have been claimed to serve.

Ostensive definitions have been alleged by some to be the "primary" or "primitive" definitions, in the sense that it is (allegedly) in this way that we first learn the meanings of words and that other definitions rely on the meanings of words first learned in this way. But that claim of primacy is mistaken, since the significance of gestures themselves must be learned. When a finger is pointed to the side of a baby's crib, the attention of the baby, if attracted at all, is as likely to be attracted to the finger as to the thing pointed at. And the same difficulty arises if we seek to define gestures with other gestures. If one is to understand the definition of any sign, some signs must already be understood. The primary way in which we learn to use language is by observation and imitation, not by definition.

One might construe the phrase "ostensive definition" very broadly, as some logicians have done, so as to include the process of "frequently hearing the word when the object it denotes is present." But such a process would not be a definition at all, as we have been using the term here. It would be the primitive, predefinitional way of learning to use language.

Finally, there are words that, although perfectly meaningful, do not denote anything at all and therefore *cannot* be defined extensionally. When we say, for example, that there are no unicorns, we are asserting that the term "unicorn" does not denote, that it has an "empty" extension. Such terms do more than exhibit a limitation of extensional definition; they show that "meaning" really pertains more to intension than to extension. For although the term "unicorn" has an empty extension, this is certainly not to say that it is meaningless. True, it does not denote anything, since there are no unicorns, but if the term "unicorn" were meaningless it also would be meaningless to say, "There are no unicorns." This statement, however, is very far from being meaningless; we fully understand its meaning, and it is true. Clearly, intension is the real key to definition, and to it we turn in the following section.

Exercises

I.   Define the following terms by example, enumerating three examples for each term.

*1.	actor	6.	flower
2.	boxer	7.	general (officer)
3.	composer	8.	harbor
4.	dramatist	9.	inventor
*5.	element	*10.	poet

II.   For each of the terms given in Exercise I, find a nonsynonymous general term that your three examples serve equally well to illustrate.

3.5   INTENSIONAL DEFINITIONS

The intension of a term, we have said, consists of the attributes shared by *all* the objects denoted by the term, and shared *only* by those objects. Thus, if the attributes that define "chair" are *being a single raised seat and having a back*, then *every* chair is a single raised seat with a back, and *only* chairs are single raised seats with backs.

But the concept of intensional definition is complicated by our need to distinguish three different senses of intension: the *subjective*, the *objective*, and the *conventional*.

The **subjective intension** of a word for a speaker is the *set* of all the attributes that the speaker believes to be possessed by objects denoted by that word. This set plainly varies from individual to individual and even from time to time for the same individual, and thus it cannot serve the purposes of definition. After all, it is the public meanings of words, not their private interpretations, in which we are interested.

The **objective intension** is the total set of characteristics shared by all the objects in the term's extension. Thus the term "circle" may have, within its objective intension, a universal feature of circles (for instance, that a circle encloses a greater area than any other closed plane figure having an equal perimeter) that many who use the word are completely unaware of. It would require complete omniscience to know all the attributes shared by the objects denoted by most terms—and since no one possesses such omniscience, the objective intension cannot be the public meaning whose explanation we seek.

Yet it is plain that there must be publicly available and widely understood intensions for most general terms (intensions that are neither subjective nor objective)—because we do communicate with one another, and we do usually understand the terms in common use. Terms have stable meanings because we have *agreed to use the same criterion (or criteria)* in deciding, about any object, whether it is part of the term's extension. Thus, what makes a thing a circle as that term is commonly used is its being a closed plane curve, all points of which are equidistant from a point within called the center. This criterion is established by *convention*. **By informal agreements we establish the conventional intension of general terms.** This is the most important sense of intension, for purposes of definition, since it is public and does not require omniscience to use. Indeed, the term "intension" is generally used to mean "conventional intension"—and this will be our usage, unless otherwise specified.

How does one actually go about defining a word? What techniques does one use to identify its conventional intension, the agreed-upon set of attributes common and peculiar to objects denoted by the word? Several methods are common.

The simplest and most frequently used—but one having limited power— is **providing another word, whose meaning is already understood, that has the same meaning as the word being defined.** Two words with the same meaning are called "synonyms," so a definition of this sort is called a **synonymous definition.** Dictionaries, especially smaller ones, rely heavily on this method of defining terms. Thus, a pocket dictionary may define "adage" as meaning "proverb"; "bashful," as meaning "shy"; and so on. Synonymous definitions are particularly useful—often essential—when it is the meanings of words in another language that call for explanation. In French, *chat* means "cat"; in Spanish, *amigo* means "friend"; and so on. One learns the vocabulary of a foreign language by studying definitions using synonyms.

This is a good method of defining terms; it is easy, efficient, and helpful— but its limitations are serious. Many words have no exact synonym, and hence synonymous definitions are often less than fully accurate and can mislead. From this realization comes the Italian proverb: *"Traduttore, traditore"* ("Translator, traitor").

A more serious limitation of synonymous definitions is this: If the concept alluded to by the word we seek to define is wholly foreign to us, and utterly puzzling, every simple synonym will be as puzzling to the hearer or reader as the *definiendum* itself. Thus, one who asks for a definition of "tylotoxea" but is totally unfamiliar with that to which this noun refers, will not be much helped when the definition given is a simple synonym. What is a tylotoxea, you ask? Oh, it's nothing more than a tylostyle. More needs to be done in such cases, more explanation provided than can be provided by a single word. Essentially the same difficulty arises when what is sought is a definition that will explain a known but fuzzy concept more fully, or with more precision. Synonyms are not likely to be sufficient when what is sought is a theoretical or a precising definition, which were explained in section 3.2.

"Operational definition"—a term first used by the Nobel prize–winning physicist P. W. Bridgeman in his influential book *The Logic of Modern Physics*

(1927)—was introduced by some scientists in order to tie the *definiendum* to some describable set of actions or operations. For example: "Space" and "time," in the wake of the success and widespread acceptance of Einstein's theory of relativity, could no longer be defined in the abstract way that Newton had used. It was then proposed to define them "operationally," that is, by means of the operations used in measuring distances and durations. **An *operational definition* of a term states that the term is correctly applied to a given case if and only if the performance of specified operations in that case yields a specified result.** The numerical value given for length would then be operationally defined by reference to the results of specified measuring procedures, and so on. Only public and repeatable operations are referred to in the *definiens* of an operational definition.

Some social scientists have sought to incorporate this technique of defining into their disciplines also, so as to avoid the confusion and disagreement that have surrounded more traditional definitions of some key terms. Thus, for example, some psychologists have sought to replace abstract definitions of "sensation" and "mind" by operational definitions referring exclusively to behavior or to physiological observations; reliance on operational definitions in psychology and other social sciences has tended to be associated with behaviorism. Extreme empiricists sometimes have insisted that a term is meaningful only if it is susceptible of operational definition, but to evaluate such claims is beyond the scope of this book.

Where a synonymous definition is unavailable and an operational definition is inappropriate, we can often use a "definition by genus and difference" to explain the conventional intension of a term. This method is also called "definition by division," "analytical definition," "definition *per genus et differentiam*," or simply "intensional definition." It would be wrong to say, as some do, that this is the only "genuine" kind of definition, but it is the technique more widely applicable than any other.

The possibility of defining terms by genus and difference depends on the fact that some attributes are complex; that is, they are analyzable into two or more other attributes. This complexity and analyzability can best be explained in terms of *classes*.

Classes having members may have their memberships divided into subclasses. For example, the class of all triangles may be divided into three nonempty subclasses: equilateral triangles, isosceles triangles, and scalene triangles. The terms "genus" and "species" are often used in this connection: the class whose membership is divided into subclasses is the *genus*, and the various subclasses are *species*. As used here, the words "genus" and "species" are *relative* terms, like "parent" and "offspring." Just as the same persons may be parents in relation to their children and offspring in relation to their parents, so one and the same class may be a genus in relation to its own subclasses, as well as a species in relation to some larger class of which it is a subclass. Thus the class of all triangles is a genus relative to the species scalene triangle and a species relative to the genus polygon. The logician's use of the words "genus" and "species" as relative terms is different from the biologist's use of them as absolute terms, and the two should not be confused.

Since a class is a collection of entities having some common characteristic, all the members of a given genus have some characteristic in common. Thus all members of the genus polygon share the characteristic of being closed plane figures bounded by straight line segments. This genus may be divided into different species or subclasses, so that all the members of each subclass have some further attribute in common that is shared by no member of any other subclass. The genus polygon is divided into triangles, quadrilaterals, pentagons, hexagons, and so on. Each species of the genus polygon differs from all the rest; the specific difference between members of the subclass hexagon and the members of any other subclass is that only members of the subclass of hexagons have precisely six sides. In general, all members of all species of a given genus share some attribute that makes them members of the genus, but the members of any one species share some further attribute that differentiates them from the members of every other species of that genus. The characteristic that serves to distinguish them is called the "specific difference." Thus, having six sides is the specific difference between the species hexagon and all other species of the genus polygon.

In this sense, the attribute of being a hexagon is analyzable into the attribute of being a polygon and the attribute of having six sides. To someone who did not know the meaning of the word "hexagon" or of any synonym of it, but who did know the meanings of the words "polygon," "sides," and "six," the meaning of the word "hexagon" could be explained by means of a *definition by genus and difference:*

> The word "hexagon" means "polygon having six sides."

Another example is the following definition of "prime number":

> A prime number is any natural number greater than one that can be divided exactly, without remainder, only by itself or by one.

Thus, **one defines a term by genus and difference in two steps: First, a genus must be named, the larger class in which the species being defined is included; then the specific difference must be named, the attribute that distinguishes the members of the species being defined from the members of all other species in that genus.** In the example immediately preceding, the genus is the class of natural numbers greater than one: 2, 3, 4, and so on; the specific difference is the quality of being divisible without remainder only by itself or by 1. Definitions by genus and difference can be very precise and are often exceedingly useful.

Yet another example of definition by genus and difference is the ancient definition of "human" as meaning "rational animal." Here the genus is "animal"; the species "human" is subsumed under it, differentiated from all other species by rationality. In this case, one could regard the class of all rational beings as the genus, and "animal" as the specific difference. The order is not absolute from the point of view of logic, although there may be extralogical reasons for considering one the genus rather than the other.

The method of definition by genus and difference also has its limitations. First, the method is applicable only to words that connote complex attributes. If there are any simple, *unanalyzable* attributes, then the words connoting them cannot be defined by genus and difference. Some have suggested that the sensed qualities of specific shades of colors are examples of simple attributes of this kind. Whether there are any such unanalyzable attributes remains an open question, but if there are, they limit the applicability of definition by genus and difference. The second limitation has to do with words conveying *universal* attributes, such as the words "being," "entity," "existent," and "object." These cannot be defined by the method of genus and difference, because the class of all entities, for example, is not a species of some broader genus; a universal class would constitute the very highest class, or *summum genus,* as it is called. The same applies to words referring to ultimate metaphysical categories, such as "substance" or "attribute." These limitations, however, are of little practical importance in the appraisal of this method of definition.

Intensional definitions, especially definitions by genus and difference, can serve any of the purposes for which definitions are constructed: They may help to eliminate ambiguity, to reduce vagueness, to explain theoretically, and even to influence attitudes. They may also be used simply to increase and enrich the vocabulary of those to whom they are provided. In section 3.2, we noted that, in achieving these different objectives, five different types of definition may be distinguished: lexical, stipulative, precising, theoretical, and persuasive. For each of these kinds, the techniques of intensional definition may be used.

FIVE TYPES OF DEFINITION

1. Stipulative
2. Lexical
3. Precising
4. Theoretical
5. Persuasive

SIX TECHNIQUES FOR DEFINING TERMS

A. *Extensional Techniques*	B. *Intensional Techniques*
1. Definitions by Example	4. Synonymous Definitions
2. Ostensive Definitions	5. Operational Definitions
3. Semi-ostensive Definitions	6. Definitions by Genus and Difference

---

Exercises

I.   Give synonymous definitions for each of the following terms.

*1.	absurd	2.	buffoon
3.	cemetery	4.	dictator
*5.	egotism	6.	feast
7.	garret	8.	hasten
9.	infant	*10.	jeopardy

11. kine	**12.** labyrinth		
13. mendicant	**14.** novice		
*15. omen	**16.** panacea		
17. quack	**18.** rostrum		
19. scoundrel	*20. tepee		

II.   Construct definitions for the following terms by matching the *definiendum* with an appropriate genus and difference.

DEFINIENDUM		DEFINIENS	
		Genus	*Difference*
*1. banquet **11.** lamb		**1.** offspring	**1.** female
2. boy **12.** mare		**2.** horse	**2.** male
3. brother **13.** midget		**3.** man	**3.** very large
4. child **14.** mother		**4.** meal	**4.** very small
*5. foal *15. pony		**5.** parent	**5.** young
6. daughter **16.** ram		**6.** sheep	
7. ewe **17.** sister		**7.** sibling	
8. father **18.** snack		**8.** woman	
9. giant **19.** son		**9.** person	
*10. girl *20. stallion			

3.6 RULES FOR DEFINITION BY GENUS AND DIFFERENCE

Certain rules have traditionally been laid down for definition by genus and difference. They do not by themselves enable us to construct good intensional definitions, because such definitions require the thoughtful selection of the appropriate genus, and the identification of the most helpful specific differences. But these rules, intended to apply chiefly to lexical definitions, are useful as criteria for appraising definitions once they have been proposed. There are five such rules.

Rule 1: A definition should state the essential attributes of the species.

As stated, this rule is somewhat cryptic, because in itself a species has just those attributes that it has, and none is more "essential" than any other. But if we understand the rule properly, as dealing with terms, it becomes clear. We distinguished earlier between the objective intension of a term and its conventional intension, the latter being those attributes whose possession constitutes the conventional criterion by which we decide whether an object is denoted by the term. Thus it is part of the objective intension of "circle" to enclose a greater area than any other plane closed figure of equal perimeter. But to define the word "circle" by this attribute would be to violate the spirit of our first rule, because it is not *the* attribute that people have agreed to mean by that word. The conventional intension is the attribute of being a closed plane curve, all points of which are equidistant from a given point called the center. To define it in these terms would be to state its "essence" and thus to conform to this first rule. Perhaps a better way to phrase this rule, using our present terminology, would be to say: "A definition should state the conventional intension of the term being defined."

The conventional intension of a term need not be an intrinsic characteristic of the things denoted by it; it may well have to do with the origin of those things, or the relations they have to other things, or the uses to which they are put. Thus the term "Stradivarius violin," which denotes a number of violins, need not refer to any actual physical characteristic shared by all those violins and possessed by no others; rather, it has the conventional intension of being a violin made in the Cremona workshop of Antonio Stradivari. Again, "governors" or "senators" are not physically or mentally different from all other persons; they simply are related in special ways to their fellow citizens. Nor can words be defined exclusively in terms of the shapes or materials of the things denoted by them; the definition of "shoe," for example, must include reference to the use to which those things are put, as outer coverings for the foot.

Rule 2: A definition must not be circular.

If the *definiendum* itself appears in the *definiens,* the definition can explain the meaning of the term being defined only to those who already understand it. So if a definition is circular, it must fail in its purpose, which is to explain the meaning of the *definiendum.* A book on gambling contains this blatant violation of the rule:

> A compulsive gambler is a person who gambles compulsively.[17]

Definitional circularity can sometimes snare even sophisticated scientists. An article in a medical journal contains this passage:

> This review defines stress as a specific morphological, biochemical, physiological, and/or behavioral change experienced by an organism in response to a stressful event or stressor.[18]

When applied to definition by genus and difference, this principle also rules out the use (in the *definiens*) of any synonym of the *definiendum.* There is, for example, little point in defining "lexicon" as "a compilation of words like a dictionary." If the synonym "dictionary" is assumed to be understood, one could as well have given a straightforward synonymous definition of "lexicon" instead of resorting to the more powerful but more complicated technique of genus and difference. This rule is usually understood to forbid the use of antonyms as well as synonyms.

---

[17] Jay Livingston, *Compulsive Gamblers* (New York: Harper & Row, 1974), p. 2.
[18] W. H. Voge, "Stress—The Neglected Variable in Experimental Pharmacology and Toxicology," *Trends in Pharmacological Science,* January 1987.

Rule 3: A definition must be neither too broad nor too narrow.

The *definiens* should not denote more things or fewer things than are denoted by the *definiendum.* This is an easy rule to understand, but a difficult one to follow.

When Plato's successors in the Academy at Athens at last settled on the definition of "man" as "featherless biped," their critic Diogenes plucked a chicken and threw it over the wall into the Academy. A featherless biped was before them—but one that was assuredly not a man. That *definiens* was too broad. Legend has it that to narrow it, they added to the *definiens* the phrase "with broad nails."

When certain items are customarily, but not necessarily, made of a given stuff, it is a temptation to make that stuff part of the definition. It would be quite incorrect to define the word "shoe" as "a leather covering for the foot," for that definition would be too narrow, since shoes may also be made of wood or canvas. Finding or constructing the *definiens* that has precisely the correct breadth to explain the *definiendum* may prove very challenging.

Of course, in the construction of a stipulative definition, this rule cannot be violated, since in such cases the *definiendum* has no meaning apart from the *definiens* provided. And in any case, if Rule 1 is fully observed (the essence of the *definiendum* stated in the *definiens*), Rule 3 will have been obeyed, since the conventional intension of the term can be neither too broad nor too narrow.

Rule 4: A definition must not be expressed in ambiguous, obscure, or figurative language.

Ambiguous terms in the *definiens* obviously will prevent the definition from performing its function of explaining the *definiendum.* Obscure terms also will defeat that purpose, but obscurity is a relative matter. Words obscure to children are reasonably clear to most adults; words obscure to amateurs may be perfectly familiar to professionals. A "dynatron oscillator" does truly mean a circuit that employs a negative-resistance, volt-ampere curve to produce an alternating current. While this is terribly obscure to the ordinary person, the language is perfectly intelligible to the students of electrical engineering, and is justifiably technical. But using obscure language in nontechnical matters is often a futile attempt to explain the unknown by the still more unknown.

Self-defeating obscurity is well illustrated by Herbert Spencer's definition of "evolution" as

> An integration of matter and concomitant dissipation of motion, during which the matter passes from an indefinite, incoherent homogeneity to a definite, coherent heterogeneity, and during which the retained motion undergoes a parallel transformation.[19]

Another example of obscurity in definition is Dr. Samuel Johnson's celebrated definition of the word "net" as meaning "anything reticulated or decussated at equal distances with interstices between the intersections."[20]

---

[19] Herbert Spencer, *Principles of Biology,* 1864.
[20] Samuel Johnson, *Dictionary of the English Language,* 1755.

Figurative or metaphorical language used in the *definiens* may give some feeling for the use of the term being defined but cannot give a clear explanation of what the *definiendum* means. Bread may be "the staff of life," but the meaning of the word "bread" is hardly explained in such a definition. Figurative definitions may be very clever, calling attention to a common but unacknowledged use of the term defined, sometimes with satirical bite; persuasive definitions often play on the use of colorful language with a humorous barb. *The Devil's Dictionary* is a famous collection of the witty definitions of Ambrose Bierce, rich with insight and very cynical. "Fib" he defined as "a lie that has not cut its teeth," and "insurance" as "an ingenious modern game of chance in which the player is permitted to enjoy the comfortable conviction that he is beating the man who keeps the table." "Oratory" said Bierce, who trusted no one, was "a conspiracy between speech and action to cheat the understanding."[21] But any definition that contains or relies on figurative language, however entertaining or insightful, cannot serve as a serious explanation of the precise meaning of the term to be defined.

Rule 5: A definition should not be negative where it can be affirmative.
A definition should explain what a term *does* mean rather than what it does *not* mean. There are far too many things that the vast majority of terms do *not* mean for any negative definition possibly to cover. To define "couch" as "a piece of furniture that is neither a bed nor a chair" is to fail miserably to explain its meaning, for there are very many other kinds of furniture not meant by the word "couch."

Some terms are essentially negative in meaning and so *require* negative definitions. The word "orphan" means "a child who does not have parents"; the word "bald" means the state of "not having hair on one's head," and so on. Sometimes there is no basis for choosing between affirmative and negative definitions; we may define "drunkard" as "one who drinks excessively," and about equally well as "one who is not temperate in drink." Even where negatives are appropriately used, the genus must first be affirmatively mentioned; then, sometimes, the species can be characterized negatively by a rejection of all other species of the genus named. But rarely are there few enough other species so that they may be conveniently mentioned and rejected in a negative definition. And even when that is possible—as when we define "scalene triangle" as "a triangle that is neither equilateral nor isosceles"—we will comply far better with the first rule, stating the essential attributes of the species, if we affirmatively identify the attribute—"having sides of unequal length"—that marks off the class of scalene triangles. We certainly cannot define the word "quadrilateral" as "a polygon that is neither a triangle, nor a pentagon, nor a hexagon, nor . . ." because there are too many alternative species of the genus polygon to be excluded. In general, affirmative definitions are much to be preferred over negative ones.

For most purposes, intensional definitions are greatly superior to extensional definitions; and of all intensional definitions, those constructed by

---

[21] Ambrose Bierce, *The Devil's Dictionary*, 1911.

genus and difference are usually most effective and most helpful when one is reasoning or engaging in other informative uses of language.

Exercises

I. Construct a definition by genus and difference for each of the terms in Exercise I on page 000.

II. Criticize the following in terms of the rules for definition by genus and difference. After identifying the difficulty (or difficulties), state the rule (or rules) violated. If the definition is either too narrow or too broad, explain why.

*1. A genius is one who, with an innate capacity, affects for good or evil the lives of others.

> —Jacqueline Du Pre, in *Jacqueline Du Pre: Her Life, Her Music, Her Legend* (Arcade Publishing, 1999)

2. Knowledge is true opinion.

> —Plato, *Theaetetus*

3. Life is the art of drawing sufficient conclusions from insufficient premisses.

> —Samuel Butler, *Notebooks*

4. "Base" means that which serves as a base.

> —Ch'eng Wei-Shih Lun, quoted in Fung Yu-Lan, *A History of Chinese Philosophy*, 1959

*5. Alteration is combination of contradictorily opposed determinations in the existence of one and the same thing.

> —Immanuel Kant, *Critique of Pure Reason*, 1787

6. Honesty is the habitual absence of the intent to deceive.

7. Hypocrisy is the homage that vice pays to virtue.

> —François La Rochefoucauld, *Reflections*, 1665

8. The word *body*, in the most general acceptation, signifieth that which filleth, or occupieth some certain room, or imagined place; and dependeth not on the imagination, but is a real part of that we call the universe.

> —Thomas Hobbes, *Leviathan*

9. Torture is "any act by which severe pain or suffering, whether physical or mental, is intentionally inflicted on a person for such purposes as obtaining from him or a third person information or a confession."

> —United Nations Convention Against Torture, 1984

*10. "Cause" means something that produces an effect.

11. War . . . is an act of violence intended to compel our opponent to fulfill our will.

   —Carl Von Clausewitz, *On War*, 1911

12. A raincoat is an outer garment of plastic that repels water.

13. A hazard is anything that is dangerous.

   —*Safety with Beef Cattle,* U.S. Occupational Safety and Health Administration, 1976

14. To sneeze [is] to emit wind audibly by the nose.

   —Samuel Johnson, *Dictionary*, 1814

*15. A bore is a person who talks when you want him to listen.

   —Ambrose Bierce, 1906

16. Art is a human activity having for its purpose the transmission to others of the highest and best feelings to which men have risen.

   —Lev Tolstoi, *What Is Art?*

17. Murder is when a person of sound memory and discretion unlawfully killeth any reasonable creature in being, and under the king's peace, with malice aforethought, either express or implied.

   —Edward Coke, *Institutes*, 1684

18. A cloud is a large semi-transparent mass with a fleecy texture suspended in the atmosphere whose shape is subject to continual and kaleidoscopic change.

   —U. T. Place, "Is Consciousness a Brain Process?" *The British Journal of Psychology*, February 1956

19. Freedom of choice: the human capacity to choose freely between two or more genuine alternatives or possibilities, such choosing being always limited both by the past and by the circumstances of the immediate present.

   —Corliss Lamont, *Freedom of Choice Affirmed*, 1967

*20. Health is a state of complete physical, mental, and social well-being and not merely the absence of disease or infirmity.

   —World Health Organization

21. By analysis, we mean analyzing the contradictions in things.

   —Mao Zedong, *Quotations from Chairman Mao*, 1966

22. Noise is any unwanted signal.

   —Victor E. Ragosine, "Magnetic Recording," *Scientific American*, February 1970

23. To explain (explicate, *explicare*) is to strip reality of the appearances covering it like a veil, in order to see the bare reality itself.

   —Pierre Duhem, *The Aim and Structure of Physical Theory*

24. The Master said, Yu, shall I teach you what knowledge is? When you know a thing, to recognize that you know it, and when you do not know a thing, to recognize that you do not know it. That is knowledge.

    —Confucius, *The Analects*

*25. I would define political correctness as a form of dogmatic relativism, intolerant of those, such as believers in "traditional values," whose positions are thought to depend on belief in objective truth.

    —Philip E. Devine, *Proceedings of the*
    American Philosophical Association, June 1992

III. Discuss the following definitions.

*1. Faith is the substance of things hoped for, the evidence of things not seen.

    —Hebrews 11:1

2. "Faith is when you believe something that you know ain't true."

    —Definition attributed to a schoolboy
    by William James in "The Will to Believe"

3. Faith may be defined briefly as an illogical belief in the occurrence of the improbable.

    —H. L. Mencken, *Prejudice*, 1922

4. Poetry is simply the most beautiful, impressive, and widely effective mode of saying things.

    —Matthew Arnold, 1865

*5. Poetry is the record of the best and happiest moments of the happiest and best minds.

    —Percy Bysshe Shelley, *The Defence of Poetry*, 1821

6. A cynic is a man who knows the price of everything and the value of nothing.

    —Oscar Wilde, *Lady Windermere's Fan*, 1892

7. Conscience is an inner voice that warns us somebody is looking.

    —H. L. Mencken, 1949

8. A sentimentalist is a man who sees an absurd value in everything and doesn't know the market price of a single thing.

    —Oscar Wilde, *Lady Windermere's Fan*

9. "The true," to put it very briefly, is only the expedient in the way of our thinking, just as "the right" is only the expedient in the way of our behaving.

    —William James, "Pragmatism's Conception of Truth," 1907

*10. To be conceited is to tend to boast of one's own excellences, to pity or ridicule the deficiencies of others, to daydream about imaginary triumphs, to reminisce about actual triumphs, to weary quickly of conversations which reflect unfavorably upon oneself, to lavish one's society upon distinguished persons and to economize in association with the undistinguished.

—Gilbert Ryle, *The Concept of Mind*, 1949

11. Economics is the science which treats of the phenomena arising out of the economic activities of men in society.

—J. N. Keynes, *Scope and Methods of Political Economy*, 1891

12. Justice is doing one's own business, and not being a busybody.

—Plato, *Republic*

13. What, then, is the government? An intermediate body established between the subjects and the sovereign for their mutual correspondence, charged with the execution of the laws and with the maintenance of liberty both civil and political.

—Jean-Jacques Rousseau, *The Social Contract*

14. By good, I understand that which we certainly know is useful to us.

—Baruch Spinoza, *Ethics*

*15. Political power, then, I take to be a right of making laws with penalties of death, and consequently all less penalties, for the regulating and preserving of property, and of employing the force of the community in the execution of such laws, and in defense of the commonwealth from foreign injury, and all this only for the public good.

—John Locke, *Essay Concerning Civil Government*

16. And what, then, is belief ? It is the demi-cadence which closes a musical phrase in the symphony of our intellectual life.

—Charles Sanders Peirce, "How to Make Our Ideas Clear"

17. Political power, properly so called, is merely the organized power of one class for oppressing another.

—Karl Marx and Friedrich Engels, *The Communist Manifesto*, 1847

18. Grief for the calamity of another is *pity;* and ariseth from the imagination that the like calamity may befall himself.

—Thomas Hobbes, *Leviathan*

19. We see that all men mean by justice that kind of state of character which makes people disposed to do what is just and makes them act justly and wish for what is just.

—Aristotle, *Nichomachean Ethics*

*20. Inquiry is the controlled or directed transformation of an indeterminate situation into one that is so determinate in its constituent distinctions and relations as to convert the elements of the original situation into a unified whole.

—John Dewey, *Logic: The Theory of Inquiry,* 1938

21. A fanatic is one who can't change his mind and won't change the subject.

—Winston Churchill

22. Regret is the pain people feel when they compare what is with what might have been.

—Richard Gotti, "How Not to Regret Regret," *Bottom Line Personal,* 30 September 1992

23. Happiness is the satisfaction of all our desires, *extensively,* in respect of their manifoldness, *intensively,* in respect of their degree, and *potensively,* in respect of their duration.

—Immanuel Kant, *Critique of Pure Reason,* 1787

24. A tragedy is the imitation of an action that is serious and also, as having magnitude, complete in itself; in language with pleasurable accessories, each kind brought in separately in the parts of the work; in a dramatic, not in a narrative form; with incidents arousing pity and fear, wherewith to accomplish its catharsis of such emotions.

—Aristotle, *Poetics*

*25. Propaganda is manipulation designed to lead you to a simplistic conclusion rather than a carefully considered one.

—Anthony Pratkanis, *New York Times,* 27 October 1992

26. . . . the frequently celebrated female intuition . . . is after all only a faculty for observing tiny insignificant aspects of behavior and forming an empirical conclusion which cannot be syllogistically examined.

—Germaine Greer, *The Female Eunuch,* 1971

27. A fetish is a story masquerading as an object.

—Robert Stoller, "Observing the Erotic Imagination"

28. Religion is a complete system of human communication (or a "form of life") showing in primarily "commissive," "behabitive," and "exercitive" modes how a community comports itself when it encounters an "untranscendable negation of . . . possibilities."

—Gerald James Larson, "Prolegomenon to a Theory of Religion," *Journal of the American Academy of Religion*

29. Robert Frost, the distinguished New England poet, used to define a liberal as someone who refuses to take his own side in an argument.

—"Dreaming of JFK," *The Economist,* 17 March 1984

*30.   The meaning of a word is what is explained by the explanation of
the meaning.

—Ludwig Wittgenstein, *Philosophical Investigations,* 1953

Summary of Chapter 3

To explain the meaning of a term is to give the definition of it. In this chapter we
have discussed the several **kinds of definitions and their uses,** and **techniques
for constructing definitions,** with **rules for applying these techniques.**
In section 3.1, we have explained **three kinds of disputes:**

1.   **Obviously genuine disputes,** in which there is no ambiguity present and
the disputers do disagree, either in attitude or in belief.
2.   **Merely verbal disputes,** in which there is ambiguity present but there is
no genuine disagreement at all.
3.   **Apparently verbal disputes that are really genuine,** in which there is ambiguity present *and* the disputers disagree, either in attitude or in belief.

In section 3.2, we first explained that definitions are always of *symbols,* and
we introduced the terms *definiendum* (the symbol that is defined) and
definiens (the symbols used to explain the meaning of the *definiendum.)*
We also distinguished among **five kinds of definition and their principal
uses:**

1.   **Stipulative definitions,** in which a meaning is assigned to some symbol.
A stipulative definition is not a report and cannot be true or false; it is a
proposal, resolution, request, or instruction to use the *definiendum* to
mean what is meant by the *definiens.*
2.   **Lexical definitions,** which report the meaning that the *definiendum* already has and which therefore can be correct or incorrect.
3.   **Precising definitions,** which go beyond ordinary usage in such a way as
to eliminate troublesome uncertainty regarding borderline cases. Its
definiendum has an existing meaning, but that meaning is vague; what is
added to achieve precision is partly a matter of stipulation.
4.   **Theoretical definitions,** which seek to formulate a theoretically adequate
or scientifically useful description of the objects to which the term applies.
5.   **Persuasive definitions,** which seek to influence attitudes or stir the emotions, using language expressively rather than informatively.

Of these five kinds of definition the first two (stipulative and lexical) are used
chiefly to eliminate ambiguity; the third (precising) is used chiefly to reduce
vagueness; the fourth (theoretical) is used to advance theoretical understanding; and the fifth (persuasive) is used to influence conduct.
In section 3.3, we explained that a general term *denotes* the several objects
to which that term may be correctly applied. The collection of these objects
constitutes the **extension** of the term. We explained that the set of attributes

shared by all and only the objects within a term's extension is the **intension** of the term. The extension of a term is determined by its intension, but the intension is not determined by the extension; so terms may have different intensions and yet the same extension; but terms with different extensions cannot possibly have the same intension.

In section 3.4, we explained how, using the **extension** of a general term, we may construct **extensional definitions,** of which there are several varieties, whose limitations also are noted:

1. **Definitions by example,** in which we list or give examples of the objects denoted by the term.
2. **Ostensive definitions,** in which we point or indicate by gesture the extension of the term being defined.
3. **Quasi-ostensive definitions,** in which the gesture or pointing is accompanied by some descriptive phrase whose meaning is taken as being known.

In section 3.5, we explained how, using the **intension** of a general term, we can construct **intensional definitions,** of which there are also several varieties, whose limitations are also noted:

1. **Synonymous definitions,** in which we provide another word, whose meaning is already understood, that has the same meaning as the word being defined.
2. **Operational definitions,** which state that the term is correctly applied to a given case if and only if the performance of specified operations in that case yields a specified result.
3. **Definition by genus and difference,** in which we first name the genus of which the species designated by the *definiendum* is a subclass, and then name the attribute (or specific difference) that distinguishes the members of that species from members of all other species in that genus.

The techniques of intensional definition may be used in constructing definitions of any one of the five kinds identified in section 3.2: stipulative, lexical, precising, theoretical, or persuasive.

In section 3.6, we formulated and explained **five rules** traditionally laid down for definitions by genus and difference:

1. A definition should **state the essential attributes** of the species.
2. A definition must **not be circular.**
3. A definition must **be neither too broad nor too narrow.**
4. A definition must **not be expressed in ambiguous, obscure, or figurative language.**
5. A definition should **not be negative** where it can be affirmative.

*It is indeed not the least of the logician's tasks
to indicate the pitfalls laid by language
in the way of the thinker.*
—Gottlob Frege

*It would be a very good thing if every trick could receive
some short and obviously appropriate name, so that when
anyone used this or that particular trick, he could at once
be reproved for it.*
—Arthur Schopenhauer

CHAPTER 4

FALLACIES

4.1 WHAT IS A FALLACY?

An argument, whatever its subject or sphere, is generally constructed in such a way as to prove its conclusion true. But any argument can fail to fulfill this purpose in two ways. One way it can fail is by assuming a false proposition as one of its premisses. We saw, in Chapter 1, that every argument involves the claim that the truth of its conclusion follows from, or is implied by, the truth of its premisses. So if its premisses are not true, the argument fails to establish the truth of its conclusion, even if the reasoning based on those premisses is correct. To test the truth or falsehood of premisses, however, is not the special responsibility of the logician; it is rather the task of inquiry in general, since premisses may deal with any subject matter whatever.

The other way in which an argument can fail to establish the truth of its conclusion is to rely upon premisses that do not imply the conclusion. Here we are in the special province of the logician, whose chief concern is the logical relations between premisses and conclusion. An argument whose premisses do not support its conclusion is one whose conclusion *could* be false *even if* all its premisses were true. In cases of this kind, the reasoning is bad, and the argument is said to be *fallacious*. A fallacy is an error in reasoning.

The word "fallacy," however, as logicians use it, designates not any mistaken inference or false belief, but *typical* errors, that is, mistakes that arise commonly in ordinary discourse and that devastate the arguments in which they appear. Each fallacy is a type of incorrect argument. An argument in which a mistake of a given type appears is said to *commit* that fallacy. Since each fallacy is a type, we can say of two or more different arguments that they contain or commit the same fallacy; that is, they exhibit the same kind of mistake in reasoning. An argument that contains or commits a fallacy of a given type may also be said to *be* a fallacy, that is, to be an example of that typical mistake.

There are many ways in which reasoning can go astray; that is, there are many *kinds* of mistakes in argument. It is customary to reserve the term "fallacy" for arguments that, although incorrect, are psychologically persuasive. Some arguments are so obviously incorrect as to deceive and persuade no one. But fallacies are dangerous because most of us are fooled by some of them on occasion. We therefore define a **fallacy** as **a type of argument that may seem to be correct, but that proves, on examination, not to be so.** It is profitable to study these mistaken arguments, because the traps they set can best be avoided when they are well understood. To be forewarned is to be forearmed!

Whether a given argument does in fact commit a fallacy may depend on the interpretation given to the terms used by its author. In a passage that appears to be fallacious, it may be difficult to determine out of context what meanings the author intended for the terms used. Sometimes the accusation of "Fallacy!" is unjustly leveled at a passage that was intended by its author to make a point missed by the critic—perhaps even to make a joke. We should bear such unavoidable complications in mind as we apply the analysis of fallacious argument to actual discourse. Our logical standards should be high, but our application of them to arguments in ordinary life should also be generous and fair.

How many different kinds of mistakes in arguments—different fallacies—may be distinguished? Aristotle, the first systematic logician, identified 13 types;[1] recently a listing of more than 100 has been developed![2] There is no precisely determinable number of fallacies, however, since much depends, in counting them, on the system of classification used. We distinguish 17 fallacies here—the most common and most deceptive mistakes in reasoning—divided into three large groups, called (a) fallacies of *relevance;* (b) fallacies of *presumption;* and (c) fallacies of *ambiguity.*[3]

The grouping of fallacies is always in some degree arbitrary, because mistakes of one kind will bear close similarities to, and sometimes overlap with, mistakes of another kind. The placement of a given fallacious passage in one

---

[1] Aristotle, *Sophistical Refutations.*

[2] The most voluminous list of fallacies we know appears in David H. Fischer's *Historians' Fallacies* (New York: Harper & Row, 1979); he discussed and named even more than the 112 different fallacies noted in his index. In *Fallacy: The Counterfeit of Argument* (Englewood Cliffs, NJ: Prentice-Hall, 1959), W. W. Fernside and W. B. Holther named and illustrated 51 fallacies. A historical and theoretical treatment of the topic was given by C. L. Hamblin in *Fallacies* (London: Methuen, 1970), and another excellent treatment of the topic is to be found in *Argument: The Logic of the Fallacies* (Scarborough, Ont.: McGraw-Hill Ryerson, 1982) by John Woods and Douglas Walton. Howard Kahane presented insightful criticism of the usual methods of classifying fallacies in "The Nature and Classification of Fallacies" in *Informal Logic,* edited by J. A. Blair and R. J. Johnson (Inverness, CA: Edgepress, 1980). All these books are warmly recommended to readers who wish to go more deeply into the subject of fallacies.

[3] Other fallacies, arising in special contexts, are discussed elsewhere in this book. Fallacies common in the misuse of syllogisms are explained in sections 6.4 and 7.7; fallacies common in symbolic logic are explained in section 8.4; some fallacies in causal reasoning are explained in Chapter 12; "the gambler's fallacy," committed in reasoning about probability, is explained in section 14.3. The kinds of mistakes made in reasoning are many and various; those discussed in this chapter are fallacies encountered in everyday, informal discourse.

specific group is also often disputable, because there may be more than one mistake of reasoning in that passage. If one remains mindful of this unavoidable imprecision, gaining an understanding of the essential features of each of the three major categories and the specific features of its several subcategories will be of much practical use. It enables one to detect the most troublesome errors in reasoning as they occur in ordinary discourse, and it promotes the logical sensitivity needed to detect related errors that may fall outside any one of these groupings.

4.2   FALLACIES OF RELEVANCE

When an argument relies on premises that are not relevant to its conclusion, and that therefore cannot possibly establish its truth, the fallacy committed is one of *relevance.* "*Ir*relevance" may perhaps better describe the problem, but the premises are often *psychologically* relevant to the conclusion, and this relevance explains their seeming correctness and persuasiveness. How psychological relevance can be confused with logical relevance can be explained in part by the different uses of language that we discussed in Chapter 2; the mechanics of these confusions will become clearer in the following analyses.

Latin names traditionally have been given to many fallacies; some of these—such as *ad hominem*—have become part of the English language. We will use here both the Latin and the English names.

R1.   The Argument from Ignorance: Argument *Ad Ignorantiam*

The argument *ad ignorantiam* (from ignorance) is the mistake that is committed **when it is argued that a proposition is true simply on the basis that it has not been proved false, or that it is false because it has not been proved true.** We realize, on reflection, that many false propositions have not yet been proved false, and many true propositions have not yet been proved true—and thus our ignorance of how to prove or disprove a proposition does not establish either truth or falsehood. This fallacious appeal to ignorance crops up most commonly in the misunderstandings incidental to developing science, where propositions whose truth cannot yet be established are mistakenly held to be false for that reason, and also in the world of pseudoscience, where propositions about psychic phenomena and the like are fallaciously held to be true because their falsehood has not been conclusively established.

Famous in the history of science is the argument *ad ignorantiam* given in criticism of Galileo, when he showed leading astronomers of his time the mountains and valleys on the moon that could be seen through his telescope. Some scholars of that age, absolutely convinced that the moon was a perfect sphere, as theology and Aristotelian science had long taught, argued against Galileo that, although we see what appear to be mountains and valleys, the moon is in fact a perfect sphere, because all its apparent irregularities are filled in by an invisible crystalline substance—an hypothesis that saves the perfection of the heavenly bodies and that Galileo could not prove false! Legend has it that Galileo, to expose the argument *ad ignorantiam,* offered another of the same kind as a caricature. Unable to prove the nonexistence of the transparent crystal supposedly filling the valleys, he put forward the equally probable hypothesis that there were, rising up from that invisible crystalline envelope, even greater mountain peaks—but made of crystal and thus invisible! And this hypothesis, he pointed out, his critics could not prove false.

Those who strongly oppose some great change are often tempted to argue against the change on the ground that it has not yet been proved workable or safe. Such proof is often impossible to provide in advance, and commonly the appeal of the objection is to ignorance mixed with fear. Such an appeal often takes the form of rhetorical questions that suggest, but do not flatly assert, that the proposed changes are full of unknown peril. Policy changes may be supported, as well as opposed, by an appeal to ignorance. When the federal government issued a waiver, in 1992, allowing Wisconsin to reduce the additional benefits it had been giving to welfare mothers for having more than one child, the governor of Wisconsin was asked if there was any evidence that unwed mothers were having additional children simply in order to gain the added income. His reply, *ad ignorantiam,* was this: "No, there isn't. There really isn't, but there is no evidence to the contrary, either."[4]

In some circumstances, of course, the fact that certain evidence or results have not been obtained, after they have been actively sought in ways calculated to reveal them, may have substantial argumentative force. New drugs being tested for safety, for example, are commonly given to rodents or other animal subjects for prolonged periods; the absence of any toxic effect on the animals is taken to be evidence (although not conclusive evidence) that the drug is probably not toxic to humans. Consumer protection often relies on evidence of this kind. In circumstances like these, we rely not on ignorance but on our knowledge, or conviction, that if the result we are concerned about were likely to arise, it would have arisen in some of the test cases. This use of the inability to prove something true supposes that investigators are highly skilled, and that they very probably would have uncovered the evidence sought had that been possible. Tragic mistakes sometimes are made in this sphere, but if the standard is set too high—if what is required is a conclusive proof of harmlessness that cannot ever be given—consumers will be denied what may prove to be valuable, even lifesaving, medical therapies.

Similarly, when a security investigation yields no evidence of improper conduct by the persons investigated, it would be wrong to conclude that the investigation has left us ignorant. A thorough investigation will properly result in their being "cleared." *Not* to draw a conclusion, in some cases, is as much a breach of correct reasoning as it would be to draw a mistaken conclusion.

The appeal to ignorance is common and often appropriate in a criminal court, where an accused person, in American jurisprudence and British common law, is presumed innocent until proved guilty. We adopt this principle because we recognize that the error of convicting the innocent is far more grave than that of acquitting the guilty—and thus the defense in a criminal case may

---

[4] "Wisconsin to Cut Welfare," *Ann Arbor News,* 11 April 1992.

legitimately claim that if the prosecution has not proved guilt beyond a reasonable doubt, the only verdict possible is not guilty. The U.S. Supreme Court strongly reaffirmed this standard of proof in these words:

> The reasonable-doubt standard . . . is a prime instrument for reducing the risk of convictions resting on factual error. The standard provides concrete substance for the presumption of innocence—that bedrock axiomatic and elementary principle whose enforcement lies at the foundation of the administration of our criminal law.[5]

But *this* appeal to ignorance succeeds only where innocence must be assumed in the absence of proof to the contrary; in other contexts, such an appeal is indeed an argument *ad ignorantiam.*

R2. The Appeal to Inappropriate Authority: Argument *Ad Verecundiam*

In attempting to make up one's mind about some difficult or complicated question, it is entirely reasonable to be guided by the judgment of an acknowledged expert. When we argue that a given conclusion is correct on the ground that an expert authority has come to that judgment, we commit no fallacy. Indeed, such recourse to authority is necessary for most of us on very many matters. Of course, an expert's judgment constitutes no conclusive proof; experts disagree, and even in agreement they may err; but expert opinion surely is one reasonable way to support a conclusion.

    The fallacy *ad verecundiam* arises **when the appeal is made to parties having no legitimate claim to authority in the matter at hand.** Thus, in an argument about morality, an appeal to the opinions of Darwin, a towering authority in biology, would be fallacious, as would be an appeal to the opinions of a great artist such as Picasso to settle an economic dispute.[6] But care must be taken in determining whose authority is reasonably to be relied on, and whose rejected. While Picasso was not an economist, his judgment might plausibly be given some weight in a dispute pertaining to the economic value of an artistic masterpiece; and if the role of biology in moral questions were in dispute, Darwin might indeed be an appropriate authority.

    The most blatant examples of misplaced appeals to authority appear in advertising "testimonials." We are urged to drive an automobile of a given make because a famous golfer or tennis player affirms its superiority; we are urged to drink a beverage of a certain brand because some movie star or football coach expresses enthusiasm about it. Wherever the truth of some proposition is asserted on the basis of the authority of one who has no special competence in that sphere, the appeal to misplaced authority is the fallacy committed.

---

[5] Justice Brennan, writing for the Court, *In re Winship,* 397 U.S. 358, 1970.

[6] Fulton J. Sheen, a well-known Catholic bishop, remarked that it would be as fatuous for Albert Einstein to make judgments about God as it would be for Sheen to make judgments about relativity theory. "Both us," Sheen wrote, "would be talking about something we know nothing about." Cited by Laurence A. Marschall, in *The Sciences,* August 2000.

This appears to be a simpleminded mistake that is easy to avoid, but there are circumstances in which the fallacious appeal is tempting, and therefore intellectually dangerous. Here are two examples. In the sphere of international relations, in which weapons and war unhappily play a major role, one opinion or another is commonly supported by appealing to those whose special competence lies in the technical design or construction of weapons. Physicists such as Robert Oppenheimer or Edward Teller, for example, may indeed have had the knowledge to give authoritative judgments regarding how certain weapons can (or cannot) function; but their knowledge in this sphere does not give them special wisdom in determining broad political goals. An appeal to the strong judgment of a distinguished physicist as to the wisdom of ratifying some international treaty would be an argument *ad verecundiam*. Similarly, we admire the depth and insight of great fiction—say, in the novels of Alexander Solzhenitsyn or Saul Bellow—but to resort to their judgment in determining the real culprit in some political dispute would be an appeal *ad verecundiam*.[7]

Many persons offer themselves, or are presented by others, as "experts" in one field or another; yet determining whose authority is truly worthy to be relied upon is often a difficult matter. Suppose we want to know whether some proposition, p, is true. Suppose that some person, A, is alleged to be an expert about p, or propositions like p, and A says that p is true. What are the conditions under which A's saying so really gives us good reason to accept the truth of p? In real cases the answer depends, of course, upon what p asserts, and on the relation between A and propositions like p. In general, the question we must answer is this: Is A, by virtue of knowledge, experience, training, or general circumstances, more able than we, who are discussing the matter, to judge whether or not p is true? If so, A's judgment has some value as evidence for us regarding the truth of p—although, of course, A's judgment may be weak evidence, perhaps more than counterbalanced by other considerations and perhaps outweighed by the testimony of still others who also have more knowledge about p than do we.

The argument *ad verecundiam* is an appeal to one who has no claim greater than our own to judge the truth of p. Even one who does have a legitimate claim to authority may well prove mistaken, of course, and we may later regret our choice of experts. But if the experts we chose deserved their reputation for knowledge about things like p (whatever p may be), it was no fallacy to rely upon them even if they erred. Our mistake becomes one of reasoning (a fallacy) when our conclusion is based upon the verdict of an authority having no rational claim to expertise in that matter.[8]

---

[7] The name was originated by John Locke, whose criticism was directed chiefly at those who think that citing learned authorities is enough to win any argument, who think it "a breach of modesty for others to derogate any way from it, and question authority," and who "style it impudence in anyone who shall stand out against them." That argument Locke named *ad verecundiam*—literally, an appeal to the *modesty* of those who might be so bold as to oppose authority (J. Locke, *An Essay Concerning Human Understanding*, 1690).

[8] For an extended and penetrating analysis of the argument *ad verecundiam*, see Jim Mackenzie, "Authority," *Journal of Philosophy of Education* 22 (1988).

R3. Argument *Ad Hominem*

The phrase *ad hominem* translates into "against the person." It names **a fallacious attack in which the thrust is directed, not at a conclusion, but at the person who asserts or defends it.** This fallacy has two major forms, because there are two major ways in which the attack can be personalized.

A. *Argument* **Ad Hominen,** *Abusive*

Participants in strenuous argument sometimes disparage the character of their opponents, deny their intelligence or reasonableness, question their integrity, and so on. But the character of an individual is logically irrelevant to the truth or falsehood of what that person says, or to the correctness or incorrectness of that person's reasoning. To contend that proposals are bad, or assertions false, because they are proposed or asserted by "radicals" or "extremists" is a typical example of the fallacy *ad hominem,* abusive.

Abusive premises are irrelevant; they may nevertheless persuade by the psychological process of transference. Where an attitude of disapproval toward a person can be evoked, the field of emotional disapproval may be extended so as to include disagreement with the assertions that person makes.

A bitter controversy among several contemporary American philosophers illustrates this fallacious attack. One of the disputants wrote:

> It is one thing to be attacked by an honorable opponent in an honorable way. This happens all the time in philosophy. But in my view Sommers's intellectual methods are dishonest. She ignores the most elementary protocols of philosophical disputation.[9]

The target of this accusation replied:

> One dishonest and unworthy tactic used by several of my detractors is to attribute to me complaints I never made and then to dismiss the "complaints" as "irresponsible and evidence of my reckless unfairness."[10]

The merits of the positions of the conflicting parties are not illuminated by argument of this character.

Ad hominem abuse has very many variations. The opponent may be abused for being of a certain persuasion, an "isolationist" or an "interventionist," a member of the "radical right" or of the "loony left," or the like. When an argument *ad hominem,* abusive, takes the form of attacking the source or genesis of the opposing position—not relevant to its truth, of course—it may be called the "genetic fallacy."

A conclusion, or its proponent, may at times be condemned because the view is also defended by persons widely believed to be of bad character. Socrates was convicted of impiety at his notorious trial partly because of his association with persons widely known to have been disloyal to Athens and

---

[9] Sandra Lee Bartky, *Proceedings of the American Philosophical Association* 65 (June 1992), 56.

[10] Christina Sommers, *Proceedings of the American Philosophical Association* 65 (June 1992), 79.

rapacious in conduct. And, in 1997, Clyde Collins Snow, called a racist because of the conclusions he reached as a forensic scientist, replied as follows:

> In the past decade my work devoted to the investigation of the disappearance, torture, and extrajudicial execution of human rights victims in many countries has often made me the target of public criticism and official outrage. To date, however, none of my critics has called me a racist. Among my detractors have been apologists for the brutal military junta in Argentina, representatives of General Pinochet's military in Chile, the Guatemalan Defense Minister, and Serbian government spokesmen. Thus Mr. Goodman [Snow's accuser] finds himself in interesting company.[11]

Unfair accusation is an exceedingly common form of personal abuse; *guilt by association* is another pattern of abuse, less widespread but equally fallacious.

In legal proceedings it is sometimes appropriate to exhibit the unreliability of the person giving testimony, to "impeach the witness." If dishonesty in other matters can be shown and credibility thus undermined, such impeachment, in that context, may not be fallacious. But it is never enough simply to assert that the witness lied; a pattern of dishonesty or duplicity must be exhibited, or inconsistencies with past testimony revealed. And even in this special context, the attack on character cannot establish the *falsehood* of the testimony given; that inference would be fallacious.

B. *Argument* Ad Hominem, *Circumstantial*

In the circumstantial form of the *ad hominem* fallacy, it is the irrelevance of the connection between the belief held and the circumstances of those holding it that gives rise to the mistake. The *circumstances* of one who makes (or rejects) some claim have no bearing on the truth of that claim.

Thus it may be argued fallaciously that *consistency* obliges an opponent to accept (or reject) some conclusion merely because of that person's employment, or nationality, or political affiliation, or other circumstances. It may be unfairly suggested that a clergyman must accept a given proposition because its denial would be incompatible with the Scriptures. Or it may be claimed that political candidates must support a given policy because it is explicitly propounded in the platform of their party. Such argument is irrelevant to the *truth* of the proposition in question; it simply urges that some persons' circumstances require its acceptance. Hunters, accused of the needless slaughter of unoffending animals, sometimes reply by noting that their critics eat the flesh of harmless cattle. Such a reply is plainly *ad hominem;* the fact that the critic eats meat does not even begin to prove that it is right for the hunter to kill animals for amusement. The Latin term *tu quoque* (meaning "you're another" or, more loosely, "look who's talking") is sometimes used to name this variety of circumstantial *ad hominem* argument.

While the circumstances of the opponent may not be the issue in a serious argument, calling attention to them may be psychologically effective in winning assent, or in persuading others. But however persuasive it may prove, argument of this kind is essentially fallacious.

---

[11] " 'Kind' Racism," *The Sciences,* June, 1997.

Circumstantial *ad hominem* arguments are sometimes used to suggest that the opponents' conclusion should be rejected because their judgment is warped, dictated by their special situation rather than by reasoning or evidence. But an argument that is favorable to some group deserves discussion on its merits; it is fallacious to attack it simply on the ground that it is presented by a member of that group and is therefore self-serving. The arguments in favor of a protective tariff (for example) may be bad, but they are not bad because they are presented by a manufacturer who benefits from such tariffs.

One argument of this kind, called "poisoning the well," is particularly perverse. The incident that gave rise to the name illustrates the argument forcefully. The British novelist and clergyman Charles Kingsley, attacking the famous Catholic intellectual John Henry Cardinal Newman, argued thus: Cardinal Newman's claims were not to be trusted because, as a Roman Catholic priest (Kingsley alleged), Newman's first loyalty was not to the truth. Newman countered that this *ad hominem* attack made it impossible for him and indeed for all Catholics to advance their arguments, since anything that they might say to defend themselves would then be undermined by others' alleging that, after all, truth was not their first concern. Kingsley, said Cardinal Newman, had poisoned the well of discourse.

Between the abusive and the circumstantial varieties of argument *ad hominem* there is a clear connection: the circumstantial may be regarded as a special case of the abusive. When a circumstantial *ad hominem* argument explicitly or implicitly charges the opponents with *inconsistency* (among their beliefs, or between what they profess and what they practice), that is clearly one kind of abuse. When a circumstantial *ad hominem* argument charges the opponents with a lack of trustworthiness by virtue of group membership or conviction, that is an accusation of *prejudice* in defense of self-interest and is clearly also an abuse. Whether of one form or the other, *ad hominem* arguments are directed fallaciously at the person of the adversary.

R4.   The Appeal to Emotion: Argument *Ad Populum*

This common fallacy and the two that follow it are so evidently fallacious that they require little explanation. In each case, the premises plainly are not relevant to the conclusion and are deliberately chosen as instruments to manipulate the beliefs of the listener or reader.

The argument *ad populum,* the appeal to emotion (literally "to the people," and by implication to the mob's easily aroused emotions) is the device of every propagandist and demagogue. It is fallacious because it **replaces the laborious task of presenting evidence and rational argument with expressive language and other devices calculated to excite enthusiasm, excitement, anger, or hate.** The speeches of Adolph Hitler, which whipped up his German listeners to a state of patriotic frenzy, may be taken as a classic example. Love of country is an honorable emotion. The manipulation of one's audience by appealing inappropriately to that love is intellectually disreputable—leading to Samuel Johnson's caustic observation that "Patriotism is the last refuge of a scoundrel."

The heaviest reliance on arguments *ad populum* is to be found in commercial advertising, where its use has been elevated almost to the status of a fine art. The products advertised are associated, explicitly or slyly, with things that we yearn for or that excite us favorably. Breakfast cereal is associated with trim youthfulness, athletic prowess, and vibrant good health; whiskey is associated with luxury and achievement, and beer with high adventure; the automobile is associated with romance, riches, and sex. The men depicted using the advertised product are generally handsome and distinguished, the women sophisticated and charming—or hardly dressed at all. So clever and persistent are the ballyhoo artists of our time that we are all influenced to some degree, in spite of our resolution to resist. Almost every imaginable device may be used to command our attention, even to penetrate our subconscious thoughts. We are manipulated by relentless appeals to emotion of every kind.

The mere association of the product and the emotion is, by itself, no argument, but an argument *ad populum* commonly lies not far beneath the surface. When advertisers make claims about their products designed to win our emotional approval, and when it is suggested that we ought to make some purchase *because* the item in question is "sexy" or "best-selling" or is associated with wealth or power, the implicit claim that this conclusion follows from such premises is plainly fallacious.

Some instances of the argument *ad populum* are brazen. Here are the exact words of a recent advertisement on ABC-TV:

> Why are so many people attracted to the Pontiac Grand Prix? It could be that so many people are attracted to the Grand Prix because—so many people are attracted to the Grand Prix!

The appeal to popular enthusiasms can be particularly pernicious in the context of public polling, where the known emotive impact (negative or positive) of certain words and phrases[12] makes possible questions designed to yield the responses sought. What, for example, is the attitude of the American public toward tax cuts and federal spending in the light of an impending budget surplus? That depends on how you ask. The question was presented to large random population samples in January 2000—with two different wordings:[13]

> Variant 1: "Should a large portion [of the money in the coming surplus] be used for a tax cut, or should it be used to fund new government programs?"

To this wording of the question, 60 percent of the sample answered "tax cut," while 25 percent answered "new programs." Not surprising: "New government programs" are distinctly unappealing to many.

---

[12] See the discussion of emotive words in section 2.4.

[13] "How Use the Coming Surplus?" *New York Times* (reporting an investigation by the Pew Research Center), 30 January 2000.

Variant 2: "Should a large portion [of the money in the coming surplus] be used for a tax cut, or should it be spent on programs for education, the environment, health care, crime fighting, and military defense?"

To this wording of the question 22 percent of the sample answered "tax cut," and 69 percent answered "new programs." Again not surprising: "education, health care, crime fighting," and so on, are words and phrases known to have substantial popular appeal.

The popular acceptance of a policy does not show it to be wise, of course; nor does the fact that many people hold a given opinion prove it to be true. Bertrand Russell condemned such argument in language that is almost too vigorous:

> The fact that an opinion has been widely held is no evidence whatever that it is not utterly absurd; indeed, in view of the silliness of the majority of mankind, a wide-spread belief is more likely to be foolish than sensible.[14]

R5. The Appeal to Pity: Argument *Ad Misericordiam*

The appeal to pity (*misericordiam* meaning literally "a pitying heart") may be viewed as **a special case of the appeal to emotion, in which the altruism and mercy of the audience are the special emotions appealed to.** The attorney for a plaintiff, seeking compensatory damages for an injury, often arranges to have the client's disability revealed in the courtroom in some heartrending way.[15] And in criminal trials, although jury sympathy has no bearing whatever on the guilt or innocence of the accused, effective defense attorneys often appeal to the pity of the jury. Sometimes that appeal is made obliquely. At his trial in Athens, Socrates referred with disdain to other defendants who had appeared before their juries accompanied by their children and families, seeking to be acquitted by evoking pity. Socrates continued:

> …I, who am probably in danger of my life, will do none of these things. The contrast may occur to his [each juror's] mind, and he may be set against me, and vote in anger because he is displeased at me on this account. Now if there be such a person among you—mind, I do not say that there is—to him I may fairly reply: My friend, I am a man, and like other men, a creature of flesh and blood, and not "of wood or stone" as Homer says; and I have a family, yes, and sons, O Athenians, three in number, one almost a man, and two others who are still young; and yet I will not bring any of them here to petition you for acquittal.[16]

There are many ways to pull heart strings, and virtually all are tried. The argument *ad misericordiam* is ridiculed in the story of the trial of a youth accused of the murder of his mother and father with an ax. Confronted with overwhelming proof of his guilt, he pleaded for leniency on the grounds that he was now an orphan.

---

[14] Bertrand Russell, *Marriage and Morals* (New York: Liveright, 1929).

[15] There is more than anecdotal evidence to support the conclusion that the appeal *ad misericordium* pays off in court. See the findings reported in *The New England Journal of Medicine,* recounted in Exercise 7, section 12.2(5).

[16] Plato, *Apology,* 34; Jowett translation.

R6. The Appeal to Force: Argument *Ad Baculum*

The appeal to force, to cause the acceptance of some conclusion, seems at first sight to be so obvious a fallacy as to need no discussion at all. The use or threat of "strong-arm methods" to coerce opponents would seem to be a last resort— a useful expedient when evidence or rational methods fail. "Might makes right" is hardly a subtle principle.

The force threatened need not be physical, of course. Two professors of law at Boise State University recently published (in a law journal of the University of Denver) an article harshly critical of the Boise Cascade Corporation, one of the world's largest producers of paper and wood products. Subsequently, the University issued a formal "errata" notice that "this article has been retracted for its lack of scholarship and false content."

Did Boise Cascade threaten the University with a lawsuit? "Well," said the University's general counsel, " 'threaten' is an interesting word. Let's just say they pointed out that the objections they raised did rise to the level of being actionable." The University, it turns out, had received a highlighted copy of the article in question from the general counsel of Boise Cascade, with a letter saying, "I have been advised to proceed with litigation against Denver University if any of these highlighted areas are republished by Denver University in any form."[17]

But there are occasions when appeals *ad baculum* (literally, "to the stick") are used with more subtlety. The arguer may not threaten directly and yet may convey a veiled threat, or a possible threat in a form calculated to win the assent (or at least the support) of those imperiled. When the attorney general in the Reagan administration was under strong attack in the press for misconduct, the White House chief of staff at the time, Howard Baker, opened one meeting of his staff by saying:

> The President continues to have confidence in the Attorney General and I have confidence in the Attorney General and you ought to have confidence in the Attorney General, because we work for the President and because that's the way things are. And if anyone has a different view of that, or any different motive, ambition, or intention, he can tell me about it because we're going to have to discuss your status.[18]

One may say that nobody is fooled by argument of this sort; the threatened party may *behave* appropriately but need not, in the end, accept the *truth* of the conclusion insisted upon. To this it was answered, by representatives of twentieth-century Italian fascism, that real persuasion can come through many different instruments, of which reason is one and the blackjack is another. But once the opponent is truly persuaded, they held, the instrument of persuasion may be forgotten. That fascist view appears to guide many of the governments of the globe to this day; but the argument *ad baculum*—reliance on the club, or on the threat of force in any form—is by reason unacceptable. The appeal to force is the abandonment of reason.

---

[17] Peter Monaghan, "A Journal Article is Expunged and Its Authors Cry Foul," *The Chronicle of Higher Education,* 8 December 2000.
[18] "White House Orders Silence on Meese," *Washington Post,* 29 April 1988.

R7.   Irrelevant Conclusion: *Ignoratio Elenchi*

The fallacy of *ignoratio elenchi* (literally, mistaken proof) is committed **when an argument purporting to establish a particular conclusion is instead directed to proving a different conclusion.** The premises "miss the point"; the reasoning may seem plausible in itself, and yet the argument misfires as a defense of the conclusion in dispute. Arguments in the sphere of social legislation frequently commit this fallacy; a program of a particular kind, designed to achieve some larger objective that is widely shared, is supported by premises that do provide reasons to share the larger end, but that tell us nothing relevant about the specific program under consideration. Sometimes this approach is deliberate; sometimes it is the result of a passionate concern for the larger objective, which blinds some advocates of the more specific proposal to the irrelevance of their premises.

For example, particular tax reforms sometimes are defended by an emphasis on the need to reduce budget deficits—when the real issue is the fairness or yield of the specific tax measure proposed. Or special programs proposed to support the building industry, or the automobile industry, may be defended with premises that show the need for assistance but do not support the need for the kind or amount of assistance the program at issue would provide. When the issue is the wisdom of developing a new and very expensive weapon system, the premises will miss the point if they simply underscore the need for a strong national defense. Whether the weapon system proposed is the one really needed is likely to be the key question. Objectives that are stated in very general terms—national security, good housing, a balanced budget— are easy to endorse; the hard questions are likely to be: Will this particular measure promote the end sought, and if so, will it do so better—more efficiently or more effectively—than the available alternatives? Bypassing these questions, by obscuring the issue with attractive generalizations about some larger or different end, commits the *ignoratio elenchi*.

How do such arguments ever fool anyone? Often they succeed by distracting attention. By urging with enthusiasm the need for the objective defended by the premises, the advocate may succeed in transferring that enthusiasm, in the minds of the audience, to the specific means fallaciously supported. The *ignoratio elenchi* also may prove effective when it is framed in highly emotional language that conceals the misfire with an *ad populum* appeal. But emotion is not the essence of this fallacy; even if the language used be cool and neutral, it is an *ignoratio elenchi* when its real thrust is a conclusion different from the one it purports to defend.

It may be said that every fallacy of relevance is, in a sense, an *ignoratio elenchi*. But as we use this term, it is the fallacy in which the argument misses the point without necessarily making one of those other mistakes—an *ad hominem* attack, or an *ad populum* appeal—that often characterize fallacies in which the premises are not relevant to the conclusion.

Political campaigns often give rise to the fallacy of irrelevant conclusion. As a candidate for the presidency of the United States in 2000, George W. Bush indicated that he was planning to grant a reprieve (under his authority as governor of Texas) to a man convicted of murder and scheduled for execution. Asked why he was telegraphing his intentions before making a final decision, he replied:

> I believe this is a case where it's important for me to send a signal about what I may do because it's a case where we're dealing with a man's innocence or guilt.[19]

The term *non sequitur* is also often applied to fallacies of relevance. That expression means no more than that the stated conclusion *does not follow from* its premiss or premisses, but it is most commonly applied when the gap between premisses and conclusion is very wide, and the claim that the conclusion does follow is a rather obvious blunder. In a speech in Chicago in 1854, Abraham Lincoln said:

> It was a great trick among some public speakers to hurl a naked absurdity at their audience, with such confidence that they should be puzzled to know if the speaker didn't see some point of great magnitude in it which entirely escaped their observation. A neatly varnished sophism would be readily penetrated, but a great, rough *non sequitur* was sometimes twice as dangerous as a well polished fallacy.[20]

But there are times when the claim that the argument presented is a *non sequitur* may itself be open to dispute. Consider this report of a historic "legal fiasco":

> The prisoner pleaded guilty. He then said he had made a mistake, and the judge allowed him to change his plea to not guilty. The case was tried. The jury acquitted. "Prisoner," said Mr. Justice Hawkins, "a few minutes ago you said you were a thief. Now the jury say you are a liar. Consequently you are discharged."[21]

Exercises

I.   Identify and explain the fallacies of relevance in the following passages.

*1.   A national organization called In Defense of Animals registered protest, in 1996, against alleged cruelty to animals being sold live or slaughtered in Chinese markets in San Francisco. Patricia Briggs, who brought the complaint to the city's Animal Welfare Commission, said: "The time of the crustaceans is coming. You'd think people wouldn't care about lobsters, because they aren't cuddly and fuzzy and they have these vacant looks and they don't vocalize. But you'd be surprised how many people care." To which response was given by Astella Kung, proprietor of Ming Kee Game Birds, where fowl are sold live: "How about the homeless people? Why don't the animal people use their energy to care for those people? They have no homes! They are hungry!"

—"Cuisine Raises Debate on Cruelty and Culture,"
New York Times, 26 August 1996.

---

[19] "Bush Expected to Grant a Stay of an Execution," *New York Times,* 1 June 2000.
[20] *The Collected Works of Abraham Lincoln,* R. R. Basler, ed., vol. 2, p. 283.
[21] Stephen Tumim, *Great Legal Fiascos* (London: Arthur Barker, 1985).

2. Nietzsche was personally more philosophical than his philosophy. His talk about power, harshness, and superb immorality was the hobby of a harmless young scholar and constitutional invalid.

   —George Santayana, *Egotism in German Philosophy*

3. Mr. Farrakhan, the Black Muslim leader, citing the example of Israel, said black Americans should also be able to form a country of their own on the African continent, and said he plans to ask African leaders to "carve out a territory for all people in the diaspora." He said black Americans should also be granted dual citizenship by all African countries. "We want dual citizenship," he said, "and because we don't know where we came from, we want dual citizenship everywhere."

   —Kenneth Noble, "U.S. Blacks and Africans Meet to Forge Stronger Ties," *New York Times*, 27 May 1993

4. However, it matters very little now what the king of England either says or does; he hath wickedly broken through every moral and human obligation, trampled nature and conscience beneath his feet, and by a steady and constitutional spirit of insolence and cruelty procured for himself an universal hatred.

   —Thomas Paine, *Common Sense*

*5. As the war in the Persian Gulf began to appear unavoidable in the late fall of 1990, Michael Moore gave a speech at the Law School of the University of Michigan condemning any American military action against the Iraqi regime of Saddam Hussein. "The day that Bush and so-called U.N. forces invade, this campus has got to be shut down. People have to take a significant stand. It's going to have to be stopped." A student asked him what he thought America should do in the light of the probability that Saddam Hussein had or was acquiring nuclear weapons. Moore replied:

   "What should we do about Israel? They have the bomb. Does Hussein have the bomb? What if he did? It keeps eyes off the depression we're heading toward or we're already in. It keeps the focus off the Palestinian cause. It does a lot of things to prevent the pickle Bush was almost finding himself in."

   —*The Michigan Daily*, 29 November 1990

6. On the Senate floor in 1950, Joe McCarthy announced that he had penetrated "Truman's iron curtain of secrecy." He had 81 case histories of persons whom he considered to be Communists in the State Department. Of Case 40, he said, "I do not have much information on this except the general statement of the agency that there is nothing in the files to disprove his Communist connections."

   —Richard H. Rovere, *Senator Joe McCarthy*

7. In a scientific journal of very high repute appeared, quite recently, the following judgment of an industrial injury:

> Summary: Whereas we cannot unequivocally eliminate other causes for the neuropsychiatric deficits noted in this case, the fact that no air samples were gathered at the worksite and no blood or urine measures were obtained at the time of exposure leads us to conclude that there is compelling evidence that this patient's workplace exposure eventuated in cerebral damage.

> —"Lead Poisoning in an Oil-Pipeline Maintenance Worker,"
> *Archives of Environmental Health,* vol. 50, no. 5, p. 391, 1995.

8. Radosh [Prof. Ronald Radosh] experienced a metaphysical lurch in 1973 during a radical junket to Cuba when his little group of revolutionary tourists were taken to one of Castro's mental hospitals and saw one ward filled with patients who had been recently lobotomized. He was disturbed enough to voice his concerns to the American tour guide who looked at him deeply for a moment and then said, "Ron, we have to understand the difference between capitalist lobotomies and socialist lobotomies."

> —Peter Collier, "The Suppression of Ronald Radosh,"
> *The Weekly Standard,* 10 June 1996

9. To ignore the possibility that America was discovered by Africans because these explorers are "unknown" is irresponsible and arrogant. If we are unaware of an event, does that mean it never happened?

> —Andrew J. Perrin, "To Search for Truth," *New York Times,*
> 16 November 1990

*10. When we had got to this point in the argument, and everyone saw that the definition of justice had been completely upset, Thrasymachus, instead of replying to me, said: "Tell me, Socrates, have you got a nurse?"

"Why do you ask such a question," I said, "when you ought rather to be answering?"

"Because she leaves you to snivel, and never wipes your nose; she has not even taught you to know the shepherd from the sheep."

> —Plato, *The Republic*

11. According to R. Grunberger, author of *A Social History of the Third Reich,* Nazi publishers used to send the following notice to German readers who let their subscriptions lapse: "Our paper certainly deserves the support of every German. We shall continue to forward copies of it to you, and hope that you will not want to expose yourself to unfortunate consequences in the case of cancellation."

12. I also admit that there are people for whom even the reality of the external world [is] a grave problem. My answer is that I do not address *them*, but that I presuppose a minimum of reason in my readers.

> —Paul Feyerabend, "Materialism and the Mind-Body Problem,"
> *The Review of Metaphysics*

13. But can you doubt that air has weight when you have the clear testimony of Aristotle affirming that all the elements have weight including air, and excepting only fire?

> —Galileo Galilei, *Dialogues Concerning Two New Sciences*

14. Like an armed warrior, like a plumed knight, James G. Blaine marched down the halls of the American Congress and threw his shining lances full and fair against the brazen foreheads of every defamer of his country and maligner of its honor.

For the Republican party to desert this gallant man now is worse than if an army should desert their general upon the field of battle.

> —Robert G. Ingersoll, nominating speech at
> the Republican National Convention, 1876

*15. I was seven years old when the first election campaign, which I can remember, took place in my district. At that time we still had no political parties, so the announcement of this campaign was received with very little interest. But popular feeling ran high when it was disclosed that one of the candidates was "the Prince." There was no need to add Christian and surname to realize which Prince was meant. He was the owner of the great estate formed by the arbitrary occupation of the vast tracts of land reclaimed in the previous century from the Lake of Fucino. About eight thousand families (that is, the majority of the local population) are still employed today in cultivating the estate's fourteen thousand hectares. The Prince was deigning to solicit "his" families for their vote so that he could become their deputy in parliament. The agents of the estate, who were working for the Prince, talked in impeccably liberal phrases: "Naturally," said they, "naturally, no one will be forced to vote for the Prince, that's understood; in the same way that no one, naturally, can force the Prince to allow people who don't vote for him to work on his land. This is the period of real liberty for everybody; you're free, and so is the Prince." The announcement of these "liberal" principles produced general and understandable consternation among the peasants. For, as may easily be guessed, the Prince was the most hated person in our part of the country.

> —Ignazio Silone, *The God That Failed*

II.   Each of the following passages may be plausibly criticized by some who conclude that it contains a fallacy, but each will be defended by some who deny
that the argument is fallacious. Discuss the merits of each argument and explain why you conclude that it does or does not contain a fallacy of relevance.

*1.   Chairman of General Electric, Jack Welch, was challenged at a
stockholder's meeting recently by a nun who argued that GE was
responsible for the cleanup of the Hudson River where pollutants
from GE's plants had for many years been allowed to collect.
Welch flatly denied the company's responsibility, saying, "Sister,
you have to stop this conversation. You owe it to God to be on the
side of truth here."

—Elizabeth Kolbert, "The River," *The New Yorker,* 4 December 2000

2.   Gender feminism is notoriously impossible to falsify: it chews up
and digests all counterevidence, transmuting it into confirming
evidence. The fact that most people, including most women, do
not see the pervasive and tenacious system of male power only
shows how thoroughly they have been socialized to perpetuate it.
The more women who reject the gender feminist perspective, the
more this proves them in thrall to the androcentric system.
Nothing and no one can refute the hypothesis of the sex-gender
system for those who . . . see it so clearly "everywhere."

—Christina Sommers, *Proceedings of the
American Philosophical Association,* June 1992

3.   As the American Revolution began to appear likely, some
Americans sought reconciliation with England; Thomas Paine opposed reconciliation bitterly. In *Common Sense* (1776), he wrote:

> . . . all those who espouse the doctrine of reconciliation may be included
> within the following descriptions. Interested men, who are not to be
> trusted, weak men who cannot see, prejudiced men who will not see, and
> a certain set of moderate men who think better of the European world
> than it deserves; and this last class, by an ill-judged deliberation, will be the
> cause of more calamities to this Continent than all the other three.

4.   "But I observe," says Cleanthes, "with regard to you, Philo, and all
speculative sceptics, that your doctrine and practice are as much at
variance in the most abstruse points of theory as in the conduct of
common life."

—David Hume, *Dialogues Concerning Natural Religion*

*5.   A press release from the National Education Association (NEA)
begins with the following statement. "America's teachers see
smaller classes as the most critical element in doing a better job, a
survey by the NEA indicates." . . . But the NEA, of course, is interested in having as many teachers in the schools as possible. For
example, in a 3,000-pupil school system with 30 pupils assigned to
each class, the teaching staff would be approximately 100. But if

class size were changed to 25 the total number of teachers would rise to 120. And in a time of shrinking enrollments, that is a way to keep teachers on the public payroll. . . .

It is unfortunate that an organization with the professional reputation the National Education Association enjoys should be so self-serving.

—Cynthia Parsons, *Christian Science Monitor Service*

6. Consider genetically engineered fish. Scientists hope that fish that contain new growth hormones will grow bigger and faster than normal fish. Other scientists are developing fish that could be introduced into cold, northern waters, where they cannot now survive. The intention is to boost fish production for food. The economic benefits may be obvious, but not the risks. Does this make the risks reasonable?

—Edward Bruggemann, "Genetic Engineering Needs Strict Regulation," *New York Times*, 24 March 1992

7. ANYTUS: "Socrates, I think that you are too ready to speak evil of men: and, if you will take my advice, I would recommend you to be careful. Perhaps there is no city in which it is not easier to do men harm than to do them good, and this is certainly the case at Athens, as I believe that you know."

—Plato, *Meno*

8. The Greek historian Thucydides, in his *History of the Peloponnesian War,* gave the following account of an Athenian's appeal to representatives of the small island of Melos, to join Athens in its war against Sparta:

> You know as well as we do that, in the logic of human nature, right only comes into question where there is a balance of power, while it is might that determines what the strong exhort and the weak concede....Your strongest weapons are hopes yet unrealized, while the weapons in your hands are somewhat inadequate for holding out against the forces already arranged against you....Reflect that you are taking a decision for your country, a country whose fate hangs upon a single decision right or wrong.

9. In that melancholy book *The Future of an Illusion,* Dr. Freud, himself one of the last great theorists of the European capitalist class, has stated with simple clarity the impossibility of religious belief for the educated man of today.

—John Strachey, *The Coming Struggle for Power*

*10. The classic trap for any revolutionary is always "What's your alternative?" But even if you *could* provide the interrogator with a blueprint, this does not mean he would use it; in most cases he is not sincere in wanting to know.

—Shulamith Firestone, *The Dialectic of Sex: The Case for Feminist Revolution*

4.3 FALLACIES OF PRESUMPTION

Some mistakes in everyday reasoning are the consequence of an unjustified assumption, often suggested by the formulation of the argument. The reader, or listener, or even the author of the passage may be caused—through oversight or by deliberate design—to assume the truth of some unproved and unwarranted proposition. When such dubious assumptions buried in the argument are crucial for the support of the conclusion, the argument is bad and can be very misleading. **Unwarranted leaps of this kind are called** *fallacies of presumption.*

In fallacious arguments of this kind the premises are, again, often not relevant to the conclusion. Indeed, in most fallacies there is a gap, an irrelevance between premises and conclusion. But the fallacies of presumption exhibit a special kind of mistake: the tacit supposition of what has not been given support and may even be insupportable. To expose such a fallacy, it is usually sufficient to call attention to that smuggled assumption, and to its doubtfulness or falsity.

P1. Complex Question

One of the most common fallacies of presumption is this: **asking a question in such a way as to presuppose the truth of some conclusion buried in that question.** The question itself is likely to be rhetorical, no answer being genuinely sought. But putting the question seriously, thereby introducing its presupposition surreptitiously, often achieves the questioner's purpose—fallaciously.

Thus an executive of a utility company may ask, "Why is the private development of resources so much more efficient than any government-owned enterprise?"—*assuming* the greater efficiency of the private sector. Or a homeowner may ask, regarding a proposed increase in the property tax, "How can you expect the majority of the voters, who rent but don't own property and don't have to pay the tax, to care if the tax burden of others is made even more unfair?"—assuming both that the burden of the proposed tax is unfair, and that those who rent rather than own their own homes are not affected by tax increases on property. Since assumptions like these are not openly asserted, the questioners evade the need to defend them forthrightly.

The complex question often is a deceitful device. The speaker may pose some question, then answer it or strongly suggest the answer with the truth of the premise that had been buried in the question simply assumed. A letter-writer asks: "If America's booming economy depends on people's using consumer credit beyond their means, thus creating poverty, do we really have a healthy economy?"[22] But the role and the results of consumer credit remain to be addressed.

One critic of research in genetics hides his assumptions in this question: "What are the consequences of reducing the world's gene pool to patented intellectual property, controlled by a handful of life-science corporations?"[23] The "consequences" asked about are never actually discussed; they are only a de-

---

[22] Barbara Commins, "The Slide into Poverty," *New York Times*, 10 September 2000.

[23] Jeremy Rifkin, "Issues in Genetic Research," *The Chronicle of Higher Education*, 3 July 1998.

vice with which the reader may be frightened by the assumptions of the question—that the world's gene pool is soon likely to be reduced to patented intellectual property, and that a handful of corporations will soon control that gene pool. But establishing the plausibility of such threats requires much more than asking questions designed to presuppose them.

The appearance of a question in an editorial or headline often has the purpose of suggesting the truth of the unstated assumptions on which it is built: JUDGE TOOK BRIBE? This technique is a common mark of what is called "yellow journalism." And in debate, whenever a question is accompanied by the aggressive demand that it be answered "yes or no," there is reason to suspect that the question is "loaded," that it is unfairly complex.

The mistake that underlies the fallacy of complex question also underlies a common problem in parliamentary procedure. Deliberative bodies sometimes confront a motion that, although not intended deceptively, is covertly complex. In such circumstances there is a need, before discussion, to simplify the issues confronting the body. This accounts for the privileged position, in parliamentary procedure governed by *Robert's Rules of Order* or like manuals, of the motion to *divide the question*. For example, a motion that the body "postpone for one year" action on some controversial matter may wisely be divided into the decision to postpone action, and *if* that is done, then to determine the length of the postponement. Some members may support the postponement itself, yet find the one-year period intolerably long; if the opportunity to divide the question were not given priority, the body might be maneuvered into taking action on a motion that, because of its complexity, cannot be decided intelligently. A presiding officer, having the duty to promote a fully rational debate, may solicit the motion to divide the question before beginning the substantive discussion.

Egregious examples of the fallacy of the complex question arise in dialogue or cross-examination in which one party poses a question that is complex, a second party answers the question, and the first party then draws a fallacious inference for which that answer was the ground. For example:

LAWYER: The figures seem to indicate that your sales increased as a result of these misleading advertisements. Is that correct?

WITNESS: They did not!

LAWYER: But you do admit, then, that your advertising was misleading. How long have you been engaging in practices like these?

When a question is complex, and all of its presuppositions are to be denied, they must be denied individually. The denial of only one presupposition may lead to the assumption of the truth of the other. In law, this has been called "the negative pregnant." Here is an illustration from a notorious murder trial:

Q: Lizzie, did you not take an axe and whack your mother forty times, and then whack your father forty-one times when faced with the prospect of cold mutton stew?

A: Not true. We were to eat brussel sprouts fondue that day.

P2.   False Cause

It is obvious that any reasoning that relies on treating as the cause of some thing or event what is not really its cause must be seriously mistaken. But often we are tempted to suppose, or led to suppose, that we understand some specific cause-and-effect relation when in fact we do not. The nature of the connection between cause and effect, and how we determine whether such a connection is present or absent, are central problems of inductive logic and scientific method. These problems are discussed in detail in Part Three of this book. Presuming the reality of a causal connection that does not really exist is a common mistake; in Latin the mistake is called the fallacy of *non causa pro causa;* we call it simply the fallacy of false cause.

Whether the causal connection alleged is indeed mistaken may sometimes be a matter in dispute. Some college faculty members, it has been argued, grade leniently because they fear that rigorous grading will cause lowered evaluations of them by their students, and would do damage to their careers. Gradual "grade inflation" is said to be the result of this fear. One college professor wrote this:

> Course evaluation forms [completed by students] are now required in many institutions, and salaries are influenced by the results. When I joined the University of Michigan 30 years ago, my salary was higher than that of any member of the anthropology department who is still active today. My standards for grading have not followed the trend toward inflation. Student complaints about grades have increased, and now my salary is at the bottom of the professorial list.[24]

Do you think the author of this passage commits the fallacy of false cause?

It sometimes happens that we presume that one event is caused by another because it *follows* that other closely in time. We know, of course, that mere temporal succession does not establish a causal connection, but it is easy to be fooled. If an aggressive move in foreign policy is followed by a distantly related international event for which we had been aiming, some may mistakenly conclude that the aggressive policy was the cause of that event. In primitive science such mistakes were common; we now reject as absurd the claim that beating drums is the cause of the sun's reappearance after an eclipse, despite the undeniable evidence that every time drums have been beaten during an eclipse the sun subsequently did reappear.

Mistakes in reasoning of this kind remain widespread: Unusual weather conditions are blamed on some unrelated celestial phenomenon that happened to precede them; an infection really caused by a virus is thought to be caused by a chill wind or wet feet, and so on. This variety of false cause is called the fallacy of *post hoc ergo propter hoc* ("after the thing, therefore because of the thing"); an example of it appeared in a recent letter to the *New York Times,* in which the correspondent wrote:

> The death penalty in the United States has given us the highest crime rate and greatest number of prisoners per 100,000 population in the industrialized world.[25]

---

[24] C. Loring Brace, "Faculty is Powerless," *New York Times,* 24 February 1998.

[25] Harvey I, "Death Penalty Ethics." *New York Times,* 13 February 1996.

Post hoc ergo propter hoc is an easy fallacy to detect when it is blatant, but even the best of scientists and statesmen are on occasion misled.

P3.   Begging the Question: *Petitio Principii*

To beg the question is to assume the truth of what one seeks to prove, in the effort to prove it. That would seem to be a silly mistake, evident to all—but how silly or obvious the mistake is depends largely on the way in which the premises of the argument are formulated. Their wording often obscures the fact that buried within one of the premises assumed lies the conclusion itself. This fallacy is illustrated by the following argument, reported long ago by the logician Richard Whately: "To allow every man unbounded freedom of speech must always be, on the whole, advantageous to the state; for it is highly conducive to the interests of the community that each individual should enjoy a liberty, perfectly unlimited, of expressing his sentiments."

Sometimes we fall into this mistake when, in the effort to establish our conclusion, we cast about in search of premises that will do the trick. Of course the conclusion itself, disguised in other language, certainly will do the trick! Most fallacies, we noted earlier, can be viewed in some light as fallacies of relevance— but the *petitio principii* cannot. The premises of the argument, in this case, are not irrelevant; they certainly do prove the conclusion—but they do so trivially. A *petitio principii* is always technically valid—but always worthless, as well.

This is another of those mistakes that often go unrecognized by those who commit them. The presumption buried in the premises may be obscured by confusing or unrecognized synonyms, or by a chain of intervening argument. Every *petitio* is a *circular argument*, but the circle that has been constructed may—if it is large or fuzzy—go quite undetected.

Powerful minds sometimes are snared by this fallacy, as is illustrated by a highly controversial issue in the history of philosophy. Logicians have long sought to establish the reliability of inductive procedures by establishing the truth of what is called the "principle of induction." This is the principle that the laws of nature will operate tomorrow as they operate today, that in basic ways nature is essentially uniform, and that therefore we may rely on past experience to guide our conduct in the future. "That the future will be essentially like the past" is the claim at issue, but this claim, never doubted in ordinary life, turns out to be very difficult to prove. Some thinkers have claimed that they could prove it by showing that, when we have in the past relied on the inductive principle, we have always found that this method has helped us to achieve our objectives. They ask, "Why conclude that the future will be like the past?" and answer, "Because it always has been like the past."

But as David Hume pointed out, this common argument is a *petitio*—it begs the question. For the point at issue is whether nature *will continue* to behave regularly; that it *has* done so in the past cannot serve as proof that it *will* do so in the future—unless one assumes the very principle that is here in question: that the future will be like the past. And so Hume, granting that in the past the future has been like the past, asked the telling question with which philosophers still tussle: How can we know that future futures will be like past futures? They *may* be so, of course, but we may not *assume* that they will be for the sake of *proving* that they will.[26]

P4. and P5.   Accident and Converse Accident

The fallacies of accident and converse accident arise as a result of the careless, or deliberately deceptive, use of generalizations. In most important affairs, and especially in political or moral argument, we rely on statements of how things generally are, how people generally behave, and the like. But even where general claims are entirely plausible, we must be careful not to apply them to particular cases mechanically or rigidly. Circumstances alter cases; a generalization that is true by and large may not apply in a given case, for good reasons having to do with the special (or "accidental") circumstances of that case. **When we presume the applicability of a generalization to individual cases that it does not properly govern, we commit the fallacy of** *accident.* When we do the reverse, and carelessly or by design **presume that what is true of a particular case is true of the great run of cases, we commit the fallacy of** *converse accident.*

Experience teaches us that generalizations, even those widely applicable and useful, often have exceptions against which we must be on guard. In the law, principles that are sound in general sometimes have very specifically identified exceptions. For example, the rule that hearsay testimony may not be accepted as evidence in court is not applicable when the party whose oral communications are reported is dead, or when the party reporting the hearsay does so in conflict with his own best interest. Almost every good rule has appropriate exceptions; we are likely to argue fallaciously when we reason on the supposition that some rule applies with universal force.

In a dialogue with the young Euthydemus, who planned to become a statesman, Socrates drew from Euthydemus a commitment to many of the conventionally accepted moral truths: that it is wrong to deceive, unjust to steal, and so on. Then Socrates (as recounted by Xenophon in his report of the dialogue) presented a series of hypothetical cases in which Euthydemus reluctantly agreed that it would appear right to deceive (to rescue our compatriots) and just to steal (to save a friend's life), and so on. To all those who may try to decide specific and complicated issues by appealing mechanically to general rules, the fallacy of accident is a genuine and serious threat. The logician H. W. B. Joseph observed that "there is no fallacy more insidious than that of treating a statement which in many connections is not misleading as if it were true always and without qualification."

Accident is the fallacy we commit when we move carelessly or too quickly *from* a generalization; converse accident is the fallacy we commit when we move carelessly or too quickly *to* a generalization. We are all familiar with those who draw conclusions about all persons in a given category because of what may be true about one or a few persons in that category; we know, and

---

[26] See David Hume, "Sceptical Doubts Concerning the Operations of the Understanding," in *An Enquiry Concerning Human Understanding,* sec. 4 (1747).

need to remember, that although a certain drug or food may be harmless in some circumstance, it is not therefore harmless in all circumstances. For example: Eating deep-fried foods has a generally adverse impact on one's cholesterol level, but that bad outcome may not arise in some persons. The owner of a "fish and chips" shop in England recently defended the healthfulness of his deep-fried cookery with this argument:

> Take my son, Martyn. He's been eating fish and chips his whole life, and he just had a cholesterol test, and his level is below the national average. What better proof could there be than a frier's son?[27]

Converse accident is a kind of fallacious reasoning whose error is plain to everyone once that error has been exposed; yet it may serve as a convenient deception, on which many persons are tempted to rely when they argue inattentively or with great passion.

Exercises

Identify and explain any fallacies of presumption found in the following passages.

*1.   My generation was taught about the dangers of social diseases, how they were contracted, and the value of abstinence. Our schools did not teach us about contraception. They did not pass out condoms, as many of today's schools do. And not one of the girls in any of my classes, not even in college, became pregnant out of wedlock. It wasn't until people began teaching the children about contraceptives that our problems with pregnancy began.

—Frank Webster, "No Sex Education, No Sex," *Insight,* 17 November 1997

2.   A national mailing in 1992, soliciting funds by People for the Ethical Treatment of Animals (PETA), contains a survey in which questions are to be answered yes or no. Two of the questions asked are these:

"Do you realize that the vast majority of painful animal experimentation has no relation at all to human survival or the elimination of disease?"

"Are you aware that product testing on animals does *not* keep unsafe products off the market?"

3.   If you want a life full of sexual pleasures, don't graduate from college. A study to be published next month in *American Demographics* magazine shows that people with the most education have the least amount of sex.

—*The Chronicle of Higher Education,* 15 January 1998

---

[27] John Bedder, reported in "Fried and Salty, Yessir, Matey, but Truly English," *New York Times,* 9 March 1993.

4. There is no surprise in discovering that acupuncture can relieve pain and nausea. It will probably also be found to work on anxiety, insomnia, and itching, because these are all conditions in which placebos work. Acupuncture works by suggestion, a mechanism whose effects on humans are well known.

    The danger in using such placebo methods is that they will be applied by people inadequately trained in medicine in cases where essential preliminary work has not been done and where a correct diagnosis has not been established.

    —Fred Levit, M.D., "Acupuncture is Alchemy, Not Medicine,"
    New York Times, 12 November 1997

*5. In a motion picture featuring the famous French comedian Sacha Guitry, some thieves are arguing over division of seven pearls worth a king's ransom. One of them hands two to the man on his right, then two to the man on his left. "I," he says, "will keep three." The man on his right says, "How come you keep three?" "Because I am the leader." "Oh. But how come you are the leader?" "Because I have more pearls."

6. ". . . I've always reckoned that looking at the new moon over your left shoulder is one of the carelessest and foolishest things a body can do. Old Hank Bunker done it once, and bragged about it; and in less than two years he got drunk and fell off of the shot tower, and spread himself out so that he was just a kind of a layer, as you may say; and they slid him edgeways between two barn doors for a coffin, and buried him so, so they say, but I didn't see it. Pap told me. But anyway it all come of looking at the moon that way, like a fool."

    —Mark Twain, *The Adventures of Huckleberry Finn*

7. Former Senator Robert Packwood of Oregon became so angry at the state's leading newspaper, the Portland *Oregonian,* that in response to a request from that paper for a quote he offered this: "Since I quit talking to the *Oregonian,* my business has prospered beyond all measure. I assume that my business has prospered because I don't talk to the Oregonian. Therefore I will continue that policy. Thanks."

    —*New York Times*, 7 February 1999

8. There is no such thing as knowledge which cannot be carried into practice, for such knowledge is really no knowledge at all.

    —Wang Shou-Jen, *Record of Instructions*

9. In 1960 this great country had the finest public schools in the world. After 35 years and spending billions of dollars of Federal money, our public schools rank near the bottom of the industrialized world. What happened? The Federal Government intruded

into public education. We now have the largest number of functional illiterates in the industrialized world.

—Ross Perot, 14 September 1996, in a speech to the Christian Coalition in Washington, DC, during the presidential campaign of 1996

*10. Hiroyuki Suzuki was formerly a member of the Sakaume gumi, an independent crime family in Japan known for its role in gambling. Mr. Suzuki's wife Mariko broke her kneecap, and when Mariko went to church the next Sunday, the minister put his hands on her broken knee and pronounced it healed. She walked away from church that day. Mr. Suzuki regarded her religion as a silly waste of time—but he was fascinated by the recovery of her knee. "In gambling," he said, "you use dice. Dice are made from bone. If God could heal her bone, I figured he could probably assist my dice and make me the best dice thrower in all of Japan." Mr. Suzuki's gambling skills did improve, enabling him to pay off his debts. He now says his allegiance is to Jesus.

—Stephanie Strom, "He Watched Over His Rackets," *New York Times*, 22 June 1999.

4.4 FALLACIES OF AMBIGUITY

The meaning of words or phrases may shift as a result of inattention, or may be deliberately manipulated within the course of an argument. A term may have one sense in a premiss, but quite a different sense in the conclusion. When the inference drawn depends upon such changes it is, of course, fallacious. Mistakes of this kind are called "fallacies of ambiguity" or sometimes "sophisms." The deliberate use of such devices is usually crude and readily detected—but at times the ambiguity may be obscure, the error accidental, the fallacy subtle. Five varieties are distinguished in the following.

A1. Equivocation

Most words have more than one literal meaning, and most of the time we have no difficulty in keeping those meanings apart by noting the context and using our good sense when reading and listening. **Yet when we confuse the several meanings of a word or phrase—accidentally or deliberately—we are using the word equivocally. If we do that in the context of an argument, we commit the fallacy of** *equivocation.*

Sometimes the equivocation is obvious and absurd and is used in a joking line or passage. Lewis Carroll's account of the adventures of Alice in *Through the Looking Glass* is replete with clever and amusing equivocations. One of them goes like this:

"Who did you pass on the road?" the King went on, holding his hand out to the messenger for some hay.

"Nobody," said the messenger.

"Quite right," said the King; "this young lady saw him too. So of course Nobody walks slower than you."

The equivocation in this passage is in fact rather subtle. As it is first used here, the word "nobody" simply means "no person." But reference is then made using a pronoun ("him"), as though that word ("nobody") had *named* a person. And when subsequently the same word is capitalized and plainly used as a name ("Nobody"), it putatively names a person having a characteristic (not being passed on the road) derived from the first use of the word. Equivocation is sometimes the tool of wit—and Lewis Carroll was a very witty logician.[28]

Equivocal arguments are always fallacious, but they are not always silly or comic, as will be seen in the example discussed in the following excerpt:

> There is an ambiguity in the phrase "have faith in" that helps to make faith respectable. When a man says that he has faith in the president he is assuming that it is obvious and known to everybody that there is a president, that the president exists, and he is asserting his confidence that the president will do good work on the whole. But, if a man says he has faith in telepathy, he does not mean that he is confident that telepathy will do good work on the whole, but that he believes that telepathy really occurs sometimes, that telepathy exists. Thus the phrase "to have faith in *x*" sometimes means to be confident that good work will be done by *x*, who is assumed or known to exist, but at other times means to believe that *x* exists. Which does it mean in the phrase "have faith in God"? It means ambiguously both; and the self-evidence of what it means in the one sense recommends what it means in the other sense. If there is a perfectly powerful and good god it is self-evidently reasonable to believe that he will do good. In this sense "have faith in God" is a reasonable exhortation. But it insinuates the other sense, namely "believe that there is a perfectly powerful and good god, no matter what the evidence." Thus the reasonableness of trusting God if he exists is used to make it seem also reasonable to believe that he exists.[29]

One kind of equivocation deserves special mention. This is the mistake that arises from the misuse of "relative" terms, which have different meaning in different contexts. For example, the word "tall" is a relative word; a tall man and a tall building are in quite different categories. A tall man is one who is taller than most men, a tall building is one that is taller than most buildings. Certain forms of argument that are valid for nonrelative terms break down when relative terms are substituted for them. The argument "an elephant is an animal; therefore a gray elephant is a gray animal" is perfectly valid. The word "gray" is a nonrelative term. But the argument "an elephant is an animal; therefore a small elephant is a small animal" is ridiculous. The point here is that "small" is a relative term: a small elephant is a very large animal. The fallacy is one of equivocation with regard to the relative term "small." Not all equivocation on relative terms is so obvious, however. The word "good" is a relative term and

---

[28] This passage from *Alice in Wonderland* very probably inspired David Powers, who formally changed his name to Absolutely Nobody, and ran as an independent candidate for lieutenant governor of the State of Oregon. His campaign slogan was: "Hi, I'm Absolutely Nobody. Vote for me." In the general election of 1992, he drew 7 percent of the vote.

[29] Richard Robinson, *An Atheist's Values* (Oxford University Press, Oxford, 1964), p. 121.

is frequently equivocated on when it is argued, for example, that so-and-so is a good general and would therefore be a good president, or is a good scholar and must therefore be a good teacher.

A2. Amphiboly

The fallacy of amphiboly occurs when one is arguing from premises whose formulations are ambiguous because of their grammatical construction. The word "amphiboly" is derived from the Greek, its meaning in essence being "two in a lump," or the "doubleness" of a lump. **A statement is amphibolous when its meaning is indeterminate because of the loose or awkward way in which its words are combined.** An amphibolous statement may be true in one interpretation and false in another. **When it is stated as premiss with the interpretation that makes it true, and a conclusion is drawn from it on the interpretation that makes it false, then the fallacy of amphiboly has been committed.**

In guiding electoral politics, amphiboly can mislead as well as confuse. During the 1990s, while he sat in the U.S. House of Representatives as a Democrat from California, Congressman Tony Coelho is reported to have said: "Women prefer Democrats to men." Amphibolous statements make dangerous premisses—but they are seldom encountered in serious discourse.

What grammarians call "dangling" participles and phrases often present amphiboly of an entertaining sort, as in "The farmer blew out his brains after taking affectionate farewell of his family with a shotgun." And tidbits in *The New Yorker* make acid fun of writers and editors who overlook careless amphiboly:

> "Leaking badly, manned by a skeleton crew, one infirmity after another overtakes the little ship." (The *Herald Tribune*, book section)
> Those game little infirmities![30]

A3. Accent

An argument may prove deceptive, and invalid, when the shift of meaning within it arises from changes in the emphasis given to its words or parts. **When a premiss relies for its apparent meaning on one possible emphasis, but a conclusion is drawn from it that relies on the meaning of the same words accented differently, the fallacy of *accent* is committed.**

Consider, as illustration, the different meanings that can be given to the statement

> *We should* not *speak* ill of *our friends.*

At least five distinct meanings—or more?—can be given to those eight words, depending on which one of them is emphasized. When read without any undue stresses the injunction is perfectly sound. If the conclusion is drawn from it, however, that we should feel free to speak ill of someone who is *not* our friend, this conclusion follows only if the premiss has the meaning it acquires

---

[30] *The New Yorker,* 8 November, 1958.

when its last word is accented. But when the last word of the sentence is accented, it is no longer acceptable as a moral rule; it then has a different meaning, and it is, in fact, a different premiss. The argument is a case of the fallacy of accent. So, too, would be the argument that drew from the same premiss the conclusion that we are free to *work* ill on our friends if only we do not speak it—and similarly with the other fallacious inferences that suggest themselves.

A phrase or passage can often be understood correctly only in its context, which makes clear the *sense* in which it is intended. The fallacy of accent may be construed broadly to include the distortion produced by pulling a quoted passage out of its context, putting it in another context, and there drawing a conclusion that could never have been drawn in the original context. This business of quoting out of context is sometimes done with deliberate craftiness. In the presidential election campaign of 1996 the Democratic vice-presidential candidate, Al Gore, was quoted by a Republican press aide as having said that "there is no proven link between smoking and lung cancer." Those were indeed Mr. Gore's exact words, uttered during a television interview in 1992. But they were only part of a sentence. In that interview, Mr. Gore's full statement was that some tobacco company scientists *"will claim with a straight face that* there is no proven link between smoking and lung cancer. . . . But the weight of the evidence accepted by the overwhelming preponderance of scientists is, yes, smoking does cause lung cancer."[31]

The omission of the words "will claim with a straight face" and of Gore's express conviction that cancer is caused by smoking, unfairly reversed the sense of the passage from which the quotation was pulled. The argument suggested by the abbreviated quotation, having the apparent conclusion that Mr. Gore seriously doubts the causal link between smoking and cancer, is an egregious example of the fallacy of accent.

Similarly, the deliberate omission of some qualification made by an author that plays a key role in giving the meaning intended for some written passage may be a damaging use of accent. In a critical essay about conservative thinkers, Sidney Blumenthal (1985) wrote about one such thinker, Gregory A. Fossedal, that "On the right, Fossedal is widely regarded as his generation's most promising journalist." A 1989 advertisement for a later book by Mr. Fossedal contained several "blurbs," including this one attributed to Mr. Blumenthal: "Many consider Fossedal the most promising journalist of his generation." The omission of the critic's phrase "on the right" very greatly distorts the sense of the original passage, leading the reader to draw a mistaken conclusion about the critic's judgment of the author. Mr. Blumenthal was understandably infuriated.[32]

Similarly, a theater critic who says of a new play that it is far from the funniest appearing on Broadway this year may be quoted in an ad for the play: "Funniest appearing on Broadway this year!" To avoid such distortions, and the fallacies of accent that may be built upon them, the responsible writer must be

---

[31] *New York Times,* 18 June 1996.

[32] "You Write the Facts, I'll Write the Blurbs," *New York Times,* 18 April 1989. The original passage appeared in the *Washington Post,* 22 November, 1985; the offending advertisement appeared in *The New Republic* in March 1989. Mr. Fossedal subsequently apologized to Mr. Blumenthal.

scrupulously accurate in quotation, always indicating whether italics were in the original, indicating (with dots) whether passages have been omitted, and so on.

Physical manipulation of print or pictures is commonly used to mislead deliberately through accent. Sensational words in large letters appear in the headlines of newspaper reports, deliberately suggesting mistaken conclusions to those who glance hastily at the account. Later in the report the headline is likely to be qualified by other words in much smaller letters. To avoid being tricked, by news reports or in contracts, one is well advised to give careful attention to "the small print." In political propaganda the misleading choice of a sensational heading or the use of a clipped photograph, in what purports to be a factual report, will use accent shrewdly so as to encourage the drawing of conclusions known by the propagandist to be false. An account that may not be an outright lie may yet distort by accent in ways that are deliberately manipulative or dishonest.

In advertising, such practices are hardly rare. A remarkably low price often appears in very large letters, followed by "and up" in tiny print. Wonderful bargains in airplane fares are followed by an asterisk, with a distant footnote explaining that the price is available only three months in advance for flights on Thursdays following a full moon, or that there may be other "applicable restrictions." Costly items with well-known brand names are advertised at very low prices, with a small note elsewhere in the ad that "prices listed are for limited quantities in stock." Readers are drawn into the store but are likely to be unable to make the purchase at the advertised price. Accented passages, by themselves, are not strictly fallacies; they become embedded in fallacies when one interpretation of a phrase, flowing from its accent, is relied upon to suggest a conclusion (*e.g.,* that the plane ticket or brand item can be advantageously purchased at the listed price) that is very doubtful when account is taken of the misleading accent.

Even the literal truth can be made use of, through manipulation of its placement, to deceive with accent. Disgusted with his first mate who was repeatedly inebriated on duty, the captain of a ship noted in the ship's logbook, almost every day, "The mate was drunk today." The angry mate took his revenge. Keeping the log himself on a day when the captain was ill, the mate recorded, "The captain was sober today."

A4.   Composition

The term "fallacy of composition" is applied to both of two closely related types of invalid argument. The first may be described as **reasoning fallaciously from the attributes of the parts of a whole to the attributes of the whole itself.** A particularly flagrant example would be to argue that, since every part of a certain machine is light in weight, the machine "as a whole" is light in weight. The error here is manifest when we recognize that a very heavy machine may consist of a very large number of lightweight parts. Not all examples of this kind of fallacious composition are so obvious, however. Some are misleading. One may hear it seriously argued that, since each scene of a certain play is a model of artistic perfection, the play as a whole is artistically perfect. But this is as much a fallacy of composition as it would be to argue that, since every ship is ready for battle, the whole fleet must be ready for battle.

The other type of composition fallacy is strictly parallel to that just described. **Here, the fallacious reasoning is from attributes of the individual elements or members of a collection to attributes of the collection or totality of those elements.** For example, it would be fallacious to argue that because a bus uses more gasoline than an automobile, therefore all buses use more gasoline than all automobiles. This version of the fallacy of composition turns on a confusion between the "distributive" and the "collective" use of general terms. Thus, although college students may enroll in no more than six different classes each semester, it is also true that college students enroll in hundreds of different classes each semester. This verbal conflict is easily resolved. It may be true of college students, distributively, that each of them may enroll in no more than six classes each semester. This is a distributive use of the term "college students," in that we are speaking of college students taken *singly.* But it is true of college students, taken collectively, that they enroll in hundreds of different classes each semester. This is a collective use of the term "college students" in that we are speaking of college students all together, as a totality. Thus, buses use more gasoline than automobiles, distributively, but collectively automobiles use more gasoline than buses, because there are so many more of them.

This second kind of composition fallacy may be defined as "the invalid inference that what may truly be predicated of a term distributively may also be truly predicated of the term collectively." Thus, the atomic bombs dropped during World War II did more damage than did the ordinary bombs dropped—but only distributively. The matter is exactly reversed when the two kinds of bombs are considered collectively, because there were so many more conventional bombs dropped than atomic ones. Ignoring this distinction in an argument would permit the fallacy of composition.

These two varieties of composition, although parallel, are really distinct because of the difference between a mere collection of elements and a whole constructed out of those elements. Thus, a mere collection of parts is no machine; a mere collection of bricks is neither a house nor a wall. A whole, such as a machine, a house, or a wall, has its parts organized or arranged in certain definite ways. And since organized wholes and mere collections are distinct, so are the two versions of the composition fallacy, one proceeding invalidly to wholes from their parts, the other proceeding invalidly to collections from their members or elements.

A5.   Division

The fallacy of division is simply the reverse of the fallacy of composition. In it the same confusion is present, but the inference proceeds in the opposite direction. As in the case of composition, two varieties of the fallacy of division may be distinguished. **The first kind of division consists in arguing fallaciously that what is true of a whole must also be true of its parts.** To argue that, since a certain corporation is very important and Mr. Doe is an official of that corporation, therefore Mr. Doe is very important, is to commit the fallacy of division. This first variety of the division fallacy would be committed in any such argument, as in moving from the premise that a certain machine is heavy, or complicated, or valuable, to the conclusion that this or any other part of the machine must be heavy, or complicated, or valuable. To argue that a student must have a large room because it is located in a large dormitory would be still another instance of the first kind of fallacy of division.

The second type of division fallacy is committed when one argues from the attributes of a collection of elements to the attributes of the elements themselves. To argue that, since university students study medicine, law, engineering, dentistry, and architecture, therefore each, or even any, university student studies medicine, law, engineering, dentistry, and architecture would be to commit the second kind of division fallacy. It is true that university students, collectively, study all these various subjects, but it is false that university students, distributively, do so. Instances of this fallacy of division often look like valid arguments, for what is true of a class distributively is certainly true of each and every member. Thus the argument

> Dogs are carnivorous.
> Afghan hounds are dogs.
> Therefore Afghan hounds are carnivorous.

is perfectly valid. Closely resembling this argument is another,

> Dogs are frequently encountered in the streets.
> Afghan hounds are dogs.
> Therefore Afghan hounds are frequently encountered in the streets.

which is invalid, committing the fallacy of division. Some instances of division are obviously jokes, as when the classical example of valid argumentation

> Humans are mortal.
> Socrates is a human.
> Therefore Socrates is mortal.

is parodied by the fallacious

> American Indians are disappearing.
> That man is an American Indian.
> Therefore that man is disappearing.

The old riddle "Why do white sheep eat more than black ones?" turns on the confusion involved in the fallacy of division, for the answer, "Because there are more of them," treats collectively what seemed to be referred to distributively in the question.

The fallacy of division, which springs from a kind of ambiguity, resembles the fallacy of accident (discussed previously in section 4.3), which springs from unwarranted presumption. Likewise, the fallacy of composition, also flowing from ambiguity, resembles the hasty generalization we call "converse accident." But these likenesses are superficial. An explanation of the differences between the two pairs of fallacies will be helpful in grasping the errors committed in all four.

If we were to infer, from looking at one or two parts of a large machine, that because they happen to be well designed, every one of its many parts is well designed, we would commit the fallacy of converse accident, for what is true about one or two surely may not be true of all. If we were to examine every single part and find each carefully made, and from that finding infer that the entire machine is carefully made, we would also reason fallaciously, because however carefully the parts were produced, they may have been *assembled* awkwardly or carelessly. But here the fallacy is one of composition. In converse accident, one argues that some atypical members of a class have a specified attribute, and therefore that all members of the class, distributively, have that attribute; in composition, one argues that, since each and every member of the class has that attribute, the class *itself* (collectively) has that attribute. The difference is great. In converse accident, all predications are distributive, whereas in the composition fallacy, the mistaken inference is from distributive to collective predication.

Similarly, division and accident are two distinct fallacies; their superficial resemblance hides the same kind of underlying difference. In division, we argue (mistakenly) that, since the class itself has a given attribute, each of its members also has it. Thus, it is the fallacy of division to conclude that, because an army as a whole is nearly invincible, each of its units is nearly invincible. But in accident, we argue (also mistakenly) that, because some rule applies in general, there are no special circumstances in which it might not apply. Thus, we commit the fallacy of accident when we insist that a person should be fined for ignoring a "No Swimming" sign when jumping into the water to rescue someone from drowning.

Accident and converse accident are fallacies of presumption in which we assume what we have no warrant for. Composition and division are fallacies of *ambiguity*, resulting from the multiple meanings of terms. Wherever the words or phrases used may mean one thing in one part of the argument and another thing in another part, and those different meanings are deliberately or accidentally confounded, we may expect the argument to be fallacious.

THE MAJOR INFORMAL FALLACIES

Fallacies of Relevance
    R1   Argument from Ignorance
    R2   Appeal to Inappropriate Authority
    R3   Argument *Ad Hominem:* (a) abusive and (b) circumstantial
    R4   Appeal to Emotion
    R5   Appeal to Pity
    R6   Appeal to Force
    R7   Irrelevant Conclusion
Fallacies of Presumption
    P1   Complex Question
    P2   False Cause
    P3   Begging the Question
    P4   Accident
    P5   Converse Accident

Fallacies of Ambiguity
- A1   Equivocation
- A2   Amphiboly
- A3   Accent
- A4   Composition
- A5   Division

Exercises

I.   Identify and explain the fallacies of ambiguity that appear in the following passages.

*1.   . . . the universe is spherical in form . . . because all the constituent parts of the universe, that is the sun, moon, and the planets, appear in this form.

> —Nicolaus Copernicus, "The New Idea of the Universe"

2.   Robert Toombs is reputed to have said, just before the Civil War, "We could lick those Yankees with cornstalks." When he was asked after the war what had gone wrong, he is reputed to have said, "It's very simple. Those damnyankees refused to fight with cornstalks."

> —E. J. Kahn, Jr., "Profiles (Georgia)," *The New Yorker,*
> 13 February 1978

3.   To press forward with a properly ordered wage structure in each industry is the first condition for curbing competitive bargaining; but there is no reason why the process should stop there. What is good for each industry can hardly be bad for the economy as a whole.

> —Edmond Kelly, *Twentieth Century Socialism*

4.   No man will take counsel, but every man will take money: therefore money is better than counsel.

> —Jonathan Swift

*5.   I've looked everywhere in this area for an instruction book on how to play the concertina without success. (Mrs. F. M., Myrtle Beach, S.C., Charlotte Observer)
You need no instructions. Just plunge ahead boldly.

> —*The New Yorker,* 21 February 1977

6.   . . . each person's happiness is a good to that person, and the general happiness, therefore, a good to the aggregate of all persons.

> —John Stuart Mill, *Utilitarianism*

7.   If the man who "turnips!" cries
Cry not when his father dies,
'Tis a proof that he had rather
Have a turnip than his father.

> —Mrs. Piozzi, *Anecdotes of Samuel Johnson*

8. Fallaci wrote her: "You are a bad journalist because you are a bad woman."

> —Elizabeth Peer, "The Fallaci Papers," *Newsweek*, 1 December 1980

9. A Worm-eating Warbler was discovered by Hazel Miller in Concord, while walking along the branch of a tree, singing, and in good view. *(New Hampshire Audubon Quarterly)*

    That's our Hazel—surefooted, happy, and with just a touch of the exhibitionist.

> —*The New Yorker*, 2 July 1979

*10. The basis of logic is the syllogism, consisting of a major and a minor premiss and a conclusion—thus:

> *Major Premiss:* Sixty men can do a piece of work sixty times as quickly as one man;
> *Minor Premiss:* One man can dig a post-hole in sixty seconds; therefore—
> *Conclusion:* Sixty men can dig a post-hole in one second.

This may be called the syllogism arithmetical, in which, by combining logic and mathematics, we obtain a double certainty and are twice blessed.

> —Ambrose Bierce, *The Devil's Dictionary*

II. Each of the following passages may be plausibly criticized by some who conclude that it contains a fallacy, but each will be defended by some who deny that the argument is fallacious. Discuss the merits of the argument in each passage, and explain why you conclude that it does (or does not) contain a fallacy of ambiguity.

*1. Seeing that eye and hand and foot and every one of our members has some obvious function, must we not believe that in like manner a human being has a function over and above these particular functions?

> —Aristotle, *Nicomachean Ethics*

2. Mr. Stace says that my writings are "extremely obscure," and this is a matter as to which the author is the worst of all possible judges. I must therefore accept his opinion. As I have a very intense desire to make my meaning plain, I regret this.

> —Bertrand Russell, "Reply to Criticisms," in P. A. Schilpp, ed.,
> *The Philosophy of Bertrand Russell* (Evanston, IL:
> The Library of Living Philosophers), p. 707

3. The only proof capable of being given that an object is visible, is that people actually see it. The only proof that a sound is audible, is that people hear it: and so of the other sources of our experience. In like manner, I apprehend, the sole evidence it is possible to produce that anything is desirable, is that people actually desire it.

> —John Stuart Mill, *Utilitarianism*, ch. 4

4. Thomas Carlyle said of Walt Whitman that he thinks he is a big poet because he comes from a big country.

> —Alfred Kazin, "The Haunted Chamber," *The New Republic,*
> 23 June 1986, p. 39

*5. Mr. Levy boasts many excellent *bona fides* for the job [of Chancellor of the New York City Public Schools]. But there is one bothersome fact: His two children attend an elite private school on Manhattan's Upper East Side. Mr. Levy . . . should put his daughter and son in the public schools. I do not begrudge any parent the right to enroll a child in a private school. My wife and I considered several private schools before sending our children to a public school in Manhattan. Mr. Levy is essentially declaring the public schools unfit for his own children.

> —Samuel G. Freedman, "Public Leaders, Private Schools,"
> *New York Times,* 15 April 2000.

6. All phenomena in the universe are saturated with moral values. And, therefore, we can come to assert that the universe for the Chinese is a moral universe.

> —T. H. Fang, *The Chinese View of Life*

III. Identify and explain the fallacies of relevance, or presumption, or ambiguity as they occur in the following passages. Explain why, in the case of some, it may be plausibly argued that what appears at first to be a fallacy is not when the argument is correctly interpreted.

*1. John Angus Smith, approaching an undercover agent, offered to trade his firearm, an automatic, for two ounces of cocaine that he planned to sell at a profit. Upon being apprehended, Smith was charged with "using" a firearm "during and in relation to . . . a drug trafficking crime." Ordinarily conviction under this statute would result in a prison sentence of five years; however, if the firearm, as in this case, is "a machine gun or other automatic weapon" the mandatory sentence is 30 years. Smith was convicted and sentenced to 30 years in prison. The case was appealed to the U.S. Supreme Court.

  Justice Scalia argued that, although Smith certainly did intend to trade his gun for drugs, that was not the sense of "using" intended by the statute. "In the search for statutory meaning we give nontechnical terms their ordinary meanings . . . to speak of 'using a firearm' is to speak of using it for its distinctive purpose, as a weapon." If asked whether you use a cane, he pointed out, the question asks whether you walk with a cane, not whether you display "your grandfather's silver-handled walking stick in the hall."

  Justice O'Connor retorted that we may do more than walk with a cane. "The most infamous use of a cane in American history had nothing to do with walking at all—the caning (in 1856) of Senator Charles Sumner in the United States Senate."

Justice Scalia rejoined that the majority of the Court "does not appear to grasp the distinction between how a word can be used and how it is ordinarily used. . . . I think it perfectly obvious, for example, that the falsity requirement for a perjury conviction would not be satisfied if a witness answered 'No' to a prosecutor's enquiry whether he had ever 'used a firearm' even though he had once sold his grandfather's Enfield rifle to a collector."

Justice O'Connor prevailed; Smith's conviction was affirmed.

—*John Angus Smith v. United States,* 508 U.S. 223, 1 June 1993

2. After deciding to sell his home in Upland, California, novelist Whitney Stine pounded a "For Sale" sign into his front yard. But he deliberately waited to do so until 2:22 p.m. one Thursday. The house sold three days later for his asking price—$238,000. And Mr. Stine credits the quick sale to the advice of his astrologer, John Bradford, whom he has consulted for 12 years in the sale of five houses.

"He always tells me the exact time to put out the sign according to the phases of the moon, and the houses have always sold within a few months." Mr. Stine says.

—"Thinking of Buying or Selling a House? Ask Your Astrologer," *Wall Street Journal,* 12 October 1986

3. In the Miss Universe Contest of 1994 Miss Alabama was asked: If you could live forever, would you? And why? She answered:

> I would not live forever, because we should not live forever, because if we were supposed to live forever, then we would live forever, but we cannot live forever, which is why I would not live forever.

4. Order is indispensable to justice because justice can be achieved only by means of a social and legal order.

—Ernest Van Den Haag, *Punishing Criminals*

*5. The Inquisition must have been justified and beneficial, if whole peoples invoked and defended it, if men of the loftiest souls founded and created it severally and impartially, and its very adversaries applied it on their own account, pyre answering to pyre.

—Benedetto Croce, *Philosophy of the Practical*

6. The following advertisement for a great metropolitan newspaper appears very widely in the State of Pennsylvania:

> In Philadelphia nearly everybody reads the *Bulletin.*

7. . . . since it is impossible for an animal or plant to be indefinitely big or small, neither can its parts be such, or the whole will be the same.

—Aristotle, *Physics*

8. For the benefit of those representatives who have not been here before this year, it may be useful to explain that the item before the General Assembly is that hardy perennial called the "Soviet item." It

is purely a propaganda proposition, not introduced with a serious purpose of serious action, but solely as a peg on which to hang a number of speeches with a view to getting them into the press of the world. This is considered by some to be very clever politics. Others, among whom the present speaker wishes to be included, consider it an inadequate response to the challenge of the hour.

> —Henry Cabot Lodge, speech to the United Nations General Assembly, 30 November 1953

9. The war-mongering character of all this flood of propaganda in the United States is admitted even by the American press. Such provocative and slanderous aims clearly inspired today's speech by the United States Representative, consisting only of impudent slander against the Soviet Union, to answer which would be beneath our dignity. The heroic epic of Stalingrad is impervious to libel. The Soviet people in the battles at Stalingrad saved the world from the fascist plague and that great victory which decided the fate of the world is remembered with recognition and gratitude by all humanity. Only men dead to all shame could try to cast aspersions on the shining memory of the heroes of that battle.

> —Anatole M. Baranovsky, speech to the United Nations General Assembly, 30 November 1953

*10. Prof. Leon Kass reports a notable response to an assignment he had given students at the University of Chicago. Compose an essay, he asked, about a memorable meal you have eaten. One student wrote as follows:

> I had once eaten lunch with my uncle and my uncle's friend. His friend had once eaten lunch with Albert Einstein. Albert Einstein was once a man of great spirituality. Therefore, by the law of the syllogism, I had once eaten lunch with God.

> —Leon Kass, *The Hungry Soul: Eating and the Perfecting of Our Nature*, 1995

11. Clarence Darrow, renowned criminal trial lawyer, began one shrewd plea to a jury thus:

> You folks think we city people are all crooked, but we city people think you farmers are all crooked. There isn't one of you I'd trust in a horse trade, because you'd be sure to skin me. But when it comes to having sympathy with a person in trouble, I'd sooner trust you folks than city folks, because you come to know people better and get to be closer friends.

> —Irving Stone, *Clarence Darrow for the Defense*

12. The most blatant occurrence of recent years is all these knuckleheads running around protesting nuclear power—all these stupid people who do no research at all and who go out and march, pretending they care about the human race, and then go off in their automobiles and kill one another.

> —Ray Bradbury, in *Omni*, October 1979

13. When Copernicus argued that the Ptolemaic astronomy (holding that the celestial bodies all revolved around the earth) should be replaced by a theory holding that the earth (along with all the other planets) revolved around the sun, he was ridiculed by many of the scientists of his day, including one of the greatest astronomers of that time, Clavius, who wrote in 1581:

> Both [Copernicus and Ptolemy] are in agreement with the observed phenomena. But Copernicus's arguments contain a great many principles that are absurd. He assumed, for instance, that the earth is moving with a triple motion … [but] according to the philosophers a simple body like the earth can have only a simple motion. … Therefore it seems to me that Ptolemy's geocentric doctrine must be preferred to Copernicus's doctrine.

14. All of us cannot be famous, because all of us cannot be well known.

—Jesse Jackson, quoted in *The New Yorker*, 12 March 1984

*15. The God that holds you over the pit of hell, much as one holds a spider or some loathsome insect over the fire, abhors you, and is dreadfully provoked; his wrath towards you burns like fire; he looks upon you as worthy of nothing else but to be cast into the fire; you are ten thousand times so abominable in his eyes as the most hateful and venomous serpent is in ours. You have offended him infinitely more than a stubborn rebel did his prince; and yet it is nothing but his hand that holds you from falling into the fire every moment.

—Jonathan Edwards, "The Pit of Hell" (1741)

16. Mysticism is one of the great forces of the world's history. For religion is nearly the most important thing in the world, and religion never remains for long altogether untouched by mysticism.

—John Mctaggart Ellis Mctaggart, "Mysticism," *Philosophical Studies*

17. If science wishes to argue that we cannot know what was going on in [the gorilla] Binti's head when she acted as she did, science must also acknowledge that it cannot prove that nothing was going on. It is because of our irresolvable ignorance, as much as fellow-feeling, that we should give animals the benefit of doubt and treat them with the respect we accord ourselves.

—Martin Rowe and Mia Macdonald, "Let's Give Animals Respect They Deserve," *New York Times*, 26 August 1996.

18. If we want to know whether a state is brave we must look to its army, not because the soldiers are the only brave people in the community, but because it is only through their conduct that the courage or cowardice of the community can be manifested.

—R. L. Nettleship, *Lectures on the Republic of Plato*

19. Whether we are to live in a future state, as it is the most important question which can possibly be asked, so it is the most intelligible one which can be expressed in language.

> —Joseph Butler, "Of Personal Identity"

*20. Which is more useful, the Sun or the Moon? The Moon is more useful since it gives us light during the night, when it is dark, whereas the Sun shines only in the daytime, when it is light anyway.

> —George Gamow (inscribed in the entry hall of the Hayden Planetarium, New York City)

Summary of Chapter 4

In this chapter, we have seen that **a fallacy is a type of argument that may seem to be correct, but that proves on examination not to be so.** Types of reasoning mistakes that commonly deceive have been given traditional names; three large groups of informal fallacies have been distinguished: the **fallacies of relevance,** the **fallacies of presumption,** and the **fallacies of ambiguity.**

Fallacies of Relevance

In these, the mistaken arguments rely on premisses that may seem to be relevant to the conclusion but in fact are not. We have explained the types of reasoning mistakes in seven fallacies of relevance:

R1. Argument from ignorance *(ad ignorantiam):* When it is argued that a proposition is true on the ground that it has not been proved false, or when it is argued that a proposition is false because it has not been proved true.

R2. Appeal to inappropriate authority *(ad verecundiam):* When the premisses of an argument appeal to the judgment of some party or parties having no legitimate claim to authority in the matter at hand.

R3. Argument against the person *(ad hominem):* When an attack is leveled not at the claims being made or the merits of the argument, but at the person of the opponent.

Arguments *ad hominem* take two forms. When the attack is directly against persons, seeking to defame or discredit them, it is called an "**abusive** *ad hominem.*" When the attack is indirectly against persons, suggesting that they hold their views chiefly because of their special circumstances or interests, it is called a "**circumstantial** *ad hominem.*"

R4. Appeal to emotion *(ad populum):* When careful reasoning is replaced with devices calculated to elicit enthusiasm and emotional support for the conclusion advanced.

R5. Appeal to pity *(ad misericordiam):* When careful reasoning is replaced by devices calculated to elicit sympathy on the part of the hearer for the objects of the speaker's concern.

R6. Appeal to force *(ad baculum):* When careful reasoning is replaced with direct or insinuated threats in order to bring about the acceptance of some conclusion.

R7. **Irrelevant conclusion** *(ignoratio elenchi):* When the premises miss the point, purporting to support one conclusion while in fact supporting or establishing another.

Fallacies of Presumption

In these the mistaken arguments arise from reliance upon some proposition that is assumed to be true, but is in fact false, or dubious, or without warrant. We have explained the types of reasoning mistakes in five fallacies of presumption:

P1. **Complex question:** When a question is asked in such a way as to pre-suppose the truth of some assumption buried in that question.

P2. **False cause:** When one treats as the cause of a thing what is not really the cause of that thing, or more generally, when one blunders in reasoning that is based upon causal relations.

P3. **Begging the question** *(petitio principii):* When one assumes in the pre-misses of an argument the truth of what one seeks to establish in the con-clusion of that argument.

P4. **Accident:** When one applies a generalization to an individual case that it does not properly govern.

P5. **Converse Accident:** When one moves carelessly or too quickly from a sin-gle case to an indefensibly broad generalization.

Fallacies of Ambiguity

In these, the mistaken arguments are formulated in such a way as to rely on shifts in the meaning of words or phrases, from their use in the premises to their use in the conclusion. We have explained the types of reasoning mistakes in five fallacies of ambiguity:

A1. **Equivocation:** When the same word or phrase is used with two or more meanings, deliberately or accidentally, in the formulation of an argument.

A2. **Amphiboly:** When one of the statements in an argument has more than one plausible meaning, because of the loose or awkward way in which the words in that statement have been combined.

A3. **Accent:** When a shift of meaning arises within an argument as a conse-quence of changes in the emphasis given to its words or parts.

A4. **Composition:** This fallacy is committed (a) when one reasons mistakenly from the attributes of a part to the attributes of the whole, or (b) when one reasons mistakenly from the attributes of an individual member of some collection to the attributes of the totality of that collection.

A5. **Division:** This fallacy is committed (a) when one reasons mistakenly from the attributes of a whole to the attributes of one of its parts, or (b) when one reasons mistakenly from the attributes of a totality of some collection of en-tities to the attributes of the individual entities within that collection.

PART TWO

DEDUCTION

For as one may feel sure that a chain will hold when he is assured that each separate link is of good material and that it clasps the two neighboring links, viz., the one preceding and the one following it, so we may be sure of the accuracy of the reasoning when the matter is good, that is to say, when nothing doubtful enters into it, and when the form consists in a perpetual concatenation of truths which allows of no gap.

—Gottfried Leibniz

Like Molière's M. Jourdain who found that he had long been speaking prose, I found that I had long been forming propositions. I said to myself, "Yes, I form propositions when my tongue does more than wag. I form them out of terms. I say something about something. Therefore I ought to be able, in serious talk, to pinpoint those two parts of my proposition. I ought to know exactly what I am talking about, and exactly what I am saying about it."
—A. A. Luce

CATEGORICAL PROPOSITIONS

5.1 THE THEORY OF DEDUCTION

Preceding chapters have dealt chiefly with language and its influence on argumentation. We turn now to argument itself, and first to the analysis of that special kind of argument called "deduction." **A deductive argument is one whose premisses are claimed to provide conclusive grounds for the truth of its conclusion.** If it does provide such conclusive grounds, the deductive argument is valid. Every deductive argument is either valid or invalid: valid if it is impossible for its premisses to be true without its conclusion being true also, and invalid otherwise.

The theory of deduction is intended to explain the relationship between premisses and conclusion of a valid argument, and to provide techniques for the appraisal of deductive arguments, that is, for discriminating between valid and invalid deductions. To accomplish this, two great bodies of theory have been developed. The first of these is called "classical" or "Aristotelian" logic, after the great Greek philosopher who initiated this study. The second is called "modern" or "modern symbolic" logic. Classical logic will be the topic of this and the following two chapters (chapters 5, 6, and 7); modern logic will be the topic of chapters 8, 9, and 10.

Aristotle was one of the towering intellects of the ancient world. After studying for 20 years in Plato's Academy, he became tutor to Alexander the Great; later he founded his own school, the Lyceum, where he contributed substantially to nearly every field of human knowledge. After Aristotle's death, his treatises on reasoning were gathered together and came to be called the *Organon*. The word "logic" did not acquire its modern meaning until the second century A.D., but the subject matter of logic was long determined by the content of the *Organon*.

5.2 CATEGORICAL PROPOSITIONS AND CLASSES

The Aristotelian study of deduction focused on arguments containing propositions of a special kind, called "categorical propositions" because they are about categories or classes. To understand the classical theory of deduction, we must begin with a very careful analysis of these propositions, which are the building blocks of that theory. Consider the argument:

> No athletes are vegetarians.
> All football players are athletes.
> Therefore no football players are vegetarians.

All three of the propositions in this argument, both premises and the conclusion, are *categorical* propositions. **Such propositions affirm, or deny, that some class S is included in some other class P, in whole or in part.** In the example above, the three categorical propositions are about the class of all athletes, the class of all vegetarians, and the class of all football players.

Classes were mentioned briefly in our discussion of definition in Chapter 3, where a class was explained to be the collection of all objects that have some specified characteristic in common. There are various ways in which two classes may be related to each other.

1. If every member of one class is also a member of a second class, like the class of dogs and the class of mammals, then the first class is said to be included or contained in the second.

2. If some but perhaps not all members of one class are also members of another, like the class of females and the class of athletes, then the first class may be said to be partially contained in the second class.

3. If the two classes have no members in common, like the class of all triangles and the class of all circles, the two classes may be said to exclude one another.

These various relationships between classes are affirmed or denied by categorical propositions. The result is that there can be just four different *standard forms* of categorical propositions. They are illustrated by the four following propositions:

1. All politicians are liars.
2. No politicians are liars.
3. Some politicians are liars.
4. Some politicians are not liars.

Let us examine these four standard-form categorical propositions in greater detail.

The first example—All politicians are liars—is a *universal affirmative* proposition. It is about two classes, the class of all politicians and the class of all liars, saying that the first class is included or contained in the second. *A universal affirmative proposition says that every member of the first class is also a member of the second class.* In the present example, the subject term "politicians" designates the class of all politicians, and the predicate term "liars" designates the class of all liars. Any universal affirmative proposition may be written schematically as

All *S* is *P.*

where the letters *S* and *P* represent the subject and predicate terms, respectively. The name "universal affirmative" is appropriate, because the proposition *affirms* that the relationship of class inclusion holds between the two classes and says that the inclusion is *complete* or universal: All members of *S* are said to be members of *P* also.

The second example—No politicians are liars—is a *universal negative* proposition. It denies of politicians universally that they are liars. Concerned with two classes, *a universal negative proposition says that the first class is wholly excluded from the second,* which is to say that there is no member of the first class that is also a member of the second. Any universal negative proposition may be written schematically as

No *S* is *P.*

where, again, the letters *S* and *P* represent the subject and predicate terms. The name "universal negative" is appropriate because the proposition *denies* that the relation of class inclusion holds between the two classes—and denies it *universally:* No members at all of *S* are members of *P.*

The third example—Some politicians are liars—is a *particular affirmative* proposition. Clearly, what the present example affirms is that some members of the class of all politicians are (also) members of the class of all liars. But it does not affirm this of politicians universally: Not all politicians universally, but, rather, some particular politician or politicians, are said to be liars. This proposition neither affirms nor denies that *all* politicians are liars; it makes no pronouncement on the matter. It does not literally say that some politicians are *not* liars, although in some contexts it might be taken to suggest it. The literal, minimal interpretation of the present proposition is that the class of politicians and the class of liars have some member or members in common. For definiteness, we adopt that minimal interpretation here.

The word "some" is indefinite. Does it mean "at least one" or "at least two" or "at least a hundred"? Or how many? For the sake of definiteness, although this position may depart from ordinary usage in some cases, it is customary to regard the word "some" as meaning "at least one." Thus a particular affirmative proposition, written schematically as

Some *S* is *P.*

says that at least one member of the class designated by the subject term S *is also a member of the class designated by the predicate term* P. The name "particular affirmative" is appropriate because the proposition *affirms* that the relationship of class inclusion holds, but does not affirm it of the first class universally but only *partially, i.e.,* of some particular member or members of the first class.

The fourth example—Some politicians are not liars—is a *particular negative* proposition. This example, like the one preceding it, does not refer to politicians universally but only to some member or members of that class; it is particular. But unlike the third example it does not affirm that the particular members of the first class referred to are included in the second class; this is precisely what is denied. A particular negative proposition, schematically written as

Some S is not P.

says that at least one member of the class designated by the subject term S *is excluded from the whole of the class designated by the predicate term* P.

Not all standard-form categorical propositions are as simple and straightforward as the four examples just considered. The subject and predicate terms of a standard-form categorical proposition always designate classes, but those terms may be complicated expressions rather than single words. For example, the proposition "All candidates for the position are persons of honor and integrity" has the phrase "candidates for the position" as its subject term and the phrase "persons of honor and integrity" as its predicate term.

It was traditionally held that all deductive arguments were analyzable in terms of classes, categories, and their relations. Thus the four standard-form categorical propositions just explained:

universal affirmative propositions	(called **A** propositions)
universal negative propositions	(called **E** propositions)
particular affirmative propositions	(called **I** propositions)
particular negative propositions	(called **O** propositions)

were thought to be the building blocks of all deductive arguments. A great deal of logical theory—as we shall see—has been built up concerning these four kinds of propositions.

Exercises

Identify the subject and predicate terms in, and name the form of, each of the following propositions.

*1. Some historians are extremely gifted writers whose works read like first-rate novels.

2. No athletes who have ever accepted pay for participating in sports are amateurs.

3. No dogs that are without pedigrees are candidates for blue ribbons in official dog shows sponsored by the American Kennel Club.

4. All satellites that are currently in orbits less than ten thousand miles high are very delicate devices that cost many thousands of dollars to manufacture.

*5. Some members of families that are rich and famous are not persons of either wealth or distinction.

6. Some paintings produced by artists who are universally recognized as masters are not works of genuine merit that either are or deserve to be preserved in museums and made available to the public.

7. All drivers of automobiles that are not safe are desperadoes who threaten the lives of their fellows.

8. Some politicians who could not be elected to the most minor positions are appointed officials in our government today.

9. Some drugs that are very effective when properly administered are not safe remedies that all medicine cabinets should contain.

*10. No people who have not themselves done creative work in the arts are responsible critics on whose judgment we can rely.

5.3 QUALITY, QUANTITY, AND DISTRIBUTION

A. Quality

Every standard-form categorical proposition is said to have a **quality,** either affirmative or negative. **If the proposition** *affirms* **some class inclusion, whether complete or partial, its quality is affirmative.** Thus both universal affirmative propositions and particular affirmative propositions are affirmative in quality, and their letter names, **A** and **I** respectively, are thought to come from the Latin word, "**Aff**I**rmo,**" meaning "I affirm." **If the proposition** *denies* **class inclusion, whether complete or partial, its quality is negative.** Thus both universal negative propositions and particular negative propositions are negative in quality, and their letter names, **E** and **O,** respectively, are thought to come from the Latin word "n**E**g**O,**" meaning "I deny."

B. Quantity

Every standard-form categorical proposition is said to have a **quantity** also, universal or particular. **If the proposition refers to** *all* **members of the class designated by its subject term, its quantity is universal.** Thus the **A** and **E** propositions are universal in quantity. **If the proposition refers only to** *some* **members of the class designated by its subject term, its quantity is particular.** Thus the **I** and **O** propositions are particular in quantity.

Every standard-form categorical proposition begins with one of the words "all," "no," or "some." These words show the quantity of the proposition. "All" and "no" indicate that the proposition is universal; "some" indicates that the quantity is particular. The quantifier "no" serves additionally to indicate the negative quality of the **E** proposition.

We observe that the names "universal affirmative," "universal negative," "particular affirmative," and "particular negative" uniquely describe each of the four standard forms by mentioning first its quantity and then its quality.

C. General Schema of Standard-Form Categorical Propositions

Between the subject and predicate terms of every standard-form categorical proposition occurs some form of the verb "to be" (accompanied by the word "not" in the case of the **O** proposition). This verb serves to connect the subject and predicate terms and is called the "copula." In the schematic formulations given in the preceding section, only "is" and "is not" appear, but depending on how the proposition is worded otherwise, some other form of the verb "to be" may be more appropriate. For example, in the following three propositions,

> Some Roman emperors were monsters.
> All squares are rectangles.
> Some soldiers will not be heroes.

"were," "are," and "will not be" serve as copulas. The general skeleton or schema of a standard-form categorical proposition consists of four parts: first the quantifier, then the subject term, next the copula, and finally the predicate term. This schema may be written as

> Quantifier (subject term) copula (predicate term).

D. Distribution

On the class interpretation, the subject and predicate terms of a standard-form categorical proposition designate classes of objects, and the proposition is regarded as being about these classes. Propositions may refer to classes in different ways, of course. A proposition may refer to *all* members of a class, or it may refer to only *some* members of that class. Thus the proposition

> All senators are citizens.

refers to or is about *all* senators but does not refer to all citizens. It asserts that each and every member of the class of senators is a citizen, but it makes no assertion about all citizens. It does not affirm that each and every citizen is a senator, but it does not deny it either. Any **A** proposition, of this form,

All S is P.

is thus seen to refer to *all* members of the class designated by its subject term, *S*, but does not refer to all members of the class designated by its predicate term, *P*.

The technical term "distribution" is introduced to characterize the ways in which terms can occur in categorical propositions. **A proposition *distributes* a term if it refers to all members of the class designated by the term.** Let us examine each of the standard-form categorical propositions, to see which terms are distributed or undistributed in them.

First, consider the **A** Proposition. As we noted above, using the example "All senators are citizens," the *subject* term of an **A** proposition *is distributed* in (or by) that proposition. But the *predicate* term of an **A** proposition is **undistributed** in (or by) it.

Next consider the **E** proposition. An **E** proposition such as

No athletes are vegetarians.

asserts of each and every athlete that he or she is not a vegetarian. The whole of the class of athletes is said to be excluded from the class of vegetarians. All members of the class designated by its subject term are referred to by an **E** proposition, which is therefore said to distribute its subject term. At the same time, in asserting that the whole class of athletes is excluded from the class of vegetarians, it is also asserted that the whole class of vegetarians is excluded from the class of athletes. The given proposition clearly asserts of each and every vegetarian that he or she is not an athlete. An **E** proposition, therefore, refers to all members of the class designated by its predicate term and is said to distribute its predicate term also. **E** *propositions distribute both their subject and their predicate terms.*

The situation is different with respect to **I** propositions. Thus,

Some soldiers are cowards.

makes no assertion about all soldiers and makes no assertion about all cowards either. It says nothing about each and every soldier, nor about each and every coward. Neither class is said to be either wholly included or wholly excluded from the other. *Both subject and predicate terms are undistributed in any particular affirmative proposition.*

The particular negative or **O** proposition is similar in that it, too, does not distribute its subject term. Thus the proposition

Some horses are not thoroughbreds.

says nothing about *all* horses but refers to *some* members of the class designated by the subject term. It says of this part of the class of all horses that it is excluded from the class of all thoroughbreds, that is, from the *whole* of the latter class. Given the particular horses referred to, it says that each and every member of the class of thoroughbreds is *not* one of those particular horses. When something is said to be excluded from a class, the whole of the class is referred to, just as, when a person is excluded from a country, all parts of that country are forbidden to that person. *The particular negative proposition does distribute its predicate term, but not its subject term.*

We may summarize these remarks on distribution as follows: Universal propositions, both affirmative and negative, distribute their subject terms, whereas particular propositions, whether affirmative or negative, do not distribute their subject terms. Thus the *quantity* of any standard-form categorical proposition determines whether its *subject* term is distributed or undistributed. Affirmative propositions, whether universal or particular, do not distribute their predicate terms, whereas negative propositions, both universal and particular, do distribute their predicate terms. Thus the *quality* of any standard-form categorical proposition determines whether its predicate term is distributed or undistributed.

The following diagram summarizes this information and may be useful in helping one to remember which propositions distribute which of their terms.

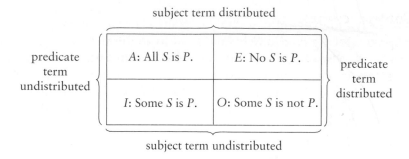

subject term distributed

predicate term undistributed · predicate term distributed

| A: All S is P. | E: No S is P. |
| I: Some S is P. | O: Some S is not P. |

subject term undistributed

Exercises

Name the quality and quantity of each of the following propositions, and state whether their subject and predicate terms are distributed or undistributed.

*1. Some presidential candidates will be sadly disappointed people.

2. All those who died in Nazi concentration camps were victims of a cruel and irrational tyranny.

3. Some recently identified unstable elements were not entirely accidental discoveries.

4. Some members of the military-industrial complex are mild-mannered people to whom violence is abhorrent.

*5. No leader of the feminist movement is a major business executive.

6. All hard-line advocates of law and order at any cost are people who will be remembered, if at all, only for having failed to understand the major social pressures of the late twentieth century.

7. Some recent rulings of the Supreme Court were politically motivated decisions that flouted the entire history of American legal practice.

8. No harmful pesticides or chemical defoliants were genuine contributions to the long-range agricultural goals of the nation.

9. Some advocates of major political, social, and economic reforms are not responsible people who have a stake in maintaining the status quo.

*10. All new labor-saving devices are major threats to the trade union movement.

5.4 THE TRADITIONAL SQUARE OF OPPOSITION

Standard-form categorical propositions having the same subject and predicate terms may differ from each other in quality or in quantity or in both. This kind of differing was given the technical name **opposition** by older logicians, and certain important truth relations were correlated with the various kinds of opposition.

A. Contradictories

Two propositions are *contradictories* **if one is the denial or negation of the other; that is, if they cannot both be true and cannot both be false.** It is clear that two standard-form categorical propositions having the same subject and predicate terms but differing from each other in *both* quantity and quality are contradictories. Thus the **A** and **O** propositions

> All judges are lawyers.

and

> Some judges are not lawyers.

which are opposed both in quantity and in quality, are clear contradictories. Exactly one of the pair is true, and exactly one is false. Similarly, the **E** and **I** propositions

> No politicians are idealists.

and

> Some politicians are idealists.

are opposed in both quantity and quality and are contradictories. Schematically, we may say that the contradictory of "All *S* is *P*" is "Some *S* is not *P*," and the contradictory of "No *S* is *P*" is "Some *S* is *P*"; **A** and **O** are contradictories, as are **E** and **I**.

B. Contraries

Two propositions are said to be *contraries* **if they cannot both be true; that is, if the truth of one entails the falsity of the other.** Thus, "Texas will win the coming game with Oklahoma" and "Oklahoma will win the coming game with Texas" are contraries; if either of these propositions (referring to the same game, of course) is true, then the other must be false. But the two propositions are not contradictories; both would be false if the game is a draw. Contraries, although they cannot both be true, may both be false. The traditional or Aristotelian account of categorical propositions held that universal propositions having the same subject and predicate terms, but differing in quality, were contraries.[1] Thus it was said that an **A** proposition and its corresponding **E** proposition, such as "All poets are idlers" and "No poets are idlers," cannot both be true but can both be false, and are therefore to be regarded as contraries.

---

[1] This traditional view will be examined critically in section 5.6.

This claim that **A** and **E** propositions are contraries is *not* correct if either the **A** or the **E** proposition is a necessary—that is, a logical or mathematical—truth, such as "All squares are rectangles" or "No squares are circles." For if a proposition is necessarily true—that is, cannot possibly be false—it cannot have a contrary, because propositions that are contraries *can* both be false. A proposition that is neither necessarily true nor necessarily false is said to be *contingent*. The claim that **A** and **E** propositions having the same subject and predicate terms are contraries may be correct if both are contingent propositions, and we shall assume that they are throughout the remainder of this chapter.

C. Subcontraries

Two propositions are said to be *subcontraries* if they cannot both be false, although they both may be true. The traditional account held that particular propositions having the same subject and predicate terms but differing in quality were subcontraries. It was affirmed that **I** and **O** propositions such as

Some diamonds are precious stones.

and

Some diamonds are not precious stones.

could both be true but could not both be false, and must therefore be regarded as subcontraries.

This claim that **I** and **O** propositions are subcontraries is *not* correct if either the **I** or the **O** proposition is necessarily false; for example, "Some squares are circles" or "Some squares are not rectangles." For if a proposition is necessarily false—that is, cannot possibly be true—it cannot have a subcontrary, because propositions that are subcontraries *can* both be true. However, if both the **I** and **O** are contingent propositions, then they can both be true, and, as noted in the preceding discussion of contraries, we shall assume that they are contingent throughout the remainder of this chapter.

D. Subalternation

Whenever two propositions have the same subject and the same predicate terms and agree in quality (*i.e.,* both are affirmative or both are negative) **but differ only in quantity** (*i.e.,* one is universal while the other is particular), **they are called *corresponding propositions*.** Thus the **A** proposition

All spiders are eight-legged animals.

has a corresponding **I** proposition

Some spiders are eight-legged.

And the **E** proposition

> No whales are fishes.

has a corresponding **O** proposition

> Some whales are not fishes.

Thus far, the examples provided of opposition between propositions have suggested disagreement. But "opposition" in the present context is a technical term, and applies even where disagreement in the ordinary sense is not present. In the case of corresponding propositions, where no disagreement between the **A** and the **I**, or between the **E** and the **O** propositions was implied, there is *opposition* nevertheless, but of a special kind. **The opposition between a universal proposition and its corresponding particular is known as** *subalternation.* In any pair of corresponding propositions, like the two pairs just given, the universal proposition is called the "superaltern," and the particular is called the "subaltern."

In subalternation, it was traditionally held, the superaltern implies the truth of the subaltern. Thus, for example, from the universal affirmative, "All birds have feathers," the corresponding particular affirmative, "Some birds have feathers," was held to follow; and from the universal negative, "No whales are fishes," the corresponding particular negative, "Some whales are not fishes," was held to follow. But the implication does *not* hold from subaltern to superaltern. From the particular affirmative proposition "Some animals are cats," we certainly may not infer that "All animals are cats." And likewise, from the particular negative proposition "Some animals are not cats," we certainly may not infer that no animals are cats.

E. The Square of Opposition

These four ways in which propositions may be "opposed"—as *contradictories,* as *contraries,* as *subcontraries,* and as *sub-* and *superalterns*—are represented by an important and widely used diagram, called the "Square of Opposition," which is reproduced as Figure 5-1.

The relationships diagrammed by this Square of Opposition were believed to provide a logical basis for the validating of certain elementary forms of argument. This may be more readily understood if we make the customary distinction between *immediate* inferences and *mediate* inferences.

Any inference is the drawing of a conclusion from one or more premises. **The inference is said to be mediate where more than one premiss is involved,** as in a syllogism, because the conclusion is supposed to be drawn from the first premiss through the mediation of the second. But **where a conclusion is drawn from only one premiss there is no such mediation, and the inference is said to be** *immediate.* A number of very useful immediate inferences may be readily drawn from the information embodied in the traditional Square of Opposition.

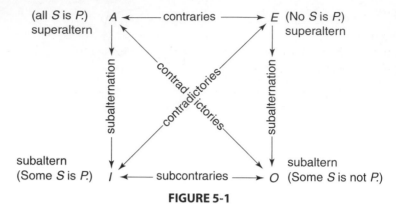

FIGURE 5-1

Here are some examples. If an **A** proposition is taken as premiss, then according to the Square of Opposition, one can validly infer that the corresponding **O** proposition (*i.e.*, the **O** proposition having the same subject and predicate terms as that **A**) is false. And from the same premiss one can immediately infer that the corresponding **I** proposition is true. Of course, from the truth of an **I** proposition, the truth of its corresponding **A** proposition does not follow, but the falsehood of its contradictory **E** proposition does. The traditional Square of Opposition provides the basis for a considerable number of such immediate inferences. Given the truth or falsehood of any one of the four standard-form categorical propositions, the truth or falsehood of some or all of the others can be inferred immediately. The immediate inferences based on the traditional Square of Opposition may be listed as follows:

A being given as true: **E** is false, **I** is true, **O** is false.
E being given as true: **A** is false, **I** is false, **O** is true.
I being given as true: **E** is false, while **A** and **O** are undetermined.
O being given as true: **A** is false, while **E** and **I** are undetermined.
A being given as false: **O** is true, while **E** and **I** are undetermined.
E being given as false: **I** is true, while **A** and **O** are undetermined.
I being given as false: **A** is false, **E** is true, **O** is true.
O being given as false: **A** is true, **E** is false, **I** is true.[2]

---

[2]If it be given that a proposition is undetermined, additional inferences may be drawn, as Prof. Joseph Gilbert, of the State University of New York at Brockport, in private correspondence, has shown. If it be given that an **A** proposition is undetermined, we may infer that its contradictory **O** proposition must be undetermined also, for if the **O** were known true, or known false, the **A** proposition could not be undetermined. The same is true of an **E** and its contradictory; so generally, if a proposition is undetermined, its contradictory must be undetermined. And if an **A** proposition is undetermined, its contrary **E** proposition must be false, for if the **E** were true, the **A** proposition could not be undetermined. And thus if the **A** proposition be given as undetermined, its corresponding **I** proposition must be true.

When it is the **E,** or the **I,** or the **O** proposition that is given as undetermined, an analysis of this same type will apply. The resultant set of inferences may be listed thus:

A being given as undetermined: **O** is undetermined, **E** is false, **I** is true.
E being given as undetermined: **I** is undetermined, **A** is false, **O** is true.
I being given as undetermined: **E** is undetermined, **A** is false, **O** is true.
O being given as undetermined: **A** is undetermined, **E** is false, **I** is true.

Exercises

What can be inferred about the truth or falsehood of the remaining propositions in each of the following sets (1) if we assume the first to be true, and
(2) if we assume the first to be false?

*1.   a.   All successful executives are intelligent people.
    b.   No successful executives are intelligent people.
    c.   Some successful executives are intelligent people.
    d.   Some successful executives are not intelligent people.

2.   a.   No animals with horns are carnivores.
    b.   Some animals with horns are carnivores.
    c.   Some animals with horns are not carnivores.
    d.   All animals with horns are carnivores.

3.   a.   Some uranium isotopes are highly unstable substances.
    b.   Some uranium isotopes are not highly unstable substances.
    c.   All uranium isotopes are highly unstable substances.
    d.   No uranium isotopes are highly unstable substances.

4.   a.   Some college professors are not entertaining lecturers.
    b.   All college professors are entertaining lecturers.
    c.   No college professors are entertaining lecturers.
    d.   Some college professors are entertaining lecturers.

5.5 FURTHER IMMEDIATE INFERENCES

There are other kinds of immediate inference, in addition to those associated
with the traditional Square of Opposition. In this section we shall present three
of these other types.

A.   Conversion

The first kind of immediate inference, called **conversion,** proceeds by simply
interchanging the subject and predicate terms of the proposition. Conversion is
perfectly valid in the case of **E** and **I** propositions. Clearly, "No men are angels"
can be uttered to make the same assertion as "No angels are men," and either
can be validly inferred from the other by the immediate inference called conversion. Just as clearly, "Some writers are women" and "Some women are writers" are logically equivalent, so by conversion either can be validly inferred
from the other. **One standard-form categorical proposition is said to be the**
converse **of another when it is formed by simply interchanging the subject**
and predicate terms of that other proposition. Thus "No idealists are politicians" is the converse of "No politicians are idealists," and each can validly be
inferred from the other by conversion. The term **convertend** is used to refer to
the premiss of an immediate inference by conversion, and the conclusion of
that inference is called the **converse.**

Note that the converse of an **A** proposition does not in general follow
validly from that **A** proposition. Thus, if our original proposition is "All dogs

are animals," its converse, "All animals are dogs," does not follow from the original proposition at all, the convertend being true while its converse is false. Traditional logic recognized this fact, of course, but asserted that something *like* conversion was valid for **A** propositions. From an **A** proposition *(All S is P)*, its subaltern **I** proposition *(Some S is P)* can be validly inferred on the traditional Square of Opposition, as explained in Section 5.3. The **A** proposition says something about *all* members of *S,* but the **I** proposition makes a more limited claim, about only *some* members of **S.** We have just seen that conversion of an **I** proposition is perfectly valid.

So, given the **A** proposition *(All S is P)*, its subaltern *(Some S is P)* can validly be inferred by subalternation, and from that subaltern the proposition *(Some P is S)* can validly be inferred by conversion. Hence by a combination of subalternation and conversion, *Some P is S* can validly be inferred from *All S is P*. This pattern of inference, called **conversion by limitation (or "conversion *per accidens"), proceeds by interchanging subject and predicate terms *and* changing the quantity of the proposition from universal to particular.** Thus it was traditionally claimed that from the premiss "All dogs are animals" the conclusion "Some animals are dogs" could validly be inferred, the inference being called "conversion by limitation." This type of conversion will be considered further in the next section.

Observe that the converse obtained as the outcome of conversion by limitation is *not equivalent* to the **A** proposition from which it is derived. The reason is that conversion by limitation requires a change in quantity, from universal to particular. The proposition that results from this conversion by limitation is therefore not an **A** but an **I** proposition; it cannot have the same meaning as its convertend, and hence cannot be logically equivalent to it. But the converse of an **E** proposition is an **E** proposition, and the converse of an **I** proposition is an **I** proposition; in these cases, the convertend and the converse do have the same quantity and are logically equivalent.

Finally, note that the conversion of an **O** proposition is not, in general, valid. The **O** proposition "Some animals are not dogs" is plainly true; its converse is the proposition "Some dogs are not animals," which is plainly false. An **O** proposition and its converse are not, in general, equivalent.

The converse of a given proposition always contains exactly the same terms as the given proposition (their order being reversed) and always has the same quality. The following table was traditionally held to give a complete picture of this immediate inference:

TABLE OF VALID CONVERSIONS	
CONVERTEND	CONVERSE
A: All *S* is *P.*	**I:** Some *P* is *S* (by limitation)
E: No *S* is *P.*	**E:** No *P* is *S.*
I: Some *S* is *P.*	**I:** Some *P* is *S.*
O: Some *S* is not *P.*	(conversion not valid)

B.   Obversion

The next type of immediate inference to be discussed is called **obversion.** Before explaining it, we shall return briefly to the notion of a "class" and introduce some new ideas that will enable us to discuss obversion more easily. **A *class* is the collection of all objects having a certain common attribute that we refer to as the "class-defining characteristic."** Thus the class of all humans is the collection of all things that have the characteristic of being human, and its class-defining characteristic is the attribute of being human. The class-defining characteristic need not be a "simple" attribute in any sense, for *any* attribute determines a class. Thus the complex attribute of being left-handed and red-headed and a student determines a class—the class of all left-handed, red-headed students.

Every class has associated with it a complementary class, or *complement*, which is the collection of all things that do not belong to the original class. Thus the complement of the class of all people is the class of all things that are *not* people. The class-defining characteristic of the complementary class is the (negative) attribute of *not being a person*. The complement of the class of all people contains no people but contains everything else: shoes and ships and sealing wax, and cabbages—but no kings, since kings are people. It is sometimes convenient to speak of the complement of the class of all persons as "the class of all nonpersons." The complement of the class designated by the term S is then designated by the term *non-S*, and we may speak of the term *non-S* as being the complement of the term S.[3]

We are using the word "complement" in two senses: one being the sense of class complement, the other the sense of the complement of a term. The two senses, although different, are very closely connected. One term is the (term) complement of another just in case the first term designates the (class) complement of the class designated by the second term. It should be noted that just as a class is the (class) complement of its own complement, a term is the (term) complement of its own complement. A sort of "double negative" rule is involved here, so that we need not have strings of "non's" prefixed to a term. Thus we should write the complement of the term "voter" as "nonvoter," but we should write the complement of "nonvoter" simply as "voter" rather than "nonnonvoter." One must be careful not to mistake contrary terms for complementary terms, as in identifying "cowards" and "nonheroes." The terms "coward" and "hero" are contraries, in that no person can be both a coward and a hero, but not everyone—and certainly not everything—need be either one or the other. Thus the complement of the term "winner" is not "loser" but "nonwinner," for although not everything—or even everyone—is either a winner or a loser, absolutely everything is either a winner or a nonwinner.

---

[3] Sometimes we reason using what is called the *relative complement* of a class, its complement within some other class. For example: within the class of "children of mine" there is a subclass, "daughters of mine," whose relative complement is another subclass, "children of mine who are not daughters" or "sons of mine." But obversion and other immediate inferences normally rely upon the absolute complement of classes, as defined above.

Now that we understand what is meant by the complement of a term, the process of obversion is easy to describe. In **obversion,** the subject term remains unchanged, and so does the quantity of the proposition being obverted. **To obvert a proposition, we change its quality and replace the predicate term by its complement.** Thus the **A** proposition

All residents are voters.

has as its obverse the **E** proposition

No residents are nonvoters.

These two propositions, it is clear, are logically equivalent, and therefore either one can validly be inferred from the other. Obversion is a valid immediate inference when applied to *any* standard-form categorical proposition. Thus the **E** proposition

No umpires are partisans.

has as its obverse the logically equivalent **A** proposition

All umpires are nonpartisans.

Similarly, the obverse of the **I** proposition

Some metals are conductors.

is the **O** proposition

Some metals are not nonconductors.

And finally the **O** proposition

Some nations were not belligerents.

has as its obverse the **I** proposition

Some nations were nonbelligerents.

The term **obvertend** is used to refer to the premiss of an immediate inference by obversion, and the conclusion is called the **obverse.** Every standard-form categorical proposition is logically equivalent to its obverse, so obversion is a valid form of immediate inference for any standard-form categorical proposition. To obtain the obverse of a proposition, we leave the quantity and the subject term unchanged, change the quality of the proposition, and replace the predicate term by its complement. The following table gives a complete picture of all valid obversions:

TABLE OF OBVERSIONS	
OBVERTEND	**OBVERSE**
A: All *S* is *P*.	**E:** No *S* is non-*P*.
E: No *S* is *P*.	**A:** All *S* is non-*P*.
I: Some *S* is *P*.	**O:** Some *S* is not non-*P*.
O: Some *S* is not *P*.	**I:** Some *S* is non-*P*.

C.   Contraposition

The third variety of immediate inference to be discussed introduces no new principles, for it can be reduced, in a sense, to the first two. **To form the *contrapositive* of a given proposition, we replace its subject term by the complement of its predicate term and replace its predicate term by the complement of its subject term.** Thus the contrapositive of the **A** proposition

> All members are voters.

is the **A** proposition

> All nonvoters are nonmembers.

That these two are logically equivalent will be evident upon a moment's reflection, and from this it is clear that contraposition is a valid form of immediate inference when applied to **A** propositions. Contraposition introduces nothing new, for we can get from any **A** proposition to its contrapositive by first obverting it, next applying conversion, and then applying obversion again. Thus, beginning with "All *S* is *P*," we obvert it to obtain "No *S* is non-*P*," which converts validly to "No non-*P* is *S*," whose obverse is "All non-*P* is non-*S*." Thus the contrapositive of any **A** proposition is the obverse of the converse of the obverse of that proposition.

Contraposition is most useful in working with **A** propositions, but it is a valid form of immediate inference when applied to **O** propositions also. Thus the contrapositive of the **O** proposition

> Some students are not idealists.

is the somewhat cumbersome **O** proposition

> Some nonidealists are not nonstudents.

which is logically equivalent to the first. Their logical equivalence can be shown by deriving the contrapositive a step at a time through obverting, converting, and then obverting again, as in the following schematic derivation: "Some *S* is not *P*" obverts to "Some *S* is non-*P*," which converts to "Some non-P is S," which obverts to "Some non-P is not non-S" (the contrapositive).

Contraposition is not, in general, valid for **I** propositions. This can be seen by noting that the true **I** proposition

Some citizens are nonlegislators.

has as its contrapositive the false proposition

Some legislators are noncitizens.

The reason that contraposition is not generally valid when applied to **I** propositions can be seen when we attempt to derive the contrapositive of an **I** proposition by successively obverting, converting, and obverting. The obverse of the **I** proposition "Some S is P" is the **O** proposition "Some S is not non-P," whose converse does not in general follow validly from it.

The contrapositive of the **E** proposition "No S is P" is "No non-P is non-S," which does not in general follow validly from the original, as can be seen by observing that the **E** proposition

No wrestlers are weaklings.

which is true, has as its contrapositive the false proposition

No nonweaklings are nonwrestlers.

If we attempt to derive the contrapositive of an **E** proposition by successive obversion, conversion, and obversion, we find the reason for this invalidity. The obverse of the **E** proposition "No S is P" is the **A** proposition "All S is non-P," and in general it cannot validly be converted except *by limitation*. If we do convert it by limitation to obtain "Some non-P is S," then the latter can be obverted to obtain "Some non-P is not non-S," which we may call the *contrapositive by limitation*. This type of contraposition will be considered further in the next section.

Note that contraposition by limitation, in which we infer an **O** proposition from an **E** proposition—that is, in which we infer "Some non-P is non-S" from "No S is P"—has the same peculiarity as conversion by limitation, on which it depends. Because a particular proposition was inferred from a universal proposition, the resulting contrapositive cannot have the same meaning and cannot be logically equivalent to the **E** proposition that was the original premiss. But the contrapositive of an **A** proposition is an **A** proposition, and the contrapositive of an **O** proposition is an **O** proposition, and in each of these cases, the contrapositive and the premiss from which it is derived are equivalent.

Thus we see that contraposition is a valid form of inference only when applied to **A** and **O** propositions. Contraposition is not valid at all for **I** propositions and is valid for **E** propositions only by limitation. The complete picture of this immediate inference also may be presented in the form of a table:

TABLE OF CONTRAPOSITION	
PREMISS	**CONTRAPOSITIVE**
A: All *S* is *P*.	**A:** All non-*P* is non-*S*.
E: No *S* is *P*.	**O:** Some non-*P* is not non-*S*. (by limitation)
I: Some *S* is *P*.	(contraposition not valid)
O: Some *S* is not *P*.	**O:** Some non-*P* is not non-*S*.

There are other types of immediate inference that have been classified and given special names, but since they involve no new principles we shall not discuss them here.

Some questions about the relations between propositions are best answered by explaining the various immediate inferences that can be drawn from one or the other of them. For example, given that the proposition "All surgeons are physicians" is true, what can be said about the truth or falsehood of the proposition "No nonsurgeons are nonphysicians"? Here one useful procedure is to draw as many valid inferences from the *given* proposition as one can, in order to discover whether the problematic proposition—or its contradictory or contrary—follows validly from the one given as true. In this example, given that "All *S* is *P*" we validly infer its contrapositive, "All non-*P* is non-*S*," from which conversion by limitation gives us "Some non-*S* is non-*P*,"—which is, according to the traditional logic, a valid consequence of the given proposition and therefore true. But according to the Square of Opposition it is the contradictory of the problematic proposition "No non-*S* is non-*P*," which is thus no longer problematic but known to be false.

As was pointed out in section 1.9, although a valid argument whose premisses are true *must* have a true conclusion, a valid argument whose premisses are false *can* have a true conclusion. Examples of the latter come easily to mind for conversion by limitation, contraposition by limitation, and subalternation in following the Square of Opposition. Thus, from the false premiss "All animals are cats," the true proposition "Some animals are cats" follows by subalternation. And from the false proposition "All parents are students," conversion by limitation yields the true proposition, "Some students are parents." Hence if a proposition is given to be false and the question is raised about the truth or falsehood of *another* (somehow related) proposition, the recommended procedure is to begin drawing immediate inference either from the contradictory of the proposition given to be false or from the problematic proposition itself. For the contradictory of a false proposition must be true, and all valid inferences from it will also be true propositions. And if the problematic proposition can be shown to imply the proposition that is given to be false, it must itself be false.

IMMEDIATE INFERENCES: CONVERSION, OBVERSION, CONTRAPOSITION	

CONVERSION

CONVERTEND		CONVERSE	
A:	All S is P.	**I:**	Some P is S (by limitation)
E:	No S is P.	**E:**	No P is S.
I:	Some S is P.	**I:**	Some P is S.
O:	Some S is not P.		(conversion not valid)

OBVERSION

OBVERTEND		OBVERSE	
A:	All S is P.	**E:**	No S is non-P.
E:	No S is P.	**A:**	All S is non-P.
I:	Some S is P.	**O:**	Some S is not non-P.
O:	Some S is not P.	**I:**	Some S is non-P.

CONTRAPOSITION

PREMISS		CONTRAPOSITIVE	
A:	All S is P.	**A:**	All non-P is non-S.
E:	No S is P.	**O:**	Some non-P is not non-S. (by limitation)
I:	Some S is P.		(contraposition not valid)
O:	Some S is not P.	**O:**	Some non-P is not non-S.

Exercises

I. State the converses of the following propositions, and indicate which of them are equivalent to the given propositions.

   *1. No people who are considerate of others are reckless drivers who pay no attention to traffic regulations.

   2. All graduates of West Point are commissioned officers in the U.S. Army.

   3. Some European cars are overpriced and underpowered automobiles.

   4. No reptiles are warm-blooded animals.

   *5. Some professional wrestlers are elderly persons who are incapable of doing an honest day's work.

II. State the obverses of the following propositions.

   *1. Some college athletes are professionals.

   2. No organic compounds are metals.

   3. Some clergy are not abstainers.

   4. No geniuses are conformists.

   *5. All objects suitable for boat anchors are objects weighing at least fifteen pounds.

III. State the contrapositives of the following propositions and indicate which of them are equivalent to the given propositions.

    *1. All journalists are pessimists.

    2. Some soldiers are not officers.

    3. All scholars are nondegenerates.

    4. All things weighing less than 50 pounds are objects not more than four feet high.

    *5. Some noncitizens are not nonresidents.

IV. If "All socialists are pacifists" is true, what may be inferred about the truth or falsehood of the following propositions? That is, which could be known to be true, which known to be false, and which would be undetermined?

    *1. Some nonpacifists are not nonsocialists.

    2. No socialists are nonpacifists.

    3. All nonsocialists are nonpacifists.

    4. No nonpacifists are socialists.

    *5. No nonsocialists are nonpacifists.

    6. All nonpacifists are nonsocialists.

    7. No pacifists are nonsocialists.

    8. Some socialists are not pacifists.

    9. All pacifists are socialists.

    *10. Some nonpacifists are socialists.

V. If "No scientists are philosophers" is true, what may be inferred about the truth or falsehood of the following propositions? That is, which could be known to be true, which known to be false, and which would be undetermined?

    *1. No nonphilosophers are scientists.

    2. Some nonphilosophers are not nonscientists.

    3. All nonscientists are nonphilosophers.

    4. No scientists are nonphilosophers.

    *5. No nonscientists are nonphilosophers.

    6. All philosophers are scientists.

    7. Some nonphilosophers are scientists.

    8. All nonphilosophers are nonscientists.

    9. Some scientists are not philosophers.

    *10. No philosophers are nonscientists.

VI. If "Some saints were martyrs" is true, what may be inferred about the truth or falsehood of the following propositions? That is, which could be known to be true, which known to be false, and which would be undetermined?

    *1. All saints were martyrs.

    2. All saints were nonmartyrs.

   3.   Some martyrs were saints.

   4.   No saints were martyrs.

  *5.   All martyrs were nonsaints.

   6.   Some nonmartyrs were saints.

   7.   Some saints were not nonmartyrs.

   8.   No martyrs were saints.

   9.   Some nonsaints were martyrs.

  *10. Some martyrs were nonsaints.

  11.   Some saints were not martyrs.

  12.   Some martyrs were not saints.

  13.   No saints were nonmartyrs.

  14.   No nonsaints were martyrs.

  *15. Some martyrs were not nonsaints.

VII. If "some merchants are not pirates" is true, what may be inferred about the truth of falsehood of the following propositions? That is, which could be known to be true, which known to be false, and which would be undetermined?

  *1.   No pirates are merchants.

   2.   No merchants are nonpirates.

   3.   Some merchants are nonpirates.

   4.   All nonmerchants are pirates.

  *5.   Some nonmerchants arc nonpirates.

   6.   All merchants are pirates.

   7.   No nonmerchants are pirates.

   8.   No pirates are nonmerchants.

   9.   All nonpirates are nonmerchants.

  *10. Some nonpirates are not nonmerchants.

  11.   Some nonpirates are merchants.

  12.   No nonpirates are merchants.

  13.   Some pirates are merchants.

  14.   No merchants are nonpirates.

  *15. No merchants are pirates.

5.6 EXISTENTIAL IMPORT AND THE INTERPRETATION OF CATEGORICAL PROPOSITIONS

We will now diagram and symbolize categorical propositions, so that we can go on to analyze and evaluate the arguments of which they are built. But before we can symbolize the **A, E, I,** and **O** propositions we must confront and re-

solve a deep logical problem—one that has been a source of controversy for literally thousands of years. In this section we will explain this problem, and provide a resolution upon which a coherent analysis of syllogisms may be built.

It is only fair to advise the reader that this matter is far from simple. The
later analysis of syllogisms will not require that the depths of this controversy
be plumbed—so long as the resulting interpretation of categorical propositions
(called the Boolean interpretation of them) is understood. If the outcome of the
controversy—summarized in the final two paragraphs of this section—is fully
grasped, the complexities in the first pages of this section may be safely by-
passed.

To understand this outcome it must be seen that some propositions have
existential import, and some do not. **A proposition is said to have existential
import if it typically is uttered to assert the existence of objects of some kind.**

Why should this seemingly abstruse matter be of concern to the student of
logic? Because whether the propositions of which any given argument is built
do or do not have existential import directly affects the correctness of the reasoning in that argument. We must arrive at a clear and consistent *interpretation*
of categorical propositions in order that we may determine with confidence
what may be rightly inferred from them, and thereby also guard against incorrect inferences.

We begin with **I** and **O** propositions, which surely do have existential   ■**Advanced Material**
import. Thus the **I** proposition "Some soldiers are heroes" says that
there exists at least one soldier who is a hero. And the **O** proposition, "Some
dogs are not companions" says that there exists at least one dog that is not a
companion. Particular propositions, **I** and **O** propositions, plainly *do* assert that
the classes designated by their subject terms (e.g., soldiers and dogs) are not
empty—the class of soldiers, and the class of dogs (if the examples given here
are true) has at least one member.[4]

But if this is so, if **I** and **O** propositions have existential import (as no one
would wish to deny) wherein lies the problem? The problem arises from the *consequences* of this fact, which are very awkward. Earlier we said that an **I** proposition follows validly from its corresponding **A** proposition by subalternation.
That is, from "All spiders are eight-legged animals," we infer validly that some
spiders are eight-legged animals. And similarly, we said that an **O** proposition
follows validly from its corresponding **E** proposition. But if **I** and **O** propositions
have existential import, and they follow validly from their corresponding **A** and
E propositions, then **A** and **E** propositions must *also* have existential import,

---

[4]A few propositions appear to be exceptions. "Some ghosts appear in Shakespeare's plays"
and "Some Greek gods are described in the *Iliad*" are particular propositions that are certainly true even though there are neither ghosts nor Greek gods. But it is the formulation
that misleads in such cases. These statements do not themselves affirm the existence of
ghosts or Greek gods; they say only that there are certain other propositions that are affirmed or implied in Shakespeare's plays and in the *Iliad*. The propositions of Shakespeare
and Homer may not be true, but it is certainly true that their writings contain or imply those
propositions. And that is all that is affirmed by these apparent exceptions, which arise
chiefly in literary or mythological contexts. **I** and **O** propositions do have existential import.

because a proposition with existential import could not be derived validly from another that did not have such import.[5]

This consequence creates a very serious problem. We know that **A** and **O** propositions, on the traditional Square of Opposition, are contradictories. "All Danes speak English" is contradicted by "Some Danes do not speak English." Contradictories cannot both be true, since one of the pair must be false, nor can they both be false since one of the pair must be true. But *if* corresponding **A** and **O** propositions do have existential import, as we concluded in the paragraph just above, then both contradictories *could* be false! To illustrate: The **A** proposition "All inhabitants of Mars are blond" and its corresponding **O** proposition "Some inhabitants of Mars are not blond" are contradictories; if they have existential import—that is, if we were to interpret them as asserting that there *are* inhabitants of Mars—then both these propositions are false if Mars has no inhabitants. And, of course, we know that Mars has no inhabitants; the class of its inhabitants is empty, so both of the propositions in the example just given are false. But if they could both be false, they *could not be contradictories!*

Something seems to have gone wrong with the traditional Square of Opposition in cases of this kind. If the traditional square is correct when it tells us that **A** and **E** propositions validly imply their corresponding **I** and **O** propositions, then the square is not correct when it tells us that corresponding **A** and **O** propositions are contradictories. And in that case, the square would also be mistaken in holding that the corresponding **I** and **O** propositions are subcontraries.

What is to be done? Can the traditional Square of Opposition be rescued? Yes, it can, but the price would be high. We could rehabilitate the traditional Square of Opposition by introducing the notion of a *presupposition.* Much earlier, we observed (in section 4.3) that some complex questions are properly answered "yes" or "no" only if the answer to a prior question has been presupposed. "Did you spend the money you stole?" can be reasonably answered "yes" or "no" only if the presupposition that you stole some money be granted. Now, to rescue the Square of Opposition, we might insist that *all* propositions—that is, the four standard-form categorical propositions **A, E, I,** and **O**—presuppose (in the sense indicated above) that the classes to which they refer do have members, are not empty. That is, questions about the truth or falsehood of propositions, and about the logical relations holding among them, are admissible and may be reasonably answered (on this interpretation) only if we presuppose that they never refer to empty classes. In this way, we may save all of the relationships set forth in the traditional Square of Opposition: **A** and **E** will remain contraries, **I** and **O** will remain subcontraries, subalterns will follow validly from their superalterns, and **A** and **O** will remain contradictories, as will **I** and **E.** To achieve this result, however, we must pay by making the

---

[5] There is another way to show that the existential import of **A** and **E** propositions must follow from that of **I** and **O** propositions, on the traditional Square of Opposition. In the case of the **A** proposition, we could show it by relying on the (traditionally assumed) validity of conversion by limitation; in the case of the **E** proposition, we could show it by relying on the (traditionally assumed) validity of contraposition by limitation. The result is always the same as that reached above: On the traditional Square of Opposition, if **I** and **O** propositions have existential import, **A** and **E** propositions must have existential import also.

blanket presupposition that all classes designated by our terms (and the complements of these classes) do have members, are not empty.[6]

Well, why not do just that? This existential presupposition is both necessary and sufficient to rescue Aristotelian logic. It is, moreover, a presupposition in full accord with the ordinary use of modern languages like English in very many cases. If you are told, "All the apples in the barrel are Delicious," and find when you look into the barrel that it is empty, what would you say? You would probably not say that the claim was false, or true, but would instead point out that there *are* no apples in the barrel. You would thus be explaining that the speaker had made a mistake, that in this case the existential presupposition (that there exist apples in the barrel) was false. And the fact that we would respond in this corrective fashion shows that we do understand, and do generally accept, the existential presupposition of propositions ordinarily uttered.

Unfortunately, however, this blanket existential presupposition, introduced to rescue the traditional Square of Opposition, imposes intellectual penalties too heavy to bear. There are very good reasons *not* to do it. Here are three such reasons.

First, this rescue preserves the traditional relations among **A, E, I,** and **O** propositions, but only at the cost of reducing their power to formulate assertions that we may need to formulate. If we invariably presuppose that the class designated has members, *we will never be able to formulate the proposition that denies that it has members!* And such denials may sometimes be very important and must surely be made intelligible.

Second, even ordinary usage of language is not in complete accord with this blanket presupposition. *Sometimes what we say does not suppose that there are members in the classes we are talking about.* If you say, for example, "All trespassers will be prosecuted," far from presupposing that the class of trespassers has members, you will ordinarily be intending to ensure that the class will become and remain empty!

Third, in science, and in other theoretical spheres, *we often wish to reason without making any presuppositions about existence.* Newton's First Law of Motion, for example, asserts that certain things are true about bodies that are not acted on by any external forces: that they persevere in rest, or in their straight-line motion. The law may be true; a physicist may wish to express and defend it without wanting to presuppose that there actually are any bodies that are not acted on by external forces.

Objections of this kind make the blanket existential presupposition unacceptable for modern logicians. The Aristotelian interpretation of categorical propositions long thought to be correct must be abandoned, and a more modern interpretation employed. ■

---

[6] Phillip H. Wiebe argues that Aristotelian logic does not require the assumption that the class designated by the complement of the subject term be nonempty. See "Existential Assumptions for Aristotelian Logic," *Journal of Philosophical Research* 16 (1990–1991): 321–328. But Aristotelian logic certainly does require the assumption that at least the classes designated by the other three terms (the subject term, the predicate term, and the complement of the predicate term) are not empty—and this existential assumption gives rise to all the difficulties noted in the remarks to follow.

The modern treatment of categorical propositions does not assume that the classes of which we speak and write always have members. The interpretation that rejects that assumption is called **Boolean,** after the English logician and mathematician George Boole (1815–1864), one of the founders of modern symbolic logic.[7]

In this book, we adopt the Boolean interpretation of categorical propositions in all that follows. Therefore we set forth now what this Boolean interpretation of categorical propositions entails:

1. In some respects, the traditional interpretation is not upset. **I** *and* **O** *propositions continue to have existential import on the Boolean interpretation,* so the proposition "Some *S* is *P*" is false if the class *S* is empty, and the proposition "Some *S* is not *P*" is likewise false if the class *S* is empty.

2. It also remains true in this interpretation that *the universal propositions,* **A** *and* **E,** *are the contradictories of the particular propositions,* **O** *and* **I.** That is, the proposition "All men are mortal" does contradict the proposition "Some men are not mortal," and the proposition "No gods are mortal" does contradict the proposition "Some gods are mortal."

3. All this is entirely coherent because, *in the Boolean interpretation, universal propositions are interpreted as having no existential import.* Even when the *S* class is empty, therefore, the proposition "All *S* is *P*" can be true, as can the proposition "No *S* is *P*." For example, the propositions "All unicorns have horns" and "No unicorns have wings" may both be true, even if there are no unicorns. But if there are no unicorns, the **I** proposition "Some unicorns have horns" is false, as is the **O** proposition "Some unicorns do not have wings."

4. Sometimes, in ordinary discourse, we utter a universal proposition with which we do intend to assert existence. *The Boolean interpretation permits this to be expressed,* of course, but doing so requires two propositions, one existential in force but particular, the other universal but not existential in force.

5. Some very important changes result from our adoption of the Boolean interpretation. *Corresponding* **A** *and* **E** *propositions can both be true and are therefore not contraries.* This may seem paradoxical and will be explained in detail later, in sections 10.2 and 10.3. For the present it will suffice to say that, in the Boolean interpretation, "All unicorns have wings" is taken to assert that "If there is a unicorn, then it has wings" and "No unicorns have wings" is taken to assert that "If there is a unicorn, it does not have wings." And both of these "if . . . then" propositions can be true if indeed there are no unicorns.

6. In like manner, in the Boolean interpretation, corresponding **I** and **O** propositions, because they do have existential import, can both be false

---

[7] Bertrand Russell, another of the founders of modern symbolic logic, also advanced this approach in a famous essay entitled "The Existential Import of Propositions," in *Mind,* July 1905, and there referred to it as "Peano's interpretation" of propositions, after Guiseppe Peano, a great Italian mathematician of the early twentieth century.

if the subject class is empty. So *corresponding* **I** *and* **O** *propositions are not subcontraries.*

7. In the Boolean interpretation, *subalternation*—inferring an **I** proposition from its corresponding **A,** and an **O** proposition from its corresponding **E**—*is not generally valid.* Of course, one may not validly infer a proposition that has existential import from one that does not.

8. The Boolean interpretation *preserves* some immediate inferences: *conversion for* **E** *and for* **I** *propositions* is preserved; *contraposition for* **A** *and for* **O** *propositions* is preserved; *obversion for any proposition* is preserved. But conversion by limitation, and contraposition by limitation, are not generally valid.

9. The traditional Square of Opposition, in the Boolean interpretation, is transformed in the following general way: *Relations along the sides of the square are undone, but the diagonal, contradictory relations remain in force.*

In short, the blanket existential presupposition is rejected by modern logicians. It is a mistake, we hold, to *assume* that a class has members if it is not asserted explicitly that it does. Any argument that relies on this mistaken assumption is said to commit the fallacy of existential assumption, or more briefly, the *existential fallacy.* With this Boolean interpretation clearly in mind, we are now in a position to set forth a powerful system for the symbolizing and diagramming of standard-form categorical syllogisms.

Exercises

In the preceding discussion of existential import, it was shown why, in the Boolean interpretation of propositions adopted in this book, some inferences that traditionally were thought to be valid, mistakenly assume that certain classes have members; these inferences commit the existential fallacy and are not valid. In each of the following arguments, this existential fallacy is committed; explain the point at which, in each argument, the mistaken existential assumption is made.

Example:

I.   (1)   No mathematician is one who has squared the circle.
therefore, (2)   No one who has squared the circle is a mathematician;
therefore, (3)   All who have squared the circle are nonmathematicians;
therefore, (4)   Some nonmathematician is one who has squared the circle.

Solution:

Step (3) to step (4) is invalid. The inference at this point is conversion by limitation (that is, from *All S is P* to *Some P is S*), which was acceptable in the traditional interpretation but is invalid on the Boolean interpretation. This step relies on an inference from a universal proposition to a particular proposition, but the preceding discussion has shown that the classes in a universal proposition cannot be assumed to have members, while the classes in a particular proposition do have members. Thus the invalid passage from (3) to (4) would permit the inference that the predicate class in (4) is not empty, and therefore that there *is* someone who has squared the circle! In inferring (4) from (3), one commits the existential fallacy.

II.

	(1)	No citizen is one who has succeeded in accomplishing the impossible;
therefore,	(2)	No one who has succeeded in accomplishing the impossible is a citizen;
therefore,	(3)	All who have succeeded in accomplishing the impossible are noncitizens;
therefore,	(4)	Some who have succeeded in accomplishing the impossible are noncitizens;
therefore,	(5)	Some noncitizen is one who has succeeded in accomplishing the impossible.

III.

	(1)	No acrobat is one who can lift himself by his own bootstraps;
therefore,	(2)	No one who can lift himself by his own bootstraps is an acrobat;
therefore,	(3)	Some one who can lift himself by his own bootstraps is not an acrobat. (From which it follows that there is at least one being who can lift himself by his own bootstraps.)

IV.

	(1)	It is true that: No unicorns are animals found in the Bronx Zoo;
therefore,	(2)	It is false that: All unicorns are animals found in the Bronx Zoo;
therefore	(3)	It is true that: Some unicorns are not animals found in the Bronx Zoo. (From which it follows that there exists at least one unicorn.)

*V.

	(1)	It is false that: Some mermaids are members of college sororities;
therefore	(2)	It is true that: Some mermaids are not members of college sororities. (From which it follows that there exists at least one mermaid.)

5.7 SYMBOLISM AND DIAGRAMS FOR CATEGORICAL PROPOSITIONS

Since the Boolean interpretation of categorical propositions depends heavily on the notion of an empty class, it is convenient to have a special symbol to represent it. The zero symbol, 0, is used for this purpose. To say that the class designated by the term S has no members, we write an equals sign between S and 0. Thus the equation $S = 0$ says that there are no S's, or that S has no members.

To say that the class designated by S does have members is to deny that S is empty. To assert that there are S's is to deny the proposition symbolized by $S = 0$. We symbolize that denial by drawing a slanting line through the equality sign. Thus the inequality $S \neq 0$ says that there are S's, by denying that S is empty.

Standard-form categorical propositions refer to two classes, so the equations that represent them are somewhat more complicated. Where each of two classes is already designated by a symbol, the class of all things that belong to both of them can be represented by juxtaposing the symbols for the two original classes. For example, if the letter S designates the class of all satires and the letter P designates the class of all poems, then the class of all things that are both satires and poems is represented by the symbol SP, which thus designates the class of all satiric poems (or poetic satires). The common part or common membership of two classes is called the product or intersection of the two classes. The *product* of two classes is the class of all things that belong to both of them. The product of the class of all Americans and the class of all composers is the class of all American composers. (One must be on one's guard against certain oddities of the English language here. For example, the product of the class of all Spaniards and the class of all dancers is not the class of all Spanish dancers, for a Spanish dancer is not a dancer who is Spanish, but any person who performs Spanish dances. Similarly, with abstract painters, English majors, antique dealers, and so on.)

This new notation permits us to symbolize **E** and **I** propositions as equations and inequalities. The **E** proposition "No S is P" says that no members of the class S are members of the class P; that is, there are no things that belong to both classes. This can be rephrased by saying that the product of the two classes is empty, which is symbolized by the equation $SP = 0$. The **I** proposition "Some S is P" says that at least one member of S is also a member of P. This means that the product of the classes S and P is not empty and is symbolized by the inequality $SP \neq 0$.

To symbolize **A** and **O** propositions, it is convenient to introduce a new method of representing class complements. The complement of a class is the collection or class of all things that do not belong to the original class, as explained earlier in section 5.5. The complement of the class of all soldiers is the class of all things that are not soldiers, the class of all nonsoldiers. Where the letter S symbolizes the class of all soldiers, we symbolize the class of all nonsoldiers by $\bar{S}$ (read "S bar"), the symbol for the original class with a bar above it. The **A** proposition "All S is P" says that all members of the class S are also members of the class P, that is, that there are no members of the class S that are not members of P or (by obversion) that "No S is non-P." This, like any other **E** proposition, says that the product of the classes designated by its subject and predicate terms is empty. It is symbolized by the equation $S\bar{P} = 0$. The **O** proposition "Some S is not P" obverts to the logically equivalent **I** proposition "Some S is non-P," which is symbolized by the inequality $S\bar{P} \neq 0$.

In their symbolic formulations, the interrelations among the four standard-form categorical propositions appear very clearly. It is obvious that the **A** and **O** propositions are contradictories when they are symbolized as $S\bar{P} = 0$ and $S\bar{P} \neq 0$, and it is equally obvious that the **E** and **I** propositions, $SP = 0$ and $SP \neq 0$ are contradictories. The **Boolean Square of Opposition** may be represented as shown in Figure 5-2.

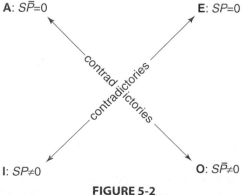

FIGURE 5-2

Propositions can be expressed diagrammatically in diagrams of the classes to which they refer. We represent a class by a circle labeled with the term that designates the class. Thus the class S is diagrammed as in Figure 5-3.

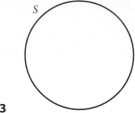

FIGURE 5-3

This diagram is of a class, not a proposition. It represents the class S, but says nothing about it. To diagram the proposition that S has no members, or that there are no S's, we shade all of the interior of the circle representing S, indicating in this way that it contains nothing and is empty. To diagram the proposition that there are S's, which we interpret as saying that there is at least one member of S, we place an x anywhere in the interior of the circle representing S, indicating in this way that there is something inside it, that it is not empty. Thus the two propositions "There are no S's" and "There are S's" are represented by the two diagrams in Figure 5-4.

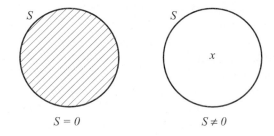

FIGURE 5-4 $S = 0$ $S \neq 0$

Note that the circle that diagrams the class S will also, in effect, diagram the class $\overline{S}$, for just as the interior of the circle represents all members of S, so the exterior of the circle represents all members of $\overline{S}$.

To diagram a standard-form categorical proposition, not one but two circles are required. The skeleton or framework for diagramming any standard-form proposition whose subject and predicate terms are abbreviated by S and P is constructed by drawing two intersecting circles, as in Figure 5-5.

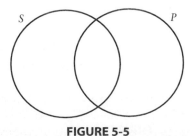

FIGURE 5-5

This figure diagrams the two classes of S and P but diagrams no proposition concerning them. It does not affirm that either or both have members, nor does it deny that they have. As a matter of fact, there are more than two classes diagrammed by the two intersecting circles. The part of the circle labeled S that does not overlap the circle labeled P diagrams all S's that are not P's and can be thought of as representing the product of the classes S and $\overline{P}$. We may label it $S\overline{P}$. The overlapping part of the two circles represents the product of the classes S and P, and diagrams all things belonging to both of them. It is labeled SP. The part of the circle labeled P that does not overlap the circle labeled S diagrams all P's that are not S's, and represents the product of the class $\overline{S}$ and P. It is labeled $\overline{S}P$. Finally, the part of the diagram external to both circles represents all things that are neither in S nor in P; it diagrams the fourth class $\overline{SP}$, so labeled. With these labels inserted, Figure 5-5 becomes Figure 5-6.

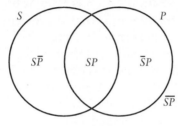

FIGURE 5-6

This diagram can be interpreted in terms of the several different classes determined by the class of all Spaniards (S) and the class of all painters (P). SP is the product of these two classes, containing all those things and only those things that belong to both of them. Every member of SP must be a member of both S and P; every member must be both a Spaniard and a painter. This product class SP is the class of all Spanish painters, which contains, among others, Velásquez and Goya. $S\overline{P}$ is the product of the first class and the complement of the second, containing all those things and only those things that belong to the class S but not to the class P. It is the class of all Spaniards who are not painters, all Spanish nonpainters, and it will contain neither Velásquez nor Goya, but it will include both the novelist Cervantes and the dictator Franco, among many others. $\overline{S}P$ is the product of the second class and the complement of the first, and is the class of all painters who are not Spaniards. This class $\overline{S}P$ of all non-Spanish painters includes, among others, both the Dutch painter Rembrandt and the American painter Georgia O'Keeffe. Finally, $\overline{SP}$ is the product of the complements of the two original classes. It contains all those things and only those things that are neither Spaniards nor painters. It is a very large class indeed, containing not merely English admirals and Swiss mountain climbers, but such things as the Mississippi River and Mount Everest. All these classes are diagrammed in Figure 6-6, where the letters S and P are interpreted as in the present paragraph.

This is what is known as a **Venn diagram,** named after the English mathematician and logician, John Venn, 1834–1923, who introduced this method of representing classes and propositions. The two-circle diagram (as in

Figure 5-6), in which the several areas are labeled but not otherwise marked, represents *classes* only. In this condition it does not represent any proposition. The fact that a circle or part of a circle is left blank signifies nothing— neither that there are, nor that there are not, members of the class represented by that space.

But, with certain additions, we can also use Venn diagrams to represent propositions; by shading some spaces, or inserting x's in various parts of the picture, we can accurately diagram any one of the four standard-form categorical propositions. Because Venn diagrams (with appropriate markings) represent categorical propositions so fully and so graphically, these diagrams have become one of the most powerful and most widely used instruments for the appraisal of syllogistic arguments. Let us consider how each of the four basic categorical propositions would be represented using this technique.

To diagram the **A** proposition "All S is P," symbolized as $S\bar{P} = 0$, we simply shade out the part of the diagram that represents the class $S\bar{P}$, thus indicating it has no members or is empty. To diagram the **E** proposition "No S is P," symbolized as $SP = 0$, we shade out that part of the diagram which represents the class SP, to indicate that it is empty. To diagram the **I** proposition "Some S is P," symbolized $SP \neq 0$, we insert an x into that part of the diagram that represents the class SP. This insertion indicates that the class product is not empty but has at least one member. Finally, for the **O** proposition "Some S is not P," symbolized $S\bar{P} \neq 0$, we insert an x into that part of the diagram that represents the class $S\bar{P}$, to indicate that it is not empty but has at least one member. Placed side by side, diagrams for the four standard-form categorical propositions display their different meanings very clearly, as shown in Figure 5-7.

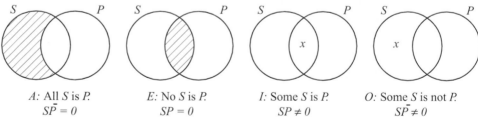

A: All S is P.
$S\bar{P} = 0$

E: No S is P.
$SP = 0$

I: Some S is P.
$SP \neq 0$

O: Some S is not P.
$S\bar{P} \neq 0$

FIGURE 5-7

We have constructed diagrammatic representations for "No S is P" and "Some S is P," and since these are logically equivalent to their converses "No P is S" and "Some P is S," the diagrams for the latter have already been shown. To diagram the **A** proposition "All P is S," symbolized as $P\bar{S} = 0$, within the same framework, we must shade out the part of the diagram that represents the class $P\bar{S}$. It should be obvious that the class $P\bar{S}$ is the same as the class $\bar{S}P$; if not immediately, then by recognizing that every object that belongs to the class of all painters and the class of all non-Spaniards must (also) belong to the class of all non-Spaniards and the class of all painters—all painting non-Spaniards are non-Spanish painters, and vice versa. And to diagram the **O** proposition "Some P is not S," symbolized by $P\bar{S} \neq 0$, we insert an x into the part of the diagram that represents the class $P\overline{S}$ ($= \overline{S}P$). Diagrams for these propositions then appear as shown in Figure 5-8.

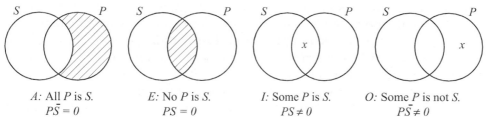

A: All P is S.　　E: No P is S.　　I: Some P is S.　　O: Some P is not S.
$P\overline{S} = 0$　　　$PS = 0$　　　$PS \neq 0$　　　$P\overline{S} \neq 0$

FIGURE 5-8

This further adequacy of the two-circle diagrams is mentioned because in the following chapter it will be important to be able to use a given pair of overlapping circles with given labels—say, S and M—to diagram any standard-form categorical proposition containing S and M as its terms, regardless of the order in which they occur in it.

The Venn diagrams constitute an *iconic* representation of the standard-form categorical propositions, in which spatial inclusions and exclusions correspond to the nonspatial inclusions and exclusions of classes. They provide an exceptionally clear method of notation. They also provide the basis for the simplest and most direct method of testing the validity of categorical syllogisms, as will be explained in the following chapter.

Exercises

Express each of the following propositions as equations or inequalities, representing each class by the first letter of the English term designating it, and symbolizing the proposition by means of a Venn diagram.

Example:

1. Some sculptors are painters.

Solution:

$SP \neq 0$

2.　No peddlers are millionaires.
3.　All merchants are speculators.
4.　Some musicians are not pianists.
*5.　No shopkeepers are members.
6.　Some political leaders of high reputation are scoundrels.
7.　All physicians licensed to practice in this state are medical school graduates who have passed special qualifying examinations.
8.　Some stockbrokers who advise their customers about making investments are not partners in companies whose securities they recommend.

9. All puritans who reject all useless pleasure are strangers to much that makes life worth living.

*10. No modern paintings are photographic likenesses of their objects.

11. Some student activists are middle-aged men and women striving to recapture their lost youth.

12. All medieval scholars were pious monks living in monasteries.

13. Some state employees are not public-spirited citizens.

14. No magistrates subject to election and recall will be punitive tyrants.

*15. Some patients exhibiting all the symptoms of schizophrenia are manic-depressives.

16. Some passengers on large jet airplanes are not satisfied customers.

17. Some priests are militant advocates of radical social change.

18. Some stalwart defenders of the existing order are not members of political parties.

19. No pipelines laid across foreign territories are safe investments.

*20. All pornographic films are menaces to civilization and decency.

Summary of Chapter 5

This chapter has presented and discussed the most basic elements of classical, or **Aristotelian, deductive logic.**

In section 5.2, we introduced the concept of classes on which traditional logic is built, and we explained the **four basic standard-form categorical propositions:**

- **A** propositions: **universal affirmative**
- **I** propositions: **particular affirmative**
- **E** propositions: **universal negative**
- **O** propositions: **particular negative**

In section 5.3, we examined these four standard-form categorical propositions in greater detail. We explored the **quality** of propositions, affirmative or negative, and the **quantity** of propositions, universal or particular; and we explained **distributed** and **undistributed terms.**

In section 5.4, we explored **the kinds of opposition** arising among the several standard-form categorical propositions: what it means for propositions to be **contradictories** of one another, or **contraries** of one another, or **subcontraries** of one another, or **sub-** and **superalterns** of one another; and we showed how these relations are exhibited in the traditional **Square of Opposition.** Some immediate inferences based on the traditional square were also noted.

In section 5.5, we explained three further immediate inferences: **conversion, obversion,** and **contraposition.**

In section 5.6, we explored the controversial issue of **existential import,** showing that the traditional Square of Opposition can be retained only if we make a blanket assumption that the classes to which the subjects of propositions refer always do have some members—an assumption that modern logicians are rightly unwilling to make. We then explained the interpretation of propositions to be adopted throughout this book, called **Boolean,** which retains much but not all of the traditional Square of Opposition, while rejecting the blanket assumption of nonempty classes. In this Boolean interpretation we explained that **particular propositions, those called I and O, are interpreted as having existential import, while universal propositions, A and E, are interpreted as not having such import.** The consequences of adopting this interpretation of propositions we carefully detailed.

In section 5.7, we introduced methods for **symbolizing and diagramming categorical propositions,** including **Venn diagrams,** in which the relations of classes are represented by overlapping circles, appropriately marked or shaded.

With these essential tools in hand we are in a position to examine—in the next two chapters—the categorical syllogisms of which standard-form propositions are the essential building blocks, as well as other central uses of traditional deductive logic in ordinary language.

I consider the invention of the form of syllogisms one of the most beautiful, and also one of the most important, made by the human mind.
—Gottfried Leibniz

Fallacious and misleading arguments are most easily detected if set out in correct syllogistic form.
—Immanuel Kant

CATEGORICAL SYLLOGISMS

STANDARD-FORM CATEGORICAL SYLLOGISMS

A syllogism is a deductive argument in which a conclusion is inferred from two premisses. A categorical syllogism is a deductive argument consisting of three categorical propositions that together contain exactly three terms, each of which occurs in exactly two of the constituent propositions.

A categorical syllogism is said to be in *standard form* when its premisses and conclusion are all standard-form categorical propositions (A, E, I, or O) and are arranged in a specified standard order. To specify that order, it will be useful to explain the logician's special names for the terms and premisses of categorical syllogisms. For brevity, in this chapter we shall refer to categorical syllogisms simply as "syllogisms," even though there are other kinds of syllogisms that will be discussed in later chapters.

A. Major, Minor, and Middle Terms

The conclusion of a standard-form syllogism is a standard-form categorical proposition that contains two of the syllogism's three terms. The conclusion is always used to identify the terms of the syllogism.

The term that occurs as the *predicate* of the conclusion is called the *major term* of the syllogism.

The term that occurs as the *subject* term of the conclusion is called the *minor term* of the syllogism.

The third term of the syllogism, which does not occur in the conclusion, appearing instead in both premisses, is called the *middle term.*

Thus, in the standard-form syllogism,

No heroes are cowards.
Some soldiers are cowards.
Therefore some soldiers are not heroes.

the term "soldiers" is the *minor term*, and the term "heroes" is the *major term*. In this example, the term "cowards," which does not appear in the conclusion, is the *middle term*.

The premisses of a standard-form syllogism are named after the terms that appear in them. The major and minor terms must each occur in a different one of the premisses. **The premiss containing the major term is called the *major premiss*, and the premiss containing the minor term is called the *minor premiss*.** In the syllogism just given, the major premiss is "No heroes are cowards," and the minor premiss is "Some soldiers are cowards."

Earlier we said that a syllogism is in standard form when its premisses are arranged in a specified standard order. We can now state that order: **In a standard-form syllogism, the major premiss is stated first, the minor premiss second, and the conclusion last.** It should be emphasized that the major premiss is defined not in terms of its position but as the premiss that contains the major term, which is by definition the predicate term of the conclusion. Likewise, the minor premiss is defined not in terms of its position but as the premiss that contains the minor term, which is defined as the subject term of the conclusion.

B.   Mood

The *mood* of a standard-form syllogism is determined by the types (identified by letter: **A, E, I,** or **O**) of the standard-form categorical propositions it contains. The mood of every syllogism is represented by three letters, in a specific order: The first letter names the type of the syllogism's major premiss, the second letter names the type of its minor premiss, and the third letter names the type of its conclusion. For example, in the illustrative syllogism given above, the major premiss is an **E** proposition, the minor premiss is an **I** proposition, and the conclusion is an **O** proposition. Hence the mood of that syllogism is **EIO.**

C.   Figure

But the mood of a standard-form syllogism does not completely characterize its form. Consider the following two syllogisms:

A.
All great scientists are college graduates.
Some professional athletes are college graduates
Therefore some professional athletes are great scientists.

and

B.
All artists are egotists.
Some artists are paupers.
Therefore some paupers are egotists.

Both are of mood **AII,** but they are of different forms. We can bring out the difference in their forms most clearly by displaying their logical "skeletons"; abbreviating the minor terms by S, the major terms by P, the middle terms by M; and using the three-dot symbol "$\therefore$" for "therefore." The forms or "skeletons" of these two syllogisms are

	All P is M.		All M is P.
A.	Some S is M.	**B.**	Some M is S.
	$\therefore$ Some S is P.		$\therefore$ Some S is P.

In the first, labeled **A,** the middle term is the predicate term of both premisses, while in the second, labeled **B,** the middle term is the subject term of both premisses. These examples show that, although the form of a syllogism is partially described by a statement of its mood, syllogisms having the same mood may differ importantly in their forms, depending on the relative positions of their middle terms.[1] We may completely describe the form of a syllogism, however, by stating both its mood and its *figure,* where **the figure indicates the position of the middle term in the premisses.**

It is clear that syllogisms can have four and only four possible different figures. The middle term may be the subject term of the major premiss and the predicate term of the minor premiss, or it may be the predicate term of both premisses, or it may be the subject term of both premisses, or it may be the predicate term of the major premiss and the subject term of the minor premiss. **These different possible positions of the middle term constitute the first, second, third, and fourth figures, respectively.** They are schematized in the following array, where only the relative positions of the terms are shown, and reference to mood is suppressed by not representing either quantifiers or copulas:

M–P	P–M	M–P	P–M
S–M	S–M	M–S	M–S
$\therefore$ S–P	$\therefore S$–P	$\therefore S$–P	$\therefore S$–P
First Figure	**Second Figure**	**Third Figure**	**Fourth Figure**

We give a complete description of the form of any standard-form syllogism by naming its mood *and* figure. Thus any syllogism of mood **AOO** in the second figure (named more briefly as **AOO–2**) will have the form

All P is M.
Some S is not M.
$\therefore$ Some S is not P.

Abstracting from the infinite variety of their possible subject matters, we obtain many different forms of standard-form syllogisms. Were we to list all possible different moods, beginning with **AAA, AAE, AAI, AAO; AEA, AEE, AEI, AEO; AIA, . . .,** and continuing through, by the time we reached **OOO** we would have enumerated 64 different moods. And since each mood can occur with each

---

[1] The difference can be huge. In this illustration, syllogism **B** is a valid argument, but syllogism **A** is not!

of the four different figures, there must be 256 distinct forms that standard-form syllogisms may assume. Only a few of them are valid, however, as we shall see.

Exercises

Rewrite each of the following syllogisms in standard form, and name its mood and figure. (*Procedure: First,* identify the conclusion; *second,* note its predicate term, which is the major term of the syllogism; *third,* identify the major premiss, which is the premiss containing the major term; *fourth,* verify that the other premiss is the minor premiss by checking to see that it contains the minor term, which is the subject term of the conclusion; *fifth,* rewrite the argument in standard form—major premiss first, minor premiss second, conclusion last; *sixth,* name the mood and figure of the syllogism.)

Example:

1. No nuclear-powered submarines are commercial vessels, so no warships are commercial vessels, since all nuclear-powered submarines are warships.

Solution:

Step 1. The conclusion is "No warships are commercial vessels."

Step 2. "Commercial vessels" is the predicate term of this conclusion, and is therefore the major term of the syllogism.

Step 3. The major premiss, the premiss that contains this term, is "No nuclear-powered submarines are commercial vessels."

Step 4. The remaining premiss, "All nuclear-powered submarines are warships," is indeed the minor premiss, since it does contain the subject term of the conclusion, "warships."

Step 5. In standard form this syllogism is written thus:

No nuclear-powered submarines are commercial vessels.
All nuclear-powered submarines are warships.
Therefore no warships are commercial vessels.

Step 6. The three propositions in this syllogism are, in order, **E, A,** and **E.** The middle term, "nuclear-powered submarines," is the subject term of both premisses, so the syllogism is in the **third** figure. The mood and figure of the syllogism therefore are: **EAE–3**

2. Some evergreens are objects of worship, because all fir trees are evergreens, and some objects of worship are fir trees.

3. All artificial satellites are important scientific achievements; therefore some important scientific achievements are not American inventions, inasmuch as some artificial satellites are not American inventions.

4. No television stars are certified public accountants, but all certified public accountants are people of good business sense; it follows that no television stars are people of good business sense.

*5. Some conservatives are not advocates of high tariff rates, because all advocates of high tariff rates are Republicans, and some Republicans are not conservatives.

6. All CD players are expensive and delicate mechanisms, but no expensive and delicate mechanisms are suitable toys for children; consequently, no CD players are suitable toys for children.

7. All juvenile delinquents are maladjusted individuals, and some juvenile delinquents are products of broken homes; hence some maladjusted individuals are products of broken homes.

8. No stubborn individuals who never admit a mistake are good teachers, so, since some well-informed people are stubborn individuals who never admit a mistake, some good teachers are not well-informed people.

9. All proteins are organic compounds, whence all enzymes are proteins, as all enzymes are organic compounds.

*10. No sports cars are vehicles intended to be driven at moderate speeds, but all automobiles designed for family use are vehicles intended to be driven at moderate speeds, from which it follows that no sports cars are automobiles designed for family use.

6.2 THE FORMAL NATURE OF SYLLOGISTIC ARGUMENT

The mood and figure of a syllogism uniquely determine its form—and the *form* of a syllogism is, from the point of view of logic, its most important aspect. The validity or invalidity of a syllogism (whose constituent propositions are all contingent) depends exclusively on its form and is completely independent of its specific content or subject matter. Thus any syllogism of the form **AAA–1**

$$\text{All } M \text{ is } P.$$
$$\underline{\text{All } S \text{ is } M.}$$
$$\therefore \text{ All } S \text{ is } P.$$

is a valid argument, regardless of its subject matter. That is, no matter what terms are substituted in this form or skeleton for the letters S, P, and M, the resulting argument will be valid. If we substitute the terms "Athenians," "humans," and "Greeks" for those letters, we obtain the valid argument

All Greeks are humans.
<u>All Athenians are Greeks.</u>
Therefore all Athenians are humans.

And if we substitute the terms "soaps," "water-soluble substances," and "sodium salts" for the letters *S, P,* and *M* in the same form, we obtain

> All sodium salts are water-soluble substances.
> <u>All soaps are sodium salts.</u>
> Therefore all soaps are water-soluble substances.

which also is valid.

A valid syllogism is a formally valid argument, valid by virtue of its form alone. This implies that if a given syllogism is valid, *any other syllogism of the same form will also be valid.* And if a syllogism is invalid, *any other syllogism of the same form will also be invalid.*[2] The common recognition of this fact is attested to by the frequent use of "logical analogies" in argumentation. Suppose that we were presented with the argument

> All liberals are proponents of national health insurance.
> <u>Some members of the administration are proponents of national health insurance.</u>
> Therefore some members of the administration are liberals.

and felt (justifiably) that regardless of the truth or falsehood of its constituent propositions, the argument was invalid. By far the best way of exposing its fallacious character would be to construct another argument having exactly the same form but whose invalidity was immediately apparent. We might seek to expose the given argument by replying, You might as well argue that

> All rabbits are very fast runners.
> <u>Some horses are very fast runners.</u>
> Therefore some horses are rabbits.

We might continue: You cannot seriously defend this argument, because here there is no question about the facts. The premises are known to be true and the conclusion is known to be false. Your argument is of the same pattern as this analogous one about horses and rabbits. This one is invalid—so *your* argument is invalid. This is an excellent method of arguing; the logical analogy is one of the most powerful weapons that can be used in debate.

Underlying the method of logical analogy is the fact that the validity or invalidity of such arguments as the categorical syllogism is a purely formal matter. Any fallacious argument can be proved invalid by finding a second argument that has exactly the same form and is known to be invalid by the fact that

---

[2] Here we assume that the constituent propositions are themselves contingent, that is, neither logically true (*e.g.,* "All easy chairs are chairs") nor logically false (*e.g.,* "Some easy chairs are not chairs"). For if it contained either a logically false premiss or a logically true conclusion, then the argument would be valid regardless of its syllogistic form—valid in that it would be logically impossible for its premises to be true and its conclusion false. We also assume that the only logical relations among the terms of the syllogism are those asserted or entailed by its premises. The point of these restrictions is to limit our considerations in this chapter and the next to syllogistic arguments alone and to exclude other kinds of arguments whose validity turns on more complex logical considerations not appropriately introduced at this place.

its premisses are known to be true while its conclusion is known to be false. (It should be remembered that an invalid argument may very well have a true conclusion—that an argument is invalid simply means that its conclusion is not logically implied or necessitated by its premisses.)

This method of testing the validity of arguments has serious limitations, however. Sometimes a logical analogy is difficult to "think up" on the spur of the moment. And there are far too many invalid forms of syllogistic argument (well over 200!) for us to prepare and remember refuting analogies of each of them in advance. Moreover, although being able to think of a logical analogy with true premisses and false conclusion proves its form to be invalid, *not* being able to think of one does not prove the form valid, for it may merely reflect the limitations of our thinking. There may be an invalidating analogy even though we are not able to think of it. A more effective method of establishing the formal validity or invalidity of syllogisms is required. It is to the explanation of effective methods of testing syllogisms that the remaining sections of this chapter are devoted.

Exercises

Refute any of the following arguments that are invalid by the method of constructing logical analogies.

Example:

1. All business executives are active opponents of increased corporation taxes, for all active opponents of increased corporation taxes are members of the chamber of commerce, and all members of the chamber of commerce are business executives.

Solution:

One possible refuting analogy is this: All bipeds are astronauts, for all astronauts are humans and all humans are bipeds.

2. No medicines that can be purchased without a doctor's prescription are habit-forming drugs, so some narcotics are not habitforming drugs, since some narcotics are medicines that can be purchased without a doctor's prescription.

3. No Republicans are Democrats, so some Democrats are wealthy stockbrokers, since some wealthy stockbrokers are not Republicans.

4. No college graduates are persons having an IQ of less than 70, but all persons having an IQ of less than 70 are morons, so no college graduates are morons.

*5. All fireproof buildings are structures that can be insured at special rates, so some structures that can be insured at special rates are not wooden houses, since no wooden houses are fireproof buildings.

6.   All blue-chip securities are safe investments, so some stocks that pay a generous dividend are safe investments, since some blue-chip securities are stocks that pay a generous dividend.

7.   Some pediatricians are not specialists in surgery, so some general practitioners are not pediatricians, since some general practitioners are not specialists in surgery.

8.   No intellectuals are successful politicians, because no shy and retiring people are successful politicians, and some intellectuals are shy and retiring people.

9.   All trade union executives are labor leaders, so some labor leaders are conservatives in politics, since some conservatives in politics are trade union executives.

*10.   All new automobiles are economical means of transportation, and all new automobiles are status symbols; therefore some economical means of transportation are status symbols.

6.3   VENN DIAGRAM TECHNIQUE FOR TESTING SYLLOGISMS

In the preceding chapter the employment of two-circle Venn diagrams to represent standard-form categorical propositions was explained. In order to test a categorical syllogism by the method of Venn diagrams, one must first represent both of its premises in one diagram. That will require drawing *three* overlapping circles, for the two premises of a standard-form syllogism contain three different terms—minor term, major term, and middle term—which we abbreviate as S, P, and M, respectively. We first draw two circles just as for the diagramming of a single proposition, and then we draw a third circle beneath, overlapping both of the first two. We label the three circles S, P, and M, in that order. Just as one circle labeled S diagrammed both the class S and the class $\bar{S}$, and as two overlapping circles labeled S and P diagrammed four classes (SP, $S\bar{P}$, $\bar{S}P$, and $\bar{S}\bar{P}$), so three overlapping circles labeled S, P, and M diagram eight classes: $S\bar{P}\bar{M}$, $SP\bar{M}$, $\bar{S}P\bar{M}$, $S\bar{P}M$, SPM, $\bar{S}PM$, $\bar{S}\bar{P}M$, and SPM. These are represented by the eight parts into which the three circles divide the plane, as shown in Figure 6-1.

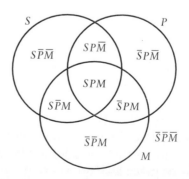

FIGURE 6-1

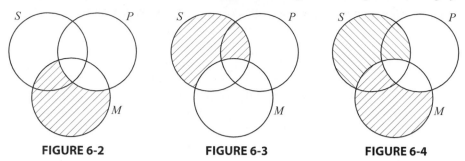

FIGURE 6-2   FIGURE 6-3   FIGURE 6-4

This can be interpreted in terms of the various different classes determined by the class of all Swedes *(S)*, the class of all peasants *(P)*, and the class of all musicians *(M)*. *SPM* is the product of these three classes, which is the class of all Swedish peasant musicians. $SP\overline{M}$ is the product of the first two and the complement of the third, which is the class of all Swedish peasants who are not musicians. $S\overline{P}M$ is the product of the first and third and the complement of the second: the class of all Swedish musicians who are not peasants. $S\overline{PM}$ is the product of the first and the complement of the others: the class of all Swedes who are neither peasants nor musicians. Next, $\overline{S}PM$ is the product of the second and third classes with the complement of the first: the class of all peasant musicians who are not Swedes. $\overline{S}P\overline{M}$ is the product of the second class with the complements of the other two: the class of all peasants who are neither Swedes nor musicians. $\overline{SP}M$ is the product of the third class and the complements of the first two: the class of all musicians who are neither Swedes nor peasants. Finally, $\overline{SPM}$ is the product of the complements of the three original classes: the class of all things that are neither Swedes nor peasants nor musicians.

If we focus our attention on just the two circles labeled *P* and *M*, it is clear that by shading out or inserting an *x* we can diagram any standard-form categorical proposition whose two terms are *P* and *M*, regardless of which is the subject term and which the predicate. Thus, to diagram the proposition "All *M* is *P*" $(M\overline{P} = 0)$, we shade out all of *M* that is not contained in (or overlapped by) *P*. This area, it is seen, includes both the portions labeled $S\overline{P}M$ and $\overline{SP}M$. The diagram then becomes Figure 6-2.

And if we focus our attention on just the two circles *S* and *M*, by shading out or inserting an *x* we can diagram any standard-form categorical proposition whose terms are *S* and *M*, regardless of the order in which they appear in it. To diagram the proposition "All *S* is *M*" $(S\overline{M} = 0)$, we shade out all of *S* that is not contained in (or overlapped by) *M*. This area, it is seen, includes both the portions labeled $S\overline{PM}$ and $SP\overline{M}$. The diagram for this proposition will appear as Figure 6-3.

Now, the advantage of having three circles overlapping is that it allows us to diagram two propositions together—on condition, of course, that only three different terms occur in them. Thus diagramming both "All *M* is *P*" and "All *S* is *M*" at the same time gives us Figure 6-4.

This is the diagram for both premises of the syllogism **AAA–1:**

All M is P.
All S is M.
∴ All S is P.

This syllogism is valid if and only if the two premises imply or entail the conclusion; that is, if together they say what is said by the conclusion. Consequently, diagramming the premises of a valid argument should suffice to diagram its conclusion also, with no further marking of the circles needed. To diagram the conclusion "All S is P" is to shade out both the portion labeled $S\overline{P}M$ and the portion labeled $S\overline{P}\overline{M}$. Inspecting the diagram that represents the two premises, we see that it does diagram the conclusion also. And from this fact we can conclude that **AAA–1** is a valid syllogism.[3]

Let us now apply the Venn Diagram test to an obviously invalid syllogism:

All dogs are mammals.
All cats are mammals.
Therefore all cats are dogs.

Diagramming both premises gives us Figure 6-5.

In this diagram, where S designates the class of all cats, P the class of all dogs, and M the class of all mammals, the portions $S\overline{P}\overline{M}$, $SP\overline{M}$, and $\overline{S}P\overline{M}$ have been shaded out. But the conclusion has not been diagrammed, because the part $S\overline{P}M$ has been left unshaded, and to diagram the conclusion *both* $S\overline{P}M$ and $S\overline{P}\overline{M}$ must be shaded. Thus we see that diagramming both the premises of a syllogism of form **AAA–2** does *not* suffice to diagram its conclusion, which proves that the conclusion says something more than is said by the premises, which shows that the premises do not imply the conclusion. But an argument whose premises do not imply its conclusion is invalid, and so our diagram proves the given syllogism to be invalid. (It proves, in fact, that *any* syllogism of the form **AAA–2** is invalid.)

When we use a Venn Diagram to test a syllogism with one universal premiss and one particular premiss, it is important to *diagram the universal premiss first*. Thus, in testing the **AII–3** syllogism

All artists are egotists.
Some artists are paupers.
Therefore some paupers are egotists.

we should diagram the universal premiss "All artists are egotists" before inserting an x to diagram the particular premiss "Some artists are paupers." Properly diagrammed, the premises appear as in Figure 6-6.

---

[3] Like every valid syllogism, this syllogism has a name. Its mood is **AAA** because it consists of three **A** propositions; it is in the first figure because its middle term is the subject of its major premiss and the predicate of its minor premiss. Any syllogism of that valid form, **AAA–1,** is called a syllogism in **Barbara.** The names of other valid syllogisms will be given in Section 6.5 below.

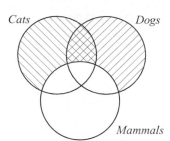

FIGURE 6-5

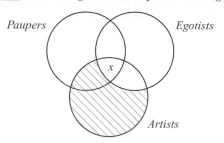

FIGURE 6-6

Had we tried to diagram the particular premiss first, before the region $S\bar{P}M$ was shaded out along with $\overline{S}PM$ in diagramming the universal premiss, we should not have known whether to insert an x in SPM or in $S\bar{P}M$ or in both. And had we put it in $S\bar{P}M$ or on the line separating it from SPM, the subsequent shading of $S\bar{P}M$ would have obscured the information the diagram was intended to contain. Now that the information contained in the premisses has been inserted into the diagram, we examine it to see whether the conclusion already has been diagrammed. If the conclusion "Some paupers are egotists" has been diagrammed, there will be an x somewhere in the overlapping part of the circles labeled "paupers" and "egotists." This overlapping part consists of both of the regions $SP\bar{M}$ and SPM, which together constitute SP. There is an x in the region SPM, so there *is* an x in the overlapping part SP. What the conclusion of the syllogism says has already been diagrammed by the diagramming of its premisses; therefore the syllogism is valid.

Let us consider still another example, the discussion of which will bring out a further important point about the use of Venn diagrams. Let's say we are testing the argument

> All great scientists are college graduates.
> Some professional athletes are college graduates.
> Therefore some professional athletes are great scientists.

After diagramming the universal premiss first (Figure 6-7) by shading out both regions $SP\bar{M}$ and $\overline{S}P\bar{M}$, we may still be puzzled about where to put the x needed in order to diagram the particular premiss. That premiss is "Some professional athletes are college graduates," so an x must be inserted somewhere in the overlapping part of the two circles labeled "professional athletes" and "college graduates." That overlapping part, however, contains two regions: SPM and $S\bar{P}M$. In which of these should an x be placed? The premisses do not tell us, and were we to make an arbitrary decision to place it in one rather than the other, we would be inserting more information into the diagram than the premisses warrant—which would spoil the diagram's use as a test for validity. Placing x's in each of them would also go beyond what the premisses assert. Yet by placing an x on the line that divides the overlapping region SM into the two parts SPM and $S\bar{P}M$, we can diagram exactly what the second premiss asserts without adding anything to it. Placing an x on the line between two regions indicates that there is something that belongs in one of them, but does

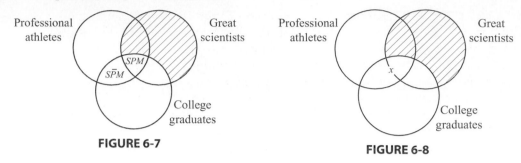

FIGURE 6-7

FIGURE 6-8

not indicate which one. The completed diagram of both premisses would appear as in Figure 6-8.

When we inspect this diagram of the premisses to see whether the conclusion of the syllogism already has been diagrammed in it, we find that it has not been. For the conclusion "Some professional athletes are great scientists" to have been diagrammed, an x would have had to occur in the overlapping part of the two upper circles, either in $S P \overline{M}$ or in SPM. The first of these is shaded out and certainly contains no x. The diagram does not show an x in SPM either. True, there must be a member of *either* SPM or $S\overline{P}M$, but the diagram does not tell us that it is in the former rather than the latter and so, for all the premisses tell us, the conclusion may be false. We do not know that the conclusion *is* false, only that it is not asserted or implied by the premisses. The latter is enough, however, to let us know that the argument is invalid. The diagram suffices to show not merely that the given syllogism is invalid, but that *all* syllogisms of the form **AII–2** are invalid.

The general technique of using Venn diagrams to test the validity of any standard-form syllogism may be summarily described as follows. First, label the circles of a three-circle Venn diagram with the syllogism's three terms. Next, diagram both premisses, diagramming the universal one first if there is one universal and one particular, being careful in diagramming a particular proposition to put an x on a line if the premisses do not determine on which side of the line it should go. Finally, inspect the diagram to see whether or not the diagram of the premisses contains a diagram of the conclusion: If it does, the syllogism is valid; if it does not, the syllogism is invalid.

■Advanced Material   What is the theoretical rationale for using Venn diagrams to distinguish valid from invalid syllogisms? The answer to this question divides into two parts. The first has to do with the formal nature of syllogistic argument as explained in section 6.2. It was there shown that one legitimate test of the validity or invalidity of a given syllogism is to establish the validity or invalidity of a different syllogism having exactly the same form. This technique is basic to the use of Venn diagrams. The explanation of *how* they serve this purpose constitutes the second part of the answer to our question.

Ordinarily, a syllogism will be about classes of objects that are not all present, such as the class of all musicians, or great scientists, or sodium salts, or the like. The relations of inclusion or exclusion among such classes may be reasoned about and may be empirically discoverable in the course of scientific investigation. But they certainly are not open to direct inspection, since not all members of the classes involved are ever present at one time to be inspected. We can, however, examine situations of our own making, in which the only classes concerned will contain by their very definitions only things that are present and directly open to inspection. And we can argue syllogistically about such situations of our own making. Venn diagrams are devices for expressing standard-form categorical propositions, but they also are situations of our own making, patterns of graphite or ink on paper, or rills of chalk raised on blackboards. And the propositions they express can be interpreted as referring to the diagrams themselves. An example can help to make this clear. Suppose we have a particular syllogism whose terms denote various kinds of people who are successful, interested in their work, and able to concentrate, and who may be scattered widely over all parts of the world:

> All successful people are people who are keenly interested in their work.
> No people who are keenly interested in their work are people whose attention is easily distracted when they are working.
> ───
> Therefore no people whose attention is easily distracted when they are working are successful people.

Its form is **AEE–4,** and it may be schematized as

$$\text{All } P \text{ is } M.$$
$$\underline{\text{No } M \text{ is } S.}$$
$$\therefore \text{ No } S \text{ is } P.$$

We may test it by constructing the Venn diagram shown in Figure 6-9, with its regions $SP\overline{M}$ and $\overline{S}P\overline{M}$ shaded out to express the first premiss, and $S\overline{P}M$ and SPM shaded out to express the second premiss.

Examining the diagram, we find that SP (which consists of the regions SPM and $SP\overline{M}$) has been shaded out, so the syllogism's conclusion already has been diagrammed. Now, how does this tell us that the given syllogism is valid? That syllogism concerns large classes of remote objects: There are many people whose attention is easily distracted while they are working, and they are scattered far and wide. However, we can construct a syllogism of the same form dealing with objects that are immediately present and directly available for our

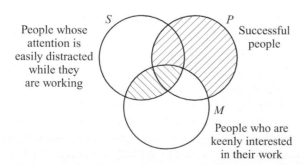

FIGURE 6-9

inspection. These objects are the points within the unshaded portions of the circles labeled *S, P,* and *M* in our Venn diagram. Here is the new syllogism:

> All points within the unshaded part of the circle labeled *P* are points within the unshaded part of the circle labeled M.
> No points within the unshaded part of the circle labeled *M* are points within the unshaded part of the circle labeled S.
> Therefore no points within the unshaded part of the circle labeled *S* are points within the unshaded part of the circle labeled *P.*

This new syllogism refers to nothing remote; it is about the parts of a situation we ourselves have created: the Venn diagram we have drawn. All the parts and all the possibilities of inclusion and exclusion among these classes are immediately present to us and directly open to inspection. We can literally see all the possibilities here, and know that since all the points of *P* are also points of *M,* and since *M* and *S* have no points in common, *S* and *P* cannot possibly have any points in common. since it refers only to classes of points in the diagram, the new syllogism is literally *seen* to be valid by looking at the things it talks about. Since the original syllogism about classes of people has exactly the same form as this second one, we are assured by the formal nature of syllogistic argument that the original syllogism also is valid. The explanation is exactly the same for Venn diagram proofs of the invalidity of invalid syllogisms; there, too, we test the original syllogism indirectly by directly testing a second syllogism having exactly the same form but referring to the diagram that exhibits that form. ∎

Exercises

I.   Write out each of the following syllogistic forms, using *S* and *P* as the subject and predicate terms of the conclusion, and *M* as the middle term. (Refer to the chart of the four syllogistic figures, if necessary, on p. 219.) Then test the validity of each syllogistic form by means of a Venn diagram.

Example:

   1.   AEE–1

Solution:

We are told that this syllogism is in the first figure, and therefore the middle term, *M,* is the subject term of the major premiss and the predicate term of the minor premiss. (See chart on p. 219.) The conclusion of the syllogism is an **E** proposition and therefore reads: *No S is P.* The first (major) premiss (which contains the predicate term of the conclusion) is an **A** proposition, and therefore reads: *All M is P.* The second (minor) premiss (which contains the subject term of the conclusion) is an **E**

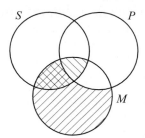

FIGURE 6-10

proposition and therefore reads: *No S is M.* This syllogism therefore reads as follows:

All *M* is *P.*
No *S* is *M.*
Therefore no *S* is *P.*

Tested by means of a Venn diagram, as in Figure 6-10, this syllogism is shown to be invalid.

2.	EIO–2	3.	OAO–3
4.	AOO–4	*5.	EIO–4
6.	OAO–2	7.	AOO–1
8.	EAE–3	9.	EIO–3
*10.	IAI–4	11.	AOO–3
12.	EAE–1	13.	IAI–1
14.	OAO–4	*15.	EIO–1

II. Put each of the following syllogisms into standard form, name its mood and figure, and test its validity by means of a Venn diagram.

*1. Some reformers are fanatics, so some idealists are fanatics, since all reformers are idealists.

2. Some philosophers are mathematicians; hence some scientists are philosophers, since all scientists are mathematicians.

3. Some mammals are not horses, for no horses are centaurs, and all centaurs are mammals.

4. Some neurotics are not parasites, but all criminals are parasites; it follows that some neurotics are not criminals.

*5. All underwater craft are submarines; therefore no submarines are pleasure vessels, since no pleasure vessels are underwater craft.

6. No criminals were pioneers, for all criminals are unsavory persons, and no pioneers were unsavory persons.

7. No musicians are astronauts; all musicians are baseball fans; consequently no astronauts are baseball fans.

8. Some Christians are not Methodists, for some Christians are not Protestants, and some Protestants are not Methodists.

9. No people whose primary interest is in winning elections are true liberals, and all active politicians are people whose primary interest is in winning elections, which entails that no true liberals are active politicians.

*10. No weaklings are labor leaders, because no weaklings are true liberals, and all labor leaders are true liberals.

6.4 SYLLOGISTIC RULES AND SYLLOGISTIC FALLACIES

A syllogism may fail to establish its conclusion in many different ways. To help avoid common errors we set forth rules—six of them—that may guide the reasoner: Any given standard-form syllogism can be evaluated by observing whether any one of these rules has been violated.

A violation of any one of these rules is a mistake. Because it is a mistake of that special *kind,* we call it a fallacy; and because it is a mistake in the *form* of the argument, we call it a formal fallacy (to be contrasted with the *in*formal fallacies described in Chapter 4). In reasoning with syllogisms, one must scrupulously avoid the fallacies that violations of the rules invariably yield. Each of these formal fallacies has a traditional name, explained below.

Rule 1. Avoid four terms.

> *A valid standard-form categorical syllogism must contain exactly three terms, each of which is used in the same sense throughout the argument.*

In every categorical syllogism the conclusion asserts a relationship between two terms, the subject (minor term) and the predicate (major term). Such a conclusion can be justified only if the premises assert the relationship of each of those two terms to the same third term (middle term). If the premises fail to do this consistently, the needed connection of the two terms in the conclusion cannot be established, and the argument will fail. So every valid categorical syllogism must involve three terms—no more and no less. If more than three terms are involved the syllogism is invalid. The fallacy then committed is called **the fallacy of four terms.**

The mistake that commonly underlies this fallacy is equivocation, using one word or phrase with two different meanings. Most often it is the middle term whose meaning is thus shifted, in one direction to connect it with the minor term, in a different direction to connect it with the major term. But by doing this the two terms of the conclusion are connected with two different terms (rather than the same middle term) and so the relationship asserted by the conclusion is not established.[4]

---

[4] Because it is the middle term that is most often manipulated, this fallacy is sometimes called "the fallacy of the ambiguous middle." But this name is not generally applicable, since one (or more) of the other terms may have its meaning shifted as well. Ambiguities may result in as many as five or six different terms involved—but the mistake retains its traditional name: the fallacy of four terms.

When the expression "categorical syllogism" was defined at the beginning of this chapter we noted that by its nature every syllogism must have three and only three terms.[5] So this rule ("Avoid four terms") may be regarded as a reminder to make sure that the argument being appraised really is a categorical syllogism.

Rule 2. Distribute the middle term in at least one premiss.

> A term is "distributed" in a proposition when (as was explained in section 5.3) the proposition refers to **all** members of the class designated by that term. If the middle term is not distributed in at least one premiss, the connection required by the conclusion cannot be made.

The historian Barbara Tuchman observed that many early critics of anarchism relied upon the following "unconscious syllogism":

> All Russians were revolutionists.
> All anarchists were revolutionists.
> Therefore, all anarchists were Russians.[6]

This syllogism is plainly invalid. Its mistake is that it asserts a connection between anarchists and Russians, relying upon the links between each of those classes and the class of revolutionists—but revolutionists is an *un*distributed term in both of the premisses. The first premiss does not refer to all revolutionists, and neither does the second. Revolutionists is the middle term in this argument, and if the middle term is not distributed in at least one premiss of a syllogism, that syllogism cannot be valid. The fallacy this syllogism commits is called **the fallacy of the undistributed middle.**

What underlies this rule is the need to *link* the minor and the major terms. But if they are to be linked by the middle term, either the subject or the predicate of the conclusion must be related to the *whole* of the class designated by the middle term. For if that is not so, it is possible that each of the terms in the conclusion may be connected with a different part of the middle term, and not necessarily connected with each other.

This is precisely what happens in the syllogism given in the example above. The Russians are included in a *part* of the class of revolutionists (by the first premiss), and the anarchists are included in a *part* of the class of revolutionists (by the second premiss)—but *different* parts of this class (the middle term of the syllogism) are involved, and so the middle term does not successfully link the minor and major terms of the syllogism. **In a valid syllogism the middle term must be distributed in at least one premiss.**

---

[5] The term "syllogism" is sometimes defined more broadly than it has been in this book. The informal fallacy of equivocation, explained and warned against in Chapter 4, may arise in many different argumentative contexts, of course.
[6] Barbara W. Tuchman, *The Proud Tower* (New York: Macmillan, 1966).

Rule 3. Any term distributed in the conclusion must be distributed in the premisses.

> *To refer to **all** members of a class is to say more about that class than is said when only **some** of its members are referred to. Therefore, when the conclusion of a syllogism distributes a term that was undistributed in the premisses, it says more about that term than the premisses did. But a valid argument is one whose premisses logically entail its conclusion, and for that to be true the conclusion must not assert any more than is asserted in the premisses. A term that is distributed in the conclusion that is not distributed in the premisses is therefore a sure mark that the conclusion has gone beyond its premisses, has reached too far. The fallacy is that of **illicit process.***

The conclusion may overreach with respect to either the minor term (its subject), or the major term (its predicate). So there are two different forms of illicit process, and different names have been given to the two formal fallacies involved. They are

Illicit process of the major term ("an illicit major"), and
Illicit process of the minor term ("an illicit minor").

To illustrate the first of these, consider this syllogism:

All dogs are mammals.
No cats are dogs.
Therefore no cats are mammals.

The reasoning is obviously bad, but where does the mistake lie? It lies in the conclusion's assertion about *all* mammals, saying that all of them fall outside the class of cats. But the premisses make no assertion whatever about *all* mammals—so the conclusion illicitly goes beyond what the premisses assert. Since "mammals" is the major term in this syllogism, the fallacy here is that of **an illicit major.**

To illustrate the second form of illicit process, consider this syllogism:

All traditionally religious people are fundamentalists.
All traditionally religious people are opponents of abortion.
Therefore all opponents of abortion are fundamentalists.

Again we sense quickly that something is wrong with this argument, and what is wrong is this: The conclusion here makes an assertion about *all* opponents of abortion. But the premisses make no such assertion; they say nothing about *all* abortion opponents. So the conclusion here goes illicitly beyond what the premisses warrant. And in this case "opponents of abortion" is the minor term, so the fallacy is that of **an illicit minor.**

Rule 4. Avoid two negative premisses.

> *Any negative proposition (**E** or **O**) denies class inclusion; it asserts that some or all of one class is excluded from the whole of the other class. But two premisses asserting such exclusion cannot yield the linkage that the conclusion asserts, and therefore cannot yield a valid argument. The mistake is named **the fallacy of exclusive premisses.***

Understanding the mistake identified here requires some reflection. Suppose we label the minor, major, and middle terms of the syllogism *S, P* and *M*, respectively. What can two negative premises tell us about the relations of these three terms? They can tell us that *S* (the subject of the conclusion) is wholly or partially excluded from all or part of *M* (the middle term), and that *P* (the predicate of the conclusion) is wholly or partially excluded from all or part of *M. But any one of these relations may very well be established no matter how S and P are related.* The negative premises cannot tell us that *S* and *P* are related by inclusion or by exclusion, partial or complete. Two negative premises (where *M* is a term in each) simply cannot justify the assertion of *any* relationship whatever between *S* and *P.* Therefore, if both premises of a syllogism are negative, the argument must be invalid.

Rule 5. If either premiss is negative, the conclusion must be negative.

> *If the conclusion is affirmative, that is, if it asserts that one of the two classes, S or P, is wholly or partly contained in the other, it could only be inferred from premises that assert the existence of a third class that contains the first and is itself contained in the second. But class inclusion can be stated only by affirmative propositions. Therefore an affirmative conclusion can follow validly only from two affirmative premises. The mistake here is called **the fallacy of drawing an affirmative conclusion from a negative premiss.***

If an affirmative conclusion requires two affirmative premises, as has just been shown, we can know with certainty that if either of the premises is negative, the conclusion must also be negative, or the argument will not be valid.

Unlike some of the fallacies identified here, this fallacy is not common, because any argument drawing an affirmative conclusion from negative premises will be instantly recognized as highly implausible. Even an illustration of the mistake will appear strained:

No poets are accountants.
Some artists are poets.
Therefore some artists are accountants.

Immediately it will be seen that the *ex*clusion of poets and accountants, asserted by the first premiss of this syllogism, cannot justify *any* valid inference regarding the *in*clusion of artists and accountants.

Rule 6. From two universal premises no particular conclusion may be drawn.

> *In the Boolean interpretation of categorical propositions (explained in section 5.6), universal propositions (**A** and **E**) have no existential import, but particular propositions (**I** and **O**) do have such import. Wherever the Boolean interpretation is supposed, as in this book, a rule is needed that precludes passage from premises that have no existential import to a conclusion that does have such import.*

This final rule is not needed in the traditional or Aristotelian account of the categorical syllogism, because that traditional account paid no attention to the problem of existential import. However, when existential import is carefully considered, it will be clear that if the premises of an argument do not assert the existence of anything at all, the conclusion will be unwarranted when, from it, the existence of some thing may be inferred. The mistake is called **the existential fallacy.**

Here is an example of a syllogism that commits this fallacy:

All household pets are domestic animals.
No unicorns are domestic animals.
Therefore some unicorns are not household pets.

If the conclusion of this argument were the universal proposition "No unicorns are household pets," the syllogism would be perfectly valid for all. And since, under the traditional interpretation, existential import may be inferred from universal as well as from particular propositions, it would not be problematic (in that view) to say that the conclusion in the example given above is simply a "weaker" version of the conclusion we all agree is validly drawn.

But in our Boolean view, the conclusion of the example ("Some unicorns are not household pets"), because it is a particular proposition, is not just "weaker," it is very different. It is an **O** proposition, a particular proposition, and thus has an existential import that the **E** proposition ("No unicorns are household pets") cannot have. Reasoning that is acceptable under the traditional view is therefore unacceptable under the Boolean view because, from the Boolean perspective, that reasoning commits the existential fallacy—a mistake that, under the traditional interpretation, cannot be made.[7]

The six rules given here are intended to apply only to standard-form categorical syllogisms. In this realm they provide an adequate test for the validity of any argument. If a standard-form categorical syllogism violates any one of these rules it is invalid; if it conforms to all of these rules it is valid.

6.5 EXPOSITION OF THE 15 VALID FORMS OF THE CATEGORICAL SYLLOGISM

The *mood* of a syllogism is its character as determined by the forms (**A, E, I,** or **O**) of the three propositions it contains. There are 64 possible moods of the categorical syllogism; that is, 64 possible sets of three propositions: **AAA, AAI, AAE,** and so on, to . . . **EOO, OOO.**

---

[7] Another interesting consequence of the difference between the traditional and the Boolean interpretation of categorical propositions is this: On the traditional view there is a need for a rule that states the converse of Rule 5 ("If either premiss is negative, the conclusion must be negative"). The converse states simply that "If the conclusion of a valid syllogism is negative, at least one premisses must be negative." And that is indisputable, for if the conclusion is negative it denies inclusion. But affirmative premises assert inclusion. Therefore affirmative premises cannot entail a negative conclusion. But this corollary is rendered unnecessary in the Boolean interpretation, because the rule precluding the existential fallacy, (Rule 6), will, in the presence of the other rules, suffice to invalidate any syllogism with affirmative premises and a negative conclusion.

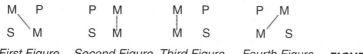

First Figure   Second Figure   Third Figure   Fourth Figure   **FIGURE 6-11**

The *figure* of a syllogism is its logical shape, as determined by the position of the middle term in its premisses. So there are four possible figures, which will be most clearly grasped if one has in mind a chart, or iconic representation, of the four possibilities, as exhibited in Figure 6-11:
It will be seen that:

- in the first figure the middle term is the subject of the major premiss and the predicate of the minor premiss;
- in the second figure the middle term is the predicate of both premisses;
- in the third figure the middle term is the subject of both premisses;
- in the fourth figure the middle term is the predicate of the major premiss and the subject of the minor premiss.

Each of the 64 moods can appear in each of the four figures. The mood and figure of a given syllogism, taken together, uniquely determine the logical form of that syllogism. Therefore there are (as noted earlier) exactly 256 (64 × 4) possible forms of the standard-form categorical syllogism.

The vast majority of these forms are not valid. We can eliminate every form that violates one or more of the syllogistic rules set forth in the preceding section. The forms that remain after this elimination are the only valid forms of the categorical syllogism. Of the 256 possible forms, there are exactly 15 forms that cannot be eliminated and thus are valid.[8]

To advance the mastery of syllogistics, classical logicians gave a unique name to every valid syllogism, each characterized completely by mood and figure. Understanding this small set of valid forms, and knowing the name of each, is very useful when putting syllogistic reasoning to work. Each name, carefully devised, contained three vowels representing (in standard-form order: major premiss, minor premiss, conclusion) the mood of the syllogism named. Where there are valid syllogisms of a given mood but in different figures, a unique name was assigned to each. Thus, for example, a syllogism of the mood **EAE** in the first figure was named **Celarent,** while a

---

[8] It should be borne in mind that here we adopt the Boolean interpretation of categorical propositions, according to which universal propositions (**A** and **E** propositions) do not have existential import. The classical interpretation of categorical propositions, according to which all the classes to which propositions refer do have members, would make acceptable some inferences that are here found to be invalid. On that older interpretation, for example, it is plausible to infer the subaltern from its corresponding superaltern—to infer an **I** proposition from its corresponding **A** proposition, and an **O** proposition from its corresponding **E** proposition. This would render plausible the claim that there are other valid syllogisms (so-called weakened syllogisms) that are not considered valid here. Compelling reasons for the rejection of that older interpretation (and hence the justification of our stricter standards for valid syllogisms) were given at some length in section 5.6.

syllogism of the mood **EAE** in the second figure, also valid, was named **Cesare.**[9]

These names had (and still have) a very practical purpose: if one knows that only certain combinations of mood and figure are valid, and can recognize by name those valid arguments, the merit of any syllogism in a given figure, or of a given mood, can be almost immediately determined. For example: the mood **AOO** is valid only in the second figure. That unique form (**AOO-2**) is known as **Baroko.**[10] One who is familiar with Baroko and able to discern it readily may be confident that a syllogism of this mood presented in any other figure may be rejected as invalid.

Classical logicians studied these forms closely, became fully familiar with their structure and their logical "feel." This elegant system, finely honed, enabled reasoners confronting syllogisms in speech or in texts to recognize immediately those that were valid, and to detect with confidence those that were not. For centuries it was common practice to defend the solidity of reasoning in progress by giving the names of the forms of the valid syllogisms being relied upon. The ability to provide these identifications even in the midst of heated oral disputes was considered a mark of learning and acumen, and it gave evidence that the chain of deductive reasoning relied upon was indeed unbroken. Once the theory of the syllogism has been fully mastered, this practical skill can be developed with profit and pleasure.

Syllogistic reasoning was so very widely employed, and so highly regarded as the most essential tool of scholarly argument, that the logical treatises of its original and greatest master, Aristotle, were venerated for more than a thousand years. His analytical account of the syllogism still carries the simple name that conveys respect and awe: the *Organon,* the *Instrument.*

As students of this remarkable logical system, our proficiency in syllogistics may be only moderate—but we will nevertheless find it useful to have before us a synoptic account of all the valid syllogisms. These 15 valid syllogisms (under the Boolean interpretation) may be divided into four groups, by figure:

---

[9] The principles that governed the construction of those traditional names, the selection and placement of consonants as well as vowels, were quite sophisticated. Some of these conventions relate to the place of the weakened syllogisms noted just above, and are therefore not acceptable on the Boolean interpretation we adopt. But some other conventions remain acceptable. For example, the letter **s** that follows the vowel **e** indicates that when that **E** proposition is converted *simpliciter,* or simply (as all **E** propositions will convert) then that syllogism reduces to, or is transformed into, another syllogism of the same mood in the first figure, which is viewed as the most basic figure. To illustrate: **Festino,** in the second figure, reduces, when its major premiss is converted simply, to **Ferio;** and **Cesare,** in the second figure, reduces to **Celarent,** and so on. The possibility of these and other reductions explains why the names of groups of syllogisms begin with the same consonant. The intricate details of the classical naming system need not be fully recounted here.

[10] Here is an example of **Baroko:**

All good mathematicians have creative intellects.
Some scholars do not have creative intellects.
Therefore some scholars are not good mathematicians.

With practice one comes to recognize the cadence of the different valid forms.

there are four valid forms in each of the first three figures, and three valid forms in the fourth figure.[11]

Here follows the exposition of the 15 valid categorical syllogisms, each with its traditional name:

THE 15 VALID FORMS OF THE STANDARD-FORM CATEGORICAL SYLLOGISM

In the first figure (in which the middle term is the subject of the major premiss and the predicate of the minor premiss):

1. **AAA–1**   **Barbara**
2. **EAE–1**   **Celarent**
3. **AII–1**   **Darii**
4. **EIO–1**   **Ferio**

In the second figure (in which the middle term is the predicate of both premisses):

5. **AEE–2**   **Camestres**
6. **EAE–2**   **Cesare**
7. **AOO–2**   **Baroko**
8. **EIO–2**   **Festino**

In the third figure (in which the middle term is the subject of both premisses):

9. **AII–3**   **Datisi**
10. **IAI–3**   **Disamis**
11. **EIO–3**   **Ferison**
12. **OAO–3**   **Bokardo**

In the fourth figure (in which the middle term is the predicate of the major premiss and the subject of the minor premiss):

13. **AEE–4**   **Camenes**
14. **IAI–4**   **Dimaris**
15. **EIO–4**   **Fresison**

Exercises

I.   Identify the rule that is broken by invalid syllogisms of the following forms, and name the fallacy that each commits.

Example:

1.   **AAA–2**

---

[11] But in the older tradition, in which reasoning from universal premisses to particular conclusions was believed correct, the number of valid syllogisms (each uniquely named) was of course greater than 15, as explained in the first footnote of this section. To illustrate: If an **I** proposition may be inferred from its corresponding **A** proposition (as we think mistaken), the valid syllogism known as *Barbara* (**AAA-1**) will have a putatively valid "weakened" sister, *Barbari* (**AAI-1**); and if an **O** proposition may be inferred from its corresponding **E** proposition (as we think mistaken), the valid syllogism known as *Camestres* (**AEE-2**) will have a putatively valid "weakened" brother, *Camestrop* (**AEO-2**).

Solution:

Any syllogism in the second figure has the middle term as predicate of both the major and the minor premiss. Thus any syllogism consisting of three **A** propositions, in the second figure, must read: All P is M; all S is M; therefore all S is P. But M is not distributed in either of the premisses in that form, and therefore it could not validly be inferred from such premisses that all S is P. Thus every syllogism of the form **AAA–2** violates the rule that the middle term must be distributed in at least one premiss, thereby committing **the fallacy of the undistributed middle.**

2.	EAA–1	3.	IAO–3
4.	OEO–4	*5.	AAA–3
6.	IAI–2	7.	OAA–3
8.	EAO–4	9.	OAI–3
*10.	IEO–1	11.	EAO–3
12.	AII–2	13.	EEE–1
14.	OAO–2	*15.	IAA–3

II. Identify the rule that is broken by any of the following syllogisms that are invalid, and name fallacy that they commit.

Example:

1. All textbooks are books intended for careful study.
   Some reference books are books intended for careful study.
   Therefore some reference books are textbooks.

Solution:

In this syllogism, "textbooks" is the major term (the predicate of the conclusion) and "reference books" is the minor term (the subject of the conclusion.) "Books intended for careful study" is therefore the middle term, and it appears as the predicate of both premisses. But in neither of the premisses is this middle term distributed, so the syllogism violates the rule that the middle term must be distributed in at least one premiss, thereby committing **the fallacy of the undistributed middle.**

2. All criminal actions are wicked deeds.
   All prosecutions for murder are criminal actions.
   Therefore all prosecutions for murder are wicked deeds.

3. No tragic actors are idiots.
   Some comedians are not idiots.
   Therefore some comedians are not tragic actors.

4. Some parrots are not pests.
   All parrots are pests.
   Therefore no pets are pests.

*5.   All perpetual motion devices are 100 percent efficient machines.
All 100 percent efficient machines are machines with frictionless
    bearings.
Therefore some machines with frictionless bearings are perpetual
    motion devices.

6.   Some good actors are not powerful athletes.
All professional wrestlers are powerful athletes.
Therefore all professional wrestlers are good actors.

7.   Some diamonds are precious stones.
Some carbon compounds are not diamonds.
Therefore some carbon compounds are not precious stones.

8.   Some diamonds are not precious stones.
Some carbon compounds are diamonds.
Therefore some carbon compounds are not precious stones.

9.   All people who are most hungry are people who eat most.
All people who eat least are people who are most hungry.
Therefore all people who eat least are people who eat most.

*10.   Some spaniels are not good hunters.
All spaniels are gentle dogs.
Therefore no gentle dogs are good hunters.

III.   Identify the rule that is broken by any of the following syllogisms that are invalid, and name the fallacy that they commit.

Example:

1.   All chocolate eclairs are fattening foods, because all chocolate eclairs are rich desserts, and some fattening foods are not rich desserts.

Solution:

In this syllogism the conclusion is affirmative ("all chocolate eclairs are fattening foods"), while one of the premisses is negative ("some fattening foods are not rich desserts"). The syllogism therefore is invalid, violating the rule that if either premiss is negative the conclusion must also be negative, thereby committing **the fallacy of affirmative conclusion from a negative premiss.**

2.   All inventors are people who see new patterns in familiar things, so all inventors are eccentrics, since all eccentrics are people who see new patterns in familiar things.

3.   Some snakes are not dangerous animals, but all snakes are reptiles, therefore some dangerous animals are not reptiles.

4.   Some foods that contain iron are toxic substances, for all fish containing mercury are foods that contain iron, and all fish containing mercury are toxic substances.

     *5. All opponents of basic economic and political changes are outspoken critics of the liberal leaders of Congress, and all right-wing extremists are opponents of basic economic and political changes. It follows that all outspoken critics of the liberal leaders of Congress are right-wing extremists.

     6. No writers of lewd and sensational articles are honest and decent citizens, but some journalists are not writers of lewd and sensational articles; consequently some journalists are honest and decent citizens.

     7. All supporters of popular government are democrats, so all supporters of popular government are opponents of the Republican Party, inasmuch as all Democrats are opponents of the Republican Party.

     8. No coal tar derivatives are nourishing foods, because all artificial dyes are coal tar derivatives, and no artificial dyes are nourishing foods.

     9. No coal tar derivatives are nourishing foods, because no coal tar derivatives are natural grain products, and all natural grain products are nourishing foods.

     *10. All people who live in London are people who drink tea, and all people who drink tea are people who like it. We may conclude, then, that all people who live in London are people who like it.

  IV. At the end of section 6.3 the ten syllogisms in group II (on p. 231–232) were to be tested using Venn diagrams. Of these ten, numbers 1, 4, 6, 7, and 10 are valid. What is the name of each of those five valid syllogisms?

Example:

    Number 1 is (**IAI–3**) *Disamis*

6.6 DEDUCTION OF THE 15 VALID FORMS OF THE CATEGORICAL SYLLOGISM

◾Advanced Material   The 15 valid forms of the categorical syllogism can be identified by eliminating from the 256 possible forms all those which cannot be valid. We can perform this elimination—*the deduction of the 15 valid forms of the syllogism*—by determining which of the possible forms violate any one of the fundamental rules of the syllogism.

It is not essential for the student of logic to undertake this detailed elimination. But those who derive satisfaction from the intricacy of analytical syllogistics are likely to find the task of eliminating the invalid syllogistic forms to be, although arduous, a pleasing challenge. Those whose chief aim is to recognize and understand the valid forms of the syllogism, as exhibited in section 6.5, may comfortably bypass this section.

The deduction will not prove easy to follow. Those who undertake to do so should have two things clearly in mind: (1) the six basic rules of the syllogism set forth in section 6.4, and (2) the pattern of the four figures of the syllogism as depicted (on p. 237) in Figure 6–11 in section 6.5.

We begin by dividing all the possible syllogistic forms into four groups, depending upon the form of the conclusion. Every conclusion will be a categorical proposition, and it is obvious that the conclusion of every possible form must be either an **A**, or an **I**, or an **E**, or an **O** proposition. There are no other alternatives. So, for each of these four cases, we will ask what characteristics a valid syllogism would need to possess. That is, we will ask what forms are excluded by one or more of the six syllogistic rules if the conclusion is an **A**, and if the conclusion is an **E**, and so on. We will take each of the four kinds of conclusion in turn.

Case 1: If the conclusion of the syllogism is an A proposition

In this case, neither premiss can be an **E** or an **O** proposition, because if either premiss is negative the conclusion would have to be negative (Rule 5). Therefore the two premisses must be **I** or **A** propositions. The minor premiss cannot be an **I** proposition because the minor term (the subject of the conclusion which is an **A**) is distributed in the conclusion, and therefore if the minor premiss were an **I** proposition, a term would be distributed in the conclusion that is not distributed in the premisses, violating Rule 3. The two premisses, major and minor, cannot be **I** and **A**, because if they were, either the distributed subject of the conclusion would not be distributed in the premiss, violating Rule 3, or the middle term of the syllogism would not be distributed in either premiss, violating Rule 2. So the two premisses (if the conclusion is an **A**) must both be **A** as well, which means that the only possible valid mood is **AAA**. But in the second figure **AAA** would again result in the middle term being distributed in neither premiss; and in both the third figure and the fourth figure **AAA** would result in a term being distributed in the conclusion that is not distributed in the premiss in which it appears. Therefore, if the conclusion of the syllogism is an **A** proposition, the only valid form it can take is **AAA** in the first figure. This valid form, **AAA–1,** is the syllogism traditionally given the name **Barbara**.

    Summary of case 1: If the syllogism has an A conclusion there is only one possibly valid form: AAA–1—Barbara.

Case 2: If the conclusion of the syllogism is an E proposition

Both the subject and the predicate of an **E** proposition are distributed, and therefore all three terms in the premisses of a syllogism having such a conclusion must be distributed, and this is possible only if one of the premisses is also an **E**. But both premisses cannot be **E** propositions, because two negative premisses are never allowed (Rule 4), and the other premiss cannot be an **O** proposition because then both premisses would also be negative. Nor can the other premiss be an **I** proposition, for if it were, a term distributed in the conclusion would then not be distributed in the premiss, violating Rule 3. So the other premiss must be an **A**, and the two premisses must be either **AE** or **EA**. The only possible moods (if the conclusion of the syllogism is an **E** proposition) would therefore be **AEE** and **EAE**.

    If the mood were **AEE,** it cannot be either in the first figure or in the third figure, since in either of those cases a term distributed in the conclusion would then not be distributed in the premisses. Therefore, the mood **AEE** is possibly valid only in the second figure, **AEE–2** (traditionally called **Camestres**), or in the fourth figure, **AEE–4** (traditionally called **Camenes**). And if the mood is **EAE** it cannot be in the third figure or in the fourth figure because again that would mean that a term distributed in the conclusion would not be distributed in the premises, which leaves as valid only the first figure, **EAE–1** (traditionally called **Celarent**), and the second figure, **EAE–2** (traditionally called **Cesare.**)

Summary of case 2: If the syllogism has an E conclusion, there are only four possibly valid forms: AEE–2, AEE–4, EAE–1, and EAE–2—Camestres, Camenes, Celarent, and Cesare, respectively.

Case 3: If the conclusion is an I proposition

In this case, neither premiss can be an **E** or an **O**, since if either premiss is negative the conclusion must be negative. The two premisses cannot both be **A**, because a syllogism with a particular conclusion cannot have two universal premisses (Rule 6). Neither can both premisses be **I**, because the middle term must be distributed in at least one premiss (Rule 2). So the premisses must be either **AI** or **IA**, and therefore the only possible moods with an **I** conclusion are **AII** and **IAI.**

AII is not possibly valid in the second figure or in the fourth figure because the middle term must be distributed in at least one premiss. The only valid forms remaining for the mood **AII**, therefore, are **AII–1** (traditionally called **Darii**) and **AII–3** (traditionally called **Datisi**). If the mood is **IAI**, it cannot be **IAI–1** or **IAI–2** since they also would violate the rule that requires the middle term to be distributed in at least one premiss. This leaves as valid only **IAI–3** (traditionally called **Disamis**), and **IAI–4** (traditionally called **Dimaris**).

Summary of case 3: If the syllogism has an I conclusion there are only four possibly valid forms: AII–1, AII–3, IAI–3, and IAI–4—Darii, Datisi, Disamis, and Dimaris, respectively.

Case 4: If the conclusion is an O proposition

In this case the major premiss cannot be an **I** proposition, because any term distributed in the conclusion must be distributed in the premisses. So the major premiss must be either an **A** or an **E** or an **O** proposition.

Suppose the major premiss were an **A**. In that case, the minor premiss could not be either an **A** or an **E**, because two universal premisses are not permitted when the conclusion (an **O**) is particular. Neither could the minor premiss then be an **I**, because if it were either, the middle term would not be distributed at all (a violation of Rule 2), or a term distributed in the conclusion would not be distributed in the premisses. So, if the major premiss were an **A**, the minor premiss would have to be an **O**, yielding the mood **AOO**. But in the fourth figure, **AOO** is not possibly valid, since in that case the middle term would not be distributed, and in the first figure and the third figure **AOO** is not possibly valid either, since that would result in terms being distributed in the conclusion that were not distributed in the premisses. For the mood **AOO** the only possibly valid form remaining, if the major premiss is an **A**, is therefore in the second figure, **AOO–2** (traditionally called **Baroko**).

But suppose (if the conclusion is an **O**) that the major premiss were an **E**. In that case, the minor premiss could not be either an **E** or an **O**, since two negative premisses are not permitted. Nor could the minor premiss be an **A**, because two universal premisses are precluded if the conclusion is particular (Rule 6). This leaves only the mood **EIO**—and this mood is valid in all four figures, traditionally known as **Ferio (EIO–1), Festino (EIO–2), Ferison (EIO–3),** and **Fresison (EIO–4).**

Finally, suppose (if the conclusion is an **O**) that the major premiss were also an **O** proposition. Then, again, the minor premiss could not be an **E** or an **O**, because two negative premisses are forbidden. And the minor premiss could not be an **I**, because then the middle term would not be distributed, or a term that is distributed in the conclusion would not be distributed in the premisses. Therefore, if the major premiss is an **O**, the minor premiss must be an **A**, and the mood must be **OAO**. But **OAO–1** is eliminated, because in that case the middle term would not be distributed. **OAO–2** and **OAO–4** are also eliminated, because in both a term distributed in the conclusion would then not be distributed in the premisses. This leaves as valid only **OAO–3** (traditionally known as **Bokardo**).

Summary of case 4: If the syllogism has an O conclusion, there are only six possibly valid forms: AOO–2, EIO–1, EIO–2, EIO–3, EIO–4, and OAO–3— Baroko, Ferio, Festino, Ferison, Fresison, and Bokardo.

This analysis has demonstrated, by elimination, that there are exactly 15 valid forms of the categorical syllogism: 1 if the conclusion is an **A** proposition, 4 if the conclusion is an **E** proposition, 4 if the conclusion is an **I** proposition, and 6 if the conclusion is an **O** proposition. Of these 15, 4 are in the first figure, 4 in the second figure, 4 in the third figure, and 3 in the fourth figure. This completes the deduction of the 15 valid forms of the standard-form categorical syllogism.

Exercises

For students who take delight in the intricacies of analytical syllogistics, here follow some theoretical questions whose answers can all be derived from the systematic application of the six rules of the syllogism set forth in 6.4. But answering them will be much easier after one has mastered the deduction of the valid syllogistic forms recounted in 6.6. Be sure to consider all possible cases.

Example:

1. Can any standard-form categorical syllogism be valid that contains exactly three terms, each of which is distributed in both of its occurrences?

Solution

No, such a syllogism cannot be valid. If each of the three terms were distributed in both of its occurrences, all three of its propositions would have to be **E** propositions, and the mood of the syllogism would thus be **EEE**, which violates Rule 4, which forbids two negative premisses.

2. In what mood or moods, if any, can a first figure standard-form categorical syllogism with a particular conclusion be valid?

3. In what figure or figures, if any, can the premisses of a valid standard-form categorical syllogism distribute both major and minor terms?

4. In what figure or figures, if any, can a valid standard-form categorical syllogism have two particular premisses?

*5.   In what figure or figures, if any, can a valid standard-form categorical syllogism have only one term distributed, and that one only once?

6.   In what mood or moods, if any, can a valid standard-form categorical syllogism have just two terms distributed, each one twice?

7.   In what mood or moods, if any, can a valid standard-form categorical syllogism have two affirmative premises and a negative conclusion?

8.   In what figure or figures, if any, can a valid standard-form categorical syllogism have a particular premiss and a universal conclusion?

9.   In what mood or moods, if any, can a second figure standard-form categorical syllogism with a universal conclusion be valid?

*10.   In what figure or figures, if any, can a valid standard-form categorical syllogism have its middle term distributed in both premisses?

11.   Can a valid standard-form categorical syllogism have a term distributed in a premiss that appears undistributed in the conclusion? ■

Summary of Chapter 6

In Chapter 6, we have examined the standard-form categorical syllogism: its elements, its forms, its validity, and the rules governing its proper use.

In section 6.1, the major, minor, and middle terms of a syllogism were identified:

- **Major term:** predicate of the conclusion
- **Minor term:** subject of the conclusion
- **Middle term:** third term appearing in both premisses but not in the conclusion.

We identified major and minor premisses as those containing the major and minor terms, respectively. We specified that a categorical syllogism is in **standard form** when its propositions appear in precisely this order: **major premiss first, minor premiss second, and conclusion last.**

We also explained in section 6.1 how the mood and figure of a syllogism are determined.

The **mood of a syllogism** is determined by the three letters identifying the types of its three propositions, **A, E, I,** or **O.** There are 64 possible different moods.

The **figure of a syllogism** is determined by the position of the middle term in its premisses. The four possible figures are described and named thus:

- **First Figure:** The middle term is **the subject term of the major premiss and the predicate term of the minor premiss.**
  Schematically: $M–P, S–M,$ therefore $S–P.$
- **Second Figure:** The middle term is **the predicate term of both premisses.**
  Schematically: $P–M, S–M,$ therefore $S–P.$
- **Third Figure:** The middle term is **the subject term of both premisses.**
  Schematically: $M–P, M–S,$ therefore $S–P.$

- **Fourth Figure:** The middle term is **the predicate term of the major premiss and the subject term of the minor premiss.**
  Schematically: *P–M, M–S, therefore S–P.*

In section 6.2, we explained how the **mood and figure** of a standard-form categorical syllogism **jointly determine its logical form.** Since each of the 64 moods may appear in all four figures, there are exactly 256 standard-form categorical syllogisms, of which only a few are valid.

In section 6.3, we explained the **Venn diagram technique for testing the validity of syllogisms,** using overlapping circles appropriately marked or shaded to exhibit the meaning of the premisses.

In section 6.4, we explained the **six essential rules for standard-form syllogisms** and **named the fallacy** that results when each of these rules is broken:

- **Rule 1.** A standard-form categorical syllogism must contain exactly three terms, each of which is used in the same sense throughout the argument.
  Violation: Fallacy of **four terms.**
- **Rule 2.** In a valid standard-form categorical syllogism, the middle term must be distributed in at least one premiss.
  Violation: Fallacy of **undistributed middle.**
- **Rule 3.** In a valid standard-form categorical syllogism, if either term is distributed in the conclusion, then it must be distributed in the premisses.
  Violation: Fallacy of the **illicit major,** or fallacy of the **illicit minor.**
- **Rule 4.** No standard-form categorical syllogism having two negative premisses is valid.
  Violation: Fallacy of **exclusive premisses.**
- **Rule 5.** If either premiss of a valid standard-form categorical syllogism is negative, the conclusion must be negative.
  Violation: Fallacy of **drawing an affirmative conclusion from a negative premiss.**
- **Rule 6.** No valid standard-form categorical syllogism with a particular conclusion can have two universal premisses.
  Violation: **Existential fallacy.**

In section 6.5, we presented an **exposition of the 15 valid forms** of the categorical syllogism, identifying their moods and figures, and explaining their traditional Latin names:

AAA–1 *(Barbara)*; **EAE–1** *(Celarent)*; **AII–1** *(Darii)*; **EIO–1** *(Ferio)*; **AEE–2** *(Camestres)*; **EAE–2** *(Cesare)*; **AOO–2** *(Baroko)*; **EIO–2** *(Festino)*; **AII–3** *(Datisi)*; **IAI–3** *(Disamis)*; **EIO–3** *(Ferison)*; **OAO–3** *(Bokardo)*; **AEE–4** *(Camenes)*; **IAI–4** *(Dimaris)*; **EIO–4** *(Fresison)*.

In section 6.6, we presented the **deduction of the 15 valid forms** of the categorical syllogism, demonstrating, through a process of elimination, that only these 15 forms can avoid all violations of the six basic rules of the syllogism.

The value, therefore, of the syllogistic form and of the rules
for using it correctly does not consist in their being the
form and the rules according to which our reasonings are
necessarily, or even usually, made, but in their furnishing
us with a mode in which those reasonings may always be
represented and which is admirably calculated, if they are
inconclusive, to bring their inconclusiveness to light.
—John Stuart Mill

CHAPTER 7

ARGUMENTS IN ORDINARY LANGUAGE

7.1 SYLLOGISTIC ARGUMENTS IN ORDINARY LANGUAGE

Standard-form categorical syllogisms, examined in the previous chapter, are often stilted and artificial. They may be thought of as being "chemically pure," free from all obscurities and irrelevancies—while, of course, in ordinary language arguments do not always occur so neatly ordered and so perfectly refined. The more general term **syllogistic argument** we introduce to refer to any argument that either *is* a standard-form categorical syllogism or *can be reformulated as* a standard-form categorical syllogism without any loss or change of meaning.

Syllogistic arguments are fairly common, and we want to be able to test their validity. But usually they appear in forms looser than the standard form, and therefore the tests for validity presented in the preceding chapter—the Venn diagram technique and the rules for categorical syllogisms—cannot be directly applied to many syllogistic arguments. So varied are the shapes taken on by syllogistic arguments in ordinary language that we could not devise special logical tests for all of them without a logical apparatus that would be hopelessly complicated. Therefore, to determine the validity of many syllogistic arguments, the wisest course often is to *reformulate* the argument as a standard-form categorical syllogism, if we can do so without changing its meaning. This process is called **reduction to standard form,** or **translation to standard form,** and the resulting syllogism is called a **standard-form translation** of the given syllogistic argument.

It will be seen that two things are required to evaluate syllogistic arguments as they appear in ordinary language. First, we need easily applicable *tests* by which we can distinguish valid from invalid standard-form categor-ical syllogisms; these (the diagrams and rules described in the preceding chapter) we already have. Second, we need *techniques for translating* syllogis-tic arguments of *any* form into *standard* form. When these techniques have been mastered, we can evaluate any syllogistic argument by first translating it into standard form, and then applying to its standard-form translation one of the tests explained earlier: the rules governing valid syllogisms or the Venn diagram method.

To describe the techniques for translation into standard form, it will be helpful first to distinguish the different ways in which a syllogistic argument in ordinary language may deviate from a standard-form categorical syllogism. There are essentially three such deviations:

1.   The *order* in which the premisses and conclusion happen to be stated may not be that of the standard-form syllogism. This is a minor problem, eas-ily remedied, since if the order of the statements is the only deviation, the three propositions may readily be reordered.

2.   *The component propositions* of the argument in ordinary language *may ap-pear to involve more than three terms,* although that appearance may prove deceptive.

3.   *The component propositions* of the syllogism in ordinary language *may not all be standard-form propositions.*

In the second and third of these deviant patterns, a proper translation of the syllogism into standard form often is possible, and the techniques for such translation are dealt with in the sections that follow.

7.2 REDUCING THE NUMBER OF TERMS IN A SYLLOGISTIC ARGUMENT

When an argument in ordinary language has an apparently syllogistic form yet also appears to involve more than three terms, the argument ought not to be immediately rejected as invalid through committing the fallacy of four terms. Frequently it is possible to translate such an argument into a standard-form syllogism that is logically equivalent to it, that contains only three terms, and that is perfectly valid. Two techniques for accomplishing this goal must be described.

(1) ELIMINATING SYNONYMS. Before attempting to apply Venn diagrams or the syllogistic rules to an argument in ordinary language, we should eliminate the synonymous terms occurring in it. Thus, for example, the argument

No wealthy persons are vagrants.
All lawyers are rich people.
Therefore no attorneys are tramps.

contains a synonym for "wealthy," a synonym for "lawyers," and a synonym for "vagrants." When those synonyms are eliminated, the argument translates into

> No wealthy persons are vagrants.
> All lawyers are wealthy persons.
> Therefore no lawyers are vagrants.

In this standard form **EAE–1** (*Celarent*) the argument is easily seen to be valid.

(2) ELIMINATING COMPLEMENTS. Sometimes, however, the simple elimination of synonyms will not suffice. Consider the following argument, all of whose propositions are standard-form categorical propositions:

> All mammals are warm-blooded animals.
> No lizards are warm-blooded animals.
> Therefore all lizards are nonmammals.

Were we to apply to this argument the six rules explained in Chapter 6 we should judge it to be invalid on more than one count. For one thing, it contains four terms: "mammals," "warm-blooded animals," "lizards," and "nonmammals." And for another, it has an affirmative conclusion drawn from a negative premiss. But it is in fact perfectly valid. Because it has *four* terms it is not a standard-form categorical syllogism, and the rules are not directly applicable to it. To test it by the syllogistic rules presented in Chapter 6, we must first translate it into standard form. This we can easily do, because two of its four terms ("mammals" and "nonmammals") are complements of one another. We can reduce the number of terms in this syllogism to three simply by obverting the conclusion—and the result is a standard-form translation of the original argument:

> All mammals are warm-blooded animals.
> No lizards are warm-blooded animals.
> Therefore no lizards are mammals.

which is logically equivalent to it, having identically the same premisses and a logically equivalent conclusion. This standard-form translation conforms to all the syllogistic rules and is thus known to be valid. Its form is **AEE–2,** *Camestres.*

The latter is not the only standard-form translation of the given argument, although it is the most easily obtainable. A different (but logically equivalent) standard-form translation can be obtained by taking the contrapositive of the first premiss and obverting the second, leaving the conclusion unchanged. This would yield

> All non (warm-blooded animals) are nonmammals.
> All lizards are non (warm-blooded animals).
> Therefore all lizards are nonmammals.

which, having the form **AAA–I,** *Barbara,* also is valid by the rules. There is no unique standard-form translation of a given syllogistic argument, but if any one is valid, all of the others must be valid also.

Any syllogistic argument containing four terms can be reduced to standard form (or translated into a logically equivalent standard-form categorical syllogism) *if* one of its four terms is the complement of one of the other three. And any containing five (or six) terms can be reduced to standard form if two (or three) of its terms are the complements of two (or three) of the others. These reductions all are effected by means of valid immediate inferences: conversion, obversion, and contraposition, explained earlier in section 5.5.

Syllogistic arguments whose constituent propositions are all in standard form may contain as many as half-a-dozen different terms and may require the drawing of more than one immediate inference for their reduction to standard form. An example of a six-term syllogistic argument that is perfectly valid is the following:

No nonresidents are citizens.
All noncitizens are nonvoters.
Therefore all voters are residents.

There are alternative ways of reducing this argument to a standard-form syllogism. One method, perhaps the most natural and obvious, requires the use of all three types of immediate inference. Converting and then obverting the first premiss and taking the contrapositive of the second premiss yields the standard-form categorical syllogism:

All citizens are residents.
All voters are citizens.
Therefore all voters are residents.

which is also in *Barbara* and easily proved valid by either of the methods set forth in Chapter 6.

Exercises

Translate the following syllogistic arguments into standard form, and test their validity by using either Venn Diagrams or the syllogistic rules set forth in Chapter 6.

Example:

1. Some preachers are persons of unfailing vigor. No preachers are nonintellectuals. Therefore some intellectuals are persons of unfailing vigor.

Solution:

This may be translated into: Some preachers are persons of unfailing vigor. (Some *P* is *V*.) All preachers are intellectuals. (By obversion: All *P* is *I*.) Therefore some intellectuals are persons of unfailing vigor. (Some *I* is *V*.) Exhibited on a Venn Diagram, this syllogism is shown to be valid:

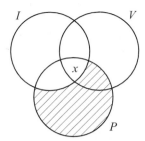

2. Some metals are rare and costly substances, but no welder's materials are nonmetals; hence some welder's materials are rare and costly substances.

3. Some Asian nations were nonbelligerents, since all belligerents were allies either of Germany or Britain, and some Asian nations were not allies of either Germany or Britain.

4. Some nondrinkers are athletes, because no drinkers are persons in perfect physical condition, and some people in perfect physical condition are not nonathletes.

*5. All things inflammable are unsafe things, so all things that are safe are nonexplosives, since all explosives are flammable things.

6. All worldly goods are changeable things, for no worldly goods are things immaterial, and no material things are unchangeable things.

7. All those who are neither members nor guests of members are those who are excluded; therefore no nonconformists are either members or guests of members, for all those who are included are conformists.

8. All mortals are imperfect beings, and no humans are immortals, whence it follows that all perfect beings are nonhumans.

9. All things present are nonirritants; therefore no irritants are invisible objects, because all visible objects are absent things.

*10. All useful things are objects no more than six feet long, since all difficult things to store are useless things, and no objects over six feet long are easy things to store.

7.3 TRANSLATING CATEGORICAL PROPOSITIONS INTO STANDARD FORM

We noted in section 7.1 that syllogistic arguments in ordinary language may deviate from standard-form categorical syllogisms not only because they may appear to contain more than three terms (as discussed in section 7.2), but also because the component propositions of the syllogism in ordinary language may not all be standard-form propositions. **A, E, I,** and **O** propositions are clearly somewhat stilted, and many syllogistic arguments in everyday life contain nonstandard-form propositions. To reduce these arguments to standard form requires that their constituent propositions be translated into standard form. But ordinary language is too rich and multiform to permit a complete set of rules for such translation. In every case what is crucial is our ability to *understand* the given nonstandard-form proposition, so that we can reformulate it without losing or changing its meaning.

Although no complete set of rules can be given, we can describe a number of conventional techniques that often prove useful in dealing with propositions of certain sorts. These methods—we will describe nine of them in this section—must be regarded as guides rather than rules, that is, as *techniques* for dealing with nonstandard propositions of certain describable kinds.

1.   **SINGULAR PROPOSITIONS.** Some propositions affirm or deny that a specific individual or object belongs to a given class; for example, "Socrates is a philosopher," and "This table is not an antique." These are called *singular propositions*. Such propositions do not affirm or deny the inclusion of one class in another (as standard-form propositions do), but we can nevertheless *interpret* a singular proposition as a proposition dealing with classes and their interrelations. We do this in the following way.

To every individual object there corresponds a unique *unit class* (one-membered class) whose only member is that object itself. Then to assert that an object s belongs to a class P is logically equivalent to asserting that the unit class S containing just that object s is wholly included in the class P. And to assert that an object s does *not* belong to a class P is logically equivalent to asserting that the unit class S containing just that object s is wholly excluded from the class P.

It is customary to make this interpretation automatically, without any notational adjustment. Thus it is customary to take any affirmative singular proposition of the form "s is P" as if it were already expressed as the logically equivalent **A** proposition "All S is P," and we similarly understand any negative singular proposition "s is not P" as an alternative formulation of the logically equivalent **E** proposition "No S is P"—in each case understanding S to designate the unit class whose only member is the object s. Thus no explicit translations have been provided for singular propositions; traditionally they have been classified as **A** and **E** propositions as they stand. As Kant remarked, "Logicians are justified in saying that, in the employment of judgments in syllogisms, singular judgments can be treated like those that are universal."[1]

---

[1] Immanuel Kant, *Critique of Pure Reason*, 1787, The Analytic of Concepts, Chapter 1, section 2. More than a century later Bertrand Russell presented a very different interpretation of singular propositions and universal propositions, and he later argued (in *My Philosophical Development*, 1959, p. 66) that logic "cannot get far" until the two forms are seen to be "completely different" because the one (the singular) attributes a predicate to a named subject, while the other (the universal) expresses a relation between two predicates. Russell's interpretation had by that time become central to the theory of quantification in modern symbolic logic, discussed at length in Chapter 10; Kant's observation pertained to the use of singular propositions in traditional syllogisms, which he knew to be very powerful logical instruments.

The situation, however, is not quite so simple. Bear in mind that, while particular propositions have existential import, universal propositions do not. Using this Boolean interpretation (for reasons explained in section 5.6), we find that if singular propositions are treated mechanically as **A** and **E** propositions in syllogistic arguments, and those arguments have their validity checked by Venn diagrams or the rules set forth in Chapter 6, serious difficulties arise.

In some cases, obviously valid two-premiss arguments containing singular propositions translate into valid categorical syllogisms, as when

All *H* is *M*.	goes into the obviously valid	All *H* is *M*.
s is an *H*.	**AAA–1** categorical syllogism in Barbara	All *S* is *H*.
∴ *s* is an *M*.		∴ All *S* is *M*.

But in other cases obviously valid two-premiss arguments containing singular propositions translate into categorical syllogisms that are *invalid*, as when

s is *M*.	goes into the invalid	All *S* is *M*.
s is *H*.	**AAI–3** categorical syllogism	All *S* is *H*.
∴ Some *H* is *M*.		∴ Some *H* is *M*.

which commits the existential fallacy, violating Rule 6.

On the other hand, if we translate singular propositions into particular propositions, there is the same kind of difficulty. In some cases obviously valid two-premiss arguments containing singular propositions translate into *valid* categorical syllogisms, as when

All *H* is *M*.	goes into the obviously valid	All *H* is *M*.
s is an *H*.	**AII–1** categorical syllogism in Darii	Some *S* is *H*.
∴ *s* is an *M*.		∴ Some *S* is *M*.

But in other cases obviously valid two-premiss arguments containing singular propositions translate into categorical syllogisms that are *invalid*, as when

s is *M*.	goes into the invalid	Some *S* is *M*.
s is *H*.	**III–3** categorical syllogism	Some *S* is *H*.
∴ Some *H* is *M*.		∴ Some *H* is *M*.

which commits the fallacy of the undistributed middle, violating Rule 2.

The difficulty arises from the fact that a singular proposition contains more information than is contained in any single one of the four standard-form categorical propositions. If "*s* is *P*" is construed as "All *S* is *P*," then what is lost is the existential import of the singular proposition, the fact that *S* is not empty. But if "*s* is *P*" is construed as "Some *S* is *P*," then what is lost is the universal aspect of the singular proposition, which distributes its subject term, the fact that *all S* is *P*.

The solution to the difficulty is to construe singular propositions as conjunctions of standard-form categorical propositions. An affirmative singular proposition is equivalent to the conjunction of the related **A** and

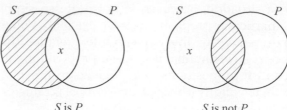

FIGURE 7-1   *S* is *P*   *S* is not *P*

I categorical propositions. Thus "*s* is *P*" is equivalent to "All *S* is *P*" *and* "Some *S* is *P*." A negative singular proposition is equivalent to the conjunction of the related **E** and **O** categorical propositions. Thus "*s* is not *P*" is equivalent to "No *S* is *P*" *and* "Some *S* is not *P*." Venn diagrams for affirmative and negative singular propositions are shown in Figure 7-1. And in applying the syllogistic rules to evaluate a syllogistic argument containing singular propositions, we must take account of *all* the information contained in those singular propositions, both distribution and existential import.

Provided that we keep in mind the existential import of singular propositions when we invoke the syllogistic rules or apply Venn Diagrams to test the validity of syllogistic arguments, it is acceptable practice to regard singular propositions as universal (**A** or **E**) propositions.

2. **CATEGORICAL PROPOSITIONS THAT HAVE ADJECTIVES OR ADJECTIVAL PHRASES AS PREDICATES, RATHER THAN SUBSTANTIVES OR CLASS TERMS.** For example, "Some flowers are beautiful" and "No warships are available for active duty" are categorical propositions, and yet they must be translated into standard-form categorical propositions; they deviate from standard form only in that their predicates "beautiful" and "available for active duty" designate *attributes* rather than classes. But every attribute *determines* a class, the class of things having that attribute, so to every such proposition corresponds a logically equivalent proposition that is in standard form. The two examples cited correspond to the **I** and **E** propositions "Some flowers are beauties" and "No warships are things available for active duty." Where a categorical proposition is in standard form except that it has an adjectival predicate instead of a predicate term, the translation into standard form is made by replacing the adjectival predicate with a term designating the class of all objects of which the adjective may truly be predicated.

3. **CATEGORICAL PROPOSITIONS WHOSE MAIN VERBS ARE OTHER THAN THE STANDARD-FORM COPULA "TO BE."** Examples of this very common type are "All people seek recognition" and "Some people drink Greek wine." The usual method of translating such a statement into standard form is to regard all of it, except the subject term and the quantifier, as naming a class-defining characteristic. Those words can then be replaced by a term designating the class determined by that class-defining characteristic and may be linked to the subject with a standard copula. Thus the two examples given translate into

the standard-form categorical propositions "All people are seekers of recognition" and "Some people are Greek-wine drinkers."

4. **STATEMENTS IN WHICH THE STANDARD-FORM INGREDIENTS ARE ALL PRESENT BUT NOT ARRANGED IN STANDARD-FORM ORDER.** Two examples are "Racehorses are all thoroughbreds" and "All is well that ends well." In such cases, we first decide which is the subject term and then rearrange the words to express a standard-form categorical proposition. Such translations are usually quite straightforward. It is clear that the preceding two statements translate into the **A** propositions "All racehorses are thoroughbreds" and "All things that end well are things that are well."

5. **CATEGORICAL PROPOSITIONS WHOSE QUANTITIES ARE INDICATED BY WORDS OTHER THAN THE STANDARD-FORM QUANTIFIERS "ALL," "NO," AND "SOME."** Statements beginning with the words "every" and "any" are easily translated. The propositions "Every dog has its day" and "Any contribution will be appreciated" reduce to "All dogs are creatures that have their days" and "All contributions are things that are appreciated." Similar to "every" and "any" are "everything" and "anything." Paralleling these, but clearly restricted to classes of persons, are "everyone," "anyone," "whoever," "whosoever," "who," "one who," and the like. These should occasion no difficulty.

The grammatical particles "a" and "an" may also serve to indicate quantity, but whether they are being used to mean "all" or "some" depends largely on the context. Thus "A bat is a mammal" and "An elephant is a pachyderm" are reasonably interpreted as meaning "All bats are mammals" and "All elephants are pachyderms." But "A bat flew in the window" and "An elephant escaped" quite clearly do not refer to all bats or all elephants; they are properly reduced to "Some bats are creatures that flew in the window" and "Some elephants are creatures that escaped."

The particle "the" may be used to refer either to a particular individual or to all the members of a class. But there is little danger of ambiguity here, for such a statement as "The whale is a mammal" translates in almost any context into the **A** proposition "All whales are mammals," whereas the singular proposition "The first president was a military hero" is already in standard form as an **A** proposition (a singular proposition having existential import) as discussed in the first subparagraph of this section.[2]

Although affirmative statements beginning with "every" and "any" are translated into "All *S* is *P*," negative statements beginning with "not every" and "not any" are quite different. Their translations are much less

---

[2] But in some contexts the article "the" is deliberately omitted to achieve desired ambiguity. When United Nations Resolution 242 was adopted, calling for the return of "territory" captured by Israel in the Six-Day War in 1967, it was formally agreed that the English version of the Resolution would be authoritative, because the Resolution when expressed in French would require the definite article (*le territoire*), of which the English translation is "the territory," meaning *all* the territory captured, which is precisely what the agreed-upon English version carefully refrains from saying. The omission of the definite article in English can be logically significant.

obvious and require great care. Thus, for example, "Not every *S* is *P*" means that *some S is not P*, whereas "Not any *S* is *P*" means that *no S is P*.

6. **EXCLUSIVE PROPOSITIONS.** Categorical propositions involving the words "only" or "none but" are often called "exclusive propositions" because in general they assert that the predicate applies exclusively to the subject named. Examples of such usages are "Only citizens can vote" and "None but the brave deserve the fair." The first translates into the standard-form categorical proposition "All those who can vote are citizens," and the second into the standard-form categorical proposition "All those who deserve the fair are those who are brave." Propositions beginning with "only" or "none but" usually translate into **A** propositions using this general rule: reverse the subject and the predicate, and replace the "only" with "all." Thus "Only *S* is *P*" and "None but *S*'s are *P*'s" are usually understood to express "All *P* is *S*."

However, there are some contexts in which "only" and "none but" are used to convey some further meaning. "Only *S* is *P*" or "None but *S*'s are *P*'s" may suggest either that "All *S* is *P*" or that "Some *S* is *P*." This is not always the case, however. Where context helps to determine meaning, attention must be paid to it, of course. But in the absence of such additional information, the translations first suggested are adequate.

7. **CATEGORICAL PROPOSITIONS THAT CONTAIN NO WORDS AT ALL TO INDICATE QUANTITY.** Two examples are "Dogs are carnivorous" and "Children are present." Where there is no quantifier, what the sentence is intended to express may be doubtful. We may be able to determine its meaning only by examining the context in which it occurs, and that examination usually will clear up our doubts. In the first example it is very probable that "Dogs are carnivorous" refers to *all* dogs, and is to be translated as "All dogs are carnivores." In the second example, on the other hand, it is plain that only *some* children are referred to, and thus the standard-form translation of "Children are present" is "Some children are beings who are present."

8. **PROPOSITIONS THAT DO NOT RESEMBLE STANDARD-FORM CATEGORICAL PROPOSITIONS AT ALL, BUT CAN BE TRANSLATED INTO STANDARD FORM.** Some examples are "Not all children believe in Santa Claus," "There are white elephants," "There are no pink elephants," and "Nothing is both round and square." On reflection these propositions will be seen to be logically equivalent to, and therefore to translate into, the following standard-form propositions: "Some children are not believers in Santa Claus," "Some elephants are white things," "No elephants are pink things," and "No round objects are square objects."

9. **EXCEPTIVE PROPOSITIONS.** Some examples of these are "All except employees are eligible," "All but employees are eligible," and "Employees alone are not eligible." Translating exceptive propositions into standard form is somewhat complicated, because propositions of this kind (much like singular propositions) make *two* assertions rather than one. Each of the logically equivalent examples just given asserts not

merely that *all nonemployees are eligible* but also (in the usual context) that *no employees are eligible.* Where "employees" is abbreviated to S and "eligible persons" to P, these two propositions can be written as "All non-S is P" and "No S is P." These are clearly independent and together assert that S and P are complementary classes.

Each of these exceptive propositions is *compound* and therefore cannot be translated into a single standard-form categorical proposition. Rather, each must be translated into an explicit conjunction of two standard-form categoricals. Thus the three illustrative propositions about eligibility translate identically into "All nonemployees are eligible persons, and no employees are eligible persons."

It should be noted that some arguments depend for their validity upon numerical or quasi-numerical information that cannot be put into standard form. Such arguments may have constituent propositions that mention quantity more specifically than standard-form propositions do, usually by the use of quantifiers such as "one," "two," "three," "many," "a few," "most," and so on. Where such specific quantitative information is critical to the validity of the arguments in which it is mentioned, the arguments themselves are *asyllogistic* and therefore require a more complicated analysis than that contained in the simple theory of the categorical syllogism. Yet some quasi-numerical quantifiers occur in arguments that do lend themselves to syllogistic analysis. These include "almost all," "not quite all," "all but a few," and "almost everyone." Propositions in which these phrases appear as quantifiers may be treated like the explicitly exceptive propositions just described. Thus the following exceptive propositions with quasi-numerical quantifiers are also compound: "Almost all students were at the dance," "Not quite all students were at the dance," "All but a few students were at the dance," and "Only some students were at the dance." Each of these *affirms* that *some students were at the dance* and *denies* that *all students were at the dance.* The quasi-numerical information they present is irrelevant from the point of view of syllogistic inference, and all are translated indifferently as "Some students are persons who were at the dance, and some students are not persons who were at the dance."

Because exceptive propositions are not categorical propositions but conjunctions, arguments containing them are not syllogistic arguments as we are using that term. But they may nevertheless be susceptible to syllogistic analysis and appraisal. How an argument containing an exceptive proposition should be tested depends on the exceptive proposition's position in the argument. If it is a premiss, then the argument may have to be given two separate tests. For example, consider the argument

> Everyone who saw the game was at the dance.
> Not quite all the students were at the dance.
> So some students didn't see the game.

Its first premiss and its conclusion are categorical propositions, which are easily translated into standard form. But its second premiss is an exceptive proposition, not simple but compound. To discover whether its premises imply its conclusion, one first tests the syllogism composed of the first premiss of the given argument, the first half of its second premiss, and its conclusion. In standard form, we have

> All persons who saw the game are persons who were at the dance.
> Some students are persons who were at the dance.
> Therefore some students are not persons who saw the game.

The standard-form categorical syllogism is of form AIO–2 and it commits the fallacy of the undistributed middle, violating Rule 2. But the original argument is not yet proved to be invalid, because the syllogism just tested contains only part of the premisses of the original argument. One now has the task of testing the categorical syllogism composed of the first premiss and the conclusion of the original argument together with the second half of the second premiss. In standard form we then get a very different argument:

> All persons who saw the game are persons who were at the dance.
> Some students are not persons who were at the dance.
> Therefore some students are not persons who saw the game.

This is a standard-form categorical syllogism in *Baroko,* **AOO–2,** and it is easily shown to be valid. Hence the original argument is valid, for the conclusion is the same, and the premisses of the original argument include the premisses of this valid standard-form syllogism. Thus to test the validity of an argument, one of whose premisses is an exceptive proposition, may require the testing of two different standard-form categorical syllogisms.

If the premisses of an argument are both categorical propositions, and its conclusion is exceptive, then we know it to be invalid, for although the two categorical premisses may imply one or the other half of the compound conclusion, they cannot imply them both. Finally, if an argument contains exceptive propositions as both premisses and conclusion, all possible syllogisms constructable out of the original argument may have to be tested if we are to determine its validity. Enough has been explained to enable the student to cope with such situations.

It is important to acquire facility in translating the many varieties of nonstandard-form propositions into standard form, for the tests of validity that we have developed—Venn diagrams and the syllogistic rules—can be applied directly only to standard-form categorical syllogisms.

Exercises

Translate the following into standard-form categorical propositions.

Example:

1. Roses are fragrant.

   Standard-form translation: All roses are fragrant things.

2. Orchids are not fragrant.

3. Many a person has lived to regret a misspent youth.

4. Not everyone worth meeting is worth having as a friend.

*5. If it's a Junko, it's the best that money can buy.

6. If it isn't a real Havana, it isn't a Ropo.

7. Nothing is both safe and exciting.

8. Only brave people have ever won the Congressional Medal of Honor.

9. Good counselors are not universally appreciated.

*10. He sees not his shadow who faces the sun.

11. To hear her sing is an inspiration.

12. He who takes the sword shall perish by the sword.

13. Only members can use the front door.

14. Nobody doesn't like Sara Lee.

*15. The Young Turks support no candidate of the Old Guard.

16. All styles are good, except the tiresome.

17. They also serve who only stand and wait.

18. Happy indeed is she who knows her own limitations.

19. A thing of beauty is a joy forever.

*20. He prayeth well who loveth well.

21. All that glitters is not gold.

22. None think the great unhappy but the great.

23. He jests at scars that never felt a wound.

24. Whatsoever a man soweth, that shall he also reap.

*25. A soft answer turneth away wrath.

7.4   UNIFORM TRANSLATION

For a syllogistic argument to be tested, it must be expressed in propositions that together contain exactly three terms. Sometimes this aim is difficult to accomplish and requires a more subtle approach than that suggested in the preceding sections. Consider the proposition "The poor always you have with you." It clearly does not assert that *all* the poor are with you, or even that *some* (particular) poor are *always* with you. There are alternative methods of reducing this proposition to standard form, but one perfectly natural route is by way of the key word "always." This word means "at all times" and suggests the standard-form categorical proposition "All times are times when you have the poor with you." The word "times," which appears in both the subject and the predicate terms, may be regarded as a **parameter, an auxiliary symbol that is of aid in expressing the original assertion in standard form.**

Care should be taken not to introduce and use parameters in a mechanical, unthinking fashion. One must be guided always by an understanding of the proposition to be translated. Thus the proposition "Smith always wins at billiards" pretty clearly does not assert that Smith is incessantly, at all times, winning at billiards! It is more reasonable to interpret it as meaning that Smith wins at billiards whenever he plays. And so understood, it translates directly into "All times when Smith plays billiards are times when Smith wins at billiards." Not all parameters need be temporal. To translate some propositions into standard form, the words "places" and "cases" can be introduced as parameters. Thus "Where there is no vision the people perish" and "Jones loses a sale whenever he is late" translate into "All places where there is no vision are places where the people perish" and "All cases in which Jones is late are cases in which Jones loses a sale."

The introduction of parameters often is requisite for the *uniform translation* of all three constituent propositions of a syllogistic argument into standard form. Since a categorical syllogism contains exactly three terms, to test a syllogistic argument we must translate its constituent propositions into standard-form categorical propositions that contain just three terms. The elimination of synonyms and the applications of conversion, obversion, and contraposition have already been discussed in section 7.2. However, there are many syllogistic arguments that cannot have the number of their terms reduced to three, either by eliminating synonyms or by applying conversion, obversion, or contraposition. Here uniform translation requires the introduction of a parameter—the *same* parameter—into all three of the constituent propositions. Consider the following argument:

> Soiled paper plates are scattered only where careless people have picnicked.
> There are soiled paper plates scattered about here.
> Therefore careless people must have been picnicking here.

This argument is perfectly valid, but before it can be proved valid by our diagrams or rules, its premises and conclusion must be translated into standard-form categorical propositions involving only three terms. The second premiss and the conclusion may be translated most naturally into "Some soiled paper plates are things that are scattered about here" and "Some careless people are those who have been picnicking here." But these two statements contain four different terms. To reduce the given argument to standard form, we begin with the first premiss, which requires a parameter for its standard-form expression, and then we use the same parameter in translating the second premiss and the conclusion into standard form. The word "where" in the first premiss suggests that the parameter "places" can be used. If this parameter is used to obtain uniform standard-form translations of all three propositions, the argument translates into

All places where soiled paper plates are scattered are places where careless people have picnicked.
This place is a place where soiled paper plates are scattered.
Therefore this place is a place where careless people have picnicked.

This standard-form categorical syllogism is in Barbara with mood and figure **AAA–1** and has already been proved valid.

The notion of standardizing expressions through the use of a parameter is not an altogether easy one to grasp, but some syllogistic arguments cannot be translated into standard-form categorical syllogisms by any other method. Another example may help to make clear the technique involved. Let us take the argument

The hounds bay wherever a fox has passed, so the fox must have taken another path, since the hounds are quiet.

First, we must understand what is asserted in the given argument. We may take the statement that the hounds are quiet as asserting that the hounds are not baying here and now. This step is part of the necessary process of eliminating synonyms, since the first assertion makes explicit reference to the baying of hounds. And in the same manner we may understand the conclusion that the fox must have taken another path as asserting that the fox did not pass here. The word "wherever" in the first assertion should suggest that the parameter "places" can be used in its translation. The standard-form translation thus arrived at is

All places where a fox has passed are places where the hounds bay.
This place is not a place where the hounds bay.
Therefore this place is not a place where a fox has passed.

This standard-form categorical syllogism is in Camestres, with mood and figure **AEE–2,** and its validity is easy to establish.

Exercises

I.   Translate the following propositions into standard form, using parameters where necessary.

Example:

  1.   He groans whenever he is reminded of his loss.

Solution:

Standard-form translation: All times when he is reminded of his loss are times when he groans.

  2.   She never drives her car to work.

  3.   He walks where he chooses.

4.   He always orders the most expensive item on the menu.

*5. She does not give her opinion unless she is asked to do so.

6.   She tries to sell life insurance wherever she may happen to be.

7.   His face gets red when he gets angry.

8.   If he is asked to say a few words, he talks for hours.

9.   Error of opinion may be tolerated where reason is left free to combat it.

*10. People are never so likely to settle a question rightly as when they discuss it freely.

II. For each of the following arguments:

   a.   Translate the argument into standard form.
   b.   Name the mood and figure of its standard-form translation.
   c.   Test its validity using a Venn Diagram. If it is valid, give its traditional name.
   d.   If it is invalid, name the fallacy it commits.

Example:

1.   Since all knowledge comes from sensory impressions and since there's no sensory impression of substance itself, it follows logically that there is no knowledge of substance.

   —Robert M. Pirsig, *Zen and the Art of Motorcycle Maintenance*

Solution:

   a.   Standard-form translation:

No things derived from sensory impressions are items of knowledge of substance itself.
<u>All items of knowledge are things derived from sensory impressions.</u>
Therefore, no items of knowledge are items of knowledge of substance itself.

   b.   Mood and figure: **EAE–1**
   c.   Valid; **Celarent**

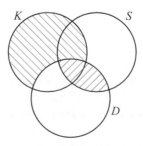

2.   . . . no names come in contradictory pairs; but all predicables come in contradictory pairs; therefore no name is a predicable.

   —Peter Thomas Geach, *Reference and Generality*

3. Everyone who smokes marijuana goes on to try heroin. Everyone who tries heroin becomes hopelessly addicted to it. Therefore, everyone who smokes marijuana becomes hopelessly addicted to it.

4. A body on which a freely swinging pendulum of fixed length has periods of oscillation which decrease slightly with increasing latitude from the equator to both poles is an oblate spheroid slightly flattened at the poles.

   But the earth is a body on which a freely swinging pendulum of fixed length has periods of oscillation which decrease slightly with increasing latitude from the equator to both poles.

   Therefore the earth is an oblate spheroid slightly flattened at the poles.

   —W. A. Wallace, *Einstein, Galileo, and Aquinas:*
   Three Views of Scientific Method

*5. Barcelona Traction was unable to pay interest on its debts; bankrupt companies are unable to pay interest on their debts; therefore, Barcelona Traction must be bankrupt.

   —John Brooks, "Annals of Finance," *The New Yorker,* 28 May 1979

6. Extremism in defense of liberty, or virtue, or whatever is *always* a vice—because extremism is but another name for fanaticism which is a vice by definition.

   —Irving Kristol, "The Environmentalist Crusade," *Wall Street Journal,*
   16 December 1974

7. When teachers' values conflict with social norms, particularly those of the local community or with those of administrators or students or other teachers, a pervasive tension marks their professional life. . . .

   In a pluralistic society dedicated, in principle at least, to respect for differences among people and to universal education for all, teachers' values will inevitably be in conflict with those of some segment or segments of the community in which they teach. Therefore, tension is a fact of professional life in our public schools.

   —David W. Adams, "Tired and Frustrated Teachers,"
   Today's Education, January 1975

8. All syllogisms having two negative premises are invalid. Some valid syllogisms are sound. Therefore some unsound arguments are syllogisms having two negative premises.

9. Any two persons who contradict each other cannot both be lying. Hence the first and third natives cannot both be lying, since they contradict each other.

*10. Not all is gold that glitters, for some base metals glitter, and gold is not a base metal.

11.   All who are frequently intoxicated are undependable, so all who are dependable are nonalcoholics, since all alcoholics are frequently intoxicated.

12.   Where there's smoke there's fire, so there's no fire in the basement, because there's no smoke there.

13.   It seems that mercy cannot be attributed to God. For mercy is a kind of sorrow, as Damascene says. But there is no sorrow in God; and therefore there is no mercy in Him.

—Thomas Aquinas, *Summa Theologiae*, I, question 21, art. 3

14.   . . . because intense heat is nothing else but a particular kind of painful sensation; and pain cannot exist but in a perceiving being; it follows that no intense heat can really exist in an unperceiving corporeal substance.

—George Berkeley, *Three Dialogues between Hylas and Philonous,
in Opposition to Sceptics and Atheists*

*15.   Only those who ignore the facts are likely to be mistaken. No one who is truly objective is likely to be mistaken. Hence no one who ignores the facts is truly objective.

16.   All bridge players are people. All people think. Therefore all bridge players think.

—Oswald and James Jacoby, "Jacoby on Bridge," *Syndicated Column,*
5 November 1966

17.   Whenever I'm in trouble, I pray. And since I'm always in trouble, there is not a day when I don't pray.

—Isaac Bashevis Singer, interview in the *New York Times*

18.   The after-image is not in physical space. The brain-process is. So the after-image is not a brain-process.

—J. J. C. Smart, "Sensations and Brain Processes,"
Philosophical Review, April 1959

19.   It must have rained lately, because the fish are not biting, and fish never bite after a rain.

*20.   . . . it is obvious that irrationals are uninteresting to engineers, since they are concerned only with approximations, and all approximations are rational.

—G. H. Hardy, *A Mathematician's Apology*

21.   All practice is theory; all surgery is practice; ergo, all surgery is theory.

—Lanfranc, *Chirurgia Magna*

22.   Since then to fight against neighbors is an evil, and to fight against the Thebans is to fight against neighbors, it is clear that to fight against the Thebans is an evil.

—Aristotle, *Prior Analytics*

23. According to Aristotle, none of the products of Nature are due to chance. His proof is this: That which is due to chance does not reappear constantly nor frequently, but all products of Nature reappear either constantly or at least frequently.

    —Moses Maimonides, *The Guide for the Perplexed*

24. She told me that she had a very simple attitude toward her students which was in fact no different from her feelings about people in general. That was, all her life she'd spoken only to people who were ladies and gentlemen. Since none of the students of 9D were ladies and gentlemen, she never spoke to them, never had, and never would.

    —James Herndon, *The Way It Spozed to Be*

*25. Not all who have jobs are temperate in their drinking. Only debtors drink to excess. So not all the unemployed are in debt.

26. It will be a good game tomorrow, for the conference title is at stake, and no title contest is ever dull.

27. Bill didn't go to work this morning, because he wore a sweater, and he never wears a sweater to work.

28. Cynthia must have complimented Henry, because he is cheerful whenever Cynthia compliments him, and he's cheerful now.

29. Every boy who meets Alice falls in love with her. Every boy who dates Betty meets Alice. Therefore every boy who dates Betty falls in love with her.

*30. There must be a strike at the factory, for there is a picket line there, and pickets are present only at strikes.

31. As epidemiologists often point out, epidemiology is not merely the study of epidemics of infectious disease; it is the broad examination of the rates and patterns of disease in the community. By almost any standard drug abuse can be regarded as a disease; accordingly it can be profitably investigated by the methods of epidemiology.

    —"Science and the Citizen," *Scientific American*, February 1975

32. And no man can be a rhapsodist who does not understand the meaning of the poet. For the rhapsodist ought to interpret the mind of the poet to his hearers, but how can he interpret him well unless he knows what he means?

    —Plato, *Ion*

33. Since morals, therefore, have an influence on the actions and affections, it follows, that they cannot be deriv'd from reason; and that because reason alone, as we have already prov'd, can never have any such influence.

    —David Hume, *A Treatise of Human Nature*

34. Any argument worthy of logical recognition must be such as would occur in ordinary discourse. Now it will be found that no argument occurring in ordinary discourse is in the fourth figure. Hence, no argument in the fourth figure is worthy of logical recognition.

*35. All valid syllogisms distribute their middle terms in at least one premiss, so this syllogism must be valid, for it distributes its middle term in at least one premiss.

36. The express train alone does not stop at this station, and as the last train did not stop, it must have been the express train.

37. No valid syllogisms have two negative premisses. No syllogisms on this page are invalid. Therefore no syllogisms on this page have two negative premisses.

38. Good poll numbers raise money. Good press gets you good poll numbers. Good press gets you money.

> —an advisor to Elizabeth Dole, during her campaign for the Republican presidential nomination, quoted in the *New York Times*, 15 April 2000.

39. There are plants growing here, and since vegetation requires water, water must be present.

*40. No one present is out of work. No members are absent. Therefore all members are employed.

41. The competition is stiff, for there is a great deal of money involved, and there is never easy competition where much money is at stake.

42. There are handsome men, but only man is vile, so it is false that nothing is both vile and handsome.

43. Also, what is simple cannot be separated from itself. The soul is simple; therefore, it cannot be separated from itself.

> —Duns Scotus, *Oxford Commentary on the Sentences of Peter Lombard*

44. All that glitters is not gold, so gold is not the only precious metal, since only precious metals glitter.

*45. Although he complains whenever he is sick, his health is excellent, so he won't complain.

46. No sane witnesses incriminate themselves. But some witnesses incriminate themselves, so some witnesses are insane.

47. We . . . define a metaphysical sentence as a sentence which purports to express a genuine proposition, but does, in fact, express neither a tautology nor an empirical hypothesis. And as tautologies and empirical hypotheses form the entire class of significant propositions, we are justified in concluding that all metaphysical assertions are nonsensical.

> —Alfred J. Ayer, *Language, Truth, and Logic*

48. This syllogism is valid, for all invalid syllogisms commit an illicit process, and this syllogism commits no illicit process.

49. All who were penniless were convicted. Some of the guilty were acquitted. Therefore some who had money were not innocent.

*__*50.__ All buildings over 300 feet tall are skyscrapers, but not all examples of modern architecture are buildings over 300 feet tall, since skyscrapers are not the only examples of modern architecture.

7.5 ENTHYMEMES

Syllogistic arguments occur frequently, but their premises and conclusions are not always stated explicitly. Often only part of the argument is expressed, the rest being "understood." Thus one may justify the conclusion that "Jones is a citizen" by mentioning only the one premise: "Jones is a native-born American." As stated the argument is incomplete, but the missing premise is easily supplied from the Constitution of the United States. Were the missing premise to be stated, the completed argument would appear as

All native-born Americans are citizens.
Jones is a native-born American.
Therefore Jones is a citizen.

Fully stated, the argument is a categorical syllogism of form **AAA–1,** Barbara, and is perfectly valid. **An argument that is stated incompletely, part being "understood" or only "in the mind," is called an** *enthymeme.* An incompletely stated argument is characterized as being *enthymematic.*

In everyday discourse, and even in science, many inferences are expressed enthymematically. The reason is easy to understand. A large body of propositions can be presumed to be common knowledge, and many speakers and writers save themselves trouble by not repeating well-known and perhaps trivially true propositions that their hearers or readers can perfectly well be expected to supply for themselves. Moreover, it is not at all unusual for an argument to be *rhetorically* more powerful and persuasive when stated enthymematically than when enunciated in complete detail. As Aristotle wrote in his *Rhetoric:* "Speeches that . . . rely on enthymemes excite the louder applause."

Because it is incomplete, an enthymeme must have its suppressed parts taken into account when testing its validity. When a necessary premise is missing, without that premise the inference is invalid. But where the unexpressed premise is easily supplied, in all fairness it ought to be included as part of the argument when one is appraising it. In such a case, one assumes that the maker of the argument did have more in mind than was stated explicitly. In most cases there is no difficulty in supplying the tacit premise that the speaker (or writer) intended but did not express. Thus, for example, as he explains the solution to the mystery in "The Adventure of Silver Blaze,"

Sherlock Holmes formulates an argument of which one critical premiss is left unstated, yet is very plainly supposed:

> A dog was kept in the stalls, and yet, though someone had been in and fetched out a horse, the dog had not barked. . . . Obviously the visitor was someone whom the dog knew well.

We all understand very well what is tacit here, that the dog would have barked had the visitor been a stranger. In fairness to the author, A. Conan Doyle, that premiss must be seen as part of Holmes's argument.

In supplying a suppressed premiss, a cardinal principle is that the proposition must be one that speakers can safely presume their hearers to accept as true. Thus it would be foolish to suggest taking the conclusion itself as a suppressed premiss, for if the arguer could have expected the auditors to accept that proposition as a premiss, without proof, it would have been idle to present it to them as the conclusion of an argument.

Any kind of argument can be expressed enthymematically, but the kinds of enthymemes that have been most extensively studied are incompletely expressed syllogistic arguments. We confine our attention to these in the remainder of this section. Enthymemes traditionally have been divided into different *orders,* according to which part of the syllogism is left unexpressed. **A first-order enthymeme is one in which the syllogism's major premiss is not stated.** The preceding example is of the first order. **A second-order enthymeme is one in which only the major premiss and the conclusion are stated, the minor premiss being suppressed.** An example of this type is "All students are opposed to the new regulations, so all sophomores are opposed to them." Here the minor premiss is easily supplied, being the obviously true proposition "All sophomores are students." **A third-order enthymeme is one in which both premisses are stated, but the conclusion is left unexpressed.** An example of this type is the following:

> Our ideas reach no farther than our experience: we have no experience of divine attributes and operations: I need not conclude my syllogism: you can draw the inference yourself.[3]

In testing an enthymeme for validity, two steps are involved: the first is to supply the missing part of the argument, the second is to test the resulting syllogism. Formulating the unstated proposition fairly may require sensitivity to the context, and an understanding of the intentions of the speaker. Consider the following argument: "No true Christian is vain, but some churchgoers are vain." It is the conclusion that remains unstated, so this is plainly a third order syllogism. But what *is* the intended conclusion? If the speaker intends to imply only that "Some churchgoers are not true Christians," the argument is valid. (**EIO–2,** *Festino*). But if the speaker's intention is to establish that "Some true Christians are not churchgoers" the en-

---

[3] David Hume, *Dialogues Concerning Natural Religion,* Pt. 2 (1779).

thymeme is invalid (**IEO–2**), for in that case the fallacy of illicit process of the major term would be committed.

Usually, however, the context indicates unambiguously what the unstated proposition is. In a Supreme Court opinion, for example, in which federal legislation regulating intrastate violence motivated by gender (the "Violence Against Women Act") was held unconstitutional, the critical argument of the majority was expressed thus:

> Gender-motivated crimes of violence are not, in any sense of the phrase, economic activity....Thus far in our nation's history our cases have upheld Commerce Clause regulation of intrastate activity only where that activity is economic in nature.[4]

The proposition that is understood but not stated in this argument is assuredly its conclusion: that gender-motivated crimes of violence may not be regulated by Congress under the long-existing rule of Supreme Court cases.

To test this third order enthymeme, we reformulate the argument so that its premisses and (tacit) conclusion are in standard form. The major premiss (the premiss containing the predicate of the conclusion) is stated first; then mood and figure are identified:

> Major premiss: All activities that may be regulated by Congress under the rule of Supreme Court cases are economic activities.
> Minor premiss: No intrastate gender-motivated crimes of violence are economic activities.
> Conclusion (unstated but clearly indicated by the context): No intrastate gender-motivated crimes of violence may be regulated by Congress under the rule of Supreme Court cases.

The mood of this syllogism is **AEE;** it is in the second figure because the middle term is the predicate of both premisses. Its form is therefore *Camestres*—a valid syllogistic argument.

In some cases a third order enthymeme may seem to be invalid without regard to context—where, for example, both premisses are negative, or where both premisses are particular propositions, or where their common term is undistributed. In such cases, no syllogistic conclusion could follow validly, and hence such enthymemes are invalid in any context.

It is possible—if it is one of the premisses of the argument that is missing—that the argument can be made valid only by adding a premiss that is highly implausible—and pointing this out is certainly a legitimate criticism of an enthymematic argument. But an even more crushing criticism, of course, would be to show that no additional premiss, however implausible, can turn the enthymeme into a valid categorical syllogism.

The difference between enthymemes and normal syllogisms is essentially rhetorical, not logical. No new logical principles need be introduced in dealing with enthymemes, and they must be tested, ultimately, by the same methods that apply to standard-form categorical syllogisms.

---

[4] *U.S. v. Morrison*, decided 15 May 2000.

Exercises

For each of the following enthymematic arguments, do the following:

- **a.** Formulate the plausible premiss or conclusion, if any, that is missing but understood.
- **b.** Write the argument in standard form, including the missing premiss or conclusion needed to make the completed argument valid—if possible—and using parameters if necessary.
- **c.** Name the order of the enthymeme.
- **d.** If the argument, even with the understood premiss included, is not valid, name the fallacy that it commits.

Example:

1. Transgenic animals are manmade and as such are patentable.

> —Alan E. Smith, cited in *Genetic Engineering*
> (San Diego, CA: Greenhaven Press, 1990).

- **a.** The premiss understood but not stated here is that whatever is manmade is patentable.
- **b.** Standard-form translation:

  All manmade things are patentable things.
  All transgenic animals are manmade things.
  Therefore, all transgenic animals are patentable things.

- **c.** The enthymeme is of the first order, since the premiss taken as understood was the major premiss of the completed argument.
- **d.** This is a valid syllogism of the form **AAA–1,** *Barbara.*

2. The soul through all her being is immortal, for that which is ever in motion is immortal.

> —Plato, *Phaedrus*

3. Abraham Beame . . . campaigned for mayor—as has been mentioned in recent weeks more often and with more irony than he might have wished—on the slogan "If you don't know the buck, you don't know the job—and Abe knows the buck."

> —*The New Yorker,* 26 August 1974

4. Although these textbooks purport to be a universal guide to learning of great worth and importance—there is a single clue that points to another direction. In the six years I taught in city and country schools, no one ever stole a textbook.

> —W. Ron Jones, *Changing Education,* Winter 1974

*5. As a matter of fact, man, like woman, is flesh, therefore passive, the plaything of his hormones and of the species, the restless prey of his desires.

> —Simone De Beauvoir, *The Second Sex*

6. You never lose respect for a man who is a vicious competitor, and you never hate a man you respect.

> —Pancho Gonzalez, former U.S. Tennis Champion

7. . . . I am an Idealist, since I believe that all that exists is spiritual.

> —John McTaggart Ellis McTaggart, *Philosophical Studies*

8. And why not become a perfect anthropomorphite? Why not assert the deity or deities to be corporeal, and to have eyes, a nose, mouth, ears, etc.? Epicurus maintained that no man had ever seen reason but in a human figure; therefore, the gods must have a human figure. And this argument, which is deservedly so much ridiculed by Cicero, becomes, according to you, solid and philosophical.

> —David Hume, *Dialogues Concerning Natural Religion*, Part V

9. However, the legal propriety of Manchester's book is at this writing before the courts and is accordingly not an appropriate subject for discussion.

> —Arnold L. Fain, "The Legal Right to Privacy,"
> *Saturday Review*, 21 January 1967

*10. I do not believe we can have any freedom at all in the philosophical sense, for we act not only under external compulsion but also by inner necessity.

> —Albert Einstein

11. All physicians are college graduates, so all members of the American Medical Association must be college graduates.

12. Small countries tend to remember history especially well, since it often turns out badly for them.

> —Marc Falcoff, "Semper Fidel," *The New Republic*, 3 July 1989

13. It must have rained lately, because the fish just aren't biting.

14. Yond Cassius has a lean and hungry look . . . such men are dangerous.

> —William Shakespeare, *Julius Caesar*, act 1, sc. 2

*15. Henry is interested only in making money, but you cannot serve both God and Mammon!

16. The Adamsons can't have a telephone, because their name isn't listed in the phone book.

17. No enthymemes are complete, so this argument is incomplete.

18. He would not take the crown
Therefore 'tis certain he was not ambitious.

> —William Shakespeare, *Julius Caesar*, act 3, sc. 2

19. Any reader who completes this argument is a good student, for it is difficult.

*20. He knows his own child, so he must be a wise father.

21. . . . we possess some immaterial knowledge. No sense knowledge, however, can be immaterial; therefore, etc.

—Duns Scotus, *Oxford Commentary on the Sentences of Peter Lombard*

22. It could hardly be denied that a tax laid specifically on the exercise of these freedoms would be unconstitutional. Yet the license tax imposed by this ordinance is in substance just that.

—Justice William O. Douglas, for the Court,
Murdock v. Commonwealth of Pennsylvania, 319 U.S. 105, 1943

23. He who is without sin should cast the first stone. There is no one here who does not have a skeleton in his closet. I know, and I know them by name.

—Representative Adam Clayton Powell,
speech in the U.S. House of Representatives, 1967

24. Only demonstrative proof should be able to make you abandon the theory of the Creation; but such a proof does not exist in Nature.

—Moses Maimonides, *The Guide for the Perplexed*

*25. It is probably true that the least destructive nuclear weapons are the most dangerous, because they make it easier for a nuclear war to begin.

—Freeman Dyson, "Reflections: Weapons and Hope,"
The New Yorker, 6 February 1984

26. Man tends to increase at a greater rate than his means of subsistence; consequently he is occasionally subject to a severe struggle for existence.

—Charles Darwin, *The Descent of Man*

27. No internal combustion engines are free from pollution; but no internal combustion engine is completely efficient. You may draw your own conclusion.

28. A nation without a conscience is a nation without a soul. A nation without a soul is a nation that cannot live.

—Winston Churchill

29. Liberty means responsibility. That is why most men dread it.

—George Bernard Shaw, *Maxims for Revolutionists*

*30. It is always possible to pretend to motives and abilities other than one's real ones, or to pretend to strengths of motives and levels of ability other than their real strengths and levels. The theatre could not exist if it was not possible to make such pretences and to make them efficiently.

—Gilbert Ryle, *The Concept of Mind*

31. Who controls the past controls the future. Who controls the present controls the past.

—George Orwell, *1984*

32. Productivity is desirable because it betters the condition of the vast majority of the people.

—Stephen Miller, "Adam Smith and the Commercial Republic," *The Public Interest*, Fall 1980

33. Advertisements perform a vital function in almost any society, for they help to bring buyers and sellers together.

—Burton M. Leiser, *Liberty, Justice, and Morals*

34. Logic is a matter of profound human importance precisely because it is empirically founded and experimentally applied.

—John Dewey, *Reconstruction in Philosophy*

*35. *Iphigeneia at Aulis* is a tragedy because it demonstrates inexorably how human character, with its itch to be admired (*philotimia* in Greek), combines with the malice of heaven to produce wars which no one in his right mind would want and which turn out to be utterly disastrous for everybody.

—George E. Dimock, Jr., Introduction to *Iphigeneia at Aulis* by Euripides

36. . . . the law does not expressly permit suicide, and what it does not expressly permit it forbids.

—Aristotle, *Nichomachean Ethics*

37. The man who says that all things come to pass by necessity cannot criticize one who denies that all things come to pass by necessity: for he admits that this too happens of necessity.

—Epicurus, Fragment XL, Vatican Collection

7.6 SORITES

■ **Advanced Material**

There are occasions when a single categorical syllogism will not suffice to account for our ability to draw a desired conclusion from a group of premisses. Thus from the premisses

All diplomats are tactful.
Some government officials are diplomats.
All government officials are people in public life.

one cannot draw the conclusion

Some people in public life are tactful.

by a *single* syllogistic inference. Yet the indicated conclusion is entailed by the stated premisses. To derive it requires two syllogisms rather than one. A stepwise process of argumentation must be resorted to, in which each step is a separate categorical syllogism. When stated explicitly, the required argument will be

> All diplomats are tactful individuals.
> Some government officials are diplomats.
> _____
> Therefore some government officials are tactful individuals.
> All government officials are people in public life.
> _____
> Therefore some people in public life are tactful individuals.

This argument is not a syllogism but a *chain* of categorical syllogisms, connected by the conclusion of the first, which is a premiss of the second. This chain has only two links, but more extended arguments may consist of a greater number. Since a chain is no stronger than its weakest link, an argument of this type is valid if, and only if, all of its constituent syllogisms are valid.

Where such an argument is expressed enthymematically, with only the premisses and the final conclusion stated, it is called a *sorites* (pronounced *sō-rī'-tēz*). Sorites may have three, four, or *any* number of premisses. Some are very lengthy indeed. The following example is drawn from the works of the philosopher Gottfried Leibniz:

> The human soul is a thing whose activity is thinking. A thing whose activity is thinking is one whose activity is immediately apprehended, and without any representation of parts therein. A thing whose activity is immediately apprehended without any representation of parts therein is a thing whose activity does not contain parts. A thing whose activity does not contain parts is one whose activity is not motion. A thing whose activity is not motion is not a body. What is not a body is not in space. What is not in space is insusceptible of motion. What is insusceptible of motion is indissoluble (for dissolution is a movement of parts). What is indissoluble is incorruptible. What is incorruptible is immortal. Therefore the human soul is immortal.[5]

This sorites contains no less than ten premisses. Any sorites may be tested by making its intermediate conclusions or steps explicit, then testing separately the various categorical syllogisms thus obtained. If we ignore the possibility that an equivocation is present, then the validity of Leibniz's sorites is easily verified.

It will be convenient, in connection with the exercises provided for this section, to say that a sorites is in standard form when all of its propositions are in standard form, when each term occurs exactly twice, and when every proposition (except the last) has a term in common with the proposition that immediately follows it. Thus one standard-form translation of Lewis Carroll's sorites

> (1) Every one who is sane can do Logic.
> (2) No lunatics are fit to serve on a jury.
> (3) None of your sons can do Logic.
> _____
> Therefore none of your sons is fit to serve on a jury.

---

[5] From H. W. B. Joseph, *An Introduction to Logic* (New York: Oxford University Press, 1916).

is

(2′) All persons fit to serve on a jury are sane persons.
(1′) All sane persons are persons who can do Logic.
(3′) No sons of yours are persons who can do Logic.
Therefore no sons of yours are persons fit to serve on a jury.

One can test it by stating the suppressed subconclusion explicitly and then testing the resulting categorical syllogisms.

Exercises

I. Translate each of the following sorites into standard form, and test its validity.[6]

Example:

1. (1) Babies are illogical.
(2) Nobody is despised who can manage a crocodile.
(3) Illogical persons are despised.
Therefore babies cannot manage crocodiles.

Solution:

Standard-form translation:
(1′) All babies are illogical persons.
(3′) All illogical persons are despised persons.
(2′) No persons who can manage crocodiles are despised persons.
Therefore, no babies are persons who can manage crocodiles.

This sorites consists of two syllogisms, as follows:

All *I* is *D*.	No *M* is *D*.
All *B* is *I*.	All *B* is *D*.
Therefore all *B* is *D*.	Therefore no *B* is *M*.

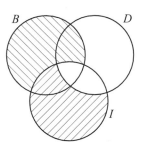

Valid, Barbara

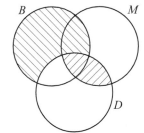

Valid, Cesare

2. (1) No experienced person is incompetent.
(2) Jenkins is always blundering.
(3) No competent person is always blundering.
Therefore Jenkins is inexperienced.

---

[6]All the following exercises, except 4 and 6 under I, are taken, with little or no modification, from Lewis Carroll's *Symbolic Logic* (New York: C. N. Potter, 1977).

3. (1) The only books in this library that I do not recommend for reading are unhealthy in tone.
(2) The bound books are all well written.
(3) All the romances are healthy in tone.
(4) I do not recommend that you read any of the unbound books.

Therefore all the romances in this library are well written.

4. (1) Only profound scholars can be dons at Oxford.
(2) No insensitive souls are great lovers of music.
(3) No one whose soul is not sensitive can be a Don Juan
(4) There are no profound scholars who are not great lovers of
music.

Therefore all Oxford dons are Don Juans.

*5. (1) No interesting poems are unpopular among people of real taste.
(2) No modern poetry is free from affectation.
(3) All your poems are on the subject of soap bubbles.
(4) No affected poetry is popular among people of real taste.
(5) Only a modern poem would be on the subject of soap bubbles.

Therefore all your poems are uninteresting.

6. (1) None but writers are poets.
(2) Only military officers are astronauts.
(3) Whoever contributes to the new magazine is a poet.
(4) Nobody is both a military officer and a writer.

Therefore not one astronaut is a contributor to the new magazine.

II. Each of the following sets of propositions can serve as premises for a valid
sorites. For each, find the conclusion and establish the argument as valid.

*1. (1) No one reads the *Times* unless he is well educated.
(2) No hedgehogs can read.
(3) Those who cannot read are not well educated.

2. (1) All puddings are nice.
(2) This dish is a pudding.
(3) No nice things are wholesome.

3. (1) The only articles of food that my doctor allows me are such as
are not very rich.
(2) Nothing that agrees with me is unsuitable for supper.
(3) Wedding cake is always very rich.
(4) My doctor allows me all articles of food that are suitable for supper.

4. (1) All my daughters are slim.
(2) No child of mine is healthy who takes no exercise.
(3) All gluttons who are children of mine are fat.
(4) No son of mine takes any exercise.

*5. (1) When I work a logic example without grumbling, you may be sure it is one that I can understand.

(2) These sorites are not arranged in regular order, like the examples I am used to.

(3) No easy example ever makes my head ache.

(4) I can't understand examples that are not arranged in regular order, like those I am used to.

(5) I never grumble at an example, unless it gives me a headache. ∎

7.7 DISJUNCTIVE AND HYPOTHETICAL SYLLOGISMS

Up to this point we have been discussing the analysis of categorical syllogisms; we turn now to syllogisms of other kinds. Syllogisms are called *categorical* when the propositions they contain are categorical, that is, propositions that affirm or deny the inclusion or exclusion of categories or classes. But a syllogism—a deductive argument consisting of two premises and a conclusion—may contain propositions that are not categorical, and in such cases it is not called a categorical syllogism but is instead named on the basis of the kind of propositions it contains. Before completing this account of syllogistic reasoning, therefore, we must attend briefly to some other kinds of propositions and the syllogisms to which they give rise.

Categorical propositions, with which we are well familiar, may be thought of as *simple;* they have a single component which affirms or denies some class relation. In contrast, some propositions used in syllogistic argument are *compound,* containing more than one component, each of which is some other proposition.

The first kind of compound proposition to be considered is the *disjunctive* (or *alternative*) proposition. An example is: "Either Fido ran away or Fido got hit by a car." Its two component propositions are "Fido ran away" and "Fido got hit by a car." The disjunctive proposition, or disjunction, contains two component propositions, which are its *disjuncts.* The disjunction does not categorically affirm the truth of either one of its disjuncts but says that at least one of them is true, allowing for the possibility that both may be true.

If we have a disjunction as one premiss, and as another premiss the denial or contradictory of one of its two disjuncts, then we can validly infer that the disjunction's other disjunct is true. Any argument of this form is a valid **disjunctive syllogism;** for example,

Either Fido ran away or Fido got hit by a car.
Fido did not run away.
Therefore Fido got hit by a car.

As we use the term in this section, not every disjunctive syllogism is valid. For example, the argument

> Either Fido ran away or Fido got hit by a car.
> Fido ran away.
> Therefore Fido did not get hit by a car.

may be classified as an invalid disjunctive syllogism. It bears a superficial resemblance to the preceding example, but it is easily seen to be fallacious. Consistently with the premises, Fido might have run away *and* gotten hit by a car. The truth of one disjunct of a disjunction does not imply the falsehood of the other disjunct, since both disjuncts of a disjunction can be true. Hence we have a valid disjunctive syllogism only where the categorical premiss contradicts one disjunct of the disjunctive premiss and the conclusion affirms the other disjunct of the disjunctive premiss.

An objection might be raised at this point, based on such an argument as the following:

> Either Smith is in New York or Smith is in Paris.
> Smith is in New York.
> Therefore Smith is not in Paris.

Here the categorical premiss affirms one disjunct of the stated disjunction, and the conclusion contradicts the other disjunct, yet the conclusion seems to follow validly. Closer analysis shows, however, that the stated disjunction plays no role in the argument. The conclusion follows enthymematically from the categorical premiss, with the unexpressed additional premiss being the obviously true proposition that "Smith can't be both in New York and in Paris," which can be stated in disjunctive form as

> Either Smith is not in New York or Smith is not in Paris.

When this tacit premiss is supplied and the superfluous original disjunction is discarded, the resulting argument is easily seen to be a valid disjunctive syllogism. The apparent exception is not really an exception, and the objection is groundless.

The second kind of compound proposition to be considered is the *conditional* (or *hypothetical*) proposition, an example of which is "If the first native is a politician, then the first native lies." A conditional proposition contains two component propositions: The one following the "if" is the *antecedent,* and the one following the "then" is the *consequent.* A syllogism that contains conditional propositions exclusively is called a **pure hypothetical syllogism;** for example,

> If the first native is a politician, then he lies.
> If he lies, then he denies being a politician.
> Therefore if the first native is a politician, then he denies being a politician.

In this argument it can be observed that the first premiss and the conclusion have the same antecedent, that the second premiss and the conclusion have the same consequent, and that the consequent of the first premiss is the same as the antecedent of the second premiss. It should be clear that any pure hypothetical syllogism whose premisses and conclusion have their component parts so related is a valid argument.

A syllogism having one conditional premiss and one categorical premiss is called a **mixed hypothetical syllogism.** There are two valid forms of the mixed hypothetical syllogism that have been given special names. The first is illustrated by

> If the second native told the truth, then only one native is a politician.
> The second native told the truth.
> Therefore only one native is a politician.

Here the categorical premiss affirms the antecedent of the conditional premiss, and the conclusion affirms its consequent. Any argument of this form is valid and is said to be in the *affirmative mood* or **modus ponens** (from the Latin *ponere*, meaning "to affirm"). One must not confuse the valid form *modus ponens* with the clearly invalid form displayed by the following argument:

> If Bacon wrote *Hamlet*, then Bacon was a great writer.
> Bacon was a great writer.
> Therefore Bacon wrote *Hamlet*.

This argument differs from *modus ponens* in that its categorical premiss affirms the consequent, rather than the antecedent, of the conditional premiss. Any argument of this form is said to commit the **fallacy of affirming the consequent.**

The other valid form of mixed hypothetical syllogism is illustrated by

> If the one-eyed prisoner saw two red hats, then he could tell the color of the hat on his own head.
> The one-eyed prisoner could not tell the color of the hat on his own head.
> Therefore the one-eyed prisoner did not see two red hats.

Here the categorical premiss denies the consequent of the conditional premiss, and the conclusion denies its antecedent. Any argument of this form is valid and is said to be in the form **modus tollens** (from the Latin *tollere*, meaning "to deny"). One must not confuse the valid form *modus tollens* with the clearly invalid form displayed by the following argument:

> If Carl embezzled the college funds, then Carl is guilty of a felony.
> Carl did not embezzle the college funds.
> Therefore Carl is not guilty of a felony.

This argument differs from *modus tollens* in that its categorical premiss denies the antecedent, rather than the consequent, of the conditional premiss. Any argument of this form is said to commit the **fallacy of denying the antecedent.**

PRINCIPAL KINDS OF SYLLOGISMS

1. **Categorical syllogisms,** which contain only categorical propositions affirming or denying the inclusion or exclusion of categories. Example:

   All *M* is *P*
   All *S* is *M*
   Therefore all *S* is *P*.

2. **Disjunctive syllogisms,** which contain a compound, disjunctive (or alternative) premiss asserting the truth of at least one of two alternatives, and a premiss that asserts the falsity of one of those alternatives. Example:

   Either *P* is true or *Q* is true
   P is not true
   Therefore *Q* is true.

3. **Hypothetical syllogisms,** which contain one or more compound, hypothetical (or conditional) propositions, affirming that if one of its components (the antecedent) is true then the other of its components (the consequent) is true. Two subtypes are distinguished:

   A) **Pure hypothetical syllogisms** contain conditional propositions only. Example:

   If *P* is true then *Q* is true
   If *Q* is true then *R* is true
   Therefore if *P* is true then *R* is true.

   B) **Mixed hypothetical syllogisms** contain both a conditional premiss and a premiss asserting the truth of the antecedent of that conditional premiss. Example:

   If *P* is true then *Q* is true
   P is true
   Therefore *Q* is true.

Exercises

Identify the form and discuss the validity or invalidity of each of the following arguments.

Example:

  1.   If a man could not have done otherwise than he in fact did, then he is not responsible for his action. But if determinism is true, it is true of every action that the agent could not have done otherwise.

Therefore, if determinism is true, no one is ever responsible for what he does.

—Winston Nesbit and Stewart Candlish,
"Determinism and the Ability to Do Otherwise," *Mind*, July 1978

Solution:

This is a pure hypothetical syllogism. Valid.

2. I can't have anything more to do with the operation. If I did, I'd have to lie to the Ambassador. And I can't do that.

—Henry Bromell, "I Know Your Heart, Marco Polo,"
The New Yorker, 6 March 1978

3. "J. J.," I replied, "if it was any of your business, I would have invited you. It is not, and so I did not."

—Paul Erdman, *The Crash of '79*

4. Men, it is assumed, act in economic matters only in response to pecuniary compensation or to force. Force in the modern society is largely, although by no means completely, obsolete. So only pecuniary compensation remains of importance.

—John Kenneth Galbraith, *The New Industrial State*

*5. If each man had a definite set of rules of conduct by which he regulated his life he would be no better than a machine. But there are no such rules, so men cannot be machines.

—A. M. Turing, "Computing Machinery and Intelligence,"
Mind, vol. 59, 1950

6. Smith is the fireman or Smith is the engineer. Smith is not the fireman. Therefore Smith is the engineer.

7. If the first native is a politician, then the first native denied being a politician. The first native denied being a politician. Therefore the first native is a politician.

8. If the first native denied being a politician, then the second native told the truth. If the second native told the truth, then the second native is not a politician. Therefore if the first native denied being a politician, then the second native is not a politician.

9. If Mr. Jones lives in Chicago, then Jones is the brakeman. Mr. Jones lives in Chicago. Therefore Jones is the brakeman.

*10. If the second native told the truth, then the first native denied being a politician. If the third native told the truth, then the first native denied being a politician. Therefore if the second native told the truth, then the third native told the truth.

11. If Robinson is the brakeman, then Mr. Robinson lives in Chicago. Mr. Robinson does not live in Chicago. Therefore Robinson is not the brakeman.

12.   If Robinson is the brakeman, then Smith is the engineer. Robinson is not the brakeman. Therefore Smith is not the engineer.

13.   If Mr. Jones is the brakeman's next-door neighbor, then $20,000 is exactly divisible by 3. But $20,000 is not exactly divisible by 3. Therefore Mr. Jones is not the brakeman's next-door neighbor.

14.   If the one-eyed prisoner does not know the color of the hat on his own head, then the blind prisoner cannot have on a red hat. The one-eyed prisoner does not know the color of the hat on his own head. Therefore the blind prisoner cannot have on a red hat.

*15.   Mr. Smith is the brakeman's next-door neighbor or Mr. Robinson is the brakeman's next-door neighbor. Mr. Robinson is not the brakeman's next-door neighbor. Therefore Mr. Smith is the brakeman's next-door neighbor.

16.   If all three prisoners have on white hats, then the one-eyed prisoner does not know the color of the hat on his own head. The one-eyed prisoner does not know the color of the hat on his own head. Therefore all three prisoners have on white hats.

17.   Mr. Robinson lives in Detroit or Mr. Robinson lives in Chicago. Mr. Robinson lives in Detroit. Therefore Mr. Robinson does not live in Chicago.

18.   The stranger is either a knave or a fool. The stranger is a knave. Therefore the stranger is no fool.

19.   If this syllogism commits the fallacy of affirming the consequent, then it is invalid. This syllogism does not commit the fallacy of affirming the consequent. Therefore this syllogism is valid.

*20.   If the first native is a politician, then the third native tells the truth. If the third native tells the truth, then the third native is not a politician. Therefore if the first native is a politician, then the third native is not a politician.

21.   Mankind, he said, judging by their neglect of him, have never, as I think, at all understood the power of Love. For if they had understood him they would surely have built noble temples and altars, and offered solemn sacrifices in his honor; but this is not done.

—Plato, *Symposium*

22.   I have already said that he must have gone to King's Pyland or to Capleton. He is not at King's Pyland, therefore he is at Capleton.

—A. Conan Doyle, *The Adventure of Silver Blaze*

23.   If Pluto, according to Halliday's calculations, had a diameter of more than 4,200 miles, then an occultation would have occurred at McDonald [Observatory at Fort Davis, Texas], and the records

clearly indicated that it did not. Thus Pluto must be that size or smaller; it cannot be larger.

> —Thomas D. Nicholson, "The Enigma of Pluto,"
> *Natural History,* March 1967

24. If then, it is agreed that things are either the result of coincidence or for an end, and these cannot be the result of coincidence or spontaneity, it follows that they must be for an end.

> —Aristotle, *Physics*

*25. There is no case known (neither is it, indeed, possible) in which a thing is found to be the efficient cause of itself; for in such a case it would be prior to itself, which is impossible.

> —Thomas Aquinas, *Summa Theologiae,* I, question 2, art. 3

26. Either wealth is an evil or wealth is a good; but wealth is not an evil; therefore wealth is a good.

> —Sextus Empiricus, *Against the Logicians*

27. And certainly if its essence and power are infinite, its goodness must be infinite, since a thing whose essence is finite has finite goodness.

> —Roger Bacon, *The Opus Majus*

28. I *do* know that this pencil exists; but I could not know this, if Hume's principles were true; *therefore,* Hume's principles, one or both of them, are false.

> —G. E. Moore, *Some Main Problems of Philosophy*

29. A theoryless position is possible only if there are no theories of evidence. But there are theories of evidence. Therefore, a theoryless position is impossible.

> —Henry W. Johnstone, Jr., "The Law of Non-Contradiction,"
> *Logique et Analyse,* n.s. vol. 3, 1960

*30. It is clear that we mean something, and something different in each case, by such words [as *substance, cause, change,* etc.]. If we did not we could not use them consistently, and it is obvious that on the whole we do consistently apply and withhold such names.

> —C. D. Broad, *Scientific Thought*

31. If number were an idea, then arithmetic would be psychology. But arithmetic is no more psychology than, say, astronomy is. Astronomy is concerned, not with ideas of the planets, but with the planets themselves, and by the same token the objects of arithmetic are not ideas either.

> —Gottlob Frege, *The Foundations of Arithmetic*

32. If error were something positive, God would be its cause, and by Him it would continually be procreated [per Prop. 12: All existing

things are conserved by God's power alone.] But this is absurd [per Prop. 13: God is never a deceiver, but in all things is perfectly true.] Therefore error is nothing positive. Q.E.D.

—Baruch Spinoza, *The Principles of Philosophy Demonstrated by the Method of Geometry*

33. ... If a mental state is to be identical with a physical state, the two must share all properties in common. But there is one property, spatial localizability, that is not so shared; that is, physical states and events are located in space, whereas mental events and states are not. Hence, mental events and states are different from physical ones.

—Jaegwon Kim, "On the Psycho-Physical Identity Theory," *American Philosophical Quarterly*, 1966

34. When we regard a man as morally responsible for an act, we regard him as a legitimate object of moral praise or blame in respect of it. But it seems plain that a man cannot be a legitimate object of moral praise or blame for an act unless in willing the act he is in some important sense a "free" agent. Evidently free will in some sense, therefore, is a precondition of moral responsibility.

—C. Arthur Campbell, *In Defence of Free Will*

*35. Syllogism [is] not the great instrument of reason ... If syllogisms must be taken for the only proper instrument and means of knowledge, it will follow, that before Aristotle there was not one man that did or could know anything by reason, and that since the invention of syllogisms there is not one of ten thousand that doth. But God has not been so sparing to men to make them barely two-legged creatures, and left it to Aristotle to make them rational.

—John Locke, *An Essay Concerning Human Understanding*

36. "It's going to be a very cold winter for housing and for the economy in general," said Michael Sumichrast, chief economist for the National Association of Home Builders.

"You cannot have a general economic recovery without housing doing reasonably well and housing will not be doing reasonably well."

—United Press report, 18 November 1980

37. In spite of the popularity of the finite-world picture, however, it is open to a devastating objection. In being finite the world must have a limiting boundary, such as Aristotle's outermost sphere. That is impossible, because a boundary can only separate one part of space from another. This objection was put forward by the Greeks, reappeared in the scientific skepticism of the early Renaissance and probably occurs to any schoolchild who thinks

about it today. If one accepts the objection, one must conclude that the universe is infinite.

—J. J. Callahan, "The Curvature of Space in a Finite Universe," *Scientific American*, August 1976

38.   If he prayed for Stalin—prayed that Stalin should mend his ways—then Stalin might become commendable, and if he was commendable, Vadim would logically be obliged to revere him. But all he could ever do was hate the monster, so he must *not* pray for him, otherwise he would face a terrible dilemma.

—William F. Buckley, Jr., *Who's on First?*

39.   Total pacifism might be a good principle if everyone were to follow it. But not everyone does, so it isn't.

—Gilbert Harman, *The Nature of Morality*

7.8 The Dilemma

The *dilemma*, a common form of argument in ordinary language, is a legacy from older times when logic and rhetoric were more closely connected than they are today. From a strictly logical point of view the dilemma is not of special importance. But rhetorically the dilemma is one of the most powerful instruments of persuasion—and a devastating weapon in controversy.

We say somewhat loosely that a person is "in" a dilemma (or "impaled on the horns of a dilemma") when that person must choose between two alternatives, both of which are bad or unpleasant. The dilemma is a form of argument intended to put one's opponent in just that kind of position. In debate, one uses a dilemma to offer alternative positions to one's adversary, from which a choice must be made, and then to prove that no matter which choice is made, the adversary is committed to an unacceptable conclusion.

The distinguished physicist Richard Feynman, recounting his experiences in the 1986 investigation of the catastrophic explosion of the Challenger rocket, was caustic in his criticism of mismanagement by administrators in the National Aeronautics and Space Administration (NASA). He said:

> Every time we talked to higher level managers, they kept saying they didn't know anything about the problems below them....Either the group at the top didn't know, in which case they should have known, or they did know, in which case they were lying to us.[7]

An attack of this kind is designed to push the adversaries (in this case the NASA administrators) into a corner and there annihilate them. The only explicitly stated premiss of the argument is a disjunction, but one of the disjuncts must obviously be true; either they knew or they didn't know about the problems below them. And whichever disjunct is choosen, the result for the adversary is very

---

[7] James Gleick, *Genius: The Life and Science of Richard Feynman* (New York: Pantheon Books, 1992).

bad. The conclusion of a dilemma can itself be a disjunction (for example, "Either the NASA administrators did not know what they should have known, or they lied") in which case we call it *complex.* But the conclusion may also be a categorical proposition, in which case we call it *simple.*

A dilemma need not always have an unpleasant conclusion. An example of one with a happy conclusion is provided by the following simple dilemma:

> If the blest in heaven have no desires, they will be perfectly content; so they will be also if their desires are fully gratified; but either they will have no desires, or have them fully gratified; therefore they will be perfectly content.

The premisses of a dilemma need not be stated in any special order; the disjunctive premiss, which offers the alternatives, may either precede or follow the other. And the consequences of those alternatives may be stated in a conjunctive proposition or in two separate propositions. An argument in dilemma form is often expressed enthymematically; that is, its conclusion generally is thought so obvious that it scarcely needs to be spelled out. This is well illustrated in a passage from a letter of President Lincoln, defending the Emancipation Proclamation that freed the slaves in the Confederacy:

> But the proclamation, as law, either is valid, or is not valid. If it is not valid, it needs no retraction, If it is valid, it cannot be retracted, any more than the dead can be brought to life.[8]

Three ways of evading or refuting the conclusion of a dilemma have been given special names, all relating to the fact that a dilemma has two (or more) "horns." These three ways of defeating a dilemma are known as "going (or escaping) between the horns," "taking (or grasping) it by the horns," and "rebutting it by means of a counterdilemma." Note that these are not ways to prove the dilemma invalid; rather, they are ways in which one seeks to avoid its conclusion without challenging the formal validity of the argument.

One escapes between the horns of a dilemma by rejecting its disjunctive premiss. This method is often the easiest way to evade the conclusion of a dilemma, for unless one half of the disjunction is the explicit contradictory of the other, the disjunction may very well be false. One justification sometimes offered for giving grades to students is that recognizing good work will stimulate the student to study harder. Students may criticize this theory, using the following dilemma:

> If students are fond of learning, they need no stimulus, and if they dislike learning, no stimulus will be of any avail. But any student is either fond of learning or dislikes it. Therefore a stimulus is either needless or of no avail.

This argument is formally valid, but we can evade its conclusion by *going between the horns.* The disjunctive premiss is false, for students have all kinds of attitudes toward learning: Some may be fond of it, many dislike it, and many are indifferent. For them, a stimulus may be both needed and of some avail. Going between

---

[8] Letter of Abraham Lincoln to James C. Conkling, 26 August 1863.

the horns does not prove the conclusion to be false but shows merely that the argument does not provide adequate grounds for accepting that conclusion.

Where the disjunctive premiss is unassailable, as when the alternatives exhaust the possibilities, it is impossible to escape between the horns. Another method of evading the conclusion must be sought. One such method is to *grasp the dilemma by the horns,* which involves rejecting the premiss that is a conjunction. To deny a conjunction, we need only deny one of its parts. When we grasp the dilemma by the horns, we attempt to show that at least one of the conditionals is false. The dilemma just above, attacking the use of grades in school, relies upon the conditional "If students are fond of learning, they need no stimulus." The proponent of grading may grasp this dilemma by the horns and argue that even students who are fond of learning may sometimes need stimulus, and that the additional stimulus provided by grades promotes careful study by even the most diligent students. There may be good response to this, of course—but the original dilemma has been grasped firmly by the horns.

Rebutting a dilemma by means of a counterdilemma is the most ingenious method of all, but it is seldom cogent, for reasons that will appear presently. To rebut a given dilemma in this way, one constructs another dilemma whose conclusion is opposed to the conclusion of the original. *Any* counterdilemma may be used in rebuttal, but ideally it should be built up out of the same ingredients (categorical propositions) that the original dilemma contained.

A classical example of this elegant kind of rebuttal concerns the legendary argument of an Athenian mother attempting to persuade her son not to enter politics:

> If you say what is just, men will hate you; and if you say what is unjust, the gods will hate you; but you must either say the one or the other; therefore you will be hated.

Her son rebutted that dilemma with the following one:

> If I say what is just, the gods will love me; and if I say what is unjust, men will love me. I must say either the one or the other. Therefore I shall be loved!

In public discussion, where the dilemma is one of the strongest weapons of controversy, the use of a rebuttal of this kind, which derives an opposite conclusion from almost the same premisses, is a mark of great rhetorical skill. But if we examine the dilemma and rebutting counterdilemma more closely, we see that their conclusions are not as opposed as they might at first have seemed.

The conclusion of the first dilemma is that the son will be hated (by men or by the gods), whereas that of the rebutting dilemma is that the son will be loved (by the gods or by men). But these two conclusions are perfectly compatible. The rebutting counterdilemma serves merely to establish a conclusion different from that of the original. Both conclusions may very well be true together, so no refutation has been accomplished. But in the heat of controversy analysis is unwelcome, and if such a rebuttal occurred in a public debate, the average audience might overwhelmingly agree that the rebuttal demolished the original argument.

That this sort of rebuttal does not refute the argument but only directs attention to a different aspect of the same situation is perhaps more clearly shown in the case of the following dilemma, advanced by an "optimist":

> If I work, I earn money, and if I am idle, I enjoy myself. Either I work or I am idle. Therefore either I earn money or I enjoy myself.

A "pessimist" might offer the following counterdilemma:

> If I work, I don't enjoy myself, and if I am idle, I don't earn money. Either I work or I am idle. Therefore either I don't earn money or I don't enjoy myself.

These conclusions represent merely different ways of viewing the same facts; they do not constitute a disagreement over what the facts are.

No discussion of dilemmas would be complete unless it mentioned the celebrated lawsuit between Protagoras and Euathlus. Protagoras was a teacher who lived in Greece during the fifth century B.C. He taught many subjects but specialized in the art of pleading before juries. Euathlus wanted to become a lawyer, but not being able to pay the required tuition, he made an arrangement according to which Protagoras would teach him but not receive payment until Euathlus won his first case. When Euathlus finished his course of study, he delayed going into practice. Tired of waiting for his money, Protagoras brought suit against his former pupil for the tuition money that was owed. Unmindful of the adage that the lawyer who tries his own case has a fool for a client, Euathlus decided to plead his own case in court. When the trial began, Protagoras presented his side of the case in a crushing dilemma:

> If Euathlus loses this case, then he must pay me (by the judgment of the court); if he wins this case, then he must pay me (by the terms of the contract). He must either lose or win this case. Therefore Euathlus must pay me.

The situation looked bad for Euathlus, but he had learned well the art of rhetoric. He offered the court the following counterdilemma in rebuttal:

> If I win this case, I shall not have to pay Protagoras (by the judgment of the court); if I lose this case, I shall not have to pay Protagoras (by the terms of the contract, for then I shall not yet have won my first case). I must either win or lose this case. Therefore I do not have to pay Protagoras!

Had you been the judge, how would you have decided?

Note that the conclusion of Euathlus' rebutting dilemma is *not* compatible with the conclusion of Protagoras' original dilemma. One conclusion is the explicit denial of the other. But it is a rare case in which a counter dilemma stands in this relation to the dilemma against which it is directed. When it does so, the premises involved are themselves inconsistent, and it is this implicit contradiction that the two dilemmas serve to make explicit.

Exercises

Discuss the various arguments that might be offered to refute each of the following.

Example:

1. If we interfere with the publication of false and harmful doctrines, we shall be guilty of suppressing the liberties of others, whereas if we do not interfere with the publication of such doctrines, we run the risk of losing our own liberties. We must either interfere or not interfere with the publication of false and harmful doctrines. Hence we must either be guilty of suppressing the liberties of others or else run the risk of losing our own liberties.

Solution:

Impossible to go between the horns. It would be plausible to grasp it by either horn, arguing either (a) that liberties do not properly include the right to publish false and harmful doctrines or (b) that we run no risk of losing our own liberties if we vigorously oppose false and harmful doctrines with true and helpful ones. And it could plausibly be rebutted (but not refuted) by the use of its ingredients to prove that "we must either be guiltless of suppressing the liberties of others or else run no risk of losing our own liberties."

2. Circuit Courts are useful, or they are not useful. If useful, no State should be denied them; if not useful, no State should have them. Let them be provided for all, or abolished as to all.

   —Abraham Lincoln, annual message to Congress, 3 December 1861

3. If you tell me what I already understand, you do not enlarge my understanding, whereas if you tell me something that I do not understand, then your remarks are unintelligible to me. Whatever you tell me must be either something I already understand or something that I do not understand. Hence whatever you say either does not enlarge my understanding or else is unintelligible to me.

4. If what you say does not enlarge my understanding, then what you say is without value to me, and if what you say is unintelligible to me, then it is without value to me. Whatever you say either does not enlarge my understanding or else is unintelligible to me. Therefore nothing you say is of any value to me.

*5. If the conclusion of a deductive argument goes beyond the premisses, then the argument is invalid, while if the conclusion of a deductive argument does not go beyond the premises, then the argument brings nothing new to light. The conclusion of a deductive argument must either go beyond the premises or not go beyond them. Therefore either deductive arguments are invalid or they bring nothing new to light.

6. If a deductive argument is invalid, it is without value, whereas a deductive argument that brings nothing new to light is also without value. Either deductive arguments are invalid or they bring nothing new to light. Therefore deductive arguments are without value.

7. If the general was loyal, he would have obeyed his orders, and if he was intelligent, he would have understood them. The general either disobeyed his orders or else he did not understand them. Therefore the general must have been either disloyal or unintelligent.

8. If he was disloyal, then his dismissal was justified, and if he was unintelligent, then his dismissal was justified. He was either disloyal or unintelligent. Therefore his dismissal was justified.

9. If the several nations keep the peace, the United Nations is unnecessary, while if the several nations go to war, the United Nations will have been unsuccessful in its purpose of preventing war. Now, either the several nations keep the peace or they go to war. Hence the United Nations is unnecessary or unsuccessful.

*10. If people are good, laws are not needed to prevent wrongdoing, whereas if people are bad, laws will not succeed in preventing wrongdoing. People are either good or bad. Therefore either laws are not needed to prevent wrongdoing or laws will not succeed in preventing wrongdoing.

11. Archbishop Morton, Chancellor under Henry VII, was famous for his method of extracting "contributions" to the king's purse. A person who lived extravagantly was forced to make a large contribution, because it was obvious that he could afford it. Someone who lived modestly was forced to make a large contribution because it was clear that he must have saved a lot of money on living expenses. Whichever way he turned he was said to be "caught on Morton's fork."

—Dorothy Hayden, *Winning Declarer Play*

12. If any member of our party is guilty in that matter, you know it or you do not know it. If you do know it, you are inexcusable for not designating the man and proving the fact. If you do not know it, you are inexcusable for asserting it, and especially for persisting in the assertion after you have tried and failed to make the proof.

—Abraham Lincoln, address at Cooper Institute,
New York City, 27 February 1860

13. There is a dilemma to which every opposition to successful iniq-
uity must, in the nature of things, be liable. If you lie still, you are
considered as an accomplice in the measures in which you silently
acquiesce. If you resist, you are accused of provoking irritable
power to new excesses. The conduct of a losing party never appears right.

   —Edmund Burke, A Letter to a Member of the National Assembly

14. And we seem unable to clear ourselves from the old dilemma.
If you predicate what is different, you ascribe to the subject what
it is *not*; and if you predicate what is *not* different, you say nothing at all.

   —F. H. Bradley, *Appearance and Reality*

*15. All political action aims at either preservation or change. When
desiring to preserve, we wish to prevent a change to the worse;
when desiring to change, we wish to bring about something better. All political action is then guided by some thought of better
and worse.

   —Leo Strauss, *What Is Political Philosophy?*

16. If a thing moves, it moves either in the place where it is or in that
where it is not; but it moves neither in the place where it is (for it
remains therein) nor in that where it is not (for it does not exist
therein); therefore nothing moves.

   —Sextus Empiricus, *Against the Physicists*

17. And what a life should I lead, at my age, wandering from city to
city, ever changing my place of exile, and always being driven out!
For I am quite sure that wherever I go, there, as here, the young
men will flock to me; and if I drive them away, their elders will
drive me out at their request; and if I let them come, their fathers
and friends will drive me out for their sakes.

   —Plato, *Apology*

18. If Socrates died, he died either when he was living or
when he was dead. But he did not die while living; for
assuredly he was living, and as living he had not died. Nor
when he died, for then he would be twice dead. Therefore
Socrates did not die.

   —Sextus Empiricus, *Against the Physicists*

19. Inevitably, the use of the placebo involved built-in contradictions.
A good patient–doctor relationship is essential to the process,
but what happens to that relationship when one of the partners

conceals important information from the other? If the doctor tells the truth, he destroys the base on which the placebo rests. If he doesn't tell the truth, he jeopardizes a relationship built on trust.

—Norman Cousins, *Anatomy of an Illness*

*20. The "paradox of analysis," which postulates the dilemma that an analysis is either a mere synonym and hence trivial, or more than a synonym and hence false, has its equivalent in Linguistic Philosophy: a neologism can either be accounted for in existing terms, in which case it is redundant, or it cannot, in which case it has not "been given sense."

—Ernest Gellner, *Words and Things*

21. In discussing Allan Bloom's *The Closing of the American Mind,* an enormously successful, best-selling book whose message is that "Our culture is going downhill. Thought has been vanquished," along with several other widely selling books with much the same message, all of which received much critical acclaim, the reviewer wrote: ". . . if the books really are good, then the public, far from being boorish and uncultivated, knows how to appreciate quality—and the books' central argument is false. On the other hand, if the argument is true, and the public can appreciate only books aimed at its own low level and the mass media can glorify nothing but marketability, then these books do not embody the high culture they extol, and are therefore not good."

—Tzvetan Todorov, "The Philosopher and the Everyday,"
The New Republic, 14 September 1987

22. The dilemma of permissible novelty is interesting . . . we may put it thus: for an interpretation to be valuable, it must do more than merely duplicate the ideas of the thinker being interpreted. Yet if it is to be just, it cannot deviate significantly from the original formulation.

—George Kimball Plochman, Foreword to *Frege's Logical Theory*
by Robert Sternfeld

23. The decision of the Supreme Court in *U.S. v. Nixon* (1974), handed down the first day of the Judiciary Committee's final debate, was critical. If the President defied the order, he would be impeached. If he obeyed the order, it was increasingly apparent, he would be impeached on the evidence.

—Victoria Schuck, "Watergate," *The Key Reporter,* Winter 1975–1976

24. Kamisar . . . seeks to impale the advocates of euthanasia on an old dilemma. Either the victim is not yet suffering pain, in which case his consent is merely an uninformed and anticipatory one—and he cannot bind himself by contract to be killed in the future—or he is

crazed by pain and stupefied by drugs, in which case he is not of sound mind.

—Glanville Williams, " 'Mercykilling' Legislation—A Rejoinder,"
Minnesota Law Review, 1958

*25. If we are to have peace, we must not encourage the competitive spirit, whereas if we are to make progress, we must encourage the competitive spirit. We must either encourage or not encourage the competitive spirit. Therefore we shall either have no peace or make no progress.

26. The argument under the present head may be put into a very concise form, which appears altogether conclusive. Either the mode in which the federal government is to be constructed will render it sufficiently dependent on the people, or it will not. On the first supposition, it will be restrained by that dependence from forming schemes obnoxious to their constituents. On the other supposition, it will not possess the confidence of the people, and its schemes of usurpation will be easily defeated by the State governments, who will be supported by the people.

—James Madison, *The Federalist Papers,* no. 46

27. Does the gentleman from Coles know that there is a statute standing in full force, making it highly penal, for an individual to loan money at a higher rate of interest than twelve per cent? If he does not he is too ignorant to be placed at the head of the committee which his resolution proposes; and if he does, his neglect to mention it shows him to be too uncandid to merit the respect or confidence of any one.

—Abraham Lincoln, speech in the Illinois legislature, 11 January 1837

28. . . . a man cannot enquire either about that which he knows, or about that which he does not know; for if he knows, he has no need to enquire; and if not, he cannot; for he does not know the very subject about which he is to enquire.

—Plato, *Meno*

29. Dissidents confined to asylums are caught up in an insoluble dilemma. "If you recant, they say, it proves that he was crazy. If you refuse to recant, and protest, they say that it proves he is still crazy."

—Lewis H. Gann, "Psychiatry: Helpful Servant or Cruel Master?"
The Intercollegiate Review, Spring 1982

*30. We tell clients to try to go through the entire first interview without even mentioning money. If you ask for a salary that is too high, the employer concludes that he can't afford you. If you ask for one that is too low, you're essentially saying,

"I'm not competent enough to handle the job that you're offering."

—James Challenger, "What to Do—and Not to Do—When Job Hunting," *U.S. News & World Report*, 6 August 1984

31. "Pascal's wager [is]" justifiably famous in the history of religion and also of betting. Pascal was arguing that agnostics—people unsure of God's existence—are best off betting that He does exist. If He does but you end up living as an unbeliever, then you could be condemned to spend eternity in the flames of Hell. If, on the other hand, He doesn't exist but you live as a believer, you suffer no corresponding penalty for being in error. Obviously, then, bettors on God start out with a big edge.

—Daniel Seligman, "Keeping Up," *Fortune*, 7 January 1985

Summary of Chapter 7

In this chapter we have examined syllogistic argument as it is used in ordinary language, exhibiting the different guises in which syllogisms appear and showing how they may be best understood, used, and evaluated.

In section 7.1, we explained the need for techniques to translate syllogistic arguments of any form into standard form. And we identified **the ways in which syllogistic arguments may deviate from standard-form categorical syllogisms.**

In section 7.2, we explained **how syllogisms in ordinary language appearing to have more than three terms may sometimes have the number of terms in them appropriately reduced to three**—by elimination of synonyms, and by elimination of complementary classes.

In section 7.3, we explained **how the propositions of a syllogistic argument, when not in standard form, may be translated into standard form so as to allow the syllogism to be tested** either by Venn diagrams or by use of the rules governing syllogisms. Nonstandard propositions of **nine different kinds** were examined, and the methods for translating each kind were explained and illustrated:

1. Singular propositions
2. Propositions having adjectives as predicates
3. Propositions having main verbs other than the copula "to be"
4. Statements having standard-form ingredients, but not in standard-form order
5. Propositions having quantifiers other than "all," "no," and "some"
6. Exclusive propositions, using "only" or "none but"
7. Propositions without words indicating quantity
8. Propositions not resembling standard-form propositions at all
9. Exceptive propositions, using "all except" or similar expressions

In section 7.4, we explained how the **uniform translation** of propositions into standard form, essential for testing, may be assisted by the use of **parameters.**

In sections 7.5 and 7.6, we explained **enthymemes,** syllogistic arguments in which one of the constituent propositions has been suppressed, and **sorites,** in which a chain of syllogisms may be compressed into a cluster of linked propositions.

In section 7.7, we explained syllogisms other than categorical: **disjunctive syllogisms** and **hypothetical syllogisms,** so called because they contain disjunctive or hypothetical premisses.

In section 7.8, we discussed the rhetorical use of **dilemmas,** disjunctive arguments that give to the adversary a choice of alternatives neither of which is acceptable. We explained and illustrated the three possible patterns of rhetorical response: going between the horns of the dilemma, grasping the dilemma by its horns, or devising a counterdilemma.

Because language is misleading, as well as because it is diffuse and inexact when applied to logic (for which it was never intended), logical symbolism is absolutely necessary to any exact or thorough treatment of our subject.
—Bertrand Russell

In order to avoid the inadequacies of the natural languages for purposes of logical analysis, it is necessary first to translate into a more exact notation.
—Alonzo Church

CHAPTER 8

SYMBOLIC LOGIC

8.1 THE SYMBOLIC LANGUAGE OF MODERN LOGIC

We seek techniques for the analysis and appraisal of deductive arguments. The theory of deduction aims to provide these techniques, and two different branches of this theory have been developed to do this: the *classical* or *Aristotelian logic*, examined in the three preceding chapters, and *modern symbolic logic*, which we will be our subject in this and the following two chapters.

The analyzing and appraising of arguments is often made difficult, however, by the peculiarities of the language—English, or any natural language—in which the arguments are presented. The words used may be vague or equivocal, the construction of the arguments may be ambiguous, metaphors and idioms may confuse or mislead, emotional appeals may distract—problems that were discussed in Part One. To avoid these difficulties, and thus move directly to the logical heart of an argument, logicians construct an artificial symbolic language, free of linguistic defects. With a symbolic language we can formulate an argument with precision.

Symbols also facilitate our thinking about an argument. "By the aid of symbolism," wrote one of the greatest of modern logicians, "we can make transitions in reasoning almost mechanically by the eye, which otherwise would call into play the higher faculties of the of the brain."[1] It may seem paradoxical, but a symbolic language helps us to accomplish some intellectual tasks without having to think too much.

The ancient and classical logicians also recognized the value of a special logical notation. Aristotle used variables in his own analyses, and the refined Aristotelian logic uses symbols in very sophisticated ways, as the preceding

---

[1] Alfred North Whitehead, *An Introduction to Mathematics*, 1911.

chapters have shown.[2] During the twentieth century very great steps have been taken to advance this process.

In modern logic, it is not syllogisms (as in the Aristotelian tradition) that are central, but logical *connectives,* the relations between elements that every deductive argument, syllogism or not, must employ. The *internal structure* of propositions and arguments is the focus of modern logic. To understand this structure we must first master the special symbols that are used in modern logical analysis.

Modern symbolic logic is not encumbered (as Aristotelian logic was) by the need to transform deductive arguments into syllogistic form. That task can be laborious, as we have seen in Chapter 7. Freed from the need to make such transformations, we can pursue the aims of deductive analysis more directly. The symbolic notation of modern logic set forth here is an exceedingly powerful tool for the analysis of arguments. With it we can more fully achieve the central aim of deductive logic: to discriminate valid arguments from invalid arguments.

8.2 THE SYMBOLS FOR CONJUNCTION, NEGATION, AND DISJUNCTION

In this chapter we shall be concerned with relatively simple arguments such as

> The blind prisoner has a red hat or the blind prisoner has a white hat.
> The blind prisoner does not have a red hat.
> Therefore the blind prisoner has a white hat.

and

> If Mr. Robinson is the brakeman's next-door neighbor, then Mr. Robinson lives halfway between Detroit and Chicago.
> Mr. Robinson does not live halfway between Detroit and Chicago.
> Therefore Mr. Robinson is not the brakeman's next-door neighbor.

Every argument of this general type contains at least one compound statement. In studying such arguments we divide all statements into two general categories, simple and compound. **A simple statement is one that does not contain any other statement as a component.** For example, "Charlie's neat" is a simple statement. **A compound statement is one that**

---

[2] The Arabic numerals we use today also illustrate very nicely how symbols can facilitate our reasoning. These numerals (1, 2, 3, . . .) replaced the old Roman numerals (i, ii, iii, . . .), which were much more cumbersome to manipulate. To multiply 113 by 9 is easy, but to multiply CXIII by IX is not so easy. Think of the difficulties of multiplying MCCCXLVIII by DCCLXIV! So awkward is calculation using the old numerals that even the ancient Romans were driven to devise a more efficient symbolism for arithmetic; some scholars contend that they actually relied on a Western version of the Oriental abacus, which they called a "counting board." We too must manipulate concepts. The more efficient our logical notation, the easier will be the tasks of deductive analysis, and the more likely that the resulting analyses will be accurate.

does contain another statement as a component. For example, "Charlie's neat and Charlie's sweet" is a compound statement, for it contains two simple statements as components. Of course, the components of a compound statement may themselves be compound.[3]

A.   Conjunction

There are several types of compound statements, each requiring its own logical notation. The first type of compound statement to be considered is the *conjunction.* **We can form the *conjunction* of two statements by placing the word "and" between them; the two statements so combined are called *conjuncts.*** Thus the compound statement "Charlie's neat and Charlie's sweet" is a conjunction whose first conjunct is "Charlie's neat" and whose second conjunct is "Charlie's sweet."

The word "and" is a short and convenient word, but it has other uses besides that of connecting statements. For example, the statement "Lincoln and Grant were contemporaries" is *not* a conjunction but a simple statement expressing a relationship. To have a unique symbol whose only function is to connect statements conjunctively, we introduce the dot "•" as our symbol for conjunction. Thus the previous conjunction can be written as "Charlie's neat • Charlie's sweet." More generally, where p and q are any two statements whatever, their conjunction is written $p • q$.

We know that every statement is either true or false. Therefore we say that **every statement has a *truth value,* where the truth value of a true statement is *true,* and the truth value of a false statement is *false.*** Using this concept of "truth value" we can divide compound statements into two distinct categories, according to whether or not the truth value of the compound statement is determined wholly by the truth values of its components, or determined by anything other than the truth values of its components.

---

[3] In formulating definitions and principles in logic one must be very precise. What appears simple often proves more complicated than had been supposed. The notion of a "component of a statement" is a good illustration of this need for caution.

One might have supposed that a *component* of a statement is simply a part of a statement that is itself a statement. But this account does not define the term with enough precision, because one statement may be a *part* of a larger statement and yet not a *component* of it in the strict sense. For example, consider the statement: "The man who shot Lincoln was an actor." Plainly the last four words of this statement are a part of it, and could indeed be regarded as a statement; it is either true or it is false that Lincoln was an actor. But the statement that "Lincoln was an actor," although undoubtedly a part of the larger statement, is not a *component* of that larger statement.

We can explain this by noting that, for part of a statement to be a component of that statement, two conditions must be satisfied: (1) The part must be a statement in its own right; *and* (2) If the part is replaced in the larger statement by any other statement, the result of that replacement must be meaningful, must make sense.

The first of these conditions is satisfied in the Lincoln example just above, but the second is not. Suppose the part "Lincoln was an actor" were replaced by "there are lions in Africa." The result of this replacement would be nonsense: "The man who shot there are lions in Africa." The term *component* is not a difficult one to understand but—like all logical terms—it must be defined accurately and applied carefully.

We apply this distinction to conjunctions. The truth value of the conjunction of two statements is determined wholly and entirely by the truth values of its two conjuncts. If both its conjuncts are true, the conjunction is true; otherwise it is false. For this reason a conjunction is said to be a *truth-functional* compound statement, and its conjuncts are said to be *truth-functional* components of it.

Not every compound statement is truth-functional, however. For example, the truth value of the compound statement "Othello believes that Desdemona loves Cassio" is not in any way determined by the truth value of its component simple statement "Desdemona loves Cassio," for it could be true that Othello believes that Desdemona loves Cassio regardless of whether she does so or not. So the component "Desdemona loves Cassio" is not a truth-functional component of the statement "Othello believes that Desdemona loves Cassio," and the statement itself is not a truth-functional compound statement.

For our present purposes we define a *component* of a compound statement as being a **truth-functional component of it provided that, if the component is replaced in the compound by any different statements having the same truth value as each other, the different compound statements produced by those replacements will also have the same truth values as each other.** And now we define a *compound statement* as being a **truth-functional compound statement if all of its components are truth-functional components of it.**[4]

We shall be concerned only with those compound statements that are truth-functionally compound. In the remainder of this book, therefore, we shall use the term *simple statement* to refer to **any statement that is not truth-functionally compound.**

A conjunction is a truth-functional compound statement, so our dot symbol is a **truth-functional connective.** Given any two statements, p and q, there are only four possible sets of truth values they can have. These four possible cases, and the truth value of the conjunction in each, can be displayed as follows:

Where p is true and q is true, $p \bullet q$ is true.
Where p is true and q is false, $p \bullet q$ is false.
Where p is false and q is true, $p \bullet q$ is false.
Where p is false and q is false, $p \bullet q$ is false.

If we represent the truth values "true" and "false" by the capital letters **T** and **F,** the determination of the truth value of a conjunction by the truth values of its conjuncts can be represented more briefly and more clearly by means of a "truth table":

p	q	$p \bullet q$
T	T	T
T	F	F
F	T	F
F	F	F

---

[4] Somewhat more complicated definitions have been proposed by David H. Sanford in his "What Is a Truth Functional Component?" *Logique et Analyse* 14 (1970), 483–486.

This truth table can be taken as defining the dot symbol, since it explains what truth values are assumed by $p \cdot q$ in every possible case.

We shall find it convenient to abbreviate simple statements by capital letters, generally using for this purpose a letter that will help us remember which statement it abbreviates. Thus we should abbreviate "Charlie's neat and Charlie's sweet" as $N \cdot S$. Some conjunctions both of whose conjuncts have the same subject term—for example, "Byron was a great poet and Byron was a great adventurer"—are more briefly and perhaps more naturally stated in English by placing the "and" between the predicate terms and not repeating the subject term, as in "Byron was a great poet and a great adventurer." For our purposes, we regard the latter as formulating the same statement as the former and symbolize either one indifferently as $P \cdot A$. If both conjuncts of a conjunction have the same predicate term, as in "Lewis was a famous explorer and Clark was a famous explorer," again the conjunction usually would be stated in English by placing the "and" between the subject terms and not repeating the predicate, as in "Lewis and Clark were famous explorers." Either formulation is symbolized as $L \cdot C$.

As shown by the truth table defining the dot symbol, a conjunction is true if and only if both of its conjuncts are true. But the word "and" has another use in which it signifies not *mere* (truth-functional) conjunction but has the sense of "and subsequently," meaning temporal succession. Thus the statement "Jones entered the country at New York and went straight to Chicago" is significant and might be true, whereas "Jones went straight to Chicago and entered the country at New York" is hardly intelligible. And there is quite a difference between "He took off his shoes and got into bed" and "He got into bed and took off his shoes."[5] Consideration of such examples emphasizes the desirability of having a special symbol with an exclusively truth-functional conjunctive use.

Note that the English words "but," "yet," "also," "still," "although," "however," "moreover," "nevertheless," and so on, and even the comma and the semicolon, can also be used to conjoin two statements into a single compound statement, and in their conjunctive sense they can all be represented by the dot symbol.

B.   Negation

The *negation* (or contradictory or denial) of a statement in English is often formed by the insertion of a "not" in the original statement. Alternatively, one can express the negation of a statement in English by prefixing to it the phrase "it is false that" or "it is not the case that." It is customary to use the symbol "~" (called a "curl" or a "tilde") to form the negation of a statement. Thus, where M symbolizes the statement "All humans are mortal," the various statements "Not all humans are mortal," "Some humans are not mortal," "It is false that all humans are mortal," and "It is not the case that all humans are mortal"

---

[5]And in *The Victoria Advocate*, Victoria, Texas, 27 October 1990, appeared the following report: "Ramiro Ramirez Garza, of the 2700 block of Leary Lane, was arrested by police as he was threatening to commit suicide and flee to Mexico."

are all indifferently symbolized as ~*M*. More generally, where *p* is any statement whatever, its negation is written ~*p*. It is obvious that the curl is a truth-functional operator. The negation of any true statement is false, and the negation of any false statement is true. This fact can be presented very simply and clearly by means of a truth table:

p	~*p*
T	F
F	T

This truth table may be regarded as the definition of the negation symbol "~".

C.   Disjunction

The *disjunction* (or alternation) of two statements is formed in English by inserting the word "or" between them. The two component statements so combined are called "disjuncts" (or "alternatives").

The English word "or" is ambiguous, having two related but distinguishable meanings. One of them is exemplified in the statement "Premiums will be waived in the event of sickness or unemployment." The intention here is obviously that premiums are waived not only for sick persons and for unemployed persons, but also for persons who are *both* sick *and* unemployed. This sense of the word "or" is called *weak* or *inclusive*. An inclusive disjunction is true in case one or the other or both disjuncts are true; only if both disjuncts are false is their inclusive disjunction false. The inclusive "or" has the sense of "either, possibly both." Where precision is at a premium, as in contracts and other legal documents, this sense is made explicit by the use of the phrase "and/or."

The word "or" is also used in a *strong* or *exclusive* sense, in which the meaning is not "at least one" but "at least one and at most one." Where a restaurant lists "salad or dessert" on its dinner menu, it is clearly meant that, for the stated price of the meal, the diner may have one or the other *but not both.* Where precision is at a premium and the exclusive sense of "or" is intended, the phrase "but not both" is usually added.

We interpret the inclusive disjunction of two statements as an assertion that at least one of the statements is true, and we interpret their exclusive disjunction as an assertion that at least one of the statements is true but not both are true. Note that the two kinds of disjunction have a part of their meanings in common. This partial common meaning, that at least one of the disjuncts is true, is the *whole* meaning of the inclusive "or" and a *part* of the meaning of the exclusive "or."

Although disjunctions are stated ambiguously in English, they are unambiguous in Latin. Latin has two different words corresponding to the two different senses of the English word "*or.*" The Latin word *vel* signifies weak or inclusive disjunction, and the Latin word *aut* corresponds to the word "or" in its strong or exclusive sense. It is customary to use the initial letter of the word *vel* to stand for "or" in its weak, inclusive sense. Where *p* and *q* are any two statements whatever, their weak or inclusive disjunction is written *p* ∨ *q*. Our symbol for inclusive disjunction (called a "wedge" or, less frequently, a "vee") is also a truth-functional connective. A weak disjunction is false only in case both of its disjuncts are false. We may regard the wedge as being defined by the following truth table:

p	q	$p \vee q$
T	T	T
T	F	T
F	T	T
F	F	F

The first specimen argument presented in this section was a Disjunctive Syllogism.[6]

> The blind prisoner has a red hat or the blind prisoner has a white hat.
> The blind prisoner does not have a red hat.
> Therefore the blind prisoner has a white hat.

Its form is characterized by saying that its first premiss is a disjunction; its second premiss is the negation of the first disjunct of the first premiss; and its conclusion is the same as the second disjunct of the first premiss. It is evident that the disjunctive syllogism, so defined, is valid on either interpretation of the word "or"; that is, regardless of whether an inclusive or exclusive disjunction is intended.[7] Since the typical valid argument that has a disjunction for a premiss is, like the disjunctive syllogism, valid on either interpretation of the word "or," a simplification may be effected by translating the English word "or" into our logical symbol "∨"—*regardless of which meaning of the English word "or" is intended.* In general, only a close examination of the context, or an explicit questioning of the speaker or writer, can reveal which sense of "or" is intended. This problem, often impossible to resolve, can be avoided if we agree to treat *any* occurrence of the word "or" as inclusive. On the other hand, if it is explicitly stated that the disjunction is intended to be exclusive, by means of the added phrase "but not both" for example, we have the symbolic machinery to formulate that additional sense, as will be shown directly.

Where both disjuncts have either the same subject term or the same predicate term, it is often natural to compress the formulation of their disjunction in English by so placing the "or" that there is no need to repeat the common part of the two disjuncts. Thus "Either Smith is the owner or Smith is the manager" might equally well be stated as "Smith is either the owner or the manager," and either one is properly symbolized as $O \vee M$. And "Either Red is guilty or Butch is guilty" would often be stated as "Either Red or Butch is guilty," either one being symbolized as $R \vee B$.

---

[6] A *syllogism* is a deductive argument consisting of two premises and a conclusion.
[7] Note that the term "disjunctive syllogism" is being used in a narrower sense here than it was in the preceding chapter.

The word "unless" is often used to form the disjunction of two statements. Thus, "You will do poorly on the exam unless you study" is correctly symbolized as $P \vee S$. The reason is that we use "unless" to mean that if the one proposition is not true, the other is or will be true. The sentence above can be understood to mean "If you don't study, you will do poorly on the exam"—and that is the thrust of the disjunction, since it asserts that one of the disjuncts is true, and hence that if one of them is false, the other must be true. Of course you may study *and* do poorly on the exam.

But the word "unless" is sometimes used to convey more information than that; it may mean that one or the other proposition is true but that not both are true. That is, "unless" may be intended as an *exclusive* disjunction. Thus Jeremy Bentham wrote, "What is politically good cannot be morally bad, unless the rules of arithmetic, which are good for a large number, are bad for a small one."[8] Here the author did mean that at least one of the two disjuncts is true, but he plainly also suggested that they cannot both be true. Other uses of "unless" are somewhat ambiguous. When we say, "The picnic will be held unless it rains" (or, "Unless it rains, the picnic will be held"), we surely do mean that the picnic will be held if it does not rain. But do we mean that it will not be held if it does rain? That may be uncertain. Here, as elsewhere, it is wise policy to treat every disjunction as weak or inclusive; "unless" is best symbolized simply with the wedge ($\vee$).

D. Punctuation

In English, punctuation is absolutely required if complicated statements are to be clear. A great many different punctuation marks are used, without which many sentences would be highly ambiguous. For example, quite different meanings attach to "The teacher says John is a fool" when it is given different punctuations. Other sentences require punctuation for their very intelligibility, as, for example, "Jill where Jack had had had had had had had had had had had the teacher's approval." Punctuation is equally necessary in mathematics. In the absence of a special convention, no number is uniquely denoted by $2 \times 3 + 5$, although when it is made clear how its constituents are to be grouped, it denotes either 11 or 16: the first when punctuated $(2 \times 3) + 5$, the second when punctuated $2 \times (3 + 5)$. To avoid ambiguity, and to make meaning clear, punctuation marks in mathematics appear in the form of parentheses, ( ), which are used to group individual symbols; brackets, [ ], which are used to group expressions that include parentheses; and braces, { }, which are used to group expressions that include brackets.

In the language of symbolic logic those same punctuation marks—parentheses, brackets, and braces—are equally essential, because in logic compound statements are themselves often compounded together into more complicated ones. Thus $p \bullet q \vee r$ is ambiguous: It might mean the conjunction of p with the disjunction of q with r, or it might mean the disjunction whose first disjunct is

---

[8] Jeremy Bentham, *Principles of Legislation* (1802).

the conjunction of p and q and whose second disjunct is r. We distinguish between these two different senses by punctuating the given formula as $p \bullet (q \vee r)$ or else as $(p \bullet q) \vee r$. That the different ways of punctuating the original formula do make a difference can be seen by considering the case in which p is false and q and r are both true. In this case the second punctuated formula is true (since its second disjunct is true), whereas the first one is false (since its first conjunct is false). Here the difference in punctuation makes all the difference between truth and falsehood, for different punctuations can assign different truth values to the ambiguous $p \bullet q \vee r$.

The word "either" has a variety of different meanings and uses in English. It has conjunctive force in the sentence "There is danger on either side." More often it is used to introduce the first disjunct in a disjunction, as in "Either the blind prisoner has a red hat or the blind prisoner has a white hat." There it contributes to the rhetorical balance of the sentence, but it does not affect its meaning. Perhaps the most important use of the word "either" is to punctuate a compound statement. Thus the sentence

> The organization will meet on Thursday and Anand
> will be elected or the election will be postponed.

can have its ambiguity resolved in one direction by placing the word "either" at its beginning, or in the other direction by inserting the word "either" before the name "Anand." Such punctuation is effected in our symbolic language by parentheses. The ambiguous formula $p \bullet q \vee r$ discussed in the preceding paragraph corresponds to the ambiguous sentence just examined. The two different punctuations of the formula correspond to the two different punctuations of the sentence effected by the two different insertions of the word "either."

The negation of a disjunction is often formed by use of the phrase "neither–nor." Thus the statement "Either Fillmore or Harding was the greatest American president" can be contradicted by the statement "Neither Fillmore nor Harding was the greatest American president." The disjunction would be symbolized as $F \vee H$, and its negation as either $\sim(F \vee H)$ or as $(\sim F) \bullet (\sim H)$. (The logical equivalence of these two symbolic formulas will be discussed in section 8.5.) It should be clear that to deny a disjunction stating that one or another statement is true requires that both be stated to be false.

The word "both" in English has a very important role in logical punctuation, and it deserves the most careful attention. When we say "Both Jamal and Derek are not . . ." we are saying, as noted just above, that "Neither Jamal nor Derek is . . ."; we are applying the negation to each of them. But when we say "Jamal and Derek are not both . . ." we are saying something very different; we are applying the negation to the pair of them taken together, saying that it is not the case that they are both . . ." This difference is very substantial. Entirely different meanings arise when the word both is placed differently in the English sentence. Consider the great difference between the meanings of

> Jamal and Derek will not both be elected.

and

Jamal and Derek will both not be elected.

The first denies the conjunction $J \bullet D$ and may be symbolized as $\sim(J \bullet D)$. The second says that each one of the two will not be elected, and is symbolized as $\sim(J) \bullet \sim(D)$. Merely changing the *position* of the two words "both" and "not" alters the logical force of what is asserted.

Of course the word "both" does not always have this role; sometimes we use it only to add emphasis. When we say that "Both Lewis and Clark were great explorers," we use the word only to state more emphatically what is said by "Lewis and Clark were great explorers." But when the task is that of logical analysis, the punctuational role of "both" must be very carefully determined.

In the interest of brevity—that is, to decrease the number of parentheses required—it is convenient to establish the convention that **in any formula the negation symbol will be understood to apply to the smallest statement that the punctuation permits.** Without this convention, the formula $\sim p \vee q$ is ambiguous, meaning either $(\sim p) \vee q$, or $\sim(p \vee q)$. But by our convention we take it to mean the first of these alternatives, for the curl *can* (and therefore by our convention *does*) apply to the first component, p, rather than to the larger formula $p \vee q$.

Given a set of punctuation marks for our symbolic language, it is possible to write not merely conjunctions, negations, and weak disjunctions in it, but exclusive disjunctions as well. The exclusive disjunction of p and q asserts that at least one of them is true but not both are true, which is written quite simply as $(p \vee q) \bullet \sim(p \bullet q)$.

Any compound statement constructed from simple statements using only the truth-functional connectives—dot, curl, and wedge—has its truth value completely determined by the truth or falsehood of its component simple statements. If we know the truth values of simple statements, the truth value of any truth-functional compound of them is easily calculated. In working with such compound statements we always begin with their inmost components and work outward. For example, if A and B are true and X and Y are false statements, we calculate the truth value of the compound statement $\sim[\sim(A \bullet X) \bullet (Y \vee \sim B)]$ as follows. Since X is false, the conjunction $A \bullet X$ is false, and so its negation $\sim(A \bullet X)$ is true. B is true; so its negation $\sim B$ is false, and since Y is false also, the disjunction of Y with $\sim B$, $Y \vee \sim B$, is false. The bracketed formula $[\sim(A \bullet X) \bullet (Y \vee \sim B)]$ is the conjunction of a true with a false statement and is therefore false. Hence its negation, which is the entire statement, is true. Such a stepwise procedure always enables us to determine the truth value of a compound statement from the truth values of its components.

In some circumstances we may be able to determine the truth value of a truth-functional compound statement even if we cannot determine the truth or falsehood of one or more of its component simple statements. We do this by first calculating the truth value of the compound statement on the assumption that a given simple component is true, and then by calculating the truth value of the compound statement on the assumption that that same simple component is false, doing the same for each component whose truth value is unknown. If both these calculations yield the *same* truth value for the compound statement in question, we will have determined the truth value of the compound statement without having had to determine the truth value of its components, because we know that the truth value cannot be other than true or false.

Exercises

I.   Using the truth table definitions of the dot, the wedge, and the curl, determine which of the following statements are true.

*1.   Rome is the capital of Italy ∨ Rome is the capital of Spain.

2.   ~(London is the capital of England • Stockholm is the capital of Norway).

3.   ~London is the capital of England • ~Stockholm is the capital of Norway.

4.   ~(Rome is the capital of Spain ∨ Paris is the capital of France).

*5.   ~Rome is the capital of Spain ∨ ~Paris is the capital of France.

6.   London is the capital of England ∨ ~London is the capital of England.

7.   Stockholm is the capital of Norway • ~Stockholm is the capital of Norway.

8.   (Paris is the capital of France • Rome is the capital of Spain) ∨ (Paris is the capital of France • ~Rome is the capital of Spain).

9.   (London is the capital of England ∨ Stockholm is the capital of Norway) • (~Rome is the capital of Italy • ~Stockholm is the capital of Norway).

*10.   Rome is the capital of Spain ∨ ~(Paris is the capital of France • Rome is the capital of Spain).

11.   Rome is the capital of Italy • ~(Paris is the capital of France ∨ Rome is the capital of Spain).

12.   ~(~Paris is the capital of France • ~Stockholm is the capital of Norway).

13.   ~[~(~Rome is the capital of Spain ∨ ~Paris is the capital of France) ∨ ~(~Paris is the capital of France ∨ Stockholm is the capital of Norway)].

14.   ~[~(~London is the capital of England • Rome is the capital of Spain) • ~(Rome is the capital of Spain • ~Rome is the capital of Spain)].

*15.   ~[~(Stockholm is the capital of Norway ∨ Paris is the capital of France) ∨ ~(~London is the capital of England • ~Rome is the capital of Spain)].

16.   Rome is the capital of Spain ∨ (~London is the capital of England ∨ London is the capital of England).

17. Paris is the capital of France • ~(Paris is the capital of France • Rome is the capital of Spain).

18. London is the capital of England • ~(Rome is the capital of Italy • Rome is the capital of Italy).

19. (Stockholm is the capital of Norway ∨ ~Paris is the capital of France) ∨ ~(~Stockholm is the capital of Norway • ~London is the capital of England).

*20. (Paris is the capital of France ∨ ~Rome is the capital of Spain) ∨ ~(~Paris is the capital of France • ~Rome is the capital of Spain).

21. ~[~(Rome is the capital of Spain • Stockholm is the capital of Norway) ∨ ~(~Paris is the capital of France ∨ ~Rome is the capital of Spain)].

22. ~[~(London is the capital of England • Paris is the capital of France) ∨ ~(~Stockholm is the capital of Norway ∨ ~Paris is the capital of France)].

23. ~[(~Paris is the capital of France ∨ Rome is the capital of Italy) • ~(~Rome is the capital of Italy ∨ Stockholm is the capital of Norway)].

24. ~[(~Rome is the capital of Spain ∨ Stockholm is the capital of Norway) • ~(~Stockholm is the capital of Norway ∨ Paris is the capital of France)].

*25. ~[(~London is the capital of England • Paris is the capital of France) ∨ ~(~Paris is the capital of France • Rome is the capital of Spain)].

II. If *A*, *B*, and *C* are true statements and *X*, *Y*, and *Z* are false statements, which of the following are true?

*1. $\sim A \lor B$ 2. $\sim B \lor X$

3. $\sim Y \lor C$ 4. $\sim Z \lor X$

*5. $(A \bullet X) \lor (B \bullet Y)$ 6. $(B \bullet C) \lor (Y \bullet Z)$

7. $\sim(C \bullet Y) \lor (A \bullet Z)$ 8. $\sim(A \bullet B) \lor (X \bullet Y)$

9. $\sim(X \bullet Z) \lor (B \bullet C)$ *10. $\sim(X \bullet \sim Y) \lor (B \bullet \sim C)$

11. $(A \lor X) \bullet (Y \lor B)$ 12. $(B \lor C) \bullet (Y \lor Z)$

13. $(X \lor Y) \bullet (X \lor Z)$ 14. $\sim(A \lor Y) \bullet (B \lor X)$

*15. $\sim(X \lor Z) \bullet (\sim X \lor Z)$ 16. $\sim(A \lor C) \lor \sim(X \bullet \sim Y)$

17. $\sim(B \lor Z) \bullet \sim(X \lor \sim Y)$ 18. $\sim[(A \lor \sim C) \lor (C \lor \sim A)]$

19. $\sim[(B \bullet C) \bullet \sim(C \bullet B)]$ *20. $\sim[(A \bullet B) \lor \sim(B \bullet A)]$

21. $[A \lor (B \lor C)] \bullet \sim[(A \lor B) \lor C]$

22. $[X \lor (Y \bullet Z)] \lor \sim[(X \lor Y) \bullet (X \lor Z)]$

23. $[A \bullet (B \lor C)] \bullet \sim[(A \bullet B) \lor (A \bullet C)]$

24. $\sim\{[(\sim A \bullet B) \bullet (\sim X \bullet Z)] \bullet \sim[(A \bullet \sim B) \lor \sim(\sim Y \bullet \sim Z)]\}$

*25. $\sim\{\sim[(B \bullet \sim C) \lor (Y \bullet \sim Z)] \bullet [(\sim B \lor X) \lor (B \lor \sim Y)]\}$

III. If *A* and *B* are known to be true and *X* and *Y* are known to be false, but the truth values of *P* and *Q* are not known, of which of the following statements can you determine the truth values?

*1. $A \lor P$ 2. $Q \bullet X$

 3. $Q \lor \sim X$ 4. $\sim B \bullet P$

*5. $P \lor \sim P$ 6. $\sim P \lor (Q \lor P)$

 7. $Q \bullet \sim Q$ 8. $P \bullet (\sim P \lor X)$

 9. $\sim (P \bullet Q) \lor P$ *10. $\sim Q \bullet [(P \lor Q) \bullet \sim P]$

11. $(P \lor Q) \bullet \sim (Q \lor P)$ 12. $(P \bullet Q) \bullet (\sim P \lor \sim Q)$

13. $\sim P \lor [\sim Q \lor (P \bullet Q)]$ 14. $P \lor \sim (\sim A \lor X)$

*15. $P \bullet [\sim (P \lor Q) \lor \sim P]$ 16. $\sim (P \bullet Q) \lor (Q \bullet P)$

17. $\sim [\sim (\sim P \lor Q) \lor P] \lor P$ 18. $(\sim P \lor Q) \bullet \sim [\sim P \lor (P \bullet Q)]$

19. $(\sim A \lor P) \bullet (\sim P \lor Y)$

*20. $\sim [P \lor (B \bullet Y)] \lor [(P \lor B) \bullet (P \lor Y)]$

21. $[P \lor (Q \bullet A)] \bullet \sim [(P \lor Q) \bullet (P \lor A)]$

22. $[P \lor (Q \bullet X)] \bullet \sim [(P \lor Q) \bullet (P \lor X)]$

23. $\sim [\sim P \lor (\sim Q \lor X)] \lor [\sim (\sim P \lor Q) \lor (\sim P \lor X)]$

24. $\sim [\sim P \lor (\sim Q \lor A)] \lor [\sim (\sim P \lor Q) \lor (\sim P \lor A)]$

*25. $\sim [(P \bullet Q) \lor (Q \bullet \sim P)] \bullet \sim [(P \bullet \sim Q) \lor (\sim Q \bullet \sim P)]$

IV. Using the letters *E, I, J, L,* and *S* to abbreviate the simple statements "Egypt's food shortage worsens," "Iran raises the price of oil," "Jordan requests more American aid," "Libya raises the price of oil," and "Saudi Arabia buys 500 more warplanes," symbolize these statements.

*1. Iran raises the price of oil but Libya does not raise the price of oil.

 2. Either Iran or Libya raises the price of oil.

 3. Iran and Libya both raise the price of oil.

 4. Iran and Libya do not both raise the price of oil.

*5. Iran and Libya both do not raise the price of oil.

 6. Iran or Libya raises the price of oil but they do not both do so.

 7. Saudi Arabia buys 500 more warplanes and either Iran raises the price of oil or Jordan requests more American aid.

 8. Either Saudi Arabia buys 500 more warplanes and Iran raises the price of oil or Jordan requests more American aid.

 9. It is not the case that Egypt's food shortage worsens, and Jordan requests more American aid.

*10. It is not the case that either Egypt's food shortage worsens or Jordan requests more American aid.

11. Either it is not the case that Egypt's food shortage worsens or Jordan requests more American aid.

12. It is not the case that both Egypt's food shortage worsens and Jordan requests more American aid.

13. Jordan requests more American aid unless Saudi Arabia buys 500 more warplanes.

14. Unless Egypt's food shortage worsens, Libya raises the price of oil.

*15. Iran won't raise the price of oil unless Libya does so.

16. Unless both Iran and Libya raise the price of oil neither of them does.

17. Libya raises the price of oil and Egypt's food shortage worsens.

18. It is not the case that neither Iran nor Libya raises the price of oil.

19. Egypt's food shortage worsens and Jordan requests more American aid, unless both Iran and Libya do not raise the price of oil.

*20. Either Iran raises the price of oil and Egypt's food shortage worsens, or it is not the case both that Jordan requests more American aid and that Saudi Arabia buys 500 more warplanes.

21. Either Egypt's food shortage worsens and Saudi Arabia buys 500 more warplanes, or either Jordan requests more American aid or Libya raises the price of oil.

22. Saudi Arabia buys 500 more warplanes, and either Jordan requests more American aid or both Libya and Iran raise the price of oil.

23. Either Egypt's food shortage worsens or Jordan requests more American aid, but neither Libya nor Iran raises the price of oil.

24. Egypt's food shortage worsens, but Saudi Arabia buys 500 more warplanes and Libya raises the price of oil.

*25. Libya raises the price of oil and Egypt's food shortage worsens; however, Saudi Arabia buys 500 more warplanes and Jordan requests more American aid.

8.3 CONDITIONAL STATEMENTS AND MATERIAL IMPLICATION

Where two statements are combined by placing the word "if" before the first and inserting the word "then" between them, the resulting compound statement is a *conditional* **(also called a "hypothetical," an "implication," or an "implicative statement").** In a conditional, the component statement that follows the "if" is called the **antecedent** (or the "implicans" or—rarely—the "protasis"), and the component statement that follows the "then" is the **consequent** (or the "implicate" or—rarely—the "apodosis"). For example, "If Mr. Jones is the brakeman's next-door neighbor, then Mr. Jones earns exactly three times as much as the brakeman" is a conditional statement in which "Mr. Jones is the brakeman's next-door neighbor" is the antecedent and "Mr. Jones earns exactly three times as much as the brakeman" is the consequent.

A conditional statement asserts that in any case in which its antecedent is true, its consequent is true also. It does not assert that its antecedent is true, but only that *if* its antecedent is true, its consequent is true also. It does not assert that its consequent is true, but only that its consequent is true *if* its antecedent is true. The essential meaning of a conditional statement is the *relationship* asserted to hold between its antecedent and consequent, in that order. To understand the meaning of a conditional statement, then, we must understand what the relationship of implication is.

"Implication" plausibly appears to have more than one meaning. We found it useful to distinguish different senses of the word "or" before introducing a special logical symbol to correspond exactly to a single one of the meanings of the English word. Had we not done so, the ambiguity of the English would have infected our logical symbolism and prevented it from achieving the clarity and precision aimed at. It will be equally useful to distinguish the different senses of "implies" or "if–then" before we introduce a special logical symbol in this connection.

Consider the following four conditional statements, each of which seems to assert a different type of implication, and to each of which corresponds a different sense of "if–then":

A. If all humans are mortal and Socrates is a human, then Socrates is mortal.
B. If Leslie is a bachelor, then Leslie is unmarried.
C. If this piece of blue litmus paper is placed in acid, then this piece of blue litmus paper will turn red.
D. If State loses the homecoming game, then I'll eat my hat.

Even a casual inspection of these four conditional statements reveals that they are of quite different types. The consequent of **A** follows *logically* from its antecedent, whereas the consequent of **B** follows from its antecedent by the very *definition* of the term "bachelor," which means unmarried man. The consequent of **C** does not follow from its antecedent either by logic alone or by the definition of its terms; the connection must be discovered empirically, for the implication stated here is *causal*. Finally, the consequent of **D** does not follow from its antecedent either by logic or by definition, nor is there any causal law involved—in the usual sense of the term. Most causal laws, those discovered in physics and chemistry, for example, describe what happens in the world regardless of people's hopes or desires. There is no such law connected with statement **D**, of course. That statement reports a *decision* of the speaker to behave in the specified way under the specified circumstances.

The four conditional statements examined in the preceding paragraph are different in that each asserts a different type of implication between its antecedent and consequent. But they are not completely different; all assert types of implication. Is there any identifiable common meaning, any partial meaning that is common to these admittedly different types of implication, although perhaps not the whole or complete meaning of any one of them?

The search for a common partial meaning takes on added significance when we recall our procedure in working out a symbolic representation for the

English word "or." In that case, we proceeded as follows. First, we emphasized the difference between the two senses of that word, contrasting inclusive with exclusive disjunction. The inclusive disjunction of two statements was observed to mean that at least one of the statements is true, and the exclusive disjunction of two statements was observed to mean that at least one of the statements is true but not both are true. Second, we noted that these two types of disjunction had a common *partial* meaning. This partial common meaning, that at least one of the disjuncts is true, was seen to be the *whole* meaning of the weak, inclusive "or," and a *part* of the meaning of the strong, exclusive "or." We then introduced the special symbol "∨" to represent this common partial meaning (which was the entire meaning of "or" in its inclusive sense). Third, we noted that the symbol representing the common partial meaning was an adequate translation of either sense of the word "or" for the purpose of retaining the Disjunctive Syllogism as a valid form of argument. It was admitted that translating an exclusive "or" into the symbol "∨" ignored and lost part of the word's meaning. But the part of its meaning that is preserved by this translation is all that is needed for the Disjunctive Syllogism to remain a valid form of argument. Since the Disjunctive Syllogism is typical of arguments involving disjunction, with which we are here concerned, this partial translation of the word "or," which may abstract from its "full" or "complete" meaning in some cases, is wholly adequate for our present purposes.

Now we wish to proceed in the same way, this time in connection with the English phrase "if–then." The first part is already accomplished: We have already emphasized the differences among some four senses of the "if–then" phrase, corresponding to four different types of implication. We are now ready for the second step, which is to discover a sense that is at least a part of the meaning of all four different types of implication.

One way of approaching this problem is to ask what circumstances would suffice to establish the falsehood of a given conditional statement. Under what circumstances should we agree that the conditional statement

> If this piece of blue litmus paper is placed in that solution, then this piece of blue litmus paper will turn red.

is *false?* It is important to realize that this conditional does not assert that any blue litmus paper is actually placed in the solution, or that any litmus paper actually turns red. It asserts merely that *if* this piece of blue litmus paper is placed in the solution, *then* this piece of blue litmus paper will turn red. It is proved false if this piece of blue litmus paper is actually placed in the solution and does not turn red. The acid test, so to speak, of the falsehood of a conditional statement is available when its antecedent is true, for if its consequent is false while its antecedent is true, the conditional itself is thereby proved false.

Any conditional statement "If p then q" is known to be false in case the conjunction $p \bullet \sim q$ is known to be true; that is, in case its antecedent is true and its consequent is false. For a conditional to be true, then, the indicated conjunction must be false; that is, its negation ~($p \bullet$ ~q) must be true. In other words, for any conditional "If p then q" to be true, ~($p \bullet$ ~q), the negation of the conjunction of its antecedent with the negation of its consequent, must also be true. We may, then, regard ~($p \bullet$ ~q) as a part of the meaning of "If p then q."

Every conditional statement means to deny that its antecedent is true and its consequent false, but this need not be the whole of its meaning. A conditional such as **A** on page 313 also asserts a logical connection between its antecedent and consequent, as **B** asserts a definitional connection, **C** a causal connection, and **D** a decisional connection. But no matter what type of implication is asserted by a conditional statement, part of its meaning is the negation of the conjunction of its antecedent with the negation of its consequent.

We now introduce a special symbol to represent this common partial meaning of the "if–then" phrase. **We define the new symbol "⊃" (called a "horseshoe") by taking $p \supset q$ as an abbreviation of** ~($p \bullet$ ~q). The exact significance of the "⊃" symbol can be indicated by means of a truth table:

p	q	~q	$p \bullet$ ~q	~($p \bullet$ ~ q)	$p \supset q$
T	T	F	F	T	T
T	F	T	T	F	F
F	T	F	F	T	T
F	F	T	F	T	T

Here the first two columns are the guide columns; they simply lay out all possible combinations of truth and falsehood for p and q. The third column is filled in by reference to the second, the fourth by reference to the first and third, the fifth by reference to the fourth, and the sixth is identical to the fifth by definition.

The symbol "⊃" is not to be regarded as denoting *the* meaning of "if–then," or standing for *the* relation of implication. That would be impossible, for there is no single meaning of "if–then"; there are several meanings. There is no unique relation of implication to be thus represented; there are several different implication relations. Nor is the symbol "⊃" to be regarded as somehow standing for *all* the meanings of "if–then." These are all different, and any attempt to abbreviate all of them by a single logical symbol would render that symbol ambiguous—as ambiguous as the English phrase "if–then" or the English word "implication." The symbol "⊃" is completely unambiguous. What $p \supset q$ abbreviates is ~($p \bullet$ ~ q), whose meaning is included in the meanings of each of the various kinds of implications considered but which does not constitute the entire meaning of any of them.

We can regard the symbol "⊃" as representing another kind of implication, and it will be expedient to do so, since a convenient way to read $p \supset q$ is "If p then q." But it is not the same kind of implication as any of those mentioned earlier. It is called *material implication* by logicians, who in giving it a special name admit that it is a special notion, not to be confused with other, more usual, types of implication.

Not all conditional statements in English need assert one of the four types of implication previously considered. Material implication constitutes a fifth type that may be asserted in ordinary discourse. Consider the remark "If Hitler was a military genius, then I'm a monkey's uncle." It is quite clear that it does not assert logical, definitional, or causal implication. It cannot represent a decisional implication, since it scarcely lies in the speaker's power to make the consequent true. No "real connection," whether logical, definitional, or causal, obtains between antecedent and consequent here. A conditional of this sort is often used as an emphatic or humorous method of denying its antecedent. The consequent of such a conditional is usually a statement that is obviously or ludicrously false. And since no true conditional can have both its antecedent true and its consequent false, to affirm such a conditional amounts to denying that its antecedent is true. The full meaning of the present conditional seems to be the denial that "Hitler was a military genius" is true when "I'm a monkey's uncle" is false. And since the latter is so obviously false, the conditional must be understood to deny the former.

The point here is that no "real connection" between antecedent and consequent is suggested by a material implication. All it asserts is that, as a matter of fact, it is not the case that the antecedent is true when the consequent is false. Note that the material implication symbol is a truth-functional connective, like the symbols for conjunction and disjunction. As such, it is defined by the truth table

p	q	$p \supset q$
T	T	T
T	F	F
F	T	T
F	F	T

As thus defined by the truth table, the horseshoe symbol "$\supset$" has some features that may at first appear odd: The assertion that a false antecedent materially implies a true consequent is true; and the assertion that a false antecedent materially implies a false consequent is also true. This apparent strangeness can be dissipated in part by the following considerations. Because the number 2 is smaller than the number 4 (a fact noted symbolically as $2 < 4$), it follows that *any* number smaller than 2 is smaller than 4. The conditional formula

If $x < 2$ *then* $x < 4$

is true for any number x whatsoever. If we focus on the numbers 1, 3, and 4, and replace the number variable x in the preceding conditional formula by each of them in turn, we can make the following observations. In

If $1 < 2$ then $1 < 4$

both antecedent and consequent are true, and of course the conditional is true. In

$$\text{If } 3 < 2 \text{ then } 3 < 4$$

the antecedent is false and the consequent is true, and of course the conditional is again true. In

$$\text{If } 4 < 2 \text{ then } 4 < 4$$

both antecedent and consequent are false, but the conditional remains true. These three cases correspond to the first, third, and fourth rows of the table defining the horseshoe symbol "⊃". So it is not particularly remarkable or surprising that a conditional should be true where both antecedent and consequent are true, where the antecedent is false and the consequent is true, or where antecedent and consequent are both false. Of course, there is no number that is smaller than 2 but not smaller than 4; that is, there is no true conditional statement with true antecedent and false consequent. This is exactly what the defining truth table for "⊃" lays down.

Now we propose to translate any occurrence of the "if–then" phrase into our logical symbol "⊃". This proposal means that in translating conditional statements into our symbolism, we treat them all as merely material implications. Of course most conditional statements assert that more than a merely material implication holds between their antecedents and consequents. So our proposal amounts to suggesting that we ignore, or put aside, or "abstract from," part of the meaning of a conditional statement when we translate it into our symbolic language. How can this proposal be justified?

The previous proposal to translate both inclusive and exclusive disjunctions by means of the "∨" symbol was justified on the grounds that the validity of the Disjunctive Syllogism was preserved even if the additional meaning that attaches to the exclusive "or" was ignored. Our present proposal to translate all conditional statements into the merely material implication symbolized by "⊃" may be justified in exactly the same way. Many arguments contain conditional statements of various different kinds, but the validity of all valid arguments of the general type with which we will be concerned is preserved even if the additional meanings of their conditional statements are ignored. This remains to be proved, of course, and will occupy our attention in the next section.

Conditional statements can be formulated in a variety of ways. The statement

If he has a good lawyer then he will be acquitted.

can equally well be stated without the use of the word "then" as

If he has a good lawyer he will be acquitted.

Antecedent and consequent can have their order reversed, provided that the "if" still directly precedes the antecedent, as

He will be acquitted if he has a good lawyer.

It should be clear that, in any of the examples just given, the word "if" can be replaced by such phrases as "in case," "provided that," "given that," or "on condition that," without any change in meaning. Minor adjustments in the phrasings of antecedent and consequent permit such alternative phrasings of the same conditional as

> That he has a good lawyer implies that he will be acquitted.

or

> His having a good lawyer entails his acquittal.

A shift from active to passive voice accompanies a reversal of order of antecedent and consequent, to yield the logically equivalent

> His being acquitted is implied (or entailed) by his having a good lawyer.

Any of these is symbolized as $L \supset A$.

The notions of necessary and sufficient conditions provide other formulations of conditional statements. For any specified event, there are many circumstances necessary for its occurrence. Thus, for a normal car to run, it is necessary that there be fuel in its tank, its spark plugs properly adjusted, its oil pump working, and so on. So if the event occurs, every one of the conditions necessary for its occurrence must have been fulfilled. Hence to say

> That there is fuel in its tank is a necessary condition for the car to run.

can equally well be stated as

> The car runs only if there is fuel in its tank.

which is another way of saying that

> If the car runs then there is fuel in its tank.

Any of these is symbolized as $R \supset F$. In general, "*q* **is a necessary condition for** *p*" **and** "*p* **only if** *q*" **are symbolized as** $p \supset q$.

For a specified situation there are many alternative circumstances, any one of which is sufficient to produce that situation. Thus, for a purse to contain over a dollar, it would be sufficient for it to contain one hundred and one pennies, twenty-one nickels, eleven dimes, five quarters, and so on. If any one of these circumstances obtains, the specified situation will be realized. Hence, to say "That the purse contains five quarters is a sufficient condition for it to contain over a dollar" is to say the same as "If the purse contains five quarters then it contains over a dollar." In general, "*p* **is a sufficient condition for** *q*" **is symbolized as** $p \supset q$.

If *p* is a sufficient condition for *q*, we have $p \supset q$, and *q* must be a necessary condition for *p*. If *p* is a necessary condition for *q*, we have $q \supset p$, and *q* must be a sufficient condition for p. Hence, if p is necessary *and* sufficient for q, then q is sufficient *and* necessary for p.

Not every statement containing the word "if" is a conditional. None of the following statements is a conditional: "There is food in the refrigerator if you want some," "Your table is ready, if you please," "There is a message for you if you're interested," "The meeting will be held even if no permit is obtained." The presence or absence of particular words is never decisive. In every case, one must understand what a given sentence means, and then restate that meaning in a symbolic formula.

There is no necessary or logical relation between the words "if" and "iffy," though there is often a suggestion that what is preceded by the word "if" is somewhat doubtful. This is illustrated by the following anecdote:

> George Bernard Shaw once sent Winston Churchill two tickets for the opening night of one of his new plays, noting, "Bring a friend—if you have one"; to which Churchill wrote back to say that he was otherwise engaged opening night, but would appreciate tickets for the second performance, "if there is one."[9]

Exercises

I.   If A, B, and C are true statements and X, Y, and Z are false statements, determine which of the following are true, using the truth tables for the horseshoe, the dot, the wedge, and the curl.

   *1. $A \supset B$

   2. $A \supset X$

   3. $B \supset Y$

   4. $Y \supset Z$

   *5. $(A \supset B) \supset Z$

   6. $(X \supset Y) \supset Z$

   7. $(A \supset B) \supset C$

   8. $(X \supset Y) \supset C$

   9. $A \supset (B \supset Z)$

   *10. $X \supset (Y \supset Z)$

   11. $[(A \supset B) \supset C] \supset Z$

   12. $[(A \supset X) \supset Y] \supset Z$

   13. $[A \supset (X \supset Y)] \supset C$

   14. $[A \supset (B \supset Y)] \supset X$

   *15. $[(X \supset Z) \supset C] \supset Y$

   16. $[(Y \supset B) \supset Y] \supset Y$

   17. $[(A \supset Y) \supset B] \supset Z$

   18. $[(A \bullet X) \supset C] \supset [(A \supset C) \supset X]$

   19. $[(A \bullet X) \supset C] \supset [(A \supset X) \supset C]$

   *20. $[(A \bullet X) \supset Y] \supset [(X \supset A) \supset (A \supset Y)]$

   21. $[(A \bullet X) \vee (\sim A \bullet \supset X)] \supset [(A \supset X) \bullet (X \supset A)]$

   22. $\{[A \supset (B \supset C)] \supset [(A \bullet B) \supset C]\} \supset [(Y \supset B) \supset (C \supset Z)]$

   23. $\{[(X \supset Y) \supset Z] \supset [Z \supset (X \supset Y)]\} \supset [(X \supset Z) \supset Y]$

   24. $[(A \bullet X) \supset Y] \supset [(A \supset X) \bullet (A \supset Y)]$

   *25. $[A \supset (X \bullet Y)] \supset [(A \supset X) \vee (A \supset Y)]$

---

[9] Andreas I. Aristides, "The Gentle Art of the Resounding Put-Down," *The American Scholar* (Summer 1987).

II. If *A* and *B* are known to be true, and *X* and *Y* are known to be false, but the truth values of *P* and *Q* are not known, of which of the following statements can you determine the truth values?

*1. $P \supset A$ 2. $X \supset Q$

3. $(Q \supset A) \supset X$ 4. $(P \bullet A) \supset B$

*5. $(P \supset P) \supset X$ 6. $(X \supset Q) \supset X$

7. $X \supset (Q \supset X)$ 8. $(P \bullet X) \supset Y$

9. $[P \supset (Q \supset P)] \supset Y$ *10. $(Q \supset Q) \supset (A \supset X)$

11. $(P \supset X) \supset (X \supset P)$ 12. $(P \supset A) \supset (B \supset X)$

13. $(X \supset P) \supset (B \supset Y)$ 14. $[(P \supset B) \supset B] \supset B$

*15. $[(X \supset Q) \supset Q] \supset Q$ 16. $(P \supset X) \supset (\sim X \supset \sim P)$

17. $(X \supset P) \supset (\sim X > Y)$ 18. $(P \supset A) \supset (A \supset \sim B)$

19. $(P \supset Q) \supset (P \supset Q)$ *20. $(P \supset \sim\sim P) \supset (A \supset \sim B)$

21. $\sim(A \bullet P) \supset (\sim A \vee \sim P)$ 22. $\sim(P \bullet X) \supset \sim(P \vee \sim X)$

23. $\sim(X \vee Q) \supset (\sim X \bullet \sim Q)$

24. $[P \supset (A \vee X)] \supset [(P \supset A) \supset X]$

*25. $[Q \vee (B \bullet Y)] \supset [(Q \vee B) \bullet (Q \vee Y)]$

III. Symbolize the following, using capital letters to abbreviate the simple statements involved.

*1. If Argentina mobilizes then if Brazil protests to the UN then Chile will call for a meeting of all the Latin American states.

2. If Argentina mobilizes then either Brazil will protest to the UN or Chile will call for a meeting of all the Latin American states.

3. If Argentina mobilizes then Brazil will protest to the UN and Chile will call for a meeting of all the Latin American states.

4. If Argentina mobilizes then Brazil will protest to the UN, and Chile will call for a meeting of all the Latin American states.

*5. If Argentina mobilizes and Brazil protests to the UN then Chile will call for a meeting of all the Latin American states.

6. If either Argentina mobilizes or Brazil protests to the UN then Chile will call for a meeting of all the Latin American states.

7. Either Argentina will mobilize or if Brazil protests to the UN then Chile will call for a meeting of all the Latin American states.

8. If Argentina does not mobilize then either Brazil will not protest to the UN or Chile will not call for a meeting of all the Latin American states.

9. If Argentina does not mobilize then neither will Brazil protest to the UN nor will Chile call for a meeting of all the Latin American states.

*10. It is not the case that if Argentina mobilizes then both Brazil will protest to the UN and Chile will call for a meeting of all the Latin American states.

11. If it is not the case that Argentina mobilizes then Brazil will not protest to the UN, and Chile will call for a meeting of all the Latin American states.

12. Brazil will protest to the UN if Argentina mobilizes.

13. Brazil will protest to the UN only if Argentina mobilizes.

14. Chile will call for a meeting of all the Latin American states only if both Argentina mobilizes and Brazil protests to the UN.

*15. Brazil will protest to the UN only if either Argentina mobilizes or Chile calls for a meeting of all the Latin American states.

16. Argentina will mobilize if either Brazil protests to the UN or Chile calls for a meeting of all the Latin American States.

17. Brazil will protest to the UN unless Chile calls for a meeting of all the Latin American States.

18. If Argentina mobilizes, then Brazil will protest to the UN unless Chile calls for a meeting of all the Latin American States.

19. Brazil will not protest to the UN unless Argentina mobilizes.

*20. Unless Chile calls for a meeting of all the Latin American States, Brazil will protest to the UN.

21. Argentina's mobilizing is a sufficient condition for Brazil to protest to the UN.

22. Argentina's mobilizing is a necessary condition for Chile to call for a meeting of all the Latin American states.

23. If Argentina mobilizes and Brazil protests to the UN, then both Chile and the Dominican Republic will call for a meeting of all the Latin American states.

24. If Argentina mobilizes and Brazil protests to the UN, then either Chile or the Dominican Republic will call for a meeting of all the Latin American states.

*25. If neither Chile nor the Dominican Republic calls for a meeting of all the Latin American states, then Brazil will not protest to the UN unless Argentina mobilizes.

8.4 ARGUMENT FORMS AND ARGUMENTS

A. Refutation by Logical Analogy

In this section, we specify more precisely what is meant by the term "valid." We relate our formal definition to more familiar and intuitive notions by considering the method of refutation by logical analogy.[10] Presented with the argument

---

[10] Just as in analyzing the categorical syllogism, we discuss refutation by logical analogy in section 6.2.

If Bacon wrote the plays attributed to Shakespeare, then Bacon was a great writer.
Bacon was a great writer.
Therefore Bacon wrote the plays attributed to Shakespeare.

we may agree with the premises but disagree with the conclusion, judging the argument to be invalid. One way of proving invalidity is by the method of logical analogy. "You might as well argue," we could retort, "that

If Washington was assassinated, then Washington is dead.
Washington is dead.
Therefore Washington was assassinated.

And you cannot seriously defend this argument," we should continue, "because here the premises are known to be true and the conclusion known to be false. This argument is obviously invalid; your argument is of the *same form:* so yours is invalid also." This type of refutation is very effective.

This method of refutation by logical analogy, points the way to an excellent general technique for testing arguments. To prove the invalidity of an argument, it suffices to formulate another argument that (1) has exactly the same form as the first and (2) has true premises and a false conclusion. This method is based upon the fact that validity and invalidity are purely *formal* characteristics of arguments, which is to say that any two arguments having exactly the same form are either both valid or both invalid, regardless of any differences in the subject matter with which they are concerned.[11]

A given argument exhibits its form very clearly when the simple statements that appear in it are abbreviated by capital letters. Thus we may abbreviate the statements "Bacon wrote the plays attributed to Shakespeare," "Bacon was a great writer," "Washington was assassinated," and "Washington is dead" by the letters B, G, A, and D, respectively, and using the familiar three dot symbol " $\therefore$ " for "therefore," symbolize the two preceding arguments as

$$
\begin{array}{ccc}
B \supset G & & A \supset D \\
G & \quad\text{and}\quad & D \\
\therefore\ B & & \therefore\ A
\end{array}
$$

So written, their common form is easily seen.

To discuss forms of arguments rather than particular arguments having those forms, we need some method of symbolizing argument forms themselves. To achieve such a method, we introduce the notion of a *variable.* In the preceding sections we used capital letters to symbolize particular simple statements. To avoid confusion, we use small, or lowercase, letters from the middle part of the alphabet $p, q, r, s, \ldots$ as *statement variables.* A **statement variable,** as

---

[11] Here we assume that the simple statements involved are neither logically true (*e.g.,* "All chairs are chairs") nor logically false (*e.g.,* "Some chairs are nonchairs"). We also assume that the only logical relations among the simple statements involved are those asserted or entailed by the premises. The point of these restrictions is to limit our considerations, in this chapter and the next, to truth-functional arguments alone, and to exclude other kinds of arguments whose validity turns on more complex logical considerations not appropriately introduced at this place.

we shall use the term, **is simply a letter for which, or in place of which, a statement may be substituted.** Compound statements as well as simple statements may be substituted for statement variables.

We define an *argument form* as **any array of symbols containing statement variables but no statements, such that when statements are substituted for the statement variables—the same statement being substituted for the same statement variable throughout—the result is an argument.** For definiteness, we establish the convention that in any argument form p shall be the first statement variable that occurs in it, q shall be the second, r the third, and so on. Thus the expression

$$p \supset q$$
$$q$$
$$\therefore p$$

is an argument form, for when the statements B and G are substituted for the statement variables p and q, respectively, the result is the first argument in this section. If the statements A and D are substituted for the variables p and q, the result is the second argument. **Any argument that results from the substitution of statements for statement variables in an argument form is called a** *substitution instance* **of that argument form.** It is clear that any substitution instance of an argument form may be said to have that form, and that any argument that has a certain form is a substitution instance of that form.

For any argument there are usually several argument forms that have the given argument as a substitution instance. For example, the first argument of this section

$$B \supset G$$
$$G$$
$$\therefore B$$

is a substitution instance of each of the four argument forms

$p \supset q$	$p \supset q$	$p \supset q$	p
q	r	r	q
$\therefore p$	$\therefore p$	$\therefore s$	$\therefore r$

Thus we obtain the given argument by substituting B for p and G for q in the first argument form; by substituting B for p and G for both q and r in the second; B for both p and s and G for both q and r in the third; and $B \supset G$ for p, G for q, and B for r in the fourth. Of these four argument forms, the first corresponds more closely to the structure of the given argument than do the others. It does so because the given argument results from the first argument form by substituting a different simple statement for each different statement variable in it. We call the first argument form the *specific form* of the given argument. Our definition of the specific form of a given argument is the following: **In case an argument is produced by substituting consistently a different simple statement for each different statement variable in an argument form, that argument form is the *specific form* of that argument.** For any given argument, there is a unique argument form that is the specific form of that argument.

The technique of refutation by logical analogy can now be described more precisely. If the specific form of a given argument has any substitution instance whose premises are true and whose conclusion is false, then the given argument is invalid. We may define the term "invalid" as applied to argument forms as follows: **An argument form is invalid if and only if it has at least one substitution instance with true premises and a false conclusion.** Refutation by logical analogy is based on the fact that any argument whose specific form is an *invalid argument form* is an *invalid argument.* Any argument form that is not invalid must be valid. Hence **an argument form is valid if and only if it has no substitution instances with true premises and a false conclusion.** And since validity is a formal notion, **an argument is valid if and only if the specific form of that argument is a valid argument form.**

A given argument is proved invalid if a refuting analogy for it can be found, but "thinking up" such refuting analogies may not always be easy. Happily, it is not necessary, because for arguments of this type there is a simpler, purely mechanical test based upon the same principle. Given any argument, we test the specific form of that argument, because its validity or invalidity determines the validity or invalidity of the argument.

B.   Testing Arguments on Truth Tables

To test an argument form, we examine all possible substitution instances of it to see if any one of them has true premises and a false conclusion. Of course any argument form has an infinite number of substitution instances, but we need not worry about having to examine them one at a time. Because we are interested only in the truth or falsehood of their premises and conclusions, we need consider only the truth values involved. The arguments that concern us here contain only simple statements and compound statements that are built up out of simple statements by means of the truth-functional connectives symbolized by the dot, curl, wedge, and horseshoe. Hence we obtain all possible substitution instances whose premises and conclusions have different truth values by examining all possible different arrangements of truth values for the statements that can be substituted for the different statement variables in the argument form to be tested.

Where an argument form contains just two different statement variables, p and q, all of its substitution instances are the result of either substituting true statements for both p and q, or a true statement for p and a false one for q, or a false one for p and a true one for q, or false statements for both p and q. These different cases are assembled most conveniently in the form of a truth table. To decide the validity of the argument form

$$p \supset q$$
$$q$$
$$\therefore p$$

we construct the following truth table:

p	q	$p \supset q$
T	T	T
T	F	F
F	T	T
F	F	T

Each row of this table represents a whole class of substitution instances. The **T**'s and **F**'s in the two initial or guide columns represent the truth values of the statements substituted for the variables p and q in the argument form. We fill in the third column by referring back to the initial or guide columns and the definition of the horseshoe symbol. The third column heading is the first "premiss" of the argument form, the second column is the second "premiss," and the first column is the "conclusion." In examining this truth table, we find that in the third row there are **T**'s under both premisses and an **F** under the conclusion, which indicates that there is at least one substitution instance of this argument form that has true premisses and a false conclusion. This row suffices to show that the argument form is invalid. Any argument of this specific form (that is, any argument the specific argument form of which is the given argument form) is said to commit the fallacy of affirming the consequent, since its second premiss affirms the consequent of its conditional first premiss.

Truth tables, although simple in concept, are powerful tools. In using them to establish the validity or the invalidity of an argument form, it is critically important that the table first be constructed correctly. To construct the truth table correctly there must be a guide column for each statement variable in the argument form, p, q, r, etc. The array must exhibit all the possible combinations of the truth and falsity of all these variables, so there must be a number of horizontal rows sufficient to do this: four rows if there are two variables, eight rows if there are three variables, and so on. And there must be an additional vertical column for each of the premisses and for the conclusion, and also a column for each of the symbolic expressions out of which the premisses and conclusion are built. The construction of a truth table in this fashion is essentially a mechanical task; it requires only careful counting and the careful placement of **T**'s and **F**'s in the appropriate columns, all governed by our understanding of the several truth-functional connectives—the dot, the wedge, the horseshoe—and the circumstances under which each truth-functional compound is true and the circumstances under which it is false.

Once the table has been constructed and the completed array is before us, it is essential to *read* it correctly, that is, to use it correctly to make the appraisal of the argument form in question. We must note carefully which columns are those representing the premisses of the argument being tested, and which column represents the conclusion of that argument. In testing the argument just above, which we found invalid, we noted that it was the second and third columns of the truth table that represent the premisses, while the conclusion was represented by the first (leftmost) column. But, depending upon which argument form we are testing, and the order in which we have placed the columns as the table was built, it is possible for the premises and the conclusion to appear in any order at the top of the table. Their position to the right or to the left is not significant; we, who use the table, must understand which column represents what, and we must understand what we are in search of. *Is there any one case*, we ask ourselves, *any single row in which all the premises are true and the conclusion false?* If there is such a row the argument form is invalid; if there is no such row the argument form must be valid. After the full array has been neatly and accurately set forth, great care in reading the truth table accurately is of the utmost importance.

C. Some Common Valid Argument Forms

Disjunctive Syllogism

One of the simplest valid argument forms relies on the fact that, in every true disjunction, at least one of the disjuncts must be true. Therefore, if one of them is false, the other must be true. We symbolize the Disjunctive Syllogism as follows:

$$p \vee q$$
$$\sim p$$
$$\therefore q$$

And to show its validity we construct the following truth table:

p	q	$p \vee q$	$\sim p$
T	T	T	F
T	F	T	F
F	T	T	T
F	F	F	T

Here, too, the initial or guide columns exhibit all possible different truth values of statements that may be substituted for the variables p and q. We fill in the third column by referring back to the first two, and the fourth by reference to the first alone. Now the third row is the only one in which **T**'s appear under both premises (the third and fourth columns), and there a **T** appears under the conclusion also (the second column). The truth table thus shows that the argument form has no substitution instance having true premises and a false conclusion, and thereby proves the validity of the argument form being tested.[12]

---

[12]As used in this chapter, the term "Disjunctive Syllogism" is the name of an elementary argument form, here proved valid. This form is always valid, of course, and therefore, in modern logic "Disjunctive Syllogism" always refers to an elementary argument form that is valid. But in traditional logic the expression "disjunctive syllogism" is used more broadly, to refer to any syllogism that contains a disjunctive premise; some such syllogisms may of course be invalid. One must be clear whether the expression is being used in the broader or the narrower sense. Here we use it in the narrower sense.

Here as always it is essential that the truth table be *read* accurately; the column representing the conclusion (second from the left) and the columns representing the premises (third and fourth from the left) being carefully identified. Only by using those three columns correctly can we reliably determine the validity (or invalidity) of the argument form in question. Note that the very same truth table could be used to test the validity of a very different argument form, one whose premises are represented by the second and third columns and whose conclusion is represented by the fourth column. That argument form, as we can see from the top row of the table, is invalid.

The truth-table technique provides a completely mechanical method for testing the validity of any argument of the general type here considered. We are now in a position to justify our proposal to translate any occurrence of the "if–then" phrase into our material implication symbol "⊃". In the preceding section, the claim was made that all valid arguments of the general type with which we are here concerned that involve "if–then" statements remain valid when those statements are interpreted as affirming merely material implications. Truth tables can be used to substantiate this claim, and will justify our translation of "if–then" into the horseshoe symbol.

Modus Ponens

The simplest type of intuitively valid argument involving a conditional statement is illustrated by the argument:

> If the second native told the truth, then only one native is a politician.
> The second native told the truth.
> Therefore only one native is a politician.

The specific form of this argument, known as *modus ponens* ("the method of putting, or affirming") is

$$p \supset q$$
$$p$$
$$\therefore q$$

and is proved valid by the following truth table:

p	q	$p \supset q$
T	T	T
T	F	F
F	T	T
F	F	T

Here the two premises are represented by the third and first columns, and the conclusion is represented by the second. Only the first row represents substitution instances in which both premises are true, and the **T** in the second column shows that in these arguments the conclusion is true also. This truth table establishes the validity of any argument of the form *modus ponens.*

Modus Tollens

We have seen that if a conditional statement is true, then if the consequent is false the antecedent must be false. This form of argument is very commonly used to establish the falsehood of some proposition in doubt. To illustrate: In a recent match for the world Scrabble championship, the team of Matt Graham and Joel Sherman met the computer program called Maven. At one point in the match the men's tiles permitted the word "triduum," which they found; but for a bingo—using of all eight tiles in one word—their remaining "s" would also have to be used. "Triduum" is definitely a word, said Joel to his partner, but is "triduums" the right plural? Matt's answer was in the form of a very common valid argument: "It has to be. If the plural were "tridua," we'd know that word, and we don't."[13]

The argument would be symbolized as:

$$p \supset q$$
$$\sim q$$
$$\therefore \sim p$$

The validity of this argument form, called ***modus tollens*** ("the method of taking away or denying"), may be shown by the following truth table:

p	*q*	*p* ⊃ *q*	~*q*	~*p*
T	T	T	F	F
T	F	F	T	F
F	T	T	F	T
F	F	T	T	T

Here again there is no substitution instance, no line, on which the premisses, $p \supset q$ and $\sim q$, are both true and the conclusion, $\sim p$, is false.

Hypothetical Syllogism

Another common type of intuitively valid argument contains only conditional statements. Here is an example:

If the first native is a politician, then the first native lies.
If the first native lies, then the first native denies being a politician.
Therefore if the first native is a politician, then the first native denies being a politician.

The specific form of this argument is

---

[13] "Humankind Battles for Scrabble Supremacy," *New York Times Magazine,* 24 May 1998. A "triduum" is a period of three days, especially a three-day period of prayers. "Triduums" was indeed a bingo—but the match was won by the computer, 6–3.

$$p \supset q$$
$$q \supset r$$
$$\therefore p \supset r$$

Since this argument, called *Hypothetical Syllogism,*[14] contains three distinct statement variables, the truth table here must have three initial or guide columns and will require eight rows for the listing of all possible substitution instances. Besides the initial columns, three additional columns are required: two for the premises, the third for the conclusion. The table appears as

p	q	r	$p{\supset}q$	$q{\supset}r$	$p{\supset}r$
T	T	T	T	T	T
T	T	F	T	F	F
T	F	T	F	T	T
T	F	F	F	T	F
F	T	T	T	T	T
F	T	F	T	F	T
F	F	T	T	T	T
F	F	F	T	T	T

In constructing it, we fill in the fourth column by referring back to the first and second, the fifth by reference to the second and third, and the sixth by reference to the first and third. Examining the completed table, we observe that the premises are true only in the first, fifth, seventh, and eighth rows, and that in all of these the conclusion is true also. This truth table establishes the validity of the argument form and proves that the Hypothetical Syllogism also remains valid when its conditional statements are translated by means of the horseshoe symbol.

Enough examples have been provided to illustrate the proper use of the truth-table technique for testing arguments. And perhaps enough have been given to show that the validity of any valid argument involving conditional statements is preserved when its conditionals are translated into merely material implications. Any doubts that remain can be allayed by the reader's providing, translating, and testing any similar examples.

As more complicated argument forms are considered, larger truth tables are required to test them, because a separate initial or guide column is required for each different statement variable in the argument form. Only two are required for a form with just two variables, and that table will have four rows. But three initial columns are required for a form with three variables, such as the Hypothetical Syllogism, and such truth tables will have eight rows. To test the validity of an argument form such as that of the Constructive Dilemma,

$$(p \supset q) \bullet (r \supset s)$$
$$p \lor r$$
$$\therefore q \lor s$$

---

[14] Called a "pure hypothetical syllogism" in Chapter 7.

which contains four distinct statement variables, a truth table with four initial columns and 16 rows is required. In general, in order to test an argument form containing n distinct statement variables we require a truth table with n initial columns and 2^n rows.

D.   Some Common Invalid Argument Forms

Two invalid argument forms deserve special notice, because they bear superficial resemblances to valid forms and therefore often tempt careless writers or readers. The **fallacy of affirming the consequent,** discussed also in section 7.7, is symbolized as

$$p \supset q$$
$$q$$
$$\therefore p$$

Although the shape of this form is something like that of *modus ponens,* the two argument forms are, in fact, very different, and this form certainly is not valid. When it is argued, for example, that since membership in the American Civil Liberties Union is indicative of strong support for freedom of speech, one who defends that freedom must be a supporter of the ACLU, the fallacy of affirming the consequent has been committed.

Another invalid form, called the **fallacy of denying the antecedent,** has a shape somewhat like that of *modus tollens* and may be symbolized as

$$p \supset q$$
$$\sim p$$
$$\therefore \sim q$$

An example of this fallacy is the campaign slogan used by a candidate for mayor of New York city some years ago: "If you don't know the buck, you don't know the job—and Abe knows the buck." The unstated conclusion to which the voter was deliberately tempted was that "Abe knows the job"—a proposition that does not follow from the stated premises.

Both of these common fallacies may readily be shown to be invalid by means of truth tables. In each case there is one line of the truth table on which the premises of these fallacious arguments are all true, but the conclusion false.

E.   Substitution Instances and Specific Forms

A given argument can be a substitution instance of several different argument forms, as we noted earlier when defining "argument form." Hence the valid disjunctive syllogism examined on page 305, which may be symbolized as

$$R \vee W$$
$$\sim R$$
$$\therefore W$$

is a substitution instance of the valid argument form

$$p \vee q$$
$$\sim p$$
$$\therefore q$$

and is *also* a substitution instance of the *in*valid argument form

$$p$$
$$q$$
$$\therefore r$$

It is obvious, in this last form, that from two premisses, p and q, we could not validly infer r. So it is clear that an invalid argument form *can* have a valid argument, *or* an invalid argument, as a substitution instance. Therefore, in determining whether any given argument is valid, *we must look to the specific form of the argument* in question. Only the specific form of the argument accurately reveals the full logical structure of that argument, and because it does, we can know that if the specific form of an argument is valid, the argument itself must be valid.

In the illustration just given, we see an argument (R $\vee$ W, $\sim$R, therefore W), and two argument forms of which that argument could be a substitution instance. The first of these argument forms ($p \vee q$, $\sim p$, therefore q) is valid, and because that form is the *specific* form of the given argument, its validity establishes that the given argument is valid. The second of those argument forms is invalid, but because it is *not* the specific form of the given argument it cannot be used to show that the given argument is invalid.

This point should be emphasized: An argument form that is valid can have only valid arguments as substitution instances. That is, all of the substitution instances of a valid form *must* be valid. This is proved by the truth-table proof of validity for the valid argument form, which shows that there is no possible substitution instance of a valid form that has true premisses and a false conclusion.

Exercises

I. Following will be found a group of arguments (Group A, lettered a–o) and a group of argument forms (Group B, numbered 1–24). For each of the arguments (in Group A), indicate which of the argument forms (in Group B), if any, have the given argument as a *substitution instance*. In addition, for each given argument (in Group A), indicate which of the argument forms (in Group B), if any, is the *specific form* of that argument.

Examples:

Argument **a** in Group A: Examining all the argument forms in Group B, we find that the only one of which Argument **a** is a **substitution instance** is Number 3. Number 3 *is* also the **specific form** of Argument **a.**

Argument **j** in Group A: Examining all the argument forms in Group B, we find that Argument **j** is a **substitution instance** *both* of Number 6 and of Number 23. But *only* number 23 is the **specific form** of Argument **j**.

Argument **m** in Group A: Examining all the argument forms in Group B, we find that Argument **m** is a **substitution instance** *both* of Number 3 and of Number 24. But there is *no* argument form in Group B that is the **specific form** of Argument **m**.

Group A—Arguments

a. $A \bullet B$
 $\therefore A$

b. $C \supset D$
 $\therefore C \supset (C \bullet D)$

c. E
 $\therefore E \vee F$

d. $G \supset H$
 $\sim H$
 $\therefore \sim G$

*e. I
 J
 $\therefore I \bullet J$

f. $(K \supset L) \bullet (M \supset N)$
 $K \vee M$
 $\therefore L \vee N$

g. $O \supset P$
 $\sim O$
 $\therefore \sim P$

h. $Q \supset R$
 $Q \supset S$
 $\therefore R \vee S$

i. $T \supset U$
 $U \supset V$
 $\therefore V \supset T$

j. $(W \bullet X) \supset (Y \bullet Z)$
 $\therefore (W \bullet X) \supset [(W \bullet X) \bullet (Y \bullet Z)]$

k. $A \supset B$
 $\therefore (A \supset B) \vee C$

l. $(D \vee E) \bullet \sim F$
 $\therefore D \vee E$

m. $[G \supset (G \bullet H)] \bullet [H \supset (H \bullet G)]$
 $\therefore G \supset (G \bullet H)$

n. $(I \vee J) \supset (I \bullet J)$
 $\sim(I \vee J)$
 $\therefore \sim(I \bullet J)$

*o. $(K \supset L) \bullet (M \supset N)$
 $\therefore K \supset L$

Group B—Argument Forms

*1. $p \supset q$
 $\therefore \sim q \supset \sim p$

2. $p \supset q$
 $\therefore \sim p \supset \sim q$

3. $p \bullet q$
 $\therefore p$

4. p
 $\therefore p \vee q$

*5. p
 $\therefore p \supset q$

6. $p \supset q$
 $\therefore p \supset (p \bullet q)$

7. $(p \vee q) \supset (p \bullet q)$
 $\therefore (p \supset q) \bullet (q \supset p)$

8. $p \supset q$
 $\sim p$
 $\therefore \sim q$

9. $p \supset q$
 $\sim q$
 $\therefore \sim p$

*10. p
 q
 $\therefore p \bullet q$

11. $p \supset q$
 $p \supset r$
 $\therefore q \vee r$

12. $p \supset q$
 $q \supset r$
 $\therefore r \supset p$

13. $p \supset (q \supset r)$
  $p \supset q$
  $\therefore p \supset r$

14. $p \supset (q \bullet r)$
  $(q \vee r) \supset \sim p$
  $\therefore \sim p$

*15. $p \supset (q \supset r)$
  $q \supset (p \supset r)$
  $\therefore (p \vee q) \supset r$

16. $(p \supset q) \bullet (r \supset s)$
  $p \vee r$
  $\therefore q \vee s$

17. $(p \supset q) \bullet (r \supset s)$
  $\sim q \vee \sim s$
  $\therefore \sim p \vee \sim s$

18. $p \supset (q \supset r)$
  $q \supset (r \supset s)$
  $\therefore p \supset s$

19. $p \supset (q \supset r)$
  $(q \supset r) \supset s$
  $\therefore p \supset s$

*20. $(p \supset q) \bullet [(p \bullet q) \supset r]$
  $p \supset (r \supset s)$
  $\therefore p \supset s$

21. $(p \vee q) \supset (p \bullet q)$
  $\sim (p \vee q)$
  $\therefore \sim (p \bullet q)$

22. $(p \vee q) \supset (p \bullet q)$
  $(p \bullet q)$
  $\therefore p \vee q$

23. $(p \bullet q) \supset (r \bullet s)$
  $\therefore (p \bullet q) \supset [(p \bullet q) \bullet (r \bullet s)]$

24. $(p \supset q) \bullet (r \supset s)$
  $\therefore p \supset q$

II. Use truth tables to prove the validity or invalidity of each of the argument forms in Group B, in Exercise 1.

III. Use truth tables to determine the validity or invalidity of each of the following arguments.

*1. $(A \vee B) \supset (A \bullet B)$
  $A \vee B$
  $\therefore A \bullet B$

2. $(C \vee D) \supset (C \bullet D)$
  $C \bullet D$
  $\therefore C \vee D$

3. $E \supset F$
  $F \supset E$
  $\therefore E \vee F$

4. $(G \vee H) \supset (G \bullet H)$
  $\sim (G \bullet H)$
  $\therefore \sim (G \vee H)$

*5. $(I \vee J) \supset (I \bullet J)$
  $\sim (I \vee J)$
  $\therefore \sim (I \bullet J)$

6. $K \vee L$
  K
  $\therefore \sim L$

7. $M \vee (N \bullet \sim N)$
  M
  $\therefore \sim (N \bullet \sim N)$

8. $(O \vee P) \supset Q$
  $Q \supset (O \bullet P)$
  $\therefore (O \vee P) \supset (O \bullet P)$

9. $(R \vee S) \supset T$
  $T \supset (R \bullet S)$
  $\therefore (R \bullet S) \supset (R \vee S)$

*10. $U \supset (V \vee W)$
  $(V \bullet W) \supset \sim U$
  $\therefore \sim U$

IV. Use truth tables to determine the validity or invalidity of the following arguments.

*1. If Angola achieves stability, then both Botswana and Chad will adopt more liberal policies. But Botswana will not adopt a more liberal policy. Therefore Angola will not achieve stability.

2. If Denmark refuses to join the European Community, then, if Estonia remains in the Russian sphere of influence, then Finland will reject a free trade policy. Estonia will remain in the Russian sphere of influence. So if Denmark refuses to join the European community, then Finland will reject a free trade policy.

3. If Greece strengthens its democratic institutions, then Hungary will pursue a more independent policy. If Greece strengthens its democratic institutions, then the Italian government will feel less threatened. Hence, if Hungary pursues a more independent policy, then the Italian government will feel less threatened.

4. If Japan continues to increase the export of automobiles, then either Korea or Laos will suffer economic decline. Korea will not suffer economic decline. It follows that if Japan continues to increase the export of automobiles, then Laos will suffer economic decline.

*5. If Montana suffers a severe drought, then, if Nevada has its normal light rainfall, Oregon's water supply will be greatly reduced. Nevada does have its normal light rainfall. So if Oregon's water supply is greatly reduced, then Montana suffers a severe drought.

6. If equality of opportunity is to be achieved, then those people previously disadvantaged should now be given special opportunities. If those people previously disadvantaged should now be given special opportunities, then some people receive preferential treatment. If some people receive preferential treatment, then equality of opportunity is not to be achieved. Therefore equality of opportunity is not to be achieved.

7. If terrorists' demands are met, then lawlessness will be rewarded. If terrorists' demands are not met, then innocent hostages will be murdered. So either lawlessness will be rewarded or innocent hostages will be murdered.

8. If people are entirely rational, then either all of a person's actions can be predicted in advance or the universe is essentially deterministic. Not all of a person's actions can be predicted in advance. Thus, if the universe is not essentially deterministic, then people are not entirely rational.

9. If oil consumption continues to grow, then either oil imports will increase or domestic oil reserves will be depleted. If oil imports increase and domestic oil reserves are depleted, then the nation eventually will go bankrupt. Therefore, if oil consumption continues to grow, then the nation eventually will go bankrupt.

*10. If oil consumption continues to grow, then oil imports will increase and domestic oil reserves will be depleted. If either oil imports increase or domestic oil reserves are depleted, then the nation will soon be bankrupt. Therefore, if oil consumption continues to grow, then the nation will soon be bankrupt.

8.5 STATEMENT FORMS AND MATERIAL EQUIVALENCE

A. Statement Forms and Statements

We now make explicit a notion tacitly assumed in the preceding section, the notion of a "statement form." There is an exact parallel between the relation of argument to argument form, on the one hand, and the relation of statement to statement form, on the other. The definition of "statement form" makes this evident: **A *statement form* is any sequence of symbols containing statement variables but no statements, such that when statements are substituted for the statement variables—the same statement being substituted for the same statement variable throughout—the result is a statement.** Thus $p \lor q$ is a statement form, for when statements are substituted for the variables p and q, a statement results. Since the resulting statement is a disjunction, $p \lor q$ is called a "disjunctive statement form." Analogously, $p \bullet q$ and $p \supset q$ are called "conjunctive" and "conditional statement forms," and $\sim p$ is called a "negation form" or "denial form." Just as any argument of a certain form is said to be a substitution instance of that argument form, so **any statement of a certain form is said to be a substitution instance of that statement form.** And just as we distinguished the *specific form* of a given argument, so we distinguish the *specific form* **of a given statement as that statement form from which the statement results by substituting consistently a different simple statement for each different statement variable.** Thus $p \lor q$ is the *specific form* of the statement "The blind prisoner has a red hat or the blind prisoner has a white hat."

B. Tautologous, Contradictory, and Contingent Statement Forms

It is perfectly natural to feel that, although the statements "Lincoln was assassinated" (symbolized as L) and "Either Lincoln was assassinated or else he wasn't" (symbolized as $L \lor \sim L$) are both *true*, they are true "in different ways" or have "different kinds" of truth. Similarly, it is perfectly natural to feel that, although the statements "Washington was assassinated" (symbolized as W) and "Washington was both assassinated and not assassinated" (symbolized as $W \bullet \sim W$) are both *false*, they are false "in different ways" or have "different kinds" of falsehood. While not pretending to give any psychological explanation of these "feelings," we can nevertheless point out certain logical differences to which they are appropriate.

The statement L is true and the statement W is false; these are historical facts. There is no logical necessity about them. Events might have occurred differently, and the truth values of such statements as L and W must be discovered by an empirical study of history. But the statement $L \vee \sim L$, although true, is not a truth of history. There is logical necessity here: Events could not have been such as to make it false, and its truth can be known independently of any particular empirical investigation. The statement $L \vee \sim L$ is a logical truth, a formal truth, true in virtue of its form alone. It is a substitution instance of a statement form all of whose substitution instances are true statements.

A statement form that has only true substitution instances is called a *tautologous statement form,* or a *tautology.* To show that the statement form $p \vee \sim p$ is a tautology, we construct the following truth table:

p	$\sim p$	$p \vee \sim p$
T	F	T
F	T	T

There is only one initial or guide column to this truth table, since the form under consideration contains only one statement variable. Consequently, there are only two rows, which represent all possible substitution instances. There are only **T**'s in the column under the statement form in question, and this fact shows that all of its substitution instances are true. Any statement that is a substitution instance of a tautologous statement form is true in virtue of its form, and is itself said to be tautologous, or a tautology.

A statement form that has only false substitution instances is said to be *self-contradictory,* or a *contradiction,* and is logically false. The statement form $p \bullet \sim p$ is self-contradictory, for in its truth table only **F**'s occur under it, signifying that all of its substitution instances are false. Any statement, such as $W \bullet \sim W$, which is a substitution instance of a self-contradictory statement form, is false in virtue of its form and is itself said to be self-contradictory, or a contradiction.

Statement forms that have both true and false statements among their substitution instances are called *contingent statement forms.* Any statement whose specific form is contingent is called a "contingent statement."[15] Thus p, $\sim p$, $p \bullet q$, $p \vee q$, and $p \supset q$ are all contingent statement forms. And such statements as L, $\sim L$, $L \bullet W$, $L \vee W$, and $L \supset W$ are contingent statements, since their truth values are dependent or contingent on their contents rather than on their forms alone.

Not all statement forms are so obviously tautological or self-contradictory or contingent as the simple examples cited. For example, the statement form $[(p \supset q) \supset p] \supset p$ is not at all obvious, though its truth table will show it to be a tautology. It even has a special name, "Peirce's law."

---

[15] It will be recalled that we are assuming here that no simple statements are either logically true or logically false. Only contingent simple statements are admitted here. See footnote 11 in this chapter, on page 322.

C.   Material Equivalence

Material equivalence is a truth functional connective, just as disjunction and material implication are truth functional connectives. The truth value of any truth functional connective, as earlier explained, depends upon (is a function of) the truth or falsity of the statements it connects. Thus, we say that the disjunction of A and B is true if either A is true or B is true or if they are both true. Material equivalence is the truth functional connective that asserts that the statements it connects have the *same* truth value. Two statements that are equivalent in truth value, therefore, are materially equivalent. One straightforward definition is this: **Two statements are "materially equivalent" when they are both true, or both false.**

Just as the symbol for disjunction is the wedge, and the symbol for material implication is the horseshoe, there is also a special symbol for material equivalence, the three-bar sign "≡". And just as we gave truth-table definitions for the wedge and the horseshoe, we can do so for the three-bar sign as well. Here is the truth table for material equivalence, "≡":

p	q	$p \equiv q$
T	T	T
T	F	F
F	T	F
F	F	T

Any two true statements materially imply one another; that is a consequence of the meaning of material implication. And any two false statements also materially imply one another. Therefore any two statements that are materially equivalent must imply one another, since they are either both true, or both false.

Since any two statements, A and B, that are materially equivalent imply one another, we may infer from their material equivalence that B is true *if* A is true, and also that B is true *only if* A is true. Since both of these relations are entailed by material equivalence, we can read the three-bar sign, ≡, to say "*if and only if.*"

In everyday discourse we use this logical relation only occasionally. I will go to the championship game, one may say, if and only if I can acquire a ticket. I will go *if* I do acquire a ticket, but I can go *only if* I acquire a ticket. So my going to the game, and my acquiring a ticket to the game, are materially equivalent.

Every implication is a *conditional* statement, as we earlier noted. Two statements, A and B, that are materially equivalent entail the truth of the conditional A ⊃ B, and also entail the truth of the conditional B ⊃ A. Since the implication goes both ways when material equivalence holds, a statement of the form A ≡ B is often called a *biconditional.*

There are four truth-functional connectives upon which deductive argument commonly depends: *conjunction, disjunction, material implication,* and *material equivalence.* Our discussion of the set of four is now complete.

TRUTH-FUNCTIONAL CONNECTIVES

A truth-functional connective is a logical connective within a truth-functionally compound proposition. A truth-functionally compound proposition is one whose truth (or falsity) depends *wholly* upon the truth or falsity of the components of that compound. Four truth-functional connectives are of central importance:

- **The Dot.** Symbolizes **conjunction.** Read as: "P and Q."
  P • Q is true if and only if P is true *and* Q is true.

∨ **The Wedge.** Symbolizes **disjunction.** Read as: "P or Q."
  P ∨ Q is true if and only if P is true, *or* Q is true,
  or P and Q are both true.

⊃ **The Horseshoe.** Symbolizes **material implication.** Read as: "P implies Q."
  P ⊃ Q is true if and only if it is not the case that P is true and Q is false; that is, if and only if P is false or Q is true.

≡ **Three bars.** Symbolizes **material equivalence.** Read as: "P if and only if Q."
  P ≡ Q is true if and only if P and Q have the same truth value, that is, if and only if P is true and Q is true *or* P is false and Q is false.

D. Arguments, Conditional Statements, and Tautologies

To every argument there corresponds a conditional statement whose antecedent is the conjunction of the argument's premises and whose consequent is the argument's conclusion. Thus, an argument having the form of *modus ponens*

$$p \supset q$$
$$p$$
$$\therefore q$$

may be expressed as a conditional statement of the form $[(p \supset q) \bullet p] \supset q$. If the argument expressed as a conditional has a valid argument form, then its conclusion must in every case follow from its premises, and therefore the conditional statement of it may be shown on a truth table to be a tautology. That is, the statement that the conjunction of the premises implies the conclusion will (if the argument is valid) have all and only true instances.

Truth tables are powerful devices for the evaluation of arguments. **An argument form is valid if and only if its truth table has a T under the conclusion in every row in which there are T's under all of its premises.** This follows from the precise meaning of "validity." Now, if the conditional statement expressing that argument form is made the heading of one column of the truth table, an **F** can occur in that column only in a row in which there are **T**'s under all the premises and an **F** under the conclusion. But there will be no such row if the argument is valid. Hence only **T**'s will occur under a conditional statement that corresponds to a valid argument, and that conditional statement *must* be a tautology. We may therefore say that **an argument form is valid if, and only if, its expression in the form of a conditional statement** (of which the antecedent is the conjunction of the premises of the given argument form and the consequent is the conclusion of the given argument form) **is a tautology.**

For every *invalid* argument of the truth-functional variety, however, the corresponding conditional statement will not be a tautology. The statement that the conjunction of its premises implies its conclusion is (for an invalid argument) either contingent or contradictory.

Exercises

I. For each statement in the left-hand column, indicate which, if any, of the statement forms in the right-hand column have the given statement as a substitution instance, and indicate which, if any, is the specific form of the given statement.

   *1. $A \vee B$ **a.** $p \bullet q$

    2. $C \bullet {\sim}D$ **b.** $p \supset q$

    3. ${\sim}E \supset (F \bullet G)$ **c.** $p \vee q$

    4. $H \supset (I \bullet J)$ **d.** $p \bullet {\sim}q$

   *5. $(K \bullet L) \vee (M \bullet N)$ **e.** $p \equiv q$

    6. $(O \vee P) \supset (P \bullet Q)$ **f.** $(p \supset q) \vee (r \bullet s)$

    7. $(R \supset S) \vee (T \bullet {\sim}U)$ **g.** $[(p \supset q) \supset r] \supset s$

    8. $V \supset (W \vee {\sim}W)$ **h.** $[(p \supset q) \supset p] \supset p$

    9. $[(X \supset Y) \supset X] \supset X$ **i.** $(p \bullet q) \vee (r \bullet s)$

 *10. $Z \equiv {\sim}{\sim}Z$ **j.** $p \supset (q \vee {\sim}r)$

II. Use truth tables to characterize the following statement forms as tautologous, self-contradictory, or contingent.

   *1. $[p \supset (p \supset q)] \supset q$ **2.** $p \supset [(p \supset q) \supset q]$

    3. $(p \bullet q) \bullet (p \supset {\sim}q)$ **4.** $p \supset [{\sim}p \supset (q \vee {\sim}q)]$

   *5. $p \supset [p \supset (q \bullet {\sim}q)]$ **6.** $(p \supset p) \supset (q \bullet {\sim}q)$

    7. $[p \supset (q \supset r)] \supset [(p \supset q) \supset (p \supset r)]$

    8. $[p \supset (q \supset p)] \supset [(q \supset q) \supset {\sim}(r \supset r)]$

    9. $\{[(p \supset q) \bullet (r \supset s)] \bullet (p \vee r)\} \supset (q \vee s)$

 *10. $\{[(p \supset q) \bullet (r \supset s)] \bullet (q \vee s)\} \supset (p \vee r)$

III. Use truth tables to decide which of the following biconditionals are tautologies.

   *1. $(p \supset q) \equiv ({\sim}q \supset {\sim}p)$ **2.** $(p \supset q) \equiv ({\sim}p \supset {\sim}q)$

    3. $[(p \supset q) \supset r] \equiv [(q \supset p) \supset r]$ **4.** $[p \supset (q \supset r)] \equiv [q \supset (p \supset r)]$

   *5. $p \equiv [p \bullet (p \vee q)]$ **6.** $p \equiv [p \vee (p \bullet q)]$

    7. $p \equiv [p \bullet (p \supset q)]$ **8.** $p \equiv [p \bullet (q \supset p)]$

9. $p \equiv [p \vee (p \supset q)]$ *10. $(p \supset q) \equiv [(p \vee q) \equiv q]$

11. $p \equiv [p \vee (q \bullet \sim q)]$ 12. $p \equiv [p \bullet (q \bullet \sim q)]$

13. $p \equiv [p \bullet (q \vee \sim q)]$ 14. $p \equiv [p \vee (q \vee \sim q)]$

*15. $[p \bullet (q \vee r)] \equiv [(p \bullet q) \vee (p \bullet r)]$

16. $[p \bullet (q \vee r)] \equiv [(p \vee q) \bullet (p \vee r)]$

17. $[p \vee (q \bullet r)] \equiv [(p \bullet q) \vee (p \bullet r)]$

18. $[p \vee (q \bullet r)] \equiv [(p \vee q) \bullet (p \vee r)]$

19. $[(p \bullet q) \supset r] \equiv [p \supset (q \supset r)]$

*20. $[(p \supset q) \bullet (q \supset p)] \equiv [(p \bullet q) \vee (\sim p \bullet \sim q)]$

8.6 LOGICAL EQUIVALENCE

At this point we introduce a new relation, important and very useful, but not a connective, and somewhat more complicated than any of the truth-functional connectives just discussed.

Statements are materially equivalent when they have the same truth value. Because two materially equivalent statements are either both true, or both false, we can readily see that they must (materially) imply one another, since a false antecedent (materially) implies any statement, and a true consequent is (materially) implied by any statement. We may therefore read the three-bar sign, $\equiv$, as "if and only if."

But statements that are materially equivalent most certainly cannot be substituted for one another. Knowing that they are materially equivalent, we know only that their truth values are the same. The statements "Jupiter is larger than the Earth" and "Tokyo is the capital of Japan" are materially equivalent because they are both true, but we obviously cannot replace one with the other. Similarly, the statements "All spiders are poisonous" and "No spiders are poisonous" are materially equivalent simply because they are both false, and they certainly cannot replace one another!

But there are many circumstances in which we must express the relationship that does permit mutual replacement. Two statements can be equivalent in a sense much stronger than that of material equivalence; they may be equivalent in *meaning* as well as having the same truth value. If they do have the same meaning, any proposition that incorporates one of them could just as well incorporate the other; there will not be—there cannot then be—any case in which one of these statements is true while the other is false. Statements equivalent in this very strong sense we call *logically equivalent*.

Of course, any two statements that are logically equivalent will be materially equivalent as well, for they would obviously have to have the same truth value. Indeed, if two statements are logically equivalent, they are materially equivalent under *all* circumstances—and this explains the short but powerful definition of logical equivalence: **two statements are logically equivalent when the statement of their material equivalence is a tautology.** That is, the statement that they do have the same truth value is itself necessarily true. And this why we use, to express this very strong logical relationship, the three bar symbol with a small **T** immediately above it, $\overset{\text{T}}{\equiv}$, indicating that the logical relationship is of such a nature that the material equivalence of the two statements is a tautology. And because material equivalence is a "biconditional" (the two statements implying one another) we may think of this symbol of logical equivalence, $\overset{\text{T}}{\equiv}$, as expressing a tautological biconditional.

Some simple logical equivalences very commonly employed will make this relation, and its great power, very clear. It is a commonplace that p and $\sim\sim p$ mean the same thing; "he is aware of that difficulty" and "he is not unaware of that difficulty" are two statements with the same content. In substance, either of these expressions may be replaced by the other because they both say the same thing. This principle of *double negation,* whose truth is obvious to all, may be exhibited on a truth table, where the material equivalence of two statement forms is shown to be a tautology, thus:

p	$\sim p$	$\sim\sim p$	$p \overset{\text{T}}{\equiv} \sim\sim p$
T	F	T	T
F	T	F	T

This truth table proves that p and $\sim\sim p$ are *logically equivalent.* This very useful logical equivalence, double negation, is symbolized thus:

$$p \overset{\text{T}}{\equiv} \sim\sim p$$

The difference between *material equivalence* on the one hand and *logical equivalence* on the other hand is very great and very important. The former is a truth-functional connective, $\equiv$, which may be true or false depending only upon the truth or falsity of the elements it connects. But the latter, logical equivalence, $\overset{\text{T}}{\equiv}$, is not a mere connective, and it expresses a relation between two statements that is not truth-functional. Two statements are logically equivalent only when it is absolutely impossible for them to have different truth values. But if they *always* have the same truth value, logically equivalent statements must have the same meaning, and in that case they may be substituted for one another in any truth-functional context without changing the truth value of that context. By contrast, two statements are materially equivalent if they merely *happen* to have the same truth value, even if there are no factual connections between them. Statements that are merely materially equivalent certainly may not be substituted for one another!

There are two well-known logical equivalences (*i.e.,* logically true biconditionals) of great importance because they express the interrelations among conjunction and disjunction, and their negations. Let us examine these two logical equivalences more closely.

First, what will serve to deny that a disjunction is true? Any disjunction $p \vee q$ asserts no more than that at least one of its two disjuncts is true. One cannot contradict it by asserting that at least one is false; we must (to deny it) assert that both disjuncts are false. Therefore, asserting the *negation of the disjunction (p ∨ q)* is logically equivalent to asserting the *conjunction of the negations of p and of q*. To show this on a truth table, we may formulate the biconditional, $\sim(p \lor q) \equiv (\sim p \bullet \sim q)$, place it at the top of its own column, and examine its truth value under all circumstances, that is, in each row.

p	q	$p \lor q$	$\sim(p \lor q)$	$\sim p$	$\sim q$	$\sim p \bullet \sim q$	$\sim(p \lor q) \equiv (\sim p \bullet \sim q)$
T	T	T	F	F	F	F	T
T	F	T	F	F	T	F	T
F	T	T	F	T	F	F	T
F	F	F	T	T	T	T	T

Of course we see that, whatever the truth values of p and of q, this biconditional must always be true. It is a tautology. Because the statement of that material equivalence *is* a tautology, we conclude that the two statements are logically equivalent. We have proved that

$$\sim(p \lor q) \overset{\text{T}}{\equiv} (\sim p \bullet \sim q)$$

Similarly, since asserting the conjunction of p and q asserts that both are true, to contradict this assertion we need merely assert that at least one is false. Thus, asserting the negation of the conjunction, $(p \bullet q)$, is logically equivalent to asserting the disjunction of the negations of p and of q. In symbols, the biconditional, $\sim(p \bullet q) \equiv (\sim p \lor \sim q)$ may be shown, on a truth table, to be a tautology. Such a table proves

$$\sim(p \bullet q) \overset{\text{T}}{\equiv} (\sim p \lor \sim q)$$

These two tautologous biconditionals, or logical equivalences, are known as De Morgan's theorems, because they were formally stated by the mathematician and logician Augustus De Morgan (1806–1871). De Morgan's theorems can be formulated in English thus:

(a) The negation of the disjunction of two statements is logically equivalent to the conjunction of the negations of the two statements;

and

(b) The negation of the conjunction of two statements is logically equivalent to the disjunction of the negations of the two statements.

These theorems of De Morgan prove to be exceedingly useful.

Another important logical equivalence is very helpful when we seek to manipulate truth-functional connectives. Material implication, ⊃, was defined earlier in this chapter (in section 8.3) as an abbreviated way of saying $\sim(p \bullet \sim q)$. That is, "p materially implies q" simply means, by definition, that it is not the case that p is true while q is false. In this definition we see that the *definiens*, $\sim(p \bullet \sim q)$, is the denial of a conjunction. And by De Morgan's theorem we know that any such denial is logically equivalent to the disjunction of the denials of the conjuncts; that is, we know that $\sim(p \bullet \sim q)$ is logically equivalent to $(\sim p \vee \sim \sim q)$; and this expression in turn, applying the principle of double negation, is logically equivalent to $\sim p \vee q$. Logically equivalent expressions mean the same thing, and therefore the original *definiens* of the horseshoe, $\sim(p \bullet \sim q)$, may be replaced with no change of meaning by the simpler expression $\sim p \vee q$. This gives us a very useful *definition of material implication: $p \supset q$ is logically equivalent to $\sim p \vee q$.* In symbols we write:

$$(p \supset q) \stackrel{\underline{\underline{T}}}{=} (\sim p \vee q)$$

This definition of material implication is widely relied upon in the formulation of logical statements and the analysis of arguments. Manipulation is often essential, and manipulation is more efficient when the statements we are working with have the same central connective. With the simple definition of the horseshoe we have just established, $(p \supset q) \stackrel{\underline{\underline{T}}}{=} (\sim p \vee q)$, statements in which the horseshoe is the connective can be conveniently replaced by statements in which the wedge is the connective; and likewise, statements in disjunctive form may be readily replaced by statements in implicative form. When we seek to present a formal proof of the validity of deductive arguments, replacements of this kind prove very useful indeed.

8.7 THE PARADOXES OF MATERIAL IMPLICATION

There are two forms of statements, $p \supset (q \supset p)$ and $\sim p \supset (p \supset q)$, that are easily proved to be tautologies. Trivial as these statement forms may be in their symbolic formulation, when stated in ordinary English they seem surprising and even paradoxical. The first may be stated as "If a statement is true, then it is implied by any statement whatever." Since it is true that the earth is round, it follows that "The moon is made of green cheese implies that the earth is round"; and this is very curious indeed, especially since it also follows that "The moon is *not* made of green cheese implies that the earth is round." The second tautology may be stated as "If a statement is false, then it implies any statement whatever." Since it is false that the moon is made of green cheese, it follows that "The moon is made of green cheese implies that the earth is round"; and this is all the more curious when we realize that it also follows that "The moon is made of green cheese implies that the earth is *not* round."

These seem paradoxical because we believe that the shape of the earth and the matter of the moon are utterly irrelevant to each other, and we believe further that no statement, true or false, can really imply any other statement, false or true, to which it is utterly irrelevant. And yet truth tables establish that a false statement implies any statement, and that a true statement is implied by any statement. This paradox is easily resolved, however, when we acknowledge the ambiguity of the word "implies." In several senses of the word "implies," it is perfectly true that no contingent statement can imply any other contingent statement with unrelated subject matter. It is true in the case of *logical* implication and of *definitional* and *causal* implications. It may even be true of *decisional* implications, although here the notion of relevance may have to be construed more broadly.

But subject matter or *meaning* is strictly irrelevant to *material implication,* which is a truth function. Only truth and falsehood are relevant here. There is nothing paradoxical in stating that any disjunction is true which contains at least one true disjunct, and this fact is all that is asserted by statements of the forms $p \supset (\sim q \vee p)$ and $\sim p \supset (\sim p \vee q)$, which are logically equivalent to the "paradoxical" ones. We have already given a justification of treating material implication as *a* sense of "if–then," and of the logical expediency of translating *every* occurrence of "if–then" into the "$\supset$" notation. That justification was the fact that translating "if–then" into the "$\supset$" preserves the validity of all valid arguments of the type with which we are concerned in this part of our logical studies. There are other proposed symbolizations, adequate to other types of implication, but they belong to more advanced parts of logic, beyond the scope of this book.

8.8   THE THREE "LAWS OF THOUGHT"

For Enrichment   Some early thinkers, after having defined logic as "the science of the laws of thought," went on to assert that there are exactly three *basic* laws of thought, laws so fundamental that obedience to them is both the necessary and the sufficient condition of correct thinking. These three have traditionally been called:

- The principle of identity.
  This principle asserts that *if any statement is true, then it is true.* Using our notation we may rephrase it by saying that the principle of identity asserts that every statement of the form $p \supset p$ must be true, that every such statement is a tautology.
- The principle of noncontradiction.
  This principle asserts that *no statement can be both true and false.* Using our notation we may rephrase it by saying that the principle of noncontradiction asserts that every statement of the form $p \bullet \sim p$ must be false, that every such statement is self-contradictory.
- The principle of excluded middle.
  This principle asserts that *every statement is either true or false.* Using our notation we may rephrase it by saying that the principle of excluded middle asserts that every statement of the form $p \vee \sim p$ must be true, that every such statement is a tautology.

It is obvious that these three principles are indeed true, logically true—but the claim that they deserve a privileged status as the most fundamental laws of thought is doubtful. The first (identity) and the third (excluded middle) are tautologies, but there are many other tautologous forms whose truth is equally certain. And the second (noncontradiction) is by no means the only self-contradictory form of statement.

We do use these principles in completing truth tables. In the initial columns of each row of a table we place either a **T** or an **F**, being guided by the principle of excluded middle. Nowhere do we put both **T** and **F** together, being guided by the principle of noncontradiction. And once having put a **T** under a symbol in a given row, then (being guided by the principle of identity) when we encounter that symbol in other columns of that row we regard it as still being assigned a **T**. So we could regard the three laws of thought as principles governing the construction of truth tables.

Nevertheless, in regarding the entire system of deductive logic, these three principles are no more important or fruitful than many others. Indeed, there are tautologies that are more fruitful than they for purposes of deduction, and in that sense more important than these three. A more extended treatment of this point lies beyond the scope of this book.[16]

Some thinkers, believing themselves to have devised a new and different logic, have claimed that these three principles are in fact not true, and that obedience to them has been needlessly confining. But these criticisms have been based on misunderstandings.

The principle of identity has been attacked on the ground that things change, and are always changing. Thus, for example, statements that were true of the United States when it consisted of the 13 original states are no longer true of the United States today with 50 states. But this does not undermine the principle of identity. The sentence "There are only thirteen states in the United States" is incomplete, an elliptical formulation of the statement that "There were only 13 states in the United States *in 1790*"—and that statement is as true today as it was in 1790. When we confine our attention to complete, nonelliptical formulations of propositions, we see that their truth (or falsity) does not change over time. The principle of identity is true, and it does not interfere with our recognition of continuing change.

The principle of noncontradiction has been attacked by Hegelians and Marxists on the grounds that genuine contradiction is everywhere pervasive, that the world is replete with the inevitable conflict of contradictory forces. That there are conflicting forces in the real word is true, of course—but to call these conflicting forces "contradictory" is a loose and misleading use of that term. Labor unions and the private owners of industrial plants may indeed find themselves in conflict—but neither the owner nor the union is the "negation" or the "denial" or the "contradictory" of the other. The principle of contradiction, understood in the straightforward sense in which it is intended by logicians, is unobjectionable and perfectly true.

The principle of excluded middle has been the object of much criticism, on the grounds that it leads to a "two-valued orientation," which implies that

---

[16] For further discussion of these matters, the interested reader can consult I. M. Copi and J. A. Gould, eds., *Readings on Logic*, 2d ed., New York, Macmillan, 1972, part 2; and I. M. Copi and J. A. Gould, eds., *Contemporary Philosophical Logic*, New York, St. Martin's Press, 1978, part 8.

things in the world must be either "white or black," and which thereby hinders the realization of compromise and less than absolute gradations. This objection also arises from misunderstanding. Of course the statement "This is black" cannot be jointly true with the statement "This is white"—where "this" refers to exactly the same thing. But although these two statements cannot both be true, they can both be false. "This" may be neither black nor white; the two statements are *contraries,* not contradictory. The contradictory of the statement "This is white" is the statement "It is not the case that this is white" and (if "white" is used in precisely the same sense in both of these statements) one of them must be true and the other false. The principle of excluded middle is inescapable.

All three of these "laws of thought" are unobjectionable—so long as they are applied to statements containing unambiguous, nonelliptical, and precise terms. They may not deserve the honorific status assigned to them by some philosophers,[17] but they are indubitably true.

Summary of Chapter 8

This chapter has presented the most fundamental concepts of modern symbolic logic.

In section 8.1, we explained the value of special symbols.

In section 8.2, we introduced and defined the symbols for **negation** (the curl: ~), and for the truth-functional connectives **conjunction** (the dot: •) and **disjunction** (the wedge: ∨). We also explained logical punctuation.

In section 8.3, we discussed conditional statements and defined the truth-functional connective **material implication** (the horseshoe: ⊃).

In section 8.4, we explained **the formal structure of arguments** and defined essential terms for dealing with **argument forms.** We gave a precise account of validity and invalidity as characteristics of argument forms and arguments. We explained **truth tables** and showed how the validity or invalidity of an argument form may be determined by use of a truth table.

In section 8.5, we explained **the formal structure of statements** and defined essential terms for dealing with **statement forms.** We introduced **tautologous, contradictory,** and **contingent statement forms** and defined a fourth truth-functional connective, **material equivalence** (three bars: ≡).

In section 8.6 we introduced and defined a powerful new relation, **logical equivalence,** using the symbol $\overset{T}{=}$. We explained why statements that are logically equivalent may be substituted for one another, while statements that are

---

[17] Plato appealed explicitly to the principle of noncontradiction in Book IV of his *Republic* (at nos. 436 and 439); Aristotle discussed all three of these principles in Books IV and XI of his *Metaphysics.* Of the principle of noncontradiction Aristotle wrote: "That the same attribute cannot at the same time belong and not belong to the same subject and in the same respect" is a principle "which everyone must have who understands anything that is," and which "every one must already have when he comes to a special study." It is, he concluded, "the most certain of all principles."

merely materially equivalent cannot replace one another. We introduced several logical equivalences of special importance: **De Morgan's theorems,** the **definition of material implication,** and **the principle of double negation.**

In section 8.7, we explained why the so-called **paradoxes of material implication** are thought to be paradoxes only because the nature of the connective we call material implication is often imperfectly understood.

In section 8.8, we discussed certain logical equivalences that have been thought by many to be fundamental in all reasoning: the principle of **identity,** the principle of **noncontradiction,** and the principle of the **excluded middle.**

It cannot be demanded that we should prove everything, because that is impossible; but we can require that all propositions used without proof be expressly declared to be so. . . . Furthermore I demand—and in this I go beyond Euclid—that all of the methods of inference used must be specified in advance.
—Gottlob Frege

CHAPTER 9

THE METHOD OF DEDUCTION

9.1 FORMAL PROOF OF VALIDITY

In theory, truth tables are adequate to test the validity of any argument of the general type here considered. But in practice they grow unwieldy as the number of component statements increases. A more efficient method of establishing the validity of an extended argument is to deduce its conclusion from its premises by a sequence of elementary arguments each of which is known to be valid. This technique accords fairly well with ordinary methods of argumentation.

Consider, for example, the following argument:

If Anderson was nominated, then she went to Boston.
If she went to Boston, then she campaigned there.
If she campaigned there, she met Douglas.
Anderson did not meet Douglas.
Either Anderson was nominated or someone more eligible was selected.
Therefore someone more eligible was selected.

Its validity may be intuitively obvious, but let us consider the matter of proof. The discussion will be facilitated by translating the argument into symbolism as

$$A \supset B$$
$$B \supset C$$
$$C \supset D$$
$$\sim D$$
$$A \vee E$$
$$\therefore E$$

349

To establish the validity of this argument by means of a truth table would require a table with 32 rows, since there are five different simple statements involved. But we can prove the given argument valid by deducing its conclusion from its premises by a sequence of just four elementary valid arguments. From the first two premises, $A \supset B$ and $B \supset C$, we validly infer $A \supset C$ by a Hypothetical Syllogism. From $A \supset C$ and the third premiss $C \supset D$, we validly infer $A \supset D$ by another Hypothetical Syllogism. From $A \supset D$ and the fourth premiss $\sim D$, we validly infer $\sim A$ by *modus tollens*. And from $\sim A$ and the fifth premiss $A \vee E$, by a Disjunctive Syllogism we validly infer E, the conclusion of the original argument. That the conclusion can be deduced from the five premisses of the original argument by four elementary valid arguments proves the original argument to be valid. Here the elementary valid argument forms Hypothetical Syllogism (H.S.), *modus tollens* (M.T.), and Disjunctive Syllogism (D.S.) are used as *rules of inference* in accordance with which conclusions are validly inferred or deduced from premises.

A more formal proof of validity is given by writing the premises and the statements that we deduce from them in a single column, and setting off in another column, to the right of each such statement, its "justification," or the reason we can give for including it in the proof. It is convenient to list all the premisses first and to write the conclusion either on a separate line, or slightly to one side and separated by a diagonal line from the premisses. If all the statements in the column are numbered, the "justification" for each statement consists of the numbers of the preceding statements from which it is inferred, together with the abbreviation for the rule of inference by which it follows from them. The formal proof of the argument above is written as

1. $A \supset B$
2. $B \supset C$
3. $C \supset D$
4. $\sim D$
5. $A \vee E$
   $\therefore E$
6. $A \supset C$ 1,2, H.S.
7. $A \supset D$ 6,3, H.S.
8. $\sim A$ 7,4, M.T.
9. E 5,8, D.S.

We define a formal proof that a given argument is valid as a sequence of statements each of which is either a premiss of that argument or follows from preceding statements of the sequence by an elementary valid argument, such that the last statement in the sequence is the conclusion of the argument whose validity is being proved.

We define an elementary valid argument as any argument that is a substitution instance of an elementary valid argument form. One matter to be emphasized is that *any* substitution instance of an elementary valid argument form is an elementary valid argument. Thus the argument

$$(A \bullet B) \supset [C \equiv (D \vee E)]$$
$$A \bullet B$$
$$\therefore C \equiv (D \vee E)$$

is an elementary valid argument because it is a substitution instance of the elementary valid argument form *modus ponens* (M.P.). It results from

$$p \supset q$$
$$p$$
$$\therefore q$$

by substituting $A \bullet B$ for p and $C \equiv (D \vee E)$ for q, and is therefore of that form even though *modus ponens* is not *the specific form* of the given argument.

Modus ponens is a very elementary valid argument form indeed, but what *other* valid argument forms are to be included as rules of inference? We begin with a list of just nine rules of inference to be used in constructing formal proofs of validity.

Rules of Inference

1. **Modus Ponens (M.P.)**
   $$p \supset q$$
   $$p$$
   $$\therefore q$$

2. **Modus Tollens (M.T.)**
   $$p \supset q$$
   $$\sim q$$
   $$\therefore \sim p$$

3. **Hypothetical Syllogism (H.S.)**
   $$p \supset q$$
   $$q \supset r$$
   $$\therefore p \supset r$$

4. **Disjunctive Syllogism (D.S.)**
   $$p \vee q$$
   $$\sim p$$
   $$\therefore q$$

5. **Constructive Dilemma (C.D.)**
   $$(p \supset q) \bullet (r \supset s)$$
   $$p \vee r$$
   $$\therefore q \vee s$$

6. **Absorption (Abs.)**
   $$p \supset q$$
   $$\therefore p \supset (p \bullet q)$$

7. **Simplification (Simp.)**
   $$p \bullet q$$
   $$\therefore p$$

8. **Conjunction (Conj.)**
   $$p$$
   $$q$$
   $$\therefore p \bullet q$$

9. **Addition (Add.)**
   $$p$$
   $$\therefore p \vee q$$

These nine rules of inference correspond to elementary argument forms whose validity is easily established by truth tables. With their aid, formal proofs of validity can be constructed for a wide range of more complicated arguments. The names listed are for the most part standard, and the use of their abbreviations permits formal proofs to be set down with a minimum of writing.

Exercises

I. For each of the following elementary valid arguments, state the rule of inference by which its conclusion follows from its premiss or premisses.

*1. $(A \bullet B) \supset C$
∴ $(A \bullet B) \supset [(A \bullet B) \bullet C]$

2. $(D \lor E) \bullet (F \lor G)$
∴ $D \lor E$

3. $H \supset I$
∴ $(H \supset I) \lor (H \supset {\sim}I)$

4. ${\sim}(J \bullet K) \bullet (L \supset {\sim}M)$
∴ ${\sim}(J \bullet K)$

*5. $[N \supset (O \bullet P)] \bullet [Q \supset (O \bullet R)]$
$N \lor Q$
∴ $(O \bullet P) \lor (O \bullet R)$

6. $(X \lor Y) \supset {\sim}(Z \bullet {\sim}A)$
${\sim}{\sim}(Z \bullet {\sim}A)$
∴ ${\sim}(X \lor Y)$

7. $(S \equiv T) \lor [(U \bullet V) \lor (U \bullet W)]$
${\sim}(S \equiv T)$
∴ $(U \bullet V) \lor (U \bullet W)$

8. ${\sim}(B \bullet C) \supset (D \lor E)$
${\sim}(B \bullet C)$
∴ $D \lor E$

9. $(F \equiv G) \supset {\sim}(G \bullet {\sim}F)$
${\sim}(G \bullet {\sim}F) \supset (G \supset F)$
∴ $(F \equiv G) \supset (G \supset F)$

*10. ${\sim}(H \bullet {\sim}I) \supset (H \supset I)$
$(I \equiv H) \supset {\sim}(H \bullet {\sim}I)$
∴ $(I \equiv H) \supset (H \supset I)$

11. $(A \supset B) \supset (C \lor D)$
$A \supset B$
∴ $C \lor D$

12. $[E \supset (F \equiv {\sim}G)] \lor (C \lor D)$
${\sim}[E \supset (F \equiv {\sim}G)]$
∴ $C \lor D$

13. $(C \lor D) \supset [(J \lor K) \supset (J \bullet K)]$
${\sim}[(J \lor K) \supset (J \bullet K)]$
∴ ${\sim}(C \lor D)$

14. ${\sim}[L \supset (M \supset N)] \supset {\sim}(C \lor D)$
${\sim}[L \supset (M \supset N)]$
∴ ${\sim}(C \lor D)$

*15. $(J \supset K) \bullet (K \supset L)$
$L \supset M$
∴ $[(J \supset K) \bullet (K \supset L)] \bullet (L \supset M)$

16. $N \supset (O \lor P)$
$Q \supset (O \lor R)$
∴ $[Q \supset (O \lor R)] \bullet [N \supset (O \lor P)]$

17. $(S \supset T) \supset (U \supset V)$
∴ $(S \supset T) \supset [(S \supset T) \bullet (U \supset V)]$

18. $(W \bullet {\sim}X) \equiv (Y \supset Z)$
∴ $[(W \bullet {\sim}X) \equiv (Y \supset Z)] \lor (X \equiv {\sim}Z)$

19. $[(H \bullet {\sim}I) \supset C] \bullet [(I \bullet {\sim}H) \supset D]$
$(H \bullet {\sim}I) \lor (I \bullet {\sim}H)$
∴ $C \lor D$

*20. $[(O \supset P) \supset Q] \supset {\sim}(C \lor D)$
$(C \lor D) \supset [(O \supset P) \supset Q]$
∴ $(C \lor D) \supset {\sim}(C \lor D)$

II. Each of the following is a formal proof of validity for the indicated argument. State the "justification" for each numbered line that is not a premiss.

*1. 1. $A \bullet B$
2. $(A \lor C) \supset D$
∴ $A \bullet D$
3. A

2. 1. $(E \lor F) \bullet (G \lor H)$
2. $(E \supset G) \bullet (F \supset H)$
3. ${\sim}G$
∴ H

4. $A \lor C$
5. D
6. $A \bullet D$

3.
1. $I \supset J$
2. $J \supset K$
3. $L \supset M$
4. $I \lor L$
   $\therefore K \lor M$
5. $I \supset K$
6. $(I \supset K) \bullet (L \supset M)$
7. $K \lor M$

*5.
1. $Q \supset R$
2. $\sim S \supset (T \supset U)$
3. $S \lor (Q \lor T)$
4. $\sim S$
   $\therefore R \lor U$
5. $T \supset U$
6. $(Q \supset R) \bullet (T \supset U)$
7. $Q \lor T$
8. $R \lor U$

7.
1. $(A \lor B) \supset C$
2. $(C \lor B) \supset [A \supset (D \equiv E)]$
3. $A \bullet D$
   $\therefore D \equiv E$
4. A
5. $A \lor B$
6. C
7. $C \lor B$
8. $A \supset (D \equiv E)$
9. $D \equiv E$

9.
1. $I \supset J$
2. $I \lor (\sim\sim K \bullet \sim\sim J)$
3. $L \supset \sim K$
4. $\sim(I \bullet J)$
   $\therefore \sim L \lor \sim J$
5. $I \supset (I \bullet J)$
6. $\sim I$
7. $\sim\sim K \bullet \sim\sim J$
8. $\sim\sim K$
9. $\sim L$
10. $\sim L \lor \sim J$

4.
4. $E \lor F$
5. $G \lor H$
6. H

4.
1. $N \supset O$
2. $(N \bullet O) \supset P$
3. $\sim(N \bullet P)$
   $\therefore \sim N$
4. $N \supset (N \bullet O)$
5. $N \supset P$
6. $N \supset (N \bullet P)$
7. $\sim N$

6.
1. $W \supset X$
2. $(W \supset Y) \supset (Z \lor X)$
3. $(W \bullet X) \supset Y$
4. $\sim Z$
   $\therefore X$
5. $W \supset (W \bullet X)$
6. $W \supset Y$
7. $Z \lor X$
8. X

8.
1. $F \supset \sim G$
2. $\sim F \supset (H \supset \sim G)$
3. $(\sim I \lor \sim H) \supset \sim\sim G$
4. $\sim I$
   $\therefore \sim H$
5. $\sim I \lor \sim H$
6. $\sim\sim G$
7. $\sim F$
8. $H \supset \sim G$
9. $\sim H$

*10.
1. $(L \supset M) \supset (N \equiv O)$
2. $(P \supset \sim Q) \supset (M \equiv \sim Q)$
3. $\{[(P \supset \sim Q) \lor (R \equiv S)] \bullet$
   $(N \lor O)\} \supset [(R \equiv S) \supset (L \supset M)]$
4. $(P \supset \sim Q) \lor (R \equiv S)$
5. $N \lor O$
   $\therefore (M \equiv \sim Q) \lor (N \equiv O)$
6. $[(P \supset \sim Q) \lor (R \equiv S)] \bullet (N \lor O)$
7. $(R \equiv S) \supset (L \supset M)$
8. $(R \equiv S) \supset (N \equiv O)$
9. $[(P \supset \sim Q) \supset (M \equiv \sim Q)] \bullet$
   $[(R \equiv S) \supset (N \equiv O)]$
10. $(M \equiv \sim Q) \lor (N \equiv O)$

III.   For each of the following, adding just two statements to the premises will produce a formal proof of validity. Construct a formal proof of validity for each of the following arguments.

*1. A
      B
      $\therefore (A \lor C) \bullet B$

2. $D \supset E$
     $D \bullet F$
     $\therefore E$

3. G
     H
     $\therefore (G \bullet H) \lor I$

4. $J \supset K$
     J
     $\therefore K \lor L$

*5. $M \lor N$
      $\sim M \bullet \sim O$
      $\therefore N$

6. $P \bullet Q$
     R
     $\therefore P \bullet R$

7. $S \supset T$
     $\sim T \bullet \sim U$
     $\therefore \sim S$

8. $V \lor W$
     $\sim V$
     $\therefore W \lor X$

9. $Y \supset Z$
     Y
     $\therefore Y \bullet Z$

*10. $A \supset B$
       $(A \bullet B) \supset C$
       $\therefore A \supset C$

11. $D \supset E$
      $(E \supset F) \bullet (F \supset D)$
      $\therefore D \supset F$

12. $(G \supset H) \bullet (I \supset J)$
      G
      $\therefore H \lor J$

13. $\sim(K \bullet L)$
      $K \supset L$
      $\therefore \sim K$

14. $(M \supset N) \bullet (M \supset O)$
      $N \supset O$
      $\therefore M \supset O$

*15. $(P \supset Q) \bullet (R \supset S)$
       $(P \lor R) \bullet (Q \lor R)$
       $\therefore Q \lor S$

16. $(T \supset U) \bullet (T \supset V)$
      T
      $\therefore U \lor V$

17. $(W \lor X) \supset Y$
      W
      $\therefore Y$

18. $(Z \bullet A) \supset (B \bullet C)$
      $Z \supset A$
      $\therefore Z \supset (B \bullet C)$

19. $D \supset E$
      $[D \supset (D \bullet E)] \supset (F \supset \sim G)$
      $\therefore F \supset \sim G$

*20. $(\sim H \lor I) \lor J$
       $\sim(\sim H \lor I)$
       $\therefore J \lor \sim H$

21. $(K \supset L) \supset M$
      $\sim M \bullet \sim(L \supset K)$
      $\therefore \sim(K \supset L)$

22. $(N \supset O) \supset (P \supset Q)$
      $[P \supset (N \supset O)] \bullet [N \supset (P \supset Q)]$
      $\therefore P \supset (P \supset Q)$

23. $R \supset S$
     $S \supset (S \bullet R)$
     $\therefore [R \supset (R \bullet S)] \bullet [S \supset (S \bullet R)]$

24. $[T \supset (U \vee V)] \bullet [U \supset (T \vee V)]$
     $(T \vee U) \bullet (U \vee V)$
     $\therefore (U \vee V) \vee (T \vee V)$

*25. $(W \bullet X) \supset (Y \bullet Z)$ 26. $A \supset B$
      $\sim[(W \bullet X) \bullet (Y \bullet Z)]$ $A \vee C$
      $\therefore \sim(W \bullet X)$ $C \supset D$
                                       $\therefore B \vee D$

27. $(E \bullet F) \vee (G \supset H)$ 28. $J \vee \sim K$
      $I \supset G$ $K \vee (L \supset J)$
      $\sim(E \bullet F)$ $\sim J$
      $\therefore I \supset H$ $\therefore L \supset J$

29. $(M \supset N) \bullet (O \supset P)$ *30. $Q \supset (R \vee S)$
      $N \supset P$ $(T \bullet U) \supset R$
      $(N \supset P) \supset (M \vee O)$ $(R \vee S) \supset (T \bullet U)$
      $\therefore N \vee P$ $\therefore Q \supset R$

IV.   For each of the following, adding just three statements to the premises will produce a formal proof of validity. Construct a formal proof of validity for each of the following arguments.

*1. $A \vee (B \supset A)$ 2. $(D \vee E) \supset (F \bullet G)$
     $\sim A \bullet C$ D
     $\therefore \sim B$ $\therefore F$

3. $(H \supset I) \bullet (H \supset J)$ 4. $(K \bullet L) \supset M$
     $H \bullet (I \vee J)$ $K \supset L$
     $\therefore I \vee J$ $\therefore K \supset [(K \bullet L) \bullet M]$

*5. $N \supset [(N \bullet O) \supset P]$ 6. $Q \supset R$
      $N \bullet O$ $R \supset S$
      $\therefore P$ $\sim S$
                                       $\therefore \sim Q \bullet \sim R$

7. $T \supset U$ 8. $\sim X \supset Y$
     $V \vee \sim U$ $Z \supset X$
     $\sim V \bullet \sim W$ $\sim X$
     $\therefore \sim T$ $\therefore Y \bullet \sim Z$

9. $(A \vee B) \supset \sim C$ *10. $E \vee \sim F$
     $C \vee D$ $F \vee (E \vee G)$
     A $\sim E$
     $\therefore D$ $\therefore G$

11. $(H \supset I) \bullet (J \supset K)$ 12. $L \vee (M \supset N)$
      $K \vee H$ $\sim L \supset (N \supset O)$
      $\sim K$ $\sim L$
      $\therefore I$ $\therefore M \supset O$

13. $(P \supset Q) \cdot (Q \supset P)$
     $R \supset S$
     $P \lor R$
     $\therefore Q \lor S$

14. $(T \supset U) \cdot (V \supset W)$
     $(U \supset X) \cdot (W \supset Y)$
     T
     $\therefore X \lor Y$

*15. $(Z \cdot A) \supset B$
      $B \supset A$
      $(B \cdot A) \supset (A \cdot B)$
      $\therefore (Z \cdot A) \supset (A \cdot B)$

V. Construct a formal proof of validity for each of the following arguments.

*1. $A \supset B$
     $A \lor (C \cdot D)$
     $\sim B \cdot \sim E$
     $\therefore C$

2. $(F \supset G) \cdot (H \supset I)$
    $J \supset K$
    $(F \lor J) \cdot (H \lor L)$
    $\therefore G \lor K$

3. $(\sim M \cdot \sim N) \supset (O \supset N)$
    $N \supset M$
    $\sim M$
    $\therefore \sim O$

4. $(K \lor L) \supset (M \lor N)$
    $(M \lor N) \supset (O \cdot P)$
    K
    $\therefore O$

*5. $(Q \supset R) \cdot (S \supset T)$
     $(U \supset V) \cdot (W \supset X)$
     $Q \lor U$
     $\therefore R \lor V$

6. $W \supset X$
    $(W \cdot X) \supset Y$
    $(W \cdot Y) \supset Z$
    $\therefore W \supset Z$

7. $A \supset B$
    $C \supset D$
    $A \lor C$
    $\therefore (A \cdot B) \lor (C \cdot D)$

8. $(E \lor F) \supset (G \cdot H)$
    $(G \lor H) \supset I$
    E
    $\therefore I$

9. $J \supset K$
    $K \lor L$
    $(L \cdot \sim J) \supset (M \cdot \sim J)$
    $\sim K$
    $\therefore M$

*10. $(N \lor O) \supset P$
      $(P \lor Q) \supset R$
      $Q \lor N$
      $\sim Q$
      $\therefore R$

VI. Construct a formal proof of validity for each of the following arguments, using the abbreviations suggested.

*1. If either Gertrude or Herbert wins, then both Jane and Kenneth lose. Gertrude wins. Therefore Jane loses. (G—Gertrude wins; H—Herbert wins; J—Jane loses; K—Kenneth loses.)

2. If Adams joins, then the club's social prestige will rise; and if Baker joins, then the club's financial position will be more secure. Either Adams or Baker will join. If the club's social prestige rises, then Baker will join; and if the club's financial position becomes more secure, then Wilson will join. Therefore either Baker or Wilson will join. (A—Adams joins; S—The club's social prestige rises; B—Baker joins; F—The club's financial position is more secure; W—Wilson joins.)

3. If Brown received the wire, then she took the plane; and if she took the plane, then she will not be late for the meeting. If the telegram was incorrectly addressed, then Brown will be late for the meeting. Either Brown received the wire or the telegram was incorrectly addressed. Therefore either Brown took the plane or she will be late for the meeting. (*R*—Brown received the wire; *P*—Brown took the plane; *L*—Brown will be late for the meeting; *T*—The telegram was incorrectly addressed.)

4. If Neville buys the lot, then an office building will be constructed; whereas if Payton buys the lot, then it quickly will be sold again. If Rivers buys the lot, then a store will be constructed; and if a store is constructed, then Thompson will offer to lease it. Either Neville or Rivers will buy the lot. Therefore either an office building or a store will be constructed. (*N*—Neville buys the lot; *O*—An office building will be constructed; *P*—Payton buys the lot; *Q*—The lot quickly will be sold again; *R*—Rivers buys the lot; *S*—A store will be constructed; *T*—Thompson will offer to lease it.)

*5. If rain continues, then the river rises. If rain continues and the river rises, then the bridge will wash out. If continuation of rain would cause the bridge to wash out, then a single road is not sufficient for the town. Either a single road is sufficient for the town or the traffic engineers have made a mistake. Therefore the traffic engineers have made a mistake. (*C*—Rain continues; *R*—The river rises; *B*—The bridge washes out; *S*—A single road is sufficient for the town; *M*—The traffic engineers have made a mistake.)

6. If Jacobson goes to the meeting, then a complete report will be made; but if Jacobson does not go to the meeting, then a special election will be required. If a complete report is made, then an investigation will be launched. If Jacobson's going to the meeting implies that a complete report will be made, and the making of a complete report implies that an investigation will be launched, then either Jacobson goes to the meeting and an investigation is launched or Jacobson does not go to the meeting and no investigation is launched. If Jacobson goes to the meeting and an investigation is launched, then some members will have to stand trial. But if Jacobson does not go to the meeting and no investigation is launched, then the organization will disintegrate very rapidly. Therefore either some members will have to stand trial or the organization will disintegrate very rapidly. (*J*—Jacobson goes to the meeting; *R*—A complete report is made; *E*—A special election is required; *I*—An investigation is launched; *T*—Some members have to stand trial; *D*—The organization disintegrates very rapidly.)

7. If Ann is present, then Bill is present. If Ann and Bill are both present, then either Charles or Doris will be elected. If either Charles or Doris is elected, then Elmer does not really dominate the club.

If Ann's presence implies that Elmer does not really dominate the club, then Florence will be the new president. So Florence will be the new president. (*A*—Ann is present; *B*—Bill is present; *C*—Charles will be elected; *D*—Doris will be elected; *E*—Elmer really dominates the club; *F*—Florence will be the new president.)

8. If Mr. Jones is the brakeman's next-door neighbor, then Mr. Jones's annual earnings are exactly divisible by 3. If Mr. Jones's annual earnings are exactly divisible by 3, then $20,000 is exactly divisible by 3. But $20,000 is not exactly divisible by 3. If Mr. Robinson is the brakeman's next-door neighbor, then Mr. Robinson lives halfway between Detroit and Chicago. If Mr. Robinson lives in Detroit, then he does not live halfway between Detroit and Chicago. Mr. Robinson lives in Detroit. If Mr. Jones is not the brakeman's next-door neighbor, then either Mr. Robinson or Mr. Smith is the brakeman's next-door neighbor. Therefore Mr. Smith is the brakeman's next-door neighbor. (*J*—Mr. Jones is the brakeman's next-door neighbor; *E*—Mr. Jones's annual earnings are exactly divisible by 3; *T*—$20,000 is exactly divisible by 3; *R*—Mr. Robinson is the brakeman's next-door neighbor; *H*—Mr. Robinson lives halfway between Detroit and Chicago; *D*—Mr. Robinson lives in Detroit; *S*—Mr. Smith is the brakeman's next-door neighbor.)

9. If Mr. Smith is the brakeman's next-door neighbor, then Mr. Smith lives halfway between Detroit and Chicago. If Mr. Smith lives halfway between Detroit and Chicago, then he does not live in Chicago. Mr. Smith is the brakeman's next-door neighbor. If Mr. Robinson lives in Detroit, then he does not live in Chicago. Mr. Robinson lives in Detroit. Mr. Smith lives in Chicago or else either Mr. Robinson or Mr. Jones lives in Chicago. If Mr. Jones lives in Chicago, then the brakeman is Jones. Therefore the brakeman is Jones. (*S*—Mr. Smith is the brakeman's next-door neighbor; *W*—Mr. Smith lives halfway between Detroit and Chicago; *L*—Mr. Smith lives in Chicago; *D*—Mr. Robinson lives in Detroit; *I*—Mr. Robinson lives in Chicago; *C*—Mr. Jones lives in Chicago; *B*—The brakeman is Jones.)

*10. If Smith once beat the fireman at billiards, then Smith is not the fireman. Smith once beat the fireman at billiards. If the brakeman is Jones, then Jones is not the fireman. The brakeman is Jones. If Smith is not the fireman and Jones is not the fireman, then Robinson is the fireman. If the brakeman is Jones and Robinson is the fireman, then Smith is the engineer. Therefore Smith is the engineer. (*O*—Smith once beat the fireman at billiards; *M*—Smith is the fireman; *B*—The brakeman is Jones; *N*—Jones is the fireman; *F*—Robinson is the fireman; *G*—Smith is the engineer.)

9.2 THE RULE OF REPLACEMENT

There are many valid truth-functional arguments whose validity cannot be proved using only the nine rules of inference given thus far. For example, to construct a formal proof of validity for the obviously valid argument

$$A \supset B$$
$$C \supset {\sim}B$$
$$\therefore A \supset {\sim}C$$

additional rules are required.

In any truth-functional compound statement, if a component statement in it is replaced by another statement having the same truth value, the truth value of the compound statement will remain unchanged. But the only compound statements that concern us here are truth-functional compound statements. We may accept, therefore, as an additional principle of inference, the **Rule of Replacement,** which permits us to infer from any statement the result of replacing any component of that statement by any other statement *logically* equivalent to the component replaced. For example, using the principle of Double Negation (D.N.), which asserts that p is logically equivalent to ${\sim}{\sim}p$, we can infer from $A \supset {\sim}{\sim}B$ any of the following

$$A \supset B, \quad {\sim}{\sim}A \supset {\sim}{\sim}B, \quad {\sim}{\sim}(A \supset {\sim}{\sim}B), \quad \text{or } A \supset {\sim}{\sim}{\sim}{\sim}B$$

by replacement.

To make the new rule definite, we list ten tautologous or logically true biconditionals with which it can be used. These biconditionals provide additional rules of inference to be used in proving the validity of extended arguments. We number them consecutively to follow the first nine rules already stated in section 9.1.

> **Rule of Replacement: Any of the following logically equivalent expressions may replace each other wherever they occur:**
>
> 10. **De Morgan's Theorems** (De M.): $\quad {\sim}(p \cdot q) \stackrel{\mathrm{T}}{=} ({\sim}p \vee {\sim}q)$
> $\quad {\sim}(p \vee q) \stackrel{\mathrm{T}}{=} ({\sim}p \cdot {\sim}q)$
>
> 11. **Commutation** (Com.): $\quad (p \vee q) \stackrel{\mathrm{T}}{=} (q \vee p)$
> $\quad (p \cdot q) \stackrel{\mathrm{T}}{=} (q \cdot p)$
>
> 12. **Association** (Assoc.): $\quad [p \vee (q \vee r)] \stackrel{\mathrm{T}}{=} [(p \vee q) \vee r]$
> $\quad [p \cdot (q \cdot r)] \stackrel{\mathrm{T}}{=} [(p \cdot q) \cdot r]$
>
> 13. **Distribution** (Dist.): $\quad [p \cdot (q \vee r)] \stackrel{\mathrm{T}}{=} [(p \cdot q) \vee (p \cdot r)]$
> $\quad [p \vee (q \cdot r)] \stackrel{\mathrm{T}}{=} [(p \vee q) \cdot (p \vee r)]$
>
> 14. **Double negation** (D.N.): $\quad p \stackrel{\mathrm{T}}{=} {\sim}{\sim}p$
>
> 15. **Transposition** (Trans.): $\quad (p \supset q) \stackrel{\mathrm{T}}{=} ({\sim}q \supset {\sim}p)$
>
> 16. **Material implication** (Impl.): $\quad (p \supset q) \stackrel{\mathrm{T}}{=} ({\sim}p \vee q)$
>
> 17. **Material equivalence** (Equiv.): $\quad (p \equiv q) \stackrel{\mathrm{T}}{=} [(p \supset q) \cdot (q \supset p)]$
> $\quad (p \equiv q) \stackrel{\mathrm{T}}{=} [(p \cdot q) \vee ({\sim}p \cdot {\sim}q)]$

18. **Exportation** (Exp.): $[(p \cdot q) \supset r] \overset{\text{T}}{\equiv} [p \supset (q \supset r)]$

19. **Tautology** (Taut.):[1] $p \overset{\text{T}}{\equiv} (p \vee p)$
$p \overset{\text{T}}{\equiv} (p \cdot p)$

The process of replacement is very different from that of substitution: We substitute statements for statement variables, whereas we replace statements by other statements. In moving from a statement form to a substitution instance of it, or from an argument form to a substitution instance of it, we can substitute any statement for any statement variable, provided that if a statement is substituted for one occurrence of a statement variable it must be substituted for every other occurrence of that statement variable. But in moving from one statement to another by way of replacement, we can replace a component of the first only by a statement certified to be logically equivalent to that component by one of the logical equivalences 10 through 19, and we can replace one occurrence of that component without having to replace any other occurrence of it.

These 19 rules of inference are somewhat redundant, in the sense that they do not constitute a bare minimum which would suffice for the construction of formal proofs of validity for extended arguments. For example, *modus tollens* could be dropped from the list without any real weakening of our proof apparatus, for any line depending upon *modus tollens* can be justified by appealing to other rules in the list instead. Thus in the first formal proof given in this chapter on page 350, line 8, $\sim A$, was deduced from lines 4 and 7, $\sim D$ and $A \supset D$, by *modus tollens*, but if *modus tollens* were eliminated as a rule of inference we still could deduce $\sim A$ from $A \supset D$ and $\sim D$. This could be done by inserting the intermediate line $\sim D \supset \sim A$, which follows from $A \supset D$ by the principle of Transposition (Trans.), and then obtaining $\sim A$ from $\sim D \supset \sim A$, and $\sim D$ by *modus ponens* (M.P.). But *modus tollens* is such a commonly used and intuitively obvious rule of inference that it has been included anyway. Others of the 19 also are redundant in this same sense.

The list of 19 rules of inference is characterized not only by redundancy, but also by a certain sort of deficiency. For example, although the argument

$$A \vee B$$
$$\sim B$$
$$\therefore A$$

is intuitively valid, its form

$$p \vee q$$
$$\sim q$$
$$\therefore p$$

has not been included as a rule of inference. The conclusion A does not follow from the premises $A \vee B$ and $\sim B$ by any single rule of inference, although it

---

[1] Note that the word "tautology" is used in three difference senses; it can mean (1) a statement form all of whose substitution instances are true; (2) a statement whose specific form is a tautology in sense (1); and (3) the particular logical equivalences numbered 19 in our list of rules of inference.

can be deduced from them by two rules of inference. A formal proof of validity for the given argument can be written as

1. $A \lor B$
2. $\sim B$
$\therefore A$
3. $B \lor A$ 1, Com.
4. A 3,2, D.S.

We could eliminate the indicated deficiency by adding another rule to our list, but if we made additions for all such cases we should end up with a list that was much longer and therefore less manageable.

The present list of 19 rules of inference constitutes a *complete* system of truth-functional logic, in the sense that it permits the construction of a formal proof of validity for *any* valid truth-functional argument.[2]

The notion of *formal proof* is an *effective* notion, which means that it can be decided quite mechanically, in a finite number of steps, whether or not a given sequence of statements constitutes a formal proof (with reference to a given list of rules of inference). No thinking is required, either in the sense of thinking about what the statements in the sequence "mean" or in the sense of using logical intuition to check any step's validity. Only two things are required, of which the first is the ability to see that a statement occurring in one place is precisely the same as a statement occurring in another, for we must be able to check that some statements in the proof are premisses of the argument being proved valid and that the last statement in the proof is the conclusion of that argument. The second thing required is the ability to see whether a given statement has a certain pattern or not; that is, to see if it is a substitution instance of a given statement form.

Thus any question about whether the preceding sequence of statements is a formal proof of validity can easily be settled in a completely mechanical fashion. That lines 1 and 2 are the premisses and line 4 is the conclusion of the given argument is obvious on inspection. That 3 follows from preceding lines by one of the given rules of inference can be decided in a finite number of steps—even where the notation "1, Com." is not written at the side. The explanatory notation in the second column is a help and should always be included, but it is not, strictly speaking, a necessary part of the proof itself. At every line, there are only finitely many preceding lines and only finitely many rules of inference or reference forms to be consulted. Although time-consuming, it can be verified by inspection and comparison of shapes that 3 does not follow from 1 and 2 by *modus ponens*, or by *modus tollens*, or by a Hypothetical Syllogism, . . . , and so on, until in following this procedure we come to the question of whether or not 3 follows from 1 by the principle of Commutation, and there we see, simply by looking at the forms, that it does. In the same way the legitimacy of *any* statement in *any* formal proof can be tested in a finite number of steps, none of

---

[2]A method of proving this kind of completeness for a set of rules of inference can be found in I. M. Copi, *Symbolic Logic*, 5th ed. (New York: Macmillan, 1979), chap. 8. See also John A. Winnie, "The Completeness of Copi's System of Natural Deduction," *Notre Dame Journal of Formal Logic* 11 (July 1970), 379–382.

which involves anything more than comparing forms or shapes. It is to pre-serve this effectiveness that we require that only one step should be taken at a time. One might be tempted to shorten a proof by combining steps, but the space and time saved are negligible. More important is the effectiveness we achieve by taking each step by means of one single rule of inference at a time.

Although a formal proof of validity is effective in the sense that it can be me-chanically decided of any given sequence whether it is a proof, *constructing* a for-mal proof is not an effective procedure. In this respect formal proofs differ from truth tables. The making of truth tables is completely mechanical: given any ar-gument of the sort with which we are now concerned, we can always construct a truth table to test its validity by following the simple rules of procedure set forth in the preceding chapter. But we have no effective or mechanical rules for the construction of formal proofs. Here we must think or "figure out" where to begin and how to proceed. Nevertheless, proving an argument valid by con-structing a formal proof of its validity is much easier than the purely mechanical construction of a truth table with perhaps hundreds or even thousands of rows.

There is an important difference between the first nine and the last ten rules of inference. *The first nine rules can be applied only to whole lines of a proof.* Thus in a formal proof of validity, the statement A can be inferred from the statement $A \bullet B$ by Simplification only if $A \bullet B$ constitutes a whole line. It is obvious that A cannot be inferred validly either from $(A \bullet B) \supset C$ or from $C \supset (A \bullet B)$, be-cause the latter two statements can be true while A is false. And the statement $A \supset C$ does not follow from the statement $(A \bullet B) \supset C$ by Simplification or by any other rule of inference. It does not follow at all, for if A is true and B and C are both false, $(A \bullet B) \supset C$ is true but $A \supset C$ is false. Again, although $A \vee B$ fol-lows from A by Addition, we cannot infer $(A \vee B) \supset C$ from $A \supset C$ by Addition or by any other rule of inference. For if A and C are both false and B is true, $A \supset C$ is true but $(A \vee B) \supset C$ is false. On the other hand, *any of the last ten rules can be applied either to whole lines or to parts of lines.* Not only can the statement $A \supset (B \supset C)$ be inferred from the whole line $(A \bullet B) \supset C$ by Exportation, but from the line $[(A \bullet B) \supset C] \vee D$ we can infer $[A \supset (B \supset C)] \vee D$ by Exportation. By replacement, logically equivalent expressions can replace each other wher-ever they occur, even where they do not constitute whole lines of a proof. But the first nine rules of inference can be used only with whole lines of a proof serving as premises.

Although we have no purely mechanical rules for constructing formal proofs, some rough-and-ready rules of thumb or hints on procedure may be suggested. The first is simply to begin deducing conclusions from the given premises by the given rules of inference. As more and more of these subconclusions become avail-able as premises for further deductions, the greater is the likelihood of being able to see how to deduce the conclusion of the argument to be proved valid. Another hint is to try to eliminate statements that occur in the premises but not in the con-clusion. Such elimination can proceed, of course, only in accordance with the rules of inference. But the rules contain many techniques for eliminating state-ments. Simplification is such a rule, whereby the right-hand conjunct can be dropped from a whole line that is a conjunction. And Commutation is a rule that permits switching the left-hand conjunct of a conjunction over to the right-hand side, from which it can be dropped by Simplification. The "middle" term q can be eliminated by a Hypothetical Syllogism given two statements of the patterns $p \supset q$ and $q \supset r$. Distribution is a useful rule for transforming a disjunction of the pattern $p \vee (q \bullet r)$ into the conjunction $(p \vee q) \bullet (p \vee r)$, whose right-hand conjunct can then be eliminated by Simplification. Another rule of thumb is to introduce by means of Addition a statement that occurs in the conclusion but not in any premiss. Yet another method, often very productive, is to work backward from the conclusion by looking for some statement or statements from which it can be deduced, and then trying to deduce those intermediate statements from the premisses. There is, however, no substitute for practice as a method of acquiring facility in the construction of formal proofs.

THE RULES OF INFERENCE

Nineteen rules of inference are specified for use in constructing proofs of validity. They are as follows:

ELEMENTARY VALID ARGUMENT FORMS:

1. Modus Ponens (M.P.):
$p \supset q, p, \therefore q$

2. Modus Tollens (M.T.):
$p \supset q, \sim q, \therefore \sim p$

3. Hypothetical Syllogism (H.S.):
$p \supset q, q \supset r, \therefore p \supset r$

4. Disjunctive Syllogism (D.S.):
$p \vee q, \sim p, \therefore q$

5. Constructive Dilemma (C.D.):
$(p \supset q) \bullet (r \supset s), p \vee r, \therefore q \vee s$

6. Absorption (Abs.):
$p \supset q, \therefore p \supset (p \bullet q)$

7. Simplification (Simp.):
$p \bullet q, \therefore p$

8. Conjunction (Conj.):
$p, q, \therefore p \bullet q$

9. Addition (Add.):
$p, \therefore p \vee q$

LOGICALLY EQUIVALENT EXPRESSIONS:

10. De Morgan's Theorems (De M.):
$\sim(p \bullet q) \overset{\text{T}}{=} (\sim p \vee \sim q)$
$\sim(p \vee q) \overset{\text{T}}{=} (\sim p \bullet \sim q)$

11. Commutation (Com.):
$(p \vee q) \overset{\text{T}}{=} (q \vee p)$
$(p \bullet q) \overset{\text{T}}{=} (q \bullet p)$

12. Association (Assoc.):
$[p \vee (q \vee r)] \overset{\text{T}}{=} [(p \vee q) \vee r]$
$[p \bullet (q \bullet r)] \overset{\text{T}}{=} [(p \bullet q) \bullet r]$

13. Distribution (Dist.):
$[(p \bullet (q \vee r)] \overset{\text{T}}{=} [(p \bullet q) \vee (p \bullet r)]$
$[p \vee (q \bullet r)] \overset{\text{T}}{=} [(p \vee q) \bullet (p \vee r)]$

14. Double Negation (D.N.):
$p \overset{\text{T}}{=} \sim\sim p$

15. Transposition (Trans.):
$(p \supset q) \overset{\text{T}}{=} (\sim q \supset \sim p)$

16. Material Implication (Impl.):
$(p \supset q) \overset{\text{T}}{=} (\sim p \vee q)$

17. Material Equivalence (Equiv.):
$(p \equiv q) \overset{\text{T}}{=} [(p \supset q) \bullet (q \supset p)]$
$(p \equiv q) \overset{\text{T}}{=} [(p \bullet q) \vee (\sim p \bullet \sim q)]$

18. Exportation (Exp.):
$[(p \bullet q) \supset r] \overset{\text{T}}{=} [p \supset (q \supset r)]$

19. Tautology (Taut.):
$p \overset{\text{T}}{=} (p \vee p)$
$p \overset{\text{T}}{=} (p \bullet p)$

Exercises

I. For each of the following arguments, state the rule of inference by which its conclusion follows from its premiss.

*1. $(A \supset B) \bullet (C \supset D)$
$\therefore (A \supset B) \bullet (\sim D \supset \sim C)$

2. $(E \supset F) \bullet (G \supset \sim H)$
$\therefore (\sim E \vee F) \bullet (G \supset \sim H)$

3. $[I \supset (J \supset K)] \bullet (J \supset \sim I)$
$\therefore [(I \bullet J) \supset K] \bullet (J \supset \sim I)$

4. $[L \supset (M \vee N)] \vee [L \supset (M \vee N)]$
$\therefore L \supset (M \vee N)$

*5. $O \supset [(P \supset Q) \bullet (Q \supset P)]$
$\therefore O \supset (P \equiv Q)$

6. $\sim(R \vee S) \supset (\sim R \vee \sim S)$
$\therefore (\sim R \bullet \sim S) \supset (\sim R \vee \sim S)$

7. $(T \vee \sim U) \bullet [(W \bullet \sim V) \supset \sim T]$
$\therefore (T \vee \sim U) \bullet [W \supset (\sim V \supset \sim T)]$

8. $(X \vee Y) \bullet (\sim X \vee \sim Y)$
$\therefore [(X \vee Y) \bullet \sim X] \vee [(X \vee Y) \bullet \sim Y]$

9. $Z \supset (A \supset B)$
$\therefore Z \supset (\sim\sim A \supset B)$

*10. $[C \bullet (D \bullet \sim E)] \bullet [(C \bullet D) \bullet \sim E]$
$\therefore [(C \bullet D) \bullet \sim E] \bullet [(C \bullet D) \bullet \sim E]$

11. $(\sim F \vee G) \bullet (F \supset G)$
$\therefore (F \supset G) \bullet (F \supset G)$

12. $(H \supset \sim I) \supset (\sim I \supset \sim J)$
$\therefore (H \supset \sim I) \supset (J \supset I)$

13. $(\sim K \supset L) \supset (\sim M \vee \sim N)$
$\therefore (\sim K \supset L) \supset \sim(M \bullet N)$

14. $[(\sim O \vee P) \vee \sim Q] \bullet [\sim O \vee (P \vee \sim Q)]$
$\therefore [\sim O \vee (P \vee \sim Q)] \bullet [\sim O \vee (P \vee \sim Q)]$

*15. $[(R \vee \sim S) \bullet \sim T] \vee [(R \vee \sim S) \bullet U]$
$\therefore (R \vee \sim S) \bullet (\sim T \vee U)$

16. $[V \supset \sim(W \vee X)] \supset (Y \vee Z)$
$\therefore \{[V \supset \sim(W \vee X)] \bullet [V \supset \sim(W \vee X)]\} \supset (Y \vee Z)$

17. $[(\sim A \bullet B) \bullet (C \vee D)] \vee [\sim(\sim A \bullet B) \bullet \sim(C \vee D)]$
$\therefore (\sim A \bullet B) \equiv (C \vee D)$

18. $[\sim E \vee (\sim\sim F \supset G)] \bullet [\sim E \vee (F \supset G)]$
$\therefore [\sim E \vee (F \supset G)] \bullet [\sim E \vee (F \supset G)]$

19. $[H \bullet (I \vee J)] \vee [H \bullet (K \supset \sim L)]$
$\therefore H \bullet [(I \vee J) \vee (K \supset \sim L)]$

*20. $(\sim M \vee \sim N) \supset (O \supset \sim\sim P)$
$\therefore \sim(M \bullet N) \supset (O \supset \sim\sim P)$

II. Each of the following is a formal proof of validity for the indicated argument. State the "justification" for each numbered line that is not a premiss.

*1. 1. $A \supset B$
2. $C \supset \sim B$
$\therefore A \supset \sim C$
3. $\sim\sim B \supset \sim C$
4. $B \supset \sim C$
5. $A \supset \sim C$

2. 1. $(D \bullet E) \supset F$
2. $(D \supset F) \supset G$
$\therefore E \supset G$
3. $(E \bullet D) \supset F$
4. $E \supset (D \supset F)$
5. $E \supset G$

3. 1. $(H \lor I) \supset [J \bullet (K \bullet L)]$
    2. I
       $\therefore J \bullet K$
    3. $I \lor H$
    4. $H \lor I$
    5. $J \bullet (K \bullet L)$
    6. $(J \bullet K) \bullet L$
    7. $J \bullet K$

4. 1. $(M \lor N) \supset (O \bullet P)$
    2. $\sim O$
       $\therefore \sim M$
    3. $\sim O \lor \sim P$
    4. $\sim (O \bullet P)$
    5. $\sim (M \lor N)$
    6. $\sim M \bullet \sim N$
    7. $\sim M$

*5. 1. $(Q \lor \sim R) \lor S$
    2. $\sim Q \lor (R \bullet \sim Q)$
       $\therefore R \supset S$
    3. $(\sim Q \lor R) \bullet (\sim Q \lor \sim Q)$
    4. $(\sim Q \lor \sim Q) \bullet (\sim Q \lor R)$
    5. $\sim Q \lor \sim Q$
    6. $\sim Q$
    7. $Q \lor (\sim R \lor S)$
    8. $\sim R \lor S$
    9. $R \supset S$

6. 1. $T \bullet (U \lor V)$
    2. $T \supset [U \supset (W \bullet X)]$
    3. $(T \bullet V) \supset \sim (W \lor X)$
       $\therefore W \equiv X$
    4. $(T \bullet U) \supset (W \bullet X)$
    5. $(T \bullet V) \supset (\sim W \bullet \sim X)$
    6. $[(T \bullet U) \supset (W \bullet X)] \bullet$
       $[(T \bullet V) \supset (\sim W \bullet \sim X)]$
    7. $(T \bullet U) \lor (T \bullet V)$
    8. $(W \bullet X) \lor (\sim W \bullet \sim X)$
    9. $W \equiv X$

7. 1. $Y \supset Z$
    2. $Z \supset [Y \supset (R \lor S)]$
    3. $R \equiv S$
    4. $\sim (R \bullet S)$
       $\therefore \sim Y$
    5. $(R \bullet S) \lor (\sim R \bullet \sim S)$
    6. $\sim R \bullet \sim S$
    7. $\sim (R \lor S)$
    8. $Y \supset [Y \supset (R \lor S)]$
    9. $(Y \bullet Y) \supset (R \lor S)$
    10. $Y \supset (R \lor S)$
    11. $\sim Y$

8. 1. $A \supset B$
    2. $B \supset C$
    3. $C \supset A$
    4. $A \supset \sim C$
       $\therefore \sim A \bullet \sim C$
    5. $A \supset C$
    6. $(A \supset C) \bullet (C \supset A)$
    7. $A \equiv C$
    8. $(A \bullet C) \lor (\sim A \bullet \sim C)$
    9. $\sim A \lor \sim C$
    10. $\sim (A \bullet C)$
    11. $\sim A \bullet \sim C$

9. 1. $(D \bullet E) \supset \sim F$
    2. $F \lor (G \bullet H)$
    3. $D \equiv E$
       $\therefore D \supset G$
    4. $(D \supset E) \bullet (E \supset D)$
    5. $D \supset E$
    6. $D \supset (D \bullet E)$
    7. $D \supset \sim F$
    8. $(F \lor G) \bullet (F \lor H)$
    9. $F \lor G$
    10. $\sim \sim F \lor G$
    11. $\sim F \supset G$
    12. $D \supset G$

*10. 1. $(I \lor \sim \sim J) \bullet K$
    2. $[\sim L \supset \sim (K \bullet J)] \bullet$
      $[K \supset (I \supset \sim M)]$
       $\therefore \sim (M \bullet \sim L)$
    3. $[(K \bullet J) \supset L] \bullet$
      $[K \supset (I \supset \sim M)]$
    4. $[(K \bullet J) \supset L] \bullet$
      $[(K \bullet I) \supset \sim M]$
    5. $(I \lor J) \bullet K$
    6. $K \bullet (I \lor J)$
    7. $(K \bullet I) \lor (K \bullet J)$
    8. $(K \bullet J) \lor (K \bullet I)$
    9. $L \lor \sim M$
    10. $\sim M \lor L$
    11. $\sim M \lor \sim \sim L$
    12. $\sim (M \bullet \sim L)$

III. For each of the following, adding just two statements to the premises will produce a formal proof of validity. Construct a formal proof of validity for each of the following arguments.

*1. $A \supset \sim A$
  $\therefore \sim A$

2. $B \bullet (C \bullet D)$
  $\therefore C \bullet (D \bullet B)$

3. E
  $\therefore (E \vee F) \bullet (E \vee G)$

4. $H \vee (I \bullet J)$
  $\therefore H \vee I$

*5. $\sim K \vee (L \supset M)$
  $\therefore (K \bullet L) \supset M$

6. $(N \bullet O) \supset P$
  $\therefore (N \bullet O) \supset [N \bullet (O \bullet P)]$

7. $Q \supset [R \supset (S \supset T)]$
  $Q \supset (Q \bullet R)$
  $\therefore Q \supset (S \supset T)$

8. $U \supset \sim V$
  V
  $\therefore \sim U$

9. $W \supset X$
  $\sim Y \supset \sim X$
  $\therefore W \supset Y$

*10. $Z \supset A$
  $\sim A \vee B$
  $\therefore Z \supset B$

11. $C \supset \sim D$
  $\sim E \supset D$
  $\therefore C \supset \sim\sim E$

12. $F \equiv G$
  $\sim(F \bullet G)$
  $\therefore \sim F \bullet \sim G$

13. $H \supset (I \bullet J)$
  $I \supset (J \supset K)$
  $\therefore H \supset K$

14. $(L \supset M) \bullet (N \supset M)$
  $L \vee N$
  $\therefore M$

*15. $(O \vee P) \supset (Q \vee R)$
  $P \vee O$
  $\therefore Q \vee R$

16. $(S \bullet T) \vee (U \bullet V)$
  $\sim S \vee \sim T$
  $\therefore U \bullet V$

17. $(W \bullet X) \supset Y$
  $(X \supset Y) \supset Z$
  $\therefore W \supset Z$

18. $(A \vee B) \supset (C \vee D)$
  $\sim C \bullet \sim D$
  $\therefore \sim(A \vee B)$

19. $(E \bullet F) \supset (G \bullet H)$
  $F \bullet E$
  $\therefore G \bullet H$

*20. $I \supset [J \vee (K \vee L)]$
  $\sim[(J \vee K) \vee L]$
  $\therefore \sim I$

21. $(M \supset N) \bullet (\sim O \vee P)$
  $M \vee O$
  $\therefore N \vee P$

22. $(\sim Q \supset \sim R) \bullet (\sim S \supset \sim T)$
  $\sim\sim(\sim Q \vee \sim S)$
  $\therefore \sim R \vee \sim T$

23. $\sim[(U \supset V) \bullet (V \supset U)]$
  $(W \equiv X) \supset (U \equiv V)$
  $\therefore \sim(W \equiv X)$

24. $(Y \supset Z) \bullet (Z \supset Y)$
  $\therefore (Y \bullet Z) \vee (\sim Y \bullet \sim Z)$

*25. $A \vee B$
  $C \vee D$
  $\therefore [(A \vee B) \bullet C] \vee [(A \vee B) \bullet D]$

26. $[(E \vee F) \bullet (G \vee H)] \supset (F \bullet I)$
  $(G \vee H) \bullet (E \vee F)$
  $\therefore F \bullet I$

27. $(J \bullet K) \supset [(L \bullet M) \vee (N \bullet O)]$
  $\sim(L \bullet M) \bullet \sim(N \bullet O)$
  $\therefore \sim(J \bullet K)$

28. $(P \supset Q) \supset [(R \vee S) \bullet (T \equiv U)]$
  $(R \vee S) \supset [(T \equiv U) \supset Q]$
  $\therefore (P \supset Q) \supset Q$

29. $[V \bullet (W \lor X)] \supset (Y \supset Z)$
$\sim(Y \supset Z) \lor (\sim W \equiv A)$
$\therefore [V \bullet (W \lor X)] \supset (\sim W \equiv A)$

*30. $\sim[(B \supset \sim C) \bullet (\sim C \supset B)]$
$(D \bullet E) \supset (B \equiv \sim C)$
$\therefore \sim(D \bullet E)$

IV. For each of the following, adding just three statements to the premises will produce a formal proof of validity. Construct a formal proof of validity for each of the following arguments.

*1. $\sim A \supset A$
$\therefore A$

2. $\sim B \lor (C \bullet D)$
$\therefore B \supset C$

3. $E \lor (F \bullet G)$
$\therefore E \lor G$

4. $H \bullet (I \bullet J)$
$\therefore J \bullet (I \bullet H)$

*5. $[(K \lor L) \lor M] \lor N$
$\therefore (N \lor K) \lor (L \lor M)$

6. $O \supset P$
$P \supset \sim P$
$\therefore \sim O$

7. $Q \supset (R \supset S)$
$Q \supset R$
$\therefore Q \supset S$

8. $T \supset U$
$\sim(U \lor V)$
$\therefore \sim T$

9. $W \bullet (X \lor Y)$
$\sim W \lor \sim X$
$\therefore W \bullet Y$

*10. $(Z \lor A) \lor B$
$\sim A$
$\therefore Z \lor B$

11. $(C \lor D) \supset (E \bullet F)$
$D \lor C$
$\therefore E$

12. $G \supset H$
$H \supset G$
$\therefore (G \bullet H) \lor (\sim G \bullet \sim H)$

13. $(I \supset J) \bullet (K \supset L)$
$I \lor (K \bullet M)$
$\therefore J \lor L$

14. $(N \bullet O) \supset P$
$(\sim P \supset \sim O) \supset Q$
$\therefore N \supset Q$

*15. $[R \supset (S \supset T)] \bullet [(R \bullet T) \supset U]$
$R \bullet (S \lor T)$
$\therefore T \lor U$

V. The exercises in this set represent frequently recurring patterns of inference found in longer formal proofs of validity. Familiarity with them will be useful in subsequent work. Construct a formal proof of validity for each of the following arguments.

*1. $\sim A$
$\therefore A \supset B$

2. C
$\therefore D \supset C$

3. $E \supset (F \supset G)$
$\therefore F \supset (E \supset G)$

4. $H \supset (I \bullet J)$
$\therefore H \supset I$

*5. $K \supset L$
$\therefore K \supset (L \lor M)$

6. $N \supset O$
$\therefore (N \bullet P) \supset O$

7. $(Q \lor R) \supset S$
$\therefore Q \supset S$

8. $T \supset U$
$T \supset V$
$\therefore T \supset (U \bullet V)$

9. $W \supset X$
   $Y \supset X$
   $\therefore (W \vee Y) \supset X$

*10. $Z \supset A$
   $Z \vee A$
   $\therefore A$

VI. Construct a formal proof of validity for each of the following arguments.

*1. $A \supset {\sim}B$
   ${\sim}(C \bullet {\sim}A)$
   $\therefore C \supset {\sim}B$

2. $(D \bullet {\sim}E) \supset F$
   ${\sim}(E \vee F)$
   $\therefore {\sim}D$

3. $(G \supset {\sim}H) \supset I$
   ${\sim}(G \bullet H)$
   $\therefore I \vee {\sim}H$

4. $(J \vee K) \supset {\sim}L$
   L
   $\therefore {\sim}J$

*5 $[(M \bullet N) \bullet O] \supset P$
   $Q \supset [(O \bullet M) \bullet N]$
   $\therefore {\sim}Q \vee P$

6. $R \vee (S \bullet {\sim}T)$
   $(R \vee S) \supset (U \vee {\sim}T)$
   $\therefore T \supset U$

7. $({\sim}V \supset W) \bullet (X \supset W)$
   ${\sim}({\sim}X \bullet V)$
   $\therefore W$

8. $[(Y \bullet Z) \supset A] \bullet [(Y \bullet B) \supset C]$
   $(B \vee Z) \bullet Y$
   $\therefore A \vee C$

9. ${\sim}D \supset ({\sim}E \supset {\sim}F)$
   ${\sim}(F \bullet {\sim}D) \supset {\sim}G$
   $\therefore G \supset E$

*10. $[H \vee (I \vee J)] \supset (K \supset J)$
   $L \supset [I \vee (J \vee H)]$
   $\therefore (L \bullet K) \supset J$

11. $M \supset N$
   $M \supset (N \supset O)$
   $\therefore M \supset O$

12. $(P \supset Q) \bullet (P \vee R)$
   $(R \supset S) \bullet (R \vee P)$
   $\therefore Q \vee S$

13. $T \supset (U \bullet V)$
   $(U \vee V) \supset W$
   $\therefore T \supset W$

14. $(X \vee Y) \supset (X \bullet Y)$
   ${\sim}(X \vee Y)$
   $\therefore {\sim}(X \bullet Y)$

*15. $(Z \supset Z) \supset (A \supset A)$
   $(A \supset A) \supset (Z \supset Z)$
   $\therefore A \supset A$

16. ${\sim}B \vee [(C \supset D) \bullet (E \supset D)]$
   $B \bullet (C \vee E)$
   $\therefore D$

17. ${\sim}F \vee {\sim}[{\sim}(G \bullet H) \bullet (G \vee H)]$
   $(G \supset H) \supset [(H \supset G) \supset I]$
   $\therefore F \supset (F \bullet I)$

18. $J \vee ({\sim}J \bullet K)$
   $J \supset L$
   $\therefore (L \bullet J) \equiv J$

19. $(M \supset N) \bullet (O \supset P)$
   ${\sim}N \vee {\sim}P$
   ${\sim}(M \bullet O) \supset Q$
   $\therefore Q$

*20. $(R \vee S) \supset (T \bullet U)$
   ${\sim}R \supset (V \supset {\sim}V)$
   ${\sim}T$
   $\therefore {\sim}V$

VII. Construct a formal proof of validity for each of the following arguments, in each case using the suggested notation.

*1. Either the manager didn't notice the change or else he approves of it. He noticed it all right. So he must approve of it. (N, A)

2. The oxygen in the tube either combined with the filament to form an oxide or else it vanished completely. The oxygen in the tube could not have vanished completely. Therefore the oxygen in the tube combined with the filament to form an oxide. (C, V)

3. If a political leader who sees her former opinions to be wrong does not alter her course, she is guilty of deceit; and if she does alter her course, she is open to a charge of inconsistency. She either alters her course or she doesn't. Therefore either she is guilty of deceit or else she is open to a charge of inconsistency. *(A, D, I)*

4. It is not the case that she either forgot or wasn't able to finish. Therefore she was able to finish. *(F, A)*

*5. If the litmus paper turns red, then the solution is acid. Hence if the litmus paper turns red, then either the solution is acid or something is wrong somewhere. *(R, A, W)*

6. She can have many friends only if she respects them as individuals. If she respects them as individuals, then she cannot expect them all to behave alike. She does have many friends. Therefore she does not expect them all to behave alike. *(F, R, E)*

7. If the victim had money in his pockets, then robbery wasn't the motive for the crime. But robbery or vengeance was the motive for the crime. The victim had money in his pockets. Therefore vengeance must have been the motive for the crime. *(M, R, V)*

8. Napoleon is to be condemned if he usurped power that was not rightfully his own. Either Napoleon was a legitimate monarch or else he usurped power that was not rightfully his own. Napoleon was not a legitimate monarch. So Napoleon is to be condemned. *(C, U, L)*

9. If we extend further credit on the Wilkins account, they will have a moral obligation to accept our bid on their next project. We can figure a more generous margin of profit in preparing our estimates if they have a moral obligation to accept our bid on their next project. Figuring a more generous margin of profit in preparing our estimates will cause our general financial condition to improve considerably. Hence a considerable improvement in our general financial condition will follow from our extension of further credit on the Wilkins account. *(C, M, P, I)*

*10. If the laws are good and their enforcement is strict, then crime will diminish. If strict enforcement of laws will make crime diminish, then our problem is a practical one. The laws are good. Therefore our problem is a practical one. *(G, S, D, P)*

11. Had Roman citizenship guaranteed civil liberties, then Roman citizens would have enjoyed religious freedom. Had Roman citizens enjoyed religious freedom, there would have been no persecution of the early Christians. But the early Christians were persecuted. Hence Roman citizenship could not have guaranteed civil liberties. *(G, F, P)*

12. If the first disjunct of a disjunction is true, the disjunction as a whole is true. Therefore if both the first and second disjuncts of the disjunction are true, then the disjunction as a whole is true. *(F, W, S)*

13. If the new courthouse is to be conveniently located, it will have to be situated in the heart of the city; and if it is to be adequate to its function, it will have to be built large enough to house all the city offices. If the new courthouse is situated in the heart of the city and is built large enough to house all the city offices, then its cost will run to over 10 million dollars. Its cost cannot exceed 10 million dollars. Therefore either the new courthouse will have an inconvenient location or it will be inadequate to its function. *(C, H, A, L, O)*

14. Jones will come if she gets the message, provided that she is still interested. Although she didn't come, she is still interested. Therefore she didn't get the message. *(C, M, I)*

*15. If the Mosaic account of the cosmogony (the account of the creation in *Genesis*) is strictly correct, the sun was not created till the fourth day. And if the sun was not created till the fourth day, it could not have been the cause of the alternation of day and night for the first three days. But either the word "day" is used in Scripture in a different sense from that in which it is commonly accepted now or else the sun must have been the cause of the alternation of day and night for the first three days. Hence it follows that either the Mosaic account of the cosmogony is not strictly correct or else the word "day" is used in Scripture in a different sense from that in which it is commonly accepted now. *(M, C, A, D)*

16. If the teller or the cashier had pushed the alarm button, the vault would have locked automatically and the police would have arrived within three minutes. Had the police arrived within three minutes, the robbers' car would have been overtaken. But the robbers' car was not overtaken. Therefore the teller did not push the alarm button. *(T, C, V, P, O)*

17. If people are always guided by their sense of duty, they must forgo the enjoyment of many pleasures; and if they are always guided by their desire for pleasure, they must often neglect their duty. People are either always guided by their sense of duty or always guided by their desire for pleasure. If people are always guided by their sense of duty, they do not often neglect their duty; and if they are always guided by their desire for pleasure, they do not forgo the enjoyment of many pleasures. Therefore people must forgo the enjoyment of many pleasures if and only if they do not often neglect their duty. *(D, F, P, N)*

18. Although world population is increasing, agricultural production is declining and manufacturing output remains constant. If agricultural production declines and world population increases then either new food sources will become available or else there will be a radical redistribution of food resources in the world unless human nutritional requirements diminish. No new food sources will become available, yet neither will family planning be encouraged

nor will human nutritional requirements diminish. Therefore there will be a radical redistribution of food resources in the world. *(W, A, M, N, R, H, P)*

19.   Either the robber came in the door, or else the crime was an inside one and one of the servants is implicated. The robber could come in the door only if the latch had been raised from the inside; but one of the servants is surely implicated if the latch was raised from the inside. Therefore one of the servants is implicated. *(D, I, S, L)*

*20.   If I pay my tuition, I won't have any money left. I'll buy a computer only if I have money. I won't learn to program computers unless I buy a computer. But if I don't pay tuition, I can't enroll in classes; and if I don't enroll in classes I certainly won't buy a computer. I must either pay my tuition or not pay my tuition. So I surely will not learn to program computers! *(P, M, C, L, E)*

VIII. The five arguments that follow are also valid, and a proof of the valid- ■**Advanced Material**
ity of each of them is called for. But these proofs will be somewhat more difficult to construct than those in earlier exercises, and students who find themselves stymied from time to time ought not become discouraged. What may appear difficult on first appraisal may come to seem much less difficult with continuing efforts. Familiarity with the 19 rules of inference, and repeated practice in applying those rules, are the keys to the construction of these proofs.

1.   If you study the humanities then you will develop an understanding of people, and if you study the sciences then you will develop an understanding of the world about you. So if you study either the humanities or the sciences then you will develop an understanding either of people or of the world about you. *(H, P, S, W)*

2.   If you study the humanities then you will develop an understanding of people, and if you study the sciences then you will develop an understanding of the world about you. So if you study both the humanities and the sciences then you will develop an understanding both of people and of the world about you. *(H, P, S, W)*

3.   If you have free will then your actions are not determined by any antecedent events. If you have free will then if your actions are not determined by any antecedent events then your actions cannot be predicted. If your actions are not determined by any antecedent events then if your actions cannot be predicted then the consequences of your actions cannot be predicted. Therefore if you have free will then the consequences of your actions cannot be predicted. *(F, A, P, C)*

4.   Socrates was a great philosopher. Therefore either Socrates was happily married or else he wasn't. *(G, H)*

*5.   If either Socrates was happily married or else he wasn't, then Socrates was a great philosopher. Therefore Socrates was a great philosopher. *(H, G)* ■

9.3 PROOF OF INVALIDITY

For an invalid argument there is, of course, no formal proof of validity. But if we fail to discover a formal proof of validity for a given argument, this failure does not prove that the argument is invalid and that no such proof can be constructed. It may mean only that we have not tried hard enough. Our inability to find a proof of validity may be caused by the fact that the argument is not valid, but it may be caused instead by our own lack of ingenuity—as a consequence of the noneffective character of the process of proof construction. Not being able to construct a formal proof of its validity does not prove an argument to be invalid. What *does* constitute a proof that a given argument is invalid?

The method about to be described is closely related to the truth-table method, although it is a great deal shorter. It will be helpful to recall how an invalid argument form is proved invalid by a truth table. If a single case (row) can be found in which truth values are assigned to the statement variables in such a way that the premises are made true and the conclusion false, then the argument form is invalid. If we can somehow make an assignment of truth values to the simple component statements of an argument that will make its premises true and its conclusion false, then making that assignment will suffice to prove the argument invalid. To make such an assignment is, in effect, what the truth table does. But if we can make such an assignment of truth values without actually constructing the whole truth table, much work will be eliminated.

Consider this argument:

> If the governor favors public housing, then he is in favor of restricting the scope of private enterprise.
> If the governor were a socialist, then he would be in favor of restricting the scope of private enterprise.
> Therefore if the governor favors public housing, then he is a socialist.

It is symbolized as

$$F \supset R$$
$$S \supset R$$
$$\therefore F \supset S$$

and we can prove it invalid without having to construct a complete truth table. First we ask, "What assignment of truth values is required to make the conclusion false?" It is clear that a conditional is false only if its antecedent is true and its consequent false. Hence assigning the truth value "true" to F and "false" to S will make the conclusion $F \supset S$ false. Now if the truth value "true" is assigned to R, both premises are made true, because a conditional is true whenever its consequent is true. We can say, then, that if the truth value "true" is assigned to F and to R, and the truth value "false" is assigned to S, the argument will have true premises and a false conclusion and is thus proved to be invalid.

This method of proving invalidity is an alternative to the truth-table method of proof. The two methods are closely related, however, and the essential connection between them should be noticed. In effect, what we did when we made the indicated assignment of truth values was to construct one row of the given argument's truth table. The relationship can perhaps be seen more clearly when the truth-value assignments are written out horizontally:

F	R	S	$F \supset R$	$S \supset R$	$F \supset S$
true	true	false	true	true	false

in which configuration they constitute one row (the second) of the truth table for the given argument. **An argument is proved invalid by displaying at least one row of its truth table in which all its premises are true but its conclusion is false.** Consequently we need not examine *all* rows of its truth table to discover an argument's invalidity: the discovery of a single row in which its premises are all true and its conclusion false will suffice. The present method of proving invalidity is a method of constructing such a row without having to construct the entire truth table.[3]

The present method is shorter than writing out an entire truth table, and the amount of time and work saved is proportionally greater for arguments involving a greater number of component simple statements. For arguments with a considerable number of premises, or with premises of considerable complexity, the needed assignment of truth values may not be so easy to make. There is no mechanical method of proceeding, but some hints may prove helpful.

It is most efficient to proceed by assigning those values seen immediately to be essential if invalidity is to be proved. Thus, any premiss that simply asserts the truth of some statement S would suggest the immediate assignment of T to S (or F if the falsehood of S had been asserted as premiss), since we know that all the premises must be made true. The same principle applies to the statements in the conclusion, save that the assignments of truth values there must make the conclusion false. Thus a conclusion of the form A $\supset$ B would suggest the immediate assignment of T to A and F to B, and a conclusion in the form A $\vee$ B would suggest the immediate assignment of F to A and F to B, since only those assignments could result in a proof of invalidity.

---

[3]The whole truth table (were we to construct it) would of course test the validity of the *specific form* of the argument in question. If it can be shown that the specific form of an argument is invalid, we may infer that the argument having that specific form is an invalid argument. The method described here differs only in that truth values here are assigned directly to premises and conclusion; nonetheless, the relation between this method and the truth-table method applied in the preceding chapter is very close.

Whether one ought to begin by seeking to make the premisses true or by seeking to make the conclusion false depends upon the structure of those propositions; usually it is best to begin wherever assignments can be made with greatest confidence. Of course there will be many circumstances in which the first assignments will have to be arbitrary and tentative. A certain amount of trial and error is likely to be needed. But even so, this method of proving invalidity is almost always shorter and easier than writing out a complete truth table.

Exercises

Prove the invalidity of each of the following by the method of assigning truth values.

*1. $A \supset B$
     $C \supset D$
     $A \lor D$
     $\therefore B \lor C$

2. $\sim(E \bullet F)$
    $(\sim E \bullet \sim F) \supset (G \bullet H)$
    $H \supset G$
    $\therefore G$

3. $I \lor \sim J$
    $\sim(\sim K \bullet L)$
    $\sim(\sim I \bullet \sim L)$
    $\therefore \sim J \supset K$

4. $M \supset (N \lor O)$
    $N \supset (P \lor Q)$
    $Q \supset R$
    $\sim(R \lor P)$
    $\therefore \sim M$

*5. $S \supset (T \supset U)$
     $V \supset (W \supset X)$
     $T \supset (V \bullet W)$
     $\sim(T \bullet X)$
     $\therefore S \equiv U$

6. $A \equiv (B \lor C)$
    $B \equiv (C \lor A)$
    $C \equiv (A \lor B)$
    $\sim A$
    $\therefore B \lor C$

7. $D \supset (E \lor F)$
    $G \supset (H \lor I)$
    $\sim E \supset (I \lor J)$
    $(I \supset G) \bullet (\sim H \supset \sim G)$
    $\sim J$
    $\therefore D \supset (G \lor I)$

8. $K \supset (L \bullet M)$
    $(L \supset N) \lor \sim K$
    $O \supset (P \lor \sim N)$
    $(\sim P \lor Q) \bullet \sim Q$
    $(R \lor \sim P) \lor \sim M$
    $\therefore K \supset R$

9. $(S \supset T) \bullet (T \supset S)$
    $(U \bullet T) \lor (\sim T \bullet \sim U)$
    $(U \lor V) \lor (S \lor T)$
    $\sim U \supset (W \bullet X)$
    $(V \supset \sim S) \bullet (\sim V \supset \sim Y)$
    $X \supset (\sim Y \supset \sim X)$
    $(U \lor S) \bullet (V \lor Z)$
    $\therefore X \bullet Z$

*10. $A \supset (B \supset \sim C)$
      $(D \supset B) \bullet (E \supset A)$
      $F \lor C$
      $G \supset \sim H$
      $(I \supset G) \bullet (H \supset J)$
      $I \equiv \sim D$
      $(B \supset H) \bullet (\sim H \supset D)$
      $\therefore E \equiv F$

9.4 INCONSISTENCY

If truth values can be assigned to make all the premises of an argument true and its conclusion false, then that shows the argument to be invalid. If a deductive argument is not invalid it must be valid. So, if no truth-value assignment can be given to the component simple statements of an argument that makes its premises true and its conclusion false, then the argument must be valid. Although this follows from the definition of "validity," it has a curious consequence. Consider the following argument, whose premises appear to be totally irrelevant to its conclusion:

> If the airplane had engine trouble, it would have landed at Bend.
> If the airplane did not have engine trouble, it would have landed at Cleveland.
> The airplane did not land at either Bend or Cleveland.
> Therefore the airplane must have landed in Denver.

and its symbolic translation:

$$A \supset B$$
$$\sim A \supset C$$
$$\sim (B \vee C)$$
$$\therefore D$$

Any attempt to assign truth values to its component simple statements in such a way as to make the conclusion false and the premises all true is doomed to failure. If we ignore the conclusion and concentrate our attention upon the other part of the objective, that of making all the premises true by an assignment of truth values to their component simple statements, we are bound to fail even here, in this apparently less ambitious project.

The reason the premises cannot be made true and the conclusion false is that the premises cannot possibly be made true in any case by *any* truth-value assignment. No truth-value assignment can make the premises true, because they are inconsistent with each other. Their conjunction is *self-contradictory,* being a substitution instance of a self-contradictory statement form. Were we to construct a truth table for the given argument, we should find that in every row at least one of the premises is false. Because there is no row in which the premises all are true, there is no row in which the premises all are true and the conclusion false. Hence the truth table for this argument would establish its validity. Its validity can also be established by the following formal proof:

1. $A \supset B$
2. $\sim A \supset C$
3. $\sim (B \vee C)$
   $\therefore D$
4. $\sim B \bullet \sim C$ 3, De M.

5.	$\sim B$	4, Simp.
6.	$\sim A$	1, 5, M.T.
7.	C	2, 6, M.P.
8.	$\sim C \cdot \sim B$	4, Com.
9.	$\sim C$	8, Simp.
10.	$C \vee D$	7, Add.
11.	D	10, 9, D.S.

In this proof, the lines from 1 through 9 are devoted to making explicit the inconsistency that was implicitly contained in the premisses. That inconsistency emerges in lines 7 and 9, which assert C and $\sim C$, respectively. Once this explicit contradiction has been expressed, the conclusion follows swiftly using the principles of Addition and Disjunctive Syllogism.

Thus we see that if a set of premisses is inconsistent, those premisses will validly yield *any* conclusion, no matter how irrelevant. The essence of the matter is more simply shown in the case of the following argument, whose openly inconsistent premisses allow us validly to infer an irrelevant and fantastic conclusion:

Today is Sunday.
Today is not Sunday.
Therefore the moon is made of green cheese.

In symbols, we have

1. S
2. $\sim S$
   $\therefore M$

The formal proof of its validity is almost immediately obvious:

3.	$S \vee M$	1, Add.
4.	M	3, 2, D.S.

What is wrong here? How can such meager and even inconsistent premisses make any argument in which they occur valid? Note first that if an argument is valid because of an inconsistency in its premisses, it cannot possibly be a sound argument. If premisses are inconsistent with each other, they cannot possibly all be true. No conclusion can be established to be true by an argument with inconsistent premisses, because its premisses cannot possibly all be true themselves.

The present situation is closely related to the so-called paradox of material implication. In discussing the latter, we observed (in section 8.7) that the statement form $\sim p \supset (p \supset q)$ is a tautology, having all its substitution instances true. Its formulation in English asserts that "If a statement is false then it materially implies any statement whatever," which is easily proved by means of truth tables. What has been established in the present discussion is that the argument form

$$p$$
$$\sim p$$
$$\therefore q$$

is valid. We have proved that *any argument with inconsistent premises is valid, regardless of what its conclusion may be.* Its validity may be established either by a truth table or by the kind of formal proof given above.

The premises of a valid argument imply its conclusion not merely in the sense of "material" implication, but *logically* or "strictly." In a valid argument, it is logically impossible for the premises to be true when the conclusion is false. And this situation obtains whenever it is logically impossible for the premises to be true, even when the question of the truth or falsehood of the conclusion is ignored. Its analogy with the corresponding property of material implication has led some writers on logic to call this a "paradox of strict implication." In view of the logician's technical definition of "validity," however, it does not seem to be especially paradoxical. The alleged paradox arises primarily from treating a technical term as if it were a term of ordinary, everyday language.

The foregoing discussion helps to explain why consistency is so highly prized. One reason, of course, is that inconsistent statements cannot both be true. This fact underlies the strategy of cross-examination, in which an attorney may seek to maneuver a hostile witness into contradicting himself. If testimony affirms incompatible or inconsistent assertions, it cannot all be true, and the witness's credibility is destroyed—or at least shaken.[4] But another reason why inconsistency is so repugnant is that any and every conclusion follows logically from inconsistent statements taken as premises. Inconsistent statements are not "meaningless;" their trouble is just the opposite. They mean too much. They mean everything, in the sense of *implying* everything. And if *everything* is asserted, half of what is asserted is surely *false*, because every statement has a denial.

The preceding discussion incidentally provides us with an answer to the old riddle: What happens when an irresistible force meets an immovable object? The description involves a contradiction. For an irresistible force to meet an immovable object, both must exist. There must be an irresistible force and there must also be an immovable object. But if there is an irresistible force there can be no immovable object. Here is the contradiction made explicit: There is an immovable object, and there is no immovable object. Given these inconsistent premises, *any* conclusion may validly be inferred. So the correct answer to the question "What happens when an irresistible force meets an immovable object?" is "Everything!"

---

[4]A witness giving contradictory testimony testifies to some proposition that is false. When it has been once established that a witness has lied under oath (or is perhaps thoroughly confused) no sworn testimony of that witness can be fully trusted. Lawyers quote the Latin saying: *Falsus in unum, falsus in omnibus;* untrustworthy in one thing, untrustworthy in all.

Although devastating when uncovered within an argument, inconsistency can be highly amusing, as in the often-quoted remarks of the great baseball player Yogi Berra. "That restaurant is so crowded," Berra is said to have announced, "that nobody goes there any more." And, speaking of his partner in a long and happy marriage, he said "We have a great time together, even when we're not together."

Such utterances are funny because the contradictions they harbor (and therefore the nonsense of the remarks when taken literally) appear not to be recognized by their authors. So we chuckle when we read of the schoolboy who said that the climate of the Australian interior is so bad that the inhabitants don't live there any more. Such inadvertent and unrecognized inconsistencies are sometimes called "Irish Bulls."

Sets of propositions that are internally inconsistent cannot all be true, as a matter of logic. But human beings are not always logical and do utter, and sometimes may even believe, two propositions that contradict one another. This may seem difficult to do, but we are told by Lewis Carroll, a very reliable authority in such matters, that the White Queen in *Alice in Wonderland* made a regular practice of believing six impossible things before breakfast!

Exercises

I.   For each of the following, either construct a formal proof of validity or prove invalidity by the method of assigning truth values to the simple statements involved.

*1. $(A \supset B) \bullet (C \supset D)$
     $\therefore (A \bullet C) \supset (B \vee D)$

2. $(E \supset F) \bullet (G \supset H)$
     $\therefore (E \vee G) \supset (F \bullet H)$

3. $I \supset (J \vee K)$
     $(J \bullet K) \supset L$
     $\therefore I \supset L$

4. $M \supset (N \bullet O)$
     $(N \vee O) \supset P$
     $\therefore M \supset P$

*5. $[(X \bullet Y) \bullet Z] \supset A$
     $(Z \supset A) \supset (B \supset C)$
     B
     $\therefore X \supset C$

6. $[(D \vee E) \bullet F] \supset G$
     $(F \supset G) \supset (H \supset I)$
     H
     $\therefore D \supset I$

7. $(J \bullet K) \supset (L \supset M)$
     $N \supset {\sim}M$
     ${\sim}(K \supset {\sim}N)$
     ${\sim}(J \supset {\sim}L)$
     $\therefore {\sim}J$

8. $(O \bullet P) \supset (Q \supset R)$
     $S \supset {\sim}R$
     ${\sim}(P \supset {\sim}S)$
     ${\sim}(O \supset Q)$
     $\therefore {\sim}O$

9. $T \supset (U \bullet V)$
     $U \supset (W \bullet X)$
     $(T \supset W) \supset (Y \equiv Z)$
     $(T \supset U) \supset {\sim}Y$
     ${\sim}Y \supset ({\sim}Z \supset X)$
     $\therefore X$

*10. $A \supset (B \bullet C)$
      $B \supset (D \bullet E)$
      $(A \supset D) \supset (F \equiv G)$
      $A \supset (B \supset {\sim}F)$
      ${\sim}F \supset ({\sim}G \supset E)$
      $\therefore E$

II. For each of the following, either construct a formal proof of validity or prove invalidity by the method of assigning truth values to the simple statements involved.

*1.   If the linguistics investigators are correct, then if more than one dialect was present in ancient Greece, then different tribes came down at different times from the north. If different tribes came down at different times from the north, they must have come from the Danube River valley. But archaeological excavations would have revealed traces of different tribes there if different tribes had come down at different times from the north, and archaeological excavations have revealed no such traces there. Hence if more than one dialect was present in ancient Greece, then the linguistics investigators are not correct.
(C, M, D, V, A)

2.   If there are the ordinary symptoms of a cold and the patient has a high temperature, then if there are tiny spots on his skin, he has measles. Of course the patient cannot have measles if his record shows that he has had them before. The patient does have a high temperature and his record shows that he has had measles before. Besides the ordinary symptoms of a cold, there are tiny spots on his skin. I conclude that the patient has a viral infection.
(O, T, S, M, R, V)

3.   If God were willing to prevent evil, but unable to do so, he would be impotent; if he were able to prevent evil, but unwilling to do so, he would be malevolent. Evil can exist only if God is either unwilling or unable to prevent it. There is evil. If God exists, he is neither impotent nor malevolent. Therefore God does not exist.
(W, A, I, M, E, G)

4.   If I buy a new car this spring or have my old car fixed, then I'll get up to Canada this summer and stop off in Duluth. I'll visit my parents if I stop off in Duluth. If I visit my parents, they'll insist upon my spending the summer with them. If they insist upon my spending the summer with them, I'll be there till autumn. But if I stay there till autumn, then I won't get to Canada after all! So I won't have my old car fixed.
(N, F, C, D, V, I, A)

*5.   If Smith is intelligent and studies hard, then she will get good grades and pass her courses. If Smith studies hard but lacks intelligence, then her efforts will be appreciated; and if her efforts are appreciated, then she will pass her courses. If Smith is intelligent, then she studies hard. Therefore Smith will pass her courses.
(I, S, G, P, A)

6. If there is a single norm for greatness of poetry, then Milton and Edgar Guest[5] cannot both be great poets. If either Pope or Dryden is regarded as a great poet, then Wordsworth is certainly no great poet; but if Wordsworth is no great poet, then neither is Keats nor Shelley. But after all, even though Edgar Guest is not, Dryden and Keats are both great poets. Hence there is no single norm for greatness of poetry. (N, M, G, P, D, W, K, S)

7. If the butler were present, he would have been seen; and if he had been seen, he would have been questioned. If he had been questioned, he would have replied; and if he had replied, he would have been heard. But the butler was not heard. If the butler was neither seen nor heard, then he must have been on duty; and if he was on duty, he must have been present. Therefore the butler was questioned. (P, S, Q, R, H, D)

8. If the butler told the truth, then the window was closed when he entered the room; and if the gardener told the truth, then the automatic sprinkler system was not operating on the evening of the murder. If the butler and the gardener are both lying, then a conspiracy must exist to protect someone in the house and there would have been a little pool of water on the floor just inside the window. We know that the window could not have been closed when the butler entered the room. There was a little pool of water on the floor just inside the window. So if there is a conspiracy to protect someone in the house, then the gardener did not tell the truth. (B, W, G, S, C, P)

9. Their chief would leave the country if she feared capture, and she would not leave the country unless she feared capture. If she feared capture and left the country, then the enemy's espionage network would be demoralized and powerless to harm us. If she did not fear capture and remained in the country, it would mean that she was ignorant of our own agents' work. If she is really ignorant of our agents' work, then our agents can consolidate their positions within the enemy's organization; and if our agents can consolidate their positions there, they will render the enemy's espionage network powerless to harm us. Therefore the enemy's espionage network will be powerless to harm us. (L, F, D, P, I, C)

---

[5]Edgar Guest (1881–1959) was for many years the contributor of a rhyme each day to the *Detroit Free Press.* Syndicated, and as a WJR radio host, he became an American favorite with homespun verse that was unfailingly cheerful:

> With a lift of his chin, and a bit of a grin
>   Without any doubting or "quit it,"
> He started to sing, as he tackled the thing
>   That couldn't be done, and he did it.

—A Heap o' Livin'(1916)

*10.   If the investigators of extrasensory perception are regarded as honest, then considerable evidence for extrasensory perception must be admitted; and the doctrine of clairvoyance must be considered seriously if extrasensory perception is tentatively accepted as a fact. If considerable evidence for extrasensory perception is admitted, then it must be tentatively accepted as a fact and an effort must be made to explain it. The doctrine of clairvoyance must be considered seriously if we are prepared to take seriously that class of phenomena called occult; and if we are prepared to take seriously that class of phenomena called occult, a new respect must be paid to mediums. If we pursue the matter further, then if a new respect must be paid to mediums, we must take seriously their claims to communicate with the dead. We do pursue the matter further, but still we are practically committed to believing in ghosts if we take seriously the mediums' claims to communicate with the dead. Hence if the investigators of extrasensory perception are regarded as honest, we are practically committed to believing in ghosts. (*H, A, C, F, E, O, M, P, D, G*)

11.   If we buy a lot, then we will build a house. If we buy a lot, then if we build a house we will buy furniture. If we build a house, then if we buy furniture we will buy dishes. Therefore if we buy a lot, we will buy dishes. (*L, H, F, D*)

12.   If your prices are low then your sales will be high, and if you sell quality merchandise then your customers will be satisfied. So if your prices are low and you sell quality merchandise, then your sales will be high and your customers satisfied. (*L, H, Q, S*)

13.   If your prices are low then your sales will be high, and if you sell quality merchandise then your customers will be satisfied. So if either your prices are low or you sell quality merchandise, then either your sales will be high or your customers will be satisfied. (*L, H, Q, S*)

14.   If Jordan joins the alliance, then either Algeria or Syria boycotts it. If Kuwait joins the alliance, then either Syria or Iraq boycotts it. Syria does not boycott it. Therefore if neither Algeria nor Iraq boycotts it, then neither Jordan nor Kuwait joins the alliance. (*J, A, S, K, I*)

*15.   If either Jordan or Algeria joins the alliance, then if either Syria or Kuwait boycotts it then although Iraq does not boycott it Yemen boycotts it. If either Iraq or Morocco does not boycott it, then Egypt will join the alliance. Therefore if Jordan joins the alliance, then if Syria boycotts it then Egypt will join the alliance. (*J, A, S, K, I, Y, M, E*)

III.   If any truth-functional argument is valid, we have the tools to prove ■**Advanced Material**
it valid; and if it is invalid, we have the tools to prove it invalid.

Prove each of the following arguments valid or invalid. The proofs here will be more difficult to construct than in preceding exercises—but they will offer greater satisfaction.

1.   If the president cuts social security benefit payments, he will lose the support of the senior citizens; and if he cuts defense spending, he will lose the support of the conservatives. If the president loses the support of either the senior citizens or the conservatives, then his influence in the Senate will diminish. But his influence in the Senate will not diminish. Therefore the president will not cut either social security benefits or defense spending. *(B, S, D, C, I)*

2.   If inflation continues, then interest rates will remain high. If inflation continues, then if interest rates remain high then business activity will decrease. If interest rates remain high, then if business activity decreases then unemployment will rise. So if unemployment rises, then inflation will continue. *(I, H, D, U)*

3.   If taxes are reduced then inflation will rise, but if the budget is balanced then unemployment will increase. If the president keeps his campaign promises, then either taxes are reduced or the budget is balanced. Therefore if the president keeps his campaign promises, then either inflation will rise or unemployment will increase. *(T, I, B, U, K)*

4.   Weather predicting is an exact science. Therefore either it will rain tomorrow or it won't. *(W, R)*

*5.   If either it will rain tomorrow or it won't rain tomorrow, then weather predicting is an exact science. Therefore weather predicting is an exact science. *(R, W)*∎

Summary of Chapter 9

In this chapter we introduced and explained the **method of deduction** with which valid truth-functional arguments may be proved valid far more efficiently than by the use of truth tables, and we explained the method by which invalid truth-functional arguments may be shown to be invalid.

In section 9.1, **we defined a formal proof of validity for any given argument as follows: a sequence of statements each of which is either a premiss of that argument or follows from preceding statements of the sequence by an elementary valid argument, where the last statement of the sequence is the conclusion of the argument whose validity is being proved.**

We defined an elementary valid argument to be any argument that is a substitution instance of an elementary valid argument form.

We listed **nine elementary valid argument forms,** the first portion of the **rules of inference** to be used in constructing formal proofs of validity.

In section 9.2, we strengthened the machinery for constructing formal proofs of validity by introducing the **Rule of Replacement, which permits us** to infer from any statement the result of replacing any component of that statement by any other statement logically equivalent to the component replaced.

We listed ten **logically true biconditionals,** logical equivalences, which we **added to the set of rules of inference** to be used in constructing formal proofs of validity.

In section 9.3, **we explained how invalid truth-functional arguments may be proved invalid by the method of assigning truth values.** To prove invalidity, we constructed that line of a truth table that exhibits the possibility that the premisses of that argument may all be true while its conclusion is false.

In section 9.4, we discussed contradictory premisses and explained why **an argument whose premisses are inconsistent with one another must be valid,** although it is necessarily unsound.

Frege's . . . discovery of quantification, the deepest single technical advance ever made in logic.
—Michael Dummett

QUANTIFICATION THEORY

10.1 SINGULAR PROPOSITIONS

The logical techniques of the two preceding chapters permit us to discriminate between valid and invalid arguments of one certain type. Arguments of that type are roughly characterized as those whose validity depends only upon the ways in which simple statements are truth-functionally combined into compound statements. There are, however, other types of arguments for which the validity criteria of the two preceding chapters do not suffice. An example of a different type is the obviously valid argument

All humans are mortal.
Socrates is human.
Therefore Socrates is mortal.

Were we to apply to this argument the evaluation methods previously introduced, we would symbolize it as

$$A$$
$$H$$
$$\therefore M$$

But in this notation it appears to be invalid. The techniques of symbolic logic presented thus far cannot be directly applied to arguments of this new type. The validity of the given argument does not depend on the way in which simple statements are compounded, for no compound statements occur in it. Its validity depends rather upon the *inner logical structure* of the noncompound statements involved. To formulate methods for testing the validity of arguments of this new sort, techniques for describing and symbolizing noncompound statements by reference to their inner logical structure must be devised.[1]

The simplest kind of noncompound statement is illustrated by the second premiss of the preceding argument, "Socrates is human." Statements of this kind have traditionally been called *singular propositions.* **An (affirmative) singular proposition asserts that a particular individual has a specified attribute.** In the present example, ordinary grammar and traditional logic would agree in classifying "Socrates" as the *subject* term and "human" as the *predicate* term. The subject term denotes a particular individual and the predicate term designates some attribute the individual is said to have.

It is clear that one and the same subject term can occur in different singular propositions. Thus we have the term "Socrates" as subject term in each of the following: "Socrates is mortal," "Socrates is fat," "Socrates is wise," and "Socrates is beautiful." Of these, some are true (the first and third) and some are false (the second and fourth).[2] It is also clear that one and the same predicate term can occur in different singular propositions. Thus we have the term "human" as predicate term in each of the following: "Aristotle is human," "Brazil is human," "Chicago is human," and "O'Keeffe is human." Of course, some are true (the first and fourth) and some are false (the second and third).

It should be clear from the foregoing that the word "individual" is used to refer not only to persons, but to any *thing*, such as a country, a city, or in fact anything of which an attribute such as *human* or *mortal* can be meaningfully predicated. In all of the examples given thus far, the predicate term has been an *adjective.* From the point of view of grammar the distinction between adjective and noun is of considerable importance. But in the present chapter the difference is not significant, and we do not distinguish between "Socrates is mortal" and "Socrates is a mortal," or between "Socrates is wise" and "Socrates is a wise individual." A predicate may be either an adjective or a noun, or even a verb, as in "Aristotle writes," which can alternatively be expressed as "Aristotle is a writer."

Assuming that we can distinguish between individuals that have attributes and the attributes that they have, we introduce and use two different kinds of symbols for referring to them. In the following discussion we will use small or lowercase letters from *a* through *w* to denote individuals. These symbols are *individual constants.* In any particular context in which they occur, each will designate one particular individual throughout the whole of that context. It usually will be convenient to denote an individual by the first letter of its (or his or her) name. Thus in the present context we should use the letters *s, a, b, c, o* to denote the individuals Socrates, Aristotle, Brazil, Chicago, and O'Keeffe,

---

[1]It was to arguments of this type that the classical or Aristotelian logic was primarily devoted, as described in Chapters 5 and 6. The older methods, however, do not possess the generality or power of the newer symbolic logic and cannot be extended to cover all asylogistic inference.

[2]Here we shall follow the custom of ignoring the time factor, and will use the verb "is" in the tenseless sense of "is, will be, or has been." Where considerations of time change are crucial, the somewhat more complicated symbolism of the logic of relations is required for an adequate treatment.

respectively. We shall use capital letters to symbolize *attributes*, and it will be convenient to use the same guiding principles here, using the letters H, M, F, W, B to symbolize the attributes of being human, of being mortal, of being fat, of being wise, and of being beautiful, respectively.

Having two groups of symbols, one for individuals and one for attributes of individuals, we adopt the convention that writing an attribute symbol immediately to the left of an individual symbol will symbolize the singular proposition affirming that the individual named has the attribute specified. Thus the singular proposition "Socrates is human" will be symbolized as Hs. The other singular propositions mentioned involving the predicate "human" are symbolized as Ha, Hb, Hc, and Ho. All of them, it will be observed, have a certain common pattern, not to be symbolized as H by itself but, rather, as H—, where the "—" indicates that to the right of the predicate symbol another symbol, an individual symbol, occurs. Instead of using the dash symbol ("—") as a place marker, it is customary to use the letter x (which is available since only the letters a through w are used as individual constants). We use Hx [sometimes written $H(x)$] to symbolize the common pattern of all singular propositions that attribute "being human" to an individual. **The letter x, called an "individual variable," is a mere** *place marker,* **serving to indicate where the various letters a through w—our individual constants—may be written so that singular propositions will result.**

The various singular propositions Ha, Hb, Hc, Hd are either true or false; but Hx is neither true nor false, not being a statement or proposition at all. The expression Hx is **a** *propositional function,* **which may be defined as an expression that (1) contains an individual variable and (2) becomes a statement when an individual constant is substituted for the individual variable.**[3] Individual constants are to be thought of as proper names of individuals. Any singular proposition is a *substitution instance* of a propositional function, the result of substituting an individual constant for the individual variable in that propositional function. Ordinarily, a propositional function will have some true substitution instances and some false substitution instances. The propositional functions considered thus far—that is, Hx, Mx, Fx, Bx, and Wx—are all of this kind. We shall call these propositional functions "simple predicates," to distinguish them from the more complex propositional functions introduced in the following sections. **A simple predicate, then, is a propositional function having some true and some false substitution instances, each of which is an affirmative singular proposition.**

10.2 QUANTIFICATION

The substitution of individual constants for individual variables is not the only way that propositions can be obtained from propositional functions. Propositions also may be obtained by the process known as *generalization* or *quantification.* Predicate terms occur frequently in propositions other than singular ones. Thus

---

[3] Some writers have regarded "propositional functions" as the meanings of such expressions, but here we define them to be the expressions themselves.

the propositions "Everything is mortal" and "Something is beautiful" contain predicate terms but are not singular propositions, since they do not contain the names of any particular individuals. Indeed, they do not refer specifically to *any* particular individuals, being *general* propositions.

The first may be expressed in various ways that are logically equivalent: either as "All things are mortal" or as

Given any individual thing whatever, it is mortal.

In the latter formulation, the word "it" is a relative pronoun, referring back to the word "thing" that precedes it in the statement. Using the letter x, our individual variable, in place of the pronoun "it" and its antecedent, we may rewrite the first general proposition as

Given any x, x is mortal.

Or, using the notation introduced in the preceding section, we may write

Given any x, Mx.

Although the propositional function Mx is not a proposition, here we have an expression containing it that *is* a proposition. **The phrase "Given any x" is customarily symbolized by "(x)", which is called the** *universal quantifier.* Our first general proposition may be completely symbolized as

$$(x)\ Mx$$

The second general proposition, "Something is beautiful," may also be expressed as

There is at least one thing that is beautiful.

In the latter formulation, the word "that" is a relative pronoun referring back to the word "thing." Using our individual variable x in place of both the pronoun "that" and its antecedent, we may rewrite the second general proposition as

There is at least one x such that x is beautiful.

Or, using the notation at hand, we may write

There is at least one x such that Bx.

Just as before, although Bx is a propositional function and not a proposition, we have here an expression containing it that is a proposition. **The phrase "there is at least one x such that" is customarily symbolized by "$(\exists x)$", which is called the** *existential quantifier.* The second general proposition may be completely symbolized as

$$(\exists x)\ Bx$$

Thus we see that **propositions may be formed from propositional functions either by *instantiation*, that is, by substituting an individual constant for its individual variable, or by *generalization*, that is, by placing a universal or existential quantifier before it.**

Now consider: The *universal* quantification of a propositional function, *(x)Mx*, is true if and only if *all* its substitution instances are true; that is what universality means here. And it is also clear that the *existential* quantification of a propositional function, *(∃x)Mx*, is true if and only if it has *at least one* true substitution instance. Let us assume (what no one would care to deny) that there exists at least one individual. Under this very weak assumption, every propositional function must have at least one substitution instance, an instance that may or may not be true. But it is certain that, under this assumption, if the *universal* quantification of a propositional function is true, then the *existential* quantification of it must also be true. That is, if every *x* is *M*, then, if there exists at least one thing, that thing is *M*.

Up to this point only affirmative singular propositions have been given as substitution instances of propositional functions. *Mx* (*x* is mortal) is a propositional function. *Ms* is an instance of it, an affirmative singular proposition that says "Socrates is mortal." But not all propositions are affirmative. One may deny that Socrates is mortal, saying ~*Ms*, "Socrates is not mortal." If *Ms* is a substitution instance of *Mx*, then ~*Ms* may be regarded as a substitution instance of the propositional function ~*Mx*. And thus we may enlarge our conception of propositional functions, beyond the simple predicates introduced in the preceding section, to permit them to contain the negation symbol, "~".

With the negation symbol at our disposal, we may now enrich our understanding of quantification as follows. We begin with the general proposition

Nothing is perfect.

which we can paraphrase as

Everything is imperfect.

which in turn may be written as

Given any individual thing whatever, it is not perfect.

which can be rewritten as

Given any *x, x* is not perfect.

If *P* symbolizes the attribute of being perfect, we can use the notation just developed (the quantifier and the negation sign) to express this proposition ("Nothing is perfect.") as *(x)~Px.*

Now we are in a position to list and illustrate a series of important connections between universal and existential quantification.

First, the (universal) general proposition "Everything is mortal" is *denied* by the (existential) general proposition "Something is not mortal." Using symbols, we would say that $(x)Mx$ is denied by $(\exists x)\sim Mx$. Since each of these is the denial of the other, we may certainly say (prefacing the one with a negation symbol) that the biconditional

$$\sim(x)Mx \overset{\text{T}}{\equiv} (\exists x)\sim Mx$$

is necessarily true, logically true.

Second, "Everything is mortal" expresses exactly what is expressed by "There is nothing that is not mortal"—which may be formulated as another biconditional, also logically true

$$(x)Mx \overset{\text{T}}{\equiv} \sim(\exists x)\sim Mx$$

Third, it is clear that the (universal) general proposition "Nothing is mortal" is *denied* by the (existential) general proposition "Something is mortal." In symbols we would say that $(x)\sim Mx$ is denied by $(x)Mx$. And since each of these is the denial of the other we may certainly say (again prefacing the one with a negation symbol) that the biconditional

$$\sim(x)\sim Mx \overset{\text{T}}{\equiv} (\exists x)Mx$$

is necessarily, logically true.

And fourth, "Everything is not mortal" expresses exactly what is expressed by "There is nothing that is mortal"—which may be formulated as a logically true biconditional:

$$(x)\sim Mx \overset{\text{T}}{\equiv} \sim(\exists x)Mx$$

These four logically true biconditionals set forth the interrelations of universal and existential quantifiers. Any proposition in which the quantifier is prefaced by a negation sign we may replace (using these logically true biconditionals) with another logically equivalent proposition in which the quantifier is not prefaced by a negation sign. We list these four biconditionals immediately below, now replacing the illustrative predicate M (for mortal) with the symbol ϕ (the Greek letter *phi*), which will stand for *any* simple predicate whatsoever.

$$[(x)\phi x] \overset{\text{T}}{\equiv} [\sim(\exists x)\sim\phi x]$$
$$[(\exists x)\phi x] \overset{\text{T}}{\equiv} [\sim(x)\sim\phi x]$$
$$[(x)\sim\phi x] \overset{\text{T}}{\equiv} [\sim(\exists x)\phi x]$$
$$[(\exists x)\sim\phi x] \overset{\text{T}}{\equiv} [\sim(x)\phi x]$$

More graphically, the general connections between universal and existential quantification can be described in terms of the square array shown in Figure 10–1.

Continuing to assume the existence of at least one individual, we can say, referring to this square, that

1.   The two top propositions are **contraries;** that is, they might both be false but cannot both be true.

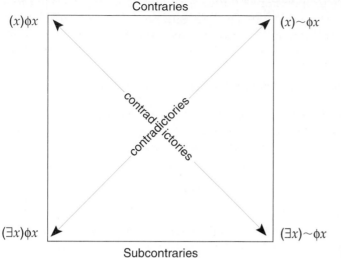

Contraries

$(x)\phi x$

$(x)\sim\phi x$

contradictories

contradictories

$(\exists x)\phi x$

$(\exists x)\sim\phi x$

Subcontraries

FIGURE 10–1

2. The two bottom propositions are **subcontraries;** that is, they might both be true but cannot both be false.
3. Propositions that are at opposite ends of the diagonals are **contradictories,** of which one must be true and the other must be false.
4. On each side of the square, the truth of the lower proposition is implied by the truth of the proposition directly above it.

10.3 TRADITIONAL SUBJECT–PREDICATE PROPOSITIONS

Using the existential and universal quantifiers, and with an understanding of the square of opposition in Figure 10–1, we are now in a position to analyze (and to use accurately in reasoning) the four types of general propositions that have been traditionally emphasized in the study of logic. The standard illustrations of these four types are the following:

All humans are mortal.   [Universal affirmative: **A**]
No humans are mortal.   [Universal negative: **E**]
Some humans are mortal.   [Particular affirmative: **I**]
Some humans are not mortal.   [Particular negative: **O**]

Each of these types is commonly referred to by its letter: the two affirmative propositions, **A** and **I** (from the Latin *affirmo,* I affirm); and the two negative propositions, **E** and **O** (from the Latin *nego,* I deny).[4]

_____

[4]An account of the traditional analysis of these four types of propositions was presented in Chapter 5.

In symbolizing these propositions by means of quantifiers, we are led to a further enlargement of our conception of a propositional function. Turning first to the **A** proposition, "All humans are mortal" we proceed by means of successive paraphrasings, beginning with

Given any individual thing whatever, if it is human then it is mortal.

The two instances of the relative pronoun "it" clearly refer back to their common antecedent, the word "thing." As in the early part of the preceding section, since those three words have the same (indefinite) reference, they can be replaced by the letter "x," and the proposition rewritten as

Given any x, if x is human then x is mortal.

Now using our previously introduced notation for "if–then," we can rewrite the preceding as

Given any x, x is human $\supset x$ is mortal.

Finally, using our now familiar notation for propositional functions and quantifiers, the original **A** proposition is expressed as

$$(x)(Hx \supset Mx)$$

In our symbolic translation, the **A** proposition appears as the universal quantification of a new kind of propositional function. The expression $Hx \supset Mx$ is a propositional function that has as its substitution instances neither affirmative nor negative singular propositions, but conditional statements whose antecedents and consequents are singular propositions having the same subject term. Among the substitution instances of the propositional function $Hx \supset Mx$ are the conditional statements $Ha \supset Ma$, $Hb \supset Mb$, $Hc \supset Mc$, $Hd \supset Md$, and so on.

There are also propositional functions whose substitution instances are conjunctions of singular propositions having the same subject terms. Thus the conjunctions $Ha \bullet Ma$, $Hb \bullet Mb$, $Hc \bullet Mc$, $Hd \bullet Md$, and so on are substitution instances of the propositional function $Hx \bullet Mx$. There are also propositional functions such as $Wx \vee Bx$, whose substitution instances are disjunctions such as $Wa \vee Ba$ and $Wb \vee Bb$. In fact, any truth-functionally compound statement whose simple component statements are singular propositions all having the same subject term may be regarded as a substitution instance of a propositional function containing some or all of the various truth-functional connectives: dot, wedge, horseshoe, three-bar equivalence, and curl, in addition to the simple predicates Ax, Bx, Cx, Dx, ... In our translation of the **A** proposition as $(x)(Hx \supset Mx)$, the parentheses serve as punctuation marks. They indicate that the universal quantifier (x) "applies to" or "has within its scope" the entire (complex) propositional function $Hx \supset Mx$.

Before going on to discuss the other traditional forms of categorical propositions, it should be observed that our symbolic formula $(x)(Hx \supset Mx)$ translates not only the standard-form proposition "All H's are M's" but any other

English sentence having the same meaning.[5] There are many ways in English of saying the same thing. A partial list of them may be set down as: "*H*'s are *M*'s," "An *H* is an *M*," "Every *H* is *M*," "Each *H* is *M*," "Any *H* is *M*," "No *H*'s are not *M*," "Everything that is *H* is *M*," "Anything that is *H* is *M*," "If anything is *H*, it is *M*," "If something is *H*, it is *M*," "Whatever is *H* is *M*," "*H*'s are all *M*'s," "Only *M*'s are *H*'s," "None but *M*'s are *H*'s," "Nothing is an *H* unless it is an *M*," and "Nothing is an *H* but not an *M*." Some English idioms are a little misleading, in using a temporal term when no reference to time is intended. Thus the proposition "*H*'s are always *M*'s" is ordinarily understood to mean simply that *all H*'s are *M*'s. Again, the same meaning may be expressed by the use of abstract nouns: "Humanity implies (or entails) mortality" is correctly symbolized as an **A** proposition. That the language of symbolic logic has a single expression for the common meaning of a considerable number of English sentences may be regarded as an advantage of symbolic logic over English for cognitive or informative purposes—although admittedly a disadvantage from the point of view of rhetorical power or poetic expressiveness.

The **E** proposition "No humans are mortal" may be successively paraphrased as

> Given any individual thing whatever, if it is human then it is not mortal.
> Given any *x*, if *x* is human then *x* is not mortal.
> Given any *x*, *x* is human $\supset$ *x* is not mortal.

and finally as

$$(x)(Hx \supset \sim Mx)$$

The preceding symbolic translation expresses not only the traditional **E** form in English, but also such diverse ways of saying the same thing as "There are no *H*'s that are *M*," "Nothing is both an *H* and an *M*," and "*H*'s are never *M*."

Similarly, the **I** proposition "Some humans are mortal" may be successively paraphrased as

> There is at least one thing that is human and mortal.
> There is at least one *x* such that *x* is human and *x* is mortal.
> There is at least one *x* such that *x* is human • *x* is mortal.

and then as

$$[(\exists x)(Hx \bullet Mx)]$$

Finally, the **O** proposition "Some humans are not mortal" is successively paraphrased as

> There is at least one thing that is human but not mortal.
> There is at least one *x* such that *x* is human and *x* is not mortal.
> There is at least one *x* such that *x* is human • $\sim$ *x* is mortal.

---

[5]A detailed explanation of the four standard forms of categorical propositions has been provided in section 5.2.

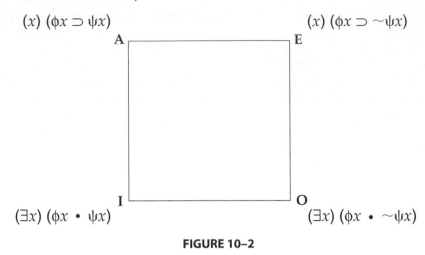

$(x) (\phi x \supset \psi x)$

$(x) (\phi x \supset {\sim}\psi x)$

$(\exists x) (\phi x \bullet \psi x)$

$(\exists x) (\phi x \bullet {\sim}\psi x)$

FIGURE 10–2

and completely symbolized as

$$[(\exists x)(Hx \bullet {\sim}Mx)]$$

Where the Greek letters *phi* (φ) and *psi* (ψ) are used to represent any predicates whatever, the four general subject-predicate propositions of traditional logic may be represented in a square array as shown in Figure 10–2.

Of these, the **A** and the **O** are contradictories, each being the denial of the other; **E** and **I** are also contradictories.

It might be thought that an **I** proposition follows from its corresponding **A** proposition, and an **O** from its corresponding **E**; but this is not so. An **A** proposition may very well be true while its corresponding **I** proposition is false. Where φx is a propositional function that has no true substitution instances, then no matter what kinds of substitution instances the propositional function ψx may have, the universal quantification of the (complex) propositional function φ$x \supset$ ψx will be true. For example, consider the propositional function "x is a centaur," which we abbreviate as Cx. Because there are no centaurs, every substitution instance of Cx is false, that is, $Ca, Cb, Cc, \ldots$ are all false. Hence every substitution instance of the complex propositional function $Cx \supset Bx$ will be a conditional statement whose antecedent is false. The substitution instances $Ca \supset Ba, Cb \supset Bb, Cc \supset Bc, \ldots$ are therefore all true, because any conditional statement asserting a material implication must be true if its antecedent is false. Because all its substitution instances are true, the universal quantification of the propositional function $Cx \supset Bx$, which is the **A** proposition $(x)(Cx \supset Bx)$, is true. But the corresponding **I** proposition $(\exists x)(Cx \bullet Bx)$ is false, because the propositional function $Cx \bullet Bx$ has no true substitution instances. That $Cx \bullet Bx$ has no true substitution instances follows from the fact that Cx has no true substitution instances. The various substitution instances of $Cx \bullet Bx$ are $Ca \bullet Ba, Cb \bullet Bb, Cc \bullet Bc, \ldots$, each of which is a conjunction whose first conjunct is false, because $Ca, Cb, Cc, \ldots$ are all false. Because all its substitution instances are false, the existential quantification of the propositional function $Cx \bullet Bx$, which is the **I** proposition $(\exists x)(Cx \bullet Bx)$, is false. Hence an **A** proposition may be true while its corresponding **I** proposition is false.

This analysis shows also why an **E** proposition may be true while its corresponding **O** proposition is false. If we replace the propositional function Bx by the propositional function $\sim Bx$ in the preceding discussion, then $(x)(Cx \supset \sim Bx)$ may be true while $(\exists x)(Cx \bullet \sim Bx)$ will be false because, of course, there are no centaurs.

The key to the matter is this: **A** propositions and **E** propositions do not assert or suppose that anything exists; they assert only that (*if* one thing *then* another) is the case. But **I** propositions and **O** propositions do suppose that some things exist; they assert that (this *and* the other) is the case. The existential quantifier in **I** and **O** propositions makes a critical difference. It would plainly be a mistake to infer the existence of anything from a proposition that does not assert or suppose the existence of anything.

If we make the general assumption that there exists at least one individual, then $(x)(Cx \supset Bx)$ does imply $(\exists x)(Cx \supset Bx)$. But the latter is not an **I** proposition. The **I** proposition "Some centaurs are beautiful" is symbolized as $(\exists x)(Cx \bullet Bx)$, which says that there is at least one centaur that is beautiful. But what is symbolized as $(\exists x)(Cx \supset Bx)$ can be rendered in English as "There is at least one thing such that, if it is a centaur, then it is beautiful." It does not say that there is a centaur, but only that there is an individual that is either not a centaur or is beautiful. And this proposition would be false in only two possible cases: first, if there were no individuals at all; and, second, if all individuals were centaurs and none of them was beautiful. We rule out the first case by making the explicit (and obviously true) assumption that there is at least one individual in the universe. And the second case is so extremely implausible that any proposition of the form $(\exists x)(\phi x \supset \psi x)$ is bound to be quite trivial, in contrast to the significant **I** form $(\exists x)(\phi x \bullet \psi x)$. The foregoing should make clear that, although in English the **A** and **I** propositions "All humans are mortal" and "Some humans are mortal" differ only in their initial words "all" and "some," their difference in meaning is not confined to the matter of universal versus existential quantification, but goes deeper than that. The propositional functions quantified to yield **A** and **I** propositions are not just differently quantified, they are different propositional functions, one containing "$\supset$", the other "$\bullet$". In other words, **A** and **I** propositions are not so much alike as they appear in English. Their differences are brought out very clearly in the notation of propositional functions and quantifiers.

For purposes of logical manipulation we can work best with formulas in which the negation sign, if one appears at all, applies only to simple predicates. So we will want to replace formulas in ways that have this result. This we can do quite readily. We know from the Rule of Replacement established in Chapter 9 that we are always entitled to replace an expression by another that is logically equivalent to it; and we have at our disposal four logical equivalences (listed in section 10.2, on page 390) in which each of the propositions in which the quantifier is negated is shown equivalent to another proposition in which the negation sign applies directly to the predicates. And using the rules of inference with which we have been long familiar, we can shift negation signs so that, in the end, they no longer apply to compound expressions but apply only to simple predicates. Thus, for example, the formula

$$\sim(\exists x)(Fx \bullet \sim Gx)$$

can be successively rewritten. First, when we apply the third logical equivalence given on page 390, it is transformed into

$$(x) \sim(Fx \bullet \sim Gx)$$

Then when we apply De Morgan's Theorem, it becomes

$$(x)(\sim Fx \vee \sim\sim Gx)$$

Next, the Principle of Double Negation gives us

$$(x)(\sim Fx \vee Gx)$$

And finally, when we invoke the definition of Material Implication, the original formula is rewritten as the **A** proposition

$$(x)(Fx \supset Gx)$$

A formula in which negation signs apply only to simple predicates we call a *normal-form formula*.

Before turning to the topic of inferences involving noncompound statements, the reader should acquire some practice in translating noncompound statements from English into our logical symbolism. The English language has so many irregular and idiomatic constructions that there can be no simple rules for translating an English sentence into logical notation. What is required in each case is that the meaning of the sentence be understood and then restated in terms of propositional functions and quantifiers.

Exercises

I. Translate each of the following into the logical notation of propositional functions and quantifiers, in each case using the abbreviations suggested and having each formula begin with a quantifier, *not* with a negation symbol.

Example:

   1. No beast is without some touch of pity. (*Bx: x* is a beast; *Px: x* has some touch of pity.)

Solution: $(x)(Bx \supset Px)$

   2. Sparrows are not mammals. (*Sx: x* is a sparrow; *Mx: x* is a mammal.)
   3. Reporters are present. (*Rx: x* is a reporter; *Px: x* is present.)
   4. Nurses are always considerate. (*Nx: x* is a nurse; *Cx: x* is considerate.)

*5. Diplomats are not always rich. (*Dx: x* is a diplomat; *Rx: x* is rich.)

6. Ambassadors are always dignified. (*Ax: x* is an ambassador; *Dx: x* is dignified.)

7. No boy scout ever cheats. (*Bx: x* is a boy scout; *Cx: x* cheats.)

8. Only licensed physicians can charge for medical treatment. (*Lx: x* is a licensed physician; *Cx: x* can charge for medical treatment.)

9. Snake bites are sometimes fatal. (*Sx: x* is a snake bite; *Fx: x* is fatal.)

*10. The common cold is never fatal. (*Cx: x* is a common cold; *Fx: x* is fatal.)

11. A child pointed his finger at the emperor. (*Cx: x* is a child; *Px: x* pointed his finger at the emperor.)

12. Not all children pointed their fingers at the emperor. (*Cx: x* is a child; *Px: x* pointed his finger at the emperor.)

13. All that glitters is not gold. (*Gx: x* glitters; *Ax: x* is gold.)

14. None but the brave deserve the fair. (*Bx: x* is brave; *Dx: x* deserves the fair.)

*15. Only citizens of the United States can vote in U.S. elections. (*Cx: x* is a citizen of the United States; *Vx: x* can vote in U.S. elections.)

16. Citizens of the United States can vote only in U.S. elections. (*Ex: x* is an election in which citizens of the United States can vote; *Ux: x* is a U.S. election.)

17. Not every applicant was hired. (*Ax: x* is an applicant; *Hx: x* was hired.)

18. Not any applicant was hired. (*Ax: x* is an applicant; *Hx: x* was hired.)

19. Nothing of importance was said. (*Lx: x* is of importance; *Sx: x* was said.)

*20. They have the right to criticize who have a heart to help. (*Cx: x* has the right to criticize; *Hx: x* has a heart to help.)

II. Translate each of the following into the logical notation of propositional functions and quantifiers, in each case having the formula begin with a quantifier, not with a negation symbol.

1. Nothing is attained in war except by calculation.

—Napoleon Bonaparte

2. No one doesn't believe in laws of nature.

—Prof. Donna Haraway *The Chronicle of Higher Education,*
28 June 1996

3. He only earns his freedom and existence who daily conquers them anew.

—Johann Wolfgang Von Goethe. *Faust,* Part II

4. No man is thoroughly miserable unless he be condemned to live in Ireland.

——Jonathan Swift

*5. Not everything good is safe, and not everything dangerous is bad.

—David Brooks, in *The Weekly Standard*, 18 August 1997

6. There isn't any business we can't improve.

—Advertising slogan, Ernst and Young, Accountants

7. A problem well stated is a problem half solved.

—Charles Kettering, former Research Director for General Motors.

8. There's not a single witch or wizard who went bad who wasn't in Slytherin.

—J. K. Rowling, in *Harry Potter and the Sorcerer's Stone*.

9. Everybody doesn't like something, but nobody doesn't like Willie Nelson.

—Steve Dollar, Cox News Service

*10. No man but a blockhead ever wrote except for money.

—Samuel Johnson

III. For each of the following, find a normal-form formula logically equivalent to the given one.

*1.	$\sim(x)(Ax \supset Bx)$	**2.**	$\sim(x)(Cx \supset \sim Dx)$
3.	$\sim(\exists x)(Ex \bullet Fx)$	**4.**	$\sim(\exists x)(Gx \bullet \sim Hx)$
*5.	$\sim(x)(\sim Ix \vee Jx)$	**6.**	$\sim(x)(\sim Kx \vee \sim Lx)$
7.	$\sim(\exists x)[\sim(Mx \vee Nx)]$	**8.**	$\sim(\exists x)[\sim(Ox \vee \sim Px)]$
9.	$\sim(\exists x)[\sim(\sim Qx \vee Rx)]$	***10.**	$\sim(x)[\sim(Sx \bullet \sim Tx)]$
11.	$\sim(x)[\sim(\sim Ux \bullet \sim Vx)]$	**12.**	$\sim(\exists x)[\sim(\sim Wx \vee Xx)]$

10.4 PROVING VALIDITY

In order to construct formal proofs of validity for arguments whose validity turns upon the inner structures of noncompound statements occurring in them, we must expand our list of rules of inference. Only four additional rules are required, and they will be introduced in connection with arguments for which they are needed.

Consider the first argument cited in the present chapter: "All humans are mortal. Socrates is human. Therefore Socrates is mortal." It is symbolized as

$$(x)(Hx \supset Mx)$$
$$Hs$$
$$\therefore Ms$$

The first premiss affirms the truth of the universal quantification of the propositional function $Hx \supset Mx$. Since the universal quantification of a propositional function is true if and only if all of its substitution instances are true, from the first premiss we can infer any desired substitution instance of the propositional function $Hx \supset Mx$. In particular we can infer the substitution instance $Hs \supset Ms$.

From that and the second premiss *Hs*, the conclusion *Ms* follows directly by *modus ponens*.

If we add to our list of rules of inference the principle that **any substitution instance of a propositional function can validly be inferred from its universal quantification,** then we can give a formal proof of the validity of the given argument by reference to the expanded list of elementary valid argument forms. This new rule of inference is the **principle of Universal Instantiation**[6] and is abbreviated as **"UI."** Using the Greek letter *nu* (ν) to represent any individual symbol whatever, we state the new rule as

$$\textbf{UI: } \begin{array}{l} (x)(\phi x) \\ \therefore \phi\nu \end{array} \quad \text{(where } \nu \text{ is any individual symbol)}$$

A formal proof of validity may now be written as

1. $(x)(Hx \supset Mx)$
2. Hs
   $\therefore Ms$
3. $Hs \supset Ms$ 1, **UI**
4. Ms 3,2, M.P.

The addition of **UI** strengthens our proof apparatus considerably, but more is required. The need for additional rules governing quantification arises in connection with arguments such as "All humans are mortal. All Greeks are human. Therefore all Greeks are mortal." The symbolic translation of this argument is

$$(x)(Hx \supset Mx)$$
$$(x)(Gx \supset Hx)$$
$$\therefore (x)(Gx \supset Mx)$$

Here both premisses and conclusion are general propositions rather than singular ones, universal quantifications of propositional functions rather than substitution instances of them. From the two premisses, by **UI,** we may validly infer the following pairs of conditional statements:

$$\begin{Bmatrix} Ga \supset Ha \\ Ha \supset Ma \end{Bmatrix} \quad \begin{Bmatrix} Gb \supset Hb \\ Hb \supset Mb \end{Bmatrix} \quad \begin{Bmatrix} Gc \supset Hc \\ Hc \supset Mc \end{Bmatrix} \quad \begin{Bmatrix} Gd \supset Hd \\ Hd \supset Md \end{Bmatrix}, \dots$$

and by successive uses of the principle of the Hypothetical Syllogism we may validly infer the conclusions:

$$Ga \supset Ma, Gb \supset Mb, Gc \supset Mc, Gd \supset Md, \dots$$

If *a, b, c, d, . . .* were all the individuals that exist, it would follow that from the truth of the premisses one could validly infer the truth of all substitution instances of the propositional function $Gx \supset Mx$. Since the universal quantification of a propositional function is true if and only if all its substitution instances are true, we can go on to infer the truth of $(x)(Gx \supset Mx)$, which is the conclusion of the given argument.

---

[6]This rule, and the three following, are variants of rules for "natural deduction" that were devised independently by Gerhard Gentzen and Stanislaw Jaskowski in 1934.

The preceding paragraph may be thought of as containing an *informal* proof of the validity of the given argument, in which the principle of the Hypothetical Syllogism and two principles governing quantification are appealed to. But it describes indefinitely long sequences of statements: the lists of all substitution instances of the two propositional functions quantified universally in the premises, and the list of all substitution instances of the propositional function whose universal quantification is the conclusion. A *formal* proof cannot contain such indefinitely, perhaps even infinitely long sequences of statements, so some method must be sought for expressing those indefinitely long sequences in some finite, definite fashion.

A method for doing this is suggested by a common technique of elementary mathematics. A geometer, seeking to prove that *all* triangles possess a certain attribute, may begin with the words "Let *ABC* be any arbitrarily selected triangle." Then the geometer begins to reason about the triangle *ABC*, and establishes that it has the attribute in question. From this he concludes that *all* triangles have that attribute. Now what justifies his final conclusion? Granted of the particular triangle *ABC* that *it* has the attribute, why does it follow that *all* triangles do? The answer to this question is easily given. If no assumption other than its triangularity is made about the triangle *ABC*, then the symbol "*ABC*" can be taken as denoting any triangle you please. Then the geometer's argument establishes that *any* triangle has the attribute in question, and if *any* triangle has it, then *all* triangles do. We now introduce a notation analogous to the geometer's in talking about "any arbitrarily selected triangle *ABC*." This will avoid the pretense of listing an indefinite or infinite number of substitution instances of a propositional function, for instead we shall talk about *any* substitution instance of the propositional function.

We shall use the (hitherto unused) lowercase letter *y* to denote any arbitrarily selected individual. We shall use it in a way similar to that in which the geometer used the letters *ABC*. Since the truth of *any* substitution instance of a propositional function follows from its universal quantification, we can infer the substitution instance that results from replacing *x* by *y*, where *y* denotes "any arbitrarily selected" individual. Thus we may begin our formal proof of the validity of the given argument as follows:

1. $(x)(Hx \supset Mx)$
2. $(x)(Gx \supset Hx)$
   $\therefore (x)(Gx \supset Mx)$
3. $Hy \supset My$ 1, **UI**
4. $Gy \supset Hy$ 2, **UI**
5. $Gy \supset My$ 4,3, H.S.

From the premises we have deduced the statement $Gy \supset My$, which in effect, since *y* denotes "any arbitrarily selected individual," asserts the truth of *any* substitution instance of the propositional function $Gx \supset Mx$. Since *any* substitution instance is true, all substitution instances must be true, and hence the universal quantification of that propositional function is true also. We may add this principle to our list of rules of inference, stating it as: **From the substitution instance of a propositional function with respect to the name of any ar-**

bitrarily selected individual, one can validly infer the universal quantifica-tion of that propositional function. Since this new principle permits us to *generalize,* that is, to go from a special substitution instance to a generalized or universally quantified expression, we refer to it as the **principle of Universal Generalization** and abbreviate it as **"UG."** It is stated as

UG: $\dfrac{\phi y}{\therefore (x)(\phi x)}$ (where y denotes "any arbitrarily selected individual")

The sixth and final line of the formal proof already begun may now be written (and justified) as

6. $(x)(Gx \supset Mx)$ 5, **UG**

Let us review the preceding discussion. In the geometer's proof the only assumption made about ABC is that it is a triangle; hence what is proved true of ABC is proved true of *any* triangle. In our proof the only assumption made about y is that it is an individual; hence what is proved true of y is proved true of *any* individual. The symbol y is an individual symbol, but it is a very special one. Typically it is introduced into a proof by using **UI.** And only the presence of y permits the use of **UG.**

Here is another valid argument, the demonstration of whose validity requires the use of **UG** as well as **UI:** "No humans are perfect. All Greeks are humans. Therefore no Greeks are perfect.[7] The formal proof of its validity is

1. $(x)(Hx \supset \sim Px)$
2. $(x)(Gx \supset Hx)$
   $\therefore (x)(Gx \supset \sim Px)$
3. $Hy \supset \sim Py$ 1, **UI**
4. $Gy \supset Hy$ 2, **UI**
5. $Gy \supset \sim Py$ 4,3, H.S.
6. $(x)(Gx \supset \sim Px)$ 5, **UG**

There may seem to be some artificiality about the foregoing. It may be urged that distinguishing carefully between $(x)(\phi x)$ and ϕy, so that they are not identified but must be inferred from each other by **UI** and **UG,** is to insist upon a distinction without a difference. But there certainly is a *formal* difference between them. The statement $(x)(Hx \supset Mx)$ is a noncompound statement, whereas $Hy \supset My$ is compound, being a conditional. From the two noncompound statements $(x)(Gx \supset Hx)$ and $(x)(Hx \supset Mx)$ no relevant inference can be drawn by means of the original list of nineteen rules of inference. But from the compound statements $Gy \supset Hy$ and $Hy \supset My$ the indicated conclusion $Gy \supset My$ follows by a Hypothetical Syllogism. The principle of **UI** is used to get from noncompound statements, to which our earlier rules of inference do not usefully apply, to compound statements, to which they *can* be applied to derive the

---

[7]This is an appropriate point to observe that, for arguments of some kinds, the traditional syllogistic analysis can establish validity as efficiently as modern quantified logic. A classical logician would quickly identify this syllogism as having the mood **EAE** in the first figure—necessarily of the form Celarent, and therefore immediately seen to be valid. See section 6.5 for a summary exposition of the valid standard-form categorical syllogisms.

desired conclusion. The quantification principles thus augment our logical apparatus to make it capable of validating arguments essentially involving noncompound (generalized) propositions as well as the other (simpler) kind of argument discussed in our earlier chapters. On the other hand, in spite of this formal difference, there must be a logical equivalence between $(x)(\phi x)$ and ϕy, or the rules **UI** and **UG** would not be valid. Both the difference and the logical equivalence are important for our purpose of validating arguments by reference to a list of rules of inference. The addition of **UI** and **UG** to our list strengthens it considerably.

The list must be expanded further when we turn to arguments involving existential propositions. A convenient example with which to begin is, "All criminals are vicious. Some humans are criminals. Therefore some humans are vicious." It is symbolized as

$$(x)(Cx \supset Vx)$$
$$(\exists x)(Hx \bullet Cx)$$
$$\therefore (\exists x)(Hx \bullet Vx)$$

The existential quantification of a propositional function is true if and only if it has at least one true substitution instance. Hence whatever attribute may be designated by ϕ, $(\exists x)(\phi x)$ says that there is at least one individual that has the attribute ϕ. If an individual constant (other than the special symbol y) is used nowhere earlier in the context, we may use it to denote either the individual that has the attribute ϕ, or some one of the individuals that have ϕ if there are several. Knowing that there is such an individual, say, a, we know that ϕa is a true substitution instance of the propositional function ϕx. Hence we add to our list of rules of inference this principle: **From the existential quantification of a propositional function, we may infer the truth of its substitution instance with respect to any individual constant (other than y) that occurs nowhere earlier in that context.** The new rule of inference is **the principle of Existential Instantiation** and is abbreviated as **"EI."** It is stated as

EI: $\dfrac{(\exists x)(\phi x)}{\therefore \phi v}$ [where v is any individual constant (other than y) having no previous occurrence in the context]

Granted the additional rule of inference **EI**, we may begin a demonstration of the validity of the stated argument:

1. $(x)(Cx \supset Vx)$
2. $(\exists x)(Hx \bullet Cx)$
   $\therefore (\exists x)(Hx \bullet Vx)$
3. $Ha \bullet Ca$ 2, **EI**
4. $Ca \supset Va$ 1, **UI**
5. $Ca \bullet Ha$ 3, Com.
6. Ca 5, Simp.
7. Va 4,6, M.P.
8. Ha 3, Simp.
9. $Ha \bullet Va$ 8,7, Conj.

Thus far we have deduced *Ha • Va*, which is a substitution instance of the propositional function whose existential quantification is asserted by the conclusion. Since the existential quantification of a propositional function is true if and only if it has at least one true substitution instance, we add to our list of rules of inference the principle that **from any true substitution instance of a propositional function we may validly infer the existential quantification of that propositional function.** This fourth and final rule of inference is the **principle of Existential Generalization,** abbreviated as **"EG"** and stated as

$$\textbf{EG:} \quad \frac{\phi v}{\therefore (\exists x)(\phi x)} \qquad \text{(where } v \text{ is any individual symbol)}$$

The tenth and final line of the demonstration already begun may now be written (and justified) as

$$10.\ (\exists x)(Hx • Vx) \qquad 9, \textbf{EG}$$

The need for the indicated restriction on the use of **EI** can be seen by considering the obviously invalid argument "Some alligators are kept in captivity. Some birds are kept in captivity. Therefore some alligators are birds." If we failed to heed the restriction on **EI** that a substitution instance of a propositional function inferred by **EI** from the existential quantification of that propositional function can contain only an individual symbol (other than *y*) *having no previous occurrence in the context,* then we might proceed to construct a "proof" of validity for this invalid argument. Such an erroneous "proof" might proceed as follows:

$$
\begin{array}{lll}
1.\ (\exists x)(Ax • Cx) & & \\
2.\ (\exists x)(Bx • Cx) & & \\
\quad \therefore (\exists x)(Ax • Bx) & & \\
3.\ Aa • Ca & 1, \textbf{EI} & \\
4.\ Ba • Ca & 2, \textbf{EI} \ (\textit{wrong!}) & \\
5.\ Aa & 3, \text{Simp.} & \\
6.\ Ba & 4, \text{Simp.} & \\
7.\ Aa • Ba & 5,6, \text{Conj.} & \\
8.\ (\exists x)(Ax • Bx) & 7, \textbf{EG} & \\
\end{array}
$$

The error in this "proof" occurs at line 4. From the second premiss $(\exists x)(Bx • Cx)$, we know that there is at least one thing that is both a bird and kept in captivity. *If* we were free to assign it the name *a* in line 4 we could, of course, assert *Ba • Ca.* But we are not free to make any such assignment of "*a*," for it has already been preempted in line 3 to serve as name for an alligator that is kept in captivity. To avoid errors of this sort, we must obey the indicated restriction whenever we use **EI.** The preceding discussion should make clear that in any demonstration requiring the use of both **EI** and **UI, EI** should always be used first.

For more complicated modes of argumentation, especially those that involve relations, certain additional restrictions must be placed on our four quantification rules. But for arguments of the present sort, traditionally called *categorical syllogisms*, the present restrictions are sufficient to prevent mistakes.

FOUR ADDITIONAL RULES OF INFERENCE

The following four rules permit the transformation of *noncompound*, generalized propositions into equivalent *compound* propositions to which the 19 Rules of Inference set forth in Chapter 9 may be applied. They also permit the transformation of compound propositions into equivalent noncompound propositions. These additional rules thus make it possible to construct formal proofs of the validity of arguments whose validity depends upon the inner structure of some noncompound statements contained in those arguments. The four additional rules are as follows:

1. Universal Instantiation
UI: $(x) (\phi x)$, $\therefore$ ϕv (where v is any individual symbol)
   In essence this rule says: Any substitution instance of a propositional function can be validly inferred from its universal quantification.

2. Universal Generalization
UG: ϕy, $\therefore$ $(x)(\phi x)$ (where y denotes "any arbitrarily selected individual")
   In essence this rule says: From the substitution instance of a propositional function with respect to the name of *any arbitrarily selected* individual, one may validly infer the universal quantification of that propositional function.

3. Existential Instantiation
EI: $(\exists x)(\phi x)$, $\therefore$ ϕv [where v is any individual constant (other than y) having no previous occurrence in the context]
   In essence this rule says: From the existential quantification of a propositional function, we may infer the truth of its substitution instance with respect to any individual constant (other than y) that occurs nowhere earlier in the context.

4. Existential Generalization
EG: ϕv, $\therefore$ $(\exists x)(\phi x)$ (where v is any individual constant)
   In essence this rules says: From any true substitution instance of a propositional function, we may validly infer the existential quantification of that propositional function.

Exercises

I.   Construct a formal proof of validity for each of the following arguments.

Example:

1. $(x)(Ax \supset \sim Bx)$
   $(\exists x)(Cx \bullet Ax)$
   $\therefore (\exists x)(Cx \bullet \sim Bx)$

Solution:

The conclusion of this argument is an existentially quantified statement. Plainly the last step will therefore be the application of **EG** (existential generalization). To obtain the line needed, we will first have to instantiate the premises, applying **EI** (existential instantiation) to the second premise and **UI** (universal instantiation) to the first premise. The restriction on the use of **EI** makes it essential that we apply **EI** *before* we apply **UI**, so that we may use the same individual constant, say *a*, for both. The proof would look like this:

1.	$(x)(Ax \supset \sim Bx)$	
2.	$(\exists x)(Cx \bullet Ax)$	
	$\therefore (\exists x)(Cx \bullet \sim Bx)$	
3.	$Ca \bullet Aa$	2, **EI**
4.	$Aa \supset \sim Ba$	1, **UI**
5.	$Aa \bullet Ca$	3, Com.
6.	Aa	5, Simp.
7.	$\sim Ba$	4,6, M.P.
8.	Ca	3, Simp.
9.	$Ca \bullet \sim Ba$	8,7, Conj.
10.	$(\exists x)(Cx \bullet \sim Bx)$	9, **EG**

2. $(x)(Dx \supset \sim Ex)$
$(x)(Fx \supset Ex)$
$\therefore (x)(Fx \supset \sim Dx)$

3. $(x)(Gx \supset Hx)$
$(x)(Ix \supset \sim Hx)$
$\therefore (x)(Ix \supset \sim Gx)$

4. $(\exists x)(Jx \bullet Kx)$
$(x)(Jx \supset Lx)$
$\therefore (\exists x)(Lx \bullet Kx)$

*5. $(x)(Mx \supset Nx)$
$(\exists x)(Mx \bullet Ox)$
$\therefore (\exists x)(Ox \bullet Nx)$

6. $(\exists x)(Px \bullet \sim Qx)$
$(x)(Px \supset Rx)$
$\therefore (\exists x)(Rx \bullet \sim Qx)$

7. $(x)(Sx \supset \sim Tx)$
$(\exists x)(Sx \bullet Ux)$
$\therefore (\exists x)(Ux \bullet \sim Tx)$

8. $(x)(Vx \supset Wx)$
$(x)(Wx \supset \sim Xx)$
$\therefore (x)(Xx \supset \sim Vx)$

9. $(\exists x)(Yx \bullet Zx)$
$(x)(Zx \supset Ax)$
$\therefore (\exists x)(Ax \bullet Yx)$

*10. $(x)(Bx \supset \sim Cx)$
$(\exists x)(Cx \bullet Dx)$
$\therefore (\exists x)(Dx \bullet \sim Bx)$

11. $(x)(Fx \supset Gx)$
$(\exists x)(Fx \bullet \sim Gx)$
$\therefore (\exists x)(Gx \bullet \sim Fx)$

II. Construct a formal proof of validity for each of the following arguments, in each case using the suggested notations.

*1. No athletes are bookworms. Carol is a bookworm. Therefore Carol is not an athlete. *(Ax, Bx, c)*

2. All dancers are exuberant. Some fencers are not exuberant. Therefore some fencers are not dancers. *(Dx, Ex, Fx)*

3. No gamblers are happy. Some idealists are happy. Therefore some idealists are not gamblers. *(Gx, Hx, Ix)*

4. All jesters are knaves. No knaves are lucky. Therefore no jesters are lucky. *(Jx, Kx, Lx)*

*5. All mountaineers are neighborly. Some outlaws are mountaineers. Therefore some outlaws are neighborly. *(Mx, Nx, Ox)*

6. Only pacifists are Quakers. There are religious Quakers. Therefore pacifists are sometimes religious. *(Px, Qx, Rx)*

7. To be a swindler is to be a thief. None but the underprivileged are thieves. Therefore swindlers are always underprivileged. *(Sx, Tx, Ux)*

8. No violinists are not wealthy. There are no wealthy xylophonists. Therefore violinists are never xylophonists. *(Vx, Wx, Xx)*

9. None but the brave deserve the fair. Only soldiers are brave. Therefore the fair are deserved only by soldiers. *(Dx: x deserves the fair; Bx: x is brave; Sx: x is a soldier)*

*10. Everyone that asketh receiveth. Simon receiveth not. Therefore Simon asketh not. *(Ax, Rx, s)*

11. *Anne:* No beast so fierce but knows some touch of pity.
    Gloucester: But I know none and therefore am no beast. *(Bx, Px, g)*

    —William Shakespeare, *Richard the Third*, act 1, sc. 2

10.5 PROVING INVALIDITY

To prove the invalidity of an argument involving quantifiers, we can use the method of refutation by logical analogy. For example, the argument "All conservatives are opponents of the administration; some delegates are opponents of the administration; therefore some delegates are conservatives" is proved invalid by the analogy "All cats are animals; some dogs are animals; therefore some dogs are cats"; which is obviously invalid, since its premises are known to be true and its conclusion known to be false. But such analogies are not always easy to devise. Some more nearly effective method of proving invalidity is desirable.

In the preceding chapter we developed a method of proving invalidity for arguments involving truth-functional compound statements. That method consisted of making truth-value assignments to the component simple statements in arguments, in such a way as to make the premises true and the conclusions false. That method can be adapted for arguments involving quantifiers. The adaptation involves our general assumption that there is at least one individual. For an argument involving quantifiers to be valid, it must be impossible for its premises to be true and its conclusion false as long as there is at least one individual.

The general assumption that there is at least one individual is satisfied if there is exactly one individual, or exactly two individuals, or exactly three individuals, or . . . If any one of these assumptions about the exact number of individuals is made, there is an equivalence between general propositions and truth-functional compounds of singular propositions. If there is exactly one individual, say *a*, then

$$(x)(\phi x) \stackrel{\text{I}}{=} \phi a \stackrel{\text{I}}{=} (\exists x)(\phi x)$$

If there are exactly two individuals, say *a* and *b*, then

$$(x)(\phi x) \stackrel{\text{I}}{=} [\phi a \bullet \phi b] \qquad \text{and} \qquad (\exists x)(\phi x) \stackrel{\text{I}}{=} [\phi a \vee \phi b]$$

If there are exactly three individuals, say *a*, *b*, and *c*, then

$$(x)(\phi x) \stackrel{\text{I}}{=} [\phi a \bullet \phi b \bullet \phi c] \qquad \text{and} \qquad (\exists x)(\phi x) \stackrel{\text{I}}{=} [\phi a \vee \phi b \vee \phi c]$$

In general, if there are exactly *n* individuals, say *a, b, c, . . . , n*, then

$$(x)(\phi x) \stackrel{\text{I}}{=} [\phi a \bullet \phi b \bullet \phi c \bullet \ldots \bullet \phi n] \qquad \text{and}$$
$$(\exists x)(\phi x) \stackrel{\text{I}}{=} [\phi a \vee \phi b \vee \phi c \vee \ldots \vee \phi n]$$

These biconditionals are true as a consequence of our definitions of the universal and existential quantifiers. No use is made here of the four quantification rules explained in the preceding section.

An argument involving quantifiers is valid if, *and only if,* it is valid no matter how many individuals there are, provided there is at least one. So an argument involving quantifiers is proved invalid if there is a possible universe or *model* containing at least one individual such that the argument's premises are true and its conclusion false *of that model.* Consider the argument "All mercenaries are undependable. No guerrillas are mercenaries. Therefore no guerrillas are undependable." It may be symbolized as

$$(x)(Mx \supset Ux)$$
$$(x)(Gx \supset \sim Mx)$$
$$\therefore (x)(Gx \supset \sim Ux)$$

If there is exactly one individual, say, *a*, this argument is logically equivalent to

$$Ma \supset Ua$$
$$Ga \supset \sim Ma$$
$$\therefore Ga \supset \sim Ua$$

The latter can be proved invalid by assigning the truth value *true* to *Ga* and *Ua* and *false* to *Ma*. (This assignment of truth values is a shorthand way of describing the *model* in question as containing only the one individual, *a*, which is a guerrilla and undependable but is not a mercenary.) Hence the original argument is not valid for a model containing exactly one individual, and is therefore *invalid.* Similarly, we can prove the invalidity of the first argument mentioned in this section (on p. 406) by describing a model containing exactly one individual, *a*, so that *Aa* and *Da* are assigned *truth* and *Ca* is assigned *falsehood*.[8]

---

[8]Here we assume that the simple predicates *Ax, Bx, Cx, Dx, . . .* occurring in our propositions are neither necessary, that is, logically true of all individuals (for example, *x* is identical with itself), nor impossible, that is, logically false of all individuals (for example, *x* is different from itself). We also assume that the only logical relations among the simple predicates involved are those asserted or logically implied by the premises. The point of these restrictions is to permit us to assign truth values arbitrarily to the substitution instances of these simple predicates without any inconsistency—for of course, a correct description of any model must be consistent.

Some arguments—for example,

$$(\exists x)Fx$$
$$\therefore (x)Fx$$

—may be valid for any model in which there is exactly one individual, but invalid for a model containing two or more individuals. Such arguments must count as invalid also, because a valid argument must be valid regardless of how many individuals there are, so long as there is at least one. Another example of this kind of argument is "All collies are affectionate. Some collies are watchdogs. Therefore all watchdogs are affectionate." Its symbolic translation is

$$(x)(Cx \supset Ax)$$
$$(\exists x)(Cx \bullet Wx)$$
$$\therefore (x)(Wx \supset Ax)$$

For a model containing exactly one individual, a, it is logically equivalent to

$$Ca \supset Aa$$
$$Ca \bullet Wa$$
$$\therefore Wa \supset Aa$$

which is valid. But for a model containing two individuals, a and b, it is logically equivalent to

$$(Ca \supset Aa) \bullet (Cb \supset Ab)$$
$$(Ca \bullet Wa) \vee (Cb \bullet Wb)$$
$$\therefore (Wa \supset Aa) \bullet (Wb \supset Ab)$$

which is proved invalid by assigning *truth* to Ca, Aa, Wa, Wb, and *falsehood* to Cb and Ab. Hence the original argument is not valid for a model containing exactly two individuals, and is therefore *invalid*. For any invalid argument of this general type it is possible to describe a model containing some definite number of individuals for which its logically equivalent truth-functional argument can be proved invalid by the method of assigning truth values.

It should be emphasized again: In moving from a given argument involving general propositions to a truth-functional argument (one that is logically equivalent to the given argument for a specified model), no use is made of our four quantification rules. Instead, each statement of the truth-functional argument is logically equivalent to the corresponding general proposition of the given argument, and that logical equivalence is shown by the biconditionals formulated earlier in this section, whose logical truth for the model in question follows from the very definitions of the universal and existential quantifiers.

The procedure for proving the invalidity of an argument containing general propositions is the following. First, consider a one-element model containing only the individual a. Then, write out the logically equivalent truth-functional argument for that model, which is obtained by moving from each general proposition (quantified propositional function) of the original argument to the substitution instance of that propositional function with respect to a. If the truth-functional argument can be proved invalid by assigning truth values to its component simple statements, that suffices to prove the original argument invalid. If that cannot be done, next consider a two-element model containing the individuals *a* and *b*. In order to obtain the logically equivalent truth-functional argument for this larger model, one can simply join to each original substitution instance with respect to *a* a new substitution instance of the same propositional function with respect to *b*. This "joining" must be in accord with the logical equivalences stated on page 407; that is, where the original argument contains a *universally* quantified propositional function $(x)(\phi x)$, the new substitution instance ϕb is combined with the first substitution instance ϕa by *conjunction* ("•"); but where the original argument contains an *existentially* quantified propositional function $(\exists x)(\phi x)$, the new substitution instance ϕb is combined with the first substitution instance ϕa by *disjunction* ("∨"). The preceding example illustrates this procedure. If the new truth-functional argument can be proved invalid by assigning truth values to its component simple statements, that suffices to prove the original argument invalid. If that cannot be done, next consider a three-element model containing the individuals *a*, *b*, and *c*. And so on. None of the exercises in this book requires a model containing more than three elements.

Exercises

In the exercises below, no model containing more than two elements is required.

I.   Prove the invalidity of the following:

Example:

1. $(\exists x)(Ax • Bx)$
   $(\exists x)(Cx • Bx)$
   $\therefore (x)(Cx \supset \sim Ax)$

Solution:

We first construct a model (or possible universe) containing exactly one individual, $\boxed{a}$. We then exhibit the logically equivalent propositions in that model. Thus:

$$\left. \begin{array}{l} (\exists x)(Ax • Bx) \\ (\exists x)(Cx • Bx) \\ \therefore (x)(Cx \supset \sim Ax) \end{array} \right\} \quad \begin{array}{l} \text{logically} \\ \text{equivalent} \\ \text{in } \boxed{a} \text{ to} \end{array} \quad \left\{ \begin{array}{l} Aa • Ba \\ Ca • Ba \\ \therefore Ca \supset \sim Aa \end{array} \right.$$

We may prove the argument invalid in this model by assigning truth values as follows:

Aa	Ba	Ca
T	T	T

Since the argument has been proved invalid in this model, the argument has been proved invalid.

2. $(x)(Dx \supset \sim Ex)$
$(x)(Ex \supset Fx)$
$\therefore (x)(Fx \supset \sim Dx)$

3. $(x)(Gx \supset Hx)$
$(x)(Gx \supset Ix)$
$\therefore (x)(Ix \supset Hx)$

4. $(\exists x)(Jx \cdot Kx)$
$(\exists x)(Kx \cdot Lx)$
$\therefore (\exists x)(Lx \cdot Jx)$

*5. $(\exists x)(Mx \cdot Nx)$
$(\exists x)(Mx \cdot Ox)$
$\therefore (x)(Ox \supset Nx)$

6. $(x)(Px \supset \sim Qx)$
$(x)(Px \supset \sim Rx)$
$\therefore (x)(Rx \supset \sim Qx)$

7. $(x)(Sx \supset \sim Tx)$
$(x)(Tx \supset Ux)$
$\therefore (\exists x)(Ux \cdot \sim Sx)$

8. $(\exists x)(Vx \cdot \sim Wx)$
$(\exists x)(Wx \cdot \sim Xx)$
$\therefore (\exists x)(Xx \cdot \sim Vx)$

9. $(\exists x)(Yx \cdot Zx)$
$(\exists x)(Ax \cdot Zx)$
$\therefore (\exists x)(Ax \cdot \sim Yx)$

*10. $(\exists x)(Bx \cdot \sim Cx)$
$(x)(Dx \supset \sim Cx)$
$\therefore (x)(Dx \supset Bx)$

II. Prove the invalidity of the following, in each case using the suggested notation.

*1. All anarchists are bearded. All communists are bearded. Therefore all anarchists are communists. *(Ax, Bx, Cx)*

2. No diplomats are extremists. Some fanatics are extremists. Therefore some diplomats are not fanatics. *(Dx, Ex, Fx)*

3. All generals are handsome. Some intellectuals are handsome. Therefore some generals are intellectuals. *(Gx, Hx, Ix)*

4. Some journalists are not kibitzers. Some kibitzers are not lucky. Therefore some journalists are not lucky. *(Jx, Kx, Lx)*

*5. Some malcontents are noisy. Some officials are not noisy. Therefore no officials are malcontents. *(Mx, Nx, Ox)*

6. Some physicians are quacks. Some quacks are not responsible. Therefore some physicians are not responsible. *(Px, Qx, Rx)*

7. Some politicians are leaders. Some leaders are not orators. Therefore some orators are not politicians. *(Px, Lx, Ox)*

8. None but the brave deserve the fair. Every soldier is brave. Therefore none but soldiers deserve the fair. *(Dx: x deserves the fair; Bx: x is brave; Sx: x is a soldier)*

9. If anything is metallic, then it is breakable. There are breakable ornaments. Therefore there are metallic ornaments. *(Mx, Bx, Ox)*

*10. Only students are members. Only members are welcome. Therefore all students are welcome. *(Sx, Mx, Wx)*

10.6 ASYLLOGISTIC INFERENCE

All the arguments considered in the preceding two sections were of the form traditionally called *categorical syllogisms.* These consist of two premises and a conclusion, each of which is analyzable either as a singular proposition or as one of the **A, E, I,** or **O** varieties. We turn now to the problem of evaluating somewhat more complicated arguments. These require no greater logical apparatus than has already been developed. Yet they are *asyllogistic* arguments; that is, they cannot be reduced to standard-form categorical syllogisms, and therefore evaluating them requires a more powerful logic than was traditionally used in testing categorical syllogisms.

In this section we are still concerned with general propositions, formed by quantifying propositional functions that contain only a single individual variable. In the categorical syllogism, the only kinds of propositional functions quantified were of the forms $\phi x \supset \psi x$, $\phi x \supset \sim\psi x$, $\phi x \bullet \psi x$, and $\phi x \bullet \sim\psi x$. But now we shall be quantifying propositional functions with more complicated internal structures. An example will help make this clear. Consider the argument

> Hotels are both expensive and depressing.
> Some hotels are shabby.
> Therefore some expensive things are shabby.

This argument, for all its obvious validity, is not amenable to the traditional sort of analysis. True enough, it could be expressed in terms of **A** and **I** propositions by using the symbols Hx, Bx, Sx, and Ex to abbreviate the propositional functions "x is a hotel," "x is both expensive and depressing," "x is shabby," and "x is expensive," respectively.[9] Using these abbreviations, we might propose to symbolize the given argument as

$$(x)(Hx \supset Bx)$$
$$(\exists x)(Hx \bullet Sx)$$
$$\therefore (\exists x)(Ex \bullet Sx)$$

But forcing the argument into the straitjacket of the traditional **A** and **I** forms in this way obscures its validity. The argument just given in symbols is invalid, although the original argument is perfectly valid. A notation restricted to categorical propositions here obscures the logical connection between Bx and Ex. A more adequate analysis is obtained by using Hx, Sx, and Ex, as explained, plus Dx as an abbreviation for "x is depressing." By using these symbols, the original argument can be translated as

1. $(x)[Hx \supset (Ex \bullet Dx)]$
2. $(\exists x)(Hx \bullet Sx)$
   $\therefore (\exists x)(Ex \bullet Sx)$

---

[9]This would, however, violate the restriction stated in footnote 8 of this chapter, p. 407.

Thus symbolized, a demonstration of its validity is easily constructed. One such demonstration proceeds as follows:

3.	$Hw \cdot Sw$	2, **EI**
4.	$Hw \supset (Ew \cdot Dw)$	1, **UI**
5.	Hw	3, Simp.
6.	$Ew \cdot Dw$	4,5, M.P.
7.	Ew	6, Simp.
8.	$Sw \cdot Hw$	3, Com.
9.	Sw	8, Simp.
10.	$Ew \cdot Sw$	7,9, Conj.
11.	$(\exists x)(Ex \cdot Sx)$	10, **EG**

In symbolizing general propositions that result from quantifying more complicated propositional functions, care must be taken not to be misled by the deceptiveness of ordinary English. One cannot translate from English into our logical notation by following any formal or mechanical rules. In every case *one must understand the meaning of the English sentence, and then symbolize that meaning in terms of propositional functions and quantifiers.*

Three locutions of ordinary English that are sometimes troublesome are the following. First, note that a statement such as "All athletes are either very strong or very quick" is *not* a disjunction, although it contains the connective "or." It definitely does *not* have the same meaning as "Either all athletes are very strong or all athletes are very quick." The former is properly symbolized—using obvious abbreviations—as

$$(x)[Ax \supset (Sx \vee Qx)]$$

whereas the latter is symbolized as

$$(x)(Ax \supset Sx) \vee (x)(Ax \supset Qx)$$

Second, note that a statement such as "Oysters and clams are delicious"—while it *can* be stated as the conjunction of two general propositions: "Oysters are delicious and clams are delicious"—also can be stated as a single noncompound general proposition; in which case the word "and" is properly symbolized by the "$\vee$" rather than by the "$\bullet$". The stated proposition is symbolized as

$$(x)[(Ox \vee Cx) \supset Dx]$$

not as

$$(x)[(Ox \bullet Cx) \supset Dx]$$

For to say that oysters and clams are delicious is to say that anything is delicious that is *either* an oyster *or* a clam, *not* to say that anything is delicious that is *both* an oyster *and* a clam.

Third, what are called *exceptive* propositions require very careful attention. Such propositions, *e.g.,* "All except previous winners are eligible," may be treated as the conjunction of two general propositions. Using the example just given, we might reasonably understand the proposition to assert both that previous winners are not eligible, *and* that those who are not previous winners are eligible. It would be symbolized thus:

$$(x)(Px \supset {\sim}Ex) \bullet (x)({\sim}Px \supset Ex)$$

But the same exceptive proposition may also be translated as a noncompound general proposition that is the universal quantification of a propositional function containing the symbol for material equivalence "≡", a biconditional, and symbolized thus:

$$(x)\ (Ex \equiv {\sim}Px)$$

which can also be rendered in English as "Anyone is eligible if and only if that person is not a previous winner." In general, exceptive propositions are most conveniently regarded as quantified biconditionals.

Whether a proposition is in fact exceptive is sometimes difficult to determine. A recent controversy requiring resolution by a federal court panel illustrates this contextual difficulty. The Census Act, a law that establishes the rules for the conduct of the national census every ten years, contains the following passage:

> Sec. 195. Except for the determination of population for purposes of apportionment of Representative in Congress among the several States, the Secretary [of Commerce] shall, if he considers it feasible, authorize the use of the statistical method known as "sampling" in carrying out the provisions of this title.

For the census of 2000, which did determine population for the purposes of apportionment, the Census Bureau sought to use the sampling technique, and was sued by the House of Representatives, which claimed that the passage quoted above prohibits sampling in such a census. The Bureau defended its plan, contending that the passage authorizes the use of sampling in some contexts, but in apportionment contexts leaves the matter undetermined. Which interpretation of that exceptive provision in the statute is correct?

The court found the House position correct, writing:

> Consider the directive "except for my grandmother's wedding dress, you shall take the contents of my closet to the cleaners." It is ... likely that the granddaughter would be upset if the recipient of her directive were to take the wedding dress to the cleaners and subsequently argue that she had left this decision to his discretion. The reason for this result ... is because of our background knowledge concerning wedding dresses: We know they are extraordinarily fragile and of deep sentimental value to family members. We therefore would not expect that a decision to take [that] dress to the cleaners would be purely discretionary.
>
> The apportionment of Congressional representatives among the states is the wedding dress in the closet ... The apportionment function is the "sole constitutional function of the decennial enumeration" The manner in which it is conducted may impact not only the distribution of representatives among the states, but also the balance of

political power within the House …This court finds that the Census Act prohibits the use of statistical sampling to determine the population for the purpose of apportionment of representatives among the states …[10]

The exceptive proposition in this statute is thus to be understood as asserting the conjunction of two propositions: (1) that the use of sampling is not permitted in the context of apportionment, and (2) that in all other contexts sampling is discretionary. A controversial sentence in exceptive form must be interpreted in its context.

In section 10.4 our list of rules of inference was expanded by four, and we showed that the expanded list was sufficient to demonstrate the validity of categorical syllogisms when they are valid. And we have just seen that the same expanded list suffices to establish the validity of asyllogistic arguments of the type described. Now we may observe that, just as the expanded list was sufficient to establish *validity* in asyllogistic arguments, so also the method of proving syllogisms invalid (explained in section 10.5) by describing possible nonempty universes, or models, is sufficient to prove the *invalidity* of asyllogistic arguments of the present type as well. The following asyllogistic argument:

Managers and superintendents are either competent workers or relatives of the owner.
Anyone who dares to complain must be either a superintendent or a relative of the owner.
Managers and foremen alone are competent workers.
Someone did dare to complain.
Therefore some superintendent is a relative of the owner.

may be symbolized as

$$(x)[(Mx \lor Sx) \supset (Cx \lor Rx)]$$
$$(x)[Dx \supset (Sx \lor Rx)]$$
$$(x)(Mx \equiv Cx)$$
$$(\exists x)\, Dx$$
$$\therefore (\exists x)(Sx \bullet Rx)$$

and we can prove it invalid by describing a possible universe or model containing the single individual *a* and assigning the truth value *true* to *Ca, Da, Fa, Ra*, and the truth value *false* to *Sa*.

Exercises

I.   Translate the following statements into logical symbolism, in each case using the abbreviations suggested.

Example:

   1.   Apples and oranges are delicious and nutritious. *(Ax, Ox, Dx, Nx)*

---

[10]Decided by a specially appointed Voting Rights Act panel of three judges on 24 August 1998.

Solution:

The meaning of this proposition clearly is that if anything is *either* an apple or an orange it is *both* delicious and nutritious. Hence it would be symbolized thus:

$$(x)[(Ax \lor Ox) \supset (Dx \bullet Nx)]$$

2. Some foods are edible only if they are cooked. *(Fx, Ex, Cx)*

3. No car is safe unless it has good brakes. *(Cx, Sx, Bx)*

4. Any tall man is attractive if he is dark and handsome. *(Tx, Mx, Ax, Dx, Hx)*

*5. A gladiator wins if and only if he is lucky. *(Gx, Wx, Lx)*

6. A boxer who wins if and only if he is lucky is not skillful. *(Bx, Wx, Lx, Sx)*

7. Not all people who are wealthy are both educated and cultured. *(Px, Wx, Ex, Cx)*

8. Not all tools that are cheap are either soft or breakable. *(Tx, Cx, Sx, Bx)*

9. Any person is a coward who deserts. *(Px, Cx, Dx)*

*10. To achieve success, one must work hard if one goes into business, or study continuously if one enters a profession. *(Ax: x* achieves success; *Wx: x* works hard; *Bx: x* goes into business; *Sx: x* studies continuously; *Px: x* enters a profession)

11. An old European joke goes like this: In America, everything is permitted that is not forbidden. In Germany, everything is forbidden that is not permitted. In France, everything is permitted even if it's forbidden. In Russia, everything is forbidden even if it's permitted. [*Ax: x* is in America; *Gx: x* is in Germany; *Fx: x* is in France; *Rx: x* is in Russia; *Px: x* is permitted; *Nx: x* is forbidden]

II. For each of the following, either construct a formal proof of validity or prove it invalid. If it is to be proved invalid, a model containing as many as three elements may be required.

*1. $(x)[(Ax \lor Bx) \supset (Cx \bullet Dx)]$
    $\therefore (x)(Bx \supset Cx)$

2. $(\exists x)\{(Ex \bullet Fx) \bullet [(Ex \lor Fx) \supset (Gx \bullet Hx)]\}$
    $\therefore (x)(Ex \supset Hx)$

3. $(x)\{[Ix \supset (Jx \bullet \sim Kx)] \bullet [Jx \supset (Ix \supset Kx)]\}$
    $(\exists x)[(Ix \bullet Jx) \bullet \sim Lx]$
    $\therefore (\exists x)(Kx \bullet Lx)$

4. $(x)[(Mx \bullet Nx) \supset (Ox \lor Px)]$
    $(x)[(Ox \bullet Px) \supset (Qx \lor Rx)]$
    $\therefore (x)[(Mx \lor Ox) \supset Rx]$

*5. $(\exists x)(Sx \cdot Tx)$
$(\exists x)(Ux \cdot \sim Sx)$
$(\exists x)(Vx \cdot \sim Tx)$
$\therefore (\exists x)(Ux \cdot Vx)$

6. $(x)[Wx \supset (Xx \supset Yx)]$
$(\exists x)[Xx \cdot (Zx \cdot \sim Ax)]$
$(x)[(Wx \supset Yx) \supset (Bx \supset Ax)]$
$\therefore (\exists x)(Zx \cdot \sim Bx)$

7. $(\exists x)[Cx \cdot \sim(Dx \supset Ex)]$
$(x)[(Cx \cdot Dx) \supset Fx]$
$(\exists x)[Ex \cdot \sim(Dx \supset Cx)]$
$(x)(Gx \supset Cx)$
$\therefore (\exists x)(Gx \cdot \sim Fx)$

8. $(x)(Hx \supset Ix)$
$(x)[(Hx \cdot Ix) \supset Jx]$
$(x)[\sim Kx \supset (Hx \vee Ix)]$
$(x)[(Jx \vee \sim Jx) \supset (Ix \supset Hx)]$
$\therefore (x)(Jx \vee Kx)$

9. $(x)\{(Lx \vee Mx) \supset \{[(Nx \cdot Ox) \vee Px] \supset Qx\}\}$
$(\exists x)(Mx \cdot \sim Lx)$
$(x)\{[(Ox \supset Qx) \cdot \sim Rx] \supset Mx\}$
$(\exists x)(Lx \cdot \sim Mx)$
$\therefore (\exists x)(Nx \supset Rx)$

*10. $(x)[(Sx \vee Tx) \supset \sim(Ux \vee Vx)]$
$(\exists x)(Sx \cdot \sim Wx)$
$(\exists x)(Tx \cdot \sim Xx)$
$(x)(\sim Wx \supset Xx)$
$\therefore (\exists x)(Ux \cdot \sim Vx)$

III. For each of the following, either construct a formal proof of its validity or prove it invalid, in each case using the suggested notation.

*1. Acids and bases are chemicals. Vinegar is an acid. Therefore vinegar is a chemical. *(Ax, Bx, Cx, Vx)*

2. Teachers are either enthusiastic or unsuccessful. Teachers are not all unsuccessful. Therefore there are enthusiastic teachers. *(Tx, Ex, Ux)*

3. Argon compounds and sodium compounds are either oily or volatile. Not all sodium compounds are oily. Therefore some argon compounds are volatile. *(Ax, Sx, Ox, Vx)*

4. No employee who is either slovenly or discourteous can be promoted. Therefore no discourteous employee can be promoted. *(Ex, Sx, Dx, Px)*

*5. No employer who is either inconsiderate or tyrannical can be successful. Some employers are inconsiderate. There are tyrannical employers. Therefore no employer can be successful. *(Ex, Ix, Tx, Sx)*

6. There is nothing made of gold that is not expensive. No weapons are made of silver. Not all weapons are expensive. Therefore not everything is made of gold or silver. *(Gx, Ex, Wx, Sx)*

7. There is nothing made of tin that is not cheap. No rings are made of lead. Not everything is either tin or lead. Therefore not all rings are cheap. *(Tx, Cx, Rx, Lx)*

8. Some prize fighters are aggressive but not intelligent. All prize fighters wear gloves. Prize fighters are not all aggressive. Any slugger is aggressive. Therefore not every slugger wears gloves. *(Px, Ax, Ix, Gx, Sx)*

9. Some photographers are skillful but not imaginative. Only artists are photographers. Photographers are not all skillful. Any journeyman is skillful. Therefore not every artist is a journeyman. *(Px, Sx, Ix, Ax, Jx)*

*10. A book is interesting only if it is well written. A book is well written only if it is interesting. Therefore any book is both interesting and well written if it is either interesting or well written. *(Bx, Ix, Wx)*

IV. Do the same (as in set III) for each of the following.

*1. All citizens who are not traitors are present. All officials are citizens. Some officials are not present. Therefore there are traitors. *(Cx, Tx, Px, Ox)*

2. Doctors and lawyers are professional people. Professional people and executives are respected. Therefore doctors are respected. *(Dx, Lx, Px, Ex, Rx)*

3. Only lawyers and politicians are members. Some members are not college graduates. Therefore some lawyers are not college graduates. *(Lx, Px, Mx, Cx)*

4. All cut-rate items are either shopworn or out of date. Nothing shopworn is worth buying. Some cut-rate items are worth buying. Therefore some cut-rate items are out of date. *(Cx, Sx, Ox, Wx)*

*5. Some diamonds are used for adornment. Only things worn as jewels or applied as cosmetics are used for adornment. Diamonds are never applied as cosmetics. Nothing worn as a jewel is properly used if it has an industrial application. Some diamonds have industrial applications. Therefore some diamonds are not properly used. *(Dx, Ax, Jx, Cx, Px, Ix)*

6. No candidate who is either endorsed by labor or opposed by the *Tribune* can carry the farm vote. No one can be elected who does not carry the farm vote. Therefore no candidate endorsed by labor can be elected. *(Cx, Lx, Ox, Fx, Ex)*

7. No metal is friable that has been properly tempered. No brass is properly tempered unless it is given an oil immersion. Some of the ash trays on the shelf are brass. Everything on the shelf is friable.

Brass is a metal. Therefore some of the ash trays were not given an oil immersion. (*Mx: x* is metal; *Fx: x* is friable; *Tx: x* is properly tempered; *Bx: x* is brass; *Ox: x* is given an oil immersion; *Ax: x* is an ash tray; *Sx: x* is on the shelf.)

8. Anyone on the committee who knew the nominee would vote for the nominee if free to do so. Everyone on the committee was free to vote for the nominee except those who were either instructed not to by the party caucus or had pledged support to someone else. Everyone on the committee knew the nominee. No one who knew the nominee had pledged support to anyone else. Not everyone on the committee voted for the nominee. Therefore the party caucus had instructed some members of the committee not to vote for the nominee. (*Cx: x* is on the committee; *Kx: x* knows the nominee; *Vx: x* votes for the nominee; *Fx: x* is free to vote for the nominee; *Ix: x* is instructed by the party caucus not to vote for the nominee; *Px: x* had pledged support to someone else.)

9. All logicians are deep thinkers and effective writers. To write effectively one must be economical if one's audience is general, and comprehensive if one's audience is technical. No deep thinker has a technical audience if he has the ability to reach a general audience. Some logicians are comprehensive rather than economical. Therefore not all logicians have the ability to reach a general audience. (*Lx: x* is a logician; *Dx: x* is a deep thinker; *Wx: x* is an effective writer; *Ex: x* is economical; *Gx: x*'s audience is general; *Cx: x* is comprehensive; *Tx: x*'s audience is technical; *Ax: x* has the ability to reach a general audience.)

*10. Some criminal robbed the Russell mansion. Whoever robbed the Russell mansion either had an accomplice among the servants or had to break in. To break in, one would either have to smash the door or pick the lock. Only an expert locksmith could have picked the lock. Had anyone smashed the door, he would have been heard. Nobody was heard. If the criminal who robbed the Russell mansion managed to fool the guard, he must have been a convincing actor. No one could rob the Russell mansion unless he fooled the guard. No criminal could be both an expert locksmith and a convincing actor. Therefore some criminal had an accomplice among the servants. (*Cx: x* is a criminal; *Rx: x* robbed the Russell mansion; *Sx: x* had an accomplice among the servants; *Bx: x* broke in; *Dx: x* smashed the door; *Px: x* picked the lock; *Lx: x* is an expert locksmith; *Hx: x* was heard; *Fx: x* fooled the guard; *Ax: x* is a convincing actor.)

11. If anything is expensive it is both valuable and rare. Whatever is valuable is both desirable and expensive. Therefore if anything is either valuable or expensive then it must be both valuable and expensive. (*Ex: x* is expensive; *Vx: x* is valuable; *Rx: x* is rare; *Dx: x* is desirable.)

12. Figs and grapes are healthful. Nothing healthful is either illaudable or jejune. Some grapes are jejune and knurly. Some figs are not knurly. Therefore some figs are illaudable. (*Fx: x* is a fig; *Gx: x* is a grape; *Hx: x* is healthful; **Ix: x** is illaudable; *Jx: x* is jejune; *Kx: x* is knurly.)

13. Figs and grapes are healthful. Nothing healthful is both illaudable and jejune. Some grapes are jejune and knurly. Some figs are not knurly. Therefore some figs are not illaudable. (*Fx: x* is a fig; *Gx: x* is a grape; *Hx: x* is healthful; *Ix: x* is illaudable; *Jx: x* is jejune; *Kx: x* is knurly.)

14. Gold is valuable. Rings are ornaments. Therefore gold rings are valuable ornaments. (*Gx: x* is gold; *Vx: x* is valuable; *Rx: x* is a ring; *Ox: x* is an ornament.)

*15. Oranges are sweet. Lemons are tart. Therefore oranges and lemons are sweet or tart. (*Ox: x* is an orange; *Sx: x* is sweet; *Lx: x* is a lemon; *Tx: x* is tart.)

16. Socrates is mortal. Therefore everything is either mortal or not mortal. (*s:* Socrates; *Mx: x* is mortal.)

Summary of Chapter 10

In Chapter 10 we have been dealing with deductive arguments whose constituent propositions are not compound, and whose validity or invalidity depends on the inner logical structure of these noncompound propositions.

In section 10.1, we explained **singular propositions** and introduced the symbols for an individual variable x, for individual constants (lowercase letters a through w), and for attributes (capital letters). We introduced the concept of a *propositional function:* **an expression that contains an individual variable and becomes a statement when an individual constant is substituted for the individual variable.** A proposition may thus be obtained from a propositional function by the process of **instantiation.**

In section 10.2, we explained how propositions also can be obtained from propositional functions by means of **generalization,** that is, by the use of **quantifiers** such as "everything," "nothing," and "some." We introduced the **universal quantifier *(x)*,** meaning "given any x," and the **existential quantifier ($\exists x$),** meaning "there is at least one x such that." On a Square of Opposition, we showed the relations between universal and existential quantification.

In section 10.3, we showed how each of the four main types of general propositions—

- **A:** Universal affirmative propositions
- **E:** Universal negative propositions
- **I:** Particular affirmative propositions
- **O:** Particular negative propositions

—is correctly symbolized by propositional functions and quantifiers. We also explained the modern interpretation of the relations of **A, E, I,** and **O** propositions.

In section 10.4, we expanded the list of rules of inference, adding four additional rules:

- Universal Instantiation, **UI**
- Universal Generalization, **UG**
- Existential Instantiation, **EI**
- Existential Generalization, **EG**

and showed how, by using these and the other 19 rules earlier set forth, we can construct **a formal proof of validity** of deductive arguments that depend on the inner structure of noncompound propositions.

In section 10.5, we explained how the method of refutation by logical analogy can be used to prove the **invalidity** of arguments involving quantifiers by creating a model, or **possible universe,** containing exactly one, or exactly two, or exactly three (etc.) individuals and the restatement of the constituent propositions of an argument in that possible universe. An argument involving quantifiers is proved invalid if we can exhibit a possible universe containing at least one individual, such that the argument's premisses are true and its conclusion is false in that universe.

In section 10.6, we explained how we can symbolize and evaluate **asyllogistic arguments,** those containing propositions **not reducible to A, E, I, and O propositions, or singular propositions.** We noted the complexity of **exceptive** propositions and other propositions whose logical meaning must first be understood and then rendered accurately with propositional functions and quantifiers.

PART THREE

INDUCTION

The contrary of every matter of fact is still possible, because it can never imply a contradiction, and is conceived by the mind with the same facility and distinctness, as if ever so conformable to reality. That the sun will not rise tomorrow is no less intelligible a proposition, and implies no more contradiction than the affirmation, that it will rise. . . . It may, therefore, be a subject worthy of curiosity, to enquire what is the nature of that evidence which assures us of any real existence and matter of fact, beyond the present testimony of our senses, or the records of our memory.

—David Hume

He that knows anything, knows this, in the first place, that he need not seek long for instances of his ignorance.

—John Locke

In reality, all arguments from experience are founded on the similarity which we discover among natural objects, and by which we are induced to expect effects similar to those which we have found to follow from such objects.
—David Hume

Though analogy is often misleading, it is the least misleading thing we have.
—Samuel Butler

Analogies prove nothing, that is quite true, but they can make one feel more at home.
—Sigmund Freud

CHAPTER 11

ANALOGY AND
PROBABLE INFERENCE

11.1 ARGUMENT BY ANALOGY

The preceding chapters have dealt with deductive arguments, which are valid if their premises establish their conclusions *demonstratively*, but invalid otherwise. There are very many good and important arguments, however, whose conclusions cannot be proved with certainty. Many causal connections in which we rightly place confidence can be established only with *probability*—though the degree of probability may be very high. Thus we can say without reservation that smoking is a cause of cancer, but we cannot ascribe to that knowledge the kind of certainty that we ascribe to our knowledge that the conclusion of a valid deductive argument is entailed by its premises. On that deductive standard, one distinguished medical investigator observes, "No one will ever be able to *prove* that smoking causes cancer, or that anything causes anything. Theoretically, you can never *prove* anything."[1] Deductive certainty is, indeed, too high a standard to impose when evaluating our knowledge of facts about the world.

In this and the following chapters we turn to the analysis of arguments that are not claimed to demonstrate the truth of their conclusions as following necessarily from their premises, but are intended merely to support their conclusions as *probable,* or probably true. Arguments of this latter kind are generally called *inductive,* and they are radically different from the deductive variety. The fundamental distinction between deduction and induction was discussed at some length in our opening chapter. Part Two of this book has been devoted to deduction; Part Three will be devoted to induction.

---

[1]Bert Vogelstein, "So, Smoking Causes Cancer: This is News?" *New York Times,* 27 October 1996. (Emphasis added.)

Of all inductive arguments there is one type that is most commonly used: argument by *analogy*. Two examples of analogical arguments are these:

> Some people look on preemployment testing of teachers as unfair—a kind of double jeopardy. "Teachers are already college graduates," they say. "Why should they be tested?" That's easy. Lawyers are college graduates and graduates of professional school, too, but they have to take a bar exam. And a number of other professions ask prospective members to prove that they know their stuff by taking and passing examinations: accountants, actuaries, doctors, architects. There is no reason why teachers shouldn't be required to do this too.[2]

> We may observe a very great similitude between this earth which we inhabit, and the other planets, Saturn, Jupiter, Mars, Venus, and Mercury. They all revolve round the sun, as the earth does, although at different distances and in different periods. They borrow all their light from the sun, as the earth does. Several of them are known to revolve around their axis like the earth, and by that means, must have a like succession of day and night. Some of them have moons, that serve to give them light in the absence of the sun, as our moon does to us. They are all, in their motions, subject to the same law of gravitation, as the earth is. From all this similitude, it is not unreasonable to think that those planets may, like our earth, be the habitation of various orders of living creatures. There is some probability in this conclusion from analogy.[3]

Most of our own everyday inferences are by analogy. Thus, I infer that a new computer will serve me well on the grounds that I got very good service from a computer earlier purchased from the same manufacturer. If a new book by a certain author is called to my attention, I infer that I will enjoy reading it on the basis of having read and enjoyed other books by that author. Analogy is at the basis of most of our ordinary reasonings from past experience to what the future will hold. Not an explicitly formulated argument, of course, but something very much like analogical inference is presumably involved in the conduct of the burned child who shuns the fire.

None of these arguments is certain or demonstratively valid. None of their conclusions follows with logical necessity from their premises. It is logically possible that what is appropriate for judging the employability of lawyers and doctors is not appropriate for judging the employability of teachers. It is logically possible that earth may be the only inhabited planet, that the new computer may not work well at all, and that I may find my favorite author's latest book to be intolerably dull. It is even logically possible that one fire may burn and not another. But no argument by analogy is intended to be mathematically certain. Analogical arguments are not to be classified as either valid or invalid. Probability is all that is claimed for them.

In addition to their frequent use in arguments, analogies very often are used nonargumentatively, for the purpose of lively description. The literary

---

[2]Albert Shanker, "Testing Teachers," *New York Times,* 8 January 1995.
[3]Thomas Reid, *Essays on the Intellectual Powers of Man,* Essay 1, 1785.

uses of analogy in metaphor and simile are tremendously helpful to the writer who strives to create a vivid picture in the reader's mind. For example:

> Life on this earth is not only without rational significance, but also apparently unintentional. The cosmic laws seem to have been set going for some purpose quite unrelated to human existence. Man is thus a sort of accidental by-product, as the sparks are an accidental by-product of the horseshoe a blacksmith fashions on his anvil. The sparks are far more brilliant than the horseshoe, but all the same they remain essentially meaningless.[4]

Analogy also is used in explanation, where something that may be unfamiliar to the reader is made somewhat more intelligible through being compared to something else, presumably more familiar, to which it has certain similarities. When the Director of the Genome Center at the Massachusetts Institute of Technology Dr. Eric Lander sought to explain the great eventual impact of the human genome project, analogy was one of the devices he used to enhance the understanding of those unfamiliar with genetic research:

> The genome project is wholly analogous to the creation of the periodic table in chemistry. Just as Mendeleev's arrangement of the chemical elements in the periodic table made coherent a previously unrelated mass of data, so the tens of thousands of genes in present-day organisms will all turn out to be made from combinations of a much smaller number of simpler genetic modules or elements, the primordial genes, so to speak.[5]

The use of analogies in description and explanation is not the same as their use in argument, though in some cases it may not be easy to decide which use is intended. But whether used argumentatively or otherwise, analogy is not difficult to define. **To draw an analogy between two or more entities is to indicate one or more respects in which they are similar.**

This explains what an analogy is, but there is still the problem of characterizing an argument by analogy. Let us examine a particular analogical argument and analyze its structure. Take the simplest of the examples cited thus far, the argument that my new computer will serve me well because my old computer, purchased from the same manufacturer, gave good service. The two things said to be similar are the two computers. There are three points of analogy involved, three respects in which the two entities are said to resemble each other: first, in being computers; second, in being purchased from the same manufacturer; and third, in serving me well.

The three points of analogy do not play identical roles in the argument, however. The first two occur in the premises, whereas the third occurs both in the premises and in the conclusion. In quite general terms, the given argument may be described as having premises that assert, first, that two things are similar in two respects and, second, that one of those things has a further

---

[4]Bertrand Russell, *Religion and Science* (London, Oxford, 1949).
[5]Quoted in an interview in the *New York Times*, 10 September 1996.

characteristic, from which the conclusion is drawn that the other thing also has that further characteristic.

Analogical argument is one of the most fundamental tools of appellate courts. Rather than laying down strict rules or principles in advance, judges very often reason that because two cases—an earlier one that has been decided, and the case at hand to be decided—share relevant characteristics, they should share the same outcome. Thus, once it has been decided that members of the Ku Klux Klan may not be restrained from speaking, a court is likely to conclude by analogical reasoning that the Nazi Party cannot be stopped from parading.[6] This argument from precedent, when it is spelled out, will identify and emphasize those respects in which the older case and the current case are closely alike.

Not every analogical argument need concern exactly two things or exactly three different characteristics, of course. Thus the argument by Thomas Reid presented earlier, suggesting that other planets may well be inhabited, draws analogies among six things (the then-known planets) in some eight respects. Apart from these numerical differences, however, all analogical arguments have the same general structure or pattern. **Every analogical inference proceeds from the similarity of two or more things in one or more respects to the similarity of those things in some further respect.** Schematically, where a, b, c, and d are any entities and P, Q, and R are any attributes or "respects," an analogical argument may be represented as having the form

> a, b, c, d all have the attributes P and Q.
> a, b, c all have the attribute R.
> Therefore d probably has the attribute R.

In identifying, and especially in appraising, analogical arguments, it may be found helpful to recast them into this form.

Exercises

All of the following passages contain analogies. Distinguish those that contain analogical arguments from those that make nonargumentative uses of analogy.

Example:

1. A Man ought no more to value himself for being wiser than a Woman, if he owes his Advantage to a better Education, than he ought to boast of his Courage for beating a Man when his hands were bound.

    —Mary Astell, *An Essay in Defence of the Female Sex*, 1721

---

[6]See Cass R. Sunstein, *Legal Reasoning and Political Conflict* (New York: Oxford University Press, 1996).

Solution:

This is an analogical argument. The analogy drawn here is between beating a man when his hands are bound and being wiser than a woman as a consequence of a better education, one party having an enormous advantage in both cases. In the first case, it is plain that one with such an advantage ought not to boast of his courage; in the second case (this argument concludes), it is equally inappropriate for one with such an advantage to boast of his relative wisdom.

2. "I'm not anti-Semitic, I'm just anti-Zionist" is the equivalent of "I'm not anti-American, I just think the United States shouldn't exist."

   —Benjamin Netanyahu, *A Place Among the Nations,*
   (Bantam Books, 1993)

3. Marriage is in the same state as the Church: Both are becoming functionally defunct, as their preachers go about heralding a revival, eagerly chalking up converts in a day of dread. And just as God has been pronounced dead quite often but has this sneaky way of resurrecting himself, so everyone debunks marriage, yet ends up married.

   —Shulamith Firestone, *The Dialectic of Sex:*
   The Case for Feminist Revolution

4. It is true that science has become so specialized, even a good education in basic science does not prepare one to be expert in all science. But the same is true of nonscientific pursuits. That historians, for example, have become experts in particular periods or areas (the history of the military, perhaps, or of science or economics) has not dissuaded us from teaching history.

   —Bruce J. Sobol, *Current Issues and Enduring Questions*
   (Boston: St. Martin's Press, 1990)

*5. Studies show that girls get better grades in high school and college than boys—yet only about 35 percent of National Merit Scholarship winners are girls. The Executive Director of FairTest contends that the "inequity is due solely to gender bias in the test used to select eligible students." But the spokeswoman for the National Merit Scholarship Corporation, Elaine Detweiler, replies "We don't really know why girls do worse on the exams. To blame the test for the difference between how boys and girls perform is like blaming a yardstick that boys are taller than girls."

   —"Merit Test Defended," *Los Angeles Times,* 26 May 1993

6. The famous chemist and biologist, Justus von Liebig, dismissed the germ theory with a shrug of the shoulders, regarding Pasteur's view that microbes could cause fermentation as ridiculous and naive as the opinion of a child "who would explain the rapidity of

the Rhine current by attributing it to the violent movement of the many millwheels at Maintz."

—René Dubos, *Pasteur and Modern Science*

7. Talking about Christianity without saying anything about sin is like discussing gardening without saying anything about weeds.

—The Rev. Lord Soper, quoted in the *New York Times,* 24 Dec 1998

8. Men and women may have different reproductive strategies, but neither can be considered inferior or superior to the other, any more than a bird's wings can be considered superior or inferior to a fish's fins.

—David M. Buss, "Where is Fancy Bred? In the Genes or in the Head?" the *New York Times,* 1 June 1999

9. "This is a matter of national spirit," said Marjorie Wilson, coordinator of the Kangaroo Protection Cooperative, an Australian wildlife group. "We believe here that we have enough meat in this country to satisfy people without them having to eat their national symbol. You Americans don't cook your bald eagles, do you?"

—"Battling over a National Symbol," *New York Times,* 10 July 1995

*10. One sure thing is that melting sea ice cannot be implicated in the coastal flooding that many global warming models have projected. Just as melting ice cubes do not cause a glass of water to overflow, melting sea ice does not increase oceanic volume. Any future rise in sea level would result from glaciers melting on land, of which there has been little evidence to date.

—Walter Gibbs, "Research Predicts Summer Doom for Northern Icecap," *New York Times,* 11 July 2000.

11. Thomas Henry Huxley, Charles Darwin's nineteenth-century disciple, presented this analogy: "Consciousness would appear to be related to the mechanism of the body simply as a collateral product of its working and to be completely without any power of modifying that working, as the steam whistle which accompanies the work of a locomotive is without influence upon its machinery."

12. The Elgin Marbles—17 figures and 56 panels that once decorated the Parthenon, on the Acropolis in Athens—were taken from the Parthenon in 1801 by Thomas Bruce, the seventh Earl of Elgin, and brought to the British Museum, in London. The Greeks say that he stole them; the British say that they were properly acquired, by purchase. Some Britons have urged that the Marbles be returned to Greece in time for the Olympic Games to be held in Athens in 2004. Said one of the leaders of the Labor Party: "The Parthenon without the Elgin Marbles is like a smile missing a tooth."

13. The Feminists decided to examine the institution of marriage as it is set up by law in order to find out whether or not it did operate in

women's favor. It became increasingly clear to us that the institution of marriage "protects" women in the same way that the institution of slavery was said to "protect" blacks—that is, that the word "protection" in this case is simply a euphemism for oppression.

> —Sheila Cronan, "Marriage," in Anne Koedt, Ellen Levine, and Anita Rapone, eds., *Radical Feminism*

14. Wittgenstein used to compare thinking with swimming: just as in swimming our bodies have a natural tendency to float on the surface so that it requires great physical exertion to plunge to the bottom, so in thinking it requires great mental exertion to force our minds away from the superficial, down into the depth of a philosophical problem.

> —George Pitcher, *The Philosophy of Wittgenstein*

*15. A person without a goal is like a computer without a program. And that's an ugly piece of furniture.

> —Steve Danish, "Getting a Life," *New York Times,* March 1998

16. The quest for usable energy from fusion involves the use of interlocked magnetic fields to contain very hot (180 million degrees Fahrenheit) and highly compressed (to a density 20 times that of lead) electrically charged plasma (a kind of gas) within a vacuum chamber. The plasma must never touch the solid walls of its container, for if it does it instantly loses its heat and can never be coaxed into undergoing fusion. One scientific report put the problem this way:

> Everything depends on keeping the plasma's magnetic bottle tightly stoppered. . . . [but] confining a dollop of super-hot compressed plasma has proved to be harder than compressing and shaping a blob of jelly using only rubber bands. Each clever idea of the plasma physicists for solving this problem has been matched by a new challenge.

> —Malcolm W. Browne, "Reviving the Quest to Tame the Energy of the Stars," *New York Times,* 8 June 1999.

17. It is important that we make clear at this point what definition is and what can be attained by means of it. It seems frequently to be credited with a creative power; but all it accomplishes is that something is marked out in sharp relief and designated by a name. Just as the geographer does not create a sea when he draws boundary lines and says: the part of the ocean's surface bounded by these lines I am going to call the Yellow Sea, so too the mathematician cannot really create anything by his defining.

> —Gottlob Frege, *The Basic Laws of Arithmetic*

18. Children in school are like children at the doctor's. He can talk himself blue in the face about how much good his medicine is going to do them; all they think of is how much it will hurt or how bad it will taste. Given their own way, they would have none of it.

> So the valiant and resolute band of travelers I thought I was leading toward a much hoped-for destination turned out instead to be more like convicts in a chain gang, forced under threat of punishment to move along a rough path leading nobody knew where and down which they could see hardly more than a few steps ahead. School feels like this to children: it is a place where *they* make you go and where *they* tell you to do things and where *they* try to make your life unpleasant if you don't do them or don't do them right.
>
> —John Holt, *How Children Fail*

19. I simply can't imagine the world will ever be normal again for us. I do talk about "after the war," but it's as if I were talking about a castle in the air, something that can never come true.

    I see the eight of us in the Annex as if we were a patch of blue sky surrounded by menacing black clouds. The perfectly round spot on which we're standing is still safe, but the clouds are moving in on us, and the ring between us and the approaching danger is being pulled tighter and tighter. We're surrounded by darkness and danger, and in our desperate search for a way out we keep bumping into each other. We look at the fighting down below and the peace and beauty up above. In the meantime, we've been cut off by the dark mass of clouds, so that we can go neither up nor down. It looms before us like an impenetrable wall, trying to crush us, but not yet able to. I can only cry out and implore, "Oh, ring, ring, open wide and let us out!"

    —Anne Frank, from *The Diary of a Young Girl*, 8 November 1943

*20. Unfortunately, the diary [of H. L. Mencken] reveals a man who was shockingly anti-Semitic and racist, to the point where his stature as a giant of American letters may be in danger. . . . I would draw a comparison with Richard Wagner, a virulent anti-Semite. One can still listen to Wagner's operas and appreciate their artistic beauty. The work is separated from the man. Or is it?

    —Gwinn Owens, "Mencken—Getting a Bum Rap?" *New York Times*, 13 December 1989

11.2   APPRAISING ANALOGICAL ARGUMENTS

No argument by analogy is ever deductively valid, in the sense of having its conclusion follow from its premises with logical necessity, but some analogical arguments are more cogent than others. Analogical arguments are evaluated as better or worse depending on the degree of probability with which their conclusions may be affirmed.

Two commonplace examples will help us to see what serves to make analogical arguments more (or less) effective. Suppose you choose to purchase a given pair of shoes because other pairs like it have given you satisfaction in the past; and suppose you select a dog of a given breed because other dogs of that same breed have exhibited the characteristics that you prize. In both cases analogical arguments have been relied upon. To appraise the strength of these sample arguments, and indeed all analogical arguments, six criteria may be distinguished.

1. **Number of entities.** If my past experience with shoes of a certain kind is limited to only one pair that I wore and liked, I will be disappointed with an apparently similar pair that I find flawed in unexpected ways. But if I have repeatedly purchased shoes just like those, I may reasonably suppose that the next pair will be as good as the ones worn earlier. Several experiences of the same kind with the same item will support the conclusion—that the purchase will be satisfying—much more than will a single instance. Each instance may be thought of as an additional entity, and the *number* of entities is the first criterion in evaluating an analogical argument.

   In general, the larger the number of entities—that is, cases in our past experience—the stronger the argument. But there is no simple ratio between that number and the probability of the conclusion. Six happy experiences with golden retrievers, intelligent and sweet-tempered dogs, will lead one to conclude that the next golden retriever will be intelligent and sweet-tempered also. But the conclusion of the analogical argument having six instances in its premisses will not be exactly three times as probable as a similar argument with two such instances in its premisses. Increasing the number of entities is important, but other factors enter as well.

2. **Variety of the instances in the premisses.** If my previous purchases of those good shoes had been both from a department store and a specialty store, and had been made both in New York and in California, by both mail order and direct sale, I may be confident that it is the shoes themselves and not their seller that accounts for my satisfaction. If my previous golden retrievers were both males and females, acquired both as puppies from breeders and as adults from the humane society, I may be more confident that it is their breed—not their sex or age or source—that accounts for my earlier satisfaction.

   We understand this criterion intuitively: *The more dissimilar the instances mentioned only in the premisses of the analogical argument, the stronger is the argument.*

3. **Number of similar respects.** Among the instances in the premisses there may have been various similarities: perhaps the shoes were of the same style, had the same price, were made of the same sort of leather; perhaps the dogs were of the same breed, came from the same breeder at the same age, and so on. All the respects in which the instances in the premisses are like one another, and also like the instance in the conclusion, increase the probability that the instance in the conclusion will have that further attribute at which the argument is aimed—giving great satisfaction in the case of the new shoes, being of a sweet disposition in the case of a new dog.

   This criterion also is rooted in common sense: *The greater the number of respects in which the entity in the conclusion is similar to the entities in the premisses, the more probable is that conclusion.* But again, of course, there is no simple numerical ratio between that conclusion and the number of similar respects identified.

4.   **Relevance.** As important as the *number* of respects shared is the *kind* of respects in which the instances in the premises are like the instance in the conclusion. If the new pair of shoes, like the previous pairs, is purchased on a Tuesday, that is a likeness that will have no bearing on the satisfaction they give; but if the new pair, like all the previous pairs, had the same manufacturer, that will of course count heavily. *Respects add to the force of the argument when they are relevant* (as style of shoe, and price, and material surely are)—*and a single highly relevant factor contributes more to the argument than a host of irrelevant similarities.*

There will sometimes be disagreement about which attributes really are relevant in establishing the likelihood of our conclusion. But the *meaning* of relevance itself is not in dispute. One attribute is relevant to another when it is connected to that other, when there is some kind of *causal relation* between them. That is why identifying causal connections of one kind or another is critical in analogical arguments, and why establishing such connections is often crucial in determining the admissibility of evidence, as relevant or irrelevant, in a court of law.

Analogical arguments can be probable whether they go from cause to effect or from effect to cause. They can even be probable when the attribute in the premiss is neither the cause nor the effect of the conclusion's attribute, provided both are the effect of the same cause. A doctor, noting the presence of a certain symptom in her patient, may predict another symptom accurately not because either symptom is the cause of the other, but because they are jointly caused by the same disorder. The color of a manufactured product is most often irrelevant to function, but it may serve as a relevant respect in an argument when that color is very unusual, and shared by the entities in the premises and the conclusion. The color itself may contribute nothing to the function of the product—but it may serve in argument if it is known to be an attribute of the manufacturing process of a unique producer.

The causal connections that are the key to the evaluation of analogical arguments can be discovered only empirically, by observation and experiment. The general theory of empirical investigation is the central concern of inductive logic, and will be discussed at length in the chapters that follow.

5.   **Disanalogies.** A disanalogy is a point of difference, a respect in which the case we are reasoning about in our conclusion is distinguishable from the cases upon which the argument is based. Returning to the example of the shoes: if the pair we plan to buy looks like those we had earlier owned, but is in fact much cheaper and made by a different company, those disanalogies will give us reason to doubt the satisfaction they will provide.

What was earlier said about relevance is important here also. Disanalogies undermine analogical arguments when the points of difference identified are relevant, causally connected to the outcome we are seeking. Investors often purchase shares of a stock mutual fund on the basis of its successful "track record," reasoning that since earlier purchases resulted in capital appreciation, a future purchase will do so as well. But if we learn that the person who had managed the fund during the period of its profitability has just been replaced, we confront a disanalogy substantially reducing the strength of that analogical argument.

Disanalogies weaken analogical arguments. They will therefore be commonly employed in *attacking* an analogical argument. As critics we may try to show that the case in the conclusion is different in important ways from the earlier cases, and that what was true of them is not likely to be true of it. In the law, where the uses of analogy are pervasive, some earlier case (or cases) will commonly be offered to a court as a precedent for deciding the case at hand. The argument is analogical. Opposing counsel will seek to *distinguish* the case at hand from the earlier cases; that is, counsel will seek to show that because there is some critical difference between the facts in the case at hand, and the facts in those earlier cases, they do not serve as good precedents in the present matter. If the differences are great, if the disanalogy is indeed critical, it may succeed in demolishing the analogical argument that had been put forward.

Because disanalogies are the primary weapon against an analogical argument, whatever can ward off any potential disanalogies will strengthen that argument. This explains why variety among the instances in the premisses adds force to an argument, as noted previously in the second criterion. The more the instances in the premisses vary from one to another, the less likely it is that the critic can point to some disanalogy between all of them and the conclusion that will weaken the argument. To illustrate: Kim Kumar comes to a university as a first year student; ten others from her secondary school had successfully completed studies at the same university. We may argue analogically that she is likely to succeed as well. If all those other students are similar to one another in some respect that bears upon college study but differ from Kim in that respect, that disanalogy will undermine the argument for Kim's success. But if we learn that the ten successful predecessors varied among themselves in many ways—in economic background, in family relations, in religious affiliation, and so on, those differences among them ward off such potential disanalogies. The argument for Kim's success is fortified—as we saw earlier—if the other students from her school serving as premisses in the argument do not resemble each other closely, but exhibit substantial variety.

A confusion must be avoided: The principle that disanalogies weaken analogical arguments is to be contrasted with the principle that differences among the premisses strengthen such arguments. In the former, the differences are between the instances in the premisses and the instance in the conclusion; in the latter differences are among the instances in the premisses only. A disanalogy is a difference between the cases with which we have had experience and the case about which a conclusion is being drawn. That conclusion (we may say in presenting the disanalogy as refutation) is not warranted because circumstances in the critical case are not similar to circumstances in earlier cases. The analogy is said to be "strained" or "does not hold." But when we point to dissimilarities among the premisses we are strengthening the argument by saying, in effect, that the analogy has wide force, that it holds in cases like this and in other cases, and that therefore the respects in which the instances in the premisses vary are not relevant to the matter with which the conclusion is concerned.

In sum: Disanalogies undermine an analogical argument; dissimilarities among the premisses reinforce it. And both considerations are tied to the question of relevance: Disanalogies tend to show that there are relevant respects in which the case in the conclusion differs from those in the premisses; dissimilarities among the premisses tend to show that what might have been thought causally relevant to the attribute of interest is not really relevant at all.

Note that the very first criterion identified, pertaining to the *number* of entities among which the analogy is said to hold, is also linked to relevance. The greater the number of instances appealed to, the greater the number of dissimilarities likely to obtain among them. Increasing the number of entities is therefore desirable—but as the number of entities increases, the impact of each additional case is reduced, since the dissimilarity it may provide is the more likely to have been provided by earlier instances—in which case it will add little or nothing to the protection of the conclusion from damaging disanalogies.

6. **Claim that the conclusion makes.** Every argument makes the claim that its premisses give reasons to accept its conclusion. It is easy to see that the more one claims, the greater the burden of sustaining that claim, and that is obviously true for every analogical argument. The *modesty of the conclusion relative to the premisses* is critical in determining the merit of the inference.

    If my friend gets 30 miles to the gallon from his new car, I may infer that were I to acquire a car of the same make and model I would get at least 20 miles to the gallon; that conclusion is modest and therefore very probable. Were my conclusion much bolder—say, that I would get at least 29 miles to the gallon—it would be less well supported by the evidence I have. In general, *the more modest the claim the less burden is placed upon the premisses and the stronger the argument; the bolder the claim the greater is burden on the premisses and the weaker the argument.*

    An analogical argument is strengthened by reducing the claim made on the basis of the premisses affirmed, or by retaining the claim unchanged while supporting it with additional or more powerful premisses. Likewise, an analogical argument is weakened if its conclusion is made bolder while its premisses remain unchanged, or if the claim remains unchanged while the evidence in its support is found to exhibit greater frailty.

Exercises

I.   For each of the following arguments by analogy, six additional premisses are suggested. For each of these alternative premisses, decide whether its addition would make the resulting argument more or less probable. Identify the criterion of appraisal that justifies this judgment, and explain how that criterion applies to the given case.

Example:

1. An investor has purchased one hundred shares of oil stock every December for the past five years. In every case the value of the stock has appreciated by about 15 percent a year, and it has paid regular dividends of about 8 percent a year on the price at which she bought it. This December she decides to buy another hundred shares of oil stock, reasoning that she will probably receive modest earnings while watching the value of her new purchase increase over the years.

    a. Suppose that she had always purchased stock in eastern oil companies before, and plans to purchase stock in an eastern oil company this year too.

    b. Suppose that she had purchased oil stocks every December for the past 15 years, instead of for only 5 years.

    c. Suppose that the oil stocks previously purchased had gone up by 30 percent a year, instead of only 15 percent.

    d. Suppose that her previous purchases of oil stock had been in foreign companies as well as in eastern, southern, and western American oil companies.

    e. Suppose she learns that OPEC has decided to meet every month instead of every six months.

    f. Suppose she discovers that tobacco stocks have just raised their dividend payments.

Solution:

    a. More probable. **Number of similar respects.** The change provides an additional respect in which the instance in the conclusion is the same as those in the premisses.

    b. More probable. **Number of entities.** With this change the number of entities in the premisses is substantially increased.

    c. More probable. **Claim made by the conclusion.** With this change in the premisses, the conclusion, although unchanged, is now, relatively speaking, substantially more modest.

    d. More probable. **Variety among the premisses.** With this change, the dissimilarity among the instances in the premisses is clearly established.

    e. Less probable. **Disanalogy.** With this change in the premisses, a significant difference between the instance in the conclusion and the instances in the premisses is introduced.

    f. Neither. **Relevance.** It is unlikely that the dividends paid by tobacco companies would have any relevance to the profitability of oil companies or the price of their shares.

2. A faithful alumnus, heartened by State's winning its last four football games, decides to bet his money that State will win its next game, too.

    a. Suppose that since the last game, State's outstanding quarterback was injured in practice and hospitalized for the remainder of the season.

    b. Suppose that two of the last four games were played away, and that two of them were home games.

c. Suppose that, just before the game, it is announced that a member of State's Chemistry Department has been awarded a Nobel Prize.

d. Suppose that State had won its last *six* games rather than only four of them.

e. Suppose that it has rained hard during each of the four preceding games, and that rain is forecast for next Saturday too.

f. Suppose that each of the last four games was won by a margin of at least four touchdowns.

3. Although she was bored by the last few foreign films she saw, Charlene agrees to go to see another one this evening, fully expecting to be bored again.

a. Suppose that Charlene also was bored by the last few American movies she saw.

b. Suppose that the star of this evening's film has recently been accused of bigamy.

c. Suppose that the last few foreign films seen by Charlene were Italian, and that tonight's film is Italian as well.

d. Suppose that Charlene was so bored by the other foreign films that she actually fell asleep during the performance.

e. Suppose that the last few foreign films she saw included an Italian, a French, an English, and a Swedish film.

f. Suppose that tonight's film is a mystery, whereas all of those she saw before were comedies.

4. Bill has taken three history courses and found them very stimulating and valuable. So he signs up for another one, confidently expecting that it too will be worthwhile.

a. Suppose that his previous history courses were in ancient history, modern European history, and American history.

b. Suppose that his previous history courses had all been taught by the same professor that is scheduled to teach the present one.

c. Suppose that his previous history courses all had been taught by Professor Smith, and the present one is taught by Professor Jones.

d. Suppose that Bill had found his three previous history courses to be the most exciting intellectual experiences of his life.

e. Suppose that his previous history courses had all met at 9 A.M., and that the present one is scheduled to meet at 9 A.M. also.

f. Suppose that, in addition to the three history courses previously taken, Bill also had taken and enjoyed courses in anthropology, economics, political science, and sociology.

*5. Dr. Brown has stayed at the Queen's Hotel every fall for the past six years on her annual visit to New York, and she has been quite satisfied with her accommodations there. On her visit to New York this fall, Dr. Brown goes again to the Queen's Hotel, confidently expecting to enjoy her stay there again.

a. Suppose that when she stayed at the Queen's Hotel before, she had occupied a single room twice, shared a double room twice, and twice occupied a suite.

    b. Suppose that last spring a new manager had been put in charge of the Queen's Hotel.

    c. Suppose that she had occupied a suite on all of her previous trips and is assigned a suite this time as well.

    d. Suppose that on her previous trips she had come to New York by train, but this time she flew.

    e. Suppose that, when she stayed at the Queen's Hotel before, her quarters had been the most luxurious she had ever known.

    f. Suppose that she had stayed at the Queen's Hotel three times a year for the past six years.

II. Analyze the structures of the analogical arguments in the following passages, and evaluate them in terms of the six criteria that have been explained.

    *1. If you cut up a large diamond into little bits, it will entirely lose the value it had as a whole; and an army divided up into small bodies of soldiers, loses all its strength. So a great intellect sinks to the level of an ordinary one, as soon as it is interrupted and disturbed, its attention distracted and drawn off from the matter in hand: for its superiority depends upon its power of concentration—of bringing all its strength to bear upon one theme, in the same way as a concave mirror collects into one point all the rays of light that strike upon it.

        —Arthur Schopenhauer, "On Noise"

    2. Every species of plant or animal is determined by a pool of germ plasm that has been most carefully selected over a period of hundreds of millions of years. We can understand now why it is that mutations in these carefully selected organisms almost invariably are detrimental. The situation can be suggested by a statement made by Dr. J. B. S. Haldane: My clock is not keeping perfect time. It is conceivable that it will run better if I shoot a bullet through it; but it is much more probable that it will stop altogether. Professor George Beadle, in this connection, has asked "What is the chance that a typographical error would improve *Hamlet?*"

        —Linus Pauling, *No More War!*

    3. Look round the world: contemplate the whole and every part of it: you will find it to be nothing but one great machine, subdivided into an infinite number of lesser machines, which again admit of subdivisions, to a degree beyond what human senses and faculties can trace and explain. All these various machines, and even their most minute parts, are adjusted to each other with an accuracy, which ravishes into admiration all men, who have ever contemplated them. The curious adapting of means to ends, throughout all nature, resembles exactly, though it much exceeds, the production of human contrivance; of human design, thought, wisdom, and intelligence. Since therefore the effects resemble each other, we are led to infer, by all the rules of analogy, that the causes also resemble; and that the Author of Nature is somewhat similar to the mind of men; though possessed of much larger faculties, proportioned to the grandeur of the work, which he has executed. By this argument *a posteriori,* and by this argument alone, do we prove at once the existence of a Deity, and his similarity to human mind and intelligence.

— David Hume, *Dialogues Concerning Natural Religion,* 1779

4. The philosopher Metrodorus of Chios, who lived in the fourth century B.C., was greatly interested in the heavenly bodies. He wrote: "To consider the Earth as the only populated world in infinite space is as absurd as to assert that in an entire field of millet, only one grain will grow."

*5. To the casual observer porpoises and sharks are kinds of fish. They are streamlined, good swimmers, and live in the sea. To the zoologist who examines these animals more closely, the shark has gills, cold blood, and scales; the porpoise has lungs, warm blood, and hair. The porpoise is fundamentally more like man than like the shark and belongs, with man, to the mammals—a group that nurses its young with milk. Having decided that the porpoise is a mammal, the zoologist can, without further examination, predict that the animal will have a four-chambered heart, bones of a particular type, and a certain general pattern of nerves and blood vessels. Without using a microscope the zoologist can say with reasonable confidence that the red blood cells in the blood of the porpoise will lack nuclei. This ability to generalize about animal structure depends upon a system for organizing the vast amount of knowledge about animals.

— Ralph Buchsbaum, *Animals without Backbones*

6. The body is the substance of the soul; the soul is the functioning of the body. . . . The relationship of the soul to its substance is like that of sharpness to a knife, while the relationship of the body to its functioning is like that of a knife to sharpness. What is called sharpness is not the same as the knife, and what is called the knife is not the same as sharpness. Nevertheless, there can be no knife if the sharpness is discarded, nor sharpness if the knife is discarded. I have never heard of sharpness surviving if the knife is destroyed, so how can it be admitted that the soul can remain if the body is annihilated?

— Fan Chen, *Essay on the Extinction of the Soul,* in Fung Yu-Lan, *A History of Chinese Philosophy*

7. If a single cell, under appropriate conditions, becomes a person in the space of a few years, there can surely be no difficulty in understanding how, under appropriate conditions, a cell may, in the course of untold millions of years, give origin to the human race.

— Herbert Spencer, *Principles of Biology*

8. An electron is no more (and no less) hypothetical than a star. Nowadays we count electrons one by one in a Geiger counter, as we count the stars one by one on a photographic plate. In what sense can an electron be called more unobservable than a star? I am not sure whether I ought to say that I have seen an electron; but I have just the same doubt whether I have seen a star. If I have seen one, I have seen the other. I have seen a small disc of light surrounded by diffraction rings which has not the least resemblance to what a star is supposed to be; but the name "star" is given to the object in the physical world which some hundreds of years ago started a chain of causation which has resulted in this particular light-pattern. Similarly in a Wilson expansion chamber I have seen a trail not in the least resembling what an electron is supposed to be; but the name "electron" is given to the object in the physical world which has caused this trail to appear. How can it possibly be maintained that a hypothesis is introduced in one case and not in the other?

—Arthur Eddington, *New Pathways in Science*

9. Just as the bottom of a bucket containing water is pressed more heavily by the weight of the water when it is full than when it is half empty, and the more heavily the deeper the water is, similarly the high places of the earth, such as the summits of mountains, are less heavily pressed than the lowlands are by the weight of the mass of the air. This is because there is more air above the lowlands than above the mountain tops; for all the air along a mountain side presses upon the lowlands but not upon the summit, being above the one but below the other.

—Blaise Pascal, *Treatise on the Weight of the Mass of the Air*

*10. Suppose that someone tells me that he has had a tooth extracted without an anaesthetic, and I express my sympathy, and suppose that I am then asked, "How do you know that it hurt him?" I might reasonably reply, "Well, I know that it would hurt me. I have been to the dentist and know how painful it is to have a tooth stopped [filled] without an anaesthetic, let alone taken out. And he has the same sort of nervous system as I have. I infer, therefore, that in these conditions he felt considerable pain, just as I should myself."

—Alfred J. Ayer, "One's Knowledge of Other Minds," *Theoria*, 1953

11. Now if we survey the universe, so far as it falls under our knowledge, it bears a great resemblance to an animal or organized body and seems actuated with a like principle of life and motion. A continual circulation of matter in it produces no disorder: a continual waste in every part is incessantly repaired; the closest sympathy is perceived throughout the entire system: and each part or member, in performing its proper offices, operates both to its own

preservation and to that of the whole. The world, therefore, I infer, is an animal, and the Deity is the *soul* of the world, actuating
it, and actuated by it.

—David Hume, *Dialogues Concerning Natural Religion*

12. One cannot require that everything shall be defined, any more than
one can require that a chemist shall decompose every substance.
What is simple cannot be decomposed, and what is logically simple cannot have a proper definition.

—Gottlob Frege, "On Concept and Object"

13. Most endangered or threatened species in the United States find
suitable habitat on private land, and the destruction of habitat is
widely recognized as the leading cause of extinctions. For these
reasons, protecting wildlife without regulating the use of private
land has been compared by biologists to playing the piano with
just the black keys.

—John H. Cushman, Jr., "Environmentalists Gain a Victory,"
New York Times, 30 June 1995

14. Opposing legislation that would restrict handgun ownership in the
United Kingdom, the husband of Queen Elizabeth II reasoned as
follows:

Look, if a cricketer, for instance, suddenly decided to go into a school and
batter a lot of people to death with a cricket bat, which he could do very easily, are you going to ban cricket bats?

—Prince Philip, the duke of Edinburgh, in an interview
on the BBC, 19 December 1996

*15. . . . The simplest form of the theological argument from design [was]
once well known under the name "Paley's watch." Paley's form of it
was just this: "If we found by chance a watch or other piece of intricate mechanism we should infer that it had been made by someone.
But all around us we do find intricate pieces of natural mechanism,
and the processes of the universe are seen to move together in complex relations; we should therefore infer that these too have a Maker."

—B. A. D. Williams, "Metaphysical Arguments,"
in D. F. Pears, ed., *The Nature of Metaphysics*

11.3   REFUTATION BY LOGICAL ANALOGY

"You should say what you mean," [said the March Hare, reproving Alice sharply.]
   "I do," Alice hastily replied; "at least—at least I mean
what I say—that's the same thing, you know."
   "Not the same thing a bit!" said the Hatter.
"Why, you might just as well say that 'I see what I
eat' is the same thing as 'I eat what I see'!"

"You might just as well say," added the March Hare, "that 'I like what I get' is the same thing as 'I get what I like'!"

"You might just as well say," added the Dormouse, which seemed to be talking in its sleep, "that 'I breathe when I sleep' is the same thing as 'I sleep when I breathe'!"

"It *is* the same thing with you," said the Hatter, and here the conversation dropped.

—Lewis Carroll, *Alice's Adventures in Wonderland,* chapter 7

The Hare, the Hatter, and the Dormouse all seek to refute Alice's claim—that meaning what you say is the same as saying what you mean—by using a *logical analogy.* The form of an argument, as distinct from its particular content, is the most important aspect of that argument from a logical point of view. Therefore, we often seek to demonstrate the weakness of a given argument by exhibiting another argument, known to be erroneous, that has the same logical form.

In the realm of deduction, a refuting analogy for a given argument is an argument having the same form as that of the given argument but whose premisses are known to be true and whose conclusion is known to be false. The refuting analogy is therefore known to be invalid, and the argument under attack, because it has the same form, is thus shown to be invalid as well. This is the same principle that underlies the testing of categorical syllogisms explained in section 6.2, and it also underlies the repeated emphasis upon the centrality of logical form, as explained in section 8.4.

In the realm of inductive argument, our present concern, the technique of refutation by logical analogy can also be used to great effect. Scientific, political, or economic arguments, not purporting to be deductive, may be countered by presenting other arguments having very similar design, whose conclusions are known to be false or are generally believed to be improbable. Inductive arguments differ fundamentally from deductive arguments in the character of the support claimed to be given to the conclusion by the premisses. But all arguments, inductive as well as deductive, may be said to have some underlying form or pattern. If, when confronted by an inductive argument we wish to attack, we can present another inductive argument having essentially the same form but one that is clearly flawed and whose conclusion is very doubtful, we throw similar doubt upon the conclusion of the argument under examination.

Consider the following illustration. One common objection to the legalization of assisted suicide is known as the *"slippery slope" argument.* It is essentially the argument that, once formal permission has been given to medical doctors to act in a certain way that is of questionable morality, that will lead to more and greater immoralities of the same general type. The first leniency ought to be avoided, the argument holds, because it must leave us insecure on a slope so slippery that our first step down cannot be our last. To this argument a contemporary critic responds as follows:

The slippery slope argument, although influential, is hard to deal with rationally. It suggests that, once we allow doctors to shorten the life of patients who request it, doctors could and would wantonly kill burdensome patients who do not want to die. This suggestion is not justified.... Physicians often prescribe drugs which, in doses greater than prescribed, would kill the patient. No one fears that the actual doses prescribed will lead to their use of lethal doses. No one objects to such prescriptions in fear of a "slippery slope." Authorizing physicians to assist in shortening the life of patients who request this assistance no more implies authority to shorten the life of patients who want to prolong it, than authority for surgery to remove the gall bladder implies authority to remove the patient's heart.[7]

This is an excellent example of refutation by logical analogy in the inductive sphere. The argument under attack is first presented: If we give physicians the authority to help patients to end their own lives, some will use that authority wantonly and abusively. Therefore, that argument concludes, we ought not take even the first step down that road; we should refuse to give to any doctor the authority to help any patient end his own life.

To this argument a refuting analogy is offered, allegedly of the same form, which relies upon common knowledge, inductively acquired, about the behavior of physicians: We do give physicians authority to take action that could be used abusively. We give physicians the authority to prescribe dangerous drugs which in low doses may be helpful, knowing that they then *could* prescribe those drugs in high doses that would kill their patients. But the fact that such abusive uses of the authority to prescribe such drugs could be the outcome, does not for a moment cause us to regret that such authority has been granted. So it may be seen that the argument which proceeds from the *possible* abuse of authority to its *likely* abuse is (this refutation suggests), at least in so far as the argument is applied to medical doctors, not very persuasive.

The passage quoted above offers a second refutation by analogy, very similar in form: Giving physicians the authority to assist patients who request help in shortening their own lives will lead (according to the argument under attack) to the giving of authority to shorten the lives of patients who really want their lives prolonged. In this case the slippery slope is taken to be one on which not physicians alone, but also the authorizing legislature, will slide.

An allegedly refuting analogy is again presented: Authority now is commonly given to physicians to remove some bodily organ with the consent of the patient. It would be absurd to conclude (the analogy suggests) that this authorization would lead anyone, legislator or physician, to suppose that the granting of such authority includes the right to remove some *other* vital organ concerning which no consent has been given.

In disputation of this kind the focus is upon argument *form*. Defenders of the slippery slope argument are likely to respond to attacks such as those we have cited by contending that the allegedly refuting analogies are not successful, because their form does not correctly mirror the form of the original argument pre-

---

[7]Ernest van den Haag, "Make Mine Hemlock," *National Review,* 12 June 1995.

sented. The controversy no doubt will continue. But the logical technique in question is of great interest: Where an argument does have the same form as that of another under attack, and where that argument offered as a responding analogy is plainly bad, the argument under attack surely is damaged.

The presentation of a refutation by logical analogy is often signaled, in the inductive as in the deductive sphere, by the appearance of some revealing phrase: "you might just as well say," or some other words having that same sense. In the passage quoted above, the telltale phrase, prefacing the (allegedly) damaging analogy there, is "no more implies . . . than . . . ." A slightly different set of words is used in the refuting analogy of a scholar attacking the argument that because Islamic culture had been brought to the country of Chad from without, it is no more than a veneer there. "Chad [you say] has only an 'Islamic overlay.' One could as sensibly say that France has only a 'Christian overlay.'"[8]

When the point of the refuting analogy is manifest, no introductory phrases may be needed. The former governor of Mississippi, Kirk Fordice, argued that "It is a simple fact that the United States is a Christian nation," because "Christianity is the predominant religion in America." The journalist Michael Kinsley, with whom he was debating on television, responded with these telling analogies: "Women are a majority in this country. Does that make us a female country? Or does it make us a white country because most people in this country are white?"[9]

Exercises

Each of the following is intended to be a refutation by logical analogy. Identify the argument being refuted in each and the refuting analogy, and decide whether they do indeed have the same argument form.

1. Steve Brill, founder of Court TV, has no doubt that cameras belong in the courtroom, and answers some critics in the following way: "Some lawyers and judges say that TV coverage makes the system look bad. They confuse the messenger with the message. If press coverage of something makes it look bad, that is a reason to have the press coverage. That criticism is like saying that because journalists were allowed to be with the troops in Vietnam, the Vietnam War was ruined."

    —Steve Brill, "Trial: A Starting Place for Reform,"
    Ann Arbor News, 12 June 1995

2. The whole history of bolshevism, both before and after the October revolution, is full of instances of maneuvering, temporizing and compromising with other parties, bourgeois

---

[8]Bassam K. Abed, in a letter to the *New York Times,* 26 June 1988.
[9]"Evangelical Update," the *New York Times,* 21 November 1992.

parties included! To carry on a war for the overthrow of the international bourgeoisie, a war which is a hundred times more difficult, prolonged and complicated than the most stubborn of ordinary wars between states, and to refuse beforehand to maneuver, to utilize the conflict of interests (even though temporary) among one's enemies, to refuse to temporize and compromise with possible (even though transitory, unstable, vacillating and conditional) allies—is this not ridiculous in the extreme? Is it not as though, when making a difficult ascent of an unexplored and hitherto inaccessible mountain, we were to refuse beforehand ever to move in zigzags, ever to retrace our steps, ever to abandon the course once selected to try others?

—V. I. Lenin, *"Left Wing" Communism: An Infantile Disorder,* 1920

3. To suggest that because early statute writers in the United States were Christians it is therefore a Christian state is like saying that because ancient Romans believed in a pantheon of gods Europeans should today bow at the feet of statues of Jupiter and Juno.

—Jeremy Gilbert, "The Roots of U.S. Law Lead to Rome,"
New York Times, 23 April 1997

4. The argument against new highways is given forceful statement by three distinguished urban planners: The authors write: "The only long term solutions to traffic are public transit and coordinated land use." New highways, they argue, bring "induced traffic." So building more highways will only cause more traffic congestion, not less.[10]

A highly critical reviewer responds to this argument as follows: "This is nonsense. . . . Long lines at a grocery store would not prompt anyone to say, "Well, we can't build any more grocery stores. That would only bring out more customers." Building more highways wouldn't lure cars. The cars come anyway."[11]

*5. America's supply of timber has been increasing for decades, and the nation's forests have three times more wood today than in 1920. "We're not running out of wood, so why do we worry so much about recycling paper?" asks Jerry Taylor, the director of natural research studies at the Cato Institute. "Paper is an agricultural product, made from trees grown specifically for paper production. Acting to conserve trees by recycling paper

---

[10]A. Duany, E. Plater-Zyberk, and J. Speck, *Suburban Nation: The Rise of Sprawl and the Decline of the American Dream* (North Point, 2000).

[11]F. Barnes, "Suburban Beauty: Why Sprawl Works," *The Weekly Standard,* 22 May 2000.

is like acting to conserve cornstalks by cutting back on corn consumption."

—John Tierney, "Recycling Is Garbage,"
New York Times Magazine, 30 June 1996

6. In 1996, heated controversy arose between the states of New Jersey and New York over formal possession of Ellis Island, located at the mouth of the Hudson River near the New Jersey shore, a tiny speck of land on which so many tens of thousands of immigrants to the United States first touched American soil. An essay defending New York's claim to the historic island appeared in the *New York Times* on 23 July 1996. The following letter appeared in the same newspaper four days later:

> Clyde Haberman is right that almost every immigrant who passed through Ellis Island was bound for New York, not New Jersey. But this fact does not determine where the island is. A significant number of passengers arriving at Newark International Airport are also on their way to New York, but it would be hard to argue that New York thus has a claim on the airport. Cincinnati International Airport is in Covington, Kentucky, and presumably, few travelers are on their way to sparsely populated northern Kentucky. Would Mr. Haberman suggest that the airport belongs to Ohio?

7. I'm getting tired of assertions like those of Rep. Ernest Istook, Jr.— "As prayer has gone out of schools, guns, knives, drugs, and gangs have come in"—with the unsupported implication that there is some causal connection between these events. This is the *post hoc ergo propter hoc* fallacy . . . We could just as well say, "After we threw God out of the schools, we put a man on the moon." Students may or may not need more faith, but Congress could certainly use more reason."

—Douglas E. McNeil, "School-Prayer Fallacy,"
New York Times, 10 June 1998

8. The big question is not whether we are a biological species; it's whether that is all we are. For E. O. Wilson in his book *Consilience,* the case is closed. "Virtually all contemporary scientists and philosophers expert on the subject agree that the mind, which comprises consciousness and rational process, is the brain at work. . . . The brain and its satellite glands have now been probed to the point where no particular site remains that can reasonably be supposed to harbor a non-physical mind."

This is on a par with Nikita Krushchev's announcement that Yuri Gagarin, the first human visitor to space, had failed to locate God. Does Wilson really suppose that if there were an immaterial component to the mind it would show up in a brain scan?

—Stephen M. Barr, "Mindless Science," *The Weekly Standard*, 6 April 1998

9. Artificial human minds will never be made (we are told) because "artificial intelligence investigation is based on advanced solid-state physics, whereas the humble human brain is a viable semiliquid system!" That is no more reassuring than the suggestion that automobiles could never replace horses because they are made of metal, while the humble horse is a viable organic system with legs of flesh and bone.

—Michael D. Rohr, *New York Times*, 27 March 1998.

*10. Modern political rhetoric [Ronald Dworkin argues] "is now extremely repetitive," and a good bit of it could be dispensed with—by law. "Every European democracy does this," the world's most highly regarded legal philosopher points out, "and Europeans are amazed that we do not."

Europeans are also amazed that we bathe as frequently as we do. What the hell kind of argument is that?

—David Tell, "Silencing Free Speech in the Name of Reform" *The Weekly Standard*, 25 November 1996

Summary of Chapter 11

In this chapter we began the analysis of inductive arguments, of which analogical arguments are one of the most common kinds.

In section 11.1, we explained argument by analogy. An **analogy is a likeness or comparison;** we draw an analogy when we indicate one or more respects in which two or more entities are similar. An **argument by analogy is an argument in which the similarity of two or more entities in one or more respects is used as the premiss(es); its conclusion is that those entities are similar in some further respect.** Not all analogies are used for purposes of argument; they also may serve some literary effect, or for purposes of explanation. **Because analogical arguments are** *inductive,* **not deductive, the terms "validity" and "invalidity" do not apply to them. The conclusion of an analogical argument, like the conclusion of every inductive argument, has** *some degree of probability,* **but is not claimed to be certain.**

In section 11.2, we explained **six criteria** used in determining whether the premisses of an analogical argument render its conclusion more or less probable. These are:

1. The *number of entities* between which the analogy is said to hold
2. The *variety, or degree of dissimilarity,* among those entities or instances mentioned only in the premisses

3.   The *number of respects* in which the entities involved are said to be analogous
4.   The *relevance* of the respects mentioned in the premisses to the further respect mentioned in the conclusion
5.   The *number and importance of disanalogies* between the instances mentioned only in the premisses and the instance mentioned in the conclusion
6.   The *modesty (or boldness)* of the conclusion relative to the premisses

In section 11.3, we explained **refutation by logical analogy,** an effective method of refuting both inductive and deductive arguments. To show that a given argument is mistaken, one may present another obviously mistaken argument that is very similar in form to the argument under attack.

The induction which proceeds by simple enumeration is childish; its conclusions are precarious, and exposed to peril from a contradictory instance; and it generally decides on too small a number of facts, and on those only which are at hand.
—Francis Bacon

CHAPTER *12*

CAUSAL CONNECTIONS: MILL'S METHODS OF EXPERIMENTAL INQUIRY

12.1 CAUSE AND EFFECT

A. The Meaning of "Cause"

To exercise any measure of control over our environment, we must have some knowledge of causal connections. To cure some disease, for example, physicians must know its *cause,* and they should understand the *effects* (including the "side effects") of the drugs they administer. The relation of cause and effect is of the deepest importance—understanding it, however, is complicated by the fact that there are several different meanings of the word "cause." Therefore we begin by distinguishing these meanings from one another.

It is a fundamental axiom in the study of nature that events do not just happen, but occur only under certain conditions. It is customary to distinguish between the *necessary* and the *sufficient* conditions for the occurrence of an event. **A necessary condition for the occurrence of a specified event is a circumstance in whose absence the event cannot occur.** For example, the presence of oxygen is a necessary condition for combustion to occur: If combustion occurs, then oxygen must have been present, for in the absence of oxygen there can be no combustion.

Although it is a necessary condition, the presence of oxygen is not a sufficient condition for combustion to occur. **A sufficient condition for the occurrence of an event is a circumstance in whose presence the event must occur.** The presence of oxygen is not a sufficient condition for combustion because oxygen can be present without combustion occurring. On the other hand, for

449

almost any substance there is some range of temperature such that *being in that range of temperature in the presence of oxygen* is a sufficient condition for combustion of that substance. It is obvious that there may be several *necessary* conditions for the occurrence of an event, and that they must all be included in the sufficient condition.

The distinction between necessary and sufficient conditions often plays a key role in legal argument. In the U. S. Supreme Court, one justice recently argued that when state funds are used to support religious institutions, that support must meet two conditions: It must be *evenhanded* (distributed on a neutral basis giving no preference to any one religion), *and* it must be *indirect,* since the Constitution bars the direct funding of religious institutions by our government. Of two such aid programs approved earlier, in which services had been provided to persons who were then free to utilize them within religious institutions if they chose to do so, this justice wrote:

> In each the fact that aid was distributed generally and on a neutral basis was a *necessary* condition for upholding the program at issue. But the significance of evenhandedness stops there. We did not, in any of these cases, hold that satisfying the condition was *sufficient,* or dispositive. Quite the contrary. Critical to our decision in these cases was the fact that the aid was indirect; it reached religious institutions only as a result of the genuinely independent and private choices of aid recipients.[1]

The justice draws this distinction because, in the case at hand (in which a state university had refused to pay printing bills for a student religious organization) the state support at issue, even if it were given evenhandedly, would be direct—and was therefore, he argued, impermissible. Acceptable programs of support have two necessary conditions in this judge's view, of which only one was satisfied.

The word "cause" sometimes is used in the sense of "necessary condition" and sometimes in the sense of "sufficient condition." It is most often used in the sense of "necessary condition" when the problem at hand is the elimination of some undesirable phenomenon. To eliminate it, one need only find some condition that is necessary to its existence and then eliminate that condition. Thus, a physician seeks to discover what kind of germ is the "cause" of a certain illness in order to cure the illness by prescribing a drug that will destroy those germs. The germs are said to be the cause of the disease in that they are a necessary condition for it, since in their absence the disease cannot occur.

Failing to attend to this sense of causation can lead to fruitless disputes. Is it genes or the environment that is really the cause of animal behaviors? Most often both play a role, of course, and while neither can by itself account for the activity, both are essential. In songbirds, usually only males sing; when scientists block testosterone in baby male songbirds, they never sing. But they also never sing if, at a precise time in their babyhood, they don't hear their relatives singing. A male baby bird hears a song which starts a process that uses testos-

---

[1] *Rosenberger v. The University of Virginia,* 29 June 1995. Justice David Souter, dissenting, pp. 18–19. (Emphasis added.)

terone to build his brain in such a way that he sings. Both nature and nurture are necessary conditions for the production of songs in birds.[2]

The word "cause" is used in the sense of "sufficient condition" when we are interested in the production of something desired, rather than the elimination of something undesirable. The metallurgist aims to discover what will produce greater strength in metal alloys, and when it is found that a certain process of mixed heating and cooling has that desired result, we say that such a process is the cause of the stronger alloy.

There is another common, but inexact, use of the word "cause" closely related to its sense as sufficient condition. It may be known that a given phenomenon tends to be associated with certain outcomes and is likely to have a causative role, as for example when we assert that "smoking causes cancer." In saying this we surely do not mean that smoking is a necessary condition of cancer, since we know that many cancers arise in the total absence of smoking. Nor is smoking sure to result in cancer, since the habit may long continue without any cancer as its outcome. But smoking, in conjunction with some biological circumstances, may so frequently play a role in the development of cancer that we think it reasonable to report that smoking is a "cause" of cancer.

This points to yet another common use of the term "cause," as the factor that is critical, or often critical, in the occurrence of some phenomenon. Suppose an insurance company were to send investigators to determine the cause of a mysterious fire. If the investigators sent back a report that the fire was caused by the presence of oxygen in the atmosphere, they would not keep their jobs very long. And yet they would be right—in the sense of necessary condition—for had there been no oxygen present, there would have been no fire. But the insurance company did not have *that* sense in mind when it sent them to investigate. Nor is the company interested in the sufficient condition. If after several weeks the investigators reported that although they had proof that the fire was deliberately ignited by the policyholder, they hadn't as yet been able to learn *all* of the necessary conditions and so hadn't been able to determine the cause (in the sense of sufficient condition), the company would recall the investigators and tell them to stop wasting their time and the company's money. The insurance company was using the word "cause" in another sense—what they wanted to find out was *the incident or action* that, in the presence of those conditions that usually prevail, *made the difference* between the occurrence or nonoccurrence of the event.

We may distinguish between two different subdivisions of this third sense of cause. These traditionally are characterized as the *remote* and the *proximate* causes. Where there is a causal sequence or chain of several events, *A* causing *B*, *B* causing *C*, *C* causing *D*, and *D* causing *E*, we can regard *E* as the effect of any or of all of the preceding events. The nearest of them, *D*, is the proximate cause of *E*, and the others are more and more remote causes, *A* more remote than *B*, and *B* more remote than *C*. Causes quite close to their effects in time

---

[2] A full discussion of this causal relation will be found in Deborah Blum, *Sex on the Brain* (Viking, 1997).

may nevertheless be considered remote in view of the number of distinct links in the causal chain. The following true account appeared in 1996:

> The train of events began on a June morning two years ago, after an overnight frost in Brazil, when a government official there announced a substantial reduction in projected coffee production. The news instantly flashed to the Chicago Board of Trade, where the price of coffee futures immediately began rising. Traders of soybeans and other products began bidding up their prices, causing the index of commodity prices to rise. This was registered on the computer screens of commodities traders in almost 200 Wall Street firms, who reported this shiver of inflation to their bond-trading colleagues, who started a sell-off of bonds, which caused bond prices to fall, which caused bond yields to rise, which put upward pressure on interest rates, which caused stock prices to fall. Elapsed time between the announcement in Brazil and the tremor on Wall Street: less than ten minutes.[3]

Poverty goes hand-in-hand with poor education. And "there is something about a person's level of education [when it is inferior] that leads to poorer medical outcomes.[4] But college study is not the *proximate* cause of good health, nor is ignorance the proximate cause of disease. A poor education is a link in the causal chain, often resulting in a less adequate understanding of the disease process, and thus a failure to make the lifestyle changes needed to promote better medical outcomes. So it is commonly and correctly observed that poverty, affecting education almost universally, is one of the "root causes" of poor health—a remote but not a proximate cause.

There are several different senses of the term "cause," as we have seen. We can legitimately infer cause from effect only in the sense of "necessary condition." And we can legitimately infer effect from cause only in the sense of "sufficient condition." Where inferences are made both from cause to effect and from effect to cause, the term "cause" must be used in the sense of "necessary and sufficient condition." In this usage, cause is identified with sufficient condition, and sufficient condition is regarded as the conjunction of all necessary conditions. It should be clear that there is no single definition of "cause" that conforms to *all* of the different uses of that word.

B.   Causal Laws and the Uniformity of Nature

But every use of the word "cause," whether in everyday life or in science, involves or presupposes the doctrine that cause and effect are *uniformly* connected. We admit that a particular circumstance caused a particular effect only if we agree that any other circumstance of that type will—if the attendant circumstances are sufficiently similar—cause another effect of the same kind as

---

[3] George Will, in a syndicated column published in the *Washington Post,* 10 October 1996.

[4] Conor O'Shea, a medical researcher from The Duke University Medical Center, who reported at the European Society of Cardiology that persons who leave school before the age of 16 are five times more likely to die from a heart attack than are university graduates, and while the death rate within one year of a heart attack is 20 percent for those with fewer than 8 years of education, it is only 3.5 percent for those with 16 years of education. London, *Daily Express,* 28 August 2000.

the first. In other words, similar causes produce similar effects. Part of the very meaning of the word "cause" as used today is that every occurrence of a cause producing an effect is an *instance* or *example* of the general causal law that such circumstances are *always* accompanied by such phenomena. Thus we are willing to relinquish a belief that circumstance *C* was the cause of effect *E* in one particular case, if it can be shown that the same (type of) circumstance was present in another situation which was the same as the first except that the effect *E did not occur* in the latter.

Since every assertion that a particular circumstance was the cause of a particular phenomenon implies the existence of some causal law, every assertion of causal connection contains a critical element of *generality*. A causal law, as we use the term, asserts that a circumstance of such-and-such kind is invariably attended by a phenomenon of a specified kind, no matter where or when it occurs. But how can we come to know such general truths?

The causal relation is not purely logical or deductive; it cannot be discovered by any *a priori* reasoning. Causal laws can be discovered only empirically, *a posteriori*, by an appeal to experience. But our experiences are always of particular circumstances, particular phenomena, and particular sequences of them. We may observe several instances of a circumstance (say, *C*), and every instance *that we observe* may be accompanied by an instance of a certain kind of phenomenon (say, *P*). But we will have experienced only some of the instances of *C* in the world, hence such observations can show us only that some cases of *C* are attended by *P*. Yet our frequent aim is to establish a general, causal relation. How are we to get from the particulars we experience to the general proposition that *all* cases of *C* are attended by *P*—which is involved in saying that *C causes P?*

C.   Induction by Simple Enumeration

The process of arriving at general or universal propositions from the particular facts of experience is called *inductive generalization.* From premisses asserting that three particular pieces of blue litmus paper turned red when dipped in acid, we may draw either a particular conclusion about what will happen to a particular fourth piece of blue litmus paper if it is dipped in acid or a general conclusion about what happens to *every* piece of blue litmus paper dipped in acid. If we draw the first, we have an argument by analogy; the second is an inductive generalization. The structure of these two types of arguments may be analyzed as follows. The premisses report a number of instances in which two attributes (or circumstances or phenomena) occur together. By analogy we may infer that a different particular instance of one attribute will also exhibit the other attribute. By inductive generalization, we may infer that *every* instance of the one attribute will also be an instance of the other. An inductive generalization of the form

Instance 1 of phenomenon *E* is accompanied by circumstance *C*.
Instance 2 of phenomenon *E* is accompanied by circumstance *C*.
Instance 3 of phenomenon E is accompanied by circumstance *C*.
Therefore every instance of phenomenon *E* is accompanied by circumstance *C*.

is an induction by *simple enumeration.* An induction by simple enumeration is very similar to an argument by analogy, differing only in having a more general conclusion.

Simple enumeration often is used in establishing causal connections. Where a number of instances of a phenomenon are invariably accompanied by a certain type of circumstance, it is only natural to infer the existence of a causal relationship between them. Since the circumstance of dipping blue litmus paper in acid is accompanied in all observed instances by the phenomenon of the paper's turning red, we infer by simple enumeration that dipping blue litmus paper in acid is the cause of its turning red. The analogical character of such an argument is quite apparent.

Because of the great similarity between argument by simple enumeration and argument by analogy, similar criteria for appraisal apply to both. Some arguments by simple enumeration may establish their conclusions with a higher degree of probability than others. The greater the number of instances appealed to, the higher the probability of the conclusion. The various instances or cases of phenomenon E accompanied by circumstance C are often called *confirming instances* of the causal law asserting that C causes E. The greater the number of confirming instances, the higher the probability of the causal law—other things being equal. Thus the first criterion for analogical arguments applies directly to arguments by simple enumeration also.

In an historical report simple enumeration can give persuasive grounds for inferring a causal relationship. To illustrate: Legislative acts designed to savage some individual or group temporarily out of favor, called bills of attainder, are known to endanger their advocates when the pendulum of political power swings. The accuser today becomes the victim tomorrow. Condemning such a bill of attainder (aimed at Thomas Osborne) in the House of Lords, the Earl of Carnarvon drove the point home in 1678 with the following enumeration:

> My Lords, I understand . . . not a little of our English history, from which I have learnt the mischiefs of prosecutions as these, and the ill fate of the prosecutors. I shall go no further back than the latter end of Queen Elizabeth's reign, at which time the Earl of Essex was run down by Sir Walter Raleigh, and your Lordships well know what became of Sir Walter Raleigh. My Lord Bacon, he ran down Sir Walter Raleigh, and your Lordships know what became of my Lord Bacon. The Duke of Buckingham, he ran down my Lord Bacon, and your Lordships know what happened to the Duke of Buckingham. Sir Thomas Wentworth, afterwards Earl of Strafford, ran down the Duke of Buckingham, and you all know what became of him. Sir Harry Vane, he ran down the Earl of Strafford, and your Lordships know what became of Sir Harry Vane. Chancellor Hyde, he ran down Sir Harry Vane, and your Lordships know what became of the Chancellor. Sir Thomas Osborne, now Earl of Danby, ran down Chancellor Hyde.
>
> What will now become of the Earl of Danby, your Lordships best can tell. But let me see that man that dare run the Earl of Danby down, and we shall soon see what will become of him.[5]

---

[5] See Zachariah Chafee, Jr., *Three Human Rights in the Constitution of 1787.*

Rhetorically effective though this recounting of instances may be, it does not provide a trustworthy argument. The conclusion, that there is a causal connection between malicious accusation and subsequent destruction, appeals to six confirming instances—but the very nature of those instances prevents them from distinguishing between confirming instances of a genuine causal law and mere historical accidents.

The heart of the difficulty is this: The method of simple enumeration takes no account—*can* take no account—of exceptions to the causal law being suggested. Any alleged causal law would be overthrown by a single negative case, for any one disconfirming instance shows that what had been proposed as a "law" was not truly general. Exceptions *disprove* the rule—for an exception (or "negative instance") is either one in which the alleged cause is found and is not followed by the alleged effect (in this historical case, a bill of attainder whose author did not suffer a like fate), or one in which the effect is encountered while the alleged cause is absent—where (using our earlier schema) C is present without E, or E is present without C. But in an argument by simple enumeration there is no place for either of these; the only legitimate premises in such an argument are reports of instances in which *both* the alleged cause and the alleged effect are present.

It is thus a grave weakness of simple enumeration arguments that, if we confine ourselves to them exclusively, we will not look for, and are therefore unlikely even to notice, the negative or disconfirming instances that might otherwise be found. For this reason, despite their fruitfulness and value in *suggesting* causal laws, inductions by simple enumeration are not at all suitable for *testing* causal laws. Yet such testing is essential; to accomplish it we must rely upon other types of inductive arguments—and to these we next turn.

12.2 MILL'S METHODS

The limitations of simple enumeration have long been appreciated. Other types of inductive procedure were recommended as early as 1605 by Sir Francis Bacon, who sought to reform the methods of scientific investigation in his great work *The Advancement of Learning*. But the careful formulation of more powerful inductive methods, and their systematization, was accomplished by another British philosopher, John Stuart Mill (in *A System of Logic*, 1843), and have come to be known as "Mill's Methods of inductive inference." Mill formulated five of these "canons," as he called them:

1.   The Method of Agreement
2.   The Method of Difference
3.   The Joint Method of Agreement and Difference
4.   The Method of Residues
5.   The Method of Concomitant Variation

We will examine these in turn, attending first to Mill's classic statement of each method (with one exception), followed by brief explication and illustration.

Although Mill's accounts of these methods are now very old, they remain penetrating analyses of the most fundamental tools used, always and everywhere, in the search for causal laws.

1. The Method of Agreement

John Stuart Mill wrote:

> If two or more instances of the phenomenon under investigation have only one circumstance in common, the circumstance in which alone all the instances agree, is the cause (or effect) of the given phenomenon.

This method goes beyond simple enumeration in that it seeks to discover not merely the repeated conjunction of cause with effect, but to identify the *only* circumstance, the *one* circumstance, that is invariably associated with the effect, or phenomenon, in which we are interested. This is an essential, and exceedingly common tool of scientific inquiry. In searching for the cause of some deadly epidemic, for example, or in searching for the cause of some geological phenomenon, the epidemiologist or geologist will seek out the special circumstances that in every instance attend that result. In what way, they ask, do apparently differing sets of circumstances *agree,* where that result is produced?

Imagine, among the residents of some dormitory, a rash of stomach upsets, whose cause we must learn. The first line of inquiry naturally will be: What food or foods were eaten by *all* those who fell ill? Foods eaten by some but not all of those afflicted are not likely to be the cause of the outbreak; we want to know what circumstance is found to be *common* to every case of the illness. Of course what turns out to be common may not be a food; it may be the use of some infected utensils, or proximity to some noxious effluent, or other circumstance. But only when some circumstance is found in which *all* the cases of the illness agree are we on the way to the solution of the problem.

Schematically, the Method of Agreement may be represented as follows, where capital letters represent circumstances and small letters denote phenomena:

> A B C D occur together with w x y z.
> A E F G occur together with w t u v.
> Therefore A is the cause (or the effect) of w.

This method is particularly useful in identifying a kind of phenomenon, or a *range* of circumstances, whose investigation holds scientific promise. It is profitably suggestive, even where it cannot be conclusive. In molecular genetics, for example, the possible causes of an inherited disease can often be greatly narrowed down using the Method of Agreement. A search is conducted for something that is unique to the genetic makeup of those persons and families among whom the targeted disease occurs with great frequency. Alzheimer's disease (a condition that results in the progressive and irreversible decline of mental processes) is believed to be genetic. Is there some circumstance common in the genetic makeup of all those afflicted? A research group at the

University of Washington first screened hundreds of afflicted families. Then, after painstaking examination of a smaller group of families with a particularly high incidence of Alzheimer's disease, the primary investigator reported:

> We took these families where the inheritance was clear and we made the assumption that there was a defective gene and our task was to find where it was. We started looking for a needle in a really big haystack containing all the human chromosomes. We found one small site on chromosome 14 where there can be a defective gene that causes Alzheimer's disease.[6]

A similar use of the Method of Agreement led, some years ago, to a discovery of enormous human benefit. The rates of dental decay were found to be much lower in several cities for reasons then unknown; investigation revealed that one circumstance was common to all of those cities: the presence of an unusually high level of fluorine in their water supplies. It was inferred that the use of fluorine can cause a decrease in the incidence of dental decay. The subsequent confirmation of this conclusion has led to the fluoridation of water supplies in cities around the globe. In short, whenever we find *a single circumstance common to all instances* of a given phenomenon, we may believe ourselves to have discovered its cause.

The Method of Agreement has serious limitations, however. Looking chiefly to confirming instances, the method by itself is often insufficient to identify the cause being sought. The data available are seldom so conveniently arranged as to permit the identification of one circumstance common to all cases. And when inquiry reveals more than one circumstance common to all cases, this technique alone cannot evaluate those alternative possibilities.

Although the presence of agreement between circumstance and phenomenon is often inconclusive, the *absence* of agreement may help us to determine what is *not* the cause of a phenomenon of interest. The Method of Agreement is in essence eliminative; it points to the fact that circumstances arising in some of the cases, but not all of the cases, of the phenomenon in which we are interested, are not likely to be its cause. Those who argue against an alleged causal relation, therefore, are likely to call attention to the absence of uniform agreement, inferring that the alleged cause can be neither the sufficient condition nor the necessary condition of that phenomenon.

To illustrate: Some argue that there is a *causal* connection between improved performance by public school students (as measured by scores on the Scholastic Assessment Tests, or SATs) and the expenditure of dollars on schools by state governments, that more money spent yields better learning. This claim is in some degree undermined by those who point out that during the years 1992–1993 none of the five states with the highest teachers' salaries was among the 15 states with the top SAT scores; and of the 10 states with the highest per-pupil expenditures, only one (Wisconsin) was among the 10 states with the highest SAT scores; and the state with the highest per-pupil expenditure, New Jersey, ranked 39th in SAT scores—all evidence tending to show that high expenditure

---

[6] Gerard Schellenberg, recounting the method of his research group that led to the landmark results reported in *Science,* 23 October 1992.

is not a *sufficient* condition of student achievement. But the 10 states with the lowest per-pupil spending included four (North Dakota, South Dakota, Tennessee, and Utah) among the 10 states with the top SAT scores; and while North Dakota ranked 44th in expenditures it ranked second in SAT scores; and while South Dakota ranked last in teachers' salaries it ranked third in SAT scores—all evidence tending to show that high expenditure is not a *necessary* condition of student achievement.[7] Senator Daniel Patrick Moynihan was moved to observe, sardonically, that what appears to be the crucial determinant in the quality of American public schools is not money, but proximity to Canada! Argument in this form is very far from conclusive—but the absence of agreement, of uniform association, does throw doubt on supposed causal connections.

After we have learned all that the Method of Agreement can teach, in any event, other inductive methods capable of greater refinement in the search for causes are sure to be required.

Exercises

Analyze each of the following scientific reports, explaining how the pattern of the Method of Agreement is manifested by each. Discuss, in each case, the limitations of the Method of Agreement as applied to that quest for a causal connection.

*1.   Neurologist Harold L. Klawans, in his book *Newton's Madness* suggests that Newton's alchemical experiments accounted for his periodic mental problems. Newton spent a lot of time around heated mercury, even sleeping in the same room with it during some of his experiments. His episodes of pathological behavior appear to coincide with those experiments. Klawans explains the neurological effects of prolonged exposure to mercury, which include the symptoms ascribed to Newton.

—Donald K. Henry, "Was Newton Nuts?" *Astronomy,* July 1998

2.   Researchers at the University of California at Irvine have theorized that listening to Mozart's piano music significantly improves performance on intelligence tests. Dr. Frances H. Rauscher and her colleagues reported:

> We performed an experiment in which students were each given three sets of standard IQ spatial reasoning tasks; each task was preceded by 10 minutes of
> (1) listening to Mozart's Sonata for Two Pianos in D major, K. 488; or
> (2) listening to a relaxation tape; or
> (3) silence.
> Performance was improved for those tasks immediately following the first condition compared to the second two.

Test scores rose an average of 8 or 9 points following the Mozart sonata. Some of the students had reported that they liked Mozart,

---

[7] From a report by the American Exchange Legislative Council, September 1993.

and some that they did not, but there were no measurable differences attributable to varying tastes. "We are testing a neurobiological model of brain function with these experiments," Dr. Rauscher said, "and we hypothesize that these patterns may be common in certain activities—chess, mathematics, and certain kinds of music. . . . Listening to such music may stimulate neural pathways important to cognition."

> —Frances H. Rauscher, Gordon L. Shaw, Katherine N. KY,
> "Music and Spatial Task Performance," *Nature,* 14 October 1993

3. Medical researchers have concluded not only that the timing of sexual intercourse in relation to ovulation strongly influences the chance of conception, but that conception occurs *only* when intercourse takes place during a specifiable period in the menstrual cycle. The researchers summarized their findings thus:

> We recruited 221 healthy women who were planning to become pregnant. At the same time the women stopped using birth control methods, they began collecting daily urine specimens and keeping daily records of whether they had sexual intercourse. We measured estrogen and progesterone metabolites in urine to estimate the day of ovulation.
>
> In a total of 625 menstrual cycles for which the dates of ovulation could be estimated, 192 pregnancies were initiated. . . . Two thirds (n = 129) ended in live births. Conception occurred only when intercourse took place during a six-day period that ended on the estimated day of ovulation. The probability of conception ranged from 0.10 when intercourse occurred five days before ovulation to 0.33 when it occurred on the day of ovulation itself.
>
> Conclusion: Among healthy women trying to conceive, nearly all pregnancies can be attributed to intercourse during a six-day period ending on the day of ovulation.

> —Allen J. Wilcox, Clarice R. Weinberg, Donna D. Baird,
> "Timing of Sexual Intercourse in Relation to Ovulation,"
> *The New England Journal of Medicine,* 7 December 1995.

4. A large extended family in the town of Cartago, Costa Rica, has long suffered an unusual affliction—an incurable form of genetically caused deafness. Children born into the family have a 50 percent chance of developing the disease, and learn their fate at about the age of ten, when those who have inherited a genetic mutation find that they are beginning to lose their hearing. Scientists from the University of Washington have recently traced the cause of the family's affliction to a previously unknown gene, named the diaphanous gene, that helps operate the delicate hair cells in the inner ear that respond to sound vibrations.

   This gene has a single mutation appearing in the Costa Rican family, whose founder arrived in Cartago from Spain in 1713, and who suffered from this form of deafness—as have half his descendants in the eight generations since. Many in the family remain in Cartago because the family's hereditary deafness is well-known and accepted there. With only a single family to be studied, and thus very few genetic differences to work with, pinpointing the gene took six years. The critical mutation involved just one of the 3,800 chemical letters that constitute the gene's DNA.

—Reported in *Science.* 14 November 1997

*5.   Researchers from the National Cancer Institute announced that they have found a number of genetic markers shared by gay brothers, indicating that homosexuality has genetic roots. The investigators, reporting in *Science*, 16 July 1993, have found that out of 40 pairs of gay brothers examined in their study, 33 pairs shared certain DNA sequences on their X chromosome, the chromosome men inherit only from their mothers. The implicit reasoning of this report is that, if brothers who have specific DNA sequences in common are both gay, these sequences can be considered genetic markers for homosexuality.

6.   A 1994 study by Dr. Stephen Moses, published in the *International Journal of Epidemiology*, showed that around the world men who were not circumcised were three to four times likelier to be infected with HIV than circumcised men. One hypothesis suggested was that the virus may be transmitted through tears in the foreskin during intercourse. A study reported in *Scientific American* in March of 1996 claimed to show that "only one factor" seemed to correlate with susceptibility to HIV infection in Africa: lack of circumcision.

2.   The Method of Difference

John Stuart Mill wrote:

> If an instance in which the phenomenon under investigation occurs and an instance in which it does not occur, have every circumstance in common save one, that one occurring only in the former, the circumstance in which alone the two instances differ, is the effect, or the cause, or an indispensable part of the cause, of the phenomenon.

This pattern focuses not on what is common among those cases in which the effect is produced, but on what is *different* between those cases in which the effect is produced and those in which it is not. If we had learned, when investigating that rash of stomach upsets earlier described, that all those who had become ill had eaten the canned pears for dessert, but that the pears had been eaten by none of those who did not become ill, we would be fairly confident that the cause of the illness had been identified.

The difference between the Method of Difference and the Method of Agreement is highlighted in a recent report about the role of the hormone testosterone in the aggressive conduct of males.

> Among many species, testes are mothballed most of the year, kicking into action and pouring out testosterone only during a very circumscribed mating season—precisely the time when male–male aggression soars. Impressive though they seem, these data

are only correlative—testosterone found on the scene repeatedly when aggression has occurred.

The proof comes with the knife, the performance of what is euphemistically known as a subtraction experiment. Remove the source of the testosterone in species after species, and levels of aggression plummet. Reinstate normal testosterone levels afterward with injections of synthetic testosterone and aggression returns.

The subtraction and replacement paradigm gives damning proof that this hormone is involved in aggression.[8]

Testosterone makes the critical difference, clearly, but the author of this report is careful not to assert that testosterone is *the cause* of male aggression. More accurately, the report states that testosterone is surely *involved* in aggression. As Mill would put it, the hormone is *an indispensable part of the cause* of male aggression. Wherever we can identify a single factor that makes the critical difference when all else remains normal—the factor that eliminates the phenomenon in question when we remove it, or the factor that produces the phenomenon in question when we introduce it—we will pretty surely have identified the cause, or an indispensable part of the cause, of the phenomenon we are investigating.

Schematically, where again capital letters denote circumstances and small letters denote phenomena, the Method of Difference may be represented as follows:

A B C D occur together with w x y z.
B C D occur together with x y z.
Therefore A is the cause, or the effect, or an indispensable part of the cause of w.

The Method of Difference is of central importance in scientific investigations of almost every kind. One vivid illustration of its use is the ongoing investigation, by medical researchers, into the effects of particular proteins suspected as implicated in the development of certain diseases. Whether the substance under investigation really is the cause (or an indispensable part of the cause) can only be determined when we create an experimental environment in which that substance has been eliminated. And investigators sometimes are able to do just that, not in humans of course, but in mice which are subject to the same disease, from whom the gene that is known to produce that suspect protein is deleted. Animals so treated are then inbred, creating populations of what are called "knockout mice," precious in the world of contemporary medical research, in which the process relevant to the disease in question can be studied in an animal exactly like other animals subject to that disease, *except for the critical difference created by the knockout*, the absence of the substance hypothesized as cause. Such studies have resulted in some remarkable medical advances.

A famous and very dramatic illustration of the Method of Difference is provided by the following account of experiments confirming the true cause of yellow fever, long one of the great plagues of mankind. The experiments

---

[8] Robert Sapolsky, "Testosterone Rules," *Discover*, March 1997.

described here were conducted by U.S. Army doctors Walter Reed, James Carroll, and Jesse W. Lazear in November of 1900. Earlier that year Dr. Carroll had contracted yellow fever by deliberately allowing himself to be bitten by an infected mosquito in another experiment; soon after, Dr. Lazear died of yellow fever, and the camp in which the following experiments took place was named for him:

> Experiments were devised to show that yellow fever was transmitted by the mosquito alone, all other reasonable opportunities for being infected being excluded. A small building was erected, all windows and doors and every other possible opening being absolutely mosquito-proof. A wire mosquito screen divided the room into two spaces. In one of these spaces fifteen mosquitoes, which had fed on yellow fever patients, were liberated. A nonimmune volunteer entered the room with the mosquitoes and was bitten by seven mosquitoes. Four days later, he suffered an attack of yellow fever. Two other non-immune men slept for thirteen nights in the mosquito-free room without disturbances of any sort.
>
> To show that the disease was transmitted by the mosquito and not through the excreta of yellow fever patients or anything which had come in contact with them, another house was constructed and made mosquito-proof. For 20 days, this house was occupied by three nonimmunes, after the clothing, bedding and eating utensils and other vessels soiled with the discharge, blood and vomitus of yellow fever patients had been placed in it. The bed clothing which they used had been brought from the beds of the patients who had died of yellow fever, without being subjected to washing or any other treatment to remove anything with which it might have been soiled. The experiment was twice repeated by other nonimmune volunteers. During the entire period all the men who occupied the house were strictly quarantined and protected from mosquitoes. None of those exposed to these experiments contracted yellow fever. That they were not immune was subsequently shown, since four of them became infected either by mosquito bites or the injection of blood from yellow fever patients.[9]

That portion of the experiment described in the first paragraph above very deliberately created a single important difference between the subjects in the two carefully enclosed spaces: the presence of mosquitoes that had fed on yellow fever patients in the one space, the absence of such mosquitoes in the other. That portion of the experiment described in the second paragraph above deliberately created a second use of the Method of Difference, in which the only significant difference between two groups of subjects, both of whom had submitted to every close contact with yellow fever victims, was the later exposure of some of them to infected mosquito bites or infected blood. Absent that circumstance, no infection arose.

In the search for causes, the Method of Difference is pervasive and powerful.

Exercises

Analyze each of the following reports, explaining the ways in which the Method of Difference has been applied in the investigations recounted. Discuss the strengths and weaknesses of the Method of Difference as it is used in each case.

---

[9] Paul Henle and William K. Frankena, *Exercises in Elementary Logic* (1940).

*1. The blackcap, a European wood warbler, appears to have developed—in just forty years—the genetic program for an entirely new migration route that shuttles it each winter from Central Europe to England rather than to the warmer climes in the Western Mediterranean normally sought by these birds. Since 1950 birdwatchers have noted a steady increase in the number of blackcaps wintering in Britain; many of these birds carry tags indicating that they spent the summer breeding in Germany and Austria.

   To test whether a genetically altered migration program was causing these birds to deviate some 800 miles from the rest of the birds leaving Central Europe each fall, researchers from the Max Planck Institute in Germany collected birds from Weston-super-Mare, about 100 miles east of London on the Bristol Channel, and removed them to Germany, where 41 experimental young birds were bred over two seasons, along with birds caught in Germany for comparison. Since all the birds in the experiment had never been out of Germany, and were subject to the same environmental cues, the only way for them to find their way to England would be through a genetically encoded map.

   The birds' preferred migratory path was tested by putting them in covered cups lined with typewriter correction paper on which, as they tried repeatedly to take off, their feet scratched out their preferred direction in tiny bird prints on the painted paper. The offspring of birds that had wintered in England left tracks in a direction northwest, toward Weston-super-Mare, England. The offspring of birds that had wintered in Germany, by contrast, left tracks headed on the birds' standard route southwest toward the Mediterranean.

   The birds' preferences for different migratory paths was clear evidence that they were guided by a map programmed into their genes. "The really surprising thing," said Dr. A. J. Helbig, one of the investigators, "was that the adaptation to this new migratory behavior developed so rapidly. It's the first demonstration that evolutionary processes can be much quicker than we thought."

   —Reported in P. Berthold, *et al.*, "Rapid Microevolution
   of Migratory Behavior in a Wild Bird Species,"
   Nature, 17 December 1992

2. The heavy use of salt is widely suspected, by experts, to be the cause of an epidemic of high blood pressure, and many resulting deaths from heart disease around the world. But how prove that salt is the culprit? There are "natural experiments" when isolated jungle or farming communities are introduced to modern civilization, move to cities, adopt high-salt diets, and commonly develop high blood pressure. But such evidence is inconclusive because many important factors change together; new stresses and many dietary changes accompany the increase in salt. How can the causal effects of salt by itself be tested?

Dr. Derek Denton, of the University of Melbourne, selected a group of normal chimpanzees, a species biologically very close to that of humans, to conduct the needed trials. A group of chimpanzees in Gabon, with normal blood pressure, were first studied in their natural state. The group was then divided in half, with one half receiving gradually increasing amounts of salt in their diet for twenty months. Normal blood pressure in a chimpanzee is 110/70. In Dr. Denton's experiment, the animals' blood pressure commonly rose as high as 150/90, and in some individuals much higher. But among animals in the control group, receiving no additional salt, blood pressure did not rise. Six months after the extra salt was withdrawn from their diet, all the chimpanzees in the experimental group had the same low blood pressure they had enjoyed before the experiment. Because there was no other change in the lifestyle of those animals, the investigators concluded that changes in salt consumption caused the changes in blood pressure.

—D. Denton *et al.,* "The Effect of Increased Salt Intake on Blood Pressure of Chimpanzees," *Nature Medicine,* October 1995

3. Does Louisiana hot sauce, the principal ingredient of the spicy New Orleans cocktail sauce commonly served with raw shellfish, kill certain bacteria found in raw oysters and clams? The answer appears to be yes. Bacteria of an infectious and sometimes fatal kind—*Vibrio vulnificus*—are found in 5 to 10 percent of raw shellfish on the market. Dr. Charles V. Sanders and his research team, from Louisiana State University Medical Center in New Orleans, added Louisiana hot sauce to cultures of *Vibrio* growing in test tubes; the sauce, even when greatly diluted, killed *V. vulnificus* in five minutes or less. "I couldn't believe what happened," Dr. Sanders said, admitting that he still eats raw oysters, "but only with plenty of hot sauce."

—Reported to the Interscience Conference on Antimicrobial Agents, New Orleans, October 1993

4. In Lithuania, rear-end auto collisions happen as they do in the rest of the world; bumpers crumple, tempers flare. But drivers there do not seem to suffer the complaints so common in other countries, the headaches and lingering neck pains known as "whiplash syndrome." Dr. Harald Schrader and colleagues from University Hospital in Trondheim, Norway, without disclosing the purpose of their study, gave health questionnaires to 202 Lithuanian drivers whose cars had been struck from behind one to three years earlier in accidents of varying severity. The drivers' reports of their symptoms were compared to the reports of a control group (of the same size, same ages, and same home towns) of drivers who had not been in an accident. Thirty-five percent of the accident victims

reported neck pain, but so did 33 percent of the controls; 53 percent of those who had been in an accident had headaches, but so did 50 percent of those in the control group. The researchers concluded: "No one in the study group had disabling or persistent symptoms as a result of the car accident."

What then can account for the explosion of whiplash cases elsewhere in the world? Drivers in the Lithuanian study did not carry personal injury insurance at the time of the study, and people there very infrequently sue one another. Most medical bills are paid by the government, and at the time of the study there were no claims to be filed, no money to be won, and nothing to be gained from a diagnosis of chronic whiplash. Chronic whiplash syndrome, the Norwegian researchers concluded, "has little validity."

> —Harald Schrader, *et al.*, "Natural Evolution of Late Whiplash
> Syndrome Outside the Medicolegal Context,"
> *The Lancet*, London, 4 May 1996

*5. Inflammation—swelling, redness, and pain—plays a key role in rheumatoid arthritis and in the process that leads to diabetes. Can the gene that causes inflammation be identified? Dr. Donald N. Cook, a pathologist at the University of North Carolina at Chapel Hill, was able to do so using what are called "knockout mice." Like humans, mice suffer inflammation as a result of many infections, and like humans they possess the gene MIP-1 alpha, suspected of producing the protein that begins the process of inflammation. Dr. Cook and his team bred mice that *lacked* the gene MIP-1 alpha, and then infected those mice, and a control group of normal mice, with the influenza virus and the coxsackie virus (which can cause heart damage in children and young adults). In response to the infection, all the normal mice developed extreme inflammation, with swelling and redness. But the mice lacking the MIP-1 alpha gene had only slight inflammation. The experiment, said Dr. Cook, proves that the MIP-1 alpha gene promotes inflammation in response to virus infection. This finding, he suggested, could lead to the development of drugs that would allow the body to fight viral infections without the damaging effects of inflammation.

> —D.N. Cook, *et al.*, "Requirement of MIP-1 Alpha for an
> Inflammatory Response to Viral Infection," *Science*, 15 September 1995

6. The cause of schizophrenia has long been mysterious. Recently, psychiatrists have hypothesized that this condition is due in significant part to abnormalities in the development of the brain in the fetus. Nerve cells are sometimes known to migrate to the wrong areas of the brain when it is first taking shape, leaving small regions of the brain permanently out of place or miswired. To test the hypothesis that there is a causal connection between these abnormalities and schizophrenia, Dr. Schahram Akbarian and colleagues conducted

autopsies on patients' brains, and examined epidemiological data including family movies taken when patients were very young. They found that in all tested patients without schizophrenia there were no such flaws in the neural architecture. But in those with schizophrenia, the misplacement of neurons in the prefrontal areas of the brain was discovered in 7 out of 20 of the brains examined. The causes of the developmental abnormalities themselves are not known, but one speculation is that the misconnections arise when the mother is infected by a virus early in the pregnancy.

—Schahram Akbarian, *et al.,* "Maldistribution of Interstitial Neurons in Prefrontal White Matter of the Brains of Schizophrenic Patients," *The Archives of General Psychiatry,* May 1996

7. El Nino, the global weather phenomenon that sent warm water in the Pacific Ocean migrating farther north than usual, also brought a bumper crop of rattlesnakes to San Diego County. Increased foliage, generated by the unusually wet winter, also created an abundant food supply for rats and mice. More rodents equal more rattlers. "It's been a jump-start this year for the rattlesnakes," said Lieut. Mary Kay Gagliardo, field supervisor for the county Animal Control Department. In the last week of April 1998, she said, the San Diego Regional Poison Center reported six people being bitten by rattlesnakes.

—*New York Times,* 12 May 1998

3. The Joint Method of Agreement and Difference

Although believed by Mill to be an additional and separate technique, this method is best understood as the combined use of the Method of Agreement and the Method of Difference in the same investigation. So it can be represented schematically (capital letters again denoting circumstances, small letters phenomena) as follows:

A B C—x y z.   A B C—x y z.
A D E—x t w.   B C—y z.
Therefore A is the effect, or the cause, or an indispensable part of the cause, of x.

Since each of the two methods (Agreement schematized above on the left, Difference schematized on the right) affords some probability to the conclusion, their joint use affords a higher probability to that conclusion. In many scientific investigations this combination serves as an extremely powerful pattern of inductive inference.

A recent and notable advance in medicine provides an illustration of the power of the joint method. Hepatitis A is a liver infection that afflicts tens of thousands of Americans; it spreads widely among children, chiefly through contaminated food or water, and sometimes is deadly. How is it to be prevented? The ideal solution, of course, would be an effective vaccine. But there is an enormous difficulty facing those who would test any vaccine for hepatitis A: It is very hard to predict where outbreaks of the infection will occur, and therefore normally it is not possible to select experimental subjects in ways that will yield reliable results. This difficulty finally was overcome in the following way.

A vaccine believed effective was tested in a community of Hasidic Jews, Kiryas Joel, in Orange County, New York, a community that is highly unusual in that it is plagued by yearly epidemics of this infection. Almost no one escapes hepatitis A in Kiryas Joel, and nearly 70 percent of the community members have been infected by the time they are nineteen years old. Dr. Alan Werzberger, of the Kiryas Joel Institute of Medicine, and his colleagues recruited 1,037 children in that community, age two to sixteen, who had not been exposed to the hepatitis A virus, as determined by a lack of antibodies to the virus in their blood. Half of them (519) received a single dose of the new vaccine, and among those vaccinated children not a single case of hepatitis A has been reported. Of the 518 children who received dummy injections, 25 soon after became infected with hepatitis A. The vaccine for hepatitis A had been found.[10]

Liver specialists in Boston and Washington greeted this study with admiration, calling it "a great breakthrough" and a "major medical advance." What is the pattern of inference on which this achievement relied? Both the Method of Agreement and the Method of Difference were employed, as is commonly done in medical investigations. Among all those young residents of the community who became safely immune to Hepatitis A there was but one circumstance *in common:* all the immunes had received the new vaccine. By itself, this strongly tends to show that the vaccine did cause that immunity. The Method of Difference supported this conclusion overwhelmingly: the circumstances of those who did become immune and those who did not were essentially alike *in every respect save one,* the administration of that vaccine to the immune residents.

The testing of new drugs or procedures is often conducted in what are called "double-arm" trials, one group receiving the new treatment while the other group does not, after which (in suitable cases) there may be a carefully executed crossover, in a second phase, in which those who originally did not receive the treatment do so, and those who originally did receive the treatment do not. The joint application of the Method of Agreement and the Method of Difference underlies such investigations, which are common and exceedingly productive.

Exercises

Analyze each of the following reports, explaining the way in which the Method of Agreement and the Method of Difference have been jointly applied, and identifying the special force, if any, of their combination.

---

[10] Reported in A. Werzberger *et al.,* "A Controlled Trial of a Formalin-Inactivated Hepatitis A Vaccine in Healthy Children" *The New England Journal of Medicine,* 13 August 1992.

1. The assumption that low birth weight is the cause of high infant mortality in the United States has been challenged by a new study of more than 7.5 million births indicating that the cause of high infant mortality is *prematurity,* not low weight. It is being born too soon, rather than too small, that appears to be the main underlying cause of stillbirths and early infant deaths.

   When the length of pregnancy is the same, American-born babies weigh, on average, less than babies born in Norway. But for any given length of pregnancy, American babies are no more likely to die than are the heavier Norwegian babies.

   Small full-term babies generally do well. That it is the term of pregnancy that is critical is supported by an earlier study of the survival rates of low-birth-weight babies of women who smoked during pregnancy, compared to the survival of babies of equal weight born to nonsmokers. Smoking, like poor nutrition, is known to interfere with prenatal weight gain. But ounce for ounce, the principal investigator reported, "the babies of smoking mothers had a higher survival rate." This paradoxical result he explained as follows: Smoking interferes with weight gain, but it does not shorten pregnancy. Thus, in a large set of low-birth-weight babies, those born to smoking mothers are more likely to be born full-term, while the smaller babies born to nonsmoking mothers are more likely to have been born prematurely. Therefore, the investigator concludes, it is their prematurity, not their smallness, that explains the higher infant mortality rate among babies of low birth weight who are born to nonsmokers.

   —Alan Wilcox, *et al.,* "Birthweight and Perinatal Mortality," *The Journal of the American Medical Association,* 1 March 1995

2. The hypothesis that the basic biological rhythms of an animal are embedded in a specific area of brain tissue has been confirmed by the studies of Dr. Martin Ralph, using hamsters which normally have a "free-running period" of about 24 hours; that is, they wake up and start running around every 24 hours, based on some internal clock. But there are mutant strains with free-running periods of about 20 hours.

   Earlier Japanese studies had shown that the clocklike regularity could be eliminated by removing the suprachiasmatic nucleus, a small area above the point where the two optic nerves cross in the brain. Such animals ran randomly at any time of day or night. When tissue containing that nucleus was reimplanted, the rhythms were restored. But scientists could not be sure whether they were reimplanting the rhythm, or only something that allowed the rhythm to be expressed. Dr. Ralph proved that it was the rhythm itself that is reimplanted, by removing the suprachiasmatic nucleus from one strain of hamster and then implanting cells with that nucleus from hamsters having different free-

running periods. In every case, he reported, the animal that received an implant subsequently exhibited the free-running period
of the *donor* animal—so that hamsters with 24-hour periods could
acquire 20-hour periods, and so on. This leaves little doubt that
the suprachiasmatic nucleus is the tissue within which the biological clock is to be found.

> —Reported at the meeting of the Society for
> Neuroscience, Toronto, 1995

3. What counts as a deformity in one organism may be a gift of evolution to another. For example, syndactyly (the webbing of the
   fingers and the toes) is a deformity in humans, but the device that
   enables ducks to thrive in water. What causes the development of
   well-defined fingers and toes in some creatures, and aquatic pad-
   dles in others? Researchers at Memorial Sloan-Kettering Cancer
   Center in Manhattan have shown that there is a biochemical signal
   that controls whether or not webbing will occur.

   The signal—bone morphogenetic proteins, or B.M.P.s—
   received normally by the developing fetus in chickens, could be
   blocked, and when blocked invariably produced the deformity,
   webbed feet. Scientists suspect that in most animals B.M.P. molecules keep webs from forming by unleashing programmed cell
   death. When signaled by the B.M.P.s, the cells between the digits
   commit mass suicide, allowing independent digits to develop, as
   in humans and normal chickens. In ducks, and apparently in people with syndactyly, this does not happen.

   To cut off the B.M.P. signal, Dr. Lee Niswander and her colleague Dr. Hongyan Zou first caused a mutation in the gene that
   makes B.M.P. receptors, then inserted that mutated gene into a
   retrovirus which smuggled the altered gene into the cells of chick
   embryos. All the embryos with the mutated gene produced defective B.M.P. receptors, which were deaf to the suicide signal. Duck-
   like webs were the invariable result. The scientists next examined
   ducks, and found that while the gene that turns the signal on had
   been activated in other parts of the duck's body, it was not turned
   on in the tissues between the digits.

   > —Hongyan Zou and Lee Niswander, "Requirement for B.M.P.
   > Signaling in Interdigital Apoptosis and Scale Formation,"
   > *Science,* 3 May 1996

4. Sixteen year-old David Merrill, of Suffolk, Virginia, hypothesized
   that the loud sounds of hard-rock music have a bad effect upon its
   devoted fans. He tested the theory on mice. Seventy-two mice
   were divided into three groups of 24, the first to be exposed to
   hard-rock music, the second to music by Mozart, and the third to
   no music at all. After becoming accustomed to their environments,
   but before exposure to the music, Merrill tested all the mice in a

maze which took them an average of 10 minutes to complete. Then the groups were exposed to the music for ten hours a day.

With repeated testing the control-group mice *reduced* their time in the maze by an average of 5 minutes. Those exposed to Mozart reduced their time by 8.5 minutes. The hard-rock mice *increased* their time in the maze by 20 minutes.

Merrill also reported that when, in an earlier attempt, he had allowed all the mice to live together, the project had to be cut short because, unlike the Mozart-listening mice, the hard-rock-listening mice killed other mice.

—Reported in *Insight,* 8 September 1997

*5. Pasteur . . . carried out at least one spectacular experiment having to do with the effect of temperature on susceptibility to infection. Puzzled by the fact that hens were refractory to anthrax, he had wondered whether this might not be explained by their body temperature, which is higher than that of animals susceptible to this disease. To test his hypothesis, he inoculated hens with anthrax bacilli and placed them in a cold bath to lower their body temperature. Animals so treated died the next day, showing numerous bacilli in their blood and organs. Another hen, similarly infected and maintained in the cold bath until the disease was in full progress, was then taken out of the water, dried, wrapped, and placed under conditions that allowed rapid return to normal body temperature. *Mirabile dictu,* this hen made a complete recovery. Thus, a mere fall of a few degrees in body temperature was sufficient to render birds almost as receptive to anthrax as were rabbits or guinea pigs.

—René Dubos, *Pasteur and Modern Science*

4. The Method of Residues

John Stuart Mill wrote:

> Subduct from any phenomenon such part as is known by previous inductions to be the effect of certain antecedents, and the residue of the phenomenon is the effect of the remaining antecedents.

The first three methods seem to suppose that we can eliminate or produce the cause (or effect) of some phenomenon in its entirety, as indeed we sometimes can. In many contexts, however, we can only deduce the causal impact of some phenomenon by observing the *change* that it makes in a set of circumstances whose cause is already understood in part.

This method, focusing upon residues, is well illustrated in the very simple device used to weigh truck cargoes. The weight of the truck when empty is known. To determine the weight of the cargo, the entire truck is weighed with its cargo—and the weight of the cargo is then known to be the weight of the whole minus the weight of the truck. The known "antecedent," in Mill's phrase, is the recorded weight of the empty truck that must be subtracted from the reading on the scale; the cause of the difference between that reading and the known antecedent is obviously attributable to the remaining "antecedents"—that is, to the cargo itself.

Schematically, the Method of Residues can be represented as follows:

A B C—x y z.
B is known to be the cause of y.
C is known to be the cause of z.
Therefore A is the cause of x.

A splendid illustration of the effectiveness of the Method of Residues is provided by one of the great chapters in the history of astronomy, the discovery of the planet Neptune:

> In 1821, Bouvard of Paris published tables of the motions of a number of planets, including Uranus. In preparing the latter he had found great difficulty in making an orbit calculated on the basis of positions obtained in the years after 1800 agree with one calculated from observations taken in the years immediately following discovery. He finally disregarded the older observations entirely and based his tables on the newer observations. In a few years, however, the positions calculated from the tables disagreed with the observed positions of the planet and by 1844 the discrepancy amounted to 2 minutes of arc. Since all the other known planets agreed in their motions with those calculated for them, the discrepancy in the case of Uranus aroused much discussion.
>
> In 1845, Leverrier, then a young man, attacked the problem. He checked Bouvard's calculations and found them essentially correct. Thereupon he felt that the only satisfactory explanation of the trouble lay in the presence of a planet somewhere beyond Uranus which was disturbing its motion. By the middle of 1846 he had finished his calculations. In September he wrote to Galle at Berlin and requested the latter to look for a new planet in a certain region of the sky for which some new star charts had just been prepared in Germany but of which Leverrier apparently had not as yet obtained copies. On the twenty-third of September Galle started the search and in less than an hour he found an object which was not on the chart. By the next night it had moved appreciably and the new planet, subsequently named Neptune, was discovered within 1° of the predicted place. This discovery ranks among the greatest achievements of mathematical astronomy.[11]

The phenomenon under investigation here is the movement of Uranus. A great part of that phenomenon, the orbit of Uranus around the sun, was well understood at the time. Observations of Uranus approximated this calculated orbit but exhibited a puzzling residue, some perturbation of what had been calculated, for which further explanation was needed. An additional "antecedent"—that is, an additional existing factor that would account for the perturbation—was hypothesized to be another (undiscovered) planet whose gravity would, together with what was already known about the

---

[11] Edward Arthur Fath, *The Elements of Astronomy* (New York: McGraw-Hill, 1926), p. 170.

orbit of Uranus, explain that residue. Once hypothesized, that new planet, Neptune, was very quickly found.

The Method of Residues differs from the other methods in that it can be used with the examination of only one case, while the others require the examination of at least two cases. And the Method of Residues, unlike the others, appears to depend upon antecedently established causal laws, while the other methods (as Mill formulated them) do not. But Residues is nevertheless an inductive, not a deductive method (as some have suggested) because it yields conclusions that are only probable and cannot be *validly deduced* from their premisses. An additional premiss or two might transform an inference by the Method of Residues into a valid deductive argument—but that can be said for other inductive methods as well.

Exercises

Analyze each of the following arguments in terms of "antecedents" and "phenomena" to show how they follow the pattern of the Method of Residues.

*1.   For 19 years space scientists, astronomers, and physicists have been puzzled by what appears to be a mysterious force pulling spacecraft in the direction of the sun. It was first noticed when the trajectories of two outward bound and very distant spacecraft (Pioneer 10 and 11, launched in 1972 and 1973) were carefully analyzed. The trajectories of two later probes (Galileo, launched toward Jupiter in 1989, and Ulysses, launched into polar orbit around the sun) have exhibited the same peculiarities: they give evidence of a weak force that perturbs their directions and velocities. This force was discovered by adding up the effects of all other known forces acting on the spacecraft and finding that something unexplained was left over.

This force is apparently slowing the outward progress of the spacecraft speeding away from or around the sun—but in contrast with the force of gravity, the strength of this mystery force does not decline proportionally to the inverse square of a spacecraft's distance from the sun, but instead at a linear rate, which makes it very unlikely that the mystery force is a gravitational effect of the sun.

Calculations were made using two independent methods, and data of different types, taking into account possible errors in the software and the hardware used in the measurements. A host of other possible errors were investigated and accounted for—and after ruling all of these out, a team of physicists from the Los Alamos National Laboratory announced, in 1998, that the mystery remains. This means that some hitherto unknown phenomenon is maybe at work—what physicists excitedly call "new physics."

—Reported in *Physical Review Letters*, September 1998

2. In H. Davies' experiments on the decomposition of water by galvanism, it was found that besides the two components of water, oxygen and hydrogen, an acid and an alkali were developed at opposite poles of the machine. Since the theory of the analysis of water did not give reason to expect these products, their presence constituted a problem. Some chemists thought that electricity had the power of producing these substances of itself. Davies conjectured that there might be some hidden cause for this part of the effect—the glass might suffer decomposition, or some foreign matter might be in the water. He then proceeded to investigate whether or not the diminution or total elimination of possible causes would change or eliminate the effect in question. Substituting gold vessels for glass ones, he found no change in the effect and concluded that glass was not the cause. Using distilled water, he found a decrease in the quantity of acid and alkali involved, yet enough remained to show that the cause was still in operation. He inferred that impurity of the water was not the sole cause, but was a concurrent cause. He then suspected that perspiration from the hands might be the cause, as it would contain salt which would decompose into acid and alkali under electricity. By avoiding such contact, he reduced the quantity of the effect still further, till only slight traces remained. These might be due to some impurity of the atmosphere decomposed by the electricity. An experiment determined this. The machine was put under an exhaust receiver and when it was thus secured from atmospheric influences, no acid or alkali was produced.

—G. Gore, *The Art of Scientific Discovery*

3. The return of the comet predicted by Professor Encke a great many times in succession, and the general good agreement of its calculated with its observed place during any one of its periods of visibility, would lead us to say that its gravitation toward the sun and planets is the sole and sufficient cause of all the phenomena of its orbital motion; but when the effect of this cause is strictly calculated and subducted from the observed motion, there is found to remain behind a *residual phenomenon,* which would never have been otherwise ascertained to exist, which is a small anticipation of the time of its reappearance, or a diminution of its periodic time, which cannot be accounted for by gravity, and whose cause is therefore to be inquired into. Such an anticipation would be caused by the resistance of a medium disseminated through the celestial regions; and as there are other good reasons for believing this to be a *vera causa* (an actually existing antecedent), it has therefore been ascribed to such a resistance.

—John Herschel, quoted in John Stuart Mill, *A System of Logic*

4. It was not merely the amount of water in circulation which was influenced by temperature. . . . It was the total amount of haemoglobin. The mystery was: "Whence came this outpouring of haemoglobin?" It was not credible that the bone-marrow could have provided the body with new corpuscles at the rate required. Moreover, there was no evidence of increase of immature corpuscles in circulation. . . .

   The question then was forced upon us: Has the body any considerable but hidden store of haemoglobin which can be drawn upon in case of emergency?. . . In searching for a locality which might fulfill such a condition, one naturally seeks in the first instance for some place where the red blood corpuscles are outside the circulatory system—some backwater outside the arteries, capillaries, and veins. There is only one such place of any considerable size in the body—that place is the spleen.

   —Joseph Barcroft, *The Lancet*, February 1925

*5. It is no longer open to discussion that the air has weight. It is common knowledge that a balloon is heavier when inflated than when empty, which is proof enough. For if the air were light, the more the balloon was inflated, the lighter the whole would be, since there would be more air in it. But since, on the contrary, when more air is put in, the whole becomes heavier, it follows that each part has a weight of its own, and consequently that the air has weight.

   —Blaise Pascal, *Treatise on the Weight of the Mass of the Air*

5. The Method of Concomitant Variation

The four methods thus far discussed are all *eliminative* in nature. By eliminating some possible cause or causes of a given phenomenon, they support some other causal account hypothesized. The Method of Agreement eliminates as possible causes those circumstances in whose absence the phenomenon can nevertheless occur; the Method of Difference permits the elimination of some possible causes by removing an antecedent factor shown to be critical; the Joint method is eliminative in both of these ways; and the Method of Residues seeks to eliminate as possible causes those circumstances whose effects have already been established by previous inductions.

But there are many situations in which no one of these methods is applicable, because there are circumstances involved that cannot possibly be eliminated. This is often the case in economics, in physics, in medicine, and wherever the general increase or decrease of one factor results in a concomitant increase or decrease of another—the complete elimination of either factor not being feasible.

John Stuart Mill wrote:

> Whatever phenomenon varies in any manner whenever another phenomenon varies in some particular manner is either a cause or an effect of that phenomenon or is connected with it through some fact of causation.

Concomitant variation is critical to the study of the causal impact of certain foods, for example. We cannot eliminate disease, no matter the diet; we can rarely eliminate foods of certain kinds from the diets of large populations. But we can note what the impact of increasing or decreasing the intake of certain foods will be upon the frequency of certain diseases in specified populations. One recent investigation of this kind examined the frequency of heart attacks as compared to the frequency with which fish had been eaten by those in the study. The inductive conclusion was striking: eating one fish meal a week reduced the risk of heart attack by 50 percent; eating just two fish meals a month reduced the risk of heart attack by 30 percent. Within some limits there appears to be a marked concomitant variation between cardiac arrests and the use of fish in the diet.[12]

Using plus and minus signs to indicate the greater or lesser degree to which a varying phenomenon is present in a given situation, the Method of Concomitant Variation can be schematized as follows:

A B C—x y z.
A+ B C—x+ y z.
Therefore A and x are causally connected.

This method is very widely used. A farmer establishes that there is a causal connection between the application of fertilizer to the soil and the size of the crop by applying different amounts to different parts of a field, then noting the concomitant variation between the amounts of the additive and the yield. A merchant seeks to verify the efficacy of advertising of different kinds by running varied advertisements at varying intervals, then noting the concomitant increase or decrease of business during some of those periods.

When the increase of one phenomenon parallels the increase of another, we say the phenomena vary *directly* with each other. But the method permits the use of variation "in any manner," and we may also infer a causal connection when the phenomena vary *inversely*—the increase of one leading to the decrease of another. Thus economists will often say that, other things remaining roughly stable, in an unregulated market an increase of the supply of some good (say, crude oil) will result in a concomitant decrease in its price. That relation does appear to be genuinely concomitant: When international tension threatens to reduce the available supply of crude oil, we note that the price of the oil almost invariably rises.

Some concomitant variations are entirely coincidental, of course. Care must be taken not to infer a causal connection from patterns of occurrence that are wholly fortuitous. But some variations that appear to be coincidental, or are otherwise puzzling, may have an obscure causal explanation. It has been shown that there is a high correlation between the number of storks found nesting in English villages and the number of babies born in each of

---

[12] Siscovick, D.S. *et al.*, "Dietary Intake and Cell Membrane Levels of Long-chain n-3 Polyunsaturated Fatty Acids and the Risk of Primary Cardiac Arrest," *Journal of the American Medical Association*, 1 November 1995, 1363–67.

those villages; the more storks, the more babies. Surely it is not possible that . . . No, it's not. Villages with high birth rates have more newly married couples, and therefore have more newly constructed houses. Storks, it turns out, prefer to nest beside chimneys that have not previously been used by other storks.[13] Tracing the causal chains of phenomena that vary concomitantly, we may find links in common, which is what Mill meant when he said that the phenomena may be "connected . . . through some fact of causation."

Because the Method of Concomitant Variation permits us to adduce, as evidence, changes in the *degree* to which circumstances and phenomena are present, it greatly strengthens our set of inductive techniques. It is a *quantitative* method of inductive inference, those earlier discussed being essentially qualitative. The use of concomitant variation therefore presupposes the existence of some method of measuring or estimating, even if only roughly, the degrees to which phenomena vary.

Exercises

Analyze each of the following arguments in terms of the variation of "phenomena," to show how they follow the pattern of the Method of Concomitant Variation.

*1.   At the largest particle accelerator in the world, the LEP [Large Electron-Positron Collider, operated by the 18-nation European Laboratory for Particle Physics (CERN)], a strange puzzle defied solution for over a year. Troublesome fluctuations in the beams of electrons and positrons (their antimatter twins) that whip around the accelerator's 17-mile ring could not be explained. Although very small, these fluctuations create serious problems when beam energies must be measured very precisely.

"We had assumed that something in our hardware was causing these fluctuations—the power supply, or something," said Dr. Lyn Evans, the Welsh physicist in charge of LEP. But Dr. Gerhard Fischer, at the Stanford Linear Accelerator Center in California, suggested that the gravitational forces exerted by the moon (called lunar tidal effects) might be responsible.

Dr. Albert Hofmann of CERN and his colleagues tested this lunar hypothesis with a long and exhausting experiment in November of 1992. They recorded a complex pattern of fluctuations in the energies of LEP's particle beams that *exactly matched* fluctuations in the tidal force exerted by the moon. The problem was solved.

The moon's gravitational pull does not affect the electrons or positrons directly, as they sweep around the underground ring at

---

[13] J. L. Casti, *Searching for Certainty* (New York: William Morrow, 1991).

LEP. But the tidal tug of the moon very slightly deforms the large tract of land in which the circular tunnel is embedded, changing the tunnel's 26.7-kilometer circumference by as much as one millimeter! This minute change in the accelerator's dimensions causes fluctuations of some 10 million electronvolts in the energies of the beams.

> —Malcolm Browne, "Moon Is Found to Be the Cause of a Real Puzzle," *New York Times*, 17 November 1992

2. Careful studies have been made of the incidence of leukemia in the survivors of the atomic bombs burst over Hiroshima and Nagasaki. These survivors received exposures ranging from a few roentgens to 1,000 roentgens or more.

    They are divided into four groups. . . . The first group, *A*, consists of the estimated 1,870 survivors who were within 1 kilometer of the hypocenter (the point on the surface of the earth directly below the bomb when it exploded). There were very few survivors in this zone, and they received a large amount of radiation.

    The second group, *B*, consists of the 13,730 survivors between 1.0 and 1.5 kilometers from the hypocenter; the third, *C*, of the 23,060 between 1.5 and 2.0 kilometers; and the fourth, *D*, of the 156,400 over 2.0 kilometers from the hypo-center.

    The survivors of zones *A*, *B*, and *C* have been dying of leukemia during the period of careful study, the eight years from 1948 to 1955, at an average rate of about 9 per year. . . . Many more cases of leukemia occurred in the 15,600 survivors of zones *A* and *B* than in the 156,400 survivors of zone *D*, who received much less radiation. There is no doubt that the increased incidence is to be attributed to the exposure to radiation.

    . . . The survivors of zone *A* received an estimated average of 650 roentgens; those of zone *B*, 250; those of zone *C*, 25; and those of zone *D*, 2.5. . . . To within the reliability of the numbers, the incidence of leukemia in the three populations *A*, *B*, and *C* is proportional to the estimated dose of radiation, even for class *C*, in which the estimated dose is only 25 roentgens.

    > —Linus Pauling, *No More War!*

3. When it comes to love, sex, and friendship, do birds of a feather flock together? Or is it more important that opposites attract? Dr. Claus Wedekind, of Bern University in Switzerland, hypothesized that body odor might signal that its owner had desirable immune genes—called MHC genes—that would help offspring to fight off diseases. He devised an experiment to see if human body odor correlated with MHC genes and if people could tell.

He and his team collected DNA samples for 49 female and 44 male university students. He asked the men to wear cotton T-shirts on two successive nights, to keep the shirt in a plastic bag, to use perfume-free detergents and soaps, and to avoid smelly rooms, smell-producing foods, and activities like smoking and sex that create odors. Meanwhile, the women were given a nasal spray to protect their nasal membranes from infection, and each received a copy of the Patrick Susskind novel *Perfume* to make them more conscious of odors.

When the T-shirts were collected, the women were asked to give ratings, for intensity, pleasantness, and sexiness, to three T-shirts from men with similar MHC genes, and three from men with dissimilar MHC genes, not knowing which was which.

Women who were dissimilar to a particular male's MHC perceived his odor as more pleasant than did women whose MHC was similar to the test man. Odors of men with dissimilar MHC reminded the women of their own mates or former mates twice as often as did the odors of men with similar MHC.

However, if a woman was taking oral contraceptives, which partly mimic pregnancy, this predilection was reversed, and they gave higher rating to men with similar MHC. "The Pill effect really surprised me," said Dr. Wedekind.

—*Proceedings* of the Royal Society of London, 1995.

4. Melatonin is secreted in a rhythm that is highly dependent on the light-dark cycle. Plasma melatonin concentrations are low throughout the day, begin to rise in the early evening before the onset of sleep, reach their peak at about midnight or soon thereafter, and then decline, whether or not the person sleeps. The duration of melatonin secretion depends on the duration of darkness, so that 24-hour melatonin secretion is greater during the winter than during the summer. Exposure to light at night inhibits melatonin secretion in a dose-dependent fashion; the brighter the light, the greater the decrease in plasma melatonin concentrations. . . . The administration of melatonin can ameliorate the symptoms of jet lag and advance the onset of sleep in persons in whom it is delayed.

—Robert D. Utiger, "Melatonin—the Hormone of Darkness,"
The New England Journal of Medicine, 5 November 1992

*5. Stanley Coren sought to plumb the connections between sleeplessness and accidents. To do that he focused on the yearly shift to daylight time in eastern North America when (because clocks are moved forward one hour) most people lose an hour of sleep. He compared the number of accidents then with the number on normal days, and found that on the day after the time change, in Canada, there was an 8 percent increase in accidents. Then, examining the day after the return to standard time, when people gain an hour of sleep, he found a corresponding decrease in accidents. "What we're looking at," says the Director of the Human Chronobiology Laboratory at the University of Pittsburgh, commenting upon Soren's results, "is national jet lag."

> —S. Coren, *Sleep Thieves* (New York: The Free Press, 1996)

6. "Perfect pitch" is the ability to hear a tone all by itself and immediately know what it is—a C-sharp, for example—or to be able to recall a specific tone. Most musicians have "relative pitch": they can identify a note by recognizing the distances or intervals between it and other notes. A recent study at the University of California at San Francisco, based on a survey of 600 musicians, reveals that the earlier the age at which they had begun their music training, the more likely they were to have perfect pitch. Among those who started music lessons before the age of 4, some 40 percent had perfect pitch. That number dropped off to 3 percent for musicians who started their training after the age of 12.

   Two other results suggest that perfect pitch probably has a genetic foundation. Musicians who do have perfect pitch were four times as likely as others to report that they had a relative with perfect pitch, suggesting that the ability may run in families. Moreover, of all musicians who had started their training before the age of 6, the majority did not have perfect pitch—suggesting that training alone, even if begun early, is not sufficient for its development.

   > —Reported in *The American Journal of Human Genetics*, February 1998

7. In a malpractice lawsuit, the size of the award to successful plaintiffs has less to do with whether a doctor has done something wrong than it does with whether the plaintiff is permanently disabled. A recent study of 46 New York State malpractice suits by the Harvard School of Public Health disclosed that, of the 13 cases in which the doctor was proved to have no culpability, the plaintiffs won 6, with awards averaging over $98,000. In contrast, of the 9 cases in which the record established some physician negligence, the plaintiffs won 5, but received on average $67,000.

   When the same cases were regrouped by the amount of disability the plaintiffs exhibited, it was found that the permanently disabled won 7 of 8 such cases regardless of fault, for a typical award of over $200,000. But where there was no disability suffered, winning plaintiffs received an average award of less than $29,000, even if the doctor had been shown at fault.

   > —Reported in *The New England Journal of Medicine*, 26 December 1996)

> ### MILL'S FIVE METHODS OF INDUCTIVE INFERENCE
>
> 1. **The Method of Agreement.** The one factor or circumstance that is *common* to all the cases of the phenomenon under investigation is likely to be the cause (or effect) of that phenomenon.
> 2. **The Method of Difference.** The one factor or circumstance whose absence or presence *distinguishes* all cases in which the phenomenon under investigation occurs from those cases in which it does not occur, is likely to be the cause, or part of the cause, of that phenomenon.
> 3. **The Joint Method of Agreement and Difference.** Although perhaps not a separate method, *the combination,* in the same investigation, *of the method of agreement and the method of difference* gives substantial probability to the inductive conclusion.
> 4. **The Method of Residues.** When some portion of the phenomenon under examination is known to be the consequence of well-understood antecedent circumstances, we may infer that *the remainder of that phenomenon is the effect of the remaining antecedents.*
> 5. **The Method of Concomitant Variation.** *When the variations in one phenomenon are highly correlated with the variations in another phenomenon,* one of the two is likely to be the cause of the other, or they may be related as the products of some third factor causing both.
>
> These are the inductive methods most commonly used by scientists in their investigation of causal laws.

12.3 CRITIQUE OF MILL'S METHODS

A. The Limitations of Mill's Methods

The techniques explained in the preceding section were believed by Mill himself to be tools with which causal relations may be *discovered,* and canons with which causal connections may be *proved.* He was wrong on both counts. The methods are indeed of the very greatest importance, but their role in science is not so majestic as he supposed.

In his statements of the methods, Mill refers to cases having "*only* one circumstance in common" and to cases having "*every* circumstance in common save one." These expressions cannot be taken literally; any two objects will have many circumstances in common however different they may appear; and no two things could ever differ in only one respect—one will be further to the north, one will be closer to the sun, etc. Nor could we even examine all possible circumstances to determine if they differ in only one way. Plainly, therefore, Mill's formulations of the methods refer to the set of all *relevant* circumstances, the ones that have some bearing on the causal connection in question.

But which are those? We cannot learn which factors are relevant by using Mill's methods alone. We must *come* to the contexts in which those methods are applied with some analysis of causal factors (thinking some relevant and some not) already in mind. The caricature of "the scientific drinker" illustrates this problem: What is causing his repeated inebriation? He carefully observes that one night his beverage is Scotch and soda, a second night bourbon and soda, on the following nights brandy and soda, rum and soda, gin and soda. He swears never to touch soda again!

The rules of the methods the scientific drinker has applied correctly, but they proved to be of no avail because the relevant factors in the antecedent circumstances had not been identified. Had *alcohol* been specified as one of the circumstances common to all the cases, that would have made it possible to eliminate soda quickly, of course, using the Method of Difference.

The heroic investigation of the causes of yellow fever, discussed earlier in connection with the Method of Difference, confirmed the conclusion that the fever is spread by the bite of an infected mosquito. We know that *now,* just as we know that it is alcohol and not soda that causes drunkenness. But the yellow fever experiments required insight as well as courage; circumstances in the real world do not come wearing tags marked "relevant" or "irrelevant." The testing of mosquito bites required some previous causal analysis, to which Mill's Methods might then be applied. With such prior analysis in hand, those methods may be exceedingly helpful. But Mill's methods plainly are not *sufficient* instruments for scientific discovery.

Likewise, Mill's methods do not constitute rules for proof. Because the methods always proceed on the basis of some antecedent hypotheses about causal factors (as noted just above), and since all circumstances cannot have been considered, attention will be confined to those believed to be the possible causes. But this judgment may prove to be in error, as when medical scientists first failed to consider the role of dirty hands in transmitting disease, or whenever scientists fail, for some reason, to break down the circumstances before them into the appropriate elements. Since the analyses that are presupposed by the application of the methods may themselves be inadequate, or incorrect, the inferences based on those analyses also may prove to be mistaken. This dependence shows that Mill's methods cannot provide demonstrative proofs.

Moreover, all of Mill's methods rely on *observed* correlations, and even when they are accurate, such observations can be deceptive. We seek causal *laws,* universal connections, whereas what we have had the opportunity to observe may not tell the whole story. The greater the number of our observations, the greater the likelihood that the correlation we record is genuinely lawlike— but no matter how great that number is, we cannot infer with certainty a causal connection among instances not yet observed.

A key point is here driven home: Between deduction and induction, there is a vast gulf. A valid deductive inference constitutes a proof, or demonstration; but every inductive argument is at best highly probable, never demonstrative. Therefore Mill's claim that his canons are "methods of proof" must be rejected, along with his claim that they are "*the* methods of discovery."

B. The Power of Mill's Methods

Although they are limited, the methods we are discussing in this chapter are central in much of science and surely are very powerful. Because it is absolutely impossible to take *all* circumstances into account, Mill's methods must be used, as we have seen, in conjunction with one or more causal *hypotheses* about the circumstances being investigated. Often we are quite unsure, and therefore formulate alternative hypotheses, under which different factors are supposed, tentatively, to be the cause of the phenomenon under investigation. Mill's methods, being eliminative, enable us to deduce that, *if* some specified analysis of the antecedent circumstances has been correct, one of these factors cannot be (or must be) the cause (or part of the cause) of the phenomenon in question. This deduction may be valid—but, again, the soundness of the argument depends upon the correctness of the antecedent analysis supposed.

The methods can yield reliable results only when the hypothesis that has been formulated does correctly identify the circumstances that are causally relevant; and the methods permit the *deduction* of those results only when that hypothesis has been added as a *premiss* in the argument. The nature of the power these methods give us may now be seen. They are not paths to discovery, not rules for proof. *They are instruments for testing hypotheses.* The statements of these methods, taken together, describe the general method of controlled experiment, which is a common and indispensable tool in all of modern science.

So important is the role of hypotheses in systematic empirical investigations that the enterprise of devising and testing hypotheses may be regarded as *the* method of science. It is with science and hypothesis that our next chapter is concerned.

Exercises

Analyze each of the following arguments in terms of "circumstances" or "antecedents" and "phenomena," and indicate which of Mill's methods are being used in each of them.

*1.   Strong links have been shown between the way people make moral judgments and their thinking about their own death. In one experiment, conducted by Dr. Jeff Greenberg of the University of Arizona and Dr. Tom Pyszcyznski of the University of Colorado, 22 municipal court judges were given a series of psychological tests. For half the judges, the tests included a question in which they were asked to write about what will happen to them physically as they die. They were also asked to describe the emotions that the thought of their own death arouses in them.

The judges were then asked to set bond for a prostitute based on a case brief describing the circumstances of her arrest. Those who did not reflect on death before setting the bond recommended, on average, that it be $50. But among those who had been thinking of their own death, the average bond recommended was $455.

"Our moral principles protect us from anxiety about death," said Dr. Pyszcyznski. "Making the judges think about their mortality presumably increased their need for faith in their moral standards. That increases the desire to punish someone who transgresses those values."

—*The Journal of Personality and Social Psychology*, November 1989

2. Repeated reports, before and after Kinsey, showed college-educated women to have a much lower-than-average divorce rate. More specifically, a massive and famous sociological study by Ernest W. Burgess and Leonard S. Cottrell indicated that women's chances of happiness in marriage increased as their career preparation increased. . . .

   Among 526 couples, less than 10 percent showed "low" marital adjustment where the wife had been employed seven or more years, had completed college or professional training, and had not married before twenty-two. Where wives had been educated *beyond college*, less than 5 percent of marriages scored "low" in happiness.

   —Betty Friedan, *The Feminine Mystique*

3. Strong evidence has been presented that a diet low in folic acid [a trace vitamin in the B complex] during pregnancy increases the chances of giving birth to a premature baby of lower than normal birth weight. Dr. Theresa Scholl [of the University of Medicine and Dentistry of New Jersey] studied the outcomes of pregnancy for 832 women from the inner city of Camden, N.J. to determine the influence of dietary and supplementary consumption of folic acid. "We found that the women who consumed less than 240 micrograms per day of folic acid had about a two to threefold greater risk of preterm delivery and low birth weight," she said. She reported that even small increases in the women's serum folic acid concentrations by the 28th week decreased the odds of preterm delivery as well as the chance of having a baby of low birth weight. Of the 219 women in the low-folic-acid category (receiving less than 240 micrograms a day), 44 had preterm, low birth weight infants. "The risks declined in direct relationship to increased serum levels of folic acid, showing that low intake is a risk factor throughout pregnancy," Dr. Scholl concluded.

   —T. O. Scholl, *et al.*, "Dietary and Serum Folate: Their Influence on the Outcome of Pregnancy," *American Journal of Clinical Nutrition*, April 1996

4. In medical centers around the country cardiologists very frequently open clogged arteries, only to have the obstructions grow back in about half the patients. No one has been able to predict which patients will have this regrowth or to prevent it. But Dr. Stephen Epstein, at the National Heart, Lung and Blood Institute, recently has accumulated evidence that the regrowth of plaque is spurred by cytomegalovirus, a virus so common that it is found in about two-thirds of elderly Americans. Examining 75 patients with

heart disease who were about to have atherectomy (which involves cutting out plaque from a clogged artery) Dr. Epstein found that 49 of these, or about 75 percent, had been infected with cytomegalovirus, as evidenced by antibodies to the virus. But when Dr. Epstein looked again at those 49 patients six months after their atherectomies, he found that 21 of them, or 43 percent, had their plaque grow back, while he found "much to our amazement" that just 2 of the 26 patients without cytomegalovirus infections, or 8 percent, had a regrowth of their plaque, called restenosis. "The risk for developing restenosis," Dr. Epstein concluded, "is nearly 10 times greater in patients who had those viral infections." When the virus is activated, he concludes, it makes a protein that releases the natural brakes on cell growth, and thus stimulates plaque development. Dr. Epstein is trying to find out, in animals, whether vaccinations against cytomegalovirus can protect those animals from restenosis. "It's very exciting," he said. "Although conventional wisdom has said that cytomegalovirus does not cause disease, what we're proposing is that it causes disease so subtle that it hasn't been recognized."

—Reported in *The New England Journal of Medicine,* 29 August 1996

*5. On the 31st of August, 1909, Paul Ehrlich and Hata stood before a cage in which sat an excellent buck rabbit. Flourishing in every way was this rabbit, excepting for the tender skin of his scrotum, which was disfigured with two terrible ulcers, each bigger than a twenty-five-cent piece. Those sores were caused by the gnawing of the pale spirochete of the disease that is the reward of sin. They had been put under the skin of that rabbit by S. Hata a month before. Under the microscope—it was a special one built for spying just such a thin rogue as that pale microbe—under this lens Hata put a wee drop of the fluid from these ugly sores. Against the blackness of the dark field of this special microscope, gleaming in a powerful beam of light that hit them sidewise, shooting backwards and forwards like ten thousand silver drills and augers, played myriads of these pale spirochetes. It was a pretty picture, to hold you there for hours, but it was sinister—for what living things can bring worse plague and sorrow to men?

Hata leaned aside. Paul Ehrlich looked down the shiny tube. Then he looked at Hata, and then at the rabbit.

"Make the injection," said Paul Ehrlich. And into the ear-vein of that rabbit went the clear yellow fluid of the solution of 606, for the first time to do battle with the disease of the loathsome name.

Next day there was not one of those spiral devils to be found in the scrotum of that rabbit. His ulcers? They were drying already! Good clean scabs were forming on them. In less than a month there was nothing to be seen but tiny scabs—it was like a cure of Bible times—no less! And a little while after that Paul Ehrlich could write:

"It is evident from these experiments that, if a large enough dose is given, the spirochetes [of syphilis] can be destroyed *absolutely and immediately with a single injection!*"

—Paul De Kruif, *Microbe Hunters,* 1926

6. Some theories arise from anecdotal evidence that is difficult to confirm. In *The Left-Hander Syndrome* (1992), Stanley Coren sought to evaluate the common belief that left-handed persons die sooner than right-handers. But death certificates or other public records very rarely mention the hand preferred by the deceased. What could serve as a reliable data source with which that hypothesis could be tested? Coren searched baseball records, noting which hand baseball pitchers threw with, and then recording their ages at death. Right-handed pitchers, he found, lived on average nine months longer than lefties. Then, in a follow-up study, he and a colleague telephoned the relatives of people named on death certificates in two California counties, to ask which hand the deceased favored. Right-handed people (that study found) lived an average of nine years longer than lefties.

7. The time-honored advice for taking care of bee stings, quoted faithfully in medical texts and first-aid manuals everywhere, is wrong. Drs. P. Kirk Visscher and Richard Vetter, of the University of California at Riverside, and Dr. Scott Camazine of Pennsylvania State University, long-time bee-keepers, hypothesized, and then proved, that speed matters more than style in removing stingers. The honeybee, after stinging, leaves its stinger in the victim, and with it the venom sac and a chunk of its abdomen which continues to twitch, working its barbs ever deeper into the flesh and continuing to pump venom from the sac.

    The researchers first experimented on themselves. To determine whether the size of the welt depended upon the amount of venom that entered the skin, Dr. Camazine gave Dr. Visscher a series of injections containing measured amounts of bee venom. As expected, the diameter of the welts, and their soreness, increased along with the amount of venom used.

    But does the time it takes to remove a stinger affect the size of the welt? Dr. Visscher, head of the research team, was again the volunteer subject, receiving a great many bee stings in the process. Dr. Visscher would catch a worker bee, grasp her by the wings and press her against the inside of his forearm until she stung. He did this repeatedly over the course of several days, scraping out the stingers at various intervals, from half a second up to 8 seconds after being stung. Dr. Vetter, unaware of how long each stinger had been left in place, measured the welt after 10 minutes. Fifty stings later the researchers had shown that time was indeed of the essence; the longer the stinger stayed in, the bigger the welt. When left in place for 8 seconds, the resulting welt was a third larger than if left only one second.

Finally, the researchers compared methods of stinger removal—the widely advised careful scraping versus grab-and-yank. Each researcher tried each method with twenty different stings otherwise identical. They found that the method of removal had no impact on welt size. Dr. Visscher and his colleagues urge those who are stung: Do not hesitate; do not fumble for a pocket knife or credit card, or stop to think about technique. Grab that stinger and yank! But he noted that the venom is pumped out so quickly that the victim must react almost instantaneously to make a difference.

—Reported in *The Lancet*, 2 August 1996

8. Medical investigators in Rhode Island and in Germany have shown that the shorter men are, the greater their risk of heart trouble and high blood pressure. Dr. Donna Parker, of Memorial Hospital in Pawtucket, Rhode Island, studied 6,589 men and women, comparing their heights and incidence of heart disease. Men under 5-foot-5 had a risk of heart disease double that of moderate-sized men [5-foot-7 to 5-foot-8], and men over 5-foot-10 had a risk 60 percent lower than that of moderate sized men. The findings did not apply to the women in this study.

At the University of Muenster, researchers found that among 5,065 men and women studied, the shorter men are, the higher their blood pressure is likely to be. Among the German men, blood pressure went up six points for each four inches shorter the men were. The shortest men, under 5-foot-7, were twice as likely to have seriously elevated blood pressure as the tallest men, those over 5-foot-11.

—Reported by The Associated Press, 15 March 1996

9. A hormone recently discovered in the brains of both humans and rats acts as a powerful appetite suppressant in the rodents, scientists are reporting today. Researchers think the hormone, urocortin, may be what causes people and animals to lose their appetites when they are under stress or in danger, and survival might depend on running away or fighting rather than stopping to eat. Dr. Mariana Spina [of the Scripps Research Institute, in San Diego] injected urocortin directly into the brains of rats and then monitored the animals' food intake, comparing it to that of rats in a control group that were not given the hormone. . . . The rats injected with urocortin ate much less than those in the control group. And the more of the hormone they were given, the less they ate. Rats receiving the highest doses ate about one-fifth of what the control group ate. Researchers suggested that drugs that could block the

action of urocortin might help patients with disorders like anorexia
nervosa that make them unable to eat.

—Reported in *Science,* 13 September 1996

*10.   We have investigated whether melatonin secretion [of the pineal
gland] differs between patients with coronary heart disease and
healthy controls. We studied 2 women and 13 men with docu-
mented coronary heart disease, and 2 healthy women and
8 healthy men. We measured melatonin in nighttime and afternoon serum.

   Melatonin was not detectable in either group in the afternoon.
Serum melatonin concentrations at night were significantly lower
in patients with coronary heart disease than in the controls. Thus,
impaired nocturnal secretion of melatonin is associated with coronary heart disease.

—P. Brugger, *et al.,* "Impaired Nocturnal Secretion of Melatonin
in Coronary Heart Disease," *The Lancet,* 3 June 1995

11.   Near the end of the Middle Ages, a few theologians (the "scientists" of that time) persuaded a king of France to give them permission for an experiment that had been forbidden by the Roman
Catholic Church. They were allowed to weigh the soul of a criminal by measuring him both before and after his hanging. As usually happens with academics, they came up with a definite result:
the soul weighed about an ounce and a half.

—John Lukacs, "Atom Smasher Is Super Nonsense,"
New York Times, 17 June 1993

12.   Undoubtedly the outstanding point of departure of industrial social psychology was the series of studies performed in the
Hawthorne plant of the Western Electric Company, starting in
1927. These were conducted by three Harvard professors, Elton
Mayo, F. J. Roethlisberger, and T. N. Whitehead, and by W. J.
Dickson of Western Electric. The original aim of the studies was to
obtain concrete data on the effects of illumination, temperature,
rest periods, hours of work, wage rate, etc., upon production. A
group of six girls, average workers, were chosen for the experiment; their task was the assembly of telephone relays. Almost from
the beginning, unexpected results appeared: The production rate
kept going up whether rest periods and hours were increased or
decreased! In each experimental period, whatever its conditions,
output was higher than in the preceding one. The answer seemed
to lie in a number of subtle social factors.

   . . . As Homans summarizes it, the increase in the girls' output
rate "could not be related to any change in their conditions of
work, whether experimentally induced or not. It could, however,
be related to what can only be spoken of as the development of an

organized social group in a peculiar and effective relation with its supervisors."

—S. Stansfeld Sargent and Robert C. Williamson, *Social Psychology*

13. Poor people have long been known to have more medical problems than affluent people of the same age, but a new study suggests that greater inequality in the distribution of income contributes to higher overall mortality rates and deaths from cancer, homicide, and heart disease. Dr. Bruce P. Kennedy and colleagues at the Harvard School of Public Health have found that for treatable conditions like tuberculosis, pneumonia, and high blood pressure, mortality rates were higher in states where the income gaps were wider. "The size of the gap between the wealthy and the less well-off, as distinct from the absolute standard of living enjoyed by the poor, appears to be related to mortality." Why this is true is not clear. "It is possible that income distribution is a proxy for other social indicators, such as the degree of investment in human capital," Dr. Kennedy said. "Communities that tolerate large degrees of income inequality may be the same ones which under-invest in social goods such as public education or accessible health care."

   Very similar conclusions were reached in a second study by Dr. George A. Kaplan of the California Department of Health Services. "Income inequality increased in all states except Alaska from 1980 to 1990," Dr. Kaplan noted, "and over the decade mortality declined in all states, but those with greater income inequality showed smaller declines." So, the California team concluded, "It would be prudent to consider health effects, and the costs associated with them, when evaluating the impact of economic policies." Dr. Kaplan, an epidemiologist, added:

   > People might assume that states with higher income inequality have more poor people, and we know that poor people have higher death rates. But the evidence in these two studies suggests that the increased death rates in those states are not due simply to their having more poor people. Income inequality seems to be increasing mortality rates among nonpoor people as well."

   —Reported in *The British Medical Journal*, 19 April 1996

14. Several small studies have previously linked baldness to heart attacks, but perhaps the most convincing evidence to support a relationship between the hair and the heart emerged recently from a two-year study of men admitted to 35 New England hospitals. [Reported in the *Journal of the American Medical Association*, 24 February 1993] Nurses collected several types of information, including hair distribution patterns, from 665 men admitted for a heart attack and 772 who were admitted with a noncardiac diagnosis. . . . The men with heart attacks were more likely than those in the comparison group to have baldness at the top (vertex) of their

heads. Vertex baldness was associated with a 40 percent increase in heart attack risk after adjustments were made for age differences between the two groups. The more severe the hair loss, the greater the risk—extreme vertex baldness was more than three times as common among the heart attack patients as among those without a cardiac diagnosis.

But there is no reason to believe that baldness causes heart attacks. Furthermore, treating baldness is unlikely to be a useful strategy for preventing heart disease. Until this association is better defined by further research, it seems prudent for bald men to do their best to control other risk factors for coronary disease, such as hypertension, smoking, diabetes, cholesterol, and obesity.

—"Baldness and Heart Attack Risk," *Harvard Heart Letter,* August 1993

15. A study by the New York Division of Criminal Justice Services has arrived at provisional but nonetheless alarming conclusions about discrimination in the courts. The study finds that members of minority groups are substantially more likely than whites to be jailed—even when they commit the same crimes and have similar criminal histories. . . . Startling differences appeared in local jail terms, which are always less than a year. A big segment of African Americans and Latinos, some 30 percent in all, received harsher sentences than whites who had committed comparable crimes. Researchers estimated that, throughout New York State, about 4,000 African Americans and Latinos are sent to jail each year for crimes and circumstances that do not lead to jail terms for whites. . . . The courts have broad discretion in lesser felonies. People who commit some burglaries, assaults or lower-level drug offenses, for example, can either be sentenced to state or local jails or be released. The study suggests that judges and police may more often award the lenient options to whites.

—"Unequal Sentencing," *New York Times,* 15 April 1996

16. Harmful strains of *E. coli* bacteria have caused scores of deaths and sickened hundreds of consumers of undercooked hamburgers. How do these bacteria survive? Studies at Cornell University disclose that a critical factor is cattle diet; when the cows were fed grains until slaughter, the acid level in their colons rose high enough to permit the growth of 100 million *E. coli* cells, of which about a million become acid resistant and thus able to withstand the acidity of the human stomach. But when the animals were fed hay for just five days, only about 10,000 *E. coli* cells remained, and virtually none of these were acid resistant, being killed easily by a dose of acid comparable to what is found in the human stomach.

The colon contents of cattle become acidic on a diet of grain because the animals incompletely digest the starch in grain, which permits some starch to reach the colon where bacteria can ferment it and produce fermentation acids. But on a diet of hay there is no residual starch to be fermented in the colon, and the *E. coli* there remain acid sensitive. If cattle were given hay for a brief period immediately before slaughter, the Cornell scientists conclude, the risk of foodborne *E. coli* infection would be substantially reduced.

—Reported in *Science,* 11 September 1998

17. Prof. Norbert Schwartz, of the University of Michigan, conducted the following experiment. He tested the attitudes of people who had just used a University of Michigan copying machine in which, for some subjects, he had planted a dime which they found, while for others there was no windfall dime. After using the copier, subjects were asked how happy they were about life. Those who had found a dime were consistently more upbeat about "their lives as a whole," and about the economy and many other matters. "We found," said Prof. Schwartz, "that a dime can make you happy for about twenty minutes. Then the mood wears off."

—N. Schwartz, *Well Being: Foundations of Hedonic Psychology,* 1999

18. To determine the role of specific genes, mice are bred in which certain genes have been deleted, called "knockout mice." When normal mice are placed in a lighted room, with dark corners, they go immediately to the dark. In one recent experiment the mice, upon entering the dark, encounter a mild electric shock, and very quickly learn to stay away from those dark regions. And mice who lack a gene called Ras-GRF learn to be wary just as quickly as do normal mice. But, unlike normal mice, the knockout mice throw caution to the winds the next day, and chance the dark corners again and yet again. It appears that the Ras-GRF gene—probably very much like the analogous gene possessed by humans—plays a critical role in the ability of the mice to remember fear. This gene is almost certainly crucial for the survival of mammals.

—Reported in *Nature,* December 1997

19. Many business people explain that golf is great for building business relationships with clients, but it is widely supposed that this only an excuse for playing hooky. Now, it turns out, skill at golf is very surely associated with business success. A rigorous study by the *New York Times* of the golfing and management prowess of America's chief executives, reveals a clear pattern: if he is a better-than-average golfer, he is also likely to deliver above-average returns to shareholders. . . . The correlations among these data are hardly a statistical fluke. Mr. Graef Crystal, who performed the complex and probably unprecedented calculations, said that the probability that the findings are due to chance alone is less than 1 percent.

—"Duffers Needn't Apply," *New York Times,* 31 May 1998

Summary of Chapter 12

In this chapter we have examined causal connections, and methods for establishing them.

In section 12.1, we explored **the various meanings of "cause"** and explained **the nature of inductive generalization.** We examined **simple enumeration,** finding that its deficiencies oblige the development of other, more reliable methods of establishing causal laws.

In section 12.2, we examined five of these inductive procedures, called **Mill's Methods,** illustrating their application and explaining their essential *eliminative* nature. These five methods are:

1.   The Method of Agreement
2.   The Method of Difference
3.   The Joint Method of Agreement and Difference
4.   The Method of Residues
5.   The Method of Concomitant Variation

In section 12.3, we discussed the deficiencies and the strengths of Mill's methods, concluding that, although they cannot do all that Mill claimed for them, they are profoundly important as **the chief means of testing scientific hypotheses.** Taken together, these inductive techniques constitute **the method of controlled experiment,** which is an essential tool in all of science.

. . . every work of science great enough to be remembered for a few generations affords some exemplification of the defective state of the art of reasoning of the time when it was written; and each chief step in science has been a lesson in logic
—Charles Sanders Peirce

CHAPTER 13

SCIENCE AND HYPOTHESIS

13.1 THE VALUES OF SCIENCE

Modern science has changed almost every aspect of our lives. Its *practical* value lies in the easier, healthier, and more abundant life it has made possible. Although some of its results have been very worrisome, most will agree that the advances of science—and their technological applications in communication, transportation, manufacturing, farming, recreation and public health—have, on balance, greatly benefited humanity.

Science also offers *intrinsic* values in the fulfillment of the desire to know. Long ago Aristotle wrote that "to be learning something is the greatest of pleasures not only to the philosophy but also to the rest of mankind."[1] And Einstein spoke for scientists of all ages when he wrote:

> What impels us to devise theory after theory? Why do we devise theories at all? The answer is simply: because we enjoy "comprehending," that is, reducing phenomena by the process of logic to something already known or (apparently) evident.[2]

The aim of science is the discovery of *general* truths. Individual facts are critical, of course; science is built up with facts as a house may be built up with stones. But a mere collection of facts no more constitutes a science than a collection of stones constitutes a house. Scientists seek to understand phenomena, and to do this they seek to uncover the patterns in which phenomena occur, and the systematic relations among them.

---

[1] Aristotle, *Poetics*, 1448b.
[2] Albert Einstein, "On the Generalized Theory of Gravitation," *Scientific American*, April, 1950.

Simply to know the facts is not enough; it is the task of science to *explain* them. This, in turn, requires the *theories* of which Einstein wrote, incorporating the natural laws that govern events, and the principles that underlie them.

13.2 EXPLANATIONS, SCIENTIFIC AND UNSCIENTIFIC

What is wanted when an *explanation* for something is requested? An account is sought, some set of statements about the world, or some story, from which the thing to be explained can be logically inferred—an account that removes or reduces the problematic aspects of what was to be explained. Explanation and inference may be thought of as the same process, viewed in opposite directions. A logical inference advances from premises *to* a conclusion; the explanation of any given fact is the identification of the premises from which that fact may be logically inferred. In the first chapter of this book (section 1.6) we illustrated how "*Q because P*" can express an argument, when we are reasoning *to* Q, but also can express an explanation, if we are reasoning *from* an already established Q to the premises that may account for it.

Every good explanation must be relevant, of course. If I offer as an explanation of my lateness in arriving at work the proposition that there is continuing political disorder in central Africa, that will be thought no explanation at all; it is *irrelevant* because from it the fact to be explained, my lateness, cannot be inferred. And of course every genuine explanation will be not only relevant but true.

Whatever the correct explanation of my lateness, it will be needed only because of questions raised about that one event, my being late. Explanations that are scientific, however, in addition to being relevant and true, must go beyond particular events to offer an understanding of *all* events of a given kind. The grandeur of Newtonian mechanics lies in the law of *universal* gravitation. Newton wrote:

> Every particle of matter in the universe attracts every other particle with a force which is directly proportional to the product of the masses of the particles and inversely proportional to the square of the distance between them.

Unscientific explanations may also be relevant and general. An engine failure may be unscientifically explained as the work of mysterious gremlins; a disease may be explained as the result of an evil spirit that invades the body. The regular motions of the planets were for centuries thought to be explained by the "intelligence" that lived in each planet and controlled its movement.

But we are interested in truly *scientific* explanations, which may be distinguished from unscientific explanations in two related ways:

The first difference is one of *attitude*. One who accepts an unscientific explanation is *dogmatic;* the account is regarded as being absolutely true and not capable of improvement. The opinions of Aristotle were for centuries accepted, unscientifically, as the ultimate authority on matters of fact. However open-minded Aristotle himself may have been, his views were adopted by some medieval scholars in a rigid and unscientific spirit.[3] In genuine science, on the other hand, the prevailing attitude is very different. Every explanation is there put forward tentatively and provisionally. Proposed scientific explanations are regarded as *hypotheses,* more or less probable in the light of available evidence.[4]

The second and most fundamental difference between scientific and unscientific explanations lies in *the basis for accepting or rejecting the view in question.* An unscientific explanation is taken simply as true, revealed from on high, perhaps, or accepted because "everyone knows" that it is so. An unscientific belief is held independently of anything we should regard as *evidence* in its favor. But in science a hypothesis is worthy of acceptance only to the extent that there is good evidence for it. Its truth or falsehood remains always subject to doubt, and the search for evidence is never ending. Science is *empirical* in holding that the test of truth lies in our experience—and therefore the essence of a scientific explanation is that it be *testable.*

The test of truth may be direct or indirect. To determine whether it is raining outside I need only glance out the window. But the general propositions offered as explanatory hypotheses are not directly testable. If my lateness at work had been explained by my claim about some traffic accident, my employer, if suspicious, might test that explanation indirectly by seeking the police accident report. An indirect test deduces, from the proposition to be tested (*e.g.* that I was involved in an accident) some other proposition (*e.g.* that an accident report had been submitted) capable of being tested directly. If that deduced proposition is false, the explanation that implied it must be false. If the deduced proposition is true, that provides some evidence (but not conclusive evidence) that the explanation is true, having been indirectly confirmed.

Indirect testing is never certain. It always relies upon some additional premisses, like the premiss that accidents of the sort I described to my employer are invariably reported to the police. But the accident report that should have been submitted in my case may not have been, so its absence does not *prove* my explanation false. And even the truth of some added premisses does not render my explanation *certain*—although the successful testing of the conclusion deduced (the reality of the accident report, in this example) does corroborate the premisses from which it was deduced.

Even an unscientific explanation has *some* evidence in its favor, namely, the very fact it is held to explain. The unscientific theory that the planets are inhabited by "intelligences" that cause them to move in their observed orbits can claim,

---

[3] One of the scholars to whom Galileo offered his telescope to view the newly discovered moons of Jupiter declined to look, expressing the certainty that no real moons could possibly be seen because no mention of them could be found in Aristotle's treatise on astronomy!

[4] The vocabulary of science is sometimes misleading on this point. When what is first suggested as an "hypothesis" is well-confirmed its status may be elevated to that of a "theory"; after universal acceptance it may be further elevated to that of "law." But descriptions vary; Newton's discovery is still called the "law of gravitation," whereas Einstein's contribution which improved and superseded it is referred to as the "theory of relativity." Whatever the terms used, the attitude of genuine scientists is not dogmatic. The general propositions of science are all in essence hypotheses, never absolutely certain.

as evidence, the fact that the planets do move in those orbits. But the great difference between that hypothesis and the reliable astronomical explanation of planetary movement lies in this: for the unscientific hypothesis there is no other directly testable proposition that can be deduced from it. Any scientific explanation of a given phenomenon, on the other hand, will have directly testable propositions deducible from it *other than the proposition stating the fact to be explained.* This is what we mean when we say that an explanation is *empirically verifiable,* and such verifiability is the most essential mark of a scientific explanation.[5]

13.3 EVALUATING SCIENTIFIC EXPLANATIONS

Different and incompatible scientific explanations may be often be put forward to account for the same phenomenon. My colleague's abrupt behavior may be explained by the hypothesis that she is angry, or by the hypothesis that she is shy. In a criminal investigation, alternative and incompatible hypotheses about the identity of the criminal may equally well account for the facts of the crime. But if the alternative hypotheses cannot both be true, how shall we choose between them?

Here we assume that we are evaluating competing scientific explanations; we suppose that both (or all) are relevant and testable. What criteria might we use to select the best of the available theories? We cannot hope for rules that will guide the *discovery* of hypotheses; devising hypotheses is the creative side of the scientific enterprise, a function of talent and imagination, in some ways like a work of art. But though there are no formulas for discovering new hypotheses, there are standards—going beyond relevance and testability—to which acceptable hypotheses may be expected to *conform.*

Three criteria are most commonly used in judging the merit of competing scientific hypotheses:

1. Compatibility with Previously Well-established Hypotheses

Science aims at achieving a *system* of explanatory hypotheses. Such a system must be self-consistent, of course, for no self-contradictory set of propositions could possibly be true. Progress is made by gradually expanding hypotheses to comprehend more and more facts. Such progress requires that each new hypothesis be consistent with those already confirmed. For example, the hypothesis that beyond the orbit of Uranus there was another planet as yet uncharted was, when proposed, perfectly consistent with the main body of astronomical theory, and it led, in 1846, to the discovery of the planet Neptune.[6] Orderly progress in scientific inquiry requires that any new theory *fit* with older theories.

---

[5] This general conception of "scientific explanation" rightly applies outside the realm of what is normally thought of as the sciences such as physics or psychology. Thus, the explanation of an event like my lateness to work as a consequence of a traffic accident, in being indirectly testable in various ways, is in this wide sense "scientific."

[6] That discovery was discussed in section 12.2 as an illustration of the use of the Method of Residues.

The scientific ideal is one of gradual growth of theoretical knowledge by the addition of one new hypothesis after another, but the actual history of scientific progress has not always followed that orderly pattern. Sometimes important new hypotheses, inconsistent with older theories, have simply replaced them, rather than fitted in with them. Einstein's relativity theory was of that sort, shattering many of the preconceptions of the older Newtonian theory. And the discovery of radioactivity in the late nineteenth century overthrew the principle of the conservation of matter which asserted that matter could be neither created nor destroyed. The hypothesis that radium atoms undergo spontaneous disintegration was simply inconsistent with that old and accepted principle, and the older principle eventually had to be relinquished.

Theories in science are not abandoned quickly or without resistance, in favor of newer and shinier ones. Indeed, older theories are not so much abandoned as corrected. Einstein himself always insisted that his own work was a modification rather than a rejection of Newton's. The principle of the conservation of matter was modified by being absorbed into the more comprehensive principle of the conservation of mass-energy. A theory gets established by being shown adequate to explain a considerable mass of data, of known facts. It cannot be dethroned by some new hypothesis unless that new hypothesis can account for those same facts as well or even better.

So the advancement of science takes the form of more comprehensive and thus more adequate explanations of the way in which the world manifests itself in our experience. There is nothing capricious about this development. Where inconsistencies arise, the greater age of one hypothesis does not automatically prove it correct, but the *presumption* is in favor of the older hypothesis if it has already been extensively confirmed. If the new one in conflict with it also received extensive confirmation, considerations of age or priority are not relevant. When two hypotheses conflict we must turn to the observable facts to decide between them. The ultimate court of appeal is experience.

This criterion, compatibility with previous well-established hypotheses, comes in the end to this: the totality of hypotheses accepted at any one time should be consistent with each other.[7] The hypothesis that fits in better with the accepted body of scientific theory is to be preferred, other things being equal. The question of what is involved in "other things being equal" takes us to the second criterion.

2. Predictive or Explanatory Power

Every scientific hypothesis must be testable, as we have seen, and it will be testable if some observable fact is deducible from it. When we confront two

---

[7] Scientists may, however, consider and even use inconsistent hypotheses for years, while awaiting the resolution of that inconsistency. This was for many years the situation with respect to the wave and corpuscular theories of lights.

testable hypotheses, of which one has a greater range of facts deducible from it than the other, we say that one has greater predictive or explanatory power.

To illustrate. Galileo Galilei (1564–1642) formulated the laws of falling bodies, which gave a very general account of the behavior of bodies near the surface of the earth. At about the same time the German astronomer Johannes Kepler (1571–1630), using the astronomical data collected by Denmark's Tycho Brahe (1546–1601), formulated the laws of planetary motion, describing the elliptical orbits traveled by the planets around the sun. Each of these scientists unified the various phenomena in his own field of investigation, Galileo in terrestrial mechanics, Kepler in celestial mechanics. Their discoveries were splendid achievements, of course, but they were isolated from one another. Isaac Newton, with his three laws of motion and his theory of universal gravitation, unified and explained these theories in turn. All the consequences explained by Galileo and by Kepler, and many more facts besides, were explained by Newton's account of universal gravitation. An observable fact that can be deduced from a given hypothesis is said to be explained by it, and also can be said to be *predicted* by it. Newton's theories had enormous predictive power. The greater the predictive power of an hypothesis the more it explains, and the better it contributes to our understanding of the phenomena with which it is concerned.[8]

This second criterion has a negative side. If a hypothesis is inconsistent with some well-attested observation, that hypothesis is false and must be rejected. When two different hypotheses both fully explain some set of facts, and both are testable, and both are compatible with the whole body of already established scientific theory, it may be possible to choose between them by deducing from them incompatible propositions that are directly testable. It may be possible to set up a *crucial experiment* to decide between the conflicting theories. Thus, if the first hypothesis entails that a given result will occur under a certain set of circumstances, and the second hypothesis entails that under those same circumstances that specified result will *not* occur, we can decide between the two hypotheses by observing the presence or the absence of that result. Its appearance disconfirms the second hypothesis; its nonappearance disconfirms the first.

A crucial experiment of this kind, to decide between competing hypotheses, may not be easy to carry out because those critical circumstances may be difficult or impossible to produce. Thus the decision between Newtonian theory and Einstein's general theory of relativity had to await a total eclipse of the

---

[8] Prediction is sometimes retrospective. In *The Descent of Man* (1871) Charles Darwin suggested consequences of his evolutionary theories that could not be confirmed at the time. He wrote: "In each great region of the world the living mammals are closely related to the extinct species of the same region. It is, therefore, probable that Africa was formerly inhabited by extinct apes closely allied to the gorilla and chimpanzee; and as these two species are now man's nearest allies, *it is somewhat more probable that our early progenitors lived on the African continent than elsewhere.*" But at the time Darwin wrote, traces of early humans were limited to some poorly understood Neanderthal remains from Europe. His prediction was verified only some sixty years later when the first discoveries of ancient hominid fossils were made in Africa.

sun—a circumstance clearly beyond our power to produce.[9] In other circumstances the crucial experiment may have to await the development of new instruments, either for the production of the required circumstances or for the observation or measurement of the predicted phenomenon. Thus proponents of rival astronomical hypotheses must sometimes bide their time while they await the construction of new and more powerful telescopes. Crucial experiments will be discussed further in section 13.6.

3.   Simplicity

Two rival hypotheses may be relevant and testable, may fit equally well with established theory, and may even have predictive power that is roughly equal. In such circumstances we are likely to favor the *simpler* of the two. The conflict of the Ptolomaic (earth-centered) and the Copernican (sun-centered) theories of celestial motion was like that. Both fit well with earlier theory, and they predicted celestial movements about equally well. Both hypotheses relied on a clumsy (and of course mistaken) device, hypothesized *epicycles* (smaller circles of movement on the larger circles), in order to explain some established astronomical observations. But the Copernican system relied upon many *fewer* such epicycles, and it was therefore much simpler, and this greater simplicity contributed substantially to its acceptance by later astronomers.[10]

Simplicity seems to be a "natural" criterion to invoke. In ordinary life also we are inclined to accept the simplest theory that fits all the facts. In a criminal trial two theories about a crime may be presented, and the case is likely to be decided—perhaps ought to be decided—in favor of the hypothesis that seems simpler, more natural.

But "simplicity" is a tricky notion; only rarely can we choose the simpler theory on the basis of the smaller required number of a given entity, as in the Ptolomaic–Copernican conflict. Two competing theories may each be simpler than the other in different ways. One may rely on a smaller number of entities, while the other may rely on simpler mathematical equations. Even "naturalness" may prove to be deceptive. Many would find it more "natural" to believe that the apparently unmoving earth really is unmoving, and that the apparently moving sun really does circle around us. Simplicity is an important criterion, even sometimes a decisive one—but it is difficult to formulate and not always easy to apply.

---

[9] But such an eclipse, and the opportunity to test general relativity, came quite soon after Einstein's predictions. Among the consequences of the theory was this: that light from a distant star would appear to bend inward as it passed through the gravitational well of the sun, and that therefore, when Earth, the sun, and that star were lined up, the star's image would appear to have moved outward from its normal position. For this experiment all that was needed were good cameras, and the right kind of solar eclipse, in which the three bodies would line up while allowing the star to be seen. The needed solar eclipse came on 29 May 1919; photographs proved that Einstein was right; we do live in a curved, four-dimensional space-time.

[10] The belief in extra-terrestrial beings is commonly contested by those who argue, given our present evidence, that the simplest explanation of the lack of success in all previous searches for extra-terrestrials is that they are simply not there, and that we humans are alone. See Robert Naeye, "OK, Where Are They?" *Astronomy*, July, 1996.

13.4 SEVEN STAGES OF SCIENTIFIC INVESTIGATION

We are now in a position to describe the general pattern of scientific research. This pattern may be broken down into seven steps, or stages. Readily distinguished in the abstract they are by no means always sharply distinct in practice, as they interpenetrate and blend in many contexts. These seven stages will first be briefly set forth in general terms. Then, with this pattern of inquiry in mind, we will examine an extended illustration of scientific investigation that exemplifies the several stages.

1. Identifying the Problem

Scientific investigation begins with a problem of some kind. A problem may be characterized as a fact or a group of facts for which we have no acceptable explanation. The detective, for example, confronts a crime; his problem is to solve it; that is, to identify and prove the guilt of the perpetrator. Sometimes—as in Conan Doyle's stories of the great Sherlock Holmes, the problem may arise from some peculiar event or circumstance that is not yet a crime. Scientists may begin an investigation with their problem sharply identified; more commonly they come gradually to discover the inconsistencies or peculiarities that evolve into a specifiable problem.

Not even Sherlock Holmes or Albert Einstein can engage in profound thought unless there is something to think about. Even a genius must have been presented with a problem before he, or she, can solve it. Reflective thinking—including a wide range of activities from criminal investigation to abstract thinking in physics and mathematics—is *problem-solving* activity, as John Dewey and many other modern philosophers have rightly insisted. The problem must be recognized, at least in some vague form, before the scientist can go to work.

2. Devising Preliminary Hypotheses

Even the most tentative consideration of alternative explanations of the problem at hand requires some preliminary theorizing. The first attempt is not likely to yield a final solution, but *some* theorizing is required in order to know what sort of evidence needs to be collected, and where or how it might best be sought. The detective examines the scene of the crime, interviews suspects, and seeks clues—but bare facts are not clues. Clues become meaningful only if they can be fitted into some pattern that is coherent, even one that is rough and tentative.

So too the scientist begins the collection of evidence with some preliminary hypothesis about the nature of the explanation sought. Some previous knowledge must be relied upon; science does not begin from absolutely nothing. Indeed there *must* have been some prior beliefs if the facts to be explained appear genuinely problematic.

For any serious problem, there are too many relevant facts, too much data in the world for anyone to collect it all. Some matters will be noticed and attended to, others not. The most patient and thorough investigator must choose, from among all the facts revealed, which are to be studied and which are to be to set aside. This requires *some* working hypothesis for which, or in the light of which, relevant data may be collected. That hypothesis need not be a complete theory—but at least the outline of a theory must be there. If it were not, the investigator could not determine which facts, from the totality of facts, to select. However incomplete and tentative, a preliminary hypothesis is needed before any serious inquiry can begin.

3.   Collecting Additional Facts

The fact or facts that initially seemed puzzling are generally too meager to suggest a wholly satisfactory explanation for themselves; if that were not the case, those facts are unlikely to have appeared problematic. But, especially to a scientist who is familiar with facts or circumstances of that general kind (say celestial, or sociological, or historical phenomena), the original problem will suggest a preliminary hypothesis that can guide the search for *additional* relevant facts. This additional evidence may serve as leads, suggestions pointing to a fuller and more nearly adequate solution. This task of collecting evidence is arduous and time-consuming; very frequently it is disappointing and frustrating. Good science is hard work. This laborious collection process is the substance of much scientific work.

Of course, steps 2 and 3 are not fully separable in real-life science; they are intimately connected and interdependent. Some preliminary hypothesis is needed to begin the collection of evidence; thus the process of gathering evidence by using that working hypothesis merges with the process of adjusting and refining the hypothesis itself, which then guides the further search . . . leading perhaps to new findings . . . which suggest yet more refined hypotheses . . . and so on and on.

4.   Formulating the Explanatory Hypothesis

In any successful investigation that point sooner or later will be reached at which the investigator—the scientist, the detective, perhaps some ordinary person—will come to believe that all the facts needed for solving the original problem are in hand. The pieces of the puzzle—more likely the *chunks,* each consisting of smaller pieces—are before him or her, and the task becomes that of assembling them in such a way as to make sense of the whole. The end-product of such thinking, if it is successful, is some hypothesis that accounts for all the data, the original set of facts that created the problem, as well as the additional facts to which the preliminary hypotheses pointed.

There is no mechanical way of arriving at some overarching theory. The actual discovery, or invention, of a truly explanatory hypothesis is a process of creation, one in which imagination as well as knowledge is involved. Some investigators, such as Sherlock Holmes and Albert Einstein, exhibit genius in this process of "reasoning backward" to the explanation of existing phenomena. But every successful scientist must undertake this challenging task of intellectual integration: constructing and formulating the final hypothesis that explains the problematic facts by which the investigation was provoked.[11]

5. Deducing Further Consequences

We have seen that predictive power is one of the criteria with which explanations may be appraised. A really fruitful hypothesis will explain not only the facts that originally inspired it, but many others as well. The good hypothesis points beyond the initial facts to new and different facts whose very existence may not earlier have been suspected. The verification of those facts confirms (but of course does not prove with certainty) the hypothesis that led to them.

An illustration of such prediction is exhibited by the cosmological theory known as "the Big Bang." If, as this theory holds, the present universe began with one extraordinary explosive event, the initial fireball would have been smooth and homogenous, lacking all structure. By contrast, the present-day universe has a great deal of structure, is very lumpy, its visible matter plainly clumped into galaxies, clusters of galaxies, and so forth. Such structure was essential for the origin and evolution of life. But when and how did this structure arise? By observing the very most distant objects in an expanding universe, astronomers can "look back" in time. They must eventually find, through those observations, evidence of the seeds of present structure. If such early structure is not detectable by the most sensitive instruments, the Big Bang theory would appear to be indefensible. If such structure is detected, the Big Bang theory is confirmed, though of course not *proved*.

6. Testing the Consequences.

In a biological context we may formulate the hypothesis that a particular protein is produced in mammals as a reaction to a particular enzyme, and that that enzyme is produced under the direction of a specifically identified gene. From that hypothesis we may deduce the further consequence that where that gene is absent, there will be an absence, or a deficiency, of the protein in question.

To test whether that biological hypothesis is correct, we construct an experiment in which the impact of that identified gene may be measured. Often this can be done by breeding mice in which that critical gene has been deleted—what are called "knockout mice." If in such mice the enzyme in question, and the protein associated with it, are indeed absent, our hypothesis will be confirmed.[12] Much very valuable information in medicine is acquired in just this way. And experiments of this general kind are typical of those conducted in a wide range of biological inquiries. We devise the experiment to determine whether what we had thought would be true, if such-and-such were the case,

---

[11] Readers who wish to test their own skills in this process, in a very narrow domain, may wish to reconsider the problems in reasoning proposed in the final section of the first chapter of this book.

[12] Testing of this particular kind relies upon the Method of Difference, as described in detail in Chapter 12. But the many methods discussed there are (as noted earlier) intellectual tools used to confirm (or disconfirm) hypotheses.

really *is* true. And to do that we must often *construct* the very special circumstances in which such-and-such has been made the case. "An experiment," as the great physicist Max Planck said, "is a question that science poses to Nature, and a measurement is the recording of Nature's answer."

Testing the consequences of some predictions like many of those of Sherlock Holmes may be straightforward. Will the bank robbers break into the vault? Holmes and Watson wait for them and they do.[13] Will the doctor slip a venomous snake through the dummy ventilator? Holmes and Watson watch from hiding, and he does.[14] Those explanatory theories were directly tested and solidly confirmed.

Most scientific theories, of course, cannot be tested by simple observation. The structure of the early universe cannot possibly be observed directly. But if there were some early structure, like that predicted by the Big Bang theory, there would have to be irregularity, unevenness in the background radiation currently encountered that stems from that early time. It is possible, in principle, to measure that background microwave radiation, and in this way to determine, *indirectly,* whether there were such irregularities very shortly after the supposed Big Bang. A few years ago, a satellite was designed that would detect those irregularities if they were present. The observations to be made through that instrument—the Cosmic Background Explorer (COBE) satellite—would be critical for the Big Bang theory. If the long-sought evidence of early structure in the universe were not eventually detected, the Big Bang account of the expanding universe would have to be considered seriously doubtful. But in the spring of 1992 the predicted irregularities, surviving from the earliest time to which astronomers can look back, were indeed detected and measured by COBE. This successful test, although of course it did not *prove* that theory correct, did confirm the Big Bang theory impressively.

7.   Applying the Theory

Through science we aim to *explain* the phenomena we encounter, but we aim also to *control* those phenomena to our advantage. The abstract theories of Newton and Einstein have played a central role in the modern exploration of our solar system. But suppose, to take an example of a very different kind, that the problem confronted is some disease, and the explanatory hypothesis devised is that the disease is caused by certain specified bacteria. Suppose that this theory has been tested by infecting mice or other rodents with those bacteria, and that such tests strongly confirm the explanatory hypothesis by producing, in the animal subjects, the very same disease. We will seek to *apply* that theory in clinical medicine, of course, and that would be done (first in experimental human groups, later as a matter of routine medical care) by eliminating those bacteria from patients suffering from that disease, thereby curing the disease itself. In just this way we have learned how to combat, and in some cases even to eliminate entirely, many terrible human diseases. We

---

[13] Arthur Conan Doyle, "The Red-Headed League."
[14] Arthur Conan Doyle, "The Adventure of the Speckled Band."

seek to understand our world through science. But through science we want also to exert some measure of *control* over the hazards the world presents.

THE SEVEN STAGES OF SCIENTIFIC INQUIRY

1. Identifying the problem
2. Selecting preliminary hypotheses
3. Collecting additional facts
4. Formulating a refined explanatory hypothesis
5. Deducing consequences from the refined hypothesis
6. Testing the consequences deduced
7. Applying the theory

These seven essential stages often overlap and interpenetrate, but they can be identified retrospectively in every investigation that is genuinely scientific.

Exercises

1. Take some detective story, and analyze its structure in terms of the seven steps discussed in the preceding sections.

2. Find an account in a popular or semipopular book on science of some specific line of research, and analyze its structure in terms of the seven steps discussed in this preceding section.

13.5 SCIENTISTS IN ACTION: THE PATTERN OF SCIENTIFIC INVESTIGATION

■**For Enrichment**   The pattern that pervades all scientific inquiry is expressible in terms of the seven steps explained in the preceding section. Of course, the methods of science are not confined to professional scientists; anyone may be said to be proceeding scientifically who follows the general pattern of reasoning from observable facts and other evidence to conclusions that can be tested by experience. The skilled detective is a scientist in this sense, as are most of us at times. We now examine an extended illustration of that pattern of rational inquiry; we follow contemporary scientists in their recent quest for the solution of the structure of deoxyribonucleic acid—DNA.[15]

1.   *The Problem.* All living things begin from a single cell, and all living things reproduce their kind; therefore the characteristics that plants and animals inherit must somehow be buried in their first cell. But where? How is the genetic message conveyed from generation to generation, and why do the parts of each developing organism take the complicated forms that they do? This deep and puzzling problem—solving "the secret of life"—

---

[15] The following account is freely adapted from James D. Watson, *The Double Helix* (1968), and Horace F. Judson, *DNA* (1978).

became an obsession of many scientists, cooperating and competing, during the middle decades of the twentieth century. The quest for the gene is one of the most exciting chapters in the recent history of science.

The solution must lie in one of the four categories of substances that make up living cells: (1) fats (lipids); (2) sugars and starches (polysaccharides); (3) proteins; and (4) nucleic acids. The first two had been eliminated definitively long before the present inquiry began. The fourth, nucleic acids, whose chemical elements were known, were also known to be quite simply constructed, their parts appearing in fixed and repeated order. One of these parts is a sugar called *ribose*; one of the omnipresent nucleic acids contained sugars with one oxygen atom missing—and was therefore called *deoxy-ribo* nucleic acid, or DNA. It was widely believed at that time that DNA was a "stupid" substance, no more than a structural stiffener in cells—like the cardboard that preserves the shape of a new shirt—and thus not a candidate to be the stuff of which genes are made.

If DNA does not carry the hereditary message, that message must be conveyed through some protein not yet identified. But there was good evidence on hand, by 1944, that whatever carried the genetic message was *not* likely to be a protein. Yet when the alpha-helix, a key structural element in proteins, was discovered by Linus Pauling in 1949, using a technique involving detection with X-rays, proteins again became exciting targets. Moreover, the extraordinary complexity of genetic messages—the enormous detail and specificity that had to be conveyed from generation to generation—persuaded many scientists that the secret of the gene could lie only in some large and very complicated protein molecules. In that direction, therefore, the hunt for the gene was widely pressed. Even were that direction correct, there are bewilderingly many proteins; but in any case, the search for the gene among them met with no success.

2.   *Preliminary hypotheses.* When James Watson and Francis Crick began their pursuit of the gene in 1951, at the Cavendish Laboratory in Cambridge, England, their data were confused and incomplete. Their puzzlement was magnified by inconsistencies among beliefs and theories widely accepted; if the observations and eliminative reasoning of Oswald Avery in 1944 were reliable, the search for the gene among the proteins was destined to fail. In that case, as Watson later wrote, "DNA would have to provide the key."[16] This was the preliminary hypothesis with which Watson and Crick began their research: that *the genetic message was somehow carried in the structure of DNA.* Two other preliminary hypotheses guided their quest: First, that its structure, as suggested by X-ray diffraction pictures taken by Rosalind Franklin, and by Maurice Wilkins (who later shared the Nobel Prize with Watson and Crick) was *regular.* Watson wrote:

> Suddenly I was excited about chemistry. . . . I had worried about the possibility that the gene might be fantastically irregular. Now, however, I knew that genes

---
[16] James P. Watson, *The Double Helix,* p. 18.

could crystallize, hence they must have a regular structure that could be solved in a straightforward fashion.[17]

Second, they hypothesized that the DNA filaments, in view of their great length and the diffraction pictures of them, probably took the form of a spiral or *helix*, perhaps similar to the alpha-helix that Pauling had earlier found in some proteins.

3.   *Collecting additional facts.* To reconcile these preliminary hypotheses with the known but confusing facts about the constituents of DNA, much more would have to be learned—some of it buried in the scientific literature, some just being discovered.

Nucleic acids were known to have a long "backbone" consisting of a *sugar* (ribose) alternating with a *phosphate* (a grouping of phosphorus with 4 oxygen atoms). At each "knuckle" of this backbone a third molecular unit, called a *base*, was somehow stuck onto the chain. Each base was one of four known kinds: adenine, guanine, cytosine, and thymine, called by their initials A, G, C, and T. The order of the appearance of these four substances on the backbone was a puzzle, and even how the bases were attached to the backbone was not known. As more data were collected, and preliminary hypotheses were refined, the problem became that of fitting the pieces of DNA together. Each three-piece unit in the chain (sugar, plus phosphate, plus one base) was called a *nucleotide.* How could the nucleotides fit together to form the acid known as DNA? The more general problem ("What is a gene?") that obsessed them had been refined, by Watson and Crick, into this more tractable problem of structure.

Progress at first was very slow. Using super-sized models made of cardboard and wire, they tried every chain-like configuration they could devise. Some specifiable conditions they knew had to be met: certain water content, certain angle of pitch, certain methods of chemical bonding. Everything had to be consistent with previously discovered facts, recent X-ray pictures, and established theories. The four bases (A, G, C, and T) were known to be flat. Watson and Crick tried models in which they were stuck like plates to the inside of the helix backbone, or to the outside, or to each other. The angle of the spiral was adjusted; the theory of bonding to sugar molecules was reexamined. Nothing worked to yield a plausible structure.

4.   *Formulating the refined explanatory hypothesis.* The solution to a large problem commonly relies upon contributions from many different quarters. It is a cooperative enterprise in great part, but becomes highly competitive at times. Other scientists also were racing toward the solution of the structure of DNA. Wilkins and Franklin were getting better X-ray diffraction pictures in their London laboratory. Pauling described what he thought to be the DNA structure as a three-chain helix, but Watson and Crick had

---

[17] *Ibid*, p. 28.

enough information to realize (with a mixture of disappointment and glee) that Pauling's account contained a fatal error. Once Pauling's manuscript was published, Watson wrote:

> it would be only a matter of days before the error would be discovered. We had anywhere up to six weeks before Linus again was in full-time pursuit of DNA.... I let Francis [Crick] buy me a whiskey. Linus had not yet won his Nobel.[18]

The refined hypothesis that would solve the problem had to account for two different powers of the gene. (1) how is the enormous detail in living structures conveyed in the genetic message? and (2) how does the genetic message duplicate itself in successive generations? Needed was a three-dimensional structure, consistent with known facts and theories, that could provide the *coding* for all the detail of life *and* that could *replicate* itself in generation after generation.

The research of Erwin Chargaff, at Columbia University, helped to put them on the right track. Chargaff had made a striking discovery: In all tested samples of DNA, the *relative* quantities of the four bases—adenine, guanine, cytosine, and thymine—were fixed. Two of these, A and G, are called *purines;* the other two, C and T, are called *pyrimidines.* Chargaff had proved that the number of A molecules always is equal to the number of T molecules, and the number of G molecules always equal to the number of C molecules. The quantity of purines (A and G) always is identical to the quantity of pyrimidines (T and C). But no one could explain why this was so.

Through calculation and the manipulation of models, Crick determined that the structures of A and T were such that they would naturally stick to one another; and that the forces which naturally would attract G and C to one another could also be specified. Then, if the DNA chain were so constructed that for every A there was a fitting T, and for every G a fitting C, the chain—if it were split down the middle—would provide an elegant system of self-replication: each side of the chain could be viewed as a lock to which the other side was a key; each would be a template for the construction of a new, matching key. And if the chain of matching pairs of bases was very long, their order and number might explain the required genetic coding of detail. The solution, they now hypothesized, would be some sort of *double* helix. They tried models with the backbone in the center and the bases sticking out; they tried models with the backbone on the outside and the bases projecting inward. Still no success. Yet they believed they were close to elucidation of the structure of DNA.

Could the remaining difficulty lie in the accepted theory of how the bases (A, G, T, and C) could bond to one another? If the accepted theory were flawed, and could be replaced by a new account of the chemical bonding of the bases to one another, a workable model of the double

---

[18] *Ibid.,* p. 104.

helix might be devised. That possibility was explored. The pieces of the puzzle began to come together in Watson's mind:

> When I got to our still empty office the following morning, I quickly cleared away the papers from my desk top so that I would have a large flat surface on which to form pairs of bases held together by hydrogen bonds.[19]

Still no success. With an A on one side matching an A on the other, and a C matching a C, and so on, the bases pointed inward and tied to one another across the hollow center of the chain, they simply could not be fitted into a double spiral.

And then at last, struggling to revise this structure so as to achieve compatibility among all the elements of the theory, Watson was able to formulate a fully refined hypothesis that proved to be correct: the DNA molecule was indeed a double helix, in which the bases did indeed extend inward—but the matching of the pairs of bases was *complementary:* every A fitted to a T, every G fitted to a C.

> I . . . began shifting the bases in and out of other various [fitting] possibilities. Suddenly I became aware that an adenine-thymine pair held together by two hydrogen bonds was identical in shape to a guanine-cytosine pair held together by at least two hydrogen bonds. All the hydrogen bonds seem to form naturally; no fudging was required to make the two types of base pairs identical in shape....
>
> [W]e now had the answer to the riddle of why the number of purine residues (A and G) exactly equaled the number of pyrimidine residues (C and T). Two irregular sequences of bases could be regularly packed in the center of a [double] helix.... Adenine would always pair with thymine, while guanine could pair only with cytosine.... the base sequences of the two intertwined chains were complementary to each other. Given the base sequence of one chain, that of its partner was automatically determined.
>
> Conceptually, it was thus very easy to visualize how a single chain could be the template for the synthesis of a chain with the complementary sequence.[20] [See Figure 13-1.]

When Francis Crick, at lunch that day at the Eagle Pub in Cambridge, told everyone within hearing that "we had found the secret of life," Watson wrote, "I felt a little queasy."[21]

5 and 6.   *Deducing and testing consequences.* The hypothesis now having been formulated, it had next to be confirmed. The first deduction was straightforward: If the double helix proposed by Watson and Crick were indeed a correct account of the structure of DNA, it should be possible to construct a three-dimensional model of that double helix in which the bases would fit together internally, and the angles of the spiral as well as all other features of the chain would satisfy

---

[19] *Ibid.,* p. 123.
[20] *Ibid.,* pp. 123–125.
[21] *Ibid,* p. 126.

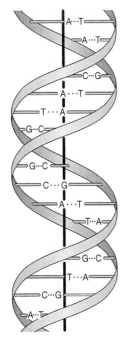

FIGURE 13-1 *A schematic illustration of the complementary double helix. The two sugar-phosphate backbones twist about on the outside. The flat bases, in pairs—A always bonding with T, C always bonding with G—make up the core. The structure resembles a spiral staircase, with the pairs of bases forming the steps. (From J. D. Watson,* The Double Helix, *p. 130.) Courtesy of the copyright holder, Gunther S. Stent.*

the requirements established by earlier X-ray pictures and other experiments. That construction quickly was achieved.

Many additional theoretical deductions were made; every test of them proved successful. One such analysis now made understandable certain data that had long puzzled and frustrated molecular biologists; the quantity of DNA in the reproductive cells coming from each parent was known to be only *half* that to be found in an ordinary cell. The reason for this was now clear: If the double helix splits in preparation for reproduction, those split cells from each parent would of course contain just one half the normal quantity of DNA. Evidence for the correctness of the Watson-Crick solution to the structure of DNA mounted quickly; soon their hypothesis was very fully confirmed.

7. *Applications.* A 128-line report by Watson and Crick on the structure of DNA[22] made scientific history; the course of biological science was dramatically and permanently altered. Extensive and powerful applications of this knowledge culminated their achievement. The codes used in DNA sequences became known in subsequent decades; a complete map of the entire human genome is virtually complete and will be widely available before long. Techniques for cutting and recombining DNA chains have been developed and are now commonly used in manufacturing new drugs, vaccines, and synthetic hormones. The applications of recombi-

---

[22] J. D. Watson and F. H. C. Crick, "A Structure for Deoxyribose Nucleic Acid," *Nature,* 25 April 1953.

nant DNA technology—possible only because the problem of the structure of DNA has at last been solved—have revolutionized biology and medicine, and are constantly expanding.∎

13.6 CRUCIAL EXPERIMENTS AND AD HOC HYPOTHESES

A. Crucial Experiments

Progress in science is rarely straightforward or easy. It would be foolish to suppose that simply by applying the several steps of the hypothetico-deductive method to any problem, the solution will be obtained. Solutions—correct explanatory hypotheses—often are obscure, may require very elaborate theoretical machinery. Devising the finally correct hypothesis may be exceedingly difficult. The process, far from being mechanical, often requires, in addition to laborious observation and experimentation, deep insight and great creativity.

Once the new hypothesis has been formulated, if it is inconsistent with some previously accepted theory it may be difficult to determine which of the alternative accounts is correct. In some cases two competing hypotheses may be tested by means of what is called a "crucial experiment," an experiment deliberately constructed so as to reveal that one but not the other of the explanations offered is in fact correct. Such crucial experiments, when they can be devised, may prove exciting and highly productive.

For example: The American physicist Albert Michelson and chemist Edward Morley collaborated in 1887 on an experiment to measure the speed of light, and by doing so to put a widely held theory (which they believed to be correct) to a crucial test. It had been long believed that space was filled with a hypothetical substance called "ether" which (supposedly) permitted waves of light to travel in much the same way as air permits sound waves to travel. Either the ether exists, or it does not exist. If it does exist, then the measured speed of light in the direction of Earth's motion should be different from the speed of light determined at right angles to Earth's motion. The experiment had what may be called a "negative" result, and yet because it was a crucial experiment testing a widely accepted theory of that time, it became one of the most famous in the history of physics. No difference could be found in the speed of light moving in the two different directions. This result effectively killed off the long-held concept of the ether.[23]

But such powerful crucial experiments are, regrettably, not always feasible. Alternative observable consequences may not be presently deducible from the alternative hypotheses; or they may be deducible but we may lack the ability to arrange circumstances so as to test which of the alternative consequences are manifested.

---

[23] The Michelson-Morley experiment also showed that the speed of light is independent of the motion of the observer. That result paved the way, in 1905, for Albert Einstein's Special Theory of Relativity.

Physics, at the opening of the twenty-first century, faces a major problem of just this kind: Between its two most powerful theories there is—as we write—an apparent conflict that cannot presently be resolved. The general theory of relativity is well confirmed, and it is an apparently inevitable consequence of its laws (describing gravity and how it shapes space and time) that some collapsing massive stars will form "black holes" from which escape would require what is known to be impossible—a speed faster than light. But the laws of quantum mechanics are also well-confirmed, and they plainly entail that information cannot ever be permanently lost, even if drawn into a black hole. Either there is some presently unknown property of space and time that can account for the retention of the information, or there is some lawlessness in physics that can account for its permanent loss. There must eventually be an amendment in one of the two theories, but we do not yet know in which, and we do not have the means to construct the needed crucial experiment.[24]

There is yet another difficulty involved in the devising of so-called crucial experiments which brings to light an important feature of scientific inquiry: The consequences of some proposed explanatory hypothesis, which we may wish to test by conducting some crucial experiment, can never be deduced from that hypothesis *by itself.* We deduce the consequence to be tested by applying the hypothesis in mind, *together with other theories* which, for this purpose, are assumed to be completely reliable. Those other theories may indeed be completely reliable. But they may not be so, and if they are not, the hypothesis in question may turn out to be correct even though the crucial experiment appeared to disconfirm it. Advancement in science depends upon *sets* of hypotheses, any one of which may be flawed.

Where hypotheses of a fairly high level of abstractness are involved, no directly testable prediction can be deduced from just a single one of them. A unified *group* of hypotheses must be used as premises for the deduction, and if the observed facts are other than those predicted we may conclude that *at least one* of the hypotheses in the group is shown to be false. But such a conclusion will not have established *which* one is in error. In the preceding account of the discovery of the structure of DNA, for example, there was a point at which Watson and Crick tested the hypothesis that the filaments of nucleic acid were in the form of a double helix, its bases pointed inward—and found that such an arrangement simply could not be made consistent with all other known facts and accepted theories. Those "known facts and accepted theories"—the water content, the pitch of the helix, the way in which the bases (adenine, gua-

---

[24] A hypothetical crucial experiment has been proposed: Throw a volume of the Encyclopedia Britannica into a black hole. Will the information it contains be forever lost? Or is such total loss indeed impossible? A wager, serious but light-hearted, between two distinguished Cal Tech physicists has been placed on the outcome. Prof. Kip Thorne bets on relativity, whose equations describe space and time and predict that from the singularity of a black hole there could *never* be any recovery; Prof. John Preskill bets on quantum mechanics whose equations precisely describe the lives of miniscule elementary particles and predict that the information can never be *totally* lost. The stakes of the wager are a set of encyclopedias, but payoff is unlikely to come soon. Says their equally distinguished colleague, Prof. Stephen Hawking of Cambridge University, "In my opinion it could go either way."

nine, cystine, and thymine) would bond—were assumed to be correct as they went about testing their hypothesis. If all of those suppositions had indeed been correct, their double helix could not have been the structure of the filament. In the actual case, however, Watson and Crick, having confidence in their hypothesis, came to suspect that the accepted theory describing the ways in which the bases (A, G, C, and T) bond to each other was not entirely correct. By relinquishing that element in the set, and replacing it with a different account, one that supposed hydrogen bonds instead, the newly hypothesized double helix (with its allied theories) could be confirmed.

Thus, an experiment may be "crucial" in showing the untenability of a *group* of hypotheses. Such a group usually will contain a considerable number of separate hypotheses, the truth of any *one* of which can be maintained in the teeth of any experimental result, however apparently unfavorable, by the expedient of rejecting some other hypothesis in the group. This consideration has led some to conclude that no individual hypothesis can ever be subjected to a crucial experiment.

B. *Ad Hoc* Hypotheses

To this critique it may be objected that an experiment can indeed be crucial in disconfirming a single new hypothesis, because the effort to "save" that hypothesis by conveniently rejecting some other element in the group (suggested as possible just above) is purely *ad hoc,* a Latin expression meaning literally "for this [special purpose]." There is one sense of the term *ad hoc* in which *all* hypotheses are *ad hoc,* since it makes no sense to speak of a hypothesis that was not devised to account *for* some antecedently established fact or other. But when used as a term of abuse, *ad hoc* suggests that the adjustment in the set of hypotheses was made *only* for the purpose of saving the hypothesis being tested, and that it has no other explanatory power or testable consequences.

No scientific hypothesis is *ad hoc* in this second sense. That "gremlins are the cause of the breakdown" would be an obviously unscientific explanation if introduced to account for the malfunction of a complicated machine; such hypotheses we rightly ridicule as *ad hoc* in this negative sense. But in any actual scientific investigation, when a new hypothesis is proposed and an older theory adjusted, it remains to determine whether the adjustment made in the set of hypotheses is indeed *ad hoc* in that negative sense.

Another illustration from the history of science will help to make this clear. In the nineteenth century, with the theory of celestial mechanics quite well understood, it became evident to astronomers that the orbits of two of the planets, Uranus and Mercury, were not what accepted theory had predicted they should be. The theory of planetary motion might then have been altered, but in fact it was retained. It was proposed that, consistent with that theory, there existed some as-yet-undiscovered planets whose gravity was causing the observed anomalies. The resultant prediction by Leverrier in 1845—of the orbit of the new planet that might account for the apparent discrepancies in the orbit of Uranus—was very soon verified by the discovery of the planet Neptune, precisely where it would have had to be to account for those discrepancies.[25] The hypothesis that there was such a planet was certainly not *ad hoc* in the negative sense, since many consequences could be deduced from that hypothesis which rendered it independently testable.

But in the case of Mercury, the hypothesis that there was another planet (prematurely named "Vulcan") perturbing its orbit could not be confirmed. If a theory supposing some imagined "mercurial forces" had then been introduced to account for the aberrations in Mercury's orbit, forces that accounted for nothing else and could be identified in no other way, such an invention certainly would have been *ad hoc*. In the actual case, the matter long remained problematic; it was not until the development of the general theory of relativity in 1915 that the observed irregularities in Mercury's orbit could be fully reconciled with other well-established astronomical accounts. The fact that the anomaly in Mercury's orbit could be predicted using the general theory of relativity became one of the most compelling confirmations of that theory. Einstein called it "the most splendid work of my life."[26] Only then had an adequate—that is, a genuinely *theoretical*—explanation of the data been given.

This problem in the history of astronomy points to a third sense, also derogatory, in which the expression *ad hoc* sometimes is used: to denote a mere descriptive generalization. A descriptive hypothesis that is *ad hoc* in this third sense will assert only that all facts of a particular sort occur in just some particular kinds of circumstances; but the hypothesis will (like those in the preceding sense) have no explanatory power or scope. The classic example of such an hypothesis is the "Fitzgerald contraction effect," introduced to account for the results of the Michelson-Morley experiment on the velocity of light. By affirming that bodies moving at extremely high velocities contract, Fitzgerald did account for the given data, and his hypothesis could be tested by repetitions of that same experiment—but his "contraction effect" explained nothing else. It was at the time generally held to be *ad hoc* rather than explanatory, and (as in the matter of the apparent discrepancies in the behavior of Mercury) it was not until relativity theory—in this case, Einstein's Special Theory of Relativity—that an adequate theoretical explanation of the experimental results of the Michelson-Morley experiment could be given.

We may conclude that it is not only because hypotheses often are *ad hoc* in the derogatory senses of that term that experiments are never crucial for a single hypothesis. More fundamental, as noted earlier in this section, experiments are never crucial for individual hypotheses because hypotheses are testable only *in groups*.[27] This limitation serves to illuminate the *systematic* character of science. Scientific progress consists in building ever-more-adequate theories so

---

[25] A brief account of the technique used in the discovery of Neptune has been given in the discussion of Mill's Method of Residues in the preceding chapter (pp. 471–472).

[26] The comment was made to his son, Hans Albert, in a letter formerly in the possession of the Einstein Correspondence Trust.

[27] This view has been argued persuasively by P. Duhem, *The Aim and Structure of Physical Theory,* trans. by P. P. Wiener, Princeton University Press, 1954. A challenging objection to it will be found in Adolf Grunbaum, "The Duhemian Argument," *Philosophy of Science* 27, January 1960. See also: Sandra G. Harding, ed., *Can Theories Be Refuted? Essays on the Duhem-Quine Thesis* (Boston: Reidel, 1976).

as to account for the enlarging body of observations made and facts experienced. Isolated, particular facts can be of great value too, for the ultimate basis of science is factual. But the structure of science grows not chiefly through the piecemeal collection of bits, but more organically, within the framework of a generally accepted body of theory. The notion that scientific hypotheses or laws are wholly discreet and independent is a naive and outdated view.

Working within such a framework of theory, one that we are not at the time concerned to question, the notion of conducting a "crucial experiment" in order to confirm or disconfirm some hypothesis can still make sense. If a negative result is obtained—that is, if some phenomenon fails to occur that had been predicted on the basis of some single dubious hypothesis, taken in tandem with accepted parts of scientific theory—then the experiment is crucial and that dubious hypothesis may be rejected. But, as we have seen, there is nothing absolute about such a procedure, for even well-accepted scientific theories come to be changed in the face of new and contradictory evidence. Science is not monolithic, either in its practices or in its aims.

The lesson to be learned from the preceding discussion is the importance to scientific progress of dragging "hidden assumptions" into the open, so that what had been tacitly assumed may, on occasion, be reconsidered. When a critical assumption is hidden there is no apparent need, and therefore no good occasion, to examine it, and to decide intelligently whether it really is true or false. Progress often is achieved by formulating explicitly an assumption that previously had been hidden, and then scrutinizing and (perhaps) rejecting it.

For example, it seems entirely unproblematic in ordinary life to refer to the occurrence of two events as taking place "at the same time." We commonly assume that events often occur simultaneously. But an important and dramatic advance in science was initiated when Einstein brought this assumption into the open, asking how an observer could determine whether or not two distant events truly occurred at the *same* time. Ultimately he was led to the conclusion that two events can be simultaneous for some observers but not for others, depending upon their locations and their velocities *relative* to the events in question. It was this rejection of the assumption of simultaneity which led Einstein to his Special Theory of Relativity, which in turn constituted a tremendous step forward in explaining such phenomena as those revealed by the Michelson-Morley experiment. But of course, an assumption must be *recognized* before it can be challenged. Hence it is enormously important in science to formulate explicitly all of the relevant assumptions at work within any theory, allowing none of them to remain hidden.

For Enrichment There may be no better way of summarizing this account of the methods of science, and to highlight the importance of its *systematic* advance, than by describing and discussing one of the most extraordinary chapters in the history of science: the observational confirmation, by Galileo Galilei, of the Copernican account of the solar system.

By the early 1600s, the movements of the planets against the backdrop of the fixed stars had been so carefully studied that their apparent movements were predictable. The moon, also much studied, was believed by theologians to be a perfect sphere. The heavenly bodies, deemed flawless in shape and movement, were widely believed to travel in perfect circles around the Earth, which was the center of the world God had created. Galileo had devised, by 1609, a telescope with 20-power magnification, its chief uses being thought at first to be maritime, or as a spyglass that could gain military advantage. With this instrument he observed the heavens, almost by accident, in January of 1610. On the 7th of that month he began a long letter, reporting in detail his observations of the moon and other bodies. He wrote:

> I have observed with one of my telescopes . . . the face of the moon, which I have been able to see very near . . . [W]hat is there can be discerned with great distinctness, and in fact it is seen that the moon is most evidently not at all of an even, smooth and regular surface, as a great many people believe of it and of the other heavenly bodies, but on the contrary it is rough and unequal. In short, it is shown to be such that sane reasoning cannot conclude otherwise than that it is full of prominences and cavities similar, but much larger, to the mountains and valleys spread over the Earth's surface . . .[28]

To save the hypothesis that the moon was indeed a perfect sphere, and thus to retain the coherence of the theological account of the heavenly bodies of which that perfection was one element, some of Galileo's critics later proposed the hypothesis—outrageously *ad hoc*—that the apparent cavities and irregularities on the surface of the moon were, in fact, filled in by a celestial substance that was flawless and crystalline, and thus invisible through Galileo's telescope!

More than the moon was examined by Galileo. His letter continued:

> And besides the observations of the Moon . . . many fixed stars are seen with the telescope that are not [otherwise] discerned; and only this evening I have seen Jupiter accompanied by three fixed stars, totally invisible [to the naked eye] by their smallness, and the configuration was in this form:[29]

At that point Galileo inserts a sketch that appears here as Figure 13-2, showing the three stars in a straight line, two to the east and one to the west of Jupiter; he reports that they did not extend more than one degree of longitude, but since at that time he supposed them to be fixed stars, their distances from Jupiter and from one another were indicated only very roughly.

On the following day, 8 January 1610, "led by I know not what," Galileo happened to observe Jupiter once again; the earlier positions of those "fixed

---

[28] This letter, dated 7 January 1610, apparently was written over a period of many days. It, and other notes taken by Galileo during these momentous days, are discussed in detail in Jean Meeus, "Galileo's First Records of Jupiter's Satellites," *Sky and Telescope*, February 1964; and in Stillman Drake, "Galileo's First Telescopic Observations," *Journal of the History of Astronomy*, 1976, p. 153; and in Dale P. Cruikshank and David Morrison, "The Galilean Satellites of Jupiter," *Scientific American*, May 1976. A copy of the photo of the original sketch Galileo made to record his observations, his notes appearing on it in Italian, is provided in Figure 13.2, through the courtesy of the library of the University of Michigan, Ann Arbor, in whose rare-book room that precious manuscript is held.

[29] That Galileo began this letter on 7 January 1610 is clear; the exact days of that month on which he continued it, with sketches and notes, is a matter about which scholars disagree.

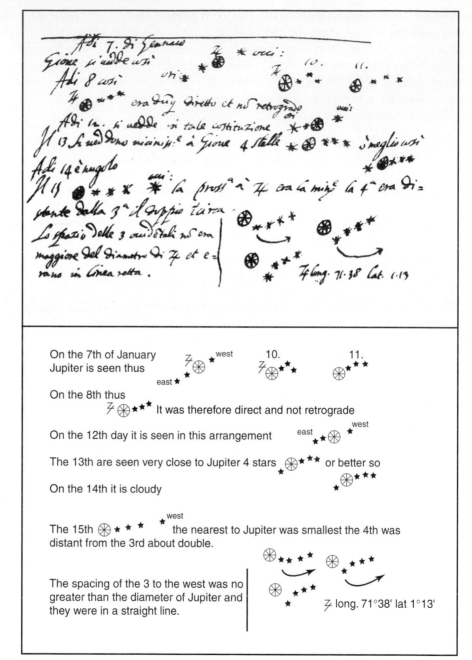

FIGURE 13-2 *A photograph of the letter begun by Galileo on 7 January 1610, on which is recorded his first monumental observations of the four major satellites of Jupiter, thus confirming the Copernican account of the movement of the celestial bodies. The letter itself was to be sent to the Doge in Venice, with a telescope that Galileo intended to present him. On a draft of that letter which he happened to have in hand, Galileo made the critical notes of his observations, which appear on the bottom half of the sheet. The translation of the bottom half into English appears below. (Courtesy of the Special Collections Library, University of Michigan.)*

stars" had fortunately been written down. His letter remained unsent; at the bottom of the sheet he wrote the following note:

> On the 8th thus: [he inserts a sketch showing Jupiter and three stars now closer to one another and nearly equidistant from one another, and *all three to the west of Jupiter!*]

This created a serious theoretical problem for Galileo, since at this time the assumption that the newly discovered stars were fixed had not been seriously doubted. Therefore their appearance on the other side of Jupiter had to be accounted for by Jupiter's movements. On the 8th he adds the note:

> It [Jupiter's movement] was therefore direct and not retrograde.

If on the 8th Jupiter was to the east of all three stars, while the day before Jupiter had been to the west of two of them, Jupiter must have moved, and moved in a way that was *contrary* to reliable astronomical calculations! One can imagine Galileo's agitation as he waited for the observations of the following night; could his direct observations and his calculations remain so sharply inconsistent? But on the 9th it was too cloudy to observe. On the 10th, Jupiter apparently had moved back to the west, now apparently obscuring the third star, and the other two were again observed to the east of the planet! On 11 January a similar pattern was observed, but on this night Galileo later wrote,

> The star nearer Jupiter was half the size of the other, and very close to the other, whereas the other evenings all three of the said stars appeared of equal size and equally far apart ...

Clearly, something had to give. From the accepted theories and beliefs a prediction confidently could be drawn, a deduction concerning the movements of Jupiter, which—if those three new stars were fixed, and Galileo's observations were accurate—did not take place. One could save the belief that those new stars were fixed by somehow revamping the entire set of astronomical calculations, but these were not in serious doubt; or, one could challenge the accuracy of Galileo's observations—which is what some of his critics later sought to do, calling his telescope an instrument of the devil. Galileo himself had no doubt about what he had seen, and he grasped quickly which element in the set of accepted hypotheses had to be relinquished, to the great distress of his dogmatic opponents. His note on the observation of the 11th continued:

> ... from which it appears that around Jupiter there are three moving stars invisible to everyone to this time.

And these three moving stars, he later wrote,

> revolved round Jupiter in the same manner as Venus and Mercury revolved round the sun.

The observations of the following nights confirmed this revolutionary conclusion, which, together with his earlier observations of the moon, cast serious doubt upon the account of celestial bodies that had been widely and dogmatically affirmed for very many centuries.

On 13 January 1610, Galileo observed a fourth "star," and the four major satellites of Jupiter had been discovered. These observations provided very strong confirmation of the Copernican hypothesis—an account of the celestial bodies difficult to reconcile with the established theological doctrine of Galileo's time. These four moons of Jupiter (many more have been discovered since)—Ganymede, Io, Europa, and Callisto—are appropriately called "the Galilean satellites." Their revolutions about that planet can be readily reconfirmed on a clear night when Jupiter is visible by anyone with an ordinary pair of binoculars. ■

13.7 CLASSIFICATION AS HYPOTHESIS

It could be objected that hypotheses play important roles only in the more advanced sciences, not in those that are relatively less advanced. It might be urged that although explanatory hypotheses are central to such sciences as physics and chemistry, they play no such role—at least not yet—in the biological or social sciences. The latter are still in their descriptive phases, and it may be felt that the method of hypothesis is not relevant to the so-called descriptive sciences, such as botany or history. This objection is easily answered. An examination of the nature of description will show that description itself is based on, or embodies, hypotheses. Hypotheses are as basic to the various systems of taxonomy or classification in biology as they are in history or any of the other social sciences.

The importance of hypothesis in the science of history may be easily shown, and will be discussed first. Some historians believe that the study of history can reveal the existence of a single cosmic purpose or pattern, either religious or naturalistic, which accounts for or explains the entire course of recorded history. Others deny the existence of any such cosmic design, but insist that the study of history will reveal certain historical laws that explain the actual sequence of past events and can be used to predict the future. On either of these views, the historian seeks explanations that must account for and be confirmed by the recorded events of the past. On either of these views, therefore, history is a theoretical rather than a merely descriptive science, and the role of hypothesis must be admitted as being central to the historian's enterprise.

There is, however, a third group of historians who set themselves what is apparently a more modest goal. According to them, the task of historians is simply to chronicle the past, to set forth a bare description of past events in their chronological order. On this view, it might seem, "scientific" historians have no need of hypotheses, since their concern is with the facts themselves, not with any theories about them.

But past events are not so easily chronicled as this view would have us believe. The past itself simply is not available for this kind of description. What *is* available are present records and traces of the past. These range all the way from official government archives of the recent past, to epic poems celebrating the exploits of half-legendary heroes; from the writings of older historians, to artifacts of bygone eras unearthed in the excavations of archaeologists. These are the only facts available to historians, and from these they must infer the nature of those past events it is their purpose to describe. Not *all* hypotheses are general; some are particular. The historian's description of the past is a particular hypothesis that is intended to account for present data, and for which the present data constitute evidence.

Historians are detectives on a grand scale.[30] Their methods are the same, and their difficulties too. The evidence is scanty, and much of it has been destroyed—if not by the bungling local constabulary, then by intervening wars and natural disasters. And just as the criminal may have left false or misleading clues to throw pursuers off the scent, so many present "records" are falsifications of the past they purport to describe; either intentional, as in the case of such forged historical documents as the "Donation of Constantine," or unintentional, as in the writings of early uncritical historians. Just as the detective must use the method of science in formulating and testing hypotheses, so too must the historian. Even those historians who seek to limit themselves to bare descriptions of past events must work with hypotheses: They are theorists in spite of themselves.

Biologists are in a somewhat more favorable position. The facts with which they deal are present, and available for inspection. To describe the flora and fauna of a given region, they need not make elaborate inferences of the sort to which historians are condemned. The data can be perceived directly. Their descriptions of these items are not casual but systematic. They are said to *classify* plants and animals, rather than merely to describe them. But classification and description are really the same process. To describe a given animal as carnivorous is to classify it as a carnivore; to classify it as a reptile is to describe it as reptilian. To describe any object as having a certain attribute is to classify it as a member of the class of objects having that attribute.

Classification, as generally understood, involves not merely a single division of objects into separate groups, but further subdivision of each group into subgroups or subclasses, and so on. This pattern is familiar to most of us, if not from our studies in school, then probably from playing the old game called "Animal, Vegetable, or Mineral?" more commonly called "Twenty Questions." Classification is a universal need. Primitive peoples were obliged to classify roots and berries as being edible or poisonous, animals as dangerous or harmless, and other tribes as friends or enemies. All people tend to draw distinctions that are of practical importance to them, and to neglect those that play a less immediate role in their affairs. A farmer will classify grains and vegetables carefully and in detail, but may call all flowers "posies," whereas florists will classify their merchandise with the greatest of care but may lump all the farmer's crops together as "produce."

Two basic motives may lead us to classify things. One is practical, the other theoretical. Having only three or four books, one could know them all well and

---

[30] See Robin W. Winks, ed., *The Historian as Detective: Essays on Evidence* (New York: Harper & Row, 1969).

could easily take them all in at a glance, so that there would be no need to classify them. But in a library containing many thousands of volumes, the situation is different. If the books there were not classified, the librarian could not find the ones that were wanted, and from a practical standpoint the collection would be useless. The larger the number of objects, the greater is the need to classify them. A practical purpose of classification is to make large collections accessible. This is especially apparent in the case of libraries, museums, and public records halls of one sort or another.

When we consider the theoretical purpose of classification, we must realize that the adoption of this or that alternative classification scheme is not a matter of truth or falsehood. Objects may be described in different ways, from different points of view. The scheme of classification adopted will depend upon the purpose or interest of the classifier. Books, for example, would be classified differently by a librarian, a bookbinder, and a bibliophile. The librarian would classify them according to their content or subject matter, the bookbinder according to their bindings, and a bibliophile according to their date of printing and perhaps their relative rarity. The possibilities are not thereby exhausted, of course: A book packer would divide books according to their shapes and sizes, and persons with still other interests would classify them differently in the light of those different interests.

Now, what special interest or purpose do scientists have, that can lead them to prefer one scheme of classification to another? The scientist's aim is knowledge, not merely of this or that particular fact for its own sake, but of the general laws to which the facts conform, and of their causal interrelations. One classification scheme is better than another, from the scientist's point of view, to the extent that it is more fruitful in suggesting scientific laws and more helpful in the formulation of explanatory hypotheses.

The theoretical or scientific motivation for classifying objects is the desire to increase our knowledge of them. Increased knowledge of things provides us with further insight into their attributes, their similarities and differences, and their interrelations. A classification scheme made for narrowly practical purposes may tend to obscure important similarities and differences. Thus, a division of animals into "dangerous" and "harmless" will assign the wild boar and the rattlesnake to one class and the domestic pig and the grass snake to the other, calling attention away from what we should today regard as more profound similarities in order to emphasize superficial resemblances. Any scientifically fruitful classification of objects will require a considerable knowledge about them. A slight acquaintance with their more obvious characteristics might lead one to classify the bat with the birds, as flying creatures, and the whale with the fishes, as creatures that live in the sea. More extensive knowledge leads us to classify both bats and whales as mammals, because their being warm-blooded, bearing their young alive, and suckling them, are more important characteristics on which to base a classificatory scheme.

A characteristic is important when it serves as a clue to the presence of other characteristics. An important characteristic, from the point of view of science, is one that is causally connected with many other characteristics, and hence relevant to the framing of a maximum number of causal laws and the formulation of very general explanatory hypotheses. That classification scheme is best, then, which is based on the most important characteristics of the objects to be classified. But we do not know in advance which causal laws obtain, and causal laws themselves partake of the nature of hypotheses, as we have emphasized. Therefore any decision as to which classification scheme is best will itself constitute a hypothesis, one that subsequent investigations may lead us to reject. If later investigations reveal *other* characteristics to be more important—that is, involved in a greater number of causal laws and explanatory hypotheses—we can reasonably expect the earlier classification scheme to be rejected in favor of a newer one based upon the more important characteristics.

This view of classification schemes as hypotheses is borne out by the actual role such schemes play in the sciences. Taxonomy is a legitimate, important, and still growing branch of biology, in which some classification schemes, such as that of Linnaeus, have been adopted, used, and subsequently abandoned in favor of better ones, which are themselves in turn subject to modification in light of new data. Classification generally is most important in the early or less developed stages of a science. It need not always diminish in importance as the science develops, however. For example, the standard classification scheme for the elements, as set forth in Mendeleeff's table, is still an important tool for the chemist.

The foregoing account of the uses of classification in the natural sciences suggests a further point of some importance regarding its use in the study of history. That the historian's descriptions of past events are themselves hypotheses based upon present data has already been noted. Yet there is an additional, equally significant role that hypotheses play in the descriptive historian's enterprise. No historical event of any magnitude can be described in *complete detail*. Even if all of its details could be known, historians could not possibly include them all in their narratives. Life is too short to permit an exhaustive description of anything. Historians must, therefore, describe the past selectively, recording only some of its features. Upon what basis shall they make their selection? Clearly, historians want to include what is significant or important in their descriptions, and to ignore what is insignificant or trivial. The subjective bias of this or that historian may lead him or her to place undue stress on the religious, the economic, the personal, or some other aspect of the historic process. But to the extent that they can make an objective or scientific appraisal, historians will regard those aspects as important which enter into the formulation of causal laws and general explanatory hypotheses. Such appraisals are, of course, subject to correction in the light of further research.

The first Western historian, Herodotus, described a great many aspects of the events he chronicled, personal and cultural as well as political and military. The so-called first scientific historian, Thucydides, restricted himself much more to the political and the military. For a long period of time most historians followed Thucydides, but now the pendulum is swinging in another direction and the economic and cultural aspects of the past are being given greatly increased emphasis. Just as biologists' classification schemes embody their hypotheses as to which characteristics of living things are implicated in a maximum number of causal laws, so historians' decisions to describe past events in terms of one rather than another set of characteristics embody their hypotheses as to which characteristics are causally related to a maximum number of others. Some such hypotheses are required, before historians can even begin to do any systematic describing of the past. It is this *hypothetical* character of classification and description, whether biological or historical, that leads us to regard hypothesis as the all-pervasive method of scientific inquiry.

Exercises

In each of the following passages,

a. What data are to be explained?
b. What hypotheses are proposed to explain them?
c. Evaluate the hypotheses in terms of the criteria presented in Section 13.3.

*1.   In a stunning discovery of new worlds, two California astronomers, Dr. Geoffrey Marcy and Dr. Paul Butler, today reported the detection of two planets orbiting Sunlike stars. The temperatures of the planets appear to be warm enough for water to exist in liquid form, a condition conducive to chemical processes that could, just possibly, be producing extraterrestrial life.

The two newly discovered extra-solar planets accompany the stars 70 Virginis, in the constellation Virgo, and 47 Ursa Majoris, in the constellation Ursa Major. They are 35 light years away, relatively close by cosmic standards. They are too small and too dim to be seen against the glare of their parent stars, but their gravitational presence has been definitely established.

Both stars are analogues of the Sun, astronomers said, with no appreciable differences in size, temperature, or age. The search for other planets has so far been focused on about 120 such Sunlike stars within 100 light years of Earth.

When Dr. Butler saw that the wobble in the motion of the star 70 Virginis fit precisely the orbit of a large planet, he reported, "I was sure of what we had in three minutes, and I almost literally fell out of my chair."

As far as scientists know, other, smaller planets may also orbit these stars. But current detection techniques may not find them. In an interview, Dr. Marcy said:

> Theorists now have a greater challenge in front of them. They have more than the solar system to explain. Other systems may be more diverse and may contain objects that defy normal classification.

—"Hints of Life in Space," *New York Times*, 18 January 1996

2.   How do genes affect the length of life? The microscopic roundworm *C. elegans* normally lives only three weeks. But it will

live up to four times that long when mutations in certain of its genes have been engineered. Might there be a longevity gene in worms? If there is and it could be found, that would give clues as to how humans might live longer. A worm gene discovered in 1999 suggests that there may indeed be a link between the mutations that affect the worm's period of hibernation and mutations affecting human longevity as influenced by stress. The new gene is called by its discoverers (at Columbia University) a "catalese gene" because when it is disabled other genes fail to prolong life in expected ways.

But evolutionary biologists have reasons to doubt the existence of any longevity gene. One reason is that natural selection does not normally increase fitness beyond reproductive age, because organisms living to a greater age than that would not leave additional descendants. Moreover, say the skeptics, a longevity gene might produce a crowd of post-reproductive animals who would then compete for food with their own progeny.

—Reported in *Nature,* 13 May 1999

3.   Population clusters—groups of persons who are found to buy the same things, get their entertainment from the same sources, exhibit similar voting patterns, and generally behave in quite similar ways—are of growing interest. Michael J. Weiss has distinguished some 62 of these clusters, which he calls "distinctive lifestyle types." He also names them, and highlights some of their peculiarities.

In the "Towns and Gowns" cluster, for example, tequila is far more popular than elsewhere, and twice as many people watch the soap opera "Another World" there than do people elsewhere. In the "Military Quarters" cluster people are four times as likely to watch the TV show "Hard Copy" as the average American. Among the young, middle-class Americans in suburbia, furniture refinishing, downhill skiing, and cats are abnormally popular, while chess and tractor pulls are abnormally unpopular.

Lifestyle clusters are found useful by businesses seeking customers, by candidates seeking votes, by nonprofit organizations seeking new contributors, and so on. What may appear trivial can be very revealing. In Washington, DC, Weiss observes, "there is a fault line between the fans of Brie cheese, who tend to hold down executive jobs and write the laws, and those of Kraft Velveeta, who maintain the service economy." He asks: "What prompts some of us to eat Brie and others to devour Velveeta cheese?"

—Michael J. Weiss, *The Clustered World* (Little, Brown, 2000).

4. One of the most challenging problems in all of social science has been untangling the environmental and genetic influences of the family on children's intellectual, occupational, and economic attainments. The educational level of parents correlates fairly well with both school achievement and mental ability test scores of their children. This correlation is usually assumed to indicate the strength of the influence of environment on school success, since parents with more years of schooling tend to expect their children to do well in school and create a richer educational environment in the home than do poorly educated parents. If the causal connection runs from the rich family environment to the academic-ability level of the child, then it makes sense to try to induce all parents to provide more educative environments, as a way of improving school performance of educationally disadvantaged children.

    If mental ability is to some extent inherited, however, a different set of causal linkages may be involved: Parents possessing high levels of mental ability will tend to spend more years in school than others do, will pass on some of their ability to their children, *and* will create more educative home environments. In this view, correlation between home environment and the child's academic performance may mask a more important genetic relation between parents' abilities and children's abilities.

    —Harry L. Miller, "Hard Realities and Soft Social Science,"
    The Public Interest, Spring 1980

*5. The mechanism of stimulus and response in geotropism has often been studied. If very young seedlings in which the root and stem are just appearing are fixed in any position whatever, the young root will invariably grow downward and the young stem upward. The English horticulturalist Knight, more than a century ago, suggested that this behavior was due to gravity. He reasoned that if this were so, it should be possible to substitute a stronger force for gravity and thus to change the direction of growth. Knight fastened young plants in various positions to the rim of a wheel, which he revolved rapidly in a horizontal plane, thus subjecting the plants to a "centrifugal force" greater than gravity. Under these conditions the roots grew outward, in the direction of the centrifugal pull, and the stems grew inward, toward the hub, in an exactly opposite direction. Knight thus proved that plant structures orient themselves to this force in just the same way that they do to gravity.

    —Edmund W. Sinnot and Katherine S. Wilson,
    Botany: Principles and Problems

6. A team of researchers recently explored the relationship between shift work and heart disease among 79,109 women enrolled in the

Nurses Health Study. In 1988 the women were asked how many years they had worked rotating night shifts. At the time none of these women had a history of coronary heart disease. Most of the women had done some shift work, 7 percent of them for 15 or more years. Compared with the women who had never worked shifts, those who had done so were slightly heavier and more likely to smoke cigarettes. Longer durations of shift work were associated with high blood pressure and diabetes. During the next four years of follow-up, 292 of the women developed evidence of coronary artery disease. The women who had done shift work were 40 percent more likely to develop heart disease, and longer periods of shift work were associated with higher overall risk. Women who had performed more than 6 years of shift work had a 51 percent increase in heart disease risk, and a 29 percent increase in the risk of dying during the follow-up period. Even when the researchers accounted for weight, smoking, and as many other cardiac risk factors as they could, the influence of shift work was still present.

But is shift work itself the culprit? Or are women who do work shifts different from women who do not, in ways this research could not detect or take into account? These questions cannot be resolved without an experiment in which large numbers of women are randomly assigned, for a prolonged period, either to shift work or to a regular schedule. That experiment is not likely to be conducted any time soon.

—I. Kawachi, *et al.*, "Prospective Study of Shift Work and Risk of Coronary Heart Disease in Women," *Circulation*, 1 December 1995

7. Ten pharmaceutical companies and the Wellcome Trust of London announced in April of 1999 that they would pool efforts to create a finescale map of the human genome. Their goal is to speed the discovery of the genetic variations that underlie disease, and hence the discovery of new drugs.

    The consortium's specific objective is to identify and locate, within two years, 300,000 "map points" along the set of human DNA molecules, or roughly 1 out of every 10,000 nucleotides, as the units of DNA are known. The map points are single nucleotide positions at which at least 1 percent of the population has a nucleotide different from that of the standard sequence. These one-letter differences are called "single nucleotide polymorphisms" or SNPs (pronounced "snips"). The genes that actually work in humans account for about 3 percent of the total genome, so most of the SNPs will fall in the nonfunctional regions, but because SNPs are easy to identify, they are ideal markers for distinguishing one region from another. The set of SNPs close to a given gene is likely to be inherited along with it, and can thus be used to identify that gene. So, by looking at a family in which (for example) diabetes is prevalent, geneticists hope to identify the many genes that probably contribute to that disease, and the work of the SNP consortium will advance this objective by enabling them to recognize patterns of SNPs that turn up in the diabetes sufferers but not in unaffected individuals.

Although the members of the consortium are profit-making firms, the SNP Consortium is a nonprofit enterprise, and the genome maps it produces will be publicly available. Dr. B. Michael Silber, a research director at Pfizer, Inc, one of the members of the consortium, emphasizes that "this kind of tool should be publicly accessible because it allows all medical researchers to add to what is being discovered."

—Reported in the *New York Times*, 15 April 1999

8. Scientists have recently embarked on their most ambitious effort yet to find and exploit one of the most elusive of the predicted phenomena of nature: gravitational waves. As long ago as 1915, Albert Einstein predicted in his general theory of relativity that the violent birth and death of stars in the universe would give off gravitational waves, bathing the earth in a unique kind of radiation. But so far, after decades of searching with increasingly sensitive detectors, scientists have not found one. A new facility, known as the laser interferometer gravitational wave observatory, has been designed to bring this search to successful culmination.

The discovery of gravitational waves would rank as one of the most important observational feats in modern physics and astronomy. It would provide a new confirmation of Einstein's General Theory of Relativity, a foundation of modern science whose validity is difficult to prove experimentally. That theory changed the concept of space from an empty void into a curving fabric of space and time. When stars collapse, the theory suggests, ripples in the space-time fabric move off in all directions at the speed of light; they do not transmit the force of gravity, but are distortions of that force.

In theory, gravity waves from distant cosmic events should move objects on earth an infinitesimal amount, measured in distances that are much smaller than the nucleus of an atom. The new observatory is designed to be sensitive enough to measure these waves and help pinpoint their cosmic origin. The risk, say skeptics, is that the apparatus will not be sensitive enough to detect the waves.

—"Ambitious Effort Aims to Find Gravity Waves,"
New York Times, 27 February 1990

9. Men born in the spring tend to be taller than those born in the fall. Researchers at the University of Vienna, after analyzing the birthdays and heights of 507,125 Austrian men during a ten-year period, concluded that men born during spring months are, on average, about a quarter of an inch (.06 centimeter) taller than their autumn-born counterparts. The scientists, led by Gerhard W. Weber of the university's Institute of Human Biology, said they could not offer "definitive explanations of why body height depends on the month of birth with such a pronounced cycle." But they did note that the regularity of the variation may be connected to the light-dependent activity of the pineal gland that produces the hormone melatonin, which in turn has an influence on the production of growth hormones.

    —Reported in *Nature*, 19 February 1998

*10. Since Venus rotates so slowly, we might be tempted to conclude that Venus, like Mercury, keeps one face always toward the Sun. If this hypothesis were correct we should expect that the dark side would be exceedingly cold. Pettit and Nicholson have measured the temperature of the dark side of Venus. They find that the temperature is not low, its value being only −9°F., much warmer than our stratosphere in broad daylight. It is unlikely that atmospheric currents from the bright side of Venus could perpetually heat the dark side. The planet must rotate fairly often to keep the dark side from cooling excessively.

    —Fred L. Whipple, *Earth, Moon and Planets*

11. The amount of sunlight during certain seasons of the year may have a variety of unexpected consequences. It may affect the height of those born during spring months, as noted in exercise 9, above. But it may also increase the likelihood of later suicide among residents of the far north. A psychiatrist at Pennsylvania State University's College of Medicine, Paul Kettl, reports that Alaskan natives born during the summer months commit more than 33 percent of the suicides there, compared to 22 percent for those born during each of the other three seasons. He speculated that, in addition to the hormonal differences that might be linked to the season of birth, children born during the summer—when many parents work very long hours—may receive less parental contact than those born during the winter, when parents can spend more time with their infants.

    —*American Indian and Alaska Native Mental Health Research*, January 1998

12. Find a sociological puzzle, and one gets, usually, a slew of esoteric explanations, couched, of course, in opaque sociological jargon. Take the question which has befuddled a number of

commentators recently: Why is it that women today seem to be marrying later than before? We shall not try to list all the ingenious explanations that have been advanced, from the rise of women's liberation to the increasing proportion of open homosexuality, male and female. Suffice to say that simple statistics, once understood, provide the most likely explanations. Here is Paul C. Glick, of the U.S. Bureau of the Census, writing in *Current Population Reports:*

> One of the tangible factors that probably helps to explain the increasing postponement of marriage is the 5 to 10-percent excess of women as compared with men during recent years in those ages when most first marriages occur (18 to 24 years for women and 20 to 26 years for men). This imbalance is a consequence of past fluctuations in the birth rate. For example, women born in 1947 after the baby boom had begun were ready to marry in 20 years, but the men they were most likely to marry were born in 1944 or 1945 (about one-half in each year) when the birth rate was still low; these men were about 8 percent less numerous than the 20-year-old women. (By contrast, girls who were born during the last 15 years, while the birth rate has been declining, will be scarce as compared with eligible men when they reach the main age for marriage.)

—Victor R. Fuchs, "The Economics of Health in a Post-Industrial Society," *The Public Interest,* Summer 1979

13. Early in the eighteenth century Edmund Halley asked: "Why is the sky dark at night?" This apparently naive question is not easy to answer, because if the universe had the simplest imaginable structure on the largest possible scale, the background radiation of the sky would be intense. Imagine a static infinite universe, that is, a universe of infinite size in which the stars and galaxies are stationary with respect to one another. A line of sight in any direction will ultimately cross the surface of a star, and the sky should appear to be made up of overlapping stellar disks. The apparent brightness of a star's surface is independent of its distance, so that everywhere the sky should be as bright as the surface of an average star. Since the sun is an average star, the entire sky, day and night, should be about as bright as the surface of the sun. The fact that it is not was later characterized as Olbers' paradox (after the eighteenth-century German astronomer Heinrich Olbers). The paradox applies not only to starlight but also to all other regions of the electromagnetic spectrum. It indicates that there is something fundamentally wrong with the model of a static infinite universe, but it does not specify what.

—Adrian Webster, "The Cosmic Radiation Background," *Scientific American,* August 1974

14.   The vast majority of fish species are cold-blooded, meaning that their body temperatures fluctuate with the surrounding water. Some 25 species, however, are endothermic–they can keep their eyes, brains, or entire bodies warm, independent of ambient temperatures, as birds and mammals do.

For years scientists have debated which of two competing theories better explains this finny ability. One was that the fish acquired their warming techniques primarily so they could expand their ranges into colder regions of the ocean, which promised new sources of food. The other hypothesis was that the techniques allowed the fish to increase their aerobic capacity so they could be more active.

Now Dr. Barbara A. Block, an animal physiologist at the University of Chicago, has concluded that new genetic evidence makes a strong case for the first theory, called niche expansion. She discovered that the warming techniques evolved not just once but on three separate occasions. "If it had evolved only once, it might not seem important," said Dr. Block, "but we're getting a clear message that keeping the central nervous system and eyes warm gives an advantage. We can see a clear correlation. The endothermic species have broad thermal niches, and the only other thing they have that others [closely related] don't have is the ability to warm their heads."

—Reported in *Science*, April 1993

*15.   Dr. Konrad Buettner of the University of California at Los Angeles has recently advanced the hypothesis that, during the lifetime of the moon, the everlasting influx of cosmic rays has slowly ground the upper-surface layers of rocks into fine dust. That the moon's skin cannot consist of solid rocks has been demonstrated through temperature measurements during lunar eclipses. As soon as the shadow of the earth creeps over the measuring area the temperature drops steeply, and after half an hour it is over 200°F. lower than it was in the full sun. When the shadow has passed by, the temperature again rises at a similarly steep rate. No solid piece of rock can cool down and heat up so quickly. These drastic temperature changes can be explained only by the existence of a thick layer of heat-insulating dust as fine as face powder. The thickness of the layer must be at least several inches. The sandblasting of meteoric dust also grinds at the moon's surface, but cosmic rays can be expected to do a much better job.

—Heinz Haber, *Man in Space*

Summary of Chapter 13

In this chapter, we saw how the scientific method, and the hypotheses and theories produced by it, is used to identify and formulate the principles that underlie the patterns encountered in our observation of the world; to resolve problematic situations by explaining the facts that create the problem; and to formulate general truths and causal laws that give us some measure of control over our world.

In section 13.1, we examined the values of science: its **practical usefulness** and its **satisfaction of our human desire to know and understand.**

In section 13.2, we distinguished scientific explanations, always **hypothetical** and uncertain in some degree, from unscientific explanations, which are characterized by **dogmatism** and a spirit of finality. Above all, **a scientific explanation is empirically verifiable;** it must be confirmed by experience; and from it there must be some propositions deducible (other than the statement of the fact to be explained) that are directly testable. But from an unscientific explanation, no other directly testable propositions can be deduced.

In section 13.3, we discussed more fully the five criteria by which scientific hypotheses are evaluated:

1. Relevance
2. Testability
3. Compatibility with previously well-established hypotheses
4. Predictive or explanatory power
5. Simplicity

In section 13.4, we described in general terms **the seven stages of any genuinely scientific investigation:**

1. Identification of the problem
2. Construction of preliminary hypotheses
3. Collection of additional data
4. Formulation of the hypothesis
5. Deduction of consequences from the hypothesis
6. Testing of the consequences deduced
7. Application of the theory developed

In section 13.5, we exhibited the operation of this hypothetical method in the conduct of a recent scientific investigation of great importance: the search for the structure of DNA. We noted the seven stages of inquiry, earlier distinguished, as manifested here in the quest for the explanation of genetic inheritance.

In section 13.6, we discussed **crucial experiments,** showing that the test of an abstract theory requires the use of a **set of hypotheses** and not just a single hypothesis; thus an experiment thought to be crucial may reveal the inadequacy of the set, yet leave uncertain which member of the set is mistaken. We discussed different senses of the term *"ad hoc* hypothesis," and explained why some, but not all, of these senses are derogatory.

In section 13.7, we showed how **classification,** although usually more prominent during the less developed stages of a science, remains a valuable instrument of scientific inquiry because it suggests general truths and permits the formulation of powerful explanatory hypotheses.

If we be, therefore, engaged by arguments to put trust in past experience, and make it the standard of our future judgment, these arguments must be probable only.
—David Hume

The theory of probabilities is simply the science of logic quantitatively treated.
—Charles Sanders Peirce

PROBABILITY

14.1   ALTERNATIVE CONCEPTIONS OF PROBABILITY

Probability is a central concept in inductive logic, as has been noted frequently in our preceding discussions of the scientific method. Even a hypothesis that fits all the available facts is not thereby established conclusively, but only with probability. The most careful uses of Mill's methods of experimental inquiry, we observed, cannot prove conclusively the truth of the causal laws to which they lead, but only tend to confirm them as highly probable. Even the very best inductive arguments fall short of that certainty which attaches to valid deductive arguments.

It is therefore fitting that our examination of inductive logic conclude with a close analysis of this key concept of probability. We begin by noting that different uses of the words "probable" and "probability" must be distinguished. The most typical of these are illustrated by the following three propositions:

1.   The probability that a tossed coin will show heads is ½.
2.   The probability that a 25-year-old woman will survive her 26th birthday is .971.
3.   On the present evidence, it is highly probable that Einstein's Theory of Relativity is correct.

There are other contexts in which the words "probable" and "probability" are used, as when we speak of "probable errors" of measurement, but these three are the most important. In the first two a number, called the *numerical coefficient of probability,* is assigned to a particular event; the third illustration differs from these in assigning no such number. When it is the probability of a scientific hypothesis that is in question, we commonly assign *degrees* of probability, as when some say that the Darwinian theory is regarded as being more probable than the account of creation given in the Book of Genesis, or that

533

the atomic theory has a higher degree of probability than some other specula-tive hypothesis concerning the inner structure of nuclei.

The numbers assigned in the first two illustrations are also very useful and seem very plausible. But where did they come from?

Coins have two sides, heads and tails, and when they fall, one side or the other must face upward. One chance out of two will place heads up, and so the probability ½ is assigned to heads. To arrive at the probability coefficient men-tioned in the second example, mortality statistics must be gathered and com-pared. Of 1,000 women who celebrated their 25th birthday, it was found that 971 lived at least one additional year, and on the basis of these findings the figure .971 was assigned to the probability of a 25-year-old woman surviving her 26th birth-day. Such probability measurements as these are utilized by life insurance com-panies, in fixing the size of premiums to be charged for their policies.

As the first two examples may suggest, studies of probability are bound up with gambling and mortality statistics; in fact, the modern study of probabil-ity had its beginning in these two fields. The theory of probability is commonly regarded as having begun with the correspondence between Blaise Pascal (1623–1662) and Pierre de Fermat (1608–1665) over the proper division of the stakes in an interrupted game of chance. Another version had it begin with Pascal's advice to the Chevalier de Mere, a notorious seventeenth-century gambler, on how to wager when throwing dice. In connection with the study of mortality, death records have been kept in London since 1592; in 1662, Captain John Graunt published a discussion of these records and what might be inferred with probability from them. Possibly as a consequence of its mixed ancestry, probability has been given two different interpretations.

A.   The *A Priori* **Theory of Probability**

The classical theory of the nature of probability, as formulated by Laplace, De Morgan, Keynes, and others, regards it as measuring degree of *rational belief.* When we are completely convinced of something, the measure of our belief may have the number 1 assigned it. And when we are utterly certain that a specified event cannot possibly happen, our belief that it *will* happen can be as-signed the number 0. Thus a rational person's belief that a tossed coin will *ei-ther* show heads or not show heads is 1, and his belief that it will *both* show heads and not show heads is 0. Where he is not sure, the degree of his reason-able belief will fall somewhere between 0 and 1. Probability is predicated of an event according to the degree to which one rationally believes that it will oc-cur. Or probability may be predicated of a statement or proposition according to the degree to which a completely rational person would believe it.

On the classical view, probability always is a result of partial knowledge and partial ignorance. If the exact motion of one's fingers in flipping a coin were known, together with the initial position, dimensions, and weight-distribution of the coin, one could predict its trajectory and final resting position with confi-dence. But such complete information is not available. Only some information is known: that the coin has only two sides, that it will fall, and so on. Consequently, our belief that it will show heads is governed by a consideration of the various possibilities, which are 2, of which heads is only 1. Therefore the probability ½ is assigned to the event of the coin showing heads. Similarly, when a deck of cards is about to be dealt, the cards are in just the order they are, and they will come off the deck, in an honest deal, in exactly the sequence of spades and hearts and diamonds and clubs, aces and kings and queens and jacks, that is determined by their arrangement in the deck. But we do not know that arrangement. We know only that there are 13 spades, out of 52 cards altogether, so the probability that the first card dealt will be a spade is exactly ¹³⁄₅₂, or ¼.

This view is known as the *a priori* theory of probability. It is so called because no trials need be run before the probability is assigned, no sample deals need to be examined. All that is required is a knowledge of the antecedent conditions: that there are only 13 spades in the deck, that there are 52 cards altogether, and that it is an honest deal so that one card has as much chance as any other of being dealt first. **In the *a priori* view, to compute the probability of an event's occurring in given circumstances, we divide the number of ways in which it can occur by the total number of possible outcomes of those circumstances, provided there is no reason to believe that any one of those possible outcomes is more likely than any other.** The probability of an event is thus expressed as a fraction, of which the denominator is the number of equipossible outcomes, and the numerator is the number of outcomes that would successfully yield the event in question. An honest lottery with 1,000 tickets sold has 1,000 equipossible outcomes. The probability of any one ticket's winning that lottery is therefore 1 over 1,000, ¹⁄₁,₀₀₀.

B.   The Relative Frequency Theory of Probability

An alternative to the *a priori* view is the theory that regards probability as being a measure of *relative frequency.* The relative frequency theory is especially well suited to take account of probability judgments arising out of statistical investigations. For instance, an actuary for an insurance company may wish to determine the mortality rate for 25-year-old women. Here we have a *reference class* and an *attribute.* The class is 25-year-old women; the attribute is surviving their 26th birthday. In this theory, the probability assigned is the measure of the relative frequency with which the members of the class exhibit the attribute in question. Here also, probability is expressed as a fraction, but in this case the denominator is the number of members in the reference class, the numerator the number of class members having the indicated attribute. If the records of 1,000 25-year-old women are examined, and 971 of them are found to survive their 26th birthday, .971 is assigned as the probability coefficient for the occurrence of this attribute in that class. Rational belief is not at issue here. **In the relative frequency theory of probability, probability is defined as the relative frequency with which members of a class exhibit a specified attribute.**

It is important to note that in both theories, the *probabilities assigned are relative to the evidence available.* This is obvious in the case of the relative frequency theory, since the probability of a given attribute must in that view vary with the reference class chosen for the computation. In the example used above, if the 1,000 women constituting the examined class are randomly selected in Egypt, the frequency with which survival to the age of 26 is found will be very different than if the 1,000 women are randomly selected in France. The probability of one-year survival for 25-year-old women is not the same in Egypt as it is in France. Similarly, the probability of blondness is higher relative to the class of Scandinavians than it is relative to the total population of the world. In using the relative frequency theory of probability, therefore, one critical step is the selection of the most appropriate reference class.

But probability is relative in the *a priori* theory also. No event, according to the classical account of this theory, has any *intrinsic* probability. An event can be assigned a probability only on the basis of the evidence available to the person making the assignment. Such relativity is to be expected in a view that regards probability as a measure of rational belief, for a reasonable person's beliefs change with the changes in that person's knowledge.

Suppose, for example, that two people are watching a deck of cards being shuffled. When the shuffle is finished, the dealer accidentally "flashes" the top card. One observer sees that the card is black, although he is not able to observe whether it is a spade or a club. But the second observer notices nothing. If the two observers are asked to estimate the probability of the first card's being a spade, the first observer will assign the probability ½, since he knows there are 26 black cards, of which half are spades. But the second observer will assign the probability ¼, since he knows only that there are 13 spades in the deck of 52 cards. The two observers thus assign different probabilities to the same event. Has one of them made a mistake? Certainly not: Each has assigned the correct probability *relative to the evidence available.* Both estimates are correct—even if the card turns out to be a club. No event has any probability *in and of itself,* which means that any prediction will have different probabilities in different contexts—that is, relevant to different sets of evidence. But of course one should always seek to gather the greatest amount of evidence available before making any probability judgment.

The two accounts of probability—the relative frequency account and the *a priori* account—are in agreement in holding that probability is relative to the evidence, and therefore adherents of both theories are also in agreement in accepting and using the *probability calculus,* an elementary presentation of which will be made in the following section.

14.2 THE PROBABILITY CALCULUS

We commonly seek to determine the probability of some complex event, an event that may be regarded as a whole of which its component events are parts. We may ask, for example: What is the probability of drawing two spades in succession from a deck of playing cards? The complex event of drawing two spades in succession is a whole, of which the two parts are the event of drawing the first spade, and the event of getting a second spade on the very next draw. Again, the complex event of a bride and groom living to celebrate their golden wedding anniversary is a whole of which the parts are the event of the bride's living an additional 50 years, the groom's living an additional 50 years, and no separation taking place. When it is known how the component events are related to each other, the probability of the complex event can be *calculated* from the probabilities of its components. We do this by using the calculus of probabilities. And thus **we define "the probability calculus" as a branch of pure mathematics that can be used in computing the probabilities of complex events from the probabilities of their component events.**

The application of the probability calculus can be extremely helpful in everyday affairs, when knowing the likelihood of certain outcomes may inform our decisions and enable us to act prudently. A mastery of its basic theorems is therefore one of the most useful products of the study of logic.

The probability calculus is most easily explained in terms of games of chance—dice, cards, and the like—because the artificially restricted universe created by such games makes possible the straightforward application of probability theorems. In this chapter, therefore, the probability calculus, although it has a very wide range of applications, will be illustrated primarily by means of problems drawn from the world of gambling. And in this exposition the *a priori* theory of probability will be used, although all of our results can, with a minimum of reinterpretation, be expressed and justified in terms of the relative frequency theory as well.

14.3 PROBABILITY OF JOINT OCCURRENCES

A *joint occurrence* is the occurrence of two or more of the component events of some complex whole. Thus, we may wish to learn the probability of drawing three successive spades from a deck of cards, or that both favorites in a horse race will finish out of the money, or of getting ten heads in ten flips of a coin. Suppose we are investigating the occurrence of only two components, called *a* and *b*; we ask about their joint occurrence when we ask the probability of getting *both a* and *b*.

A complication presents itself immediately: Does the occurrence or nonoccurrence of one of the two components have any effect whatever on the occurrence or nonoccurrence of the other component? If there is such a relation, the component events are not independent; if there is not such a relation, they are independent. **Two events are said to be independent if the occurrence or nonoccurrence of either of them has absolutely no effect on the occurrence or nonoccurrence of the other.** For example, if two coins are tossed, whether one comes down heads or tails has absolutely no effect on whether the other shows heads or tails; they are independent events.

In discussing the probability of the joint occurrence of events, we turn first to the simpler case: the joint occurrence of *independent* events. Consider this simple problem: What is the probability of getting two heads when tossing two coins? There are three possible outcomes to tossing two coins: We may get two heads, or we may get two tails, or we may get one head and one tail. *But these are not equipossible alternatives,* for there are two ways of getting one head and one tail, as contrasted with only one way of getting two heads. The first coin may be heads and the second tails, or the first coin may be tails and the second one heads; these are two distinct cases. Thus four distinct possible events may occur when two coins are tossed; they may be listed as follows:

First Coin	Second Coin
H	H
H	T
T	H
T	T

There is no reason to expect any one of these cases to occur rather than any other, so we regard them as being equipossible. The *favorable* case, that of getting two heads, is only one of four equipossible events, so the probability of getting two heads in tossing two coins is ¼. The probability for this complex event may be calculated from the probabilities of its two independent component events. The complex event of getting two heads is constituted by the joint occurrence of the event of getting a head on the first toss and the event of getting a head on the second. The probability of getting a head on the first is ½, and the probability of getting a head on the second is also ½. The events are presumed to be independent, so the *product theorem* of the probability calculus can be used to compute the probability of their joint occurrence. **The product theorem for independent events asserts that the probability of the joint occurrence of two independent events is equal to the product of their separate probabilities.** The general formula may be written

$$P(a \text{ and } b) = P(a) \times P(b)$$

where a and b are the two independent events, $P(a)$ and $P(b)$ are their separate probabilities, and $P(a \text{ and } b)$ designates the probability of their joint occurrence. In the present case, since a is the event of the first coin falling heads, and b is the event of the second coin falling heads, $P(a) = ½$ and $P(b) = ½$, so $P(a \text{ and } b) = ½ \times ½ = ¼$.

Consider a second problem of the same sort. What is the probability of getting a 12 when rolling two dice? Two dice will show twelve points only if each of them shows six points. Each die has six sides, any one of which is as likely to be face-up after a roll as any other. Where a is the event of the first die showing a 6, $P(a) = ⅙$. And where b is the event of the second die showing a 6, $P(b) = ⅙$. *The complex event of the two dice showing a 12 is constituted by the joint occurrence of a and b.* By the product theorem, then $P(a \text{ and } b) = ⅙ \times ⅙ = 1/36$, which is the probability of getting a 12 on one roll of two dice. We can arrive at the same result by taking the trouble to enumerate all the possible events that may occur when two dice are rolled. There are 36 equipossible events, which may be listed as follows, where in each pair of numbers the first stands for the number on the top face of the first die, the second for the number showing on the second die:

1—1	2—1	3—1	4—1	5—1	6—1
1—2	2—2	3—2	4—2	5—2	6—2
1—3	2—3	3—3	4—3	5—3	6—3
1—4	2—4	3—4	4—4	5—4	6—4
1—5	2—5	3—5	4—5	5—5	6—5
1—6	2—6	3—6	4—6	5—6	6—6

Of these 36 equipossible cases, only one is favorable (to getting a 12), so the probability is thus directly seen to be ⅟₃₆.

The product theorem may be *generalized* so as to cover the joint occurrence of *any* number of independent events. Thus if we draw a card from a deck, replace it and draw again, and replace it and draw once more, the event of drawing three spades is the joint occurrence of the event of getting a spade on the first draw, the event of getting a spade on the second draw, and the event of getting a spade on the third draw. Where these three events are designated by *a*, *b*, and *c*, their joint probability $P(a$ and b and $c)$ is equal to the product of the separate probabilities of the three events: $P(a) \times P(b) \times P(c)$. The probability is easily computed. A deck of cards contains 52 different cards, of which 13 are favorable to the event of drawing a spade. Thus the probability of getting a spade is ¹³⁄₅₂ or ¼. Since the card drawn is replaced before we draw again, the initial conditions for the second drawing are the same, so each $P(a)$, $P(b)$, and $P(c)$ is equal to ¼. Their joint occurrence has the probability $P(a$ and b and $c) = ¼ \times ¼ \times ¼ = ⅟₆₄$. The general product theorem allows us to compute the probability of the joint occurrence of any number of independent events.

We turn next to events that are *not* independent. Simply multiplying the probabilities of independent events, as in the examples above, does not take into account any *relationship* between component events. But if those component events are related, we may need to take that relationship into account in order to compute the joint occurrence of such events accurately. Frequently it is possible to do this. Consider a revised version of the previous example. Suppose we seek the probability of drawing three successive spades from a shuffled deck of cards, *but the cards drawn are not replaced*. If each card drawn is *not* returned to the deck before the next drawing, the outcomes of the earlier drawings *do* have an effect on the outcomes of the later drawings. If the first card drawn is a spade, then for the second draw there are only 12 spades left among a total of 51 cards, whereas if the first card is *not* a spade, then there are 13 spades left among 51 cards. Where *a* is the event of drawing a spade from the deck and not replacing it, and *b* is the event of drawing another spade from among the remaining cards, then the probability of *b*, that is, $P(b$ if $a)$, is ¹²⁄₅₁ or ⁴⁄₁₇. And if both *a* and *b* occur, the third draw will be made from a deck of 50 cards containing only 11 spades. If *c* is this last event, then $P(c$ if both a and $b)$ is ¹¹⁄₅₀. Thus, the probability that all three are spades, if three cards are drawn from a deck and not replaced, is according to the product theorem, ¹³⁄₅₂ × ¹²⁄₅₁ × ¹¹⁄₅₀, or ¹¹⁄₈₅₀. This is *less* than the probability of getting three spades in three draws when the cards drawn are replaced before drawing again, which was to be expected, since replacing a spade increases the probability of getting a spade on the next draw.

Consider another example, involving the probability of the joint occurrence of dependent events. Suppose we have an urn containing two white balls and one black ball. If two balls are drawn in succession, the first one *not* being replaced before drawing the second, what is the probability that both balls drawn will be white? Let *a* be the event of drawing a white ball on the first draw. There are three equipossible draws, one for each ball. Of these two are favorable, since two of the balls are white. The probability of getting a white ball on the first draw, $P(a)$, is therefore ⅔. If *a* occurs, then there remain only two balls in the urn, one white and one black. The probability of getting a white ball on the second draw, which event we may call *b*, is clearly ½; that is, $P(b$ if $a) =$ ½. Now, by the general product theorem, the probability of getting two white balls is the probability of the joint occurrences of *a* and (*b* if *a*), which is the product of the probabilities of their separate occurrence, ⅔ × ½ = ⅓. **The general formula here is**

$$P(a \text{ and } b) = P(a) \times P(b \text{ if } a).$$

The probability of getting two white balls in two such successive draws can also be determined, in this very simple situation, by a consideration of all possible cases. Where one white ball is designated by W_1 and the other white ball by W_2 and the black ball by B, the following list of equipossible pairs of draws is exhaustive:

First Draw	Second Draw
W_1	W_2
W_1	B
W_2	W_1
W_2	B
B	W_1
B	W_2

Of these six equipossible events, two are favorable (the first and third), which gives us ⅓ directly as the probability of getting two white balls in two successive draws with no replacement made.

The general product theorem can be applied to real-world problems of consequence, as in the following true account. A California teenager, afflicted with chronic leukemia that would soon kill her if untreated, could be saved only if a donor with matching bone marrow were found. When all efforts to locate such a donor failed, her parents decided to try to have another child, hoping that a successful bone-marrow transplant might then be possible. But the girl's father had first to have his vasectomy reversed, for which there was only a fifty percent (.50) chance of success. And if that were successful, the mother, 45 years old at the time, would have only a .73 chance of becoming pregnant. And if she did become pregnant, there was only a one-in-four chance (.25) that the baby's marrow would match that of the afflicted daughter. And if there were such a match, there would still be only a .70 chance that the leukemia patient would live through the needed chemotherapy and bone-marrow transplant.

The probability of a successful outcome was seen at the outset to be low, but not hopelessly low. The vasectomy was successfully reversed, and the mother did become pregnant—after which prospects improved. It turned out that the baby did possess matching bone marrow. Then, in 1992, the arduous bone-marrow-transplant procedure was begun. It proved to be a complete success.[1] What was the probability of this happy outcome at the time of the parents' original decision to pursue it?

THE PRODUCT THEOREM

To calculate the probability of the *joint occurrence* of two or more events:

A. If the events (say, *a* and *b*) are *independent:* The probability of their joint occurrence is the simple product of their probabilities:

$$P(a \text{ and } b) = P(a) \times P(b)$$

B. If the events (say, *a* and *b* and *c*, etc.) are *not independent:* The probability of their joint occurrence is the probability of the first event times the probability of the second event if the first occurred, times the probability of the third event if the first and the second occurred, etc.

$$P(a \text{ and } b \text{ and } c) = P(a) \times P(b \text{ if } a) \times P(c \text{ if both } a \text{ and } b)$$

Exercises

Example:

1. What is the probability of getting three aces in three successive draws from a deck of cards
    a. if each card drawn is replaced before the next drawing is made?
    b. if the cards drawn are not replaced?

Solution:

a. If each card drawn *is replaced* before the next drawing is made, the component events have absolutely no effect on one another and are therefore *independent.* In this case, $P(a \text{ and } b \text{ and } c) = P(a) \times P(b) \times P(c)$. There are 52 cards in the deck, of which four are aces. So the probability of drawing the first ace, $P(a)$, is $\frac{4}{52}$, or $\frac{1}{13}$. The probability of drawing the second ace, $P(b)$, is likewise $\frac{1}{13}$, as is the probability of drawing the third ace, $P(c)$. So the probability of the joint occurrence of *a* and *b* and *c* is $\frac{1}{13} \times \frac{1}{13} \times \frac{1}{13}$, or $\frac{1}{2,197}$.

b. If the cards drawn are *not replaced,* the component events are *dependent,* not independent. The formula is $P(a \text{ and } b \text{ and } c) = P(a) \times P(b \text{ if } a) \times P(c \text{ if } a \text{ and } b)$. In this case, the probability of drawing the first ace, $P(a)$, remains $\frac{4}{52}$, or $\frac{1}{13}$. But the probability of drawing a

---

[1] Anissa Ayala, the patient, was married one year after the successful transplant; the sister who saved her life, Marissa Ayala, was a flower girl at her wedding. Details of this case were reported in *Life* magazine, December 1993.

second ace if the first card drawn was an ace, $P(b$ if $a)$, is $\frac{3}{51}$, or $\frac{1}{17}$. And the probability of drawing a third ace if the first two cards drawn were aces, $P(c$ if a and $b)$, is $\frac{2}{50}$, or $\frac{1}{25}$. The probability of the joint occurrence of these three dependent events is therefore $\frac{1}{13} \times \frac{1}{17} \times \frac{1}{25}$, or $\frac{1}{5,525}$.

The probability of getting three successive aces in the second case is much lower than in the first, as one might expect, because, without replacement, the chances of getting an ace in each successive drawing are reduced by success in the preceding drawing.

2.   What is the probability of getting tails every time in three tosses of a coin?

3.   An urn contains 27 white balls and 40 black balls. What is the probability of getting four black balls in four successive drawings (a) if each ball drawn is replaced before making the next drawing? (b) if the balls are not replaced?

4.   What is the probability of rolling three dice so the total number of points that appear on their top faces is 3, three times in a row?

*5.   Four men whose houses are built around a square spend an evening celebrating in the center of the square. At the end of the celebration each staggers off to one of the houses, no two going to the same house. What is the probability that each one reached his own house?

6.   A dentist has her office in a building with five entrances, all equally accessible. Three patients arrive at her office at the same time. What is the probability that they all entered the building by the same door?

7.   In 1993, the probability that an American male of 25 would survive his 50th birthday was .742, and the probability that an American female of 22 would survive her 47th birthday was .801. Suppose that in that year, the probability that the marriage of such a couple would not end in divorce during the first 25 years was .702. For such a couple who married in that year, what then was the probability that they would live to celebrate their silver wedding anniversary?

8.   In each of two closets there are three cartons. Five of the cartons contain canned vegetables. The other carton contains canned fruits: ten cans of pears, eight cans of peaches, and six cans of fruit cocktail. Each can of fruit cocktail contains 300 chunks of fruit of approximately equal size, of which three are cherries. If a child goes into one of the closets, unpacks one of the cartons, opens a can and eats two pieces of its contents, what is the probability that two cherries will be eaten?

9.   A player at draw poker holds the seven of spades and the eight, nine, ten, and ace of diamonds. Aware that all the other players are drawing three cards, he figures that any hand he could win with a flush he could also win with a straight. For which should he draw? (A *straight* consists of any five cards in numerical sequence; a *flush* consists of any five cards all of the same suit.)

*10.   Four students decide they need an extra day to cram for a Monday exam. They leave town for the weekend, returning Tuesday. Producing dated receipts for hotel and other expenses, they explain that their car suffered a flat tire, and that they did not have a spare.

  The professor agrees to give them a make-up exam in the form of a single written question. The students take their seats in separate corners of the exam room, silently crowing over their deceptive triumph—until the professor writes the question on the blackboard: "Which tire?"

  Assuming that the students had not agreed in advance upon the identification of the tire in their story, what is the probability that all four students will identify the same tire?

14.4 PROBABILITY OF ALTERNATIVE OCCURRENCES

We are sometimes interested in the probability that either one or more of a set of alternative events will occur. When we toss two coins, for example, we may want to know the likelihood of *one or the other* landing as a head. And in a card game in which two cards are drawn, we may be interested in the probability of drawing *either* a spade *or* a club. The probability of alternative occurrence is always *greater* than the probability of each of the alternates taken singly—just as, in the case of joint occurrence, the probability of both events taking place will be *smaller* than the probability of one of them taken singly.

How can one calculate the probability of alternatives? In the case of joint occurrence we *multiplied* the fractions, arriving at the lower probability. In contrast, when seeking the probability of alternative occurrence, we *add* the fractions, increasing the probability. Once again we encounter a complication, however, that requires our distinguishing two types of cases.

Alternatives events may be *mutually exclusive,* or *not mutually exclusive.* Two events are mutually exclusive when they cannot both occur. If I toss two coins and get two heads, I cannot in those same tosses get two tails; two heads and two tails are mutually exclusive, obviously. But if I draw two cards from a deck, *getting a spade or getting a club* as one or the other of the two cards drawn presents a very different situation. I may get a spade on one of the draws, *and* a club on the other. "Drawing a spade" and "drawing a club" (in two draws from a deck) are not mutually exclusive events. But the method of calculating the probability of alternative events will differ importantly depending upon whether the events in question are, or are not, mutually exclusive. We take the two cases in turn.

If the events are mutually exclusive the calculation is easy and straightforward: We simply add the probabilities of the two component events. What is the probability of two heads or two tails in two tosses of a coin? It is, of course, the probability of the one plus the probability of the other. The probability of two heads is $\frac{1}{4}$, the probability of two tails is $\frac{1}{4}$, the probability of either two heads or two tails is $\frac{1}{4} + \frac{1}{4}$ or $\frac{1}{2}$.

The formula for computing the probability of complex events when they are mutually exclusive is simply:

$$P(a \text{ or } b) = P(a) + (Pb)$$

This is the addition theorem, and it may be generalized to apply to any number of alternatives, a or b or c or . . . If all are mutually exclusive, the probability of one of the other of them taking place is the sum of the probabilities of them all.

This may be well illustrated by the problem of computing the probability of being dealt a *flush* (five cards, all of the same suit) in a game of poker. There are four mutually exclusive alternatives here: the event of getting five spades, the event of getting five hearts, the event of getting five diamonds, and the event of getting five clubs. Let's first consider the probability of getting five spades. That is a joint occurrence of five subsidiary events that certainly are not independent, since each spade dealt reduces the probability of getting the next spade. Using the product theorem for dependent probabilities, we get $\frac{13}{52} \times \frac{12}{51} \times \frac{11}{50} \times \frac{10}{49} \times \frac{9}{48} = \frac{33}{66,640}$. Each of the other alternative flushes—a flush with hearts, or with diamonds, or with clubs—has the same probability. These four different flushes are mutually exclusive alternatives, so the probability of being dealt *any* flush (now we use the addition theorem) is $\frac{33}{66,640} + \frac{33}{66,640} + \frac{33}{66,640} + \frac{33}{66,640} = \frac{33}{16,660}$.

One more example. In drawing one ball from each of two urns, one containing two white balls and four black balls, the other containing three white balls and nine black balls, what is the probability of getting two balls of the same color? The event in whose probability we are interested is the alternative occurrence of two mutually exclusive events, one that of getting two white balls, the other that of getting two black balls. Their probabilities are to be computed separately, then added. The probability of getting two white balls is $\frac{2}{6} \times \frac{3}{12} = \frac{1}{12}$. And the probability of getting two black balls is $\frac{4}{6} \times \frac{9}{12} = \frac{1}{2}$. So the probability of getting two balls of the same color is $\frac{1}{12} + \frac{1}{2} = \frac{7}{12}$.

Thus far, in our discussion of alternative occurrences, we have dealt only with mutually exclusive events. But suppose we must compute the probability of a complex event that is constituted by the occurrence of at least one of two or more alternatives that are *not* mutually exclusive. For example, what is the probability of getting *at least* one head on two tosses of a coin? The events are nonexclusive, because surely it is possible to get heads on both tosses. We know that the probability of getting heads on the first toss is $\frac{1}{2}$, and the probability of getting heads on the second toss is also $\frac{1}{2}$, but the sum of these separate probabilities is 1, or certainty, and it is *not* certain that at least one toss will yield heads! This example shows that, when we compute the probability of the alternative occurrence of nonexclusive events, the addition theorem is not *directly* applicable. Two indirect methods can be used in the computing of probabilities of this type.

The first method of computing the probability that at least one of two nonexclusive events will occur requires that we break down the favorable cases into exclusive events. In the problem of finding the probability that at least one head will appear in two tosses of a coin, the equipossible cases are

H—H, H—T, T—H, T—T. These are all mutually exclusive, and each of them has the probability ¼. The first three are favorable; that is, if any one of the first three occurs, it will be true that at least one head appears in the two tosses. Hence the probability of getting at least one head is equal to the sum of the separate probabilities of all of the mutually exclusive favorable cases, which is ¼ + ¼ + ¼ = ¾.

The other method of computing the probability that at least one of two nonexclusive events will occur depends upon the fact that *no case can be both favorable and unfavorable.* If a designates an event, say, the event of getting at least one head on two tosses of a coin, then we shall use the notation $\bar{a}$ to designate the event *unfavorable* to a, that is, the event of not getting any head at all on two tosses of the coin. Since no case can be both favorable and unfavorable, a and $\bar{a}$ are *mutually exclusive;* that is, a and $\bar{a}$ cannot possibly both occur. And since every case must be either favorable or unfavorable, it is certain that either a or $\bar{a}$ must occur. Since zero is the probability coefficient we assign to an event that cannot possibly occur, and 1 is the probability coefficient assigned to an event that is certain to occur, the following two equations are true:

$$P(a \text{ and } \bar{a}) = 0$$

$$P(a \text{ or } \bar{a}) = 1$$

where $P(a \text{ and } \bar{a})$ is the probability that a and $\bar{a}$ will both occur, and $P(a \text{ or } \bar{a})$ is the probability that either a or $\bar{a}$ will occur. Since a and $\bar{a}$ are mutually exclusive, the addition theorem is applicable, and we have

$$P(a \text{ or } \bar{a}) = P(a) + P(\bar{a})$$

The last two equations combine to give

$$P(a) + P(\bar{a}) = 1$$

which yields the following very useful equation:

$$\mathbf{P(a) = 1 - P(\bar{a})}$$

Hence we can compute the probability of an event's occurrence by computing the probability that the event will *not* occur and subtracting that figure from 1. Applied to the event of tossing at least one head in two tosses of a coin, we can easily see that the only case in which the event does *not* occur is when both tosses result in tails. This is the unfavorable case, and by the product theorem, its probability is ½ × ½ = ¼, whence the probability that the event of getting at least one head in two tosses *does* occur is 1 − ¼ = ¾.

Another illustration of an event composed of alternative but nonexclusive occurrences is the following. If one ball is drawn from each of two urns, the first containing two white balls and four black balls, the second containing three white balls and nine black balls, what is the probability of getting at least one white ball? This problem can be solved using either of the two methods just explained. We can divide the favorable cases into mutually exclusive alternatives. These are a white ball from the first urn and a black ball from the second, a black ball from the first urn and a white ball from the second, and a white ball from both urns. The respective probabilities of these three are 2/6 × 9/12 = ¼, 4/6

$\times \frac{3}{12} = \frac{1}{6}$, and $\frac{6}{8} \times \frac{3}{12} = \frac{1}{2}$. Then the addition theorem for exclusive alternatives gives us $\frac{1}{4} + \frac{1}{6} + \frac{1}{12} = \frac{1}{2}$ as the probability of getting at least one white ball. The other method is somewhat simpler. The unfavorable case in which the draw does not result in at least one white ball is the event of getting two black balls. The probability of getting two black balls is $\frac{6}{8} \times \frac{5}{12} = \frac{1}{2}$, so the probability of getting at least one white ball is $1 - \frac{1}{2} = \frac{1}{2}$.

Sometimes the application of the probability calculus leads to a result which, although correct, differs from what we might have anticipated after a casual consideration of the facts given. Such a result is called *counterintuitive*. When a problem's solution is counterintuitive one may be led to judge probability mistakenly, and such "natural" mistakes encourage, at carnivals and elsewhere, the following wager. Three dice are to be thrown; the operator of the gambling booth offers to bet you even money (risk one dollar, and get that dollar back plus one more if you win) that no one of the three dice will show an ace. There are six faces on each of the dice, each with a different number; you get three chances for an ace; superficially, this looks like a fair game.

In fact it is *not* a fair game, and hefty profits are reaped by swindlers who capitalize on that counterintuitive reality. The game would be fair only if the appearance of any given number on one of the three dice precludes its appearance on either of the other two dice. That is plainly not true. The unwary player is misled by mistakenly (and subconsciously) supposing that mutual exclusivity. But of course the numbers are not mutually exclusive; some throws will result in the same number appearing on two or three of the dice. The attempt to identify and count all of the possible outcomes, and then to count the outcomes in which at least one ace appears, quickly becomes frustrating. But because the appearance of any given number does not exclude the appearance of that same number on the remaining dice, the game truly is a swindle—and this becomes evident when the chances of winning are calculated by first determining the probability of *losing* and subtracting that from 1. The probability of any single *non*-ace (a 2, or 3, or 4, or 5, or 6) showing up is $\frac{5}{6}$. The probability of losing is that of getting three non-aces, which (since the dice are independent of one another) is $\frac{5}{6} \times \frac{5}{6} \times \frac{5}{6}$, which equals $\frac{125}{216}$, or .579! The probability of the player throwing at least one ace, therefore, is $1 - \frac{125}{216} = \frac{91}{216}$, which is .421. This is a gambling game to pass by!

Let us now attempt to work out a moderately complicated problem in probability. The game of craps is played with two dice. The *shooter*, who rolls the dice, wins if a 7 or an 11 turns up on the first roll, but loses if a 2, or 3, or 12 turns up on the first roll. If one of the remaining numbers, 4, 5, 6, 8, 9, or 10, turns up on the first roll, the shooter continues to roll the dice until either that same number turns up again, in which case the shooter wins, or a 7 appears, in which case the shooter loses. Craps is widely believed to be a "fair" game, that is, a game in which the shooter has an even chance of winning. Is this true? Let us calculate the probability that the shooter will win at craps.

To do this, we must first obtain the probabilities that the various numbers will occur. There are 36 different equipossible ways for two dice to fall. Only one of these ways will show a 2, so the probability here is $\frac{1}{36}$. Only one of these ways will show a 12, so here the probability also is $\frac{1}{36}$. There are two ways to throw a 3: 1–2 and 2–1, so the probability of a 3 is $\frac{2}{36}$. Similarly, the probability of getting an 11 is $\frac{2}{36}$. There are three ways to throw a 4: 1–3, 2–2, and 3–1, so the probability of a 4 is $\frac{3}{36}$. Similarly, the probability of getting a 10 is $\frac{3}{36}$. Since there are four ways to roll a 5 (1–4, 2–3, 3–2, and 4–1), its probability is $\frac{4}{36}$, and this is also the probability of getting a 9. A 6 can be obtained in any one of five ways (1–5, 2–4, 3–3, 4–2, and 5–1), so the probability of getting a 6 is $\frac{5}{36}$, and the same probability exists for an 8. There are six different combinations that yield 7 (1–6, 2–5, 3–4, 4–3, 5–2, 6–1), so the probability of rolling a 7 is $\frac{6}{36}$.

The probability that the shooter will win on the first roll is the sum of the probability that a 7 will turn up and the probability that an 11 will turn up, which is $\frac{6}{36} + \frac{2}{36} = \frac{8}{36}$, or $\frac{2}{9}$. The probability of losing on the first roll is the sum of the probabilities of getting a 2, a 3, and a 12, which is $\frac{1}{36} + \frac{2}{36} + \frac{1}{36} = \frac{4}{36}$, or $\frac{1}{9}$. The shooter is twice as likely to win on the first roll as to lose on the first roll; however, the shooter is most likely not to do either on the first roll, but to get a 4, 5, 6, 8, 9, or 10. If one of these six numbers is thrown, the shooter is obliged to continue rolling the dice until that number is rolled again, in which case the shooter wins, or until a 7 comes up, which is a losing case. Those cases in which neither the number first thrown nor a 7 occurs can be ignored, for they are not decisive. Suppose the shooter gets a 4 on the first roll. The next *decisive* roll will show either a 4 or a 7. In a decisive roll, the equipossible cases are the three combinations that make up a 4 (1–3, 2–2, 3–1) and the six combinations that make up a 7. The probability of throwing a second 4 is therefore $\frac{3}{9}$. The probability of getting a 4 on the first roll was $\frac{3}{36}$, so the probability of winning by throwing a 4 on the first roll and then getting another 4 before a 7 occurs is $^3{}_{36} \times \frac{3}{9} = \frac{1}{36}$. Similarly, the probability of the shooter winning by throwing a 10 on the first roll and then getting another 10 before a 7 occurs is also $\frac{3}{36} \times \frac{3}{9} = \frac{1}{36}$.

By the same line of reasoning, we can find the probability of the shooter winning by throwing a 5 on the first roll and then getting another 5 before throwing a 7. In this case, there are 10 equipossible cases for the decisive roll: the four ways to make a 5 (1–4, 2–3, 3–2, 4–1) and the six ways to make a 7. The probability of winning with a 5 is therefore $\frac{4}{36} \times \frac{4}{10} = \frac{2}{45}$. The probability of winning with a 9 is also $\frac{2}{45}$. The number 6 is still more likely to occur on the first roll, its probability being $\frac{5}{36}$. And it is more likely than the others mentioned to occur a second time before a 7 appears, the probability here being $\frac{5}{11}$. So the probability of winning with a 6 is $\frac{5}{36} \times \frac{5}{11} = \frac{25}{396}$. And again, similarly, the probability of winning with an 8 is $\frac{25}{396}$.

There are eight different ways for the shooter to win: if a 7 or 11 is thrown on the first roll, or if one of the six numbers 4, 5, 6, 8, 9, or 10 is thrown on the first roll *and* again before a 7. These ways are all exclusive; so the total probability of the shooter's winning is the sum of the probabilities of the alternative ways in which winning is possible, and this is $\frac{6}{36} + \frac{2}{36} + \frac{1}{36} + \frac{2}{45} + \frac{25}{396} + \frac{25}{396} + \frac{2}{45} + \frac{1}{36} = \frac{244}{495}$. Expressed as a decimal fraction, this is .493. This shows that in a crap game the shooter has *less* than an even chance of winning—only slightly less, to be sure, but still less than .500.

THE ADDITION THEOREM

To calculate the probability of the *alternative occurrence* of two or more events:

A. If the events (say *a* or *b*) are *mutually exclusive:* The probability of at least one of them occurring is the simple addition of their probabilities:

$$P(a \text{ or } b) = P(a) + P(b)$$

B. If the events (say *a* or *b* or *c*) are *not mutually exclusive:* The probability of at least one of them occurring may be determined by either
    (1) analyzing the favorable cases into mutually exclusive events and summing the probabilities of those successful events; or
    (2) determining the probability that no one of the alternative events will occur, and then subtracting that probability from 1.

Exercises

*1.   Calculate the shooter's chances of winning in a crap game by the second method; that is, compute the chances of his losing, and subtract it from 1.

2.   In drawing three cards in succession from a standard deck, what is the probability of getting at least one spade (a) if each card is replaced before making the next drawing? (b) if the cards drawn are not replaced?

3.   What is the probability of getting at least one head in three tosses of a coin?

4.   If three balls are selected at random from an urn containing 5 red, 10 white, and 15 blue balls, what is the probability that they will all be the same color (a) if each ball is replaced before the next one is withdrawn? (b) if the balls selected are not replaced?

*5.   If someone offers to bet you even money that you will not throw either an ace or a six on either of two successive throws of a die, should you accept the wager?

6.   In a group of 30 students randomly gathered in a classroom, what is the probability that no two of those students will have the same birthday; that is, what is the probability that there will be no duplication of the same date of birth, ignoring the year and attending only to the month and the day of the month? How many students would need to be in the group in order for the probability of such a duplication to be approximately .5?

7.   If the probability that a man of 25 will survive his 50th birthday is .742, and the probability that a woman of 22 will survive her 47th birthday is .801, and such a man and woman marry, what is the probability (a) that at least one of them lives at least another 25 years? (b) that only one of them lives at least another 25 years?

8. One partly filled case contains two bottles of orange juice, four bottles of cola, and four bottles of beer; another partly filled case contains three bottles of orange juice, seven colas, and two beers. A case is opened at random and a bottle selected at random from it. What is the probability that it contains a non-alcoholic drink? Had all the bottles been in one case, what is the probability that a bottle selected at random from it would contain a nonalcoholic drink?

9. A player in a draw-poker game is dealt three jacks and two small odd cards. He discards the latter and draws two cards. What is the probability that he improves his hand on the draw? (One way to improve it is to draw another jack to make four-of-a-kind; the other way to improve it is to draw any pair to make a full house.)

Challenge to the Reader

The following problem has been a source of some controversy among probability theorists. Is the correct solution counterintuitive?

*10. Remove all cards except aces and kings from a deck, so that only eight cards remain, of which four are aces and four are kings. From this abbreviated deck, deal two cards to a friend. If she looks at her cards and announces (truthfully) that her hand contains an ace, what is the probability that both her cards are aces? If she announces instead that one of her cards is the ace of spades, what is the probability then that both her cards are aces? Are these two probabilities the same?[2]

14.5 EXPECTED VALUE

In placing bets or making investments it is important to consider not only the probability of winning or receiving a return, but also *how much* can be won on the bet or returned on the investment. These two considerations, *safety* and *productivity*, often clash; greater potential returns usually entail greater risks. The safest investment may not be the best one to make, nor may the investment that promises the greatest return *if* it succeeds. The need to reconcile safety and maximum return confronts us not only in gambling and investing, but also in choosing among alternatives in education, employment, and other spheres of life. We would like to know whether the investment—of money or of time and energy—is "worth it"; that is, whether that wager on the future is wise, all things considered. The future cannot be known, but the probabilities may be

---

[2] For some discussion of this problem see L. E. Rose, "Countering a Counter-Intuitive Probability," *Philosophy of Science* 39 (1972): 523–524; A. I. Dale, "On a Problem in Conditional Probability," *Philosophy of Science* 41 (1974): 204–206; R. Faber, "Re-Encountering a Counter-Intuitive Probability," *Philosophy of Science* 43 (1976): 283–285; and S. Goldberg, "Copi's Conditional Probability Problem," *Philosophy of Science* 43 (1976): 286–289.

estimated. When one is attempting to compare investments, or bets, or "chancy" decisions of any kind, the concept of *expected value* is a powerful tool to use.

Expected value can best be explained in the context of wagers whose outcomes have known probabilities. Any bet—say, an even-money bet of $1 that heads will appear on the toss of a coin—should be thought of as a purchase; the money is spent when the bet has been made. The dollar wagered is the price of the purchase; it buys some *expectation,* or *expected value.* If heads appears, the bettor receives a return of $2 (one his own, the other his winnings); if tails appears, the bettor receives $0 return. There are only two possible outcomes of this wager, a head or a tail; the probability of each is known to be ½; and there is a specified return ($2, or $0) associated with each outcome. **We multiply the return yielded on each possible outcome by the probability of that outcome's being realized; the sum of all such products is the expectation or expected value of the bet or investment.** The expected value of a one-dollar bet that heads will turn up when a fair coin is tossed is thus equal to (½ × $2) + (½ × $0), which is $1. In this case, as we know, the "odds" are even—which means that the expected value of the purchase was equal to the purchase price.

But such is not always the case. We seek investments in which the expected value purchased will prove greater than the cost of our investment. We want the odds to be in our favor. Yet often we are tempted by wagers of which the expected value is less, sometimes much less, than the price of the gamble.

The disparity between the price and the expected value of a bet can be readily seen in a raffle, in which the purchase of a ticket offers a small chance at a large return. How much the raffle ticket is really worth depends upon how small the chance *and* how large the return. Suppose that the return, if we win it, is an automobile, worth $20,000, and the price of the raffle ticket is $1. If 20,000 raffle tickets are sold, of which we buy one, the probability of our winning is $\frac{1}{20,000}$. The chances of winning are thus very small, but the return if we win is very large. In this hypothetical case, the expected value of the raffle ticket is ($\frac{1}{20,000}$ × $20,000) + ($\frac{19,999}{20,000}$ × $0), or precisely $1, the purchase price of the ticket. But the usual purpose of a raffle is to raise money for some worthy cause, and that can happen only if more money is collected from ticket sales than is paid out in prizes. Therefore many more than 20,000 tickets—perhaps 40,000 or 80,000 or 100,000—will be sold. Suppose that 40,000 tickets are sold. The expected value of our $1 ticket then will be ($\frac{1}{40,000}$ × $20,000) + ($\frac{39,999}{40,000}$ × $0), or 50 cents. If 80,000 tickets are sold, the expected value of the $1 ticket will be reduced to 25 cents, and so on. We may be confident that the expected value of any raffle ticket we are asked to buy will be substantially less than the amount we are asked to pay for it.

Lotteries are very popular because of the very large prizes that may be won. States and countries conduct lotteries because every ticket purchased buys an expected value equal to only a fraction of the ticket's price; those who run the lottery retain the difference, reaping huge profits.

The Michigan lottery, played by more than two-thirds of the citizens of that state, is typical. Different bets are offered. In one game, called the "Daily 3," the player may choose (in a "straight bet") any three-digit number from 000 to 999.

After all bets are placed, a number is drawn at random and announced by the State; a player who has purchased a $1 straight-bet ticket on that winning number wins a prize of $500. The probability that the correct three digits in correct order have been selected is 1 in 1,000; the expected value of a $1 "Daily 3" straight-bet ticket is therefore $\frac{1}{1,000} \times \$500$ plus $\frac{999}{1,000} \times \$0$, or 50 *cents*.[3]

Lotteries and raffles are examples of great disparity between the price and the expected value of the gambler's purchase. Sometimes the disparity is small, but the number of purchasers nevertheless ensures the profitability of the sale, as in gambling casinos, where every normal bet is one in which the purchase price is greater than the expected value bought. In the preceding section we determined, using the product theorem and the addition theorem of the calculus of probability, that the dice game called craps is one in which the shooter's chance of winning is .493—just a little less than even. But that game is widely and mistakenly believed to offer the shooting player an even chance. Betting on the shooter in craps, at even money, is therefore a leading attraction in American gambling casinos. But every such bet of $1 is a purchase of expected value equal to $(.493 \times \$2) + (.507 \times \$0)$, which is 98.6 cents. The difference of approximately a penny and a half may seem trivial; but because casinos receive that advantage (and other similar advantages on other wagers) in thousands of bets made each day on the dice tables, they are very profitable enterprises. In the gambling fraternity, those who regularly bet on the shooter to win at craps are called paradoxically "right bettors," and among professional gamblers it is commonly said that "all right bettors die broke."

Disparities of a similar kind, in which every wager costs more than the expected value it buys, are to be found when analyzing all other bets in gambling casinos. The roulette wheel, the symbol of chance all over the world, gives a further illustration of these disparities. In roulette the numbers 1 to 36 appear (not in numerical order) around the circumference of a large wheel, and behind each number is a small groove. The wheel, carefully balanced so as to favor no number or section of the wheel, is spun vigorously, and a small steel ball is set spinning in the opposite direction just outside it and behind the numbers. The groove in which the ball finally comes to rest marks the one number that wins that game. The payoff for a bet on one number is 35-to-1. However, in addition to the 36 numbers colored alternately red and black around the rim of the wheel, there are two other numbers (0 and 00) colored green. The probability of winning a bet on any one number on the roulette wheel, therefore, is 1 in 38. The expected value of a $1 bet on a given number in roulette is therefore $(\frac{1}{38} \times \$36) + (\frac{37}{38} \times \$0)$, or just under 95 cents.

In roulette one also can bet on groups of numbers, at odds that vary with the size of the group. One may wager that the ball will come to rest on any one of a group of three numbers, at the odds of 11 to 1, but the two green numbers keep the game profitable for the house. The probability of winning such a bet

---

[3] However imprudent a wager on the "Daily 3" may be, it is a very popular lottery, so popular that it is now run twice a day, midday and evening. One may infer that either those who purchase such lottery tickets have not thought through the expected value of their wagers, or that such wagering offers them satisfactions independent of the money value of their bets.

will be ³⁄₃₈, and the return, if one wagers $1 and wins, will be $12. The expected value of the bet on a group of three numbers (³⁄₃₈ × $12 = 94.7) remains just under 95 cents. Or one may bet on a group of four numbers, the bet paying 8 to 1, (⁴⁄₃₈ × $9 = 94.7) or on two numbers at odds of 17 to 1 (²⁄₃₈ × $18 = 94.7)—but the expected value of all these wagers remains a little less than 95 cents. Instead of betting on one or a few numbers, one may bet on half of them—that the winning number will be red (or black), or that it will be even (or odd), but such bets, at even money, also lose if the ball comes to rest behind either of the two greens. Of the 38 possible outcomes, 18 outcomes will yield a return of $2 on a $1 bet on red (or black, or even, or odd), and 20 outcomes will yield a return of $0. The expected value of such a bet is therefore (¹⁸⁄₃₈ × $2) + (²⁰⁄₃₈ × $0) = 94.7— again just under 95 cents! Gambling casinos are not places in which prudent people spend their money.

The concept of *expected value* is of great practical use in helping one to decide how to save (or invest) one's money most wisely. Banks pay differing rates of interest on accounts of different kinds. Let us assume that the alternative bank accounts among which we choose are all government insured, and that therefore there is no chance of a loss of the principal. At the end of a full year, the expected value of each $1,000 savings investment, at 5 percent simple interest, is ($1,000 [the principal that we know will be returned]) + (.05 × $1,000), or $1,050 in all. To complete the calculation, this return must be multiplied by the probability of our getting it—but here we assume, because the account is insured, that our getting it is certain, so we merely multiply by 1, or ¹⁰⁰⁄₁₀₀. If the rate of interest is 6 percent, the insured return will be $1,060, and so on. The expected value purchased in such savings accounts is indeed greater than the deposit, the purchase price—but to get that interest income we must give up the use of our money for some period of time. The bank pays us for its use during that time because, of course, it plans to invest that money at yet higher rates of return.

Safety and productivity are considerations always in tension. If we are prepared to sacrifice a very small degree of safety for our savings, we may achieve a modest increase in the rate of return. For example, with that $1,000 we may purchase a corporate bond, perhaps paying 8 or even 10 percent interest, in effect lending our money to the company issuing the bond. The yield on our corporate bond may be double that of a bank savings account—but we will be running the risk, small but real, that the corporation issuing the bond will be unable to make payment when the loan we made to them falls due. In calculating the expected value of such a bond, say at 10 percent, the amount to be returned to the investor of $1,000 is determined in precisely the same way in which we calculated the yield on a savings account. First we calculate the return, if we get it: ($1,000 [the principal]) + (10% × $1,000 [the interest]), or $1,100 total return. But in this case the probability of our getting that return is not ¹⁰⁰⁄₁₀₀; it may be very high, but it is not certain. The fraction by which that $1,100 return therefore must be multiplied is the probability, as best we can estimate it, that the corporation will be financially sound when its bond is due for payment. If we think this probability is very high—say, .99—we may conclude that the purchase of the corporate bond at 10 percent offers an expected value ($1,089) greater than that of the insured bank account at 5 percent ($1,050), and is therefore a wiser investment. Here is the comparison in detail:

Insured bank account at 5 percent simple interest for one year:

Return = [principal + interest] = ($1,000 + $50) = $1,050
Probability of return (assumed) = 1
Expected value of investment in this bank account:
($1,050 × 1 = $1,050 + ($0 × 0 = $0) or $1,050 *total*

Corporate bond at 10 percent interest, at the end of one year:

Return if we get it = [principal + interest] = ($1,000 + $100) = $1,100
Probability of return (estimated) = .99
Expected value of investment in this corporate bond:
($1,100 × .99 = $1,089) + ($0 × .01 = $0) or $1,089 *total*

However, if we conclude that the company to which we would be lending the money is not absolutely reliable, our estimated probability of ultimate return will drop, say, to .95, and the expected value will drop also:

Corporate bond at 10 percent interest, at the end of one year:

Return if we get it = [principal + interest] = ($1,000 + $100) = $1,100
Probability of return (new estimate) = .95
Expected value of investment in this corporate bond:
($1,100 × .95 = $1,045) + ($0 × .05 = $0) or $1,045 *total*

If this last estimate reflects our evaluation of the company selling the bond, then we will judge the bank account, paying a lower rate of interest with much greater safety, the wiser investment.

Interest rates on bonds or on bank accounts fluctuate, of course, depending on the current rate of inflation and other factors, but the interest paid on a commercial bond is always higher than that paid on an insured bank account *because* the risk of the bond is greater; that is, the probability of its anticipated return is lower. And the greater the known risk, the higher the interest rate must go to attract investors. Expected value, in financial markets as everywhere, must take into consideration both probability (risk) and outcome (return).

When the soundness of a company enters our calculation of the expected value of an investment in it, we must make some probability assumptions. Explicitly or implicitly, we estimate the fractions that we then think best represent the likelihoods of the possible outcomes foreseen. These are the fractions by which the returns that we anticipate in the event of these outcomes must be multiplied, before we sum the products. All such predictions are necessarily speculative, and all the outcomes calculated are therefore uncertain, of course.

When we can determine the approximate value of a given return *if* we achieve it, calculations of the kind here described enable us to determine what probability those outcomes *need* to have (given present evidence) so that our investment now will prove worthwhile. Many decisions in financial matters, and also many choices in ordinary life, depend (if they are to be rational) on such estimates of probability and the resultant expected value. The calculus of probability may have application whenever we must gamble on the future.

There is no gambling system that can evade the rigor of the probability calculus. It is sometimes argued, for example, that in a game in which there are even-money stakes to be awarded on the basis of approximately equiprobable alternatives (such as tossing a coin, or betting black versus red on a roulette wheel), one can be *sure to win* by making the same bet consistently—always heads, or always the same color—and doubling the amount of money wagered after each loss. Thus, if I bet $1 on heads, and tails shows, then I should bet $2 on heads the next time, and if tails shows again, my third bet, also on heads, should be $4, and so on. One cannot fail to win by following this procedure, some suppose, because extended runs (of tails, or of the color I don't bet on) are highly improbable.[4] And anyway, it is said, the longest run must *sometime* end, and when it does, the person who has regularly doubled the bet will always be money ahead.

Wonderful! Why need anyone work for a living, when we can all adopt this apparently foolproof system of winning at the gaming table? Let us ignore the fact that most gaming houses put an upper limit on the size of the wager they will accept, a limit that may block the application of the doubling system. What is the real fallacy contained in this doubling prescription? A long run of tails, say, is almost certain to end sooner or later, but it may end later rather than sooner. So an adverse run may last long enough to exhaust any finite amount of money the bettor has to wager. To be certain of being able to continue doubling the bet each time, no matter how long the adverse run may continue or how large the losses are that the run has imposed, the bettor would have to begin with an infinite amount of money. But of course, a player with an infinite amount of money could not possibly win—in the sense of increasing his wealth.

Putting aside the fanciful case of bettors with infinite wealth, let us examine the operation of this doubling system in a realistic setting, in which the amount of money available to risk is finite. If a player is resolved to double bets until all his money is lost, all the money will be lost sooner or later (provided the house has sufficient funds to cover all the bets, of course). And if the player is resolved to double bets until some antecedently specified amount of money has been won, the game may go on forever, and the player may never either reach the goal or go broke. To test the system, therefore, we examine definite cases, that is, cases in which it is decided in advance how long the doubling will continue. This definiteness may be achieved in a number of ways.

---

[4] In fact, a long random sequence of heads and tails (or reds and blacks on a roulette wheel, etc.) will include extended runs of one result (tails, or reds, etc.) with much greater frequency than is commonly supposed. A run of a dozen heads in a row—requiring a bet of $2,048 on the 12th bet if one wagers steadily on tails in a doubling series that began with $1—is very far from rare. And after a run of twelve, of course, the chances of a thirteenth tail is ½!

For the sake of simplicity, let's suppose a player begins with just $3, so that she is prepared to sustain just one loss; two in a row would wipe her out. Let's have her decide to bet on heads just twice, and consider the different possible outcomes. The $3 is her purchase price; what is the expectation purchased? If two heads come up in a row, the player, winning $1 on each, will get a return of $5. If there is a head first and then a tail, the return will be just $3. If there is tail first and then a head, having lost $1 on the first toss and having bet $2 on the second, which won, the player's return will be $4. Finally, two tails will wipe her out, yielding a return of $0. Each of these events has a probability of ¼, so the expected value is (¼ × $5) + (¼ × $3) + (¼ × $4) = $3. The player's expectation is no greater when she uses the doubling technique than when she risks her entire capital on one toss of a coin.

Let us make a different supposition, that a player decides to play three times (if his money holds out) so that with luck he can double his money. The eight equipossible outcomes can be listed in the form of a table:

First Toss	Second Toss	Third Toss	Return	Probability
H	H	H	$6	⅛
H	H	T	$4	⅛
H	T	H	$5	⅛
H	T	T	$1	⅛
T	H	H	$5	⅛
T	H	T	$3	⅛
T	T	H	$0	⅛
T	T	T	$0	⅛

The expectation in this new strategy—the return on each outcome multiplied by the probability of that outcome, and these products summed—remains the same, still $3.

Consider just one more aspect of the doubling technique. Suppose someone wants to win just a single dollar, which means that she will play until she wins just once or else goes broke. With this more modest aim, what is the probable value of her investment? If heads appears on the first toss, the return is $4 (the $1 won, and the original stake of $3), and having won her dollar, the woman stops playing. If tails appears on the first toss, $2 is bet on the second. If heads appears, the return is $4, and the player quits with her winnings. If tails appears, the return is $0, and the player quits because she has lost all her money. There are only these three possible outcomes, the first of which has a probability of ½, the second ¼, and the third ¼. Such a player, following such a strategy, is three times as likely to win as to lose. But of course, she can lose three times as much as she can win by this method. The expected value is (½ × $4) + (¼ × $4) + (¼ × $0) = $3. The expectation is not increased at all by the doubling technique. The *chances of winning* are increased, just as they would be by betting on more numbers at roulette, but the *amount* that can be won decreases rapidly enough to keep the *expected value constant*.

The inevitable failure of the doubling technique teaches an important lesson. The probability of getting a head (or of a tail) on the next fair toss of a coin cannot be affected by the outcomes of preceding tosses, because the events are independent. On the assumption that there really is no causal connection between the events in the preceding series, it is simply foolish to believe that either red or black is "due" on the roulette wheel, or that the repeated appearance of certain numbers among winning lottery entries shows that those numbers are "hot." One who bets, or invests, on the supposition that some future event is made more probable, or less probable, by the frequency of the occurrence of independent events that have preceded it, commits a blunder so old and so common that it has been given a mocking name: *the gambler's fallacy.* It is a mistake in inductive reasoning that has led to many a financial downfall.

Exercises

*1.   In the Virginia lottery in 1992, six numbers were drawn at random from 44 numbers; the winner needed to select all six, in any order; each ticket (with one such combination) cost $1. The total number of possible six-number combinations was 7,059,052. One week in February of that year, the jackpot in the Virginia lottery had risen to $27 million. (a) What was the expected value of each ticket in the Virginia lottery that week?

These unusual circumstances led an Australian gambling syndicate to try to buy all of the tickets in the Virginia lottery that week. They fell short—but they were able to acquire some 5 million of the available six-number combinations. (b) What was the expected value of their $5-million purchase? [Yes, the Aussies won!]

2.   At most crap tables in gambling houses, the house will give odds of 6 to 1 against rolling a 4 the "hard way," that is, with a pair of 2's as contrasted with a 3 and a 1, which is the "easy way." A bet made on a "hard way" 4 wins, if a pair of 2's show before either a 7 is rolled or a 4 is made the "easy way"; otherwise it loses. What is the expectation purchased by a $1 bet on a "hard-way" 4?

3.   If the odds are 8 to 1 against rolling an 8 the "hard way" (that is, with two 4's), what is the expectation purchased by a $1 bet on a "hard-way" 8?

4.   What expectation does a person with $15 have who bets on heads, beginning with a $1 bet, and uses the doubling technique, if the bettor resolves to play just four times and quit?

*5.   Anthrax is a disease nearly always deadly to cows and other animals. The nineteenth-century French veterinarian, Louvrier, devised a treatment for anthrax that was later shown to be totally without merit. His alleged "cure" was tried on two cows, selected at random from four cows that had received a powerful dose of anthrax microbes. Of the two he treated, one died and one recovered; of the two he left untreated, one died and one recovered. The reasons for recovery were unknown. Had Louvrier tested his "cure" on the two cows that happened to live, his treatment would have received impressive but spurious confirmation. What was the probability of Louvrier choosing, for his test, just those two cows that chanced to live?

6. On the basis of past performance, the probability that the favorite will win the Bellevue Handicap is .46, while there is a probability of only .1 that a certain dark horse will win. If the favorite pays even money, and the odds offered are 8 to 1 against the dark horse, which is the better bet?

7. If $100 invested in the preferred stock of a certain company will yield a return of $110 with a probability of .85, whereas the probability is only .67 that the same amount invested in common stock will yield a return of $140, which is the better investment?

8. An investor satisfies herself that a certain region contains radioactive deposits, which may be either plutonium or uranium. For $500 she can obtain an option that will permit her to determine which element is present, and to enjoy the proceeds from its extraction and sale. If only plutonium is present, she will lose four-fifths of her option money, whereas if uranium is present she will enjoy a return of $40,000. If there is only one chance in a hundred that uranium is present, what is the expected value of the option?

9. The following notice is a real one, distributed to all the parents in the school attended by the son of one of the authors of this book:

Up, Up and Away—Raffle '98
We are all winners!
4 lucky people will walk away with lots of cash!

1st Prize	$1,000
2nd Prize	$400
3rd Prize	$250
4th Prize	$100

Chances of winning are good—Only 4,000 tickets were printed!
Everyone will benefit from the great new sports equipment
we will be able to buy with the money raised!

In this raffle, supposing all the tickets were sold, what was the expected value of each ticket costing $1?

*10. The probability of the shooter winning in the dice game called "craps" is .493, slightly less than even, as we proved in the preceding section. In casinos, a bet that the shooter will win is a bet on what is called the "Pass" line. We could all become rich, it would seem, if only we bet consistently *against* the shooter, on the "Don't Pass" line. But of course there is no such line; one cannot simply bet against the shooter, because the house will not take so unprofitable a bet. Yet usually one can place a bet called "Don't Pass–Bar 3," which wins if the shooter loses, unless the shooter loses by rolling a 3, in which case this bet loses also. What is the expected value of a $100 bet on the "Don't Pass–Bar 3" line?

Challenge to the Reader

We noted in this section that if the value of the return on a wager (*if* we achieve that return) is known, and if the decision facing us is whether to make that wager (or investment), it is possible to calculate the probability that this anticipated return must have to justify the present wager. That is the situation often facing a player in the game of poker, when she must decide whether to risk additional money to retain her chances of winning the pot by staying in the game, or to drop out. Imagine yourself such a player in the following circumstances:

11.   You are playing stud poker. (In this game, one card is dealt to each player on the first round, face down; on each of the following four rounds, one card is dealt to each player face up, for all to see. Betting is done after each round.) Just before the last round is dealt—each player showing three cards and having one "in the hole"—one of the other players, who has the ace and king of spades and the six of diamonds showing, bets the limit of $2. You must decide whether to call (that is, to match his bet and stay in the game) or to drop out. No other player remains in the game, but you are certain that he has an ace or a king in the hole. The four cards in your hand are the three and five of hearts and the four and six of clubs. If your last card gives you a straight (a numerical sequence of five cards, regardless of their suit) that would beat two pairs, and it would also beat three of a kind. Suppose you are confident that, after the last round, your opponent will do no more than check and call—that is, pass and subsequently match the $2 bet you place then. How much money must there be in the pot now, for your call of his bet on this round to be worth the $2 you must now risk to stay in the game?

Summary of Chapter 14

In all inductive arguments the conclusion is supported by the premises with only some degree of probability, usually described simply as "more" or "less" probable in the case of scientific hypotheses. But we explained in this chapter how a *quantitative* measure of probability, stated as a fraction between 0 and 1, can be assigned to many inductive conclusions.

Two alternative conceptions of probability, both permitting this quantitative assignment, were presented in section 14.1:

• The **relative frequency theory,** according to which probability is defined as the relative frequency with which members of a class exhibit a specified attribute.

- The *a priori* **theory,** according to which the probability of an event's occurring is determined by dividing the number of ways in which the event can occur by the number of equipossible outcomes.

Both theories accommodate the development of a **calculus of probability,** introduced in section 14.2, with which the probability of a complex event can be computed if the probability of its component events can be determined. Two basic theorems, the **product theorem** and the **addition theorem,** are used in this probability calculus.

If the complex event of interest is a **joint occurrence,** the probability of two or more components both occurring, the *product* theorem is applied, as explained in section 14.3. The product theorem asserts that if the component events are *independent,* the probability of their joint occurrence is equal to the product of their separate probabilities. But if the component events are *not independent,* the general product theorem applies, in which the probability of (*a* and *b*) is equal to the probability of (*a*) multiplied by the probability of (*b* if *a*).

If the complex event of interest is an **alternative occurrence** (the probability of at least one of two or more events), the *addition* theorem is applied, as explained in section 14.4. The addition theorem asserts that if the component events *are mutually exclusive,* their probabilities are summed to determine their alternative occurrence. But if the component events *are not mutually exclusive,* the probability of their alternative occurrence may be computed either:

- By analyzing the favorable cases into mutually exclusive events and summing the probabilities of those successes, or
- By determining the probability that the alternative occurrence will not occur and subtracting that fraction from 1.

To compute the **expected value** of an investment or a wager, explained in section 14.5, we must consider *both* the probability of the possible outcomes *and* the return received in the event of each. For each outcome, the anticipated return is multiplied by the probability of that outcome occurring; those products are then summed to give the expected value of the investment.

SOLUTIONS TO SELECTED EXERCISES

SECTION 1.3

Exercises on pp. 9–11

5.   PREMISS: We are all sinners.
    CONCLUSION: We ought to forbear to judge.
10.   PREMISS: Light moves at a finite speed.
    CONCLUSION: Looking at objects that are millions of miles away is actually looking at light that was emitted many years ago.
15.   PREMISSES: The more poorly students perform, the more money public education asks for and gets.
    CONCLUSION: The institution of public education thrives on its own failures.
20.   PREMISSES: In 1998 AIDS was the infectious disease that killed most people around the world.
      The AIDS epidemic is not abating.
    CONCLUSION: Unquestionably, no more important goal exists in medical research today than the development of an AIDS vaccine.

SECTION 1.4

Exercises on pp. 19–21

5.   PREMISS: The divorce rate is very low where marriage is prearranged.
    CONCLUSION: If you marry without love you may later come to love the person you marry.
    PREMISS: The divorce rate is very high where marriage decisions are based on love.
    CONCLUSION: If you marry the person you love you may not have a successful marriage.
10.   PREMISSES: Petitioner argues that Congress may regulate gender-motivated crime because of its substantial economic effects. Gender-motivated violence is a subset of all violent crime, and is certain to have lesser nationwide economic impact than does the total of violent crimes.
    CONCLUSION: Petitioner's reasoning would allow Congress to regulate murder or any other type of violence.
11.   DISCUSSION: Variants of the following arguments were presented by several Supreme Court justices.
    To support the conclusion that the death sentence should be nullified in this case, premisses such as these were employed:
      The question asked by the jury on their return indicates that they were confused or uncertain about their duty with respect to the imposition of the death penalty.

The agitation of the jurors further supports the belief that they were confused.

A death sentence imposed by a jury confused or uncertain about its duty ought not be sustained.

To support the conclusion that the death sentence should not be nullified, premises such as these were employed:

The judge's instructions—that the jury "may" impose the death penalty—were clear.

The question asked by the jury was answered by directing their attention to this clear instruction.

A jury is presumed to understand a judge's answer to its questions.

(The case was *Weeks v. Angelone,* decided 19 January 2000. The death sentence was upheld in a 5–4 decision of the Court.)

SECTION 1.5

Exercises on pp. 29–34

I.

5. PREMISSES: If future scientists find a way to signal back in time, their signals would have reached us already.
But such signals have not reached us.

CONCLUSION: Future scientists never will find a way to signal back in time.

10. PREMISSES: The IRS code is inordinately complex, imposes an enormous burden on taxpayers, and thus undermines compliance with the law.
Repeated efforts to simplify and reform the law have failed.
Further patchwork will only compound the problem.

CONCLUSION: It is time to repeal the IRS code and start over.
(The first premise of this argument may be analyzed as containing an argument that has two premises and the conclusion is that the IRS code undermines compliance with the law.)

II.

5. PREMISS: Vacuum cleaners to insure clean houses are essential.
CONCLUSION: Our houses are generally clean.
PREMISS: Street cleaners to clean streets are an unfortunate expense.
CONCLUSION: Our streets are generally filthy.

10. DIAGRAMED: ① [This dichotomy between the "best" and the "best black" is not something manufactured by racists to denigrate the abilities of professionals who are not white.] ② [On the contrary, it is reinforced from time to time by those students who demand that universities commit to hiring some preset number of minority faculty members . . . saying (in effect), "Go out and hire the best blacks."] ③ [And it is further reinforced by faculty members who see these demands as nothing more than claims for simple justice.]

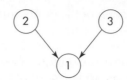

15.   PREMISSES: Because I like Nolan Myers I heard toughness and confidence in his answers.
If I hadn't liked him I would have heard arrogance and bluster.

    CONCLUSION: (and the premiss of a succeeding argument): The first impression becomes a self-fulfilling prophesy: We hear what we expect to hear.

    CONCLUSION: The interview is biased in favor of the nice.
(Each of the first two premisses may be analyzed as an argument as well.)

20.   PREMISSES: Native American beliefs about the past and the dead should not be allowed to dictate government policy on the investigation and interpretation of early American prehistory.
Only theories built on empirical evidence and capable of adjustment are scientific.

    CONCLUSION: If a choice must be made between Native American theories and scientific theories, primacy should be given to scientific theories.

SECTION 1.6

Exercises on pp. 38–42

5. This is not an argument, but a brief account of what black holes are, and an explanation of why they appear black.

10. This is an explanation of why traditionally Cupid is painted blind, and thus an explanation of why it is that so much conduct, under the influence of love, is not rational.

15. On the surface, this may be taken as an explanation of why it is that girls become afraid of science and find it less interesting than do boys. But it also serves as an argument supporting the claim that, since these outcomes are learned, parents and teachers can and should do more to encourage girls' interests in science.

20. Although this passage may be taken to explain some of what goes on in the schools, it is essentially an argument whose conclusion, stated first, is the controversial claim that Americans are simply not learning science—a conclusion supported by the five premises that follow.

25. This is essentially an explanation, an account of the unacknowledged social and political circumstances that account for the fact that "black boys tend to shoot." It may also serve indirectly as an argument in support of policies that would alter those circumstances.

SECTION 1.10

Exercises on pp. 54–57

1. ① [Democratic laws generally tend to promote the welfare of the greatest possible number] for ② [they emanate from the majority of the citizens, who are subject to error, but who cannot have an interest opposed to their own advantage.] ③ [The laws of an aristocracy tend, on the contrary, to concentrate wealth and power in the hands of the minority;] because ④ [an aristocracy, by its very nature, constitutes a minority.] It may therefore be asserted as a general proposition, that ⑤ [the purpose of a democracy in its legislation is more useful to humanity than that of an aristocracy.]

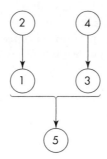

5.   "... You appeared to be surprised when I told you, on our first meeting, that you had come from Afghanistan."

"You were told, no doubt."

"Nothing of the sort. I *knew* you came from Afghanistan. From long habit the train of thoughts ran so swiftly through my mind that I arrived at the conclusion without being conscious of intermediate steps. There were such steps, however. The train of reasoning ran, ' ① [Here is a gentleman of a medical type,] but ② [with the air of a military man.] Clearly ③ [an army doctor,] then. ④ [He has just come from the tropics,] for ⑤ [his face is dark,] and ⑥ [that is not the natural tint of his skin,] for ⑦ [his wrists are fair.] ⑧ [He has undergone hardship and sickness], as ⑨ [his haggard face says clearly.] ⑩ [His left arm has been injured.] ⑪ [He holds it in a stiff and unnatural manner.] ⑫ [Where in the tropics could an English army doctor have seen much hardship and got his arm wounded? Clearly in Afghanistan.]' The whole train of thought did not occupy a second. I then remarked that you came from Afghanistan, and you were astonished."

"It is simple enough as you explain it," I said, smiling.

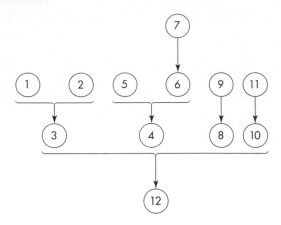

10.   ① [Nothing is demonstrable unless the contrary implies a contradiction.]
② [Nothing that is distinctly conceivable implies a contradiction.]
③ [Whatever we conceive as existent, we can also conceive as nonexistent.]
Therefore, ④ [there is no being whose nonexistence implies a contradiction.]
Consequently ⑤ [there is no being whose existence is demonstrable.]

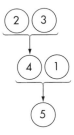

SECTION 1.11

Exercises on pp. 65–68

1. If the first native is a politician, then he lies and denies being a politician. If the first native is not a politician, then he tells the truth and denies being a politician. In either case, then, the first native denies being a politician.
   Since the second native reports that the first native denies being a politician, he tells the truth, and is, therefore, a nonpolitician.
   The third native asserts that the first native is a politician. If the first native is a politician, then the third native speaks the truth and is, therefore, a nonpolitician. If the first native is a nonpolitician, then the third native lies and is, therefore, a politician. Hence only one of the first and third natives is a politician, and since the second is a nonpolitician, there is only one politician among the three natives.
5. Since Lefty said that Spike did it, Spike's first and third statements are equivalent in meaning and therefore either both true or both false. Since only one statement is false, they are both true.

Dopey's third statement is, therefore, false, and so his first two are true. Therefore Butch's third statement is false and so his first two are true, of which the second reveals that Red is the guilty man.

(An alternative method of solving this problem is suggested by Peter M. Longley of the University of Alaska. All but Red both assert their innocence *and* accuse someone else. If their professions of innocence are false, so are their accusations of other persons. But no one makes two false statements, so their statements that they are innocent must be true. Hence Red is the guilty one. This solution, however, presupposes that only one of the men is guilty.)

(Still another method of solving this problem comes from James I. Campbell of Eisenhower College and Walter Charen of Rutgers College. Dopey's second statement and Butch's third statement are contradictory, so at least one must be false. But if Dopey's second statement were false, his third statement would be true and Spike would be guilty. However, if Spike were guilty, his first and third statements would both be false, so he cannot be guilty and hence Dopey's second statement cannot be false. Therefore, Butch's third statement must be false, whence his second statement is true and Red is the guilty man.)

10. It is not possible to distribute the strings so that no one triangle has all three sides (strings) of the same color; at least one triangle must have three sides of the same color.

    Consider any one nail, say the one on a wall we call A. From it stretch five strings, and of these five at least three must be of the same color, since only two colors (red and blue) are available. Suppose that three of the strings from the nail in wall A are red, and that they go to the other three walls, B, C, and D. Now consider the triangle formed by the nails on these three other walls, B, C, and D. They must not all be of the same color, so they cannot all be blue, so at least one of them must be red. But if any one of the strings connecting B, C, and D is red, it must complete a triangle of three red strings. (Suppose the string connecting B and D is the red one. Then there will be a triangle of three red strings connecting A, B and D, etc.) No matter which nail we begin with, there is no way to avoid at least one triangle all of whose sides are strings of the same color.

11. Challenge to the reader:

    Presenting the solution to this lovely problem would rob our readers of too much pleasure. One hint will be enough: Every correct solution (there are several!) must begin with a weighing in which four balls are weighed against four. From this point, the solution is straightforward!

SECTION 2.3

Exercises on pp. 80–86

I.   pp. 80–81

1. Directive
5. The expressive function is primary in this great poem, the poet's voice making his passion manifest. But there may be supposed some informative

function here also, insofar as the reader takes the poet to be telling about his own life.

10. Informative. The report is correct, because a small portion of Alaska lies across the international date line.

II. pp. 81–83

1. The primary purpose of this passage is informative: to instruct all who read it that the Constitution of the United States permits no system of preference by class or caste. The passage also clearly expresses Justice Harlan's approval of this guarantee of equality under the law, and directs others to respect it—although his directive was ineffective in this famous case, in which the doctrine of "separate but equal" for the races was applied and approved and was not overruled until 1954.

5. The primary function in this passage of the novel is expressive, evoking the reader's antipathy toward lawyers. Because it is a utopian novel, many of its passages have a directive function also; here the direction is: Rid yourselves of lawyers! And the passage may be said to inform the reader as well, explaining that lawyers, by profession, conceal and distort the facts.

10. The primary function of this passage is directive; Amiel wanted his readers not to delay decisions until perfect clearness is achieved. The passage may be said to inform also, teaching that perfect clearness is not required for wise decision making. And there is some expressive function here also, the author showing disapproval of those who demand perfect understanding before deciding.

15. The primary function of this passage is probably informative, Bacon teaching that philosophy, studied in depth, brings one back to religion. There is a directive function also: The author thinks his readers should be religious, and that if they study philosophy, they should study it deeply, not superficially. Perhaps exhibiting a contempt for atheism as shallow gives the passage some expressive function also.

20. The primary function of this passage is directive. A judgment is expressed in this passage concerning the function of the "notion of race," and the author's attitude toward these uses is expressed—but the plain purpose of the author is to cause his readers to attend less to race and more to the challenges of normal human interaction.

25. Directive. The author gives information concerning the letters he has received, but his chief purpose here is to encourage in his readers the will power that is needed to hold out against tyranny and vilification and murder.

III. pp. 84–86

1. Asserts that the speaker will not accept the nomination and would not serve even if elected president.

Intended to stop Republican politicians from working for his (Sherman's) nomination.

Provides evidence that the speaker is not available as a candidate and is very forthright.

5. Asserts that research requires continual reexamination of accepted beliefs; asserts further (as a conclusion) that research is critical of established practices.

   Intended to support and stimulate research, to stimulate a questioning attitude and a critical spirit, and to warn those who wish to enjoy the fruits of research that they must tolerate criticism of accepted doctrines and existing practices.

   Provides evidence that the speaker is committed to the continual reexamination of doctrines and axioms on which current thought and action are based, and is critical of existing practices.

10. Asserts that there are the classes of citizens named, having the characteristics noted.

    Intended to cause hostility toward both the rich and poor, and to produce approval of the middle class.

    Provides some evidence that the speaker probably is not rich and almost certainly is not poor.

15. Asserts that all who speak about constitutional rights, free speech, and the free press are Communists.

    Intended to cause hostility toward those who defend constitutional rights, free speech, and free press, or who call on such rights.

    Provides evidence that the speaker is hostile toward constitutional rights, free speech, free press, and Communists.

20. Asserts that the painting in question is overpriced and without merit.

    Intended to cause people to laugh, and especially to laugh at Whistler— and to refrain from buying or praising Whistler's paintings.

    Provides evidence that the speaker is hostile toward Whistler and his art and is witty and bombastic.

25. Asserts that the speaker, Socrates, is amazed to learn that his audience has been warned of his eloquence, and that this characterization of him is false. And it asserts that he, Socrates, tells the truth, as many of his critics do not.

    Intended to cause his listeners (actually his jury in Athens) to hear his defense patiently, to think him modest, to believe him—and perhaps to acquit him of the crimes with which he is charged.

    Provides evidence that the speaker is sharp in argument, ready to do battle with his critics, and very eloquent in his own way.

SECTION 2.5

Exercises on pp. 91–95

1. Disagreement in belief as to how a fool should be answered. Agreement in attitude (of contempt) toward fools.
5. Disagreement in belief as to how the physical separation of two persons affects their fondness or regard for one another. Disagreement in attitude is suggested: *a* generally approves of separation, while *b* appears to be negative (or perhaps neutral) about it.
10. Disagreement in belief is only implied or strongly suggested here: *a* clearly believes in the truth of atheism, but that *b* disbelieves the atheist doctrine is

implied by his statement that atheists are scoundrels. Disagreement in attitude is expressed: *a* approves of atheism and atheists, whereas *b* disapproves of atheists and—by implication—of atheism.

15. Disagreement in belief as to the value or propriety of the American government: *a* believes it is disgraceful, *b* believes that though it is imperfect, it is better than any other up to that time. Disagreement in attitude: *a* disapproves, *b* approves, of the American government.

20. Disagreement in belief as to how reason can and will be used: *a* believes that reason is needed to avoid disaster, *b* believes that reason never serves spiritual things and usually serves those who oppose what comes from God. Disagreement in attitude: *a* strongly approves of reason, while *b* strongly disapproves of reason and its consequences.

SECTION 3.2

Exercise on pp. 111–114

II. It would seem that the better precising definition in this case is the one that more nearly catches the sense intended by Congress when increasing the penalty imposed upon a person who, as he commits the crime "uses or carries a firearm." The gravity of the offense, one may argue, is directly affected only when there is some likelihood that the firearm, by its use during the commission of a crime, may aggravate the injury done. On this view, the precising definition of Justice Breyer, supposing the narrower sense of "carries," would be the better. But in fact the precising definition of Justice Ginsburg was that adopted in the ruling of the Supreme Court.

III.

1. An apparently verbal dispute that is really genuine. There is a verbal dispute here over the ambiguous phrase "greatest hitter," which is used by Daye to mean the one who gets the largest number of *hits* and by Knight to mean the one who hits the largest number of *home runs.* Beyond that, they really do disagree. They surely disagree in attitude about Rose and Aaron, since Daye holds Rose in highest esteem as a hitter, and Knight holds Aaron in highest esteem as a hitter. They probably also disagree in belief, defending different *criteria* for determining who is the greatest hitter.

5. A merely verbal dispute. The ambiguous phrase "business . . . good" is used by Daye in the sense of increased *sales,* and by Knight in the sense of increased *profit.* There *may* be disagreement in attitude toward the company in question, Daye approving and Knight disapproving, but this is not at all clear from their words.

10. An obviously genuine dispute. Daye affirms and Knight denies that *Dick bought himself a new car.*

15. A merely verbal dispute. The ambiguous word is "unemployed." Daye uses this word in the more usual sense of "employable person who is ready and willing to work but not able to secure employment." Knight uses the same

word in the (somewhat odd) sense of "person who is not gainfully employed." There appears to be no genuine disagreement between them.

20. This is a tricky example, for which alternative analyses are plausible. One treatment is to regard it as an obviously genuine dispute, with Daye denying and Knight affirming the proposition that *Knight should ask his wife.* Another treatment is to regard the dispute as apparently verbal but really genuine. In this analysis, the phrase "your own judgment" (about it) is ambiguous, used by Daye in the sense of deciding about it without considering anyone else's opinion, and used by Knight in the (broader) sense of deciding everything about it by oneself, including the question of whether to consult the opinion of others. In this second analysis, there remains an underlying disagreement of belief as to whether Knight should consult his wife.

SECTION 3.3

Exercises on p. 117

I.

1. animal, vertebrate, mammal, feline, wildcat, lynx
5. number, real number, rational number, integer, positive integer, prime

SECTION 3.4

Exercises on p. 120

I.

1. John Gielgud, Paul Newman, Lawrence Olivier (for example)
5. fluorine, chlorine, iodine (for example)
10. Browning, Keats, Shelley (for example)

II.

1. movie stars (using example above)
5. halogens (using example above)
10. Victorians (using example above)

SECTION 3.5

Exercises on pp. 124–125

I.

1. ridiculous;   5. vanity;   10. danger;   15. portent;   20. wigwam

II.

1. very large meal;   5. young horse;
10. young woman;   15. very small horse;   20. male horse

SECTION 3.6

Exercises on pp. 129–134

II.   pp. 129–131

1. Both too broad and too narrow. Many persons with an innate capacity who affect the lives of others for good or evil are not geniuses; and there are some geniuses who do not affect the lives of others for good or evil. This definition seriously violates Rule 3.
5. Obscure; violates Rule 4. Also it fails to state the essence of alteration, which is *changing over time,* and thus it violates Rule 1.
10. Circular, since "produces" is synonymous with "causes." Violates Rule 2.
15. Figurative language; violates Rule 4.
20. This is a tricky example. The definition may be faulted for being both too narrow and too broad. It is too narrow in that it attends to well-being, but not to the normal physiological functions with which health is most commonly associated; it is too broad in that it introduces social circumstances not ordinarily viewed as within the ambit of health; thus it violates Rule 3 and Rule 1.
25. This definition also is both too narrow and too broad. It is too narrow, in that "political correctness" may characterize a point of view that is absolutist as well as relativist. It is too broad, in that many dogmatic relativists who are intolerant of believers in "traditional values" and the like may not exhibit the censorious practices normally associated with political correctness. It violates Rule 3 and Rule 1.

III.   pp. 131–134

1. Figurative language, violates Rule 4. It also fails to state the essence, violating Rule 1.
5. Too broad, since some prose records such moments; and too narrow, since some (great) poetry is tragic; violates Rule 3. It also may be criticized as being phrased in figurative language, violating Rule 4, although this is not altogether obvious.
10. Too broad, since some persons with a very low opinion of themselves tend to behave this way; and too narrow, since some supremely conceited persons do not stoop to such vainglory or social climbing; violates Rule 3. It also may be criticized for violating Rule 1 in not stating the essence, which is a trait of character rather than a tendency to overt behavior of the kinds specified.
15. Too narrow; not all political power is exercised "for the public good," certainly not "*only* for the public good"; violates Rule 3.
20. Too broad, violates Rule 3. In his *History of Western Philosophy,* Bertrand Russell criticized this definition on the grounds that "the dealings of a drill-sergeant with a crowd of recruits, or of a bricklayer with a heap of bricks . . . exactly fulfill Dewey's definition of 'inquiry.' "
25. Figurative language, violates Rule 4. Probably the definition of "liberty" is too narrow in several respects: It is not confined to people in "good social position," or to saying what "everybody believes"; violates Rule 3. And "license" also is defined in a way that is too narrow, because people often exer-

cise license by saying what is not true; violates Rule 3. But this kind of comment runs the danger of spoiling a good joke.

30. As it stands, this definition obviously is circular. It is followed in Wittgenstein's book, however, by "*I.e.:* if you want to understand the use of the word 'meaning', look for what are called 'explanations of meaning.' " Thus emended, the definition is made consistent with Wittgenstein's tendency to identify *meaning* with *use.* Compare: "A spade is to dig."

SECTION 4.2

Exercises on pp. 150–153

I.

1. *Ignoratio elenchi*—concern for the homeless is admirable, but not relevant to the pains allegedly felt by lobsters.
5. *Ignoratio elenchi.*
10. *Ad hominem* (abusive).
15. *Ad baculum*—plainly an appeal to the threat of force.

II.

1. Mr. Welch honestly believed that this attack against General Electric was based upon a false premiss, and his response may be taken as his very emphatic way of insisting that it was false. On the other hand, since his response is aimed at the speaker in her capacity as a nun, it is also in the form of an argument *ad hominem* (circumstantial).
5. Here again the attack is leveled against the claims of the NEA on the supposition that what is contained in the press release is no more than material designed to serve the interests of its members—an argument *ad hominem* (circumstantial). It is indeed wise practice to consider the interests of organizations that issue press releases, the better to interpret the claims made; but it is unfair to suppose that the claims made are mistaken, or the facts announced are false, just because they serve the purposes of the organizations issuing the press release.
10. The writer correctly contends that one who takes a revolutionary point of view need not sustain the obligation to provide a detailed account of the changes sought, and thus (although the context is not clear) the "interrogator" referred to may be addressing a matter that is not relevant. But the writer, in questioning the sincerity of the interrogator, commits an *ad hominem* (abusive).

SECTION 4.3

Exercises on pp. 161–163

1. False Cause (*post hoc ergo propter hoc*)
5. *Petitio principii*
10. False Cause

Section 4.4

Exercises on pp. 171–177

I.

1. Composition. It cannot be inferred from the fact that the parts have a specified shape that the whole has that same shape.
5. This is only a joke, of course. The argument of the joke is that, since you need no instruction on how to play the concertina without success, you need no instruction on how to play the concertina at all. If one were thus to interpret the phrase "without success" as though it modified the phrase "how to play the concertina," when in fact it was intended to modify "looked everywhere," this silly argument would commit the fallacy of amphiboly. Our recognition of the inadvertent amphiboly gives some amusement.
10. Composition.

II.

1. It may be argued that although the parts have functions, this does not permit the inference that the whole has functions. On this view, Aristotle here commits the fallacy of composition. On the other hand, many will argue that we may reasonably infer from the patterns found in some natural objects that similar patterns may be expected in other natural objects, in which case the passage would commit no fallacy.
5. It may be argued that the passage commits an *ad hominem* (circumstantial) fallacy in supposing that the competence of the school's chancellor is suspect in view of the school placement of his own children. On the other hand, many will argue that in placing his own children in private schools, the chancellor does unavoidably undermine public confidence in his support of the public schools, and that this conclusion is not fallacious.

III.

1. Equivocation, or alleged equivocation, is the nub of this dispute. If Justice Scalia were correct, the statute that increases the severity of punishment for "using" a firearm was not meant to impose that additional sanction on one who *traded* his firearm in the commission of the crime. Justice O'Connor, on the other hand, treats the terms "using" in the statute very broadly, so that any role the firearm may have played would satisfy the condition of being "used." Justice Scalia insists that her argument commits an equivocation because it treats "use" as meaning "use in any way whatever," while statutes ought to be read so that their words carry *ordinary* meanings. There is no obvious resolution of the logical issue; the legal issue was resolved by a vote of the Court.
5. An argument *ad populum* is plainly involved here, insofar as it is believed that a conclusion may be held acceptable because it was so widely approved. But it is probable that the author (Croce) is doing no more than calling attention to widespread irrationality at the time of the Inquisition.

10. This passage plays with false cause—but mixes with that fallacy an appeal to inappropriate authority. On the other hand the author, in jesting, is also ridiculing such an argument.

15. This argument may be construed to contain no fallacy, or to contain a blatant argument *ad baculum,* a resort to the threat of force. If construed to mean that congregants ought to behave in certain ways lest they be severely punished by an angry God, the argument contains no fallacy—although its factual supposition may be questioned, of course. If construed to mean also that, because those punishments are so fearfully threatening, some propositions (having nothing directly to do with God's anger) are *true,* and should be believed, the argument is fallacious, since the threats would not be relevant to the truth or falsity of those propositions. Probably the argument was intended in both ways.

20. A fallacy of false cause lies behind the humor in this passage. The answer to the query supposes, mistakenly, that the light in the daytime is caused by something other than the sun!

Section 5.2

Exercises on p. 184–185

1. S = historians; P = extremely gifted writers whose works read like first-rate novels. Form: Particular affirmative.

5. S = members of families that are rich and famous; P = persons of either wealth or distinction. Form: Particular negative.

10. S = people who have not themselves done creative work in the arts; P = responsible critics on whose judgments we can rely. Form: Universal negative.

Section 5.3

Exercises on p. 188

1. Quality: affirmative; quantity: particular; subject and predicate terms both undistributed.

5. Quality: negative; quantity: universal; subject and predicate terms both distributed.

10. Quality: affirmative; quantity: universal; subject term distributed, predicate term undistributed.

Section 5.4

Exercises on p. 193

1. If we assume that (a) is true, then:
   (b), which is its contrary, is false, and
   (c), which is its subaltern, is true, and
   (d), which is its contradictory, is false.

If we assume that (a) is false, then:
(b), which is its contrary, is undetermined, and
(c), which is its subaltern, is undetermined, and
(d), which is its contradictory, is true.

SECTION 5.5

Exercises on pp. 200–202

I.   p. 200

1. No reckless drivers who pay no attention to traffic regulations are people who are considerate of others. Equivalent.
5. Some elderly persons who would be incapable of doing an honest day's work are professional wrestlers. Equivalent.

II.   p. 200

1. Some college athletes are not nonprofessionals.
5. No objects suitable for boat anchors are objects weighing less than 15 pounds.

III.   p. 201

1. All nonpessimists are nonjournalists. Equivalent.
5. Some residents are not citizens. Equivalent.

IV.   p. 201

1. False	5. False	10. False

V.   p. 201

1. False	5. Undetermined	10. False

VI.   pp. 201–202

1. Undetermined	5. False	10. Undetermined	15. False

VII. p. 202

1. Undetermined	5. Undetermined	10. True	15. Undetermined

SECTION 5.6

Exercises on pp. 207–208

V. Step (1) to step (2) is invalid: (1) asserts the falsehood of an **I** proposition; (2) asserts the truth of its corresponding **O** proposition. In the traditional interpretation, corresponding **I** and **O** propositions are subcontraries and cannot both be false. Therefore, if the **I** proposition in (1) is false, the **O** proposition in (2) would have to be true, in *that* interpretation. But because both **I** and **O** propositions do have existential import, both *can* be false (in the Boolean interpretation) if the subject class is empty. The subject class *is* empty in this case, because there are no mermaids. Hence the inference from the falsehood of (1) to the truth of (2) is invalid. Corresponding **I** and **O** propositions are not subcontraries in the Boolean interpretation but the inference from (1) to (2) assumes that they are.

SECTION 5.7

Exercises on pp. 213–214

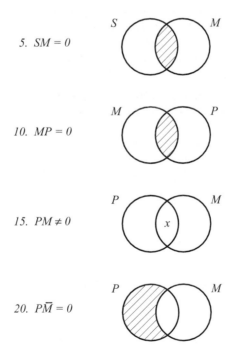

5. $SM = 0$

10. $MP = 0$

15. $PM \neq 0$

20. $P\bar{M} = 0$

SECTION 6.1

Exercises on pp. 220–221

5. Step 1: The conclusion is: Some conservatives are not advocates of high tariff rates.

Step 2: Major term: advocates of high tariff rates.

Step 3: Major premiss: All advocates of high tariff rates are Republicans.

Step 4: Minor premiss: Some Republicans are not conservatives.

Step 5: This syllogism written in standard form:

All advocates of high tariff rates are Republicans.
Some Republicans are not conservatives.
Therefore some conservatives are not advocates of high tariff rates.

Step 6: The three propositions of this syllogism are, in order: **A, O, O.** The middle term, *Republicans,* is the predicate term of the major premiss and the subject term of the minor premiss, so the syllogism is in the **fourth figure.** Thus its mood and figure are: **AOO–4.**

10. Step 1: The conclusion is: No sports cars are automobiles designed for family use.

Step 2: Major term: Automobiles designed for family use.

Step 3: Major premiss: All automobiles designed for family use are vehicles intended to be driven at moderate speeds.

Step 4: Minor premiss: No sports cars are vehicles intended to be driven at moderate speeds.

Step 5: This syllogism written in standard form:

All automobiles designed for family use are vehicles intended to be driven at moderate speeds.
No sports cars are vehicles intended to be driven at moderate speeds.
Therefore no sports cars are automobiles designed for family use.

Step 6: The three propositions of this syllogism are, in order, **A, E, E.** The middle term, *vehicles intended to be driven at moderate speeds,* is the predicate term of both the major and the minor premiss, so the syllogism is in the second figure. Thus its mood and figure are: **AEE–2.**

SECTION 6.2

Exercises on pp. 223–224

5. One possible refuting analogy is this: All unicorns are mammals, so some mammals are not animals, since no animals are unicorns.

10. One possible refuting analogy is this: All square circles are circles, and all square circles are squares, therefore some circles are squares.

SECTION 6.3

Exercises on pp. 230–232

I.   pp. 230–231

5. No *P* is *M*.
   Some *M* is *S*.
   ∴ Some *S* is not *P*.

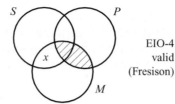

EIO-4
valid
(Fresison)

10. Some *P* is *M*.
    All *M* is *S*.
    ∴ Some *S* is *P*.

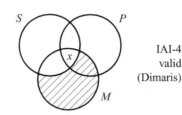

IAI-4
valid
(Dimaris)

15. No *M* is *P*.
    Some *S* is *M*.
    ∴ Some *S* is not *P*.

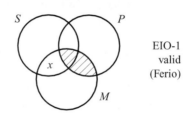

EIO-1
valid
(Ferio)

II.   pp. 231–232

1. Some reformers are fanatics.
   All reformers are idealists.
   ∴ Some idealists are fanatics.

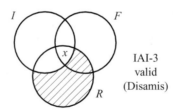

IAI-3
valid
(Disamis)

5. No pleasure vessels are underwater craft.
   All underwater craft are submarines.
   ∴ No submarines are pleasure vessels.

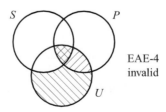

EAE-4
invalid

10. All labor leaders are true liberals.
    No weaklings are true liberals.
    ∴ No weaklings are labor leaders.

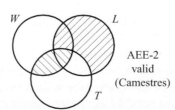

AEE-2
valid
(Camestres)

SECTION 6.5

Exercises on pp. 239–242

I. **pp. 239–240**

5. Commits the fallacy of the illicit minor. Breaks Rule 3.
10. Commits the fallacy of the illicit major. Breaks Rule 3.
15. Commits the fallacy of the illicit minor. Breaks Rule 3.

II. **pp. 240–241**

5. Commits the existential fallacy. Breaks Rule 6.
10. Commits the fallacy of the illicit minor. Breaks Rule 3.

III. **pp. 241–242**

5. Commits the fallacy of the illicit minor. Breaks Rule 3.
10. Commits the fallacy of *four terms*. (There is an equivocation on the term "people who like it," which has a very different meaning in the conclusion from the one it has in the premiss.) Breaks Rule 1.

SECTION 6.6

Exercises on pp. 245–246

5. Plainly this is **possible in the first figure,** where **AII–1,** which is valid, has only one term distributed, and that term only once. It also is **possible in the third figure,** where **AII–3** (as well as **IAI–3**) are valid and also have only one term distributed, and distributed only once. It also is **possible in the fourth figure,** where **IAI–4,** which is valid, has only one term distributed, and distributed only once. But where the middle term is the predicate term of both premisses, **in the second figure, it is not possible.** Consider: To avoid breaking Rule 2, which requires that the middle term be distributed in at least one premiss, one of the premisses in this figure must be negative. But then, by Rule 5, the conclusion would have to be negative and would distribute its predicate. Thus, if only one term could be distributed only once, in the second figure that would have to be in the conclusion; but if the distributed term could be distributed only once, that would break Rule 3, because if it is distributed in the conclusion it must be distributed in the premisses.
10. **None.** If the middle term were distributed in both premisses, then: **In the first figure,** the minor premiss would have to be negative, whence (by Rule 5) the conclusion would have to be negative, so by Rule 3 the major premiss would have to be negative, in violation of Rule 4. **In the second figure,** both premisses would have to be negative, in violation of Rule 4. **In the third figure** both premisses would have to be universal, so the minor premiss would have to be negative by Rule 3, and by Rule 5 the conclusion would be negative—so by Rule 3 the major premiss would have to be negative also in violation of Rule 4. **In the fourth figure** the major premiss would have to be negative, and so by Rule 3 the major premiss would be universal, whence (by Rule 3) the minor premiss would have to be negative also in violation of Rule 4.

SECTION 7.2

Exercises on pp. 252–253

5. Where   *E* = Explosives
    F = Flammable things (note that "flammable" and "inflammable"
        are *synonyms!*)
    S = Safe things

this syllogism translates into standard form thus:

> All *E* is *F*.
> No *F* is *S*.
> Therefore no *S* is *E*.

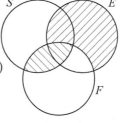

Exhibited in a Venn diagram, this syllogism (in Camenes)
is shown to be valid.

10. Where   *O* = Objects over six feet long
    D = Difficult things to store
    U = Useful things

this syllogism translates into standard form thus:

> All *O* are *D*.
> No *D* are *U*.
> Therefore no *U* are *O*.

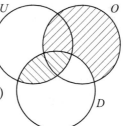

Exhibited in a Venn diagram, this syllogism (in Camenes)
is shown to be valid.

SECTION 7.3

Exercises on p. 261

5. All Junkos are the best things that money can buy.
10. No people who face the sun are people who see their own shadows.
15. No candidates of the Old Guard are persons supported by the Young Turks.
    (Or, No Young Turks are supporters of candidates of the Old Guard.)
20. All people who love well are people who pray well.
25. All soft answers are things that turn away wrath.

SECTION 7.4

Exercises on pp. 263–269

I.   **p. 264**

5. All cases in which she gives her opinion are cases in which she is asked to
   give her opinion.
10. No times when people do not discuss questions freely are times when people
    are most likely to settle questions rightly.

II. pp. 264–269

5. All bankrupt companies are companies unable to pay interest on their debts.
Barcelona Traction is a company unable to pay interest on its debts.
∴ Barcelona Traction is a bankrupt company.

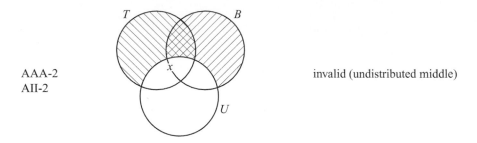

AAA-2
AII-2

invalid (undistributed middle)

10. No gold is base metal.
Some base metals are things that glitter.
∴ Some things that glitter are not gold.

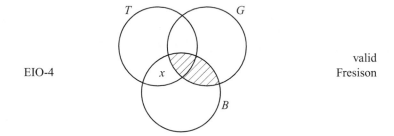

EIO-4

valid
Fresison

15. No persons who are truly objective are persons likely to be mistaken.
All persons likely to be mistaken are persons who ignore the facts.
∴ No persons who ignore the facts are persons who are truly objective.

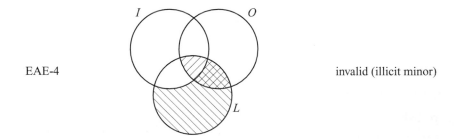

EAE-4

invalid (illicit minor)

20. All things interesting to engineers are approximations.
No approximations are irrationals.
∴ No irrationals are things interesting to engineers.

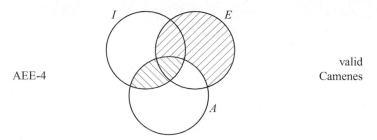

AEE-4

valid
Camenes

25. All excessive drinkers are debtors.
Some excessive drinkers are not unemployed persons.
∴ Some unemployed persons are not debtors.

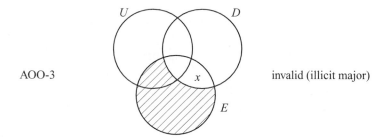

AOO-3

invalid (illicit major)

30. All places where pickets are present are places where there is a strike.
The factory is a place where pickets are present.
∴ The factory is a place where there is a strike.

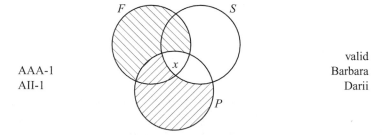

AAA-1
AII-1

valid
Barbara
Darii

35. All valid syllogisms are syllogisms that distribute their middle terms in at least one premiss.
This syllogism is a syllogism that distributes its middle term in at least one premiss.
∴ This syllogism is a valid syllogism.

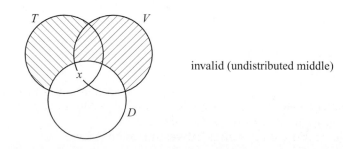

AAA-2
AII-2

invalid (undistributed middle)

40. All persons present are employed persons.
All members are persons present.
∴ All members are employed persons.

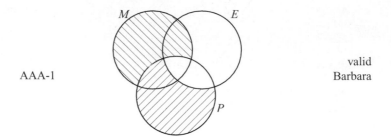

AAA-1

valid
Barbara

45. All times when he is sick are times when he complains.
This time is not a time when he is sick.
∴ This time is not a time when he complains.

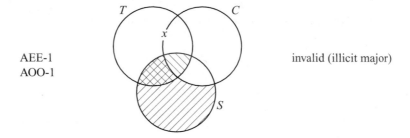

AEE-1
AOO-1

invalid (illicit major)

50. All buildings over 300 feet tall are skyscrapers.
Some examples of modern architecture are not skyscrapers.
∴ Some examples of modern architecture are not buildings over 300 feet tall.

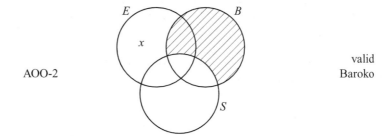

AOO-2

valid
Baroko

SECTION 7.5

Exercises on pp. 272–275

5. First order.
All flesh is passive, the plaything of its hormones and of the species, the
   restless prey of its desires.
Man is flesh.

∴ Man is passive, the plaything of his hormones and of the species, the restless prey of his desires.

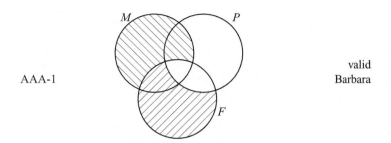

AAA-1

valid
Barbara

10. First order.
   No creatures who act not only under external compulsion, but also by inner necessity are possessors of freedom in the philosophical sense.
   All persons are creatures who act not only under external compulsion, but also by inner necessity.
   ∴ No persons are possessors of freedom in the philosophical sense.

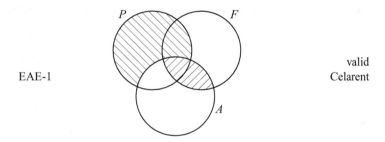

EAE-1

valid
Celarent

Valid enthymeme, whose major premiss probably would be expressed as "No one is free in the philosophical sense who acts not only under external compulsion, but also by inner necessity."

15. Third order.
   No men who serve Mammon are men who serve God.
   Henry is a man who serves Mammon.
   ∴ Henry is not a man who serves God.

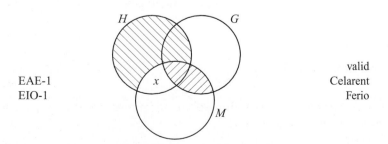

EAE-1
EIO-1

valid
Celarent
Ferio

20. First order.

All fathers who know their own children are wise fathers.

He is a father who knows his own child.

∴ He is a wise father.

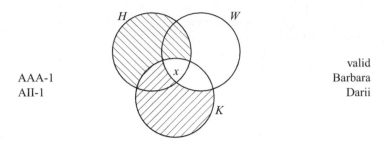

AAA-1
AII-1

valid
Barbara
Darii

Here the missing major premiss was expressed in Shakespeare's *The Merchant of Venice* as "It is a wise father that knows his own child."

25. First order.

Weapons that make it easier for a nuclear war to begin are probably the most dangerous.

The least destructive nuclear weapons make it easier for a nuclear war to begin.

∴ It is probably true that the least destructive nuclear weapons are the most dangerous.

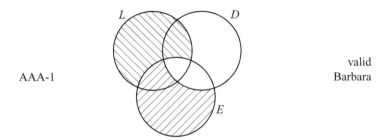

AAA-1

valid
Barbara

30. Second order.

All times in which the theater could exist are times when it is possible to pretend to motives and abilities other than one's real ones, or to pretend to strengths of motives and levels of ability other than their real strengths and levels.

All times are times in which the theater could exist.

∴ All times are times when it is possible to pretend, etc.

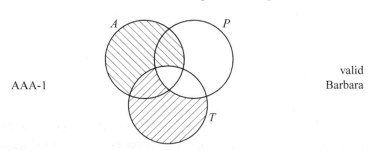

AAA-1

valid
Barbara

35. First order.

All things that demonstrate inexorably how human character, with its itch to be admired, combines with the malice of heaven to produce wars which no one in his right mind would want and which turn out to be utterly disastrous for everybody, are tragedies.

Iphigeneia at Aulis demonstrates inexorably how ... etc.

Therefore *Iphigeneia at Aulis* is a tragedy.

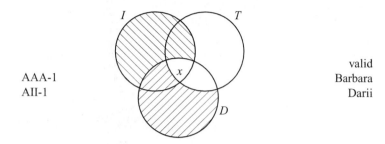

AAA-1
AII-1

valid
Barbara
Darii

Section 7.6

Exercises on pp. 277–279

I. pp. 277–278

5. (1′) All interesting poems are poems that are popular among people of real taste.

(4′) No affected poems are poems that are popular among people of real taste.

(2′) All modern poems are affected poems.

(5′) All poems on the subject of soap bubbles are modern poems.

(3′) All poems of yours are poems on the subject of soap bubbles.

∴ No poems of yours are interesting poems.

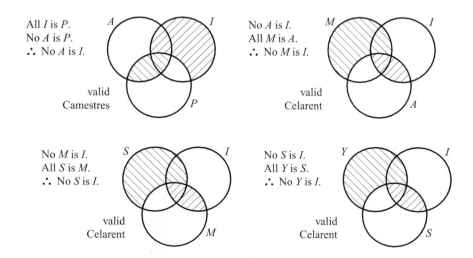

All I is P.
No A is P.
∴ No A is I.

valid
Camestres

No A is I.
All M is A.
∴ No M is I.

valid
Celarent

No M is I.
All S is M.
∴ No S is I.

valid
Celarent

No S is I.
All Y is S.
∴ No Y is I.

valid
Celarent

Valid

II. pp. 278–279

1. (1′) All those who read the *Times* are those who are well educated.
   (3′) No creatures who cannot read are those who are well educated.
   (2′) All hedgehogs are creatures who cannot read.
   ∴ No hedgehogs are those who read the *Times*.

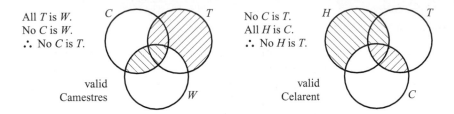

All *T* is *W*.
No *C* is *W*.
∴ No *C* is *T*.

valid
Camestres

No *C* is *T*.
All *H* is *C*.
∴ No *H* is *T*.

valid
Celarent

5. (2′) These sorites are examples not arranged in regular order, like the examples I am used to.
   (4′) No examples not arranged in regular order, like the examples I am used to, are examples I can understand.
   (1′) All examples I do not grumble at are examples I can understand.
   (5′) All examples that do not give me a headache are examples I do not grumble at.
   (3′) All easy examples are examples that do not give me a headache.
   ∴ These sorites are not easy examples.

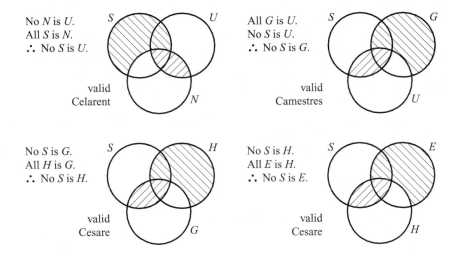

No *N* is *U*.
All *S* is *N*.
∴ No *S* is *U*.

valid
Celarent

All *G* is *U*.
No *S* is *U*.
∴ No *S* is *G*.

valid
Camestres

No *S* is *G*.
All *H* is *G*.
∴ No *S* is *H*.

valid
Cesare

No *S* is *H*.
All *E* is *H*.
∴ No *S* is *E*.

valid
Cesare

Valid

Section 7.7

Exercises on pp. 282–286

5. Fallacy of denying the antecedent. Invalid.
10. Pure hypothetical syllogism. Invalid.

15. Disjunctive syllogism. Valid.
20. Pure hypothetical syllogism. Valid.
25. Mixed hypothetical syllogism, *modus tollens.* Valid.
30. Mixed hypothetical syllogism, *modus tollens.* Valid.
35. Mixed hypothetical syllogism, *modus tollens.* Valid.

SECTION 7.8

Exercises on pp. 290–295

5. The key to refuting this dilemma lies in exposing the ambiguity of the key phrase "going beyond," which could mean "going logically beyond to what is not implied" or "going psychologically beyond to what is not suggested." When this is done, it permits grasping it by one horn or the other, depending upon which sense of "going beyond" is intended. A plausible but nonrefuting rebuttal can be constructed here.

10. It is very easy to go between the horns here, because people lie on a continuum of virtue stretching from saints to sinners. It can plausibly be grasped by the second horn, arguing that even very bad people may be deterred from wrongdoing by strictly enforced laws. A plausible but nonrefuting rebuttal can be constructed here out of the ingredients of the given dilemma.

15. Impossible to go between the horns. It is plausible to grasp it by either horn, arguing either (a) that when desiring to preserve we may be motivated simply by inertia and seek to rest in the status quo, even while admitting that a change would not be worse and might even be better—but just "not worth the trouble of changing" or (b) that when desiring to change we may be motivated simply by boredom with the status quo, and seek a change even while admitting that a change might not be better and might even be worse—but "let's have a little variety." These are psychological rather than political or moral considerations, but the original dilemma appears to be itself psychological. The usual rebutting counterdilemma could be used here: When desiring to preserve, we do not wish to bring about something better; when desiring to change, we do not wish to prevent a change to the worse. It is a question, however, how plausible this is.

20. Of the first dilemma, one must admit that as it is formulated here one cannot go between the horns, at least if "more than a synonym" is understood as "other than a synonym." But grasping the first horn is easy, especially along Fregean lines, which distinguish sense from reference. And grasping the second horn also is possible, with one plausible move turning on equivocations that need untangling, another turning on the legitimate aim of improving the terms (or concepts) being analyzed. The usual nonrefuting rebuttal can be constructed out of the original dilemma's ingredients. Of the second dilemma, one can go between the horns by remarking on the fact that directions for the proper use of a new term need not take the form of, or be reducible to, an explicit definition of it. This suggests a plausible way of grasping the first horn. The usual nonrefuting rebuttal can be constructed out of the original dilemma's ingredients.

25. Impossible to go between the horns. But either horn may plausibly be grasped. The claim that having peace requires that the competitive spirit not be encouraged may be contested; that spirit, it could be argued, results in the productivity that alone can yield the contentment that peace requires. Or the claim that progress requires the encouragement of the competitive spirit may be contested; cooperation in place of competition may produce progress of a more lasting and more satisfying kind.

30. It is easy to go between the horns here. On the continuum of possible salaries, there is surely a range (though it might be narrow) of salaries that are neither too high nor too low. And either horn may be grasped, though with different degrees of plausibility. If "too high" a salary is asked for, employers may see that the job or the applicant is worth more than they first thought. And if "too low" a salary is asked for, the applicant may also express a willingness to work at that low salary with a conviction that the employer is likely soon to recognize that a higher salary is deserved.

SECTION 8.2

Exercises on pp. 309–312

I.   1. True.   5. True.   10. True.   15. False.   20. True.   25. False.

II. 1. True.   5. False.   10. True.   15. True.   20. False.   25. False.

III. 1. True.   5. True.   10. False.   15. False.   20. True.   25. False.

IV. 1. $I \bullet \sim L$ 5. $\sim I \bullet \sim L$ 10. $\sim(E \vee J)$
     15. $\sim I \vee L$ 20. $(I \bullet E) \vee \sim(J \bullet S)$ 25. $(L \bullet E) \bullet (S \bullet J)$

SECTION 8.3

Exercises on pp. 319–321

I.   1. True.   5. False.   10. True.   15. False.   20. False.   25. True.

II. 1. True.   5. False.   10. False.   15. True.   20. False.   25. True.

III. 1. $A \supset (B \supset C)$ 5. $(A \bullet B) \supset C$ 10. $\sim[A \supset (B \bullet C)]$
     15. $B \supset (A \vee C)$ 20. $B \vee C$ 25. $(\sim C \bullet \sim D) \supset (\sim B \vee A)$

SECTION 8.4

Exercises on pp. 331–334

I.   pp. 331–333
     e. 10 is the specific form of *e*.
     o. 3 has *o* as a substitution instance, and 24 is the specific form of *o*.

II. p. 333

1.

p	q	$p \supset q$	$\sim q$	$\sim p$	$\sim q \supset \sim p$
T	T	T	F	F	T
T	F	F	T	F	F
F	T	T	F	T	T
F	F	T	T	T	T
valid

5.

p	q	$p \supset q$
T	T	T
T	F	F
F	T	T
F	F	T
invalid (shown by second row)

10.

p	q	$p \cdot q$
T	T	T
T	F	F
F	T	F
F	F	F
valid

15.

p	q	r	$q \supset r$	$p \supset (q \supset r)$	$p \supset r$	$q \supset (p \supset r)$	$p \vee q$	$(p \vee q) \supset r$
T	T	T	T	T	T	T	T	T
T	T	F	F	F	F	F	T	F
T	F	T	T	T	T	T	T	T
T	F	F	T	T	F	T	T	F
F	T	T	T	T	T	T	T	T
F	T	F	F	T	T	T	T	F
F	F	T	T	T	T	T	F	T
F	F	F	T	T	T	T	F	T
invalid (shown by fourth and sixth row)

20.

p	q	r	s	p • q	p ⊃ q	(p • q) ⊃ r	r ⊃ s	p ⊃ (r ⊃ s)	(p ⊃ q) • [(p • q) ⊃ r]	p ⊃ s
T	T	T	T	T	T	T	T	T	T	T
T	T	T	F	T	T	T	F	F	T	F
T	T	F	T	T	T	F	T	T	F	T
T	T	F	F	T	T	F	T	T	F	F
T	F	T	T	F	F	T	T	T	F	T
T	F	T	F	F	F	T	F	F	F	F
T	F	F	T	F	F	T	T	T	F	T
T	F	F	F	F	F	T	T	T	F	F
F	T	T	T	F	T	T	T	T	T	T
F	T	T	F	F	T	T	F	T	T	T
F	T	F	T	F	T	T	T	T	T	T
F	T	F	F	F	T	T	T	T	T	T
F	F	T	T	F	T	T	T	T	T	T
F	F	T	F	F	T	T	F	T	T	T
F	F	F	T	F	T	T	T	T	T	T
F	F	F	F	F	T	T	T	T	T	T

valid

III. p. 333

1. $(A \lor B) \supset (A \bullet B)$ $(p \lor q) \supset (p \bullet q)$
   $A \lor B$ has the specific $p \lor q$
   $\therefore A \bullet B$ form $\therefore p \bullet q$

p	q	p ∨ q	p • q	(p ∨ q) ⊃ (p • q)
T	T	T	T	T
T	F	T	F	F
F	T	T	F	F
F	F	F	F	T

valid

5. $(I \lor J) \supset (I \bullet J)$ $(p \lor q) \supset (p \bullet q)$
   $\sim(I \lor J)$ has the specific $\sim(p \lor q)$
   $\therefore \sim(I \bullet J)$ form $\therefore \sim(p \bullet q)$

p	q	p ∨ q	p • q	(p ∨ q) ⊃ (p • q)	∼(p ∨ q)	∼(p • q)
T	T	T	T	T	F	F
T	F	T	F	F	F	T
F	T	T	F	F	F	T
F	F	F	F	T	T	T

valid (Note: Fallacy of denying the antecedent is *not* committed here!)

10. $U \supset (V \lor W)$ $p \supset (q \lor r)$
  $(V \bullet W) \supset {\sim}U$ has the specific $(q \bullet r) \supset {\sim}p$
  $\therefore {\sim}U$ form $\therefore {\sim}p$

p	q	r	$q \lor r$	$p \supset (q \lor r)$	$q \bullet r$	${\sim}p$	$(q \bullet r) \supset {\sim}p$
T	T	T	T	T	T	F	F
T	T	F	T	T	F	F	T
T	F	T	T	T	F	F	T
T	F	F	F	F	F	F	T
F	T	T	T	T	T	T	T
F	T	F	T	T	F	T	T
F	F	T	T	T	F	T	T
F	F	F	F	T	F	T	T
Invalid (shown by second and third row)							

IV. pp. 333–334

1. $A \supset (B \bullet C)$ $p \supset (q \bullet r)$
  ${\sim}B$ has the specific ${\sim}q$
  $\therefore {\sim}A$ form $\therefore {\sim}p$

p	q	r	$q \bullet r$	$p \supset (q \bullet r)$	${\sim}q$	${\sim}p$
T	T	T	T	T	F	F
T	T	F	F	F	F	F
T	F	T	F	F	T	F
T	F	F	F	F	T	F
F	T	T	T	T	F	T
F	T	F	F	T	F	T
F	F	T	F	T	T	T
F	F	F	F	T	T	T
valid						

5. $M \supset (N \supset O)$ $p \supset (q \supset r)$
  N has the specific q
  $\therefore O \supset M$ form $\therefore r \supset p$

p	q	r	$q \supset r$	$p \supset (q \supset r)$	$r \supset p$
T	T	T	T	T	T
T	T	F	F	F	T
T	F	T	T	T	T
T	F	F	T	T	T
F	T	T	T	T	F
F	T	F	F	T	T
F	F	T	T	T	F
F	F	F	T	T	T
invalid (shown by fifth row)					

10.

symbolized	specific form	
$C \supset (I \bullet D)$	$p \supset (q \bullet r)$	valid
$(I \vee D) \supset B$	$(q \vee r) \supset s$	
$\therefore C \supset B$	$\therefore p \supset s$	

SECTION 8.5

Exercises on pp. 338–339

I.

1. c is the specific form of 1.

5. c has 5 as a substitution instance, and i is the specific form of 5.

10. e has 10 as a substitution instance.

II.

1.

p	q	$p \supset q$	$p \supset (p \supset q)$	$[p \supset (p \supset q)] \supset q$
T	T	T	T	T
T	F	F	F	T
F	T	T	T	T
F	F	T	T	F
contingent				

5.

p	q	$\sim q$	$q \bullet \sim q$	$p \supset$ $(q \bullet \sim q)$	$p \supset$ $[p \supset (q \bullet \sim q)]$
T	T	F	F	F	F
T	F	T	F	F	F
F	T	F	F	T	T
F	F	T	F	T	T
contingent					

10. Contingent.   Final column: T T T T T T T T T T F F T T F T

III.

1.

p	q	$p \supset q$	$\sim q$	$\sim p$	$\sim q \supset \sim p$	$(p \supset q) \equiv$ $(\sim q \supset \sim p)$
T	T	T	F	F	T	T
T	F	F	T	F	F	T
F	T	T	F	T	T	T
F	F	T	T	T	T	T
tautology						

5.

p	q	$p \vee q$	$p \bullet (p \vee q)$	$p \equiv [p \bullet (p \vee q)]$
T	T	T	T	T
T	F	T	T	T
F	T	T	F	T
F	F	F	F	T

tautology

10.

p	q	$p \supset q$	$p \vee q$	$(p \vee q) \equiv q$	$(p \supset q) \equiv$ $[(p \vee q) \equiv q]$
T	T	T	T	T	T
T	F	F	T	F	T
F	T	T	T	T	T
F	F	T	F	T	T

tautology

15.

p	q	r	$q \vee r$	$p \bullet$ $(q \vee r)$	$p \bullet q$	$p \bullet r$	$(p \bullet q) \vee$ $(p \bullet r)$	$[p \bullet (q \vee r)] \equiv$ $[(p \bullet q) \vee (p \bullet r)]$
T	T	T	T	T	T	T	T	T
T	T	F	T	T	T	F	T	T
T	F	T	T	T	F	T	T	T
T	F	F	F	F	F	F	F	T
F	T	T	T	F	F	F	F	T
F	T	F	T	F	F	F	F	T
F	F	T	T	F	F	F	F	T
F	F	F	F	F	F	F	F	T

tautology

20. tautology   Final column: T T T T

SECTION 9.1

Exercises on pp. 352–358

I.   p. 352

1. Absorption (Abs.)   **5.** Constructive Dilemma (C.D.)
10. Hypothetical Syllogism (H.S.)   **15.** Conjunction (Conj.)
20. Hypothetical Syllogism (H.S.)

II.   pp. 352–353

1. 3. 1, Simp.   **5. 5.** 2,4, M.P.   **10.   6.** 4,5, Conj.
   4. 3, Add.   **6.** 1,5, Conj.   **7.** 3,6, M.P.
   5. 2,4, M.P.   **7.** 3,4, D.S.   **8.** 7,1, H.S.
   6. 3,5, Conj.   **8.** 6,7, C.D.   **9.** 2,8, Conj.
                                                      10. 9,4, C.D.

III. pp. 354–355

1. **1.** A
    2. B
    ∴ $(A \vee C) \bullet B$
    3. $A \vee C$ 1, Add.
    4. $(A \vee C) \bullet B$ 3,2, Conj.

10. **1.** $A \supset B$
    2. $(A \bullet B) \supset C$
    ∴ $A \supset C$
    3. $A \supset (A \bullet B)$ 1, Abs.
    4. $A \supset C$ 3,2, H.S.

20. **1.** $(\sim H \vee I) \vee J$
    2. $\sim(\sim H \vee I)$
    ∴ $J \vee \sim H$
    3. J 1,2, D.S.
    4. $J \vee \sim H$ 3, Add.

30. **1.** $Q \supset (R \vee S)$
    2. $(T \bullet U) \supset R$
    3. $(R \vee S) \supset (T \bullet U)$
    ∴ $Q \supset R$
    4. $Q \supset (T \bullet U)$ 1,3, H.S.
    5. $Q \supset R$ 4,2, H.S.

5. **1.** $M \vee N$
    2. $\sim M \bullet \sim O$
    ∴ N
    3. $\sim M$ 2, Simp.
    4. N 1,3, D.S.

15. **1.** $(P \supset Q) \bullet (R \supset S)$
    2. $(P \vee R) \bullet (Q \vee R)$
    ∴ $Q \vee S$
    3. $P \vee R$ 2, Simp.
    4. $Q \vee S$ 1,3, C.D.

25. **1.** $(W \bullet X) \supset (Y \bullet Z)$
    2. $\sim[(W \bullet X) \bullet (Y \bullet Z)]$
    ∴ $\sim(W \bullet X)$
    3. $(W \bullet X) \supset [(W \bullet X) \bullet (Y \bullet Z)]$ 1, Abs.
    4. $\sim(W \bullet X)$ 3,2, M.T.

IV. pp. 355–356

1. **1.** $A \vee (B \supset A)$
    2. $\sim A \bullet C$
    ∴ $\sim B$
    3. $\sim A$ 2, Simp.
    4. $B \supset A$ 1,3, D.S.
    5. $\sim B$ 4,3, M.T.

10. **1.** $E \vee \sim F$
    2. $F \vee (E \vee G)$
    3. $\sim E$
    ∴ G
    4. $\sim F$ 1,3, D.S.
    5. $E \vee G$ 2,4, D.S.
    6. G 5,3, D.S.

5. **1.** $N \supset [(N \bullet O) \supset P]$
    2. $N \bullet O$
    ∴ P
    3. N 2, Simp.
    4. $(N \bullet O) \supset P$ 1,3, M.P.
    5. P 4,2, M.P.

15. **1.** $(Z \bullet A) \supset B$
    2. $B \supset A$
    3. $(B \bullet A) \supset (A \bullet B)$
    ∴ $(Z \bullet A) \supset (A \bullet B)$
    4. $B \supset (B \bullet A)$ 2, Abs.
    5 $B \supset (A \bullet B)$ 4,3, H.S.
    6. $(Z \bullet A) \supset (A \bullet B)$ 1,5, H.S.

V. p. 356

1. **1.** $A \supset B$
    2. $A \vee (C \bullet D)$
    3. $\sim B \bullet \sim E$
    ∴ C
    4. $\sim B$ 3, Simp.
    5. $\sim A$ 1,4, M.T.
    6. $C \bullet D$ 2,5, D.S.
    7. C 6, Simp.

5. **1.** $(Q \supset R) \bullet (S \supset T)$
    2. $(U \supset V) \bullet (W \supset X)$
    3. $Q \vee U$
    ∴ $R \vee V$
    4. $Q \supset R$ 1, Simp.
    5. $U \supset V$ 2, Simp.
    6. $(Q \supset R) \bullet (U \supset V)$ 4,5, Conj.
    7. $R \vee V$ 6,3, C.D.

10. **1.** $(N \lor O) \supset P$
   2. $(P \lor Q) \supset R$
   3. $Q \lor N$
   4. $\sim Q$
      $\therefore R$
   5. N 3,4, D.S.
   6. $N \lor O$ 5, Add.
   7. P 1,6, M.P.
   8. $P \lor Q$ 7, Add.
   9. R 2,8, M.P.

VI. pp. 356–358

1. **1.** $(G \lor H) \supset (J \bullet K)$
   2. G
      $\therefore J$
   3. $G \lor H$ 2, Add.
   4. $J \bullet K$ 1,3, M.P.
   5. J 4, Simp.

5. **1.** $C \supset R$
   2. $(C \bullet R) \supset B$
   3. $(C \supset B) \supset \sim S$
   4. $S \lor M$
      $\therefore M$
   5. $C \supset (C \bullet R)$ 1, Abs.
   6. $C \supset B$ 5,2, H.S.
   7. $\sim S$ 3,6, M.P.
   8. M 4,7, D.S.

10. **1.** $O \supset \sim M$
   2. O
   3. $B \supset \sim N$
   4. B
   5. $(\sim M \bullet \sim N) \supset F$
   6. $(B \bullet F) \supset G$
      $\therefore G$
   7. $\sim M$ 1,2, M.P.
   8. $\sim N$ 3,4, M.P.
   9. $\sim M \bullet \sim N$ 7,8, Conj.
   10. F 5,9, M.P.
   11. $B \bullet F$ 4,10, Conj.
   12. G 6,11, M.P.

SECTION 9.2

Exercises on pp. 364–371

I. p. 364

 1. Transposition (Trans.)
10. Association (Assoc.)
20. De Morgan's Theorem (D.M.)

 5. Material Equivalence (Equiv.)
15. Distribution (Dist.)

II. pp. 364–365

1.
3. 2, Trans.
4. 3, D.N.
5. 1,4, H.S.

5.
3. 2, Dist.
4. 3, Com.
5. 4, Simp.
6. 5, Taut.
7. 1, Assoc.
8. 7,6, D.S.
9. 8, Impl.

10.
3. 2, Trans.
4. 3, Exp.
5. 1, D.N.
6. 5, Com.
7. 6, Dist.
8. 7, Com.
9. 4,8, C.D.
10. 9, Com.
11. 10, D.N.
12. 11, De M.

III. pp. 366–367

1.
1. $A \supset \sim A$
$\therefore \sim A$
2. $\sim A \lor \sim A$ 1, Impl.
3. $\sim A$ 2, Taut.

10.
1. $Z \supset A$
2. $\sim A \lor B$
$\therefore Z \supset B$
3. $A \supset B$ 2, Impl.
4. $Z \supset B$ 1,3, H.S.

20.
1. $I \supset [J \lor (K \lor L)]$
2. $\sim[(J \lor K) \lor L]$
$\therefore \sim I$
3. $\sim[J \lor (K \lor L)]$ 2, Assoc.
4. $\sim I$ 1,3, M.T.

25.
1. $A \lor B$
2. $C \lor D$
$\therefore [(A \lor B) \bullet C] \lor [(A \lor B) \bullet D]$
3. $(A \lor B) \bullet (C \lor D)$ 1,2, Conj.
4. $[(A \lor B) \bullet C] \lor [(A \lor B) \bullet D]$ 3, Dist.

5.
1. $\sim K \lor (L \supset M)$
$\therefore (K \bullet L) \supset M$
2. $K \supset (L \supset M)$ 1, Impl.
3. $(K \bullet L) \supset M$ 2, Exp.

15.
1. $(O \lor P) \supset (Q \lor R)$
2. $P \lor O$
$\therefore Q \lor R$
3. $O \lor P$ 2, Com.
4. $Q \lor R$ 1,3, M.P.

30.
1. $\sim[(B \supset \sim C) \bullet (\sim C \supset B)]$
2. $(D \bullet E) \supset (B \equiv \sim C)$
$\therefore \sim(D \bullet E)$
3. $\sim(B \equiv \sim C)$ 1, Equiv.
4. $\sim(D \bullet E)$ 2,3, M.T.

IV. p. 367

1.
1. $\sim A \supset A$
$\therefore A$
2. $\sim\sim A \lor A$ 1, Impl.
3. $A \lor A$ 2, D.N.
4. A 3, Taut.

10.
1. $(Z \lor A) \lor B$
2. $\sim A$
$\therefore Z \lor B$
3. $(A \lor Z) \lor B$ 1, Com.
4. $A \lor (Z \lor B)$ 3, Assoc.
5. $Z \lor B$ 4,2, D.S.

5.
1. $[(K \lor L) \lor M] \lor N$
$\therefore (N \lor K) \lor (L \lor M)$
2. $[K \lor (L \lor M)] \lor N$ 1, Assoc.
3. $N \lor [K \lor (L \lor M)]$ 2, Com.
4. $(N \lor K) \lor (L \lor M)$ 3, Assoc.

15.
1. $[R \supset (S \supset T)] \bullet [(R \bullet T) \supset U]$
2. $R \bullet (S \lor T)$
$\therefore T \lor U$
3. $(R \bullet S) \lor (R \bullet T)$ 2, Dist.
4. $[(R \bullet S) \supset T] \bullet [(R \bullet T) \supset U]$ 1, Exp.
5. $T \lor U$ 4,3, C.D.

V. pp. 367–368

1.
1. $\sim A$
    $\therefore A \supset B$
2. $\sim A \lor B$ 1, Add.
3. $A \supset B$ 2, Impl.

5.
1. $K \supset L$
    $\therefore K \supset (L \lor M)$
2. $\sim K \lor L$ 1, Impl.
3. $(\sim K \lor L) \lor M$ 2, Add.
4. $\sim K \lor (L \lor M)$ 3, Assoc.
5. $K \supset (L \lor M)$ 4, Impl.

10.
1. $Z \supset A$
2. $Z \lor A$
    $\therefore A$
3. $A \lor Z$ 2, Com.
4. $\sim\sim A \lor Z$ 3, D.N.
5. $\sim A \supset Z$ 4, Impl.
6. $\sim A \supset A$ 5,1, H.S.
7. $\sim\sim A \lor A$ 6, Impl.
8. $A \lor A$ 7, D.N.
9. A 8, Taut.

VI. p. 368

1.
1. $A \supset \sim B$
2. $\sim(C \bullet \sim A)$
    $\therefore C \supset \sim B$
3. $\sim C \lor \sim\sim A$ 2, De M.
4. $C \supset \sim\sim A$ 3, Impl.
5. $C \supset A$ 4, D.N.
6. $C \supset \sim B$ 5,1, H.S.

5.
1. $[(M \bullet N) \bullet O] \supset P$
2. $Q \supset [(O \bullet M) \bullet N]$
    $\therefore \sim Q \lor P$
3. $[O \bullet (M \bullet N)] \supset P$ 1, Com.
4. $[(O \bullet M) \bullet N] \supset P$ 3, Assoc.
5. $Q \supset P$ 2,4, H.S.
6. $\sim Q \lor P$ 5, Impl.

10.
1. $[H \lor (I \lor J)] \supset (K \supset J)$
2. $L \supset [I \lor (J \lor H)]$
    $\therefore (L \bullet K) \supset J$
3. $[(I \lor J) \lor H] \supset (K \supset J)$ 1, Com.
4. $[I \lor (J \lor H)] \supset (K \supset J)$ 3, Assoc.
5. $L \supset (K \supset J)$ 2,4 H.S.
6. $(L \bullet K) \supset J$ 5, Exp.

15.
1. $(Z \supset Z) \supset (A \supset A)$
2. $(A \supset A) \supset (Z \supset Z)$
    $\therefore A \supset A$
3. $[(Z \supset Z) \supset (A \supset A)] \lor \sim A$ 1, Add.
4. $\sim A \lor [(Z \supset Z) \supset (A \supset A)]$ 3, Com.
5. $A \supset [(Z \supset Z) \supset (A \supset A)]$ 4, Impl.
6. $A \supset \{A \bullet [(Z \supset Z) \supset (A \supset A)]\}$ 5, Abs.
7. $\sim A \lor \{A \bullet [(Z \supset Z) \supset (A \supset A)]\}$ 6, Impl.
8. $(\sim A \lor A) \bullet \{\sim A \lor [(Z \supset Z) \supset (A \supset A)]\}$ 7, Dist.
9. $\sim A \lor A$ 8, Simp.
10. $A \supset A$ 9, Impl.

20. **1.** $(R \lor S) \supset (T \bullet U)$
    2. $\sim R \supset (V \supset \sim V)$
    3. $\sim T$
      $\therefore \sim V$
    4. $\sim T \lor \sim U$ 3, Add.
    5. $\sim(T \bullet U)$ 4, De M.
    6. $\sim(R \lor S)$ 1,5, M.T.
    7. $\sim R \bullet \sim S$ 6, De M.
    8. $\sim R$ 7, Simp.
    9. $V \supset \sim V$ 2,8, M.P.
    10. $\sim V \lor \sim V$ 9, Impl.
    11. $\sim V$ 10, Taut.

VII. pp. 368–371

1. **1.** $\sim N \lor A$
    2. N
      $\therefore A$
    3. $N \supset A$ 1, Impl.
    4. A 3,2, M.P.

5. **1.** $R \supset A$
      $\therefore R \supset (A \lor W)$
    2. $\sim R \lor A$ 1, Impl.
    3. $(\sim R \lor A) \lor W$ 2, Add.
    4. $\sim R \lor (A \lor W)$ 3, Assoc.
    5. $R \supset (A \lor W)$ 4, Impl.

10. **1.** $(G \bullet S) \supset D$
    2. $(S \supset D) \supset P$
    3. G
      $\therefore P$
    4. $G \supset (S \supset D)$ 1, Exp.
    5. $S \supset D$ 4,3, M.P.
    6. P 2,5, M.P.

15. **1.** $M \supset \sim C$
    2. $\sim C \supset \sim A$
    3. $D \lor A$
      $\therefore \sim M \lor D$
    4. $M \supset \sim A$ 1,2, H.S.
    5. $A \lor D$ 3, Com.
    6. $\sim\sim A \lor D$ 5, D.N.
    7. $\sim A \supset D$ 6, Impl.
    8. $M \supset D$ 4,7, H.S.
    9. $\sim M \lor D$ 8, Impl.

20. 1. $P \supset \sim M$
    2. $C \supset M$
    3. $\sim L \lor C$
    4. $(\sim P \supset \sim E) \bullet (\sim E \supset \sim C)$
    5. $P \lor \sim P$
      $\therefore \sim L$
    6. $(\sim E \supset \sim C) \bullet (\sim P \supset \sim E)$ 4, Com.
    7. $\sim P \supset \sim E$ 4, Simp.
    8. $\sim E \supset \sim C$ 6, Simp.
    9. $\sim P \supset \sim C$ 7,8, H.S.
    10. $\sim M \supset \sim C$ 2, Trans.
    11. $P \supset \sim C$ 1,10, H.S.
    12. $(P \supset \sim C) \bullet (\sim P \supset \sim C)$ 11,9, Conj.
    13. $\sim C \lor \sim C$ 12,5, C.D.
    14. $\sim C$ 13, Taut.
    15. $C \lor \sim L$ 3, Com.
    16. $\sim L$ 15,14, D.S.

VIII. p. 371

5. **1.** $(H \vee \sim H) \supset G$
   $\therefore G$
   2. $[(H \vee \sim H) \supset G] \vee \sim H$ 1, Add.
   3. $\sim H \vee [(H \vee \sim H) \supset G]$ 2, Com.
   4. $H \supset [(H \vee \sim H) \supset G]$ 3, Impl.
   5. $H \supset \{H \bullet [(H \vee \sim H) \supset G]\}$ 4, Abs.
   6. $\sim H \vee \{H \bullet [(H \vee \sim H) \supset G]\}$ 5, Impl.
   7. $(\sim H \vee H) \bullet \{\sim H \vee [(H \vee \sim H) \supset G]\}$ 6, Dist.
   8. $\sim H \vee H$ 7, Simp.
   9. $H \vee \sim H$ 8, Com.
   10. G 1,9, M.P.

SECTION 9.3

Exercises on p. 374

1.

A	B	C	D
f	f	f	t

5.

S	T	U	V	W	X
t	f	f	t	t	t

or any of 13 other truth-value assignments.

10.

A	B	C	D	E	F	G	H	I	J
t	t	f	t	f	t	f	t	f	t
or f	t	t	t	f	t	f	t	f	t
or f	t	f	t	f	t	f	t	f	t

SECTION 9.4

Exercises on pp. 378–382

I. p. 378

1. **1.** $(A \supset B) \bullet (C \supset D)$
   $\therefore (A \bullet C) \supset (B \vee D)$
   2. $A \supset B$ 1, Simp.
   3. $\sim A \vee B$ 2, Impl.
   4. $(\sim A \vee B) \vee D$ 3, Add.
   5. $\sim A \vee (B \vee D)$ 4, Assoc.
   6. $[\sim A \vee (B \vee D)] \vee \sim C$ 5, Add.
   7. $\sim C \vee [\sim A \vee (B \vee D)]$ 6, Com.
   8. $(\sim C \vee \sim A) \vee (B \vee D)$ 7, Assoc.
   9. $(\sim A \vee \sim C) \vee (B \vee D)$ 8, Com.
   10. $\sim (A \bullet C) \vee (B \vee D)$ 9, De M.
   11. $(A \bullet C) \supset (B \vee D)$ 10, Impl.

5.

X	Y	Z	A	B	C
t	f	t	f	t	f

10.

A	B	C	D	E	F	G
f	f	t	t	f	t	t
or f	f	t	f	f	t	t
or f	f	f	t	f	t	t
or f	f	f	f	f	t	t

II. pp. 379–381

1.
   1. $C \supset (M \supset D)$
   2. $D \supset V$
   3. $(D \supset A) \bullet \sim A$
       $\therefore M \supset \sim C$
   4. $D \supset A$ 3, Simp.
   5. $\sim A \bullet (D \supset A)$ 3, Com.
   6. $\sim A$ 5, Simp.
   7. $\sim D$ 4,6, M.T.
   8. $(C \bullet M) \supset D$ 1, Exp.
   9. $\sim(C \bullet M)$ 8,7, M.T.
   10. $\sim C \vee \sim M$ 9, De M.
   11. $\sim M \vee \sim C$ 10, Com.
   12. $M \supset \sim C$ 11, Impl.

5. $(I \bullet S) \supset (G \bullet P)$
   $[(S \bullet \sim I) \supset A] \bullet (A \supset P)$
   $I \supset S$
   $\therefore P$

proved invalid by

	I	S	G	P	A
	f	f	t	f	f
or	f	f	f	f	f

10. $(H \supset A) \bullet (F \supset C)$
   $A \supset (F \bullet E)$
   $(O \supset C) \bullet (O \supset M)$
   $P \supset (M \supset D)$
   $P \bullet (D \supset G)$
   $\therefore H \supset G$

proved invalid by

H	A	C	F	E	O	M	P	D	G
t	t	t	t	t	f	f	t	f	f

15.
   1. $(J \vee A) \supset [(S \vee K) \supset (\sim I \bullet Y)]$
   2. $(\sim I \vee \sim M) \supset E$
       $\therefore J \supset (S \supset E)$
   3. $\sim(J \vee A) \vee [(S \vee K) \supset (\sim I \bullet Y)]$ 1, Impl.
   4. $[(S \vee K) \supset (\sim I \bullet Y)] \vee \sim(J \vee A)$ 3, Com.
   5. $[(S \vee K) \supset (\sim I \bullet Y)] \vee (\sim J \bullet \sim A)$ 4, De M.
   6. $\{[(S \vee K) \supset (\sim I \bullet Y)] \vee \sim J\} \bullet$
       $\{[(S \vee K) \supset (\sim I \bullet Y)] \vee \sim A\}$ 5, Dist.
   7. $[(S \vee K) \supset (\sim I \bullet Y)] \vee \sim J$ 6, Simp.
   8. $[\sim(S \vee K) \vee (\sim I \bullet Y)] \vee \sim J$ 7, Impl.
   9. $\sim(S \vee K) \vee [(\sim I \bullet Y) \vee \sim J]$ 8, Assoc.
   10. $[(\sim I \bullet Y) \vee \sim J] \vee \sim(S \vee K)$ 9, Com.
   11. $[(\sim I \bullet Y) \vee \sim J] \vee (\sim S \bullet \sim K)$ 10, De M.
   12. $\{[(\sim I \bullet Y) \vee \sim J] \vee \sim S\} \bullet \{[(\sim I \bullet Y) \vee \sim J] \vee \sim K\}$ 11, Dist.
   13. $[(\sim I \bullet Y) \vee \sim J] \vee \sim S$ 12, Simp.

14. $(\sim I \bullet Y) \vee (\sim J \vee \sim S)$ 13, Assoc.
15. $(\sim J \vee \sim S) \vee (\sim I \bullet Y)$ 14, Com.
16. $[(\sim J \vee \sim S) \vee \sim I] \bullet [(\sim J \vee \sim S) \vee Y]$ 15, Dist.
17. $(\sim J \vee \sim S) \vee \sim I$ 16, Simp.
18. $[(\sim J \vee \sim S) \vee \sim I] \vee \sim M$ 17, Add.
19. $(\sim J \vee \sim S) \vee (\sim I \vee \sim M)$ 18, Assoc.
20. $\sim(J \bullet S) \vee (\sim I \vee \sim M)$ 19, De M.
21. $(J \bullet S) \supset (\sim I \vee \sim M)$ 20, Impl.
22. $(J \bullet S) \supset E$ 21,2, H.S.
23. $J \supset (S \supset E)$ 22, Exp.

III. p. 382

5. **1.** $(R \vee \sim R) \supset W$
    $\therefore W$
2. $[(R \vee \sim R) \supset W] \vee \sim R$ 1, Add.
3. $\sim R \vee [(R \vee \sim R) \supset W]$ 2, Com.
4. $R \supset [(R \vee \sim R) \supset W]$ 3, Impl.
5. $R \supset \{R \bullet [(R \vee \sim R) \supset W]\}$ 4, Abs.
6. $\sim R \vee \{R \bullet [(R \vee \sim R) \supset W]\}$ 5, Impl.
7. $(\sim R \vee R) \bullet \{\sim R \vee [(R \vee \sim R) \supset W]\}$ 6, Dist.
8. $\sim R \vee R$ 7, Simp.
9. $R \vee \sim R$ 8, Com.
10. W 1,9, M.P.

SECTION 10.3

Exercises on pp. 396–398

I.   pp. 396–397

5. $(\exists x)(Dx \bullet \sim Rx)$
10. $(x)(Cx \supset \sim Fx)$
15. $(x)(Vx \supset Cx)$
20. $(x)(Cx \equiv Hx)$

II.   pp. 397–398

5. $[(\exists x)(Gx \bullet \sim Sx)] \bullet [(\exists x)(Dx \bullet \sim Bx)]$
10. $(x)(\sim Bx > \sim Wx)$

III. p. 398

1. $(\exists x)(Ax \bullet \sim Bx)$
5. $(\exists x)(Ix \bullet \sim Jx)$
10. $(\exists x)(Sx \bullet \sim Tx)$

SECTION 10.4

Exercises on pp. 404–406

I.   **p. 405**

  5. **1.** $(x)(Mx \supset Nx)$
        2. $(\exists x)(Mx \bullet Ox)$
            $\therefore (\exists x)(Ox \bullet Nx)$
        3. $Ma \bullet Oa$ 2, **EI**
        4. $Ma \supset Na$ 1, **UI**
        5. Ma 3, Simp.
        6. Na 4,5, M.P.
        7. $Oa \bullet Ma$ 3, Com.
        8. Oa 7, Simp.
        9. $Oa \bullet Na$ 8,6, Conj.
        10. $(\exists x)(Ox \bullet Nx)$ 9, **EG**
  10. **1.** $(x)(Bx \supset \sim Cx)$
        2. $(\exists x)(Cx \bullet Dx)$
            $\therefore (\exists x)(Dx \bullet \sim Bx)$
        3. $Ca \bullet Da$ 2, **EI**
        4. $Ba \supset \sim Ca$ 1, **UI**
        5. Ca 3, Simp.
        6. $\sim\sim Ca$ 5, D.N.
        7. $\sim Ba$ 4,6, M.T.
        8. $Da \bullet Ca$ 3, Com.
        9. Da 8, Simp.
        10. $Da \bullet \sim Ba$ 9,7, Conj.
        11. $(\exists x)(Dx \bullet \sim Bx)$ 10, **EG**

II. **pp. 405–406**

  1. **1.** $(x)(Ax \supset \sim Bx)$
        2. Bc
            $\therefore \sim Ac$
        3. $Ac \supset \sim Bc$ 1, **UI**
        4. $\sim\sim Bc$ 2, D.N.
        5. $\sim Ac$ 3,4, M.T.
  5. **1.** $(x)(Mx \supset Nx)$
        2. $(\exists x)(Ox \bullet Mx)$
            $\therefore (\exists x)(Ox \bullet Nx)$
        3. $Oa \bullet Ma$ 2, **EI**
        4. $Ma \supset Na$ 1, **UI**
        5. Oa 3, Simp.
        6. $Ma \bullet Oa$ 3, Com.
        7. Ma 6, Simp.
        8. Na 4,7, M.P.
        9. $Oa \bullet Na$ 5,8, Conj.
        10. $(\exists x)(Ox \bullet Nx)$ 9, EG

10. **1.** $(x)(Ax \supset Rx)$
  2. $\sim Rs$
    $\therefore \sim As$
  3. $As \supset Rs$ 1, **UI**
  4. $\sim As$ 3,2, M.T.

Section 10.5

Exercises on pp. 409–410

I. pp. 409–410

5. $(\exists x)(Mx \bullet Nx)$ } logically { $(Ma \bullet Na) \vee (Mb \bullet Nb)$
  $(\exists x)(Mx \bullet Ox)$ } equivalent { $(Ma \bullet Oa) \vee (Mb \bullet Ob)$
  $\therefore (x)(Ox \supset Nx)$ } in $\boxed{a, b}$ to { $\therefore (Oa \supset Na) \bullet (Ob \supset Nb)$

  proved invalid by

Ma	Mb	Na	Nb	Oa	Ob
t	t	t	f	t	t

  or any of several other truth-value assignments.

10. $(\exists x)(Bx \bullet \sim Cx)$ } logically { $(Ba \bullet \sim Ca) \vee (Bb \bullet \sim Cb)$
  $(x)(Dx \supset \sim Cx)$ } equivalent { $(Da \supset \sim Ca) \bullet (Db \supset \sim Cb)$
  $\therefore (x)(Dx \supset Bx)$ } in $\boxed{a, b}$ to { $\therefore (Da \supset Ba) \bullet (Db \supset Bb)$

  proved invalid by

Ba	Bb	Ca	Cb	Da	Db
f	t	f	f	t	t

II. p. 410

1. $(x)(Ax \supset Bx)$ } logically { $Aa \supset Ba$
  $(x)(Cx \supset Bx)$ } equivalent { $Ca \supset Ba$
  $\therefore (x)(Ax \supset Cx)$ } in $\boxed{a}$ to { $\therefore Aa \supset Ca$

  proved invalid by

Aa	Ba	Ca
t	t	f

5. $(\exists x)(Mx \bullet Nx)$ } logically { $(Ma \bullet Na) \vee (Mb \bullet Nb)$
  $(\exists x)(Ox \bullet \sim Nx)$ } equivalent { $(Oa \bullet \sim Na) \vee (Ob \bullet Nb)$
  $\therefore (x)(Ox \supset \sim Mx)$ } in $\boxed{a, b}$ to { $\therefore (Oa \supset \sim Ma) \bullet (Ob \supset \sim Mb)$

  proved invalid by

Ma	Mb	Na	Nb	Oa	Ob
t	t	t	f	t	t

  or any of several other truth-value assignments.

10. $(x)(Mx \supset Sx)$ } logically { $Ma \supset Sa$
  $(x)(Wx \supset Mx)$ } equivalent { $Wa \supset Ma$
  $\therefore (x)(Sx \supset Wx)$ } in $\boxed{a}$ to { $\therefore Sa \supset Wa$

  proved invalid by

Ma	Sa	Wa
t	t	f

SECTION 10.6

Exercises on pp. 414–419

I. p. 415

5. $(x)Gx \supset (Wx \equiv Lx)$
10. $(x)\{Ax \supset [(Bx \supset Wx) \bullet (Px \supset Sx)]\}$

II. pp. 415–416

1. **1.** $(x)[(Ax \lor Bx) \supset (Cx \bullet Dx)]$
   $\therefore (x)(Bx \supset Cx)$

2. $(Ay \lor By) \supset (Cy \bullet Dy)$	1, **UI**
3. $\sim(Ay \lor By) \lor (Cy \bullet Dy)$	2, Impl.
4. $[\sim(Ay \lor By) \lor Cy] \bullet [\sim(Ay \lor By) \lor Dy]$	3, Dist.
5. $\sim(Ay \lor By) \lor Cy$	4, Simp.
6. $Cy \lor \sim(Ay \lor By)$	5, Com.
7. $Cy \lor (\sim Ay \bullet \sim By)$	6, De M.
8. $(Cy \lor \sim Ay) \bullet (Cy \lor \sim By)$	7, Dist.
9. $(Cy \lor \sim By) \bullet (Cy \lor \sim Ay)$	8, Com.
10. $Cy \lor \sim By$	9, Simp.
11. $\sim By \lor Cy$	10, Com.
12. $By \supset Cy$	11, Impl.
13. $(x)(Bx \supset Cx)$	12, **UG**

5. $(\exists x)(Sx \bullet Tx)$ logically $(Sa \bullet Ta) \lor (Sb \bullet Tb) \lor (Sc \bullet Tc)$
$(\exists x)(Ux \bullet \sim Sx)$ equivalent $(Ua \bullet \sim Sa) \lor (Ub \bullet \sim Sb) \lor (Uc \bullet \sim Sc)$
$(\exists x)(Vx \bullet \sim Tx)$ in $\boxed{a, b, c}$ $(Va \bullet \sim Ta) \lor (Vb \bullet \sim Tb) \lor (Vc \bullet \sim Tc)$
$\therefore (\exists x)(Ux \bullet Vx)$ to $\therefore (Ua \bullet Va) \lor (Ub \bullet Vb) \lor (Uc \bullet Vc)$

proved invalid by

Sa	Sb	Sc	Ta	Tb	Tc	Ua	Ub	Uc	Va	Vb	Vc
t	f	t	t	t	f	f	t	f	t	f	t

or any of several other truth-value assignments.

10.

logically equivalent in $\boxed{a, b}$ to

$(x)[(Sx \lor Tx) \supset \sim(Ux \lor Vx)]$ $[(Sa \lor Ta) \supset \sim(Ua \lor Va)] \bullet$
     $[(Sb \lor Tb) \supset \sim(Ub \lor Vb)]$
$(\exists x)(Sx \bullet \sim Wx)$ $(Sa \bullet \sim Wa) \lor (Sb \bullet \sim Wb)$
$(\exists x)(Tx \bullet \sim Xx)$ $(Ta \bullet \sim Xa) \lor (Tb \bullet \sim Xb)$
$(x)(\sim Wx \supset Xx)$ $(\sim Wa \supset Xa) \bullet (\sim Wb \supset Xb)$
$\therefore (\exists x)(Ux \bullet \sim Vx)$ $\therefore (Ua \bullet \sim Va) \lor (Ub \bullet \sim Vb)$

and proved invalid by

Sa	Sb	Ta	Tb	Ua	Ub	Va	Vb	Wa	Wb	Xa	Xb
t	t	t	t	f	f	f	f	f	f	t	t	f

or any of several other truth-value assignments.

III. pp. 416–417

1. **1.** $(x)[(Ax \lor Bx) \supset Cx]$
    2. $(x)(Vx \supset Ax)$
        $\therefore (x)(Vx \supset Cx)$
    3. $(Ay \lor By) \supset Cy$ 1, **UI**
    4. $Vy \supset Ay$ 2, **UI**
    5. $\sim Vy \lor Ay$ 4, Impl.
    6. $(\sim Vy \lor Ay) \lor By$ 5, Add.
    7. $\sim Vy \lor (Ay \lor By)$ 6, Assoc.
    8. $Vy \supset (Ay \lor By)$ 7, Impl.
    9. $Vy \supset Cy$ 8,3, H.S.
    10. $(x)(Vx \supset Cx)$ 9, **UG**

5. $(x)\{[Ex \bullet (Ix \lor Tx)] \supset \sim Sx\}$
    $(\exists x)(Ex \bullet Ix)$
    $(\exists x)(Ex \bullet Tx)$
    $\therefore (x)(Ex \supset \sim Sx)$

    This argument is logically equivalent in $\boxed{a, b}$ to

    $\{[Ea \bullet (Ia \lor Ta)] \supset \sim Sa\} \bullet \{[Eb \bullet (Ib \lor Tb)] \supset \sim Sb\}$
    $(Ea \bullet Ia) \lor (Eb \bullet Ib)$
    $(Ea \bullet Ta) \lor (Eb \bullet Tb)$
    $\therefore (Ea \supset \sim Sa) \bullet (Eb \supset \sim Sb)$

    which is proved invalid by

	Ea	Eb	Ia	Ib	Ta	Tb	Sa	Sb
	t	t	t	f	t	f	f	t
or	t	t	f	t	f	t	t	f

10. **1.** $(x)[Bx \supset (Ix \supset Wx)]$
    2. $(x)[Bx \supset (Wx \supset Ix)]$
        $\therefore (x)\{Bx \supset [(Ix \lor Wx) \supset (Ix \bullet Wx)]\}$
    3. $By \supset (Iy \supset Wy)$ 1, **UI**
    4. $By \supset (Wy \supset Iy)$ 2, **UI**
    5. $[By \supset (Iy \supset Wy)] \bullet [By \supset (Wy \supset Iy)]$ 3,4, Conj.
    6. $[\sim By \lor (Iy \supset Wy)] \bullet [\sim By \lor (Wy \supset Iy)]$ 5, Impl.
    7. $\sim By \lor [(Iy \supset Wy) \bullet (Wy \supset Iy)]$ 6, Dist.
    8. $\sim By \lor (Iy \equiv Wy)$ 7, Equiv.
    9. $\sim By \lor [(Iy \bullet Wy) \lor (\sim Iy \bullet \sim Wy)]$ 8, Equiv.
    10. $\sim By \lor [(\sim Iy \bullet \sim Wy) \lor (Iy \bullet Wy)]$ 9, Com.
    11. $\sim By \lor [\sim (Iy \lor Wy) \lor (Iy \bullet Wy)]$ 10, De M.
    12. $By \supset [(Iy \lor Wy) \supset (Iy \bullet Wy)]$ 11, Impl.
    13. $(x)\{Bx \supset [(Ix \lor Wx) \supset (Ix \bullet Wx)]\}$ 12, **UG**

IV. pp. 417–419

1. 1. $(x)[(Cx \bullet \sim Tx) \supset Px]$
   2. $(x)(Ox \supset Cx)$
   3. $(\exists x)(Ox \bullet \sim Px)$
      $\therefore (\exists x)(Tx)$
   4. $Oa \bullet \sim Pa$ 3, **EI**
   5. $Oa \supset Ca$ 2, **UI**
   6. $(Ca \bullet \sim Ta) \supset Pa$ 1, **UI**
   7. Oa 4, Simp.
   8. Ca 5,7, M.P.
   9. $\sim Pa \bullet Oa$ 4, Com.
   10. $\sim Pa$ 9, Simp.
   11. $Ca \supset (\sim Ta \supset Pa)$ 6, Exp.
   12. $\sim Ta \supset Pa$ 11,8, M.P.
   13. $\sim\sim Ta$ 12,10, M.T.
   14. Ta 13, D.N.
   15. $(\exists x)(Tx)$ 14, **EG**

5. $(\exists x)(Dx \bullet Ax)$
   $(x)[Ax \supset (Jx \vee Cx)]$
   $(x)(Dx \supset \sim Cx)$
   $(x)[(Jx \bullet Ix) \supset \sim Px]$
   $(\exists x)(Dx \bullet Ix)$
   $\therefore (\exists x)(Dx \bullet \sim Px)$

   This argument is logically equivalent in $\boxed{a, b}$ to

   $(Da \bullet Aa) \vee (Db \bullet Ab)$
   $[Aa \supset (Ja \vee Ca)] \bullet [Ab \supset (Jb \vee Cb)]$
   $(Da \supset \sim Ca) \bullet (Db \supset \sim Cb)$
   $[(Ja \bullet Ia) \supset \sim Pa] \bullet [(Jb \bullet Ib) \supset \sim Pb]$
   $(Da \bullet Ia) \vee (Db \bullet Ib)$
   $\therefore (Da \bullet \sim Pa) \vee (Db \bullet \sim Pb)$

   proved invalid by

	Da	Db	Aa	Ab	Ja	Jb	Ca	Cb	Ia	Ib	Pa	Pb
	t	t	t	f	t	f	f	f	f	t	t	t
or	t	t	f	t	f	t	f	f	t	f	t	t

10.

1. $(\exists x)(Cx \cdot Rx)$
2. $(x)[Rx \supset (Sx \vee Bx)]$
3. $(x)[Bx \supset (Dx \vee Px)]$
4. $(x)(Px \supset Lx)$
5. $(x)(Dx \supset Hx)$
6. $(x)(\sim Hx)$
7. $(x)\{[(Cx \cdot Rx) \cdot Fx] \supset Ax\}$
8. $(x)(Rx \supset Fx)$
9. $(x)[Cx \supset \sim(Lx \cdot Ax)]$
   $\therefore (\exists x)(Cx \cdot Sx)$
10. $Ca \cdot Ra$ — 1, **EI**
11. $Ra \cdot Ca$ — 10, Com.
12. Ra — 11, Simp.
13. $Ra \supset Fa$ — 8, **UI**
14. Fa — 13,12, M.P.
15. $(Ca \cdot Ra) \cdot Fa$ — 10,14, Conj.
16. $[(Ca \cdot Ra) \cdot Fa] \supset Aa$ — 7, **UI**
17. Aa — 16,15, M.P.
18. $Ca \supset \sim(La \cdot Aa)$ — 9, **UI**
19. Ca — 10, Simp.
20. $\sim(La \cdot Aa)$ — 18,19, M.P.
21. $\sim La \vee \sim Aa$ — 20, De M.
22. $\sim Aa \vee \sim La$ — 21, Com.
23. $Aa \supset \sim La$ — 22, Impl.
24. $\sim La$ — 23,17, M.P.
25. $Pa \supset La$ — 4, **UI**
26. $\sim Pa$ — 25,24, M.T.
27. $Da \supset Ha$ — 5, **UI**
28. $\sim Ha$ — 6, **UI**
29. $\sim Da$ — 27,28, M.T.
30. $\sim Da \cdot \sim Pa$ — 29,26, Conj.
31. $\sim(Da \vee Pa)$ — 30, De M.
32. $Ba \supset (Da \vee Pa)$ — 3, **UI**
33. $\sim Ba$ — 32,31, M.T.
34. $Ra \supset (Sa \vee Ba)$ — 2, **UI**
35. $Sa \vee Ba$ — 34,12, M.P.
36. $Ba \vee Sa$ — 35, Com.
37. Sa — 36,33, D.S.
38. $Ca \cdot Sa$ — 19,37, Conj.
39. $(\exists x)(Cx \cdot Sx)$ — 38, **EG**

15.

1. $(x)(Ox \supset Sx)$
2. $(x)(Lx \supset Tx)$
   $\therefore (x)[(Ox \vee Lx) \supset (Sx \vee Tx)]$
3. $Oy \supset Sy$ — 1, **UI**
4. $Ly \supset Ty$ — 2, **UI**
5. $\sim Oy \vee Sy$ — 3, Impl.
6. $(\sim Oy \vee Sy) \vee Ty$ — 5, Add.
7. $\sim Oy \vee (Sy \vee Ty)$ — 6, Assoc.
8. $(Sy \vee Ty) \vee \sim Oy$ — 7, Com.
9. $\sim Ly \vee Ty$ — 4, Impl.
10. $(\sim Ly \vee Ty) \vee Sy$ — 9, Add.
11. $\sim Ly \vee (Ty \vee Sy)$ — 10, Assoc.
12. $\sim Ly \vee (Sy \vee Ty)$ — 11, Com.
13. $(Sy \vee Ty) \vee \sim Ly$ — 12, Com.
14. $[(Sy \vee Ty) \vee \sim Oy] \cdot [(Sy \vee Ty) \vee \sim Ly]$ — 8,13, Conj.
15. $(Sy \vee Ty) \vee (\sim Oy \cdot \sim Ly)$ — 14, Dist.
16. $(\sim Oy \cdot \sim Ly) \vee (Sy \vee Ty)$ — 15, Com.
17. $\sim(Oy \vee Ly) \vee (Sy \vee Ty)$ — 16, De M.
18. $(Oy \vee Ly) \supset (Sy \vee Ty)$ — 17, Impl.
19. $(x)[(Ox \vee Lx) \supset (Sx \vee Tx)]$ — 18, **UG**

SECTION 11.1

Exercises on pp. 426–430

5. Analogical argument.

15. Nonargumentative use of analogy.

10. Analogical argument.

20. Analogical argument.

SECTION 11.2

Exercises on pp. 434–440

I.   pp. 436–437

5. (a) more, criterion 2; (b) less, criterion 5; (c) more, criterion 3; (d) neither, criterion 4; (e) more, criterion 6; (f) more, criterion 1.

II. pp. 437–440

1. Large diamonds, armies, great intellects all have the attributes of greatness [of value for diamonds, of military strength for armies, of mental superiority for intellects], and of divisibility [through cutting for diamonds; dispersion for armies; interruption, disturbance, and distraction for intellects].

Large diamonds and armies all have the attribute of having their greatness diminish when they are divided.

Therefore great intellects also have the attribute of having their greatness diminish when they are divided.

   (1) There are only three kinds of instances among which the analogies are said to hold, which is not very many. On the other hand, there are many, many instances of these kinds. By our first criterion the argument is fairly cogent.

   (2) There are but two kinds of instances in the premises with which the conclusion's instances are compared. Armies and large diamonds are, however, quite dissimilar to each other, so from the point of view of our second criterion, the argument is moderately cogent.

   (3) There are only three respects in which the things involved are said to be analogous. This is not many and the argument is accordingly rather weak.

   (4) Schopenhauer recognizes that the question of relevance is important, for he introduces a separate little discussion on this point. He urges that the superiority (the "greatness") of a great intellect "depends upon" its concentration or undividedness. Here he invokes the illustrative or explanatory (nonargumentative) analogy of the concave mirror, which focuses all its available light upon one point. There is indeed some merit in this claim, and by our fourth criterion the argument has a fairly high degree of cogency.

   (5) The instances with which the conclusion deals are enormously different from the instances mentioned in the premises. There are so many disanalogies between intellects, on the one hand, and large diamonds and armies, on the other, that by our fifth criterion Schopenhauer's argument is almost totally lacking in probative force.

(6) The conclusion states only that, when "divided," a great intellect will sink to the level of an ordinary one. This is not a terribly bold conclusion relative to the premises, and so by our sixth criterion the argument is fairly cogent.

Finally, however, it must be admitted that the whole passage might plausibly be analyzed as invoking large diamonds and armies for illustrative and explanatory rather than argumentative purposes. The plausibility of this alternative analysis, however, derives more from the weakness of the analogical argument than from what is explicitly stated in the passage in question.

5. This passage can be analyzed in two different ways. In both ways the analogical argument is presented primarily as an illustration of the biologist's reasoning.

(I) Porpoises and men all have lungs, warm blood, and hair.
Men are mammals.
Therefore porpoises also are mammals.

(1) There are many instances examined, which makes the conclusion probable.

(2) There are very few dissimilarities among men—biologically speaking—and by our second criterion this tends to weaken the argument.

(3) There are only three respects noted in the premisses in which porpoises and men resemble each other. In terms of their sheer number, this is not many: not enough to make the argument plausible.

(4) But in terms of relevance the argument is superlatively good, because biologists have found the three attributes noted in the premisses to be such remarkably dependable indicators of other mammalian characteristics.

(5) There are many disanalogies between men and porpoises: porpoises are aquatic, men are terrestrial; porpoises have tails, men do not; porpoises do not have the well-developed, highly differentiated limbs characteristic of men; and so on. These tend to weaken the argument.

(6) The conclusion is very bold relative to the premisses, because so many attributes are summarized in the term "mammal" (shown by the variety of other, specific attributes confidently predicted by the zoologist). This tends, of course, to weaken the argument.

Alternative analysis:

(II) Porpoises and humans all have lungs, warm blood, and hair.
Humans also nurse their young with milk, have a four-chambered heart, bones of a particular type, a certain general pattern of nerves and blood vessels, and red blood cells that lack nuclei.
Therefore porpoises also nurse their young with milk, have a four-chambered heart, bones of the same particular type, the same general pattern of nerves and blood vessels, and red blood cells that lack nuclei.

This version of the analogical argument contained in the given passage is evaluated in much the same way as the first one discussed. It is somewhat stronger an argument than the first one according to the sixth criterion, because in spite of the apparently greater detail in the second version's conclusion, it is more modest than that of the first version, since being a mammal entails all of these anatomical details plus many more.

Nature has a way of reminding us that such arguments are only probable, however, and never demonstrative. For the platypus resembles all other mammals in having lungs, warm blood, hair, nursing their young with milk, and so on. Other mammals are viviparous (bearing their young alive). Therefore the platypus. . .? No, the platypus lays eggs.

10. This is an example of a very strong analogical argument. Using all of the six criteria for appraisal, we are not likely to find the argument deficient. The number of instances (our past visits to the dentist) probably is considerable. The variety of work done on our teeth during these visits (variety within the cases used in the premises) is likely to be substantial. The respects in which our dental visits and the dental visit in question are similar are likely to be many and significant: the same kind of treatment, on the same bodily organs, using the same kind of dental instruments, and so on. This is a case very much like those with which we have direct experience. The causal relevance of the treatments is undoubted. The claim made in the conclusion (merely that the extraction hurt him) is modest and entirely reasonable. If the argument proves in some degree vulnerable, that is likely to be because the person whose treatment is in question differs importantly from me with respect to his or her tolerance for pain. On this fifth criterion—the identification of some significant disanalogies—the argument may be attacked, but that attack is not likely to succeed in persuading us that his tooth extraction without anesthetic did not hurt him.

15. A watch and other human artifacts display an intricacy that justifies our inference that they have been designed by their maker. Natural mechanisms also are intricate, as are the processes of the universe; hence we are justified in concluding that they also are designed by some Maker.

    (1) There is an unlimited number of manufactured mechanisms that we know to have been designed and made. On the first criterion, the argument has much support.

    (2) There are many great dissimilarities among the cases in the premises, which strengthen the argument, but these dissimilarities do not block the major disanalogies noted under (5), so the argument cannot be said to gain very much from its strength on this criterion.

    (3) There is only one respect in which the products of human design are claimed to be like the products of the divine Maker, namely, the intricacy and complexity of the designs encountered—the "curious adapting of means to ends," as Hume put it in the *Dialogues Concerning Natural Religion*. Although this is only one respect, it is a respect of great importance if established. This single (but disputable) respect leaves the argument in problematic circumstances.

    (4) Whether the analogy is relevant is difficult to say. For those who doubt the applicability of cause-and-effect reasoning beyond the range of experienced phenomena, it would not be relevant and would be held to fail on that ground. For those who accept the universal applicability of

causal analysis, going beyond human experience even to the universe itself, the analogy is indeed relevant.

(5) There are many great disanalogies between the human artifacts mentioned in the premisses and the natural mechanisms we encounter. The size, duration, and general character of the universe render it greatly and importantly different from any watch or other humanly designed machine. From this point of view also, the conclusion has only little probability.

(6) How modest this conclusion is, relative to the premisses, depends on what is included in the claim that there is a divine Maker of the natural universe. If implicit in this conclusion is the singularity, perfection, infinity, and incorporeality of a supernatural Maker (as commonly intended by such arguments), the conclusion is very bold relative to the premisses, rendering the argument weak. If the qualities normally attributed to God are not part of the conclusion, the mere claim that there is a "Maker" may be modest enough to be well supported by the premisses.

All things considered, the argument is neither worthless nor compelling. The degree of probability with which it warrants its conclusion decreases, however, as the similarity of the Maker in that conclusion to the God of traditional Western theism increases. The truth of such theism, of course, is not affected by the weakness of an argument designed to establish it.

Section 11.3

Exercises on pp. 443–446

5. The argument being refuted is the following:

Trees are cut down in very great numbers to make paper.
Using recycled paper would make it unnecessary to cut down many of those trees.
Therefore, we ought to use recycled paper to reduce the slaughter of trees.

The refuting analogy is:

Cornstalks are cut down in very great number to harvest corn.
Cutting back on corn consumption would make it unnecessary to cut down many of those cornstalks.
Therefore we ought to cut down on corn consumption in order to reduce the slaughter of cornstalks.

The refuting analogy does have the same form as the argument under attack. Moreover, its premisses are true and its conclusion surely is false. These considerations make this an effective counterargument. However, the refuting analogy supposes that the environmental status of cornstalks is essentially akin to that of trees. That plainly is disputable, and if a substantial disanalogy can be exhibited here, that would greatly weaken the purportedly refuting analogical argument.

SECTION 12.2

Exercises on pp. 458–460 (Method of Agreement)

5. This is a straightforward use of the Method of Agreement. Of all the pairs of brothers, who were gay, the one feature that was common—not to all of them, but to a very high percentage of them—was that they shared certain DNA sequences on their X chromosome. This analysis has some merit—but it falls very far short of proving that the brothers' being gay was caused by those sequences. We note in the first place that those sequences were *not* shared by *all* the gay brothers, which immediately casts some doubt on the alleged causal relation; agreement is not universal. And we note in the second place that there may very well be *other* characteristics shared by those pairs of brothers which led to their homosexuality—characteristics perhaps not yet identified, and certainly not discussed in this research. While serving as no proof, this use of the Method of Agreement does point to a range of considerations worthy of further investigation in seeking causal connections pertaining to homosexuality.

Exercises on pp. 463–466 (Method of Difference)

1. This is a vivid illustration of the Method of Difference. The *sole difference* between the blackcaps that seek to go northwest (toward England) and the blackcaps that seek to go southwest (toward the Mediterranean) lies in their breeding; the former are the birds bred from parents that had wintered in England, the latter were bred from parents that had wintered on the Mediterranean. All other circumstances are identical for all the birds.

    Where A denotes the circumstance of being bred from birds that wintered in England, and w denotes the phenomenon of attempting to migrate toward England, and B, C, D denote all the other circumstances of the birds being bred and raised in Germany, and x, y, z, denote phenomena common to all the birds other than their choice of migratory direction, the argument may be represented thus:

    $A B C D$ $w x y z$ (birds with English parents bred in Germany)
    $B C D$ $x y z$ (all other birds bred under identical circumstances in Germany)
    Therefore A is the cause of w.

5. This is a splendid illustration of the Method of Difference, and one that is typical of successful investigations in the world of medical research. A test for the causal efficacy of the gene MIP-1 alpha was devised by developing two populations of mice that differed in no important respects whatever *save only the presence or absence of that gene*. And all those with the gene, but none of those without the gene, exhibited the inflammatory response to the identical virus infection.

    We may reflect upon these results with the help of the schematic representation of the Method of Difference:

    $A B C D$ occur together with $w x y z$.
    $B C D$ occur together with $x y z$.

where A is the presence of the MIP-1 alpha gene in normal mice; where B, C, and D represent the other circumstances of the subject mice in both the experimental and the control groups; where w is the inflammatory response; and where x, y, and z are the other responses of the subject mice to the viral infection.

We may conclude, as Mill would have put it, that A (the presence of that gene) is the cause, or an indispensable part of the cause, of w (the inflammatory response).

Exercises on pp. 468–470 (Joint Method of Agreement and Difference)

5. The phenomenon under investigation here is susceptibility to the terrible disease anthrax. The Method of Agreement was applied when all the hens inoculated with anthrax bacilli were placed in a cold bath to lower their temperatures. All hens so treated died. This is a use of the Method of Agreement because, it will be remembered, hens whose body temperatures had not been lowered had been refractory to anthrax. Lowered temperature was the one circumstance in common that could be inferred as the cause of the elimination of that resistance. The Method of Difference was applied when one of the hens treated in that way was warmed; its body temperature quickly returned to normal after its cold bath. This hen recovered, and the only difference in this case was the rapid elevation of temperature. Here we have a neat illustration of the joint operation of the method of Agreement (in indicating that body temperature was likely to be critical to susceptibility) and the method of Difference (in further confirming this relation when infection is avoided by the quick re-raising of body temperature).

Exercises on pp. 472–474 (Method of Residues)

1. This is a case in which the Method of Residues does not confirm any particular hypothesis about the cause of the slowing of objects moving away from or around the sun, but it gives good reason to search for *some* cause (of the slowing phenomenon) not heretofore recognized or understood. All the calculations based upon the many known factors that enter into the determination of the trajectories or orbits of such moving bodies yield results that do not accord with observational data. Those data present a puzzling discrepancy, a "residue" needing further explanation. The natural suggestion that this discrepancy is merely the result of some error in measurement is put in serious doubt when, after accounting for possible errors investigation repeatedly produces the same results. Something theoretically new—but presently unknown—appears to be operative. If that is the case, it is likely to be identified before long, and when it is identified that discovery will be attributable in part to the provocation of this application of the Method of Residues.

5. A B occur together with a b.
   B is known to be the cause of b.
   Therefore A is the cause of a.

   Where B is the balloon by itself, uninflated, and A is the air with which the balloon is inflated, and b is the reading of the weight of the balloon when not inflated, and a b is the reading of the weight of the balloon when inflated. The conclusion is that a is the reading of the weight of the air with which the balloon is inflated, and that the air with which the balloon is inflated must therefore be the cause of that residual weight reading.

Exercises on pp. 476–479 (Method of Concomitant Variations)

1.

A	B	C	—	a	b	c
$A-$	B	C	—	$a-$	b	c
$A+$	B	C	—	$a+$	b	c

Therefore A is the cause of or causally connected with a.

Where A, $A+$, and $A-$ are the varying gravitational forces exerted by the moon upon the earth (the lunar tidal effects), B and C are other circumstances roughly constant in the operation of the Large Electron-Positron Collider (LEP), and a, $a+$, and $a-$ are the fluctuating energies of the beams of electrons and positrons in the underground ring of the LEP.

5. The concomitant variations in this pair of studies is straightforward: There appears to be an inverse relationship between the number of hours of sleep and the number of accidents on the following day. In the first study, the *reduction* of sleep by one hour (because of the shift to daylight time) resulted in a marked *increase* of accidents on the day following. In the second study, the *increase* in the hours of sleep (because of the shift back from daylight to standard time) resulted in a marked *decrease* in accidents on the day following. Other causal factors may enter in, of course, but it would be hard to deny that this concomitance of variation does tend to confirm that accidents are in some degree caused by sleep deficiency.

SECTION 12.3

Exercises on pp. 482–490

1. This may be analyzed in two ways: an application of the Method of Residues, or of the Method of Difference.

A	B	C	—	x	y	z

B is the cause of y; C is the cause of z.
Therefore A is the cause of x.

Here y is the bond usually set in the circumstances described in the brief, and also set by the judges who had not been caused to engage in any unusual reflections before setting bond; z is the set of circumstances usually attendant on such bond setting. B is the set of personal factors that normally result in judges' decisions in setting such bonds; C is the set of other circumstances, legal and societal, that lead to such action being taken. A is the circumstance of being caused to write about what will happen to one as one dies, and x is the *increment* in the bond set by those judges who had been caused to reflect on their own death just before setting bond. What B and C do not account for must be accounted for by some residual phenomena—in this case, reflections on death. It should be admitted that the causal chain suggested by the investigator, Dr. Pyszcyznski—in which thinking about mortality has this effect because it is said to have increased those judges' need for faith in moral standards and led to an increase in their desire to punish transgressors—is highly speculative.

An alternative analysis of this investigation, as representative of the Method of Difference, also is plausible. In such an account, reflection on death is one significant circumstance that differentiates the group of judges setting (on average) the high bond from the group setting (on average) the low bond.

5. *B C* occur together with *b c.*
   A B C occur together with *a b c.*
   Therefore *A* is the cause of *a.*

   The instance in the first line is the particular rabbit used by Ehrlich and Hata, already infected with syphilis. The instance in the second line is the same rabbit after being injected with 606 solution. Here *A* is the circumstance of injecting 606 solution, *B, C* are other circumstances attending the rabbit in question; *a* is the absence of spirochetes and the remission of ulcers; *b, c* are other phenomena attending the rabbit in question. This is the Method of Difference.

10. This is a straightforward illustration of the Method of Concomitant Variation. Shown here is a clear inverse relation between coronary heart disease and the nocturnal secretion of melatonin. Where that secretion is lower, heart disease is more likely; and where that secretion is higher, heart disease is less likely. It is reasonable to conclude that, while the lower levels of melatonin are not likely to be the entire cause of heart disease, those lower levels are probably (in Mill's words) "connected with it through some fact of causation."

SECTION 13.7

Exercises on pp. 522–529

1. The data to be explained here are the irregularities in the motion of the sun-like stars under observation. They wobble, and wobble in such a way and at such regular intervals that some systematic explanation is called for. The hypothesis proposed to explain this wobbling is the existence of a large planet in orbit about those stars, whose mass creates, through gravity, the observed perturbation.

   On the criteria presented in section 13.3 for the evaluation of proposed hypotheses, this planetary hypothesis fares quite well. The existence of those planets is not conclusively proved, of course; some other explanation of those unusual star movements ultimately may be revealed. But the existence of planets is, for the present at least, the best and most probable scientific explanation of the observed data.

(1) The hypothesized planets certainly would be *relevant* to the wobble noted. The gravitational forces they create would be causally related to the movements of those stars.

(2) The *testability* of the hypothesis arises from the regularity of the wobbles observed; if indeed a planet has been detected, we should be able to calculate the recurrent movements of the newly discovered bodies, and the resultant alteration in the movements of the stars they revolve about.

(3) The existence of planets outside the solar system is surely *compatible with existing theories.* No such planets have previously been found; but many astronomers have long supposed that one day they *would* be found. And there is nothing about their presence in the systems of those stars that is incompatible with what is known about stellar systems. On the contrary, these peculiarities of the stars' motions were *looked for;* the preliminary hypothesis (wholly compatible with existing theory) that there might be such observable patterns gave direction to the quest. The stars so closely observed were, therefore, those most like the Sun, which is the center of our known planetary system.

(4) The *predictive power* of the hypothesis is uncertain for the present. It may be possible to deduce many conclusions about the gravitational systems around those stars, and those planets—but with present technology we may be unable to confirm those predictions confidently. As observational techniques improve, however, with more advanced observational equipment eventually stationed outside of the earth's atmosphere, it is likely that critical tests can be devised for some of those predictions. Should such predictions be verified, the explanatory power of the hypothesis must be judged very great.

(5) The hypothesis proposed to explain the stars' movements—that there is a planet in orbit around each of them accounting for their wobble—is clear and straightforward and on the criterion of *simplicity* it is probably much superior to any other available hypothesis. Hence the remark of the investigator: "I was sure of what we had in three minutes."

5. The data to be explained are that a plant's roots grow *down* and its stem grows *up*, regardless of the orientation in which a young seedling is fixed. Knight's hypothesis to explain this data was that "this behavior was due to gravity," meaning by this that the plant's roots are positively gravity-sensitive and its stem negatively gravity-sensitive.

The hypothesis is relevant because the gravitational attraction of the earth is well established, and would exercise a constant "pull" on the gravity-sensitive roots regardless of how the seedling was placed.

The hypothesis is testable in a variety of ways, some only recently available. If the astronauts who reached the moon had been able to stay there longer, they could have arranged seedlings in various positions and then observed the direction in which their roots and stems grew. If the roots grew in the direction of the moon and their stems in the opposite direction, that would show that the earth's gravity rather than anything else about the earth (*e.g.*, its magnetic field or its iron core) was the cause of the phenomenon observed on earth. Or if in an artificial satellite far removed from all external massive bodies, the roots and stems of seedlings arranged in different positions continued to grow in quite different directions, that too would provide an affirmative test of Knight's hypothesis. Knight's own test using centrifugal force stronger than gravity was extremely ingenious.

The hypothesis seems to be perfectly compatible with previously well-established hypotheses. Its predictive power also is considerable, because it enables us to predict how plants would grow on the moon or in artificial satellites.

The hypothesis is simple, in the sense that it explains the data in terms of an already well-established theory concerning the earth's gravity. It is incomplete, of course, in that it leaves unanswered the question of what makes the roots positively gravity-sensitive, and what there is in the stem to make it negatively gravity-sensitive.

10. The first datum to be explained is the apparent slowness of rotation of the planet Venus. The first hypothesis considered is that Venus, like Mercury, rotates at the same rate that it revolves about the sun, thus keeping the same side always toward the sun and the other side always dark.

This hypothesis is surely relevant: If Venus does rotate slowly, that would explain why it appears to rotate slowly. It is testable by various means, not all of which are as yet technically feasible. It is compatible with the previously established hypothesis that Mercury behaves in the same way. It has predictive power not only to explain the original datum, but also other phenomena that can be used in testing it. It is an admirably simple hypothesis.

The first hypothesis leads to the prediction that the dark side of Venus must be exceedingly cold. But Pettit and Nicholson measured the temperature of the dark side of Venus and found it to be comparatively mild, $-9°F$. This disconfirms the first hypothesis, unless it can be salvaged by some other hypothesis that could explain the apparent discrepancy.

The second hypothesis considered as a possible way to save the first one is that atmospheric currents from the warm and bright side of Venus could perpetually heat the cold and dark side. This second hypothesis could save the first one.

The second hypothesis is clearly relevant. It is testable by various means, not all technically feasible at present. It has predictive power and is fairly simple. But it is not compatible with previously well-established hypotheses about the size of Venus and—especially—the behavior of atmospheric currents. So the second hypothesis is rejected, and with it the first.

The third hypothesis intended to replace the first two is that Venus rotates "fairly often."

This third hypothesis is relevant, for if Venus rotates only *fairly* often, that would explain the original datum that Venus appears to rotate slowly, and if it rotates fairly *often*, that would explain why the dark side does not cool excessively. This is of course very loose: the refined hypothesis in this case must ultimately be made quantitative in order to take account of the actual measurements that are made. The third hypothesis also satisfies the several other criteria discussed in the text.

15. The data to be explained here are the steep rates at which the surface of the moon cools down and heats up during and after lunar eclipses.

The hypothesis that the surface of the moon is solid rock, or composed of rocks of macroscopic size, is rejected, because it is incompatible with the previously well-established hypothesis that "no solid piece of rock can cool down and heat up so quickly."

The alternative hypothesis is that the upper surface of the moon is "a thick layer of heat-insulating dust as fine as face powder." This hypothesis is relevant, for it would certainly explain the extremely rapid changes of surface temperature: Only the few inches of dust change temperature, the insulated substratum remaining relatively constant in temperature. It is testable, though at the time it was proposed the techniques were not technically feasible. It is compatible with the previously established hypothesis. It has predictive power: It could be used to predict what would happen if a meteorite should land on the surface of the moon. And it is fairly simple.

But there is the question: How did the surface of the moon become so minutely pulverized? Here Dr. Buettner proposed his hypothesis that the moon's rocks have been ground to dust not merely by "the sandblasting of meteoric dust" but by "the everlasting influx of cosmic rays."

This hypothesis is relevant, testable, compatible with previously well-established hypotheses, has predictive and explanatory power, and is simple.

And yet moon rocks brought back to earth by our Apollo flights show that the moon is not covered by "dust as fine as face powder." This should help to emphasize the fact that scientific theories and hypotheses are continually subject to revision as new data are accumulated.

SECTION 14.3

Exercises on pp. 541–543

5. $\frac{1}{4} \times \frac{1}{3} \times \frac{1}{2} \times \frac{1}{1} = \frac{1}{24}$

The component events here are not independent, but in this case each success (in reaching the right house) *increases* rather than decreases the probability of the next success, because the number of available houses is fixed. After three men reach the correct house, the fourth (having to go to a different house) *must* succeed!

10. The probability that all four students will identify the same tire may be calculated in two different ways—just as the solution to problem 6 in this same set may be reached in two different ways.

Suppose that the first student, A, names the front left tire. The probability of his doing so, after *having* done so, is 1. Now the probability of the second student, B, naming that tire is $\frac{1}{4}$, there being four tires all (from B's point of view) equipossibly the one that A had named. The same is true of student C, and of student D. Therefore, regardless of which tire A does happen to name, (front left, or any other), the probability that all four students will name the same tire is $1 \times \frac{1}{4} \times \frac{1}{4} \times \frac{1}{4} = \frac{1}{64}$, or **.016.**

The same result could be achieved by first specifying a particular tire (say the front left tire) and asking: What is the probability of all four students naming that specified tire? This would be $\frac{1}{4} \times \frac{1}{4} \times \frac{1}{4} \times \frac{1}{4} = .004$. But the condition specified in the problem, that all four name the *same* tire, would be satisfied if all named the front left, or if all named the front right, or if all named the rear left, or if all named the rear right tire. So, if we were to approach the problem in this way, we also would need to inquire as to the probability of *either* the one or the other of these four outcomes—a calculation requiring the addition theorem, explained in section 14.4, for alternative outcomes. Since the four successful outcomes are mutually exclusive, we then would simply sum the four probabilities: $.004 + .004 + .004 + .004 = \mathbf{.016.}$ The two ways of approaching the problem must yield exactly the same result, of course.

This dual analysis applies likewise to the three patients arriving at a building with five entrances, in problem 6. One may calculate $1 \times \frac{1}{5} \times \frac{1}{5} = \frac{1}{25}$; or (using the addition theorem discussed in section 14.4) one may calculate $\frac{1}{5} \times \frac{1}{5} \times \frac{1}{5} = \frac{1}{125}$, and then add $\frac{1}{125} + \frac{1}{125} + \frac{1}{125} = \frac{1}{25}$.

SECTION 14.4

Exercises on pp. 548–549

1. Probability of losing with a 2, a 3, or a 12 is $\frac{4}{36}$ or $\frac{1}{9}$.
   Probability of throwing a 4, and then a 7 before another 4, is $\frac{3}{36} \times \frac{6}{9} = \frac{1}{18}$.
   Probability of throwing a 10, and then a 7 before another 10, is likewise $\frac{1}{18}$.
   Probability of throwing a 5, and then a 7 before another 5, is $\frac{4}{36} \times \frac{6}{10} = \frac{1}{15}$.
   Probability of throwing a 9, and then a 7 before another 9, is likewise $\frac{1}{15}$.
   Probability of throwing a 6, and then a 7 before another 6, is $\frac{5}{36} \times \frac{6}{11} = \frac{5}{66}$.
   Probability of throwing an 8, and then a 7 before another 8, is likewise $\frac{5}{66}$.
   The sum of the probabilities of the exclusive ways of the shooter's losing is $\frac{251}{495}$.
   So the shooter's chance of winning is $1 - \frac{251}{495} = \frac{244}{495}$, or **.493.**

5. Yes. You lose the bet only if you throw either a 2, or a 3, or a 4, or a 5, on *both* rolls of the die. On each throw the chance of getting one of those four numbers is $\frac{4}{6}$, or $\frac{2}{3}$. The chance of losing the bet is therefore $\frac{2}{3} \times \frac{2}{3}$, or $\frac{4}{9}$. Your chance of winning the bet, therefore, is $(1 - \frac{4}{9}) = \frac{5}{9} = \mathbf{.556}$

10. Challenge to the Reader

    This problem, which has been the focus of some controversy, may be analyzed in two different ways.

    First analysis:

    a. There are 28 possible pairs in the abbreviated deck consisting of four kings and four aces. Of these 28 possible pairs, only seven (equipossible) pairs contain the ace of spades. Of these seven pairs, three contain two aces. If we know that the pair drawn contains the ace of spades, therefore, the probability that this pair contains two aces is $\frac{3}{7}$.

    b. However, if we know only that one of the cards in the pair is an ace, we know only that the pair drawn is one of the 22 (equipossible) pairs that contain at least one ace. Of these 22 pairs, six contain two aces. Therefore, if we know only that the pair contains an ace, the probability that the pair drawn contains two aces is $\frac{6}{22}$, or $\frac{3}{11}$.

On this first analysis, the probabilities in the two cases are different.

Second analysis:

a. If one of the cards of the pair drawn is known to be the ace of spades, there are seven other possible cards with which the pair may be completed. Of these seven, three are aces. Therefore, if we know that one of the cards drawn is the ace of spades, the probability that this pair contains two aces is ³⁄₇.

b. If we know only that one of the cards drawn is an ace, we know that it is either the ace of spades, or the ace of hearts, or the ace of diamonds, or the ace of clubs. If it is the ace of spades, the analysis immediately above applies, and the probability that this pair contains two aces is again ³⁄₇. If the ace is the ace of hearts, the same analysis applies; as it does if the card drawn is the ace of diamonds, or the ace of clubs. Therefore, even if we know only that an ace is one of the cards drawn, the probability that the pair contains two aces remains ³⁄₇.

On this second analysis, the probabilities in the two cases are the same.

Which of these two analyses do you believe to be correct? Why?

SECTION 14.5

Exercises on pp. 556–558

1. (a) **$3.82**

   (b) **$19,100,000.00**

   But note: This was a *very* unusual set of circumstances!

5. This problem requires only a straightforward use of the product theorem. The probability of selecting, at random, just those two cows out of four, is the probability of selecting one of that pair on the first choosing (½), times the probability of selecting the other one of that pair on the second choosing, where the first already had been selected (⅓). So the calculation would be: ½ × ⅓ = ⅙.

10. The calculation of the bettor's chances of winning on the "Don't Pass–Bar 3" line is the probability of the player's losing when the game is played according to the normal rules, *with the provision that he does not lose if he gets a 3 on the first roll*. The probability of a 3 on the first roll is ²⁄₃₆, or .056. The probability of the player losing on the normal rules is .507, as was shown in section 16.4. Therefore the probability of the player losing, barring the loss on a first-roll 3, is .507 − .056 = **.451**. Since this is the probability of the player's losing if he cannot lose by getting a three on the first roll, it is the probability of the bettor winning on the "Don't Pass–Bar 3" line. So the expected value of a $100 bet on the "Don't Pass–Bar 3" line is .451 × $200 = **$90.20.**

    Note that this bet, which the house will gladly accept, is substantially less favorable to the bettor than simply betting on the pass line; that is, simply betting on the player to win. The expected value of such a $100 wager (*i.e.*, on the player to win according to normal rules) is .493 × $200 = **$98.60.**

SPECIAL SYMBOLS

	Page
$s = 0$	208
$s \neq 0$	208
SP	209
$S\overline{P}$	209
$\overline{S}$	209
$\bullet$	301
$\sim$	303
$\vee$	304
$\supset$	315
$\equiv$	336
$\underline{\underline{\mathrm{T}}}$	340
$\therefore$	350
(x)	388
$(\exists x)$	388
ϕ	390
ψ	394
ν	399
y	401
$P(a)$	538
$\overline{a}$	545

GLOSSARY/INDEX

Buss. David M., 428

Butler, Joseph, 177

Butler, Samuel, 129, 422

C

Calculus of probability: A branch of mathematics that can be used to compute the probabilities of complex events from the probabilities of their component events, 536–37

Callahan, Daniel, 9

Callahan, J.J., 286–87

Camenes: The traditional name of one of the 15 valid standard-form categorical syllogisms. A syllogism in the form Camenes has the mood and figure **AEE-4;** that is to say, its minor premiss and conclusion are **E** propositions, its major premiss is an **A** proposition, and it is in the fourth figure because the middle term is the predicate of the major premiss and the subject of the minor premiss, 239, 243

Camestres: The traditional name of one of the 15 valid standard-form categorical syllogisms. A syllogism in the form Camestres has the mood and figure **AEE-2;** that is to say, its minor premiss and conclusion are **E** propositions, its major premiss is an **A** proposition, and it is in the second figure because the middle term is the predicate of both the major and the minor premiss, 239, 243

Campbell, C. Arthur, 286

Candlish, Stewart, 283

Can Theories Be Refuted? Essays on the Duhem-Quine Thesis (Harding), 513

Carroll, James, 462

Carroll, Lewis, 80, 163–64, 276–77, 440–41

Carter, Stephen L., 33

Cassidy, John, 32

Categorical proposition: A proposition that can be analyzed as being about classes, or categories, affirming or denying that one class, *S*, is included in some other class, *P*, in whole or in part. Four standard forms of categorical propositions are traditionally distinguished: **A:** Universal affirmative propositions (All *S* is *P*); **E:** Universal negative propositions (No *S* is *P*); **I:** Particular affirmative propositions (Some *S* is *P*); Particular negative propositions (Some *S* is not *P*), 180–215; symbolism and diagrams for, 208–13; theory of deduction and, 181; translating into standard form, 250–53. *See also* Standard-form categorical propositions

Categorical syllogism: A deductive argument consisting of three categorical propositions that contain exactly three terms, each of which occurs in exactly two of the propositions, 217–47; Venn diagram technique for testing, 224–30. *See also* Disjunctive Syllogism; Hypothetical Syllogism; Syllogistic argument

Causal laws: Descriptive laws asserting a necessary connection between events of two kinds, of which one is the cause and the other the effect, 452–53

Causal reasoning: Inductive reasoning in which some effect is inferred from what is assumed to be its cause, or some cause is inferred from what is assumed to be its effect, 452–55

Cause: Either the *necessary* condition for the occurrence of an effect (the sense used when we seek to *eliminate* some thing or event by eliminating its cause), or the *sufficient* condition for the occurrence of an effect, understood as the conjunction of its necessary conditions. The latter meaning is more common, and is the sense of cause used when we wish to *produce* some thing or event, 449–52

Cecil, Robert, 85

Celarent: The traditional name of one of the 15 valid standard-form categorical syllogisms. A syllogism in the form Celarent has the mood and figure **EAE-1;** that is to say, its major premiss and conclusions are **E** propositions, its minor premiss is an **A** proposition, and it is in the first figure because the middle term is the subject of the major premiss and the predicate of the minor premiss, 237, 244

Ceremonial language: language with special social uses normally having a mix of expressive, directive, and informative functions, 75–76

Cesare: The traditional name of one of the 15 valid standard-form categorical syllogisms. A syllogism in the form Cesare has the mood and figure **EAE-2;** that is to say, its major premiss and conclusion are **E** propositions, its minor premiss is an **A** proposition, and it is in the second figure because the middle term is the predicate of both the major and the minor premiss, 239, 244

Chafee, Zachariah, Jr., 454

Challenger, James, 295–96

Character and Opinion in the United States (Santayana), 81

Chase, Salmon P., 85

Chen, Fan, 438

Chess Mysteries of Sherlock Holmes (Smullyan), 64

Chesterton, G.K., 95

Chirugia Magna (Lanfranc), 266

Church, Alonzo, 298

Churchill, Winston, 133, 274

Circular argument: A fallacious argument in which the conclusion is assumed in one of the premisses; begging the question. Also called a *petitio principii*, 159–60

Circular definition: A definition that is faulty because its *definiendum* (what is to be defined) appears in its *definiens* (the defining symbols) and therefore is useless, 126

Circumstantial *ad hominem* argument: An informal fallacy in which the *ad hominem* attack against the

is the subject of both the major and minor premiss, 239, 244

Debs, Eugene, 84

Decatur, Stephen, 94

Decline and Fall of the Roman Empire, The (Gibbon), 9

Deduction: One of the two major types of argument traditionally distinguished, the other being induction. A deductive argument claims to provide conclusive grounds for its conclusion; if it does so it is valid, if it does not it is invalid, 42–46; formal proof of validity and, 349–51; inconsistency and, 375–78; method of, 349–83; proof of invalidity and, 372–74; refutation by logical analogy and, 440–43; rule of replacement and, 359–63; theory of, 181

Defence of Poetry, The (Shelley), 131

Definiendum: In any definition, the word or symbol being defined, 103. *See also* specific types of definition

Definiens: In any definition, a symbol or group of symbols that is said to have the same meaning as the *definiendum*, 103. *See also* specific types of definition

Definition: An expression in which one word or set of symbols (the *definiens*) is provided, which is claimed to have the same meaning as the *definiendum*, the word or symbol defined, 98–133; disputes and, 99–102; extensional, 118–20; extension/intension and, 114–17; intensional, 120–24; lexical, 105–6; operational, 121–22; ostensive, 119; persuasive, 110–11; precising, 106–9; quasi-ostensive, 119; rules for, by genus and difference, 125–34; stipulative, 103–5; theoretical, 109–10

Definition by genus and difference: A type of intensional definition of a term that first identifies the larger class ("genus") of which the *definiendum* is a species or subclass, and then identifies the attribute ("difference") that distinguishes the members of that species from members of all other species in that genus, 122–24; rules for, 125–29

De Kruif, Paul, 485

Democracy in America (Tocqueville), 54

Demonstrative definition: An ostensive definition; one that refers by gesture to examples of the term being defined, 119

De Morgan, Augustus, 342

De Morgan's theorem (De M.): An expression of logical equivalence; a rule of inference that permits the valid mutual replacement of the negation of a disjunction, by the conjunction of the negations of the disjuncts: $\sim(p \vee q) \doteqdot (\sim p \bullet \sim q)$; and that permits the valid mutual replacement of the negation of a conjunction, by the disjunction of the negations of the conjuncts: $\sim(p \bullet q) \doteqdot (\sim p \vee \sim q)$, 342, 363

Denotation: The several objects to which a term may correctly be applied; its extension, 115–17

Denotative definition: A definition that identifies the extension of a term, by (for example) listing the members of the class of objects to which the term refers; the members of that class are thus denoted. An extensional definition, 118–20

Denton, Derek, 464

Denying the antecedent: A formal fallacy, so named because the categorical premiss in the argument, $\sim p$, denies the antecedent rather than the consequent of the conditional premiss. Symbolized as: $p \supset q, \sim p$, therefore $\sim q$, 281, 330

De Rerum Natura (Lucretius), 30

Descartes, René, 9

Descent of Man, The (Darwin), 83, 274, 498

Devil's Dictionary, The (Bierce), 128, 172

Devine, Philip E., 131

Dewan, Lawrence, 29

Dewey, John, 39, 58, 132–33, 275, 500

Diagraming arguments, 13–15

Dialectic of Sex: The Case for Feminist Revolution, The, 155

Dialectic of Sex: The Case for Feminist Revolution, The (Firestone), 427

Dialogues Concerning Natural Religion (Hume), 57–58, 154, 270, 273, 437–38, 440

Dialogues Concerning Two New Sciences (Galileo), 153

Diary in Australia (Cecil), 85

Diary of a Young Girl, The (Frank), 430

Dickens, Charles, 83

Difference, Method of: A pattern of inductive argument in which, when in cases in which the phenomenon under investigation occurs and cases in which it does not occur differ in only one circumstance, that circumstance is inferred to be causally connected to the phenomenon under investigation., 460–62, 480

Dilemma: A common form of argument in ordinary discourse in which it is claimed that a choice must be made between two alternatives, both of which are (usually) bad, 287–90; ways of evading or refuting, 288–90

Dimaris: The traditional name of one of the 15 valid standard-form categorical syllogisms. A syllogism in the form Dimaris has the mood and figure **IAI-4**; that is to say, its major premiss and conclusion are **I** propositions, its minor premiss is an **A** proposition, and it is in the fourth figure because the middle term is the predicate of the major premiss and the subject of the minor premiss, 239

Dimock, George E., Jr., 275

Directive function of language, 73

Disagreement, kinds of, 88–95

Disamis: The traditional name of one of the 15 valid standard-form categorical syllogisms. A syllogism in the form Disamis has the mood and figure **IAI-3**; that is to say, its major premiss and conclusion are **I**

Hypothetical proposition, Hypothetical statement: A compound proposition of the form *"if p then q"*; a conditional proposition or statement, 312–15

Hypothetical Syllogism (HS.): A syllogism that contains a hypothetical proposition as a premiss. If the syllogism contains hypothetical propositions exclusively it is called a "pure" hypothetical syllogism; if the syllogism contains one conditional and one categorical premiss, it is called a "mixed" hypothetical syllogism. "Hypothetical syllogism" ("H.S.") is also the name of an elementary valid argument form that permits the conclusion that *p* ⊃ *r*, if the premisses *p*⊃*q* and *q*⊃*r* are assumed to be true, 279–82, 328–30, 363

I

Iconic representation: The representation of standard-form categorical propositions, and of arguments constituted by such propositions, by means of spatial inclusions and exclusions, as in the use of Venn diagrams, 213

Identity, Principle of: A principle which asserts that if any statement is true then it is true; sometimes held to be one of the laws of thought, 343–45

Ignoratio elenchi: The informal fallacy of irrelevant conclusion, 149–50

Illicit major: Short name for the "Fallacy of Illicit Process of the Major Term," a formal mistake made when the major term of a syllogism is undistributed in the major premiss, but is distributed in the conclusion. Such a mistake breaks the rule that if either term is distributed in the conclusion, it must be distributed in the premisses, 234

Illicit minor: Short name for the "Fallacy of Illicit Process of the Minor Term," a formal mistake made when the minor term of a syllogism is undistributed in the minor premiss, but is distributed in the conclusion, 234

Immediate inference: An inference that is drawn directly from one premiss without the mediation of any other premiss. Various kinds of immediate inferences may be distinguished, traditionally including *conversion, obversion,* and *contraposition,* 193–200

Imortalie Dei (Leo XIII), 94

Implicans: The antecedent of a conditional or hypothetical statement; the protasis, 312

Implicate: The consequent of a conditional or hypothetical statement; the apodosis, 312

Implication: The relation that holds between the antecedent and the consequent of a true conditional or hypothetical statement. Because there are different kinds of hypothetical statements, there are different kinds of implication, including: logical implication, definitional implication, causal impli-

cation, decisional implication, and material implication. "Impl." is also the abbreviation for "Material Implication," the name of a rule of inference, the expression of a logical equivalence that permits the mutual replacement of a statement of the form "*p* ⊃ *q*" by one of the form " ~*p* ∨ *q*," 312–15. *See also* Material implication

Inclusive disjunction: A truth- functional connective between two components, called disjuncts; a compound statement asserting inclusive disjunction is true when at least one (or both) of the disjuncts is true. Normally called simply "disjunction" it is also called "weak disjunction" and is symbolized by the wedge, ∨ , 304–6. *See also* Exclusive disjunction

Inconsistent: Characterizing any set of propositions that cannot all be true together, or any argument having contradictory premises, 375–78

In Defence of Free Will (Campbell), 286

In Defense of Anarchism (Wolff), 30

Independent events: In probability theory, events so related that the occurrence or nonoccurrence of one has no effect upon the occurrence or nonoccurrence of the other, 537–39

Individual constant: A symbol (by convention, normally a lower case letter, *a* through *w*) used in logical notation to denote an individual, 387

Individual variable: A symbol (by convention normally the lower case *x* or *y*), which serves as a placeholder for an individual constant. The universal quantifier, *(x)*, means "for all x . . ." The existential quantifier, (∃*x*) means "there is an *x* such that. . .", 387

Induction: One of the two major types of argument traditionally distinguished, the other being deduction. An inductive argument claims that its premisses give only some degree of probability, but not certainty, to its conclusion, 42–46; argument by analogy and, 423–34; probability and, 43–46, 533–56; refutation by logical analogy and, 440–43

Induction, Principle of: The principle, underlying all inductive argument, that nature is sufficiently regular to permit the discovery of causal laws having general application, 452–53

Induction by simple enumeration: A type of inductive generalization, much criticized, where the premisses are instances in which phenomena of two kinds repeatedly accompany one another in certain circumstances, from which it is concluded that phenomena of those two kinds always accompany one another in such circumstances, 453–55. *See also* Methods of experimental inquiry

Inductive generalization: The process of arriving at general or universal propositions from the particular facts of experience, relying upon the principle of induction, 453–55. *See also* Methods of experimental inquiry

Inference: A process by which one proposition is arrived at and affirmed on the basis of some other proposition or propositions, 6. *See also* **Immediate inference**

Inference, Rules of: In deductive logic, the rules that may be used in constructing formal proofs of validity, comprising three groups: a set of elementary valid argument forms, a set of logically equivalent pairs of expressions whose members may be replaced by one another, and a set of rules for quantification, 351, 363, 398–404

Informal Logic (Blair and Johnson), 138

Informative function of language, 72

Ingersoll, Robert G., 153

Instantiation: In quantification theory, the process of substituting an individual constant for an individual variable, thereby converting a propositional function into a proposition, 389

Institutes (Coke), 130

Instructions on Christian Theology (Smith), 93

Intensional definitions, 120–24; conventional, 121; objective, 120; subjective, 120

Intension of a term: The attributes shared by all and only the objects in the class that term denotes, 114–17

Interwoven arguments, 15–21

Introduction to Logic, An (Joseph), 276

Introduction to Mathematics, An (Whitehead), 299

Introduction to the Study of Browning, An (Symons), 84

Invalid: Not valid; characterizing a deductive argument that fails to provide conclusive grounds for the truth of its conclusion; every deductive argument is either valid or invalid, 43; invalidity, proof of, 372–74

Ion (Plato), 267

Irrelevant conclusion: An informal fallacy committed when the premises of an argument purporting to establish one conclusion are actually directed toward the establishment of some other conclusion. Also called the fallacy of *ignoratio elenchi*, 149–50

J

Jacoby, James, 266

Jacoby, Oswald, 266

Jacqueline Du Pre: Her Life, Her Music, Her Legend (Du Pre), 129

Jaffe, Michael G., 39

James, William, 100–101, 131

Jefferson, Thomas, 85, 94

Jefferson's Children (Botstein), 10

Jimmy the Greek, 92

Jochnowitz, George, 33

Johnson, R.J., 138

Johnson, Samuel, 82, 127, 398

Johnston, David Cay, 20

Johnstone, Henry W., Jr., 285

Joint Method of Agreement and Difference: A pattern of inductive inference in which the Method of Agreement and the Method of Difference are used in combination, 466–67, 480

Joint occurrence: In probability theory, a compound event in which two simple events both occur. To calculate the probability of joint occurrence the product theorem is applied, 537–41

Jones, W. Ron, 272

Joseph, H.W.B., 160, 276

Journal of Blacks in Higher Education, 82

Joyce, James, 104

Judson, Horace F., 504

Julius Caesar (Shakespeare), 27, 273

K

Kahane, Howard, 138

Kahn, E.J., Jr., 171

Kant, Immanuel, 38, 129, 133, 216, 254

Karenga, Maulana Ron, 29

Karl Marx and Friedrich Engels Correspondence, 1846-1895, 15

Kass, Leon, 175

Kawachi, I., 525

Kazan, Y., 92

Kazin, Alfred, 173

Keeping Faith with the Student-Athlete: A New Model for Intercollegiate Athletics, 31

Kelly, Edmond, 171

Kepler, Johannes, 498

Kettering, Charles, 398

Keynes, J.M., 132

Kim, Jaegwon, 286

Kingsley, Charles, 145

Kinsley, Michael, 443

Knight, Jonathan, 92

Koedt, Anne, 429

Kolbert, Elizabeth, 154

Kristol, Irving, 265

Ky, Katherine N., 459

L

Lady Windermere's Fan (Wilde), 131

Lamont, Corliss, 130

Simple predicate: In quantification theory, a propositional function having some true and some false substitution instances, each of which is an affirmative singular proposition, 387

Simple statement: A statement that does not contain any other statement as a component, 300, 302

Simplification (Simp.): One of the nine elementary valid argument forms; it is a rule of inference that permits the separation of conjoined statements. If the conjunction of *p* and *q* is given, simplification permits the inference that *p*. Symbolized as $p \cdot q$, therefore *p,* 363

Sine qua non: A necessary condition for something; meaning literally: "that without which not," 318, 449–51

Singer, Isaac Bashevis, 266

Singular proposition: A proposition that asserts that a particular individual has (or has not) some specified attribute, 254–56, 385–87

Sinnot, Edmund W., 524

Siscovick, D.S., 475

Sisk, John P., 117

Six Books of the Commonwealth (Bodin), 40

Sleep Thieves (Coren), 479

"Slippery slope" argument, 441–42

Small, Meredith F., 39

Smart, J.J.C., 266

Smith, Alan E., 272

Smith, J.P., 93

Smith, Theobald, 84

Smullen, Ivor, 33

Snow, Clyde Collins, 144

Sobol, Bruce J., 427

Social Contract, The (Rousseau), 93, 132

Social Ethics (Mappes & Zembaty), 14

Socrates, 147, 160

Some Main Problems of Philosophy (Moore), 285

Sommers, Christina, 143, 154

Soper, Rev. Lord, 428

Sophism: Any of the fallacies of ambiguity, 163–71

Sophistical Refutations (Aristotle), 138

Sorites: An argument whose conclusion is inferred from its premises by a *chain* of syllogistic inferences in which the conclusion of each inference serves as a premise for the next, and the conclusion of the last syllogism is the conclusion of the entire argument, 275–77

Sound: A deductive argument that is valid *and* has true premises is said to be sound; a deductive argument is *un*sound if it is not valid, *or* if one or more of its premises is false, 49

Southerland, Thomas C., Jr., 41–42

Spadafora, David, 34

Specific form of a given argument: The argument form from which the given argument results when a different simple statement is substituted for each different statement variable in that form, 323

Specific form of a given statement: The statement form from which the statement results by substituting a different simple statement for each different statement variable, 335

Speck, Jeff, 30, 444

Spencer, Herbert, 127, 438

Spinoza, Baruch, 84, 85, 132, 285–86

Square of opposition: A diagram in the form of a square in which the four types of categorical propositions (**A, E, I,** and **O**) are situated at the corners, exhibiting the logical relations (called "oppositions") among these propositions. The traditional square of opposition, which represents the Aristotelian interpretation of these propositions and their relations, differs importantly from the square of opposition as it is used in Boolean, or modern symbolic, logic, according to which some traditional oppositions do not hold, 191–92; Boolean, 209, 210

St. Anselm, 117

St. Aubyn, Giles, 95

Standard-form categorical propositions: The four categorical propositions, named **A, E, I,** and **O**–for universal affirmative, universal negative, particular affirmative, and particular negative, respectively, 182–84; contradictories and, 189; contraries and, 189–90; distribution and, 186–88; existential import in interpretation of, 202–7; general schema of, 186; immediate inferences and, 193–200; opposition and, 188–92; quality and, 185; quantity and, 185; Square of Opposition and, 191–92; subalternation and, 190–91; subcontraries and, 190; symbolism and diagrams for, 208–13; theory of deduction and, 181

Standard-form categorical syllogism: A categorical syllogism in which the premises and conclusions are all standard-form categorical propositions (**A, E, I** or **O**) and are arranged in a specified order; major premise first, minor premise second, and conclusion last, 217–21; deduction of the 15 valid forms of, 242–45; exposition of 15 valid forms of, 236–42; figure and, 218–20; mood and, 218; rules for and fallacies of, 232–36; syllogistic argument and, 221–23; Venn diagram technique for testing, 224–30

Standard-form translation. *See* Reduction to standard form

Statement: A proposition; what is typically asserted by a declarative sentence, but not the sentence itself. Every statement must be either true or false, although the truth or falsity of a given statement may be unknown., 4–6

MILL'S METHODS OF INDUCTIVE INFERENCE

1. **The Method Of Agreement:** The one factor or circumstance that is *common* to all the cases of the phenomenon under investigation is likely to be the cause (or effect) of that phenomenon.
2. **The Method of Difference:** The one factor or circumstance whose *absence* or *presence distinguishes* all cases in which the phenomenon under investigation occurs from those cases in which it does not occur, is likely to be the cause, or part of the cause, of that phenomenon.
3. **The Joint Method of Agreement and Difference:** The *combination*, in the same investigation, of the Method of Agreement and Method of Difference.
4. **The Method of Residues:** When some portion of the phenomenon under examination is known to be the consequence of well-understood antecedent circumstances, we may infer that the *remainder* of that phenomenon is the effect of the remaining antecedents.
5. **The Method of Concomitant Variation:** When the variations in one phenomenon are highly *correlated* with the variation in another phenomenon, one of the two is likely to be the cause of the other, or they may be related as the products of some third factor causing both.

PROBABILITY CALCULATIONS

To calculate the probability of the **joint occurrence** of two or more events:

(A) If the events (say, *a and b*) are *independent*, the probability of their joint occurrence is the simple *product* of their probabilities: $P(a \text{ and } b) = P(a) \times P(b)$.

(B) If the events (say, *a and b and c*) are *not independent*, the probability of their joint occurrence is the probability of the first event, times the probability of the second event if the first occurred, times the probability of the third event if the first and second occurred, and so on: $P(a \text{ and } b \text{ and } c) = P(a) \times P(b \text{ if } a) \times P(c \text{ if both } a \text{ and } b)$.

To calculate the probability of the **alternative occurrence** of two or more events:

(A) If the events (say, *a or b*) are *mutually exclusive*, the probability of at least one of them occurring is the simple *sum* of their probabilities: $P(a \text{ or } b) = P(a) + P(b)$.

(B) If the events (say, *a or b or c*) are *not mutually exclusive*, the probability of at least one of them occurring may be determined by either:

　　(1) analyzing the favorable cases into mutually exclusive events and summing the probabilities of those successful events; or

　　(2) determining the probability that no one of the alternative events will occur and subtracting that probability from 1.

QUANTIFICATION RULES

UI:	$(x)(\phi x)$ $\therefore \phi v$	(where v is any individual symbol)
UG:	ϕy $\therefore (x)(\phi x)$	(where y denotes "any arbitrarily selected individual")
EI:	$(\exists x)(\phi x)$ $\therefore \phi v$	[where v is any individual constant (other than y) having no previous occurrence in the context]
EG:	ϕv $\therefore (\exists x)(\phi x)$	(where v is any individual symbol)